EMPIRE OF NATIONS

**CULTURE&SOCIETY
AFTER SOCIALISM**
A SERIES EDITED BY
BRUCE GRANT&NANCY RIES

EMPIRE *of* NATIONS

ETHNOGRAPHIC KNOWLEDGE *&* THE
MAKING OF THE SOVIET UNION

FRANCINE HIRSCH

CORNELL UNIVERSITY PRESS
ITHACA AND LONDON

Copyright © 2005 by Cornell University

All rights reserved. Except for brief quotations in a review, this book, or parts thereof, must not be reproduced in any form without permission in writing from the publisher. For information, address Cornell University Press, Sage House, 512 East State Street, Ithaca, New York 14850.

First published 2005 by Cornell University Press
First printing, Cornell Paperbacks, 2005

Printed in the United States of America

Library of Congress Cataloging-in-Publication Data
Hirsch, Francine, 1967–
    Empire of nations : ethnographic knowledge and the making of the Soviet Union / Francine Hirsch.
        p. cm. — (Culture and society after socialism)
    Includes bibliographical references and index.
    ISBN 0-8014-4273-7 (cloth : alk. paper)—ISBN 0-8014-8908-3 (pbk. : alk. paper)
    1. Ethnology—Soviet Union. 2. Soviet Union—Ethnic relations. 3. Minorities—Government policy—Soviet Union. 4. Soviet Union—Politics and government. I. Title. II. Series.

DK33.H57 2005
323.147'09'04—dc22
2005002722

Cornell University Press strives to use environmentally responsible suppliers and materials to the fullest extent possible in the publishing of its books. Such materials include vegetable-based, low-VOC inks and acid-free papers that are recycled, totally chlorine-free, or partly composed of nonwood fibers. For further information, visit our website at www.cornellpress.cornell.edu.

Cloth printing   10 9 8 7 6 5 4 3 2 1
Paperback printing   10 9 8 7 6 5 4 3 2 1

To Mark

CONTENTS

FIGURES AND MAPS

Figures

Maps

ACKNOWLEDGMENTS

Researching and writing this book has been an incredible journey, and I gratefully acknowledge those institutions and individuals whose generous support and assistance have made it possible.

The International Research and Exchanges Board (IREX), the MacArthur Foundation, the Social Science Research Council (SSRC), the Andrew W. Mellon Foundation, the Whiting Foundation, and the Princeton Society of Fellows of the Woodrow Wilson Foundation funded this project in its initial stages. Postdoctoral fellowships from the Davis Center for Russian Studies at Harvard University and the Social Science Research Council (SSRC), as well as a Vilas Young Investigator award from the University of Wisconsin, provided the time and the funding to do additional research in Russia and the United States and to begin reworking the manuscript. A sabbatical at the National Fellows' Program at the Hoover Institution on War, Revolution, and Peace at Stanford University in 2003–04 provided leave time and an ideal environment to bring this project to completion.

As a doctoral student at Princeton University I had the good fortune to work with Laura Engelstein and Stephen Kotkin—who have both profoundly shaped my approach to history. Laura Engelstein taught me the importance of intellectual rigor and the joy of going after the difficult questions. Over the years, she has read most of the chapters in this manuscript several times, offering honest feedback and encouragement. I thank her for her unstinting support, and for being an outstanding mentor, colleague, and friend. Stephen Kotkin taught me to think broadly and comparatively about Soviet history, and also urged me to look at local responses to Soviet policies. His thoughtful engagement with my work has been of tremendous help; his iconoclasm continues to inspire me. While at Princeton I also had the opportunity to study with Mark von Hagen at Columbia University. I thank him for sharing his vast knowledge of Soviet nationality policy and for reading and commenting on my work. I thank Philip Nord for sparking my interest in colonial exhibits and ethnography in his seminar on nineteenth-century Europe.

The time I spent in Russia was extraordinary, due in large part to my Russian colleagues. I owe a huge debt to all of the archivists at the St. Petersburg branch of the Academy of Sciences, whose unparalleled kindness and expertise made my experience doing research there a great pleasure. In particular, I thank Irina Tunkina and the late Mikhail Fainshtein for their assistance; my special thanks go to Olga Ulanova, former archivist and true friend. I owe a similar debt to the staff of the Russian Ethnographic Museum in St. Petersburg, and especially to Elena Ivanovna. I am also grateful to have had the assistance of the archivists and librarians at the State Archive of the Russian Federation, the State Archive of the Russian Economy, the Russian Center for the Preservation and Study of Documents of Recent History, the Central State Archive of Historical-Political Documents of St. Petersburg, the Archive of the Russian Geographical Society, the Russian State Library in Moscow, and the M. E. Saltykov-Shchedrin State Public Library in St. Petersburg. Special thanks to Maria Novichenok of the State Archive of the Russian Economy. The months I spent in Moscow were enriched by my friendship with Sergei Zhuravlev, a talented scholar at the Institute of Russian History.

Back in the United States I made extensive use of Firestone Library at Princeton University, Widener and Tozzer Libraries at Harvard University, Memorial Library at the University of Wisconsin–Madison, and the Hoover Institution Library and Archive at Stanford University. I thank the librarians and archivists at these fine institutions for their assistance.

At the University of Wisconsin–Madison, where I have taught since 2000, I have had the privilege to be surrounded by a group of gifted historians. I thank my colleagues for making Madison an exciting and congenial intellectual home. I am especially grateful to those colleagues who read and commented on the manuscript. Tony Michels, Brett Sheehan, Florencia Mallon, Lee Wandel, Diane Lindstrom, and Suzanne Desan read sections of the manuscript; Nan Enstad read the entire draft. David McDonald read the entire manuscript more than once and was always willing to discuss the project's ideas. I thank them all for sharing critical insights, and also for their encouragement and good humor.

Thanks also go to those colleagues at the University of Wisconsin who provided important technical assistance. Jim Escalante of the Art Department donated his time and expertise to scan images for the book. Richard Worthington of the Cartographic Lab skillfully turned my sketches into maps. Sean Gillen and Ayten Kilic were outstanding research assistants.

I have presented my ideas and arguments at conferences and workshops over the years and have reaped the benefits of colleagues' thoughtful comments and questions. In particular, I thank Jonathan Bone, Jane Burbank, Frederick Corney, Robert Crews, Michael David-Fox, Adrienne Edgar, David Hoffman, Adeeb Khalid, Nathaniel Knight, Douglas Northrop, Yuri Slezkine, Susan Solomon, Charles Steinwedel, Willard Sunderland, and Reginald Zelnik. I am especially grateful to those colleagues who read and commented on parts of the manuscript: Nancy Appelbaum, Peter Holquist, Arthur McKee, John Randolph, Rebecca Sokolovsky, and Amir Weiner. Much appreciation to Amir Weiner and Norman Naimark for welcoming me into their *kruzhok* during my sabbatical at the Hoover Institution; I thank them and their graduate students for critical feedback that made the final version of the manuscript better.

I thank Bruce Grant and Nancy Ries for inviting me to submit my manuscript to their series with Cornell University Press. Bruce Grant read unpolished chapter drafts and offered numerous suggestions that greatly improved the final manuscript; his enthusiasm for this project was a source of motivation. Yuri Slezkine was an ideal "anonymous" reader for the press, going through the manuscript with great care and suggesting ways to clarify my arguments—even when he disagreed with them. I thank him for his intellectual generosity. I also thank the editorial staff at Cornell University Press for their professionalism and patience, and for expertly guiding the manuscript through the review and production processes.

My deepest appreciation goes to those friends and family members whose love and friendship have sustained me through this journey. Maureen Waller, Suzanne Verderber, David Horwich, David Hirsch, and Erika and Lawrence Hessman have been there through the twists and turns. My parents, Mark and Lois Hirsch, have always believed in me; their love and steadfast support have been a great source of strength. Finally, my husband, Mark Hessman, has lived with this manuscript for as long as he has known me. He has read more drafts of each chapter than anyone else, offering substantive and stylistic suggestions and cheering me on. His love, sense of humor, and companionship have kept me going—and have helped me to see this project through. It is to him that I dedicate this book.

This book incorporates material that appeared in the following articles: "The Soviet Union as a Work-in-Progress: Ethnographers and the Category *Nationality* in the 1926, 1937, and 1939 Censuses," *Slavic Review* 56, no. 2 (1997): 251–78; "Toward an Empire of Nations: Border-Making and the Formation of Soviet National Identities," *The Russian Review* 59, no. 2 (2000): 201–26; "Getting to Know 'The Peoples of the USSR': Ethnographic Exhibits as Soviet Virtual Tourism, 1923–1934," *Slavic Review* 62, no. 4 (2003): 683–709; and "Toward a Soviet Order of Things: The 1926 Census and the Making of the Soviet Union," in *Categories and Contexts: Anthropological and Historical Studies in Critical Demography,* ed. Simon Szreter, Hania Sholkamy, and A. Dharmalingam (Oxford: Oxford University Press, 2004).

NOTE ON TRANSLITERATION AND DATES

In transliterating most Russian names and titles, I have used the Library of Congress system. I have made an exception in rendering the names of well-known places in non-Russian regions (such as Jalal-Abad in Kirgizia). I have also made an exception in rendering the names of some of the tribes and nationalities of the Soviet Union. Here, I have used Ronald Wixman, *The Peoples of the USSR: An Ethnographic Handbook* (Armonk, NY, 1984) as a basic guide. Wixman offers alternative spellings for most names. In some cases, I have chosen to use these alternative spellings when they are closer to the non-Russian original. Thus I discuss the Tajiks (and not the Tadzhiks) of Central Asia. Throughout the book I use contemporary, not present-day, place names.

Dates are given according to the Julian calendar—which was thirteen days behind the Western calendar—until January 31, 1918, when Russia adopted the Western calendar.

TERMS AND ABBREVIATIONS

AO:	autonomous national oblast (established within ASSRs and SSRs, and within the RSFSR)
ASSR:	autonomous national republic (established within SSRs and within the RSFSR)
bedniak (pl. *bedniaki*):	Soviet term for "poor peasant"
byt:	way of life, culture
Goskolonit:	State Colonization Research Institute
Gosplan:	State Planning Commission, responsible for union-wide economic plan
guberniia (pl. *gubernii*):	province, large administrative-territorial unit of the Russian Empire
IAE:	Institute of Anthropology and Ethnography (formed in 1933)
inorodets (pl. *inorodtsy*):	non-Russian "alien"
IRGO:	Imperial Russian Geographical Society
IPIN:	Institute for the Study of the *Narodnosti* of the USSR (formerly KIPS)
KEPS:	Commission for the Study of the Natural Productive Forces of Russia (later, of the USSR)
KIPS:	Commission for the Study of the Tribal Composition of the Population of the Borderlands of Russia (later, of Russia; of the USSR and Contiguous Countries)
kolkhoz:	collective farm
krai (pl. *kraia*):	large administrative-territorial unit in the RSFSR, comprised of oblasts and in some cases also ASSRs
kulak:	Soviet term for "wealthy peasant"
LONO:	Leningrad Department of Education
MAE:	Museum of Anthropology and Ethnography
Narkomnats:	People's Commissariat for the Affairs of the Nationalities
Narkompros:	People's Commissariat of Enlightenment
NKVD:	People's Commissariat of Internal Affairs
oblast:	large district or province, administrative-territorial unit in the Soviet republics
okrug (pl. *okruga*):	regional administrative unit, larger than a *raion* and

	smaller than an oblast
raion (pl. *raiony*):	regional administrative unit, smaller than an *okrug* or an oblast
raionirovanie:	regionalization, the process of delimiting administrative-territorial units
RSFSR:	Russian Soviet Federation of Socialist Republics
seredniak (pl. *seredniaki*):	Soviet term for "middle peasant"
SOPS:	Council for the Study of the Productive Forces of the USSR (formed in 1930)
soslovie:	social estate (status) category in the Russian Empire
sovkhoz:	state farm
SSR:	union republic
TSFSR:	Transcaucasian Soviet Federative Socialist Republic
TsIK:	Central Executive Committee of the Soviet government
TsSU:	Central Statistical Administration
TsUNKhU:	Central Administration of the National-Economic Inventory (formerly TsSU)
uezd (pl. *uezdy*):	regional administrative unit of the Russian Empire, smaller than a *guberniia*
volost' (pl. *volosty*):	local-level administrative unit of the Russian Empire, smaller than an *uezd*
VTsIK:	All-Russian Central Executive Committee (of the RSFSR government)

EMPIRE OF NATIONS

Introduction

> In the modern age history emerged as something it never had been before. It was no longer composed of the deeds and sufferings of men, and it no longer told the story of events affecting the lives of men; it became a man-made process, the only all-comprehending process which owed its existence exclusively to the human race.
>
> —Hannah Arendt, *Between Past and Future*, 1968

1991 was a year of phenomenal events—bearing witness to the collapse and dissolution of the Soviet Union and the official end of the Cold War. The geopolitical map of Europe and Asia changed rapidly and dramatically. Observers in the West looked with awe, concern, and confusion on the emergence of national movements and national conflicts, and the formation of new nation states, in the lands of the former USSR. Accustomed to seeing the Soviet state as a monolith and to thinking about "Russians" and "Soviets" as one and the same, many politicians, journalists, and scholars asked: Where had all these nations come from? What kind of state had the Soviet Union been? What was the Soviet socialist experiment all about? These were some of the questions that I had on my mind when I first set foot in the archives of the former Soviet Union in 1994 and began to research the institutional, political, social, and scientific processes that had shaped the formation of the Soviet Union. They are the questions at the heart of this book.

1991 and the Paradigm Shift

From the perspective of today, it is perhaps difficult to remember just how surprised people were by the fracturing of the Soviet Union along national lines in 1991. But even some of the most astute observers of Soviet affairs were nothing less than shocked—and with good reason. For decades, national conflicts and national tensions within the Soviet Union had been a "blank spot" on the historical record. Throughout the Cold War, most Western histories of the Soviet Union focused on Russia and the Russians. To be sure, these years saw the publication in the West of some excellent monographs about the USSR's non-Russian nationalities, and following the Soviet invasion of Afghanistan, European and American scholars wrote a number of important books about Islam under communism.[1] But such works constituted their own subfields outside of the mainstream and were not integrated into any of the "master narratives" of the Bolshevik Revolution that were then vying for dominance. Moreover, these works reflected the general biases of the time. Many portrayed the non-Russian nationalities as the hapless victims of "Soviet-Russian" rule, as inmates of the Soviet "prison of peoples," and as nonparticipants in the revolution. Most took a "top-down approach" and gave limited attention to the complex nature of local-level interests and conflicts.[2]

How can this conflation of "Russian" and "Soviet" be explained? What accounts for the relative lack of interest that most scholars in the West showed towards the non-Russian nationalities of the USSR during the Cold War? To some degree, this orientation toward "Russia" reflected practical considerations. It was difficult enough for scholars to gain access to archives in Moscow and Leningrad; it was all but impossible for them to do so in the national republics. But even more important, this orientation was the consequence of seeing the Soviet Union through the lens of the Cold War. As the Soviet Union and the United States became embroiled in conflicts across the globe, Western observers became accustomed to thinking about "the Soviets" as an undifferentiated whole, and as the polar opposite of "the Americans." The Soviet lead-

1. See, for example, Nicholas P. Vakar, *Belorussia: The Making of a Nation, A Case Study* (Cambridge, MA, 1956); John Stephen Reshetar, *The Ukrainian Revolution, 1917–1920: A Study in Nationalism* (Princeton, 1952); Alfred Senn, *The Great Powers: Lithuania and the Vilna Question, 1920–1928* (Leiden, 1966); Jurij Borys, *The Sovietization of Ukraine, 1917–1923: The Communist Doctrine and Practice of National Self-Determination* (Edmonton, 1980); Teresa Rakowska-Harmstone, *Russia and Nationalism in Central Asia: The Case of Tadzhikistan* (Baltimore, 1970); Gregory J. Massell, *The Surrogate Proletariat: Moslem Women and Revolutionary Strategies in Soviet Central Asia, 1919–1929* (Princeton, 1974); Alexandre Bennigsen and Chantal Lemercier-Quelquejay, *Islam in the Soviet Union* (London, 1967); Alexandre Bennigsen and S. Enders Wimbush, *Muslim National Communism in the Soviet Union: A Revolutionary Strategy for the Colonial World* (Chicago, 1979); and Alexandre Bennigsen and Marie Broxup, *The Islamic Threat to the Soviet State* (London, 1983). Some of the most insightful works about the Soviet approach to the nationality question were written before the start of the Cold War. See, for example, Hans Kohn, *Nationalism in the Soviet Union* (New York, 1933), and Oscar J. Janowsky, *Nationalities and National Minorities* (New York, 1945).

2. In this, many followed the approach of the "totalitarian school" which gained predominance during the Cold War. For a work that strongly aligns itself with the totalitarian school but also gives a detailed account of local-level interests see Richard Pipes, *The Formation of the Soviet Union: Communism and Nationalism, 1917–1923*, rev. ed. (Cambridge, MA, 1997). Pipes's work was first published in 1954.

ership, for its part, encouraged this view with its own claims about the existence of a unified Soviet people (*Sovetskii narod*).[3]

The end of Soviet rule brought about a major paradigm shift. As new nation states emerged out of the Soviet colossus, a new literature appeared, making what was at the time a controversial and original argument: that the Soviet regime had deliberately "made" territorial nations. As described in one of these works, the Bolsheviks had pursued a policy of "compensatory nation-building"—actively "creating" many of those nationalities (such as the Uzbeks and the Belorussians) that subsequently claimed independence in the face of the Soviet economic and political collapse.[4] Meanwhile, at the same moment that scholars in the West were writing about the unexpectedly "progressive" character of Soviet nationality policy, leaders and scholars in the post-Soviet nation states began using the language of decolonization to hail the demise of a communist empire that had subjugated non-Russians to Moscow's will.[5] In creating a postcolonial narrative, these leaders and scholars drew on Western works from the height of the Cold War that characterized the Soviet Union as a colonial empire and "breaker of nations."[6]

---

3. See, for example, D. T. Shepilov, *Velikii sovetskii narod* (Moscow, 1947), and Viktor Sherstobitov, *Sovetskii narod: Monolitnaia obshchnost' stroitelei kommunizma* (Moscow, 1976).

4. Yuri Slezkine, "The USSR as a Communal Apartment, or How a Socialist State Promoted Ethnic Particularism," *Slavic Review* 53, no. 2 (1994): 414–52. See also Ronald Grigor Suny, *The Revenge of the Past: Nationalism, Revolution, and the Collapse of the Soviet Union* (Stanford, 1993); Rogers Brubaker, *Nationalism Reframed: Nationhood and the National Question in the New Europe* (Cambridge, 1996); Ben Fowkes, *The Disintegration of the Soviet Union: A Study in the Rise and Triumph of Nationalism* (New York, 1997); Jeremy Smith, *The Bolsheviks and the National Question, 1917–23* (Houndmill, UK, 1999); and Gerhard Simon, *Nationalism and Policy toward the Nationalities in the Soviet Union: From Totalitarian Dictatorship to Post-Stalinist Society* (Boulder, 1991). Simon's work first appeared in German in 1986, *before* the Soviet collapse. Some authors such as Suny attributed the Soviet collapse to the nationality question. Others did not make that causal link. Much of this literature was influenced by works that appeared in the 1980s and 1990s, discussing the "construction" of modern nations. These include Ernest Gellner, *Nations and Nationalism* (Ithaca, 1983); E. J. Hobsbawm, *Nations and Nationalism since 1780: Programme, Myth, Reality* (Cambridge, 1990); and Benedict Anderson, *Imagined Communities: Reflections on the Origin and Spread of Nationalism*, rev. ed. (London, 1991). The authors of these works wrote from a Marxist perspective (or, in the case of Gellner, with the Soviet example in mind). Like Marx, and like the Bolsheviks, they saw "the nation" as the product of the capitalist era—arising with industrialization, the spread of print culture, and so on.

5. See, for example, Stephen Velychenko, "The Issue of Russian Colonialism in Ukrainian Thought: Dependency Identity and Development," *Ab Imperio*, no. 1 (2002): 323–67. Velychenko notes: "Eight of Ukraine's thirteen political parties referred to the country as an exploited country in their programs" in 1991. He also discusses a 1995 Ukrainian textbook that "specifically identified Soviet Ukraine as a colony and its party organization as a colonial administration serving the interests of an 'occupation regime.'" See also Rakhim Masov, *Istoriia topornogo razdeleniia* (Dushanbe, 1991), and Masov, *Tadzhiki: Istoriia s grifom "sovershenno sekretno"* (Dushanbe, 1995).

6. In particular, they drew on the work of British scholars who had been writing as the British Empire was undergoing its own painful process of decolonization. Examples of this British scholarship include Robert Conquest, *The Last Empire* (London, 1962); Olaf Caroe, *Soviet Empire:*

Empire, Nation, and the Making of the Soviet Union

Following the wave of post-1991 scholarship, historians have engaged in a lively debate about whether the Soviet Union was an empire, a new type of state that "made nations," or some combination thereof. Some scholars have addressed this question by taking a comparative approach, by sketching out typologies of "nations" and "empires" and then suggesting where the Soviet Union fits in.[7] Others have mined the theoretical literature about nation-building, nationalism, and colonialism—borrowing models or key phrases from other historical contexts to describe Soviet policies and practices, and making arguments about the Soviet case largely by means of analogy.[8] And still others have attempted to locate the roots of the Soviet approach to the "nationality question" (*natsional'nyi vopros*) within the broad context of "European modernity."[9] All of these approaches place the Soviet Union within a larger international context, refrain from making claims of Soviet exceptionalism, and (rightly) treat the Soviet regime's handling of the nationality question as fundamental to the narrative of the Bolshevik Revolution. But when it comes to discussing the unique form of the Soviet state and the nature of Soviet rule, ultimately all have more descriptive than explanatory power.

This book takes a different approach. Taking as a given that the Soviet Union bore a strong resemblance to other modernizing empires and that its constituent parts, the national republics and national oblasts (districts), looked somewhat like nation states, it sets out to explain exactly *how* and *why* this came to be so. More specifically, it investigates how European ideas about "nation" and "empire" crossed into Russia and then changed form in the Soviet context with its Marxist vision of historical development. Arguing that the

---

The Turks of Central Asia and Stalinism (London, 1953); and Walter Kolarz, *Communism and Colonialism* (London, 1964). Conquest restates and expands on his arguments in Conquest, *Stalin: Breaker of Nations* (London, 1991).

7. See, for example, Alexander J. Motyl, "Thinking About Empire," in *After Empire: Multi-ethnic Societies and Nation-Building,* ed. Karen Barkey and Mark von Hagen (Boulder, 1997), 19–29, and Karen Dawisha and Bruce Parrot, eds., *The End of Empire? The Transformation of the USSR in Comparative Perspective* (Armonk, NY, 1997). For a comparison of the Soviet Union and other empires that avoids such typologizing see Dominic Lieven, *Empire: The Russian Empire and Its Rivals* (New Haven, 2000).

8. For the application of the term *affirmative action* to the Soviet context, see Terry Martin, *The Affirmative Action Empire: Nations and Nationalism in the Soviet Union, 1923–1939* (Ithaca, 2001). Paula Michaels, in her work on medical propaganda in Soviet Kazakhstan, draws from the literature about British imperialism and medicine, but does not explain why the Soviet and the British cases were similar. See Paula A. Michaels, "Medical Propaganda and the Cultural Revolution in Soviet Kazakhstan, 1928–41," *The Russian Review* 59, no. 2 (2000): 159–78.

9. See, for example, David L. Hoffman, "European Modernity and Soviet Socialism," in *Russian Modernity: Politics, Knowledge, Practices,* ed. David L. Hoffman and Yanni Kotsonis (New York, 2000), 245–60. Hoffman draws on the ideas of Zygmunt Bauman. See Bauman, *Modernity and the Holocaust* (Ithaca, 1989).

Soviet Union took shape through a process of selective borrowing, it traces the transmission of ideas and practices from the West into the Soviet Union; the efforts of Soviet leaders, experts, and local elites to redefine those ideas and practices to pursue specific, and sometimes competing, agendas; and the "activation" of those ideas and practices "on the ground" among different population groups.

This book is about the formation of the Soviet Union. It is concerned both with the official creation of the Union of Soviet Socialist Republics in 1922 and with the far longer and more intensive process of transforming the lands and peoples within that state's borders.[10] In particular, it seeks to understand how the Bolsheviks went about changing the individual and group identities of the population of the former Russian Empire. Eschewing the "prison of peoples" view of the Soviet Union, this book treats the "Sovietization" of all of the peoples within Soviet borders (non-Russians and Russians alike) as an interactive and participatory process. The Bolsheviks did not wish to just establish control over the peoples of the former Russian Empire; they set out to bring those peoples into the revolution and secure their active involvement in the great socialist experiment. To meet such ambitious goals, the Bolsheviks could not rely on coercion and force alone. They forged alliances with former impe- rial experts, secured the loyalties of local elites, and introduced administrative and social structures that encouraged or demanded mass participation.

No issue was more central to the formation of the Soviet Union than the na- tionality question. The Bolsheviks had set themselves the task of building socialism in a vast multiethnic landscape populated by hundreds of different settled and nomadic peoples belonging to a multitude of linguistic, confessional (religious), and ethnic groups. That they were attempting to do so in an age of nationalism, against the backdrop of the Paris Peace Conference's exaltation of the "national idea," only added to this enormous challenge. Before 1917, the Bolsheviks had called for the national self-determination of all peoples and had condemned all forms of colonization as exploitative. After attaining power, however, they began to express concern that it would not be possible for Soviet Russia to survive without the cotton of Turkestan and the oil of the Caucasus. In an effort to reconcile their anti-imperialist position with their strong desire to hold on to all of the lands of the former Russian Empire, the Bolsheviks integrated the national idea into the administrative-territorial structure of the new Soviet Union. With the assistance of former imperial ethnographers and local elites, they placed all of the peoples of the former Russian Empire into a definitional grid of official nationalities—simultane-

10. On the official formation of the Soviet Union in 1922 see Pipes, *Formation of the Soviet Union*; Smith, *Bolsheviks and the National Question*; and E. H. Carr, *The Bolshevik Revolution, 1917–1923*, vol. 1 (New York, 1950). On the Soviet attempt to transform non-Russian regions see Douglas Northrop, *Veiled Empire: Gender and Power in Stalinist Central Asia* (Ithaca, 2004), and Adrienne Lynn Edgar, *Tribal Nation: The Making of Soviet Turkmenistan* (Princeton, 2004).

ously granting these peoples "nationhood" and facilitating centralized rule. With the assistance of former imperial economists, they articulated a program of "Soviet colonization," which they defined as a plan for the state-directed development of productive forces, without the imperialistic exploitation of "less-developed" peoples by "more-developed" peoples.

It is impossible to understand the Bolsheviks' approach to the nationality question without considering their Marxist-Leninist view of the world.[11] The Bolsheviks took from Karl Marx the ideas that there was a "logic" (or "telos") to history, and that it was possible to get on the "right side" of the historical process by carefully interpreting its inner dynamics and figuring out where one stood on the timeline of development.[12] They also took from Marx and from Friedrich Engels the basic precepts that all social orders were built on economic structures; that the development of "productive forces" propelled societies forward; and that societies would evolve from their primeval origins through the stages of feudalism, capitalism, and socialism before making the final transition to communism.[13] It was with these ideas in mind that the Bolsheviks made a careful study of the European nation states and their empires. They saw Western Europe as occupying a position ahead of Russia on the timeline of development, and thus as an indicator of where Russia was heading. However, the Bolsheviks hoped to do much more than follow in Europe's footsteps. They held the conviction that it was possible—and desirable—not just to interpret the inner dynamics of the historical process, but to seize control of history and push it forward.[14] Marx had suggested that changes to the "economic base" would bring about corresponding changes in social forms and culture (which he considered part of the "superstructure"). The Bolsheviks, by contrast, set out to accelerate the historical process by acting on the economic base, social forms, and culture *all at the same time*. Before the Bolsheviks could even begin to attempt this monumental task, they needed accurate information about the social forms and cultures that prevailed in the former Russian Empire.

The Bolsheviks could not have realized their goals without assistance. The leaders of the new party-state had a comprehensive worldview and a secular

---

11. An important premise of this book is that ideology mattered a great deal to the Bolsheviks. For discussions of the importance of ideology to the Soviet project see Stephen Kotkin, *Magnetic Mountain: Stalinism as a Civilization* (Berkeley, 1995); Peter Holquist, *Making War, Forging Revolution: Russia's Continuum of Crisis, 1914–1921* (Cambridge, MA, 2002); Igal Halfin, *From Darkness to Light: Class, Consciousness, and Salvation in Revolutionary Russia* (Pittsburgh, 2000); Martin Malia, *The Soviet Tragedy: A History of Socialism in Russia, 1917–1991* (New York, 1994); and Amir Weiner, *Making Sense of War: The Second World War and the Fate of the Bolshevik Revolution* (Princeton, 2001).

12. On the Bolshevik understanding of history see Halfin, *From Darkness to Light,* 82; Malia, *Soviet Tragedy;* G. A. Cohen, *Karl Marx's Theory of History: A Defense* (Princeton, 2000); and Hoffman, "European Modernity and Soviet Socialism."

13. For an elaboration of this idea see Cohen, *Karl Marx's Theory of History.*

14. See Halfin, *From Darkness to Light,* and Malia, *Soviet Tragedy.*

vision of progress, but lacked even the most basic knowledge about the lands and peoples of the former Russian Empire.[15] From the start, they found themselves relying on former imperial experts such as ethnographers and economists—who themselves looked to Europe for approaches to solving Russia's economic and social problems. Many of these experts had lived and studied in Europe. All were well versed in the politics of nationalism and in the practices of empire. Like the Bolsheviks, these experts saw Russia's problems and potential through the prism of Europe's experiences, and like the Bolsheviks they had enormous faith in the transformative power of scientific government and in the idea of progress. Vladimir Il'ich Lenin and other Bolshevik leaders had the good sense and the good fortune to forge an alliance with these experts, who helped them to spread the revolution, attain the conceptual conquest of their domain, and feel their way toward a revolutionary nationality policy.

The Commission for the Study of the Tribal Composition of the Population of Russia (*Komissiia po izucheniiu plemennogo sostava naseleniia Rossii* [KIPS]) was one group of such experts. Formed in February 1917, KIPS was made up of ethnographers who had evaluated Russia's ethnographic composition during the First World War, as the nationality question began to take on international political significance. Russia's ethnographers had long envied their Western counterparts for the influence they imagined them to have in their own governments' colonial projects. As expert-consultants to the Bolsheviks, the KIPS ethnographers would play a far greater role in the work of government than most European or American anthropologists had ever done. These ethnographers would produce all-union censuses, assist government commissions charged with delimiting the USSR's internal borders, lead expeditions to study "the human being as a productive force," and create ethnographic exhibits and civic education courses about "The Peoples of the USSR." Indeed, scholars of European colonialism who have asserted that anthropologists were "never indispensable to the grand process of imperial power" and played a "trivial" role in "maintaining structures of imperial rule" might want to reconsider their arguments in light of the Soviet case.[16]

The KIPS ethnographers did not just provide the Soviet regime with much-needed information, but also helped it formulate a unique approach to transforming the population. This approach, which I call "state-sponsored evolutionism," was a Soviet version of the civilizing mission that was grounded in the Marxist conception of development through historical stages and also drew on European anthropological theories about cultural evolutionism (which, like Marxism, subscribed to a teleological vision of "spatialized

---

15. I use the terms *party-state* and *Soviet regime* interchangeably. The Soviet Union is often referred to as a party-state because it was a one-party state with overlapping party and government personnel.

16. Quoted from Talal Asad, "Afterword: From the History of Colonial Anthropology to the Anthropology of Western Hegemony," in *Colonial Situations: Essays on the Contextualization of Ethnographic Knowledge*, ed. George W. Stocking, Jr. (Madison, 1991), 315.

time").[17] State-sponsored evolutionism put a unique spin on the national idea, gaining its impetus from the Leninist position that it was possible to speed up the evolution of the population through the stages on the Marxist timeline of historical development. Beginning in the 1920s, the Soviet regime and its ethnographers attempted to take charge of the process of nation formation in regions where clan and tribal identities prevailed and where local populations seemed to lack national consciousness. They did so on the grounds that clans and tribes were "feudal-era" social forms—and that the amalgamation and consolidation of clans and tribes into nationalities (which had taken place in Europe during the transition to capitalism) was the requisite next step on the road to socialism. Ethnographers tried to help the regime predict which clans and tribes would eventually come together and form new nationalities—a task that required great leaps of faith. Ethnographers, along with local elites, then worked with the Soviet government to create national territories and official national languages and cultures for these groups. State-sponsored evolutionism was thus premised on the belief that "primordial" ethnic groups were the building blocks of nationalities *and* on the assumption that the state could intervene in the natural process of development and "construct" modern nations. Indeed, discussions in the post-1991 literature about whether the Soviet regime had a constructivist or a primordialist conception of nationality create a false dichotomy given the Bolsheviks' Marxist-Leninist view of the world.[18]

What were the goals of state-sponsored evolutionism? First of all, state-sponsored evolutionism was not the same thing as national self-determination. Nor was it a program of "making nations" for their own sake. Even as the Soviet regime was amalgamating clans and tribes into nationalities, it reneged on (or "reinterpreted") its earlier promise of national self-determination and condemned all attempts to separate from the Soviet state as "bourgeois nationalist." Second of all, state-sponsored evolutionism was not a form of "affirmative action" intended to promote "national minorities" at the expense of "national majorities."[19] The short-term goal of state-sponsored evolutionism was to "assist" the potential victims of *Soviet* economic modernization, and thus to differentiate the Soviet state from the "imperialistic empires" it disdained. The long-term goal was to usher the *entire* population through the Marxist timeline of historical development: to transform feudal-era clans and tribes into nationalities, and nationalities into socialist-era nations—which, at

---

17. Johannes Fabian, *Time and the Other: How Anthropology Makes Its Object* (New York, 1983), chapter 1.

18. Here I disagree with Martin, who argues that during the mid-1930s "there was a dramatic turn away from the former Soviet view of nations as fundamentally modern constructs and toward an emphasis on the deep primordial roots of modern nations." *Affirmative Action Empire,* 443. See also Ronald Grigor Suny, "Constructing Primordialism: Old Histories for New Nations," *Journal of Modern History* 73, no. 4 (December 2001): 862–96.

19. Here, too, I am arguing against Martin, *Affirmative Action Empire.*

some point in the future, would merge together under communism.[20] This larger vision provides an important context for understanding the regime's effort in the 1930s to amalgamate nationalities into a smaller number of "developed" socialist nations. Some historians have characterized this later effort as a "retreat" (from an "affirmative action" agenda, for example).[21] This book, by contrast, makes the case that it was in line with the Soviet regime's long-term goals—and that it marked an attempt to further accelerate the revolution and to speed the transition to the communist future.

The Bolsheviks took state-sponsored evolutionism very seriously, putting far more effort into realizing its ends than the European colonial empires had put into their own civilizing missions.[22] Characterizing "backwardness" as the result of sociohistorical circumstances and not of innate racial or biological traits, Soviet leaders maintained that all peoples could "evolve" and thrive in new Soviet conditions. The party-state devoted significant resources to furthering the population's ethnohistorical evolution, establishing official national territories, cultures, languages, and histories. It also made a major push to "indigenize" local institutions—training Uzbek, Belorussian, and other "national communists" to serve in government and party bodies in the national republics, oblasts, and regions.

It would be a mistake, however, to idealize the Soviet approach to its population. The party-state was both high-minded and vicious at the same time—combining its more "beneficent" policies with the use of violence and terror. It attacked traditional culture and religion, destroyed local communities, and persecuted individuals and groups that exhibited "spontaneous nationalism." It imprisoned, deported, and in some cases executed individuals and entire communities for the "crime" of "bourgeois nationalism." Moreover, the policy of state-sponsored evolutionism itself did not mean that all clans and tribes would have the opportunity to develop into *separate* nations. During the 1920s, at the height of what some historians describe as the regime's period of "ethnophilia," Soviet leaders and experts endeavored to *wipe out* the languages, cultures, and separate identities of hundreds of clans and tribes in

20. On the evolution of peoples through the stages on the Marxist timeline see Yuri Slezkine, *Arctic Mirrors: Russia and the Small Peoples of the North* (Ithaca, 1994).

21. Martin argues that the regime abandoned its "affirmative action" programs in the 1930s—missing the fact that *from the start* Soviet policies were oriented toward the amalgamation of ethnohistorical groups. The 1930s saw the *acceleration* of this process, not a retreat from it. In arguing that this period saw a "retreat," Martin is drawing on the work of Nicholas S. Timasheff, *The Great Retreat: The Growth and Decline of Communism in Russia* (New York, 1946).

22. The Soviet drive to transform the most remote areas of its domain stands in marked contrast to the British Empire, where "only a minority of the subjected peoples" had real cultural, political, and economic ties with the center. Anderson, *Imagined Communities,* 92. On the British case also see George W. Stocking, Jr., *After Tylor: British Social Anthropology, 1888–1951* (Madison, 1995), and David Cannadine, *Ornamentalism: How the British Saw Their Empire* (New York, 2001).

order to "help" them to "evolve" (and/or amalgamate) into new official nationalities.[23]

Ethnographic Knowledge

A major concern of this book is the role of ethnographic knowledge in the formation of the Soviet Union. I use the term *ethnographic knowledge* to refer to two main types of information. The first is the "academic, but practical" knowledge that professional ethnographers, anthropologists, geographers, and other experts collected and compiled for the Soviet regime, often with the explicit intention of facilitating the work of government.[24] Russian and early Soviet ethnography (*etnografiia*) was a broad field of inquiry, which included under its umbrella the disciplines of geography, archaeology, physical anthropology, and linguistics. It shared important similarities with European cultural anthropology, but was distinct from Russian and Soviet anthropology (*antropologiia*), which was a narrower field, focusing on physical anthropology.[25] Former imperial ethnographers provided the party-state with ethnographic reports, inventories of lands and peoples, maps, charts of kinship structures, and other materials, which it used to make sense of local populations, spread the revolution, and consolidate Soviet rule. These experts also developed a standardized vocabulary of nationality, using specific terms (such as *narodnost'*, *natsional'nost'*, and *natsiia*) to refer to ethnic groups at different stages of development.

The second type of information is the local knowledge that local leaders and administrators supplied to central party and government institutions about the lands and peoples within their direct purview.[26] Some of these local elites were self-defined communists and held official Soviet positions. Others had a more tenuous relationship with the Soviet regime. Most were engaged in local power struggles and seized on the national idea as a means of promoting the interests of their particular communities or constituencies. In some cases, local elites and administrators did their own research, compiling old data and digging up historical materials from local archives. They provided the party-state with

23. On Soviet "ethnophilia," see Slezkine, "The USSR as a Communal Apartment," 415.

24. George W. Stocking, Jr., "Maclay, Kubary, Malinowski: Archetypes from the Dreamtime of Anthropology," in Stocking, ed., *Colonial Situations*, 64.

25. Ernest Gellner, ed., *Soviet and Western Anthropology* (London, 1980), x–xi. Before the revolution and up through the 1920s, the terms *ethnography* (*etnografiia*) and *ethnology* (*etnologiia*) were frequently used as synonyms in Russia. However, the term *ethnology* also came to refer more specifically to the study of physical or racial characteristics.

26. I use the term *local knowledge* somewhat differently from Clifford Geertz. Geertz is interested primarily in how ethnographers, lawyers, and other experts interpret, use, and influence thought and sensibilities. I am interested in how local elites and administrators put together local knowledge for official or expert use. Clifford Geertz, *Local Knowledge: Further Essays in Interpretative Anthropology* (New York, 1983).

their own maps, reports, and surveys—which sometimes confirmed, sometimes contradicted, and sometimes even drew on the experts' information.

Ethnographic knowledge is never value-neutral, although it can appear to be so when it is obtained through scholarly or scientific inquiries. In fact, it is always the product of a series of decisions and judgments, and more often than not it embodies the assumptions and ambitions of those doing the collecting, classifying, and compiling.[27] Ethnographers and other experts chose to use particular approaches or criteria to map out the population based in part on their own training, institutional ties, and preconceived ideas about different peoples and regions. Local elites, for their part, presented party and government commissions with maps or data that supported their own groups' claims to disputed land and other resources. The biases or aspirations of those individuals providing the regime with information mattered a great deal. Whether ethnographers used language, physical type, ethnic origins, or self-definition to ascertain an individual's (or a group's) national membership had an impact on the creation of ethnographic maps that were used to parcel out land. Whether they included only "pure ethnic groups" or "mixed groups" on a list of nationalities determined which peoples were entitled to national rights. Whether local elites claimed to represent local populations on the basis of a shared language, kinship ties, or cultural similarities affected the delimitation of new national territories. This book shows how all of these choices shaped the administrative-territorial structure of the Soviet Union, the allocation of resources to different population groups, and the development of "Soviet" national identities.

Much of the literature about Soviet nationality policy focuses almost exclusively on the party-state, on the grounds that party leaders in Moscow made all meaningful decisions. But in fact the production of knowledge cannot be easily disentangled from the exercise of power in the Soviet Union—or in any other modern state. To be sure, the party-state was the locus of political power. But the party-state did not have a monopoly on knowledge; on the contrary, it depended to a significant degree on the information about the population that experts and local elites provided. By compiling critical ethnographic knowledge that shaped how the regime saw its lands and peoples, and by helping the regime generate official categories and lists, these experts and local elites participated in the formation of the Soviet Union. Sometimes the party-state marshaled ethnographic knowledge to rationalize what were in essence purely political decisions. But more often the party-state used ethnographic knowledge to determine how to formulate its policies.[28]

27. For a similar argument about scientific knowledge see Helen E. Longino, *Science as Social Knowledge: Values and Objectivity in Scientific Inquiry* (Princeton, 1990). See also Michel Foucault, *The Archaeology of Knowledge and the Discourse on Language* (New York, 1972).

28. For a similar argument about the use of scientific knowledge in the Nazi state see Margit Szöllösi-Janze, "National Socialism and the Sciences: Reflections, Conclusions, and Historical Perspectives," in *Science in the Third Reich,* ed. Margit Szöllösi-Janze (Oxford, 2001), 1–35.

All this is not to suggest, however, that ethnographic knowledge can exist fully outside politics. Nor is it to suggest that the party-state and the groups supplying it with ethnographic knowledge had an equal or even reciprocal relationship. The balance of power between the Soviet regime and these groups was always uneven—and their alliance always tenuous. Former imperial experts and local elites shared with the Bolsheviks some short-term goals, but most did not share their Marxist-Leninist worldview or their dream of building socialism. Soviet leaders were willing to overlook these "faults" as long as they were in dire need of information about the population. By 1929, however, the Soviet regime had achieved the basic conceptual conquest of the lands and peoples within its borders, due in large part to the efforts of experts and local elites over the previous decade. That year, the party-state—with Joseph Stalin at the helm—launched an offensive on the "ideological front" in a push to establish control over all individuals and institutions that were engaged in the production of knowledge.[29] Over the course of the next decade, an intricate feedback loop developed: Ethnographic knowledge continued to shape Soviet policies at the same time as the coercive arm of the party-state exerted greater influence over the production of ethnographic knowledge. Ethnographers and other knowledge-producing experts re-created their disciplines from within in an effort to avoid persecution, accommodate the regime's needs, and save their professions. Local elites learned how to show that their nationalism was the correct "Soviet" kind, devoid of "bourgeois" tendencies and ambitions.

Ethnographic Knowledge and Cultural Technologies of Rule

In discussing the production of ethnographic knowledge in the Soviet Union, this book investigates what scholars of European colonialism call "cultural technologies of rule": those forms of enumeration, mapping, and surveying that "modern" states use to order and understand a complicated human and geographical landscape.[30] It argues that in the Soviet Union, as in other modern states or empires, these techniques supported and strengthened centralized

29. This offensive accompanied the industrialization and collectivization campaigns that were part of Stalin's "revolution from above." The party's campaign to seize control of scientific and cultural institutions during this period is often referred to in Western historiography as the "cultural revolution." I prefer to discuss this as a campaign on the "ideological front" for two reasons. First, the campaign was about more than just culture. Second, Soviet leaders and experts *themselves* used the term *cultural revolution* to refer to their campaign to "bring culture to" or "civilize" "backward" regions. I discuss this in detail in chapter 5. Sheila Fitzpatrick, writing not long after China's cultural revolution, was the first to use the term *cultural revolution* to refer to the party's attack on scientific and cultural institutions. See Sheila Fitzpatrick, "Cultural Revolution as Class War," in *Cultural Revolution in Russia, 1928–1931*, ed. Sheila Fitzpatrick (Bloomington, 1978), 8–40.

30. Nicholas B. Dirks is the originator of the term. See Dirks's "Foreword" to Bernard S. Cohn, *Colonialism and its Forms of Knowledge: The British in India* (Princeton, 1996), ix, and Nicholas B. Dirks, *Castes of Mind: Colonialism and the Making of Modern India* (Princeton, 2001). See also Clifton Crais, "Chiefs and Bureaucrats in the Making of Empire: A Drama from

rule, serving as a complement to force and coercion. It further argues that in the Soviet case, cultural technologies of rule were used with the intention of enacting a revolutionary agenda. Whereas the European colonial empires often used such technologies (intentionally or not) to "create new categories and oppositions between colonizers and colonized, European and Asian, modern and traditional," the Soviet party-state used them to *eliminate* these oppositions— to "modernize" and transform all the lands and peoples of the former Russian Empire and bring them into the Soviet whole.[31] In the late 1930s, the Soviet regime used these same technologies to establish a different kind of opposition—between "Soviet" and "non-Soviet" (suspect, outsider, foreign) nationalities.

This book devotes special attention to the census, the map, and the museum—three cultural technologies of rule that brought ethnographers and other experts into contact with local contexts and with state power. To be sure, these are just a small sampling of the cultural technologies of rule that are fundamental to the work of state-building.[32] I focus on them in particular because of their important role in the production and dissemination of ethnographic knowledge. The population census, the administrative-territorial map, and the ethnographic museum were crucial to the creation of an official definitional grid of nationalities in the Soviet Union. Benedict Anderson's work *Imagined Communities* first brought to my attention the possible connections among census, map, and museum in the modern state.[33] But whereas Anderson takes the "crucial intersection" or "linkage" of census, map, and museum as a given, this book explores the interconnections *and* disjunctures among them. It does so in part by focusing on a group of experts who had a significant role in all three enterprises. In the Soviet Union, the same ethnographers who were drawing up an official "List of the Nationalities of the USSR" for the Central Statistical Administration to give to its census takers were also creating new maps for government commissions and new museum exhibits about

---

the Transkei, South Africa, October 1880," *The American Historical Review* 108, no. 4 (2003) 1034–60.

31. The quote is from Dirks, "Foreword," in Cohn, *Colonialism and its Forms of Knowledge,* ix.

32. One could also look at the educational curriculum, the judicial system, print media, and so on.

33. Anderson, *Imagined Communities.* On the census also see Bernard S. Cohn, "The Census, Social Structure and Objectification in South Asia," in *An Anthropologist Among the Historians and Other Essays* (New Delhi, 1987), 224–54, and Arjun Appadurai, "Number in the Colonial Imagination," in Carol A. Breckenridge and Peter van der Veer, eds., *Orientalism and the Postcolonial Predicament: Perspectives on South Asia* (Philadelphia, 1993), 314–39. Also see the essays in David Kertzer and Dominique Arel, eds., *Census and Identity: The Politics of Race, Ethnicity, and Language in National Censuses* (Cambridge, 2002). On maps and border-making see Matthew Edney, *Mapping an Empire: The Geographical Construction of British India, 1765–1843* (Chicago, 1997). On exhibiting see Herman Lebovics, *True France: The Wars over Cultural Identity, 1900–1945* (Ithaca, 1992).

"The Peoples of the USSR." Each of these enterprises affected the others. And yet during the 1920s they did not correspond completely: many of the nationalities included on the list were not represented on the maps or in the ethnographic exhibits. The Soviet Union was a work in progress—and Soviet ethnographers working for the party-state would spend the next two decades trying to bring census, map, and museum into closer agreement.

Census, map, and museum all facilitated a process I call "double assimilation": the assimilation of a diverse population into nationality categories and, simultaneously, the assimilation of those nationally categorized groups into the Soviet state and society. Census-taking and border-making were couched in the language of self-determination but were in fact powerful "disciplining" mechanisms that facilitated administrative consolidation and control. The categorization of the entire population according to "nationality"—including clans and tribes that lacked national consciousness—helped the regime to pursue its agenda of state-sponsored evolutionism. The establishment of new national territories and national institutions proved to be an effective means to integrate the entire non-Russian population into a unified Soviet state. Finally, the ethnographic museum served as an important venue for experts and administrators to work out and disseminate an official narrative about the transformation of the Russian Empire into the Soviet Union—a narrative that highlighted the development of peoples of the USSR under the aegis of Soviet power.

It must be emphasized that double assimilation was an interactive process. The regime did not just impose official categories or narratives on the population. Instead, these categories and narratives were generated as well as activated through expert and mass participation. Preparations for the All-Union Census involved unionwide deliberations among Soviet leaders, experts, and local elites about which peoples to include on an official "List of the Nationalities of the USSR." The census itself was then conducted through one-on-one interviews between census takers and respondents. Indeed, while the census called for national "self-definition," local populations often learned *through* these interviews how to define themselves in official terms. Border-making, too, involved intense expert and local participation. Border-dispute commissions consulted with experts and local elites, and also solicited petitions from the localities. Local elites, treating border delimitation as a means to obtain territories and resources, spread the Soviet "national idea" among their populations—and helped to integrate those populations into the Soviet whole. Meanwhile, visitors to the ethnographic museum (and other cultural institutions) were encouraged to imagine themselves into the emerging official narrative about the peoples of the USSR and were also asked to give their "socialist criticism" of the exhibits and presentations.

What does this model of "double assimilation" suggest about the nature of Soviet rule? This book, like a number of works written after 1991, attempts to move beyond a Cold War-era debate between "totalitarian-model" and "revisionist-model" histories. The "totalitarian school" in many of its 1960s and 1970s incarnations assumed that the party-state had achieved total control over the population during the Stalin era, and thus that social processes did not bear studying. The "revisionist school," by contrast, tended to focus on social processes—and interpreted the airing of local grievances and the pursuit of local agendas as evidence that Soviet state control was not "total."[34] Both groups gave little credence to Hannah Arendt's argument (set out in her 1951 work *The Origins of Totalitarianism*) that the Soviet regime established and maintained power through a process of mass mobilization.[35] This book argues that it is imperative to pay close attention to the particular vocabularies, categories, and narratives that individuals and groups used when expressing their complaints and aspirations, and to whether or not they were pursuing local agendas through official channels.[36] It suggests that insofar as people used official Soviet language and interacted with Soviet institutions, their participation "from below" actually helped to assimilate the Union's disparate parts and strengthen Soviet rule. Even local populations who attempted to use official categories and vocabularies to "resist" Soviet power and pursue their own aims ended up reifying those categories and vocabularies—and were thus brought into the Soviet fold.

The Changing European Backdrop

Soviet leaders and experts formulated their ideas about "nation" and "empire" not just in dialogue with each other, but also in dialogue with other states. The European "age of empire" and the First World War (which saw the popularization of the national idea) were the critical backdrop for the early years of Soviet state formation. But neither this backdrop nor the Soviet regime's policies and practices remained static. The Soviet approach to the population continued to evolve in the 1930s, in large part in response to what I call the "dual threat": the ideological challenge of Nazi race theories and the geopolitical danger of "imperialist encirclement." The Nazi positions that cultural and behavioral traits were linked to racial traits, that racial traits derived from "immutable genetic material," and that social measures could not improve the human condition all posed direct challenges to the Bolshevik worldview. At the same time, the Bolsheviks' long-held fears of "imperialist encir-

34. Classic examples of the "totalitarian school" include Leonard Schapiro, "The Concept of Totalitarianism," *Survey*, no. 73 (1969): 93–115, and Carl J. Friedrich and Zbigniew K. Brzezinski, *Totalitarian Dictatorship and Autocracy* (Cambridge, MA, 1965). Classic examples of the "revisionist school" include Moshe Lewin, *The Making of the Soviet System: Essays in the Social History of Interwar Russia* (New York, 1985), and Sheila Fitzpatrick, *Education and Social Mobility in the Soviet Union* (Cambridge, 1979).

35. Hannah Arendt, *The Origins of Totalitarianism*, rev. ed. (San Diego, 1979).

36. On the importance of participation to the Soviet project, and on the phenomenon of people learning to "speak Bolshevik," see Kotkin, *Magnetic Mountain*.

clement" began to seem all too real as the Japanese made incursions into the Soviet Far East in the 1930s and the Nazis claimed the right to intervene in the affairs of ethnic Germans in the Soviet Union. Challenging Soviet aspirations on ideological grounds and posing a threat to Soviet borders, the Nazis and their allies thus endangered the Soviet project of socialist transformation on two fronts at once.

The spread of national socialist ideas after 1930, and the consolidation of the Nazi German state in 1933, elicited a strong response from the Soviet regime—ultimately resulting in a push to further accelerate the revolution and its process of state-sponsored evolutionism. Beginning in 1931 (as national socialist ideas spread among German scientists), the Soviet regime called on its ethnographers and anthropologists to define race in Marxist-Leninist terms and to gather evidence supporting the Soviet position that social conditions— and not racial traits—determined human development. These experts set out to prove that nurture trumped nature, that "backwardness" was the result of sociohistorical (and not biological) factors, and that state-sponsored evolutionism had already proved a success. At the same time, the Soviet regime took measures to defend its borderlands and other regions of economic and geopolitical significance from "unreliable elements," including the so-called "diaspora nationalities"—a group that included Germans, Poles, and other nationalities with homelands in other states. A line was drawn between "Soviet" and "foreign" nations, and the latter were brutally cast out of the Soviet whole. In effect, in its effort to counter the dual threat, the Soviet regime took a firm stand against biological determinism at the same time as it persecuted people with the "wrong" ethnic origins. This book explores the tension between these two policies and its implications for understanding the nature of the Soviet project.

Framework

Many works about Soviet nationality policy adopt what has become a standard chronology for thinking about Soviet history. They begin with the years of the "New Economic Policy" (1923 to 1928), continue with the era of the "Socialist Offensive" and the "Cultural Revolution" (1928 to 1932), and then move on to the period of the "Great Retreat" (1933 to 1938). This book follows a somewhat different periodization and challenges some of these conventional labels. It explores continuities and disjunctures between 1905 and 1941 from the perspective of different historical actors, and looks at major events from the perspective of different regions of the Soviet Union. It also examines how Soviet leaders and experts themselves used terms such as *cultural revolution*.

Part 1, "Empire, Nation, and the Scientific State," treats the period between 1905 and 1924 as a whole—analyzing a series of choices that the Bolsheviks made about how to "make a revolution" in a multiethnic empire and create a new type of state. Chapter 1 asks how late-imperial experts and Bolshevik leaders came to form a working relationship after the Bolshevik seizure of power, and looks at the ideas and approaches that both sides brought to the table. It places particular emphasis on the impact of the First World War on the development of these ideas and approaches. Chapter 2 analyzes the interinstitutional debate about the administrative-territorial organization of the Soviet state. It looks at two competing models for Soviet state organization: the ethnographic paradigm (which took the "national idea" as its starting point) and the economic paradigm (which drew inspiration from the European colonial economies). Together, these chapters evaluate the influence of European ideas about nation, empire, and economic development on the Bolsheviks, on the former imperial experts, and on the process of Soviet state formation.

Part 2, "Cultural Technologies of Rule and the Nature of Soviet Power," focuses on the decade from 1924 to 1934—analyzing the "Sovietization" of the new Soviet Union. It describes the period of 1924 to 1929 as one in which the regime attained the basic conceptual conquest of the lands and peoples within its borders, and the period of 1929 to 1934 as one in which the regime (now armed with critical information) attempted to make a "great break" (*velikii perelom*) with the past. Chapter 3 evaluates the First All-Union Census, which was conducted in 1926, as an important tool of state-building that provided the Soviet regime with ethnographic knowledge and also facilitated the revolutionary transformation of the population. Chapter 4 investigates the delimitation of new administrative-territorial units (national republics and oblasts) in accordance with ethnographic and economic criteria. Together, these two chapters suggest that the creation of official national categories, along with the introduction of policies that entitled nationalities (as opposed to clans and tribes) to territories and resources, encouraged people to rearticulate their identities and concerns in official "national" terms. Chapter 5 looks at the Ethnographic Department of the Russian Museum, tracing the efforts of experts and political-enlightenment activists to determine what "Soviet nationalities" should look like and to come up with an official narrative about the formation of the USSR. It examines museumgoers' written responses to exhibits and discusses how those responses were used during the period of the "great break" to fuel the campaign on the ideological front.

Part 3, "The Nazi Threat and the Acceleration of the Bolshevik Revolution," focuses on the period between 1931 and 1941, examining the Soviet regime's reaction to the Nazis. It argues that beginning in 1931, in the midst of the "great break," the regime reforged its alliance with former imperial experts in order to focus on an external foe: German race science. It depicts the period from 1934 to 1941 as one in which the regime attempted to secure the Soviet Union's borders and to push forward (*not* retreat from) the process of revolutionary transformation. Chapter 6 focuses on joint ethnographical-anthropological research expeditions to Central Asia, the Far East, and other regions; it looks at the efforts of anthropologists and ethnographers to refute

German claims about the racial inferiority of the Soviet population and to come up with an appropriate explanation for the continuing "backwardness" of some of these regions. Chapter 7 looks at the efforts of ethnographers to use the Second All-Union Census (taken first in 1937 and again in 1939) to dramatically further the amalgamation of nationalities into Soviet nations. It also looks at the spread of the internal passport—another cultural technology of rule. It argues that the census and the passport together institutionalized a distinction between "Soviet" and "foreign" nations and enabled the regime to monitor and persecute (actual or suspected) members of the latter group.

This book investigates the Soviet approach to the nationality question and the development of the field of Soviet ethnography, with the aim of gaining insight into the dynamics of Soviet rule. Rather than focus exclusively on scientific institutions or the party-state, it looks at important sites of interaction among experts, local elites, the party-state, and the general population. It is my hope that by studying how the Soviet Union was formed, and by examining the connection between national-identity formation and Sovietization during the first several decades of Soviet rule, we can begin to understand not just why the Soviet Union fell apart along particular national lines in 1991, but how it endured for more than seventy years.

PART I

Empire, Nation, and the Scientific State

CHAPTER 1

Toward a Revolutionary Alliance

I know Russia so little. Simbirsk, Kazan, Petersburg, and that's about it.
—Vladimir Lenin, 1907, quoted in *Lenin: A Biography* (2000)

When the Bolsheviks staged a successful coup in October 1917, they proclaimed the dawn of a new era. Vladimir Il'ich Ul'ianov Lenin imagined that Russia's revolution would spark European socialist revolutions, creating a new international order. In the meantime, he and his comrades turned their attention to preserving and furthering the revolution's gains within the former Russian Empire. The Bolshevik Party engaged in agitation and propaganda, denouncing enemies and rallying mass support. It also turned to work at which the revolutionaries were unpracticed: the work of government.

As Russia's new rulers, the Bolsheviks claimed vast lands with a multilingual and multiethnic population. This posed an ideological as well as a practical challenge. Karl Marx had not imagined that the socialist revolution would happen in an empire like Russia. As an underground political party, the Bolsheviks had given much attention to the Russian Empire's economic and nationality problems, writing polemics on both themes. But as the new government in power in 1917, they still had much to learn about the expanse in which they hoped to put theory into practice and build socialism. Many leading Bolsheviks had spent long years in European exile and were out of touch with actual conditions in much of Russia. They advocated economic transformation and promised national self-determination, but lacked detailed knowledge about the former empire's lands and peoples.

In late 1917, an unlikely group came to the Bolsheviks' aid. Sergei F. Ol'denburg, permanent secretary of the Academy of Sciences, offered the Bolsheviks the expertise of ethnographers, geographers, linguists, and other scholars, many of whom had loyally served the Tsar. These experts included in their ranks leading political figures from the recently deposed Provisional Government. Ol'denburg was a member of the Constitutional Democratic Party (the

Kadets) and a self-described constitutional monarchist. He and his colleagues opposed the Bolsheviks as extremists and were aware that the Bolsheviks characterized them as class enemies. But instead of fleeing Russia or collaborating with anti-Bolshevik forces, they actively sought an alliance with the Bolsheviks. They saw in this alliance the opportunity to help Russia in the war, to preserve their scientific institutions, and to pursue their own revolutionary agenda—using scientific knowledge to turn Russia into a modern state.[1] The Bolsheviks, for their part, recognized Ol'denburg and his colleagues as valuable providers of direly needed information about the lands and peoples of the Russian Empire. Two Academy of Sciences commissions were already doing the types of ethnographic and economic inventories of Russia that Lenin himself deemed necessary.

This alliance between Bolsheviks and liberal experts was facilitated by the fact that Ol'denburg and Vladimir Ul'ianov had a personal history. The two men met for the first time in 1891.[2] Ol'denburg, who had recently returned from a two-year trip to Paris, London, and Cambridge, was completing his graduate work in Oriental Studies and teaching Indian languages and literatures at St. Petersburg University. At age twenty-nine, he was a published scholar with an international reputation.[3] Ul'ianov, a law student whose revolutionary activities had led to his expulsion from Kazan University, had recently been granted permission to take the jurisprudence exams as an external student at St. Petersburg University. In March 1891, the twenty-one-year-old Ul'ianov went to St. Petersburg for the exams and while in the capital visited Ol'denburg.[4] He hoped to learn more about his older brother Aleksandr, who had been executed in 1887 for his part in an unsuccessful conspiracy to assassinate Tsar Aleksandr III. Aleksandr Ul'ianov had attended St. Petersburg University in the 1880s, where he and Ol'denburg had traveled in the same circles. Both had been members of the Student Scientific-Literary Association, a brotherhood and haven for liberal and radical idealists.[5]

1. For a similar point about the revolutionary goals of liberal experts, see Peter Holquist, *Making War, Forging Revolution: Russia's Continuum of Crisis, 1914–1921* (Cambridge, MA, 2002), introduction and chapter 1.

2. S. F. Ol'denburg, "Neskol'ko vospominanii ob A. I. i V. I. Ul'ianovykh," *Krasnaia letopis'*, no. 2 (1924): 17–18; P. N. Pospelov, *Lenin i Akademiia nauk: Sbornik dokumentov* (Moscow, 1969), 89–94; and G. I. Golikov, *Vladimir Il'ich Lenin: Biograficheskaia khronika, 1870–1924*, vol. 1 (Moscow, 1970), 55. A. P. Baziiants discusses different accounts of this meeting in "Dve vstrechi S. F. Ol'denburga s V. I. Leninym i razvitie sovetskogo vostokovedeniia," in *Sergei Fedorovich Ol'denburg*, ed. G. K. Skriabin et al. (Moscow, 1986), 21–28. (Pospelov dates the meeting to 1887, and Baziiants to 1891.)

3. I. D. Serebriakov, "Po stranitsam arkhiva akademika S. F. Ol'denburga," in *Sergei Fedorovich Ol'denburg*, 101–12.

4. Ibid., and Robert Service, *Lenin: A Biography* (Cambridge, MA, 2000), 83–84.

5. Serebriakov, "Po stranitsam arkhiva akademika S. F. Ol'denburga," 102–4, and Baziiants, "Dve vstrechi S. F. Ol'denburga s V. I. Leninym," 22. Ol'denburg and the elder Ul'ianov had been part of the association's inner circle. Ul'ianov had dropped out of the association while planning the assassination attempt.

Ol'denburg and Vladimir Ul'ianov belonged to the same small world of educated society (*obshchestvo*) which was frustrated with what it saw as Russia's
political, social, and economic "backwardness" vis-a-vis the West. Both men
were critics of the tsarist state, as well as advocates of rational government and
science-based reform. Both shared a broad European orientation, a fascination
with the French Revolution, a secular (materialistic) worldview, and a desire to
see Russia's transformation. But Ol'denburg and Ul'ianov imagined this transformation in different terms and chose different personal paths. Ul'ianov's
path took him through the Russian and European revolutionary underground:
to prison, forced Siberian exile, and eventually to Europe.[6] From Europe, he
published his strategies for revolution under the pseudonym Lenin. While
Ul'ianov dreamed of overthrowing the imperial government, Ol'denburg rapidly rose through the ranks of its scholarly institutions. He became a member
of the Academy of Sciences in 1901 and was chosen to serve as its permanent
secretary in 1904.[7] After 1905 he became increasingly active in the Imperial
Russian Geographical Society (IRGO).

By 1905, Ol'denburg and Ul'ianov had established their career paths and
their politics; over the course of the next decade, each in his own way undertook a study of the Russian Empire's "nationality question." For most of the
period between 1905 and 1917, Ul'ianov lived in Western Europe and the
Austro-Hungarian Empire, debating with other socialists and developing his
own theory about the role of national movements in a socialist revolution. Ol'-
denburg spent these years in Russia, organizing research expeditions and
studying the lands and peoples of the empire. Upon becoming reacquainted in
November 1917, the two men discovered that they had a similar appreciation
for the potential of scientific government and a shared interest in the nationality question. They forged a working relationship between radical revolutionaries and liberal experts—a relationship that shaped the very formation of the
Soviet Union.

6. Ol'denburg was born in 1863 in Zabaikalsk province in eastern Siberia, to a family of noble
German origin. Ul'ianov was born in 1870 in Simbirsk, a provincial capital on the Volga; the son
of a school inspector, he too was a hereditary noble but was not titled. Ul'ianov returned briefly to
St. Petersburg in 1905, when he learned of the widespread demonstrations in Russia; when the
workers' revolution did not come to pass he again fled abroad. Service, *Lenin: A Biography*,
13–30, 102–3, 129–30, 170–71, 181–87; Serebriakov, "Po stranitsam arkhiva akademika S. F.
Ol'denburga," 107; Loren R. Graham, *Science in Russia and the Soviet Union: A Short History*
(Cambridge, 1993), 83–85; Larry E. Holmes, "Sergei Fedorovich Ol'denburg," in Joseph L.
Wieczynski, ed., *The Modern Encyclopedia of Russian and Soviet History*, vol. 25 (Gulf Breeze,
FL, 1981), 237; Richard Pipes, ed., *The Unknown Lenin: From the Secret Archives* (New Haven,
1996), 19; and "Osnovnye daty zhizni i deiatel'nosti S. F. Ol'denburga," in *Sergei Fedorovich Ol'-
denburg*, 120.

7. Ol'denburg was an expert on India and Turkestan and chair of Indian languages and literatures at St. Petersburg University. See G. M. Bongard-Levin, "Indologicheskoe i buddologicheskoe
nasledie S. F. Ol'denburga," in *Sergei Fedorovich Ol'denburg*, 30, 41–42; B. V. Lunin, "Istorik
vostokovedeniia (Iz nauchnogo naslediia akademika S. F. Ol'denburga)," in *Sergei Fedorovich
Ol'denburg*, 78; and Baziiants, "Dve vstrechi S. F. Ol'denburga s V. I. Leninym," 26.

This chapter treats Soviet nationality policy as the product of a collaborative effort between Bolsheviks and imperial experts—two groups whose ideas took shape within a broader pan-European framework and crystallized in the wake of the First World War. Unlike many studies of Soviet nationality policy, which begin in 1917 or 1923 and treat Lenin and Joseph Stalin as the sole architects of Soviet policies and practices, this chapter takes as its focus the years between 1905 and 1917 and weaves together two separate but related stories.[8] The first of these stories traces how Bolshevik theories about nationalism and national movements evolved in response to the intense politicization of the "national idea" in Europe. The second investigates how European ideas about *Volk* and "nation" and about the scientific management of empire crossed into Russia via a group of ethnographers and other experts. The two stories converge after October 1917, when the Bolsheviks and the experts came together and began to formulate a unique "Soviet" approach to the peoples of the Russian Empire—by drawing on a range of European and Russian practices and ideas (including the theories of Marx and Friedrich Engels) as well as responding to certain "facts on the ground" such as the appearance of new national separatist movements, which themselves drew inspiration from the European context. The Bolsheviks and the experts were driven by conflicting long-term goals. But in 1917 both groups put their differences aside and began the work of transforming the former Russian Empire into a new type of multinational state based not on "God" and "Tsar," but on a secular vision of progress.

The Nationality Question and the Bolsheviks

The Russian Empire's nationality question became the focus of increasing official attention after the failed revolution of 1905. Newspapers reported that demonstrations that year had taken on a "national character" in the western borderlands, Transcaucasia, and even Siberia. Tsar Nicholas II attempted to appease the empire's non-Russian population by guaranteeing its participation in the new constitutional assembly, the State Duma.[9] But nationality-based po-

8. For examples see Gerhard Simon, *Nationalism and Policy toward the Nationalities in the Soviet Union: From Totalitarian Dictatorship to Post-Stalinist Society* (Boulder, 1991); Hélène Carrère d'Encausse, *The Great Challenge: Nationalities and the Bolshevik State, 1917–1930* (New York, 1992); Jeremy Smith, *The Bolsheviks and the National Question, 1917–1921* (Houndmills, UK, 1999); and Terry Martin, *The Affirmative Action Empire: Nations and Nationalism in the Soviet Union, 1923–1939* (Ithaca, 2001). For an exception, see Richard Pipes, *The Formation of the Soviet Union: Communism and Nationalism, 1917–1923*, rev. ed. (Cambridge, MA, 1997). Pipes begins earlier and focuses not just on the Bolsheviks, but also on the development of local nationalist movements.

9. The State Duma was the lower chamber of the bicameral parliament established in 1905. Elections to the First State Duma in 1906 were organized according to the categories *soslovie* and/or *nationality* in some regions in order to ensure that non-Russian delegates were selected. Charles Steinwedel notes that "the means used to categorize people by nationality were not specified and often not consistent." Charles Steinwedel, "The 1905 Revolution in Ufa: Mass Politics, Elections, and Nationality," *The Russian Review* 59, no. 4 (2000): 574.

litical parties, which gained visibility in 1905, had more ambitious goals: they demanded that the Tsar grant the empire's nationalities cultural and (some form of) political autonomy. These parties were relatively small and did not represent mass movements, but after 1905 they attained a disproportionately important role in the empire's civic life. Some sought and achieved representation in the Duma. Others did not participate directly in imperial politics, but instead worked out their programs in European exile; the socialists among them fraternized with Russian Social Democrats.[10]

Most of the empire's nationality-based political parties drew on proposals that had been advanced over the previous ten years for the nationalities of the Austro-Hungarian Empire. Some appropriated the argument made by the Austrian Social Democrats at the 1899 Bruenn Congress that nationalities were entitled to national-territorial autonomy—to administrative regions established on the basis of ethnographic criteria.[11] Others adopted the argument advanced by the South Slavs at the Bruenn Congress that every nationality was entitled to extraterritorial (cultural) autonomy or "self-rule in linguistic and cultural matters" regardless of territorial divisions. The South Slav proposal (later adopted and further developed by the Austrian Social Democrats Otto Bauer and Karl Renner) became a critical part of the national program of the Jewish Socialist Party, the Bund; the Bund then introduced it to other nationality-based parties in the Russian Empire.[12]

By 1905 Lenin and the Russian Social Democrats had started to formulate their own position on the nationality question. They too developed their ideas in dialogue with the Austrian Social Democrats and with the Bund. At this time, Lenin dismissed the importance of the nationality question in the Russian Empire, arguing that there was nothing particularly "nationalist" about the demonstrations of 1905: that these local populations were expressing the *universal* desire for equal rights. He was, however, concerned about the threat that nationalism posed to the international unity of the Social Democrats; this threat seemed especially acute as Jewish, Georgian, and other groups of socialists advocated the reorganization of the Social Democratic Party into national divisions.[13] Lenin critiqued the Bruenn Congress proposals that had become popular among these socialists, maintaining that they would delay the socialist revolution. Extraterritorial autonomy would erect barriers between workers of

10. Many of these political parties existed underground before the establishment of the Duma in 1905. See Pipes, *Formation of the Soviet Union*.

11. Richard Pipes, *The Russian Revolution* (New York, 1990), 19.

12. Pipes, *Formation of the Soviet Union*, 24, 27–28. Also Tom Bottomore and Patrick Goode, eds., *Austro-Marxism* (Oxford, 1978). Other nationality-based parties included the Belorussian Hromada and the Armenian Dashnaks.

13. See, for example, V. I. Lenin, "Proekt rezoliutsii o vykhode Bunda iz RSDRP," "Poslednee slovo bundovskogo natsionalizma," and "Rezoliutsiia 'Ob otnoshenii k natsional'nym sotsial-demokraticheskim organizatsiiam,'" in V. I. Lenin, KPSS, *O bor'be s natsionalizmom: Dokumenty i materialy* (Moscow, 1985), 120, 129–31, 175.

different nationalities; federalism would decentralize the state and impede economic development.[14] Yet Lenin also dismissed the argument of Polish Social Democrat Rosa Luxemburg that socialists, as committed internationalists, should not support national movements at all. According to Lenin, to not uphold the right of an oppressed nation to secede from an oppressive state would be to support despotism.[15]

By all accounts, Lenin began to take a greater interest in Russia's nationality question in 1912, when he took up residence in Krakow, a hotbed of national tension in the Austro-Hungarian Empire. In Krakow, Lenin became better acquainted with the national struggles among Austria-Hungary's multinational population.[16] These struggles seemed all the more serious against the backdrop of the Balkan wars, which were being fought by Serbs, Croats, Slovenes, and Bosnians in the name of "national liberation."[17] It was an episode in St. Petersburg, however, that most strongly impressed on Lenin the importance of clarifying the Bolshevik position. In a December 1912 speech before the Fourth State Duma, the Georgian Social Democrat Akaki Chkhenkeli, a Menshevik, demanded extraterritorial autonomy for the nationalities of the Russian Empire. Lenin was irate that the Georgian Mensheviks had adopted the "South Slav solution" (by this time espoused enthusiastically by Austrian Social Democrats) and had introduced it before the Duma as part of the Russian Social Democratic program.[18]

The following month at a party meeting in Krakow, Lenin condemned the Georgian Menshevik position and asked a young Georgian Bolshevik to write an essay critiquing the idea of extraterritorial autonomy. The Georgian Bolshevik was Iosif Vissarionovich Dzhugashvili. His article, "The Nationality Question and Social Democracy," appeared in the party journal *Prosveshchenie (Enlightenment)*, under the pseudonym Stalin, in spring 1913. It was Stalin's debut as a writer on important matters of party policy; four years later, he would be named Commissar of Nationalities of a new Soviet government.

14. Pipes, *Formation of the Soviet Union*, 33. In 1903 the Russian Social Democrats had added a clause to their program asserting their support for the "right of self-determination for all nations comprising the state." The Second International had endorsed this clause in 1896. Walker Connor, *The National Question in Marxist-Leninist Theory and Strategy* (Princeton, 1984), 30. According to Lenin, if a nation chose not to secede, it had no other rights *as a nation*. Its members, however, had the right to demand equal rights with the members of other nations in "matters of language, education, and culture." E. H. Carr, *The Bolshevik Revolution, 1917–1923*, vol. 1 (New York, 1950), 420.

15. V. I. Lenin, "Natsional'nyi vopros v nashei programme," in Lenin, KPSS, *O bor'be s natsionalizmom*, 125–28.

16. Carr, *Bolshevik Revolution*, vol. 1, 418; Connor, *National Question in Marxist-Leninist Theory and Strategy*, 30; Pipes, *Formation of the Soviet Union*, 35; and B. D. Wolfe, *Three Who Made a Revolution* (New York, 1948), 580.

17. V. I. Lenin, "Balkanskaia voina i burzhuaznyi shovinizm," in Lenin, KPSS, *O bor'be s natsionalizmom*, 20–21, and Connor, *National Question in Marxist-Leninist Theory and Strategy*, 30.

18. Pipes, *Formation of the Soviet Union*, 37.

The article (probably written at least in part under Lenin's guidance) called on Social Democrats to work "indefatigably against the fog of nationalism." It criticized the Bund and the Georgian Mensheviks for promoting "purely nationalist aims."[19]

Stalin's article attacked the principle of extraterritorial autonomy on the grounds that it strengthened national differences, which would otherwise dissipate as class consciousness grew. According to Stalin, the Austrian Social Democrats had made a critical mistake in assuming that nations (*natsii*) were permanent entities. In fact, he argued, "the nation" was a "historically-specific" temporary category that belonged to "the epoch of rising capitalism." Turning his attention to the Russian Empire, he explained that the "profound upheaval of 1905" and the "industrial boom" that followed had furthered the development of capitalism, especially in the western borderlands. It was capitalism that was leading to the "economic consolidation of the nationalities of Russia" and was "stirring them into action." It was the new State Duma, an institution of bourgeois government, that was providing "a new and wide arena" for nationality-based political parties to mobilize.[20]

Stalin also addressed the issue of "national rights." In principle, so long as a nation existed, it had the right to extraterritorial autonomy and the right to "enter into federal relations" with other nations, Stalin noted. However, this did not mean that Social Democrats would indiscriminately support these rights; Social Democrats were committed "to defend the interests of the proletariat," and nations were made up "of various classes." Stalin maintained that even Social Democratic support for the right to secession was not unconditional: separation had to benefit the "toiling strata."[21] For example, Social Democrats could not support the secession of the Transcaucasian Tatars (the Azeris of Azerbaijan) from the state, because to do so would be to deliver their masses "to the mercies of" Tatar "beys and mullahs" (religious leaders).[22] This qualification, along with the assumption that only the party could determine what was "advantageous" for the masses, was at the heart of the Bolshevik position.

Stalin did recommend a solution to the nationality question for nations choosing not to secede from the Russian Empire during the "transitional period" of rising capitalism. Suggesting that national movements had come into existence as a result of political and economic oppression—and that most people did not have deep national feelings—he argued that the "nationality question" could be "solved" by granting the population "real rights in the localities they inhabit." In particular, he proposed granting "provincial auton-

19. Ibid., and I. Stalin, "Marksizm i natsional'nyi vopros," in I. Stalin, *Marksizm i natsional'no-kolonial'nyi vopros: Sbornik izbrannykh statei i rechei* (Moscow, 1935), 4.

20. Stalin, "Marksizm i natsional'nyi vopros," 10–11.

21. Ibid., 14–15. Lenin first made this point in his 1903 "Natsional'nyi vopros v nashei programme."

22. Stalin, "Marksizm i natsional'nyi vopros," 15.

omy" (*oblastnaia avtonomiia*) to "such crystallized units" as Transcaucasia, Ukraine, and Poland. Provincial autonomy differed from extraterritorial autonomy and federalism in that it did not divide the population along strictly ethnographic lines. National majorities and minorities would live together in autonomous oblasts (districts), and their members would possess the same rights, including the right to use their native languages. To encourage the spirit of internationalism, "the workers of all nationalities" of each autonomous oblast would be organized into proletarian organizations, which would be united into "a single party"; in time, "international solidarity" would supplant national sentiment.[23]

While Stalin was writing his first major article, Lenin continued to develop his critique of the arguments of the Austrian Social Democrats and Rosa Luxemburg.[24] In early 1914 Lenin wrote the article "On the Right of Nations to Self-Determination," an important theoretical work that also appeared in *Prosveshchenie*.[25] Lenin's article, like Stalin's, was a polemic written for other Social Democrats. The Bolsheviks used such polemics to facilitate discussion on important issues. Only later would these pieces take on the status of "sacred texts" to which Soviet leaders and officials would look for appropriate passages to promote or explain different policies. The two articles had different emphases, reflecting their specific purposes. Stalin's piece was directed against the proponents of extraterritorial autonomy and was intended to rally other Social Democrats to "resist nationalism."[26] Lenin's article was aimed at those Social Democrats who disparaged the very principle of national self-determination. Lenin explained why Bolshevik support for *certain* national movements in countries at *certain* stages of historical development could facilitate worldwide socialist revolution. The article represented a theoretical breakthrough, suggesting that in some cases socialists could use the forces of nationalism to their own ends.

Alluding to Marx's theory of history (which suggested that different economic structures corresponded to different stages on a timeline of historical development), Lenin argued that Marxists were obligated to analyze all social questions with regard to "the concrete historical moment" in which they exist. When considering the nationality question, he explained, Marxists must make a strict distinction between the period of "developing [or rising] capitalism" and the period of "developed capitalism." In the period of developing capitalism, the bourgeoisie and the workers join together to overthrow an absolutist

23. Ibid., 42–44.

24. Lenin wrote "Kriticheskie zametki po natsional'nomu voprosu" in late 1913 and "O prave natsii na samoopredelenie" in early 1914. He also wrote a number of shorter pieces on the nationality question during this period. See Lenin, KPSS, *O bor'be s natsionalizmom*.

25. V. I. Lenin, "O prave natsii na samoopredelenie," in *Polnoe sobranie sochinenii*, vol. 25 (Moscow, 1961), 257–320.

26. Stalin, "Marksizm i natsional'nyi vopros," 3–4.

regime; national movements become mass movements and draw "*all* classes of the population into politics." In the period of developed capitalism, "crystallized capitalist states" are the norm and the relationship between the bourgeoisie and the workers becomes antagonistic.[27] Lenin explained that Western Europe and Russia were currently at different moments of the capitalist stage. Europe had experienced its "bourgeois-democratic revolutions" between 1789 and 1871, and had since entered the era of developed capitalism. In Russia, by contrast, "the period of bourgeois-democratic revolutions only began in 1905." It was "precisely and solely" because Russia was passing through the period of "developing capitalism" that the Bolsheviks "require an item in our program on the right of nations to self-determination." A "whole series of bourgeois-democratic national movements" are now struggling against feudalism and absolutism in Russia, Lenin explained, and are thus progressive from a Marxist perspective.[28]

Lenin cautioned, however, that it was essential not just to pinpoint where particular countries stood on the Marxist timeline but also to evaluate the concrete political conditions within those countries. In multiethnic states like the Russian Empire, he noted, it was not unusual for some groups to dominate other groups. Indeed, Lenin differentiated between two types of nationalism: oppressor-nation nationalism and oppressed-nation nationalism. He argued that the first was chauvinistic, whereas the second had a democratic impulse. According to Lenin, the "Great Russians in Russia are an oppressor nation," by virtue of the fact that the tsarist regime rejects the "equality of nationalities." The national movements in the empire's western and eastern borderlands, by contrast, were manifestations of "oppressed-nation nationalism." These movements had emerged in response to Great Russian oppression after their members were exposed to the national idea through "kindred nationalities" in neighboring states.[29] Social Democrats were obliged to support, at least in principle, the right of these oppressed nations to secede from the Russian Empire, Lenin argued. He challenged the argument made by the Kadets and numerous Social Democrats that the right to secession would result in the "disintegration of the state" and would hinder economic progress. According to Lenin, most peoples simply wanted equal rights and would "resort to secession" only if "national oppression" made "joint life intolerable."[30]

In 1913 and 1914, Lenin publicized his views on the nationality question among European Social Democrats and worked from afar to introduce them

---

27. Lenin, "O prave natsii na samoopredelenie," 264–65.

28. Ibid., 269.

29. Ibid., 271, 274. He suggested that the non-Russians of the eastern borderlands had learned about the "incipient bourgeois revolutions and national movements" of the Ottoman Empire.

30. Ibid., 287–88. He noted that if a state were to become so unstable that it ceased to function as an economic unit, then "the interests of capitalist development" (a prerequisite for socialism) would be "best served by secession."

into the debate back in Russia.[31] In a May 1914 letter to an Armenian Social Democrat, he maintained that it was imperative for the Bolsheviks to put before the Fourth State Duma their own draft law on the "equality of nations" in order to counter Menshevik proposals for extraterritorial autonomy. Such a draft law would stipulate the "rights of national minorities" and would establish measures to introduce the principle of "provincial autonomy." In particular, it would recommend that the state replace the empire's *guberniia* system (its ninety-seven provinces) with new "autonomous provinces [oblasts]" established on the basis of local "economic and cultural [*bytovye*] conditions" and "the population's national composition." Lenin noted that for such a law to be effective, the Duma would need detailed information about Russia's population. He recommended that in "areas with a mixed population" the Duma conduct a census every five years. He also suggested that local populations compile ethnographic information about themselves.[32] Unbeknownst to Lenin, Ol'denburg and his colleagues at the IRGO were at the time planning their own ethnographic study of the Russian Empire. They too were arguing that the Duma needed ethnographic knowledge to introduce effective reforms.

Ethnographic Knowledge and the Imperial Russian Geographical Society

The decade after 1905 was one of civic activity for experts throughout Russia, and Sergei F. Ol'denburg was the consummate expert-activist. Ol'denburg, who believed that a constitutional monarchy would best serve the needs of science, had reason for optimism in 1905, due to the establishment of the State Duma. That same year, Ol'denburg became a member of the Kadet Party, joining other intellectuals who posited that the development of science and culture could facilitate Russia's social and political transformation.[33] He also became active in the IRGO. The Geographical Society had long been an advocate for

---

31. Pipes, *Formation of the Soviet Union*, 46, and Lenin, "Rezoliutsii letnego 1913 goda," in *Pol'noe sobranie sochinenii*, vol. 24 (Moscow, 1961), 58.

32. Lenin called for a census "not less than once in every ten years throughout the state and not less than once in every five years in oblasts and localities with populations of a heterogeneous national composition." V. I. Lenin, "Proekt zakona o ravnopravii natsii i o zashchite prav natsional'nykh men'shinstv," in *Polnoe sobranie sochinenii*, vol. 25, 137. The proposed draft law was never introduced. The letter (addressed to Stepan Shaumian) is discussed in Wolfe, *Three Who Made a Revolution*, 585–86.

33. N. G. Dumova, *Kadetskaia partiia v period pervoi mirovoi voiny i Fevral'skoi revoliutsii* (Moscow, 1988). Katerina Clark suggests that the men of this circle saw "systematization, rationalization, and a greater role for culture and science as key items on an agenda of social transformation." See Katerina Clark, *Petersburg: Crucible of Cultural Revolution* (Cambridge, MA, 1995), 67. Also Kendall Bailes, "Natural Scientists and the Soviet System," in *Party, State, and Society in the Russian Civil War*, ed. Diane P. Koenker, William G. Rosenberg, and Ronald Grigor Suny (Bloomington, 1989), 269.

political and social reforms, including civil liberties, the spread of education, and greater professional autonomy.[34] With the establishment of the Duma, it became an outspoken proponent of scientifically informed government, and made a determined effort to orient its research toward problems with practical state significance—such as the empire's nationality question.[35]

Members of the Geographical Society's Ethnographic Division were particularly interested in investigating the recent "explosion of nationalism" among the peoples of "Asiatic Russia." Whereas the Bolsheviks focused their attention on the national movements of the western borderlands, the ethnographers looked eastward; asked to write an article for a 1910 volume about "national movements in the Russian, German, and Austro-Hungarian Empires," the ethnographer and Ethnographic Division member Lev Shternberg chose to focus on the indigenous populations (the *inorodtsy* or non-Russian "aliens") of the Kirgiz steppe (part of current-day Kazakhstan), Turkestan, and Siberia.[36] For the ethnographers, the question was as follows: How had the empire's *inorodtsy* attained national consciousness without direct exposure to the European national idea? In a 1909 article, Ol'denburg speculated that the nationality question and the colonial question were linked in Asiatic Russia: that Russian colonization policies had led to the emergence of nationalism in the Russian east.[37] Shternberg expressed a similar view. He noted that the events of 1905—Russia's embarrassing defeat by "little Japan" and the empire-wide demonstrations that followed—had "discredited the old order" and served as a catalyst for "national expression" in Asiatic Russia. But he argued that the tsarist government's colonization and Russification policies of

---

34. IRGO members shared this impulse with members of other professional organizations. See for example Joseph Bradley, "Subjects into Citizens: Societies, Civil Society, and Autocracy in Tsarist Russia," *The American Historical Review* 107, no. 4 (2002): 1094–1123. On the role of intellectuals in imagining a "modern" Russia, see Laura Engelstein, *The Keys to Happiness: Sex and the Search for Modernity in Fin-de-Siècle Russia* (Ithaca, 1992). Also see the essays in Edith Clowes, Samuel Kassow, and James West, eds., *Between Tsar and People: Educated Society and the Quest for Public Identity in Late Imperial Russia* (Princeton, 1991).

35. At their meetings, IRGO members discussed coordinating their work with "routine questions of government." See for example V. Bartol'd, "Khronika: XII s''ezd russkikh estestvoispytatelei i vrachei v Moskve," *Zhivaia starina* 19, no. 1–2 (1910): 176–87, and D. Zolotarev, "Obzor deiatel'nosti Postoiannoi Komissii po sostavleniiu etnograficheskikh kart Rossii pri I.R.G. Obshchestve (15 okt. 1910 g.—15 okt. 1915 g.)," *Zhivaia starina* 25, no. 1 (1916): xi–xxi.

36. Lev Shternberg, "Inorodtsy Obshchii obzor," in *Formy natsional'nago dvizheniia v sovremennykh gosudarstvakh: Avstro-Vengriia, Rossiia, Germaniia*, ed. A. I. Kastelianskii (St. Petersburg, 1910), 533. On the category *inorodtsy*, see John W. Slocum, "Who, and When, Were the *Inorodtsy?*: The Evolution of the Category of 'Aliens' in Imperial Russia," *The Russian Review* 57, no. 2 (1998): 173–90. On Shternberg's life and work, see N. I. Gagen-Torn, *Lev Iakovlevich Shternberg* (Moscow, 1975).

37. Serebriakov, "Po stranitsam arkhiva akademika S. F. Ol'denburga," 108. Ol'denburg also reflected on the Kirgiz and Kazakhs and the colonization question in his personal diary on May 6, 1909. The St. Petersburg Branch of the Archive of the Russian Academy of Sciences (PFA RAN) f. 208, op. 2, d. 9, ll. 12–14.

the previous decade were the more fundamental causes of the "national awakening" in the east.[38]

Shternberg took care to differentiate between two groups of *inorodtsy*. The first group were *inorodtsy* who lived in regions far from the center (such as Turkestan), and who had enjoyed relative economic and cultural independence until the introduction of new imperial colonization policies. According to Shternberg, these *inorodtsy* had developed national consciousness as a direct result of the colonization of their land. He gave the example of the tribes of the Kirgiz steppe—who had long shared a common "language, way of life, and beliefs," but had not considered themselves "a unified people [*edinyi narod*]" or "nationality [*narodnost'*]" until Russian colonization threatened their institutions, land, and access to water.[39] The Buriats, too, had "ascended to national consciousness" in the face of Russian colonial oppression, Shternberg argued; before Russian attempts to seize their land, the Buriats had considered themselves "an aggregate of clans and tribes, but not a people."[40] By contrast, Shternberg described the second group of *inorodtsy* as those who lived interspersed with Russians in regions that had been incorporated into the empire long ago (such as the Volga region). According to Shternberg, these *inorodtsy* had economic concerns similar to those of the Russian peasantry and did not see the "land question" as a matter of colonial oppression. Other issues, such as linguistic Russification and forced conversion to the Orthodox religion, had prompted the development of national sentiment among them, he argued.[41]

The ethnographers, like Bolshevik leaders, characterized national movements as a response to economic and political oppression. Shternberg, noting the "remarkable absence of national separatism" in Asiatic Russia and most of European Russia, argued that most non-Russians wanted greater economic and cultural rights, but not independence from the empire.[42] (In this, he shared Lenin's view that secession posed only a minimal danger.) But while the Bolsheviks debated the potential role of national movements in the socialist revolution, Shternberg and his colleagues sought a more liberal version of the Russian Empire. The ethnographers suggested that the imperial regime could prevent the rise of national separatism, which had become a serious issue for the Austro-Hungarian Empire, if it learned about and responded to the needs of its non-Russian subjects.[43] They imagined a new role for themselves as

38. Shternberg, "Inorodtsy," 535–38.

39. Ibid., 538, 546.

40. Ibid., 540, 546.

41. Shternberg maintained that these issues also had political and economic significance. *Inorodtsy* without the right to use their native language in public life were unable to defend themselves juridically and administratively; *inorodtsy* who had converted to Orthodoxy were being economically oppressed by the Russian clergy.

42. Shternberg, "Inorodtsy," 566.

43. Ibid. On the national idea and national separatism in the Austro-Hungarian Empire, see A. I. Kastelianskii, "Predislovie," in *Formy natsional'nago dvizheniia v sovremennykh gosudarstvakh: Avstro-Vengriia, Rossiia, Germaniia*, i–xiii.

champions of the non-Russian nationalities and defenders of a "unified Russia."[44]

The ethnographers discussed this possible new role in December 1909, at the Twelfth Congress of Russian Natural Scientists and Physicians in Moscow. The prominent IRGO members Dmitrii Anuchin, Vladimir Bogdanov, and Vsevolod Miller convened the congress's ethnographic subsection, where self-defined "professional ethnographers"—a diverse group that included anthropologists, geographers, statisticians, and linguists—called for a more active part for themselves in the work of studying and governing the empire. Contrasting the practical orientation of European and American ethnographers with their own "academicism," they called for a major reform of their discipline.[45]

At first glance, the ethnographers' comments seem disingenuous. A number of Russia's ethnographers had important roles in state-sponsored efforts to categorize the population and to celebrate the empire. Several members of the IRGO's Ethnographic Division, including Veniamin Semenov-Tian-Shanskii and Serafim Patkanov, served on the Central Statistical Committee of the Ministry of Internal Affairs; these men had helped formulate and produce the All-Russian Census of 1897. Other commission members, including Anuchin, had worked on large-scale ethnographic exhibits in Russia and at international fairs like the World Paris Exposition.[46]

But the IRGO ethnographers—who traveled widely, attended international conferences, and read European and American journals—saw themselves as far less active in the work of empire than their peers in Western Europe. And there was some truth to this. The Ministry of Internal Affairs denigrated ethnography (with its focus on nationality) as a "promoter of separatism," and considered professional ethnographers (who advocated a conciliatory approach to the non-Russian population) to be politically unreliable; it did not help matters that Shternberg, Vladimir Bogoraz, and several other ethnographers had taken up ethnography after having been exiled to Siberia in the 1890s for antigovernment activities.[47] For these reasons and others the Tsar

---

44. This position mirrored that of the Kadets, who upheld the unity of empire while calling for greater national rights. See Dumova, *Kadetskaia partiia v period pervoi mirovoi voiny*. Some of the ethnographers had a more radical orientation.

45. Bartol'd, "Khronika: XII s''ezd russkikh estestvoispytatelei i vrachei v Moskve," 176–87, and Zolotarev, "Obzor deiatel'nosti," xi–xxi. Ol'denburg did not attend the meeting. Bartol'd told him about it in a letter dated January 24, 1910. PFA RAN f. 208, op. 3, d. 33, l. 60b. These ethnographers were also pursuing the further professionalization of their discipline. The professionalization of ethnography began in earnest in the 1890s and gained momentum after 1905. The IRGO ethnographers were anxious to differentiate themselves from missionaries and other "amateurs."

46. On Anuchin's time in Europe and his participation in the World Paris Exposition see V. V. Bogdanov, *D. N. Anuchin: Antropolog i geograf, 1843–1923* (Moscow, 1940), 14–16.

47. See D. Ianovich, "K voprosu ob izuchenii byta narodnostei RSFSR," *Zhizn' natsional'nostei*, no. 29 (127) (December 14, 1921): 1. Both Shternberg and Bogoraz had spent time in New

and his ministers looked to local governors-general and military statisticians, and not to professional ethnographers, for information about the population.[48]

It is also true, however, that Russia's ethnographers idealized the position of their European counterparts, often exaggerating the involvement of British and French anthropologists in their governments' colonial projects. To be sure, European anthropologists from a number of countries were providing colonial officials with ethnographic information and helping their governments to work out "forms of administration for subject peoples."[49] But Ol'denburg and Shternberg were motivated by European discussions about "applied anthropology" and "applied ethnography" long before these fields were firmly established. Shternberg seems to have drawn inspiration from news that the British government was establishing an Imperial Bureau of Anthropology, a project that came to naught at the time.[50]

At the 1909 congress, Shternberg proposed that Russia establish its own imperial bureau of ethnography—based on the European model—to undertake empire-wide research and produce maps for official use.[51] Shternberg assured his colleagues that a bureau of this type could serve a liberal agenda, providing the Duma with information needed to improve the lives of the empire's *inorodtsy*. Other ethnographers were less enthusiastic about this proposal, cautioning that their own goals would inevitably be subordinated to those of tsarist bureaucrats. Anuchin was the most vocal critic, arguing that a government-sponsored ethnographic bureau would precipitate a loss of professional autonomy. After some deliberation, the majority sided with Anuchin and rejected Shternberg's proposal.[52]

York, working with Franz Boas. See Bruce Grant's introduction to Lev Shternberg, *The Social Organization of the Gilyak,* ed. Bruce Grant (New York, 1999).

48. On the role of governors-general in Russian imperial rule see David Alan Rich, *The Tsar's Colonels: Professionalism, Strategy, and Subversion in Late Imperial Russia* (Cambridge, MA, 1998).

49. Quoted from T. D. Solovei, " 'Korennoi perelom' v otechestvennoi etnografii (Diskussiia o predmete etnologicheskoi nauki: konets 1920-x–nachalo 1930-x-godov)," *Etnograficheskoe obozrenie,* no. 3 (2001): 102–3. Solovei argues that European anthropology benefited from the "practical demands of colonial policies": that it "enjoyed state protection and support," which "stimulated an active scientific search conducive to the advancement of new concepts and theories." He argues that, by contrast, ethnography in "prerevolutionary Russia" lacked "single-minded and large-scale state support." The literature about European colonialism suggests that Solovei perhaps overstates the *direct* role of European anthropologists in their governments' colonial projects. See, for example, Talal Asad, *Anthropology and the Colonial Encounter* (New York, 1973). Also see Talal Asad, "Afterword: From the History of Colonial Anthropology to the Anthropology of Western Hegemony," in *Colonial Situations: Essays on the Contextualization of Ethnographic Knowledge,* ed. George W. Stocking Jr. (Madison, 1991), 314–24.

50. On the British plans see George W. Stocking, Jr., *After Tylor: British Social Anthropology, 1888–1951* (Madison, 1995), 376–77.

51. Bartol'd, "Khronika: XII s''ezd russkikh estestvoispytatelei i vrachei v Moskve," 179–80.

52. Ibid.

In the wake of the Moscow congress, the Ethnographic Division met back in St. Petersburg.[53] Ol'denburg, who had just been elected its chair, moderated a discussion about the division's goals. The ethnographers called for a closer relationship between experts and the State Duma, and expressed the hope that the Duma would use expert-produced ethnographic knowledge as a tool for political and social reform.[54] It was in this context that the Ethnographic Division integrated Shternberg's suggestions into its own agenda: it would establish a new ethnographic research commission to provide the Duma with ethnographic reports and maps of the empire. In September 1910, Ol'denburg and his colleagues organized the Commission for Establishing Ethnographic Maps of Russia. For the next six years, Ol'denburg chaired or actively participated in the Ethnographic Division and the map commission.[55] Under his leadership, the map commission debated the definition of "nationality," the validity of language as a determinant of nationality, and the viability of using different criteria to categorize the peoples of European versus Asiatic Russia. It made notable progress on a comprehensive ethnographic map of the Russian Empire.[56]

The Vocabulary of Nationality

Between 1908 and 1914, the Bolsheviks and the IRGO ethnographers engaged in different intellectual and political endeavors. Lenin and Stalin participated in a heated political discussion with other socialists about the road to socialism; Ol'denburg and his colleagues gathered "scientific knowledge" about the empire. By the time that Lenin and Ol'denburg became reacquainted in 1917, the revolutionaries and the experts had worked out their own vocabularies of nationality. There was significant overlap in their terminology, which can be attributed to the fact that the Bolsheviks and the ethnographers were part of the same world: both groups, along with other Russian intellectuals, were engaged in a pan-European conversation about the national idea. Yet while the

---

53. Archive of the Russian Geographical Society (RGO) f. 24, op. 1, d. 78, l. 56. These events are recounted in "Zhurnaly zasedanii Otdeleniia Etnografii Imperatorskago Russkago Geografich-eskago Obshchestva: Zasedanie 25 fevraliia 1911 goda," *Zhivaia starina* 20, no. 1 (1911): v–vi, and Zolotarev, "Obzor deiatel'nosti," xi–xxi.

54. Zolotarev, "Obzor deiatel'nosti," xi.

55. Ol'denburg chaired both until late 1912, and reclaimed both chairs in 1915. In the interim period, Vsevolod Miller and then Aleksandr Shakhmatov served in these posts.

56. Russian Geographical Society researchers (such as Petr Keppen and Aleksandr Rittikh) had produced ethnographic maps in the nineteenth century, but these maps were primarily of European Russia. L. S. Berg, *Vsesoiuznoe geograficheskoe obshchestvo za sto let* (Moscow-Leningrad, 1946), 168, and A. N. Pypin, *Istoriia russkoi etnografii*, vol. 4 (St. Petersburg, 1892), 104–5. Veniamin Semenov-Tian-Shanskii and his father, the geographer Petr Semenov-Tian-Shanskii, included detailed ethnographic maps in their eleven-volume *Russia: A Full Geographical Description of Our Fatherland*, which evaluated the empire region by region. See V. P. Semenov-Tian-Shanskii, P. P. Semenov-Tian-Shanskii, and V. I. Lamanskii, eds., *Rossiia: Polnoe geograficheskoe opisanie nashego otechestva*, 11 vols. (St. Petersburg, 1899–1914).

Figure 1.1 Sergei F. Ol'denburg, permanent secretary of the Academy of Sciences and chair of the Imperial Russian Geographical Society's Ethnographic Division. (Archive of the Russian Academy of Sciences, St. Petersburg Branch f. 909, op. 2, d. 44, l. 1)

Bolsheviks and the experts used most of the same terms, and thus seemed to speak the same language, they actually defined these terms somewhat differently. It would later become apparent that the two groups, drawing from a number of European intellectual traditions, were often using the same words to talk about different things.

Ol'denburg and his colleagues used the designations "ethnographic group" and *plemia* (translated as "tribe" or sometimes as "ethnicity") more or less as synonyms. They also used the terms *narodnost'* and *natsional'nost'*, both of which were roughly translated as "nationality." Most frequently the ethnographers used the term *narodnost'*—which derived from *narod*, the Russian word for "people" or *Volk*. When Nikolai Nadezhdin argued in 1846 that Russia's ethnographers should take *narodnost'* as their primary category of study, what he meant was that they should study ethnographic materials reflecting the "essence" of the Russian people.[57]

57. A decade earlier, in an article called "Europeanism and *Narodnost'* in Relation to Russian Literature," Nadezhdin had characterized *narodnost'* as "the totality of all traits, external and internal, physical and spiritual, mental and moral out of which is composed the physiognomy of the Russian person, distinguishing him from all other people." Cited in Nathaniel Knight, "Ethnicity, Nationality and the Masses: *Narodnost'* and Modernity in Imperial Russia," in *Russian Moder-*

Nadezhdin, a founding member of the IRGO's then newly formed Ethnographic Division, was drawing on the ideas of the German romantic Johann Herder. According to Herder, each people had a unique spirit (*Volksgeist*) that was expressed in the language, culture, and customs of the common folk (*Volk*). Nadezhdin was also positioning himself against the "theory of official nationality" as it had been articulated in the 1830s by Sergei Uvarov, minister of education and advisor to Tsar Nicholas I. In the wake of the French Revolution (and against the backdrop of the popular national movements spreading throughout Europe in the 1820s and 1830s), Uvarov looked for a new state ideology that would show Russia to be a part of "European civilization" but would also preserve its own unique "system of social values."[58] He came up with the formula "Orthodoxy, Autocracy, Nationality [*Narodnost'*]," which imagined the Tsar as "the embodiment of" the Russian *narod* or nation.[59] In the 1840s, Russian intellectuals including Nadezhdin used the ideas of the German romantics to "recast the image of the Russian *narod*" and free it from this "autocratic embrace."[60]

Nadezhdin was primarily interested in the Russian peasantry. But other members of the Ethnographic Division subsequently used the same approach to study the non-Russian peoples of the empire, including the *inorodtsy*. Beginning in the 1850s and 1860s, the ethnographers compiled and published ethnographic materials, such as works of folklore and descriptions of *byt* (way of life), which reflected the "essence" of many of the empire's indigenous peoples.[61] By the 1890s—as cultural-evolutionary theories were coming into

---

nity: Politics, Knowledge, Practices, ed. David L. Hoffman and Yanni Kotsonis (New York, 2000), 55.

58. Andrei Zorin, "Ideologiia 'Pravoslaviia-Samoderzhaviia-Narodnosti': Opyt rekonstruktsii," *Novoe literaturnoe obozrenie,* no. 26 (1998): 71–104 (esp. 71, 81–82.) Also Benedict Anderson, *Imagined Communities: Reflections on the Origin and Spread of Nationalism,* rev. ed. (London, 1991), chapter 6.

59. Cited from Knight, "Ethnicity, Nationality and the Masses," 54. Also see Zorin, "Ideologiia 'Pravoslaviia-Samoderzhaviia-Narodnosti,'" 71–104, and Nicholas Riasanovsky, *Nicholas I and Official Nationality* (Berkeley, 1959). Benedict Anderson, in discussing Uvarov's formula, mistakenly presents it as "Autocracy, Orthodoxy, *Natsional'nost'.*" Anderson, *Imagined Communities,* 87. In fact, however, Uvarov chose *narodnost'* (with the Russian root *narod*) in order to differentiate the Russian Empire from the other European states.

60. Quoted from Knight, "Ethnicity, Nationality and the Masses," 56. Knight makes this point regarding "radical intellectuals" such as Alexander Herzen. In a separate article he suggests how Nadezdin used the science of ethnography to pursue similar goals. See Nathaniel Knight, "Science, Empire, and Nationality in the Russian Geographical Society, 1845–1855," in *Imperial Russia: New Histories for the Empire,* ed. Jane Burbank and David L. Ransel (Bloomington, 1998), 108–41. Uvarov too had been influenced by German romantic nationalism.

61. Knight, "Science, Empire, and Nationality in the Russian Geographical Society," 127, 129, 130; Berg, *Vsesoiuznoe geograficheskoe obshchestvo,* 146–47; and Pypin, *Istoriia russkoi etnografii,* 455. Also Nathaniel Knight, "Constructing the Science of Nationality: Ethnography in Mid-Nineteenth Century Russia," Ph.D. diss., Columbia University, 1994. On Herder's ideas see Matti Bunzl, "Franz Boas and the Humboldtian Tradition: From *Volksgeist* and *Nationalcharak-*

vogue in Russia—experts within the Ethnographic Division were using the term *narodnost'* in a number of ways.[62] Sometimes they used it to refer to a specific people with a distinctive language, folk or national culture, and physiognomy: ethnographers spoke about the "Russian *narodnost'*," the "Buriat *narodnost'*," the "Georgian *narodnost'*," and so on. At other times, they used it more narrowly to refer to only that segment of a people that had preserved its *narodnaia* (*völkisch*) culture.

In the early twentieth century, Russian ethnography essentially remained the science of *narodnost'*. Thus, when the IRGO's new map commission convened in 1910, it seemed natural that it should take *narodnost'* as the main category for organizing its research. And yet, as soon the ethnographer Dmitrii Zelenin suggested that it do so, a debate ensued: How should the commission define "this weak and undefined concept"? What traits were most significant in distinguishing one *narodnost'* from another?[63] A number of map commission members, including Aleksandr Shakhmatov, maintained that native language (*rodnoi iazyk*) was one of the most reliable indicators of *narodnost'*.[64] These ethnographers suggested that the commission use data from the 1897 All-Russian Census as the basis for its work. The 1897 census had not included a separate question about *narodnost'*, but had instead categorized most imperial subjects according to native language and confessional group (*veroispovedanie*); the Central Statistical Administration had used these results to compile "a list of the empire's *narodnosti*."[65] Other commission members criticized this formula, maintaining that *narodnost'* was more than just a reflection of language (or language and religion). Shternberg (who had just finished his article about the emergence of national consciousness among the empire's *inorodtsy*) maintained that the commission should look at the population's "self-definition."[66] Fedor Volkov asserted that it was essential for the commission to also map out the population's anthropological (physical or racial)

ter to an Anthropological Concept of Culture," in *Volksgeist as Method and Ethic: Essays on Boasian Ethnography and the German Anthropological Tradition*, ed. George W. Stocking, Jr. (Madison, 1996), 17–78. On Belinskii, Nadezhdin, and the influence of Herder, see Viktor Terras, *Belinskij and Russian Literary Criticism: The Heritage of Organic Aesthetics* (Madison, 1974).

62. On the cultural-evolutionary school in Russia, see T. V. Staniukovich, *Etnograficheskaia nauka i muzei* (Leningrad, 1978), chapter 3. Also see Solovei, " 'Korennoi perelom' v otechestvennoi etnografii," 101–21.

63. RGO f. 24, op. 1, d. 78, ll. 59–620b, 640b–66.

64. Ibid., ll. 65–650b. Zelenin also favored a linguistic approach.

65. A. Kotel'nikov, *Istoriia proizvodstva i razrabotki vseobshchei perepisi naseleniia* (St. Petersburg, 1909), and S. Patkanov, "K tablitsam XIII, XIV, XV i XVI," in *Obshchii svod po imperii rezul'tatov razrabotki dannykh Pervoi vseobshchei perepisi naseleniia proizvedennoi 28 ianvaria 1897 goda*, vol. 2, ed. N. A. Troinitskii (St. Petersburg, 1905), 1–39. This was in keeping with European norms as established at international statistical conferences. The Russian Empire's statisticians attended these conferences. The 1872 conference was held in St. Petersburg. On the 1897 census also see David W. Darrow, "Census as a Technology of Empire," *Ab Imperio*, no. 4 (2002): 145–76.

66. RGO f. 24, op. 1, d. 78, l. 590b.

traits.[67] Most commission members, including Nikolai Mogilianskii, wanted the commission to focus on a combination of language and other ethnographic traits, including those elements of material and spiritual culture that were expressions of a people's *byt*.[68]

These disagreements about the meaning—and the best indicators—of *narodnost'* in part reflected the fact that ethnography, sometimes called ethnology, did not have a strong heritage as a separate academic discipline in Russia (or elsewhere), but included in its purview a number of disciplines including geography, anthropology, history, linguistics, and folklore.[69] The commission's members favored different methodologies in part because they had been trained in different fields. Zelenin and Evfimii Karskii were linguists; Volkov and Sergei Rudenko were physical anthropologists; and Veniamin Semenov-Tian-Shanskii was a geographer. Not only did the commission members have different backgrounds, but they also drew their approaches from competing European traditions. Rudenko and Volkov followed Paul Broca's "French school" of anthropology and studied racial traits. Mogilianskii, taking his methodological approach from the German science of *Völkskunde*, wanted to understand how "racial particularities, geographical milieu, and historical circumstances" shaped the "material and spiritual" lives of individual peoples.[70] Shternberg, deriving his methodology in part from British and American cultural evolutionists such as Edward B. Tylor and Lewis Henry Morgan, attempted to rank the empire's peoples in accordance with their "level of culture."[71]

In the spirit of compromise, the map commission adopted a broad-based approach. Significantly, the commission agreed to consider native language as

67. Zolotarev, "Obzor deiatel'nosti," xvii–xviii.

68. RGO f. 24, op. 1, d. 78, ll. 610b–63.

69. The ethnographer and archaeologist Nikolai Kharuzin had noted in the late nineteenth century that "the science of ethnography is a new science. . . . Some call it ethnography, others ethnology, others consider it part of anthropology, or part of history, or, finally, mix it with sociology. Some scholars consider it a science of natural history, other include it as a social science." The IRGO ethnographers sometimes used the terms *ethnography* and *ethnology* as synonyms; at other times they used the terms to connote different aspects of their discipline. In general, ethnography was considered to be concerned with the study of culture and *byt*, and ethnology concerned with tracing the "possible physical connections" among different peoples. See the discussion in N. Mogilianskii, "Predmet i zadachi etnografii," *Zhivaia starina* 25, no. 1 (1916): 1–22 (esp. 7.) Also see "Zhurnal zasedaniia Otdeleniia Etnografii I.R.G.O. 4 marta 1916 goda," *Zhivaia starina* 25, no. 2–3 (1916): 1–11.

70. Ibid., 17. Also E. G. Kagarov, "Predely etnografii," *Etnografiia*, no. 1 (1928): 13–14.

71. These competing approaches are discussed in the Russian Geographical Society's journal *Zhivaia starina* between 1909 and 1916. For summaries of the major approaches see Mogilianskii, "Predmet i zadachi etnografii," 1–22, and "Zhurnal zasedaniia Otdeleniia Etnografii I.R.G.O. 4 marta 1916 goda," 1–11. On Edward B. Tylor and Russian ethnography see "Zhurnaly zasedanii Otdeleniia Etnografii Imperatorskago Russkago Geograficheskago Obshchestva: Zasedanie 28 oktiabria 1911," xxxi–xxxv. Also see Robert Geraci, "Ethnic Minorities, Anthropology, and Russian National Identity on Trial: The Multan Case, 1892–96," *The Russian Review* 59, no. 4 (2000): 530–54.

Figure 1.2 Sergei Rudenko, physical anthropologist and member of the Imperial Russian Geographical Society's Map Commission. Shown on an expedition in an Ostiak graveyard at the Ob River basin in western Siberia (1910–1911). (Archive of the Russian Academy of Sciences, St. Petersburg Branch f. 1004, op. 1, d. 466, l. 1)

the "primary category" of *narodnost'*; it formed a linguistic subcommission which, using materials from the 1897 census, started drawing up a preliminary list of the empire's *narodnosti*. The commission also agreed to consider data about anthropological type as a complement—or in some cases as a corrective—to data about language. An anthropological subcommission embarked on fieldwork to map out the distribution of particular physical traits; it recorded data about hair, eye, and skin color, and took head and body measurements. The commission also established six additional subcommissions to produce maps of different aspects of *byt* (economic practices, clothing types, dwelling types, folk art, music, and religion) for all of the peoples included on the preliminary list of nationalities. Combined, the linguistic, anthropological, and cultural-*bytovye* maps were supposed to identify the correlations among native language, physical type, and *byt* in the Russian Empire—and to allow the experts to determine which peoples had intermixed.[72]

72. F. Volkov, "Anketnye voprosy Komissii po sostavleniiu etnograficheskikh kart Rossii, sostoiashchei pri Otdelenii Etnografii Imperatorskago Russkago Geograficheskago Obshchestva," *Zhivaia starina* 23, no. 1–2 (1914): 194. Sample questionnaires are attached, 195–212. Also see "Otchet o deiatel'nosti Otdeleniia Etnografii i sostoiashchikh pri nem postoiannykh komissii za 1913 god," *Zhivaia starina* 23, no. 1–2 (1914): vii; "Otchet o deiatel'nosti Otdeleniia Etnografii i sostoiashchikh pri nem postoiannykh komissii za 1912 god," *Zhivaia starina* 22, no. 1–2 (1913): xxi–xxvi; "Zhurnaly zasedanii Otdeleniia Etnografii Imperatorskago Russkago Geograficheskago Obshchestva: Zasedanie 25 fevraliia 1911 goda"; and Zolotarev, "Obzor deiatel'nosti."

By 1912, however, the map commission had come to the realization that
language was perhaps not the best indicator of *narodnost'* in all parts of the
empire. The ethnographers had been able to use linguistic data to draw up a
preliminary list of the *narodnosti* of European Russia. But as they looked further east, it became apparent that a new approach was needed. First, census
data on native language were flawed and incomplete for large parts of
Turkestan, the Kirgiz steppe, and Siberia. Second, even Russia's preeminent
linguists did not know all the languages of the peoples of these regions. Third,
many of the empire's *inorodtsy* had been linguistically Russified in recent
decades and, when asked, claimed Russian as their "native language." Map
commission members such as the Siberian expert Serafim Patkanov argued
that it would be misleading to classify such peoples as Russians.[73]

Patkanov, a former member of the Central Statistical Administration who
had been deeply involved in the production of the All-Russian Census of 1897,
had long been concerned about the connection between language and nationality. He had addressed this issue in his published explanatory notes for the
1897 census, commenting on data about the empire's "*narodnosti* as determined by native language and confessional group." It "is well known,"
Patkanov had explained in these notes, that "many Siberian *inorodtsy*" and
countless other peoples "have been Russified" or forcibly "assimilated by
other peoples" (such as the Tatars and Bashkirs). But, Patkanov had argued,
such peoples had not necessarily lost their national identities. Just as the Irish
strongly maintained their national identity in spite of having "almost completely forgotten their native language and adopted English," many of Russia's
peoples who had "taken on the language and even the physical traits" of their
neighbors preserved a sense of themselves as members of their nationality of
origin.[74]

As the map commission puzzled over how best to differentiate between
Russified *inorodtsy* and Russians, Patkanov suggested that it look at data from
the 1897 census under the category *soslovie* ("social estate"). Almost all of the
subjects of the Russian Empire belonged to a *soslovie,* such as nobility, peasantry, merchantry, townspeople, clergy, and *inorodtsy*.[75] By comparing census
data about native language with census data about *soslovie,* Patkanov noted, it
would be possible to assess how many supposed "Russians" were in fact *in-*

73. S. Patkanov, "Proekt sostavleniia plemennoi karty Rossii," *Zhivaia starina* 24, no. 3
(1915): 239–40. After 1917, KIPS used this article in its deliberations about new ethnographic
maps. PFA RAN f. 2, op. 1–1917, d. 30, l. 79. Patkanov noted that the peoples of entire regions of
Turkestan had been registered as speakers of "Turkic" without clarification or mention of dialect.
He blamed this on the "semiliteracy and carelessness of local census takers." Patkanov, "K tablitsam XIII, XIV, XV i XVI," i–ii.

74. Patkanov, "K tablitsam XIII, XIV, XV i XVI," i–ii.

75. Each *soslovie* had certain obligations and privileges. On the category *soslovie*, see Gregory
Freeze, "The *Soslovie* (Estate) Paradigm in Russian Social History," *The American Historical Review* 91, no. 1 (1986): 11–36.

orodtsy. Patkanov further recommended that the commission look at a sampling of completed census forms from Asiatic Russia in order to get a sense of the ethnographic makeup of particular regions. In certain parts of Siberia, census takers had noted directly on the census forms the tribe or ethnographic group (for example, Buriat, Vogul, Ostiak) to which members of the *inorodtsy* belonged.[76] Patkanov cautioned, however, that the notation of such information was far from consistent. He proposed that the commission conduct extensive anthropological-ethnographical fieldwork of its own in Asiatic Russia.[77] Patkanov's colleagues upheld this proposal, agreeing that Asiatic Russia required a different approach from European Russia. To facilitate their work, the map commission split into two commissions. The first, under Volkov's leadership, focused on European Russia and parts of the Caucasus; the second, led by Shternberg, focused on Siberia, Turkestan, the Kirgiz steppe, and the Far East.[78]

While the IRGO ethnographers were organizing expeditions to Asiatic Russia, Lenin and his supporters were focusing their attention almost exclusively on the empire's "most developed" nationalities: the Poles, Finns, Lithuanians, and Ukrainians of the western borderlands, and the Georgians of Transcaucasia. These were groups with national intelligentsias, national movements, and articulated demands for national rights; Lenin theorized that they had entered the era of "developing capitalism," and that their levels of national and class consciousness were analogous to those of the Western European nationalities of the previous century. The Bolsheviks took not only their examples of national development, but also their terminology, from Western Europe, and from France in particular. While the IRGO map commission debated the meaning of the term *narodnost'*, the Bolsheviks used the two terms *natsiia* and *natsional'nost'*—derived from the French words *nation* and *nationalité*—most frequently in their writings. Unlike the map commission, which sometimes used the term *natsional'nost'* as a synonym for *narodnost'*, the Bolsheviks often used *natsional'nost'* as a synonym for *natsiia*.[79] Lenin repeatedly referred to the "equality of *natsii*," the "equality of all *natsional'nosti* without exception," the "merger of workers of all *natsional'nosti*," and the "right of a *natsiia* to self-determination."[80]

76. Patkanov, "Proekt sostavleniia plemennoi karty Rossii," 239–40.

77. "Otdel Komissii po sostavleniiu etnograficheskikh kart Rossii (Sibir' i Sredniaia Aziia): Vyderzhki iz protokolov (1914–1915 g.)," *Zhivaia starina* 25, no. 1 (1916): 19–25. Patkanov's 1915 article ("Proekt sostavleniia plemennoi karty Rossii") summed up and expanded on the main points of his presentation.

78. "Otchet o deiatel'nosti Otdeleniia Etnografii i sostoiashchikh pri nem komissii za 1914 god," and "Otdel Komissii po sostavleniiu etnograficheskikh kart Rossii (Sibir' i Sredniaia Aziia): Vyderzhki iz protokolov (1913–1914 g.)," *Zhivaia starina* 24, no. 3 (1915): v–vii, 36–38.

79. Patkanov's reports for the map commission in 1914, for example, used the terms *narodnost'* and *natsional'nost'* interchangeably to refer to Buriats, Tungus, and other *inorodtsy* of Siberia. Patkanov, "Proekt sostavleniia plemennoi karty Rossii," 240.

80. See Lenin, KPSS, *O bor'be s natsionalizmom,* 26, 29–31, 56, 66, 81.

It was Stalin who defined the term *natsiia* for the Bolsheviks in his seminal article of 1913. A *natsiia*, asserted Stalin, "is not a racial or tribal [*plemennyi*]" group, but a "historically evolved community" formed "from people of diverse races and tribes." A *natsiia* is united by "a common language, territory and economic life"; its members share a "common mentality" (or consciousness), which is the result of shared experiences and is manifested in their culture.[81] Stalin gave examples from the Western European context to illustrate the relationship between nations (*natsii*) and tribes: "The French nation was formed from Gauls, Romans, Britons, Teutons" and other tribes; "the modern Italian nation was formed from Romans, Teutons, Etruscans, Greeks, Arabs" and other tribes; the English and the German nations were formed in a similar manner.[82]

Stalin also elaborated on the connections among language, identity, and nationhood. He argued that for a group to constitute a nation, it was not necessary for its members to have their own *separate* language; he (like Patkanov) noted that the Irish and the English are "distinct nations," even though both speak English. However, according to Stalin, the members of a group had to have a language and a territory in common, as well as national consciousness, in order to be considered a nation. Repudiating the position of the Bund, he asserted that the Jews were not a nation because they "inhabit different parts of the globe" and "do not understand each other (since they speak different languages)."[83]

The Bolsheviks also used the term *narodnost'*, albeit less regularly than the ethnographers did. Whereas the ethnographers sometimes used *narodnost'* to refer to the common folk (such as the Russian peasantry) and sometimes to refer to "a people" in the generic sense, the Bolsheviks usually used it to connote "backwardness." In Lenin's usage, the term *narodnost'* often designated a less-developed people lacking national consciousness—a people at the precapitalist or early-capitalist stage on the historical timeline who had not yet formed a "bourgeois-democratic nationalist movement."[84] Lenin frequently used the term to refer to *inorodtsy,* as when describing, for example, the "Russification of non-Russian *narodnosti*." On the eve of World War I, as Lenin developed his position on the connections between imperialism and nationalism, he used the term to refer to the "downtrodden *narodnosti*" of the European colonies.[85]

While Lenin's usage of the terms *narodnost'* and *natsional'nost'* was far from systematic, it to some degree reflected the ideas of radical social thinker

81. Stalin, "Marksizm i natsional'nyi vopros," 4–6.
82. Ibid., 4.
83. Ibid., 6, 9.
84. Lenin did not always use terminology consistently. In his theses on imperialism, he frequently referred to the peoples of the Russian Empire as oppressor and oppressed nations (*natsii*). See for example "Sotsializm i voina," in Lenin, KPSS, O bor'be s natsionalizmom, 162–65.
85. For examples of Lenin's use of *narodnost'* see Lenin, KPSS, O bor'be s natsionalizmom, 19, 33, 107, 127.

and literary critic Vissarion Belinskii. In the 1840s, in what would become a famous essay about Russian history, Belinskii argued that *narodnost'* and *natsional'nost'* represented two different levels of national development. *Narodnost'*, explained Belinskii, is a reflection of "folk life"; the folk have a shared language and folk culture, but do not have a defined national consciousness. *Natsional'nost'*, by contrast, is a reflection of the developed cultural nation, whose members have national consciousness, as well as a national language and culture.[86] In his definition of *narodnost'*, Belinskii, like Nikolai Nadezhdin, was influenced by German romanticism of the early nineteenth century. However, Belinskii did not share Nadezhdin's admiration of *narodnost'*. Instead, he characterized the national culture of *natsional'nost'* as superior to the folk culture of *narodnost'*, arguing that the former (which was based on the latter) had meaning for "enlightened humanity" as a whole.[87]

Imperial ethnographers shared with the Bolsheviks the view that humankind evolved through stages on an evolutionary timeline. Moreover, prominent members of both groups saw economic structures and relationships as the determinants of cultural and social forms and as motors for change. These shared ideas were not coincidental. Some of the same anthropological theories that shaped Russian ethnography in the late nineteenth century had also inspired Marx and Engels. Lewis Henry Morgan's ideas about periodizing "progress in human history" were read with great interest by Marx and also debated by Russia's ethnographers. Edward B. Tylor's cultural-evolutionary theories—particularly his argument that all peoples irrespective of race went through similar stages of "savage, barbaric and civilized life"—influenced Engels's work on the history of culture as well as Russia's ethnographers' ideas about the stages of cultural development. (Tylor had spent time in St. Petersburg collaborating with members of the Ethnographic Division in the 1880s.)[88]

But ethnographers and Bolsheviks had different theories about evolutionary development, and they described evolutionism in different terms. Shternberg and other followers of the cultural-evolutionary school attempted to map out

86. According to Belinskii, folk songs were a product of *narodnost'*, while the poetry of Aleksandr Pushkin (embodying "the national spirit" in "universal terms") was a product of *natsional'nost'*. V. G. Belinskii, "Deianiia Petra Velikogo, mudrogo preobrazovateliia Rossii," in V. G. Belinskii, *Izbrannye filosofskie sochineniia*, vol. 1, ed. M. T. Iovchuk and Z. V. Smirnov (Moscow, 1948), 336–37. On Belinskii's use of these terms see Terras, *Belinskij and Russian Literary Criticism*, 94.

87. Terras, *Belinskij and Russian Literary Criticism*, 16–17, 98–99.

88. On Marx, Engels, Tylor, and Morgan see John J. Honigmann, *The Development of Anthropological Ideas* (Homewood, IL, 1976). On Tylor see Geraci, "Ethnic Minorities, Anthropology, and Russian National Identity on Trial." On the influence of Morgan and Tylor in Russia see L. Ia. Shternberg, "Sovremennaia etnologiia: Noveishie uspekhi, nauchnye techeniia i metody," *Etnografiia*, no. 1–2 (1926): 15–43. On the connection between Morgan and Engels (and on the influence of both on Lev Shternberg) see "Lev Iakovlevich Shternberg (Nekrolog)," *Etnografiia*, no. 3–4 (1927): 263–66.

the empire's *narodnosti* according to their places on the "universal ladder of culture." The ethnographers debated which peoples to consider *narodnosti* (peoples unified by language, culture, religion, or physical type, or only peoples with national consciousness) and attempted to understand the process through which tribes united into a *narodnost'*. Lenin and other Bolshevik theorists, by contrast, argued that different types of ethnohistorical groups corresponded to the different stages of socioeconomic organization—primitive communism, feudalism, capitalism, socialism, and communism—enumerated by Marx and Engels. Lenin wrote about "feudal era" clans and tribes, and the emergence and development of nationalities and nations (*narodnosti, natsional'nosti,* and *natsii*) in the conditions of capitalism. (However, it was not until the 1920s and 1930s that these terms came to systematically connote specific stages on the Marxist timeline.) The ethnographers drew on the work of British and American cultural evolutionists to understand the connections between "modern" cultures and their "primitive" antecedents; they studied what Marxist thinkers considered part of the superstructure—culture, kinship, and language. The Bolsheviks, by contrast, were most interested in understanding the socioeconomic conditions that gave rise to different types of national movements. Lenin theorized that national movements could be progressive forces for change in the late-feudal and early-capitalist stages of a society, but were retrogressive in the late-capitalist and socialist stages.

As Russia entered World War I, the language of nationality became increasingly important. Various constituencies and individuals, including Woodrow Wilson, the German government, and the Bolsheviks, heralded the principle of "national rights." While it was not clear what these rights were, it was even less clear to which groups—nations, *natsional'nosti, narodnosti,* or tribes—they applied.[89]

World War I and the Mobilization of Science

The economic and organizational demands of World War I facilitated a closer working relationship between experts and governments throughout Europe and led to the introduction of new and more intensive means to organize, inventory, and mobilize peoples and resources. New fields of applied social sciences, which had struggled for government support before 1914, gained recognition as useful to the state. Economists, geographers, and anthropologists in France, Germany, and Britain provided their governments with maps and inventories of their countries' resources.[90] Russia's experts—including members

89. See, for example, S. Elpat'evskii, "Natsional'nyi vopros," *Russkoe bogatstvo,* no. 11 (1910): 195–228, and Dmitrii Muratov, "O poniatii narodnosti," *Russkaia mysl',* no. 5 (1916): 111–25.

90. On World War I as a transformative moment that redefined the relationship between science and the state, see Peter Holquist, *Making War, Forging Revolution;* Alexei Kojevnikov, "The Great War, the Russian Civil War, and the Invention of Big Science," *Science in Context* 15, no. 2

of the IRGO and the Academy of Sciences—also organized themselves to help the war effort, but their involvement was more circumscribed than that of their European counterparts. The tsarist regime was disinclined to rely on Russia's professionals and continued to look primarily to military experts and bureaucrats to manage the home front.

The overwhelming demands of the war precipitated an economic crisis in the Russian Empire. Before 1914, Russia had relied heavily on the West, and on Germany in particular, for weapons, industrial machinery, technology, and even natural resources. After the war began, imports stopped.[91] The early loss to the Germans of Russia's western borderlands, where industry was concentrated, compounded the economic difficulties.[92] The imperial regime did not know if important natural resources, including those needed to produce ammunition, could be found within Russia's borders or not; Nicholas II and previous tsars had not supported comprehensive studies of the empire's productive forces.[93]

The war also worsened Russia's nationality problem, as antagonists on both sides of the conflict used the national idea—and the promise of national self-determination in particular—as a political weapon to sponsor separatist movements in the lands of their enemies. The German government stirred up non-Russian nationalism within the Russian Empire by advocating Polish independence and by assisting Ukrainian, Finnish, Jewish, and other nationalist organizations. The members of the Entente used similar tactics against the Austro-Hungarian Empire.[94] Meanwhile, measures for mass mobilization—including the deportation of Germans, Poles, Ukrainians, Jews, and other groups from the western borderlands, and the conscription of *inorodtsy*, who were formerly exempt from military service—exacerbated the disaffection of non-Russians with the imperial state.[95]

(2002): 239–75; John Horne, "Remobilizing for 'Total War': France and Britain, 1917–1918," in *State, Society, and Mobilization in Europe during the First World War*, ed. John Horne (Cambridge, 1997); Michael Geyer, "Militarization of Europe, 1914–1945," in *The Militarization of the Western World*, ed. John Gillis (New Brunswick, NJ, 1989); and Vejas Gabriel Liulevicius, *War Land on the Eastern Front* (Cambridge, 2000).

91. Alexander Vucinich, *Empire of Knowledge: The Academy of Sciences of the USSR (1917–1970)* (Berkeley, 1984), 68–69, and Clark, *Petersburg*, 67–68.

92. Alec Nove, *An Economic History of the U.S.S.R.*, rev. ed. (London, 1989), 7.

93. B. A. Lindener, *Raboty Rossiiskoi Akademii nauk v oblasti issledovaniia prirodnykh bogatstv Rossii: Obzor deiatel'nosti KEPS za 1915–21 gg.* (Petrograd, 1922), and Nove, *Economic History of the U.S.S.R.*, 20.

94. Mark Mazower, *Dark Continent: Europe's Twentieth Century* (New York, 1998), 41–64; C. A. Macartney, *National States and National Minorities* (London, 1934), 179–211; and Aviel Roshwald, *Ethnic Nationalism and the Fall of Empires: Central Europe, Russia and the Middle East, 1914–1923* (London, 2001), chapter 4.

95. Peter Gatrell, *A Whole Empire Walking: Refugees in Russia During World War I* (Bloomington, 1999), and Eric Lohr, *Nationalizing the Russian Empire: The Campaign Against Enemy Aliens during World War I* (Cambridge, MA, 2003).

In the decade before the war, many of Russia's ethnographers, geographers, and economists had embraced the position that scientific or expert knowledge could be used to "rationalize economic production," resolve the so-called nationality question, and turn the Russian Empire into a "modern" state.[96] With an eye on the European colonial empires, some of these experts had expressed interest in inventorying and "drawing into use" the rich "productive forces" of Asiatic Russia in order to become less dependent on other states.[97] After the war began, Russia's economists argued that such an approach should be taken to all of Russia, to ensure that the country meet the challenge of total war. In early 1915, the prominent geochemist Vladimir Vernadskii (a colleague of Ol'-denburg's and a member of the State Council, the upper chamber of the new Russian parliament) proposed that the government and the Academy of Sciences organize a new scientific commission to aid the war effort by studying the empire's natural productive forces.[98] The imperial regime, although initially cool, was ultimately receptive to this proposal. In May 1915, the war and naval ministries supplied funds to establish the Commission for the Study of the Natural Productive Forces of Russia (KEPS). This new commission served as a "technical advisory committee for war needs"; it inventoried resources and assisted in the wartime mobilization of the economy. Several prominent ethnographers (including Ol'denburg, Anuchin, Veniamin Semenov-Tian-Shanskii, and Lev Berg) joined geologists, geochemists, and other scientists in the new commission.[99]

When discussions about KEPS began in 1915, Anuchin proposed the establishment alongside it of a second government-sponsored commission to study "the population," Russia's "most powerful productive force." "Here there is nothing resembling the American Bureau of Ethnology or English organiza-

96. David L. Hoffman, "European Modernity and Soviet Socialism," in *Russian Modernity*, 246–47. Hoffman notes "the spread of what might be termed scientism—an effort to organize all political, social, and economic relations according to scientifically determined norms."

97. G. Gins, "Pereselenie i kolonizatsiia," *Voprosy kolonizatsii*, no. 12 (1913): 104–5.

98. Vernadskii was a member of the Kadet Central Committee. He (like Ol'denburg) belonged to the Student Scientific-Literary Association at St. Petersburg University in the 1880s, joined the Academy of Sciences in the early 1900s, and joined the new Kadet Party in 1905. D. I. Anuchin, "Izuchenie proizvoditel'nykh sil Rossii," in D. I. Anuchin, *Geograficheskie raboty*, ed. A. A. Grigoriev (Moscow, 1954), 335–42. This is a reprint of the article which appeared in *Zemlevedenie* 23, no. 1–2 (1916): 97–103. On Vernadskii and KEPS also see Kojevnikov, "The Great War, the Russian Civil War, and the Invention of Big Science," 250–54, and Kendall Bailes, *Science and Russian Culture in an Age of Revolutions: V. I. Vernadsky and His Scientific School, 1863–1945* (Bloomington, 1990).

99. Lindener, *Raboty Rossiiskoi Akademii nauk v oblasti issledovaniia prirodnykh bogatstv Rossii*, 2–7; Pospelov, *Lenin i Akademiia nauk*, 29–39; and A. V. Kol'tsov, *Lenin i stanovlenie Akademii nauk kak tsentra sovetskoi nauki* (Leningrad, 1969), 71–111. Also Vucinich, *Empire of Knowledge*, 102–6. KEPS did research in geology, chemistry, soil science, geography, and other fields and searched for deposits of rare metals. This commission would later be renamed the Commission for the Study of the Natural Productive Forces of the USSR.

tions for studying the peoples of India," Anuchin noted.[100] Some of the European governments, drawing on their experience in the colonies and responding to the demands of the war, were establishing new institutions at home to study the population as an economic resource. Anuchin wanted to follow their lead. The Academy of Sciences discussed Anuchin's proposal, but dismissed it as unrealizable. Instead, it created within KEPS a Committee for the Description of Russia by Region. This committee of ethnographers, anthropologists, geographers, and economists embarked on a region-by-region analysis of the empire's population, natural resources, and "populated places of note" (towns, villages, cities).[101]

Only six years earlier, Anuchin had opposed Shternberg's proposal for a government-sponsored central ethnographic bureau. Now, he was suggesting that a bureau of this sort was desperately needed. How can Anuchin's shift in position be accounted for? Clearly, much had changed between 1909 and 1915. After the start of World War I, scholars at research institutes and universities in Moscow and St. Petersburg (renamed Petrograd in 1914) had far fewer opportunities to do independent research. Anthropologists and ethnographers were drafted to work in military hospitals and other institutions. Research budgets were reduced and travel was restricted. Indeed, between 1914 and 1916, the IRGO's ethnographic research all but came to a standstill.[102] Anuchin came to the realization that there would be limited support for any research that was not directly part of the war effort.[103]

The ethnographers were motivated not just by professional concerns, but also by a desire to defend Russia's "state interests."[104] In their opinion, the government needed ethnographic research at least as much as ethnographers needed the government. In late 1916, Ol'denburg learned that the Germans were using their own ethnographers to map out the ethnographic composition

100. Anuchin, "Izuchenie proizvoditel'nykh sil Rossii," 337–38. Anuchin proposed that a "central institution of this sort" might work with "a corresponding central institution" engaged in "the geographical study of Russia" (such as the Russian Geographical Society).

101. This committee based its approach in large part on the model that the Semenov-Tian-Shanskiis had developed for their work describing the entire Russian Empire region by region. On this committee see Lindener, *Raboty Rossiiskoi Akademii nauk v oblasti issledovaniia prirodnykh bogatstv Rossii,* and P. M. Alampiev, *Ekonomicheskoe raionirovanie SSSR* (Moscow, 1959), 82–84. Also PFA RAN f. 135, op. 1, d. 1, l. 6; d. 3, l. 18.

102. "Otchet o deiatel'nosti Otdeleniia Etnografii i sostoiashchikh pri nem komissii za 1915 god," *Zhivaia starina* 25, no. 1 (1916), viii, ix, and "Otchet o deiatel'nosti Otdeleniia Etnografii i sostoiashchikh pri nem komissii za 1914 god," *Zhivaia starina* 24, no. 1–2 (1915): vii.

103. Anuchin, "Izuchenie proizvoditel'nykh sil Rossii," 340–42. Ol'denburg initially opposed Anuchin's proposal, arguing that the IRGO's Ethnographic Division had itself assumed such a role. As the war continued he changed his mind and concluded that such an institution was necessary.

104. Dumova, *Kadetskaia partiia v period pervoi mirovoi voiny,* 154, and William G. Rosenberg, *Liberals in the Russian Revolution: The Constitutional Democratic Party, 1917–1921* (Princeton, 1974), 38–39.

of the Russian Empire's recently German-occupied western borderlands. The Germans were citing these ethnographic data to justify the establishment of Lithuanian, Belorussian, and other nationality-based institutions and administrative units in these German-occupied territories (which included the Land Ober Ost).[105] Characterizing the German appeal to the national idea as a form of political warfare, Ol'denburg decried the Russian government's ignorance of these territories. He expressed frustration that Russia's Ministry of Foreign Affairs was relying on provincial governors-general and military statisticians—whom he characterized as inept—instead of turning to the Academy of Sciences for assistance.[106]

Ol'denburg appealed to the president of the Academy of Sciences in early February 1917, recommending the formation of a "special commission" of ethnographers to support the war effort and the future peace; he argued that expert-produced ethnographic knowledge was of tremendous importance in a war that was being "conducted to a significant degree in connection with the nationality question." Ol'denburg's entreaty resulted in the establishment of the Commission for the Study of the Tribal Composition of the Population of the Borderlands of Russia (KIPS); the Academy of Sciences gave KIPS a modest budget and suggested that Ol'denburg petition state ministries for additional support.[107]

Ol'denburg's commission, KIPS, was composed of twelve of Petrograd's leading anthropologists, ethnographers, linguists, and geographers—nine of whom had been members of the Geographical Society's (now-defunct) map commission.[108] This new commission used the map commission's research as the foundation of its work.[109] But whereas the map commission had aimed to

105. On German censuses and ethnographic studies of the western borderlands see Wiktor Sukiennicki, *East Central Europe During World War I: From Foreign Domination to National Independence*, vol. 1 (Boulder, 1984), 159–66, and Liulevicius, *War Land on the Eastern Front*, 21, 31, 94–108. The German experts were conducting censuses, collecting data about the population's native language and religion. The German military administration was using the ethnographic data to draw up a blueprint for the colonization of the occupied territories; its plans included instructions for the deportation of certain nationalities such as the Poles.

106. PFA RAN f. 2, op. 1–1917, d. 30, l. 38, and Rossiiskaia Akademiia nauk, *Ob uchrezhdenii Komissii po izucheniiu plemennogo sostava naseleniia Rossii, Izvestiia Komissii po izucheniiu plemennogo sostava naseleniia Rossii*, vol. 1 (Petrograd, 1917), 3–4, 7–8.

107. Rossiiskaia Akademiia nauk, *Ob uchrezhdenii Komissii*, 8.

108. PFA RAN f. 2, op. 1–1917, d. 30, ll. 48–50. Ol'denburg invited six representatives from the Academy of Sciences (Shakhmatov, Mikhail D'iakonov, Nikolai Marr, Vasilii Bartol'd, Vladimir Peretts, and Karskii); two representatives from the University's Anthropological Society (Rudenko and Volkov); two representatives from the University's Philological Society (Andrei Rudnev and Lev Shcherba); and two representatives from the Geographical Society's Ethnographic Division (David Zolotarev and Mogilianskii). All of these experts considered themselves ethnographers, although some saw themselves as ethnographers first and others saw themselves primarily as members of one of the related disciplines.

109. For example, PFA RAN f. 2, op. 1–1917, d. 30, ll. 49–50, 56. In 1916, Marr was already doing ethnographic studies in the occupied regions of Turkish Armenia.

create an ethnographic map of the entire empire, KIPS had a more modest goal: to produce maps of those territories which "lie on both sides" of Russia's European and Asiatic borders and "are contiguous with the lands of our enemies."[110] Some commission members worked on an ethnographic map of the western borderlands, including Lithuania, Poland, Galicia, Ruthenia, Bukovina, and part of Bessarabia; large areas of this region were occupied by German forces. Other commission members focused on the eastern borderlands, mapping out the ethnographic composition of those parts of the Caucasus and Turkestan that bordered northern Persia; as a result of the war, Russia had gained territories in these regions.[111]

The commission's ethnographers engaged in a discussion about methodology that was reminiscent of the IRGO map commission's deliberations. But now, in the midst of a war, the ethnographers made a greater point of emphasizing the practical value of their suggestions. Some ethnographers, such as Karskii, suggested that KIPS base its maps on native language, in keeping with European norms, in order to facilitate the settlement of postwar borders.[112] Others, such as Rudenko, proposed that the commission embark on anthropological studies of the population: that it collect data about physical type in order to elucidate "the degree of suitability" of different peoples "for the execution of military and other state obligations" in the war.[113]

After much discussion, KIPS resolved to take as its starting point the map commission's decision to take different approaches to European and Asiatic Russia. This would make it easier for KIPS to use the map commission's research. It also took into consideration the realities of the war. KIPS would not do fieldwork in the western borderlands, where the war still raged. Instead, it would produce maps of these regions using data about native language that the map commission had already collected. KIPS would, however, do ethnographical-anthropological fieldwork in the eastern borderlands, where census data were flawed and where great uncertainty persisted about the correlation between language and *narodnost'*.[114] This decision to use language as the main trait for mapping the peoples of the western borderlands but to use a combination of traits, including physical type, to map the peoples of the east-

---

110. Ibid., l. 38. Also, Rossiiskaia Akademiia nauk, *Ob uchrezhdenii Komissii*, 3, 7. After the war the Geographical Society's map commission reconvened and focused its efforts on the preparation of an ethnographic map of Siberia. See for example RGO f. 24, op. 1, d. 78 part 2, ll. 32–33.

111. PFA RAN f. 2, op. 1–1917, d. 30, ll. 49–50.

112. E. F. Karskii, *Etnograficheskaia karta Belorusskago plemeni, Trudy Komissii po izucheniiu plemennogo sostava naseleniia Rossii*, vol. 2 (Petrograd, 1917).

113. PFA RAN f. 2, op. 1–1917, d. 30, ll. 40–42.

114. Ibid., ll. 38, 49–50, 73–74. KIPS made plans to dispatch experts to do fieldwork in the eastern borderlands. It also negotiated agreements with local researchers who agreed to provide information about local populations, including the Syrians, Greeks, Armenians, Georgians, Turks, Persians, and Laz.

ern borderlands was reflected in new maps—which after 1917 influenced the Bolsheviks' view of their domain.

As the commission worked out its approach, Ol'denburg appealed to the Tsar's ministers for support; he emphasized the "exceptional significance" of ethnographic research for the war effort and promised completed maps within six months.[115] Ol'denburg reported back to KIPS on February 23, 1917 that Minister of Foreign Affairs N. N. Pokrovskii had expressed his enthusiasm for the commission. Ol'denburg's meeting with the minister of education, scheduled for the next day, never took place.[116] The commission's records note dryly that it was canceled due to "political events and state revolution."[117]

World War I and Bolshevik Ideology

World War I was a critical moment for experts and Bolsheviks alike, serving as a catalyst for both groups to refine their ideas and formulate programs for action. While Ol'denburg was mobilizing Russia's scholars for the war effort, Lenin remained in Europe and called for a worldwide socialist revolution—urging socialists and soldiers to use their weapons "not against the brother wage-slaves of other countries," but against "the bourgeoisie both of 'their own' and of 'foreign' countries."[118] Explaining his position on the war, Lenin maintained that the present international conflict was not a "national war" for liberation like those of the previous century which had overthrown feudalism; instead, it was an "imperialist war" that signified the end of capitalism—a war in which socialists "must not choose sides."[119] Responding to Lenin's theses on the war, a number of prominent Bolsheviks proposed that the right to national self-determination be expunged from the party program.[120] If national wars belonged to the past, if the current goal was international socialist revolution, why should socialists support national movements at all?

In 1916, Lenin addressed this question by broadening his analysis of the nationality question beyond the borders of Europe to include Europe's colonies. Europeans "often forget that colonial [colonized] peoples are *also* nations," Lenin noted. Even in colonial countries where oppressed peoples lacked class consciousness and national consciousness, it was "obligatory for every Marxist to advance the slogan of 'self-determination.'" Lenin suggested that in colonies, the right of a "nation [*natsiia*] to self-determination" was best trans-

115. Rossiiskaia Akademiia nauk, *Ob uchrezhdenii Komissii*, 7–9.

116. PFA RAN f. 2, op. 1–1917, d. 30, ll. 49–50.

117. Rossiiskaia Akademiia nauk, *Ob uchrezhdenii Komissii*, 9.

118. V. I. Lenin, "Zadachi revoliutsionnoi sotsial-demokratii v Evropeiskoi voine," in *Polnoe sobranie sochinenii*, vol. 26 (Moscow, 1961), and Service, *Lenin: A Biography*, 223–25.

119. V. I. Lenin, "Sotsializm i voina (Otnoshenie RSDRP k voine)," in *Polnoe sobranie sochinenii*, vol. 26, 307–50.

120. Pipes, *Formation of the Soviet Union*, 47.

lated as the right of a "people [*narod*] to sovereignty."[121] Now embracing a more expansive argument about self-determination, Lenin began to consider the "incipient nationalism" of the peoples of Turkestan, Siberia, and the Kirgiz steppe—the very regions that Russia's ethnographers had taken as their subject of inquiry. In particular, Lenin began to analyze the ways in which the nationality question and the colonization question were interconnected.

Lenin again emphasized the importance of the Marxist historical timeline. This time, however, he argued that the countries of the world could be divided into three main groups, each at different stages on the road to socialism: the "advanced capitalist countries of Europe and the United States," the "countries to the east of Europe," and the "semi-colonial and colonial countries."[122] For each group the nationality question needed to be evaluated differently.[123] For France, England, and other "advanced capitalist countries," the progressive national movement was "a thing of the past," argued Lenin. These countries, which "previously had led humanity forward," had "completed the process of becoming nation states"; they were now "oppressing other peoples," primarily in the colonies, in an effort to prolong their own capitalist epoch. For the peoples of Europe's colonies and of semicolonial countries like Persia, by contrast, nationalism was progressive and the "bourgeois-democratic national movement" was "largely a thing of the future."[124] Lenin argued that it was the responsibility of workers from the advanced capitalist countries to "render determined support" to the national movements of the colonies and the semicolonial countries: to "demand the unconditional and immediate liberation" of those colonial peoples that their "own" nations were subjugating.[125]

Nationalist movements in the countries "to the east of Europe"—Austria-Hungary, Russia, the Balkans—were more difficult to evaluate because these countries were populated by peoples at different stages of national development, Lenin argued. The nationalism of oppressed nations (or colonial peoples) in these countries was progressive, insofar as it contributed to the collapse of feudalism and the development of capitalism.[126] At the same time, the nationalism of the dominant nations (such as Great Russians in Russia) was a

---

121. V. I. Lenin, "O karikature na marksizm i ob 'imperialisticheskom ekonomizme,'" in *Polnoe sobranie sochinenii*, vol. 30 (Moscow, 1962), 116.

122. V. I. Lenin, "Sotsialisticheskaia revoliutsiia i pravo natsii na samoopredelenie," in *Polnoe sobranie sochinenii*, vol. 27 (Moscow, 1962), 252–66. The argument is recapitulated and expanded on in "O karikature na marksizm."

123. Lenin, "O karikature na marksizm," 123.

124. Ibid., 88, and Lenin, "Sotsialisticheskaia revoliutsiia i pravo natsii," 260–61.

125. Lenin, "Sotsialisticheskaia revoliutsiia i pravo natsii," 261. He argued that this demand, "in its political expression, signifies nothing more nor less than the recognition of the right to self-determination."

126. Lenin, "O karikature na marksizm," 119, 121. Lenin noted that the distinction between oppressed nations and colonies was "not clear" and "not vital" in these countries since, for example, there was "no economic or political difference between Russia's 'owning' Poland or Turkestan."

reactionary force that hindered the development of other peoples. In preparation for socialist revolutions, it was essential to foster solidarity between the workers of the oppressor nations and the oppressed nations within these countries' borders, Lenin argued.[127]

Looking to the future, Lenin extended his analysis of oppressor and oppressed nationalism to the era of early socialism—focusing on the relationship between workers from advanced and colonial countries (or regions). After the revolution, socialists and workers from European oppressor nations "will grant the colonies the right to free secession," but "will not recommend secession," Lenin explained. At the same time, socialists would work toward political and economic unification, by giving "unselfish cultural aid" to "backward peoples."[128] Lenin predicted that by simultaneously granting "freedom of secession" and offering aid, it would be possible to attract not just the colonies, but also the small oppressed nations of Europe, "into an alliance with the great socialist states."[129]

Lenin emphasized that Social Democrats within Russia were to continue to promote the right to national self-determination after the Russian socialist revolution. He criticized those Bolsheviks who assumed that a socialist revolution in Russia would instantly eradicate the nationality question. It is not true, maintained Lenin, "that the democratic state of victorious socialism" will "exist without boundaries," or that boundaries will "be drawn 'only' in accordance with the requirements of production." He argued that it would be essential to draw state boundaries "democratically" after the revolution, in accordance with the population's ethnographic and economic orientation.[130] Lenin continued to emphasize the importance of attaining accurate region-by-region information about the Russian Empire's ethnic and linguistic composition and about the distribution of its economic resources (productive forces).

1917

The revolution of February 1917 was a spontaneous mass uprising that took both Ol'denburg and Lenin by surprise. Demonstrations began in the capital on February 23, sparking a general strike and a mutiny of soldiers. On February 27, 1917, a newly formed Provisional Duma Committee announced that it

127. Lenin, "Sotsialisticheskaia revoliutsiia i pravo natsii," 256–58, 260–61, and "O karikature na marksizm," 89–98, 107–8. He emphasized that only by defending the principle of self-determination could revolutionaries achieve their ultimate aim: the voluntary "merger" of all nations in a socialist union. V. I. Lenin, "Itogi diskussii o samoopredelenii," in *Polnoe sobranie sochinenii*, vol. 30, 21.

128. Lenin, "O karikature na marksizm," 119–21, and "Itogi diskussii o samoopredelenii," 34–37.

129. Lenin, "Itogi diskussii o samoopredelenii," 36–37.

130. Ibid., 18, 21.

had taken power; the same day, factory workers and soldiers in Petrograd established their own representative body, the Soviet of Workers' and Soldiers' Deputies. Ol'denburg was in Petrograd as events unfolded. He watched with concern as the Provisional Duma Committee created a Provisional Government in which Kadets predominated, and as this government attempted to coexist with the Petrograd Soviet in an arrangement known as dual power.[131]

Lenin was in Switzerland during the heady days of February; from there he sent a telegram to Petrograd, urging the Bolsheviks to reject the authority of the Provisional Government.[132] Two months later, Lenin returned to Petrograd and began to actively call for socialist revolution. Bolsheviks and Mensheviks alike were unsettled by Lenin's position; most believed that Russia was experiencing a bourgeois-democratic revolution, and that it would be decades before the proletariat could be ready to take power.[133] Lenin countered that "the revolutionary-democratic dictatorship of the proletariat and the peasantry" was already being established ("in a certain form and to a certain extent") through the Petrograd Soviet. He argued that the time was right to complete the "transition from the first [bourgeois-democratic] stage of the revolution to the second [socialist] stage of the revolution."[134]

Meanwhile, news of the events in Petrograd spread throughout the empire and was met enthusiastically and expectantly. With the end of the tsarist autocracy, Russia's nationality-based political parties hoped that their demands for greater political and cultural autonomy for the empire's non-Russians would be met. Ukrainian and Georgian leaders urged the creation of a Russian federation with autonomous national regions, while Jewish and Armenian leaders called for the institutionalization of extraterritorial autonomy; Polish and Finnish leaders pressed for complete national independence.[135]

Recognizing the political volatility of the nationality question, the Provisional Government immediately introduced legislation abolishing all restrictions based on religion and nationality.[136] It also attempted to introduce a modicum of self-rule for the empire's nationalities by officially transferring

131. Dumova, *Kadetskaia partiia v period pervoi mirovoi voiny,* 93–107, and Rosenberg, *Liberals in the Russian Revolution,* 49–66.

132. Service, *Lenin: A Biography,* 253–55.

133. Carr, *Bolshevik Revolution,* vol. 1, 77–80.

134. V. I. Lenin, "Pis'ma o taktike," in *Polnoe sobranie sochinenii,* vol. 31 (Moscow, 1962), 132–33, 135. The parenthetical comment was added in a footnote. Acknowledging that he had broken with earlier ideas about the transition to socialism, Lenin urged Social Democrats to "take cognizance of real life" and not to treat their theories as "dogma."

135. See Marc Ferro, *October 1917: A Social History of the Russian Revolution* (London, 1980), 91–100. The Provisional Government issued a decree recognizing Polish autonomy, but since Poland was occupied by the German army at the time the decree had only symbolic significance. Robert Paul Browder and Alexander F. Kerensky, *The Russian Provisional Government, 1917,* vol. 1 (Stanford, 1961), 321–23 ("The Proclamation of the Provisional Government to the Poles, March 16, 1917").

136. Browder and Kerensky, *Russian Provisional Government,* vol. 1, 211–12 ("The Abolition of Restrictions Based on Religion and Nationality").

local power from governors-general to local non-Russian representatives.[137] In so doing, it disempowered some of the very bureaucrats on which the tsarist regime had been relying for information about the population. The Provisional Government was unwilling, however, to take measures to change the administrative-territorial organization of Russia. Most of its ministers opposed proposals to create a Russian federation or to grant nationalities autonomous status, arguing that doing so would further weaken the Russian state.[138] Even those ministers who supported changing the state's structure refused to act; they saw themselves as the temporary leaders of Russia, ruling only until the election of a representative body, the Constituent Assembly, could take place. Some non-Russians were not willing to wait for the Constituent Assembly. In Ukraine, radical Ukrainian nationalists demanded an autonomous Ukraine within a Russian federation.[139] In the Bashkir and Kirgiz steppe, indigenous peoples demanding autonomous status attempted to expel Russian colonists.[140]

Against a backdrop of national-political unrest, Ol'denburg attempted to convince the Provisional Government that "scientific data about Russia's ethnographic composition" could help it meet the needs of the population and guarantee that non-Russians received fair representation in the Constituent Assembly. In April, he asked the Provisional Government to support KIPS's efforts to study the peoples and territories of the borderlands and of "inner Russia." He noted that KIPS already had materials that could be used to resolve "questions that might arise" in the Assembly regarding the national composition of the population.[141] Ol'denburg, who was on cordial terms with key government figures, received a promise of state support. But KIPS was unable to resume its scholarly activities until September 1917; Ol'denburg later recalled that "the complications of political life"—war, social unrest, an attempted coup from the right—"curtailed the commission's undertakings" in the spring and the summer.[142]

While the Provisional Government implored national leaders to be patient and to wait for a Constituent Assembly, the Bolsheviks proclaimed the right of nationalities to secede from the state.[143] In late April, at Lenin's request, Stalin

137. Pipes, *Formation of the Soviet Union*, 50.

138. Browder and Kerensky, *Russian Provisional Government*, vol. 1, 317–18 ("The Kadet Policy on the National Question").

139. Ibid., vol. 1, 370, 372–73 ("Telegrams from the Ukrainian Central Rada to Prince L'vov and Kerensky, March 6, 1917" and "From the Resolutions of the Ukrainian National Congress, April 5–8, 1917"). The Ukrainian nationalists took over the Ukrainian Central Rada (Soviet or Council).

140. Pipes, *Formation of the Soviet Union*, 83–86, and Richard N. Pierce, *Russian Central Asia, 1867–1917: A Study in Colonial Rule* (Berkeley, 1960).

141. Rossiiskaia Akademiia nauk, *Ob uchrezhdenii Komissii*, 9–10.

142. Ibid., 9–11.

143. Lenin, "Rech' po natsional'nomu voprosu 29 aprelia (12 maiia)," in *Polnoe sobranie sochinenii*, vol. 31, 435.

drew up a "Report on the Nationality Question," setting out the official Bolshevik position.[144] First and foremost, the report demanded that all "oppressed nations within Russia" be "allowed the right to decide for themselves" whether "to remain part of the Russian state." At the same time, it demanded that peoples choosing not to secede (Stalin predicted that this would include 90 percent of Russia's nationalities) be granted greater autonomy within the Russian state: that the inhabitants of distinct regions such as "Transcaucasia, Turkestan, and Ukraine" be granted self-rule in the form of provincial autonomy (*oblastnaia avtonomiia*), with their borders determined on the basis of economic and ethnographic information. It stipulated that national minorities be guaranteed equal rights and "freedom of development," and it called for the unification of workers of all nationalities into a "single proletarian collective body."[145]

There was little that was new in Stalin's report, which essentially restated the main points of a party resolution from October 1913. But context is everything. In 1913, the Bolshevik position on the nationality question had done nothing more than spark debate among Social Democrats. In 1917, it had a real impact on discussions about the form of the new Russian state. The Bolshevik "solution" was discussed at workers' and soldiers' conferences throughout Russia and was well received; the proposal for provincial autonomy corresponded to the demands of many non-Russian leaders. By May 1917, the Kadets recognized that it was necessary to modify their own position on the nationality question and pledged to find their own "solution" that would enable the "various regions of Russia" to enjoy greater "provincial autonomy."[146]

In June 1917, when representatives from soviets (local government bodies) throughout Russia met for the All-Russian Congress of Soviets in Petrograd, they integrated key elements of the Bolshevik program into their own resolutions; in particular, the congress advocated provincial autonomy for regions "that differ by virtue of their ethnographic or socioeconomic characteristics." The congress agreed with the Provisional Government that all decisions concerning national self-determination should await the convocation of the Constituent Assembly. But it urged the Provisional Government to take "more vigorous action" in the interim to satisfy some of the nationalities' demands.[147] It asked the Provisional Government to introduce a decree stipulating the right of all nationalities to use their native languages "in schools, courts, organs of

144. I. Stalin, "Doklad po natsional'nomu voprosu na VII (aprel'skoi) Vserossiiskoi konferentsii RSDRP, 29 apreliia (12 maiia) 1917 g.," in Stalin, *Marksizm i natsional'no-kolonial'nyi vopros*, 46–50.

145. Ibid., 47, 49.

146. Browder and Kerensky, *Russian Provisional Government*, vol. 1, 317 ("Kadet Policy on the National Question").

147. Ibid., vol. 1, 318–19 ("Soviet Resolution on the National Question").

self-government," and in communicating with the state. It also asked the Provisional Government to create "councils on nationality affairs" (composed of "representatives of all the nationalities in Russia") which would help state ministers to prepare materials on the nationality question for the Constituent Assembly. In addition, it asked the Provisional Government to publish a declaration stating that "the right of all peoples to self-determination, including separation," would be realized on approval by the Constituent Assembly.

Ol'denburg became involved in the day-to-day affairs of the Provisional Government in late spring, upon being elected to the Central Committee of the Kadet Party. In May 1917, he witnessed the creation of a coalition cabinet comprised of Kadet and moderate socialist ministers. Two months later he watched it fall apart as the issue of Ukrainian autonomy precipitated a crisis of state authority.[148] With the government in crisis, pro-Bolshevik soldiers and workers took to the streets in Petrograd. Military units loyal to the Provisional Government and the Petrograd Soviet put down the disorder. Blaming the Bolsheviks, the Provisional Government ordered the arrest of the party's leaders. Lenin and other Bolshevik leaders fled to Finland.[149]

In the wake of the "Bolshevik threat," liberals and moderate socialists formed a second coalition cabinet. Only four Kadets served in the fifteen-person cabinet. One was Ol'denburg, the new minister of education. Ol'denburg held his post for only five weeks before this second coalition cabinet fell apart.[150] Freed from ministerial responsibilities, Ol'denburg refocused his attention on KIPS—using his contacts in the Ministry of Education to obtain funds for the commission.[151] KIPS held four meetings in September, resuming its work on ethnographic maps of Russia.[152] Then, in early October, it began to work in an official capacity with the new National Department of the Provisional Government's Ministry of Internal Affairs. KIPS and the National Department collaborated on legislation to guarantee the use of local languages in organs of local government and to protect the indigenous peoples of the Kirgiz steppe from Russian colonizers.[153]

---

148. In late June, attempting to establish its sovereignty over Ukrainian affairs, the Rada demanded that Ukrainian military detachments be placed under its command. To the Kadets' dismay, the moderate socialist ministers, along with the Petrograd Soviet, supported the Rada. Rosenberg, *Liberals in the Russian Revolution*, 171–75.

149. For an account of these events, see Alexander Rabinowitch, *Prelude to Revolution* (Bloomington, 1968).

150. Dumova, *Kadetskaia partiia v period pervoi mirovoi voiny*, 182. In late September, moderate socialists and Kadets formed a third coalition government.

151. The ministry gave KIPS twelve thousand rubles for use through January 1918. PFA RAN f. 2, op. 1–1917, d. 30, l. 56.

152. KIPS met on September 5, 8, 9, and 25. PFA RAN f. 2, op. 1–1917, d. 30, ll. 56, 58, 73–74, and Rossiiskaia Akademiia nauk, *Ob uchrezhdenii Komissii*, 11.

153. "K deiatel'nosti natsional'nogo otdela," *Vestnik Vremennogo pravitel'stva*, no. 167 (October 3, 1917).

As KIPS began its work with the National Department, the Provisional Government issued a long-awaited official statement on the nationality question. It affirmed its commitment to guarantee national minorities ("in places of their permanent residence") the right "to use their native languages in schools, courts, institutions of self-government, and in their dealings with the local State organs." The Provisional Government also promised to initiate a broad-based discussion of national self-determination."[154] In mid-October, it created a new Commission on Nationality Affairs to prepare "material on the nationality question for the Constituent Assembly." It appointed Ol'denburg to head the commission.[155]

The Commission on Nationality Affairs, like the Provisional Government itself, would not last long. Massive demonstrations shook the empire throughout September and October, and the government's remaining authority disintegrated rapidly. Lenin returned to Petrograd on October 9, and the following day attended a meeting of the Bolshevik Central Committee. The majority voted to seize power.[156] The Bolsheviks made their move on October 24, and by the following day had taken strategic points throughout the capital and had arrested key members of the Provisional Government. When the Second All-Russian Congress of Soviets convened that evening, the Bolsheviks announced that the Provisional Government had been deposed. The Bolsheviks decreed the transfer of power to soviets of workers, peasants, and soldiers throughout Russia, and on the following day named Lenin the head of a new Council of People's Commissars. The Bolsheviks had achieved a quick victory in Petrograd. The real difficulties of consolidating power and spreading the revolution were still before them.

Ol'denburg, like most of his colleagues at the Academy of Sciences, was outraged by the Bolshevik seizure of power. But in spite of his own antipathy to the Bolsheviks, Ol'denburg quickly concluded that cooperation was necessary. Russia was still in the midst of war, and Ol'denburg did not want to see it fall to foreign powers. He, like other members of the Kadet Party in leadership positions at the Academy of Sciences, held out the hope that a Bolshevik government would in time take on a less radical form.[157] Ol'denburg also recognized that the Academy's survival would depend on working with the new Soviet government and securing a promise of state support. Living and working conditions in Russia had deteriorated through the years of war and revolution. The Academy had little heat and electricity, let alone the resources to continue its research.[158]

---

154. Browder and Kerensky, *Russian Provisional Government,* vol. 3, 1716 ("Declaration of the Third Coalition Government, September 25, 1917").

155. Dumova, *Kadetskaia partiia v period pervoi mirovoi voiny,* 213.

156. Carr, *Bolshevik Revolution,* vol. 1, 94–96.

157. Bailes, "Natural Scientists and the Soviet System," 268, 270.

158. Loren R. Graham, *Science in Russia and the Soviet Union: A Short History,* 82–83, and *The Soviet Academy of Sciences and the Communist Party, 1927–1932* (Princeton, 1967), 30–31;

Lenin and Ol'denburg became reacquainted in November 1917, when Ol'-denburg arrived at the Smolny Institute, Communist Party headquarters, as part of a small delegation of professors protesting the arrest of a group of ministers of the Provisional Government. Ol'denburg returned to the Smolny one month later to talk with Lenin about the fate of the Academy of Sciences. The two men had much to discuss, and spoke for more than two hours about the role of science and the place of scholars in a new Soviet state.[159] By the end of the meeting, Lenin and Ol'denburg had reached an understanding. The Academy's scholars would aid the Soviet regime by addressing urgent questions of "state construction." In return, the Academy would receive financial and political support. In subsequent weeks Soviet leaders decided that the Academy would report to the Department for the Mobilization of Scientific Forces of the People's Commissariat of Enlightenment (Narkompros), the successor to the Provisional Government's Ministry of Education. In February 1918, Ol'denburg and six other academics (three of them members of KIPS) signed a resolution affirming the Academy's commitment to the Soviet regime.[160] Several weeks later the Bolsheviks signed the Treaty of Brest-Litovsk with the German government—and used KIPS's maps of the western borderlands.[161]

While Russia's ethnographers had aspired to work with and help the imperial regime and then the Provisional Government, it was the Bolsheviks who recognized their potential. Whereas the imperial regime had been reluctant to support scholarly studies of Russia's nationalities, and the Provisional Government had been unable to make such studies a priority, the Bolsheviks were interested in the ethnographers' maps, notes, publications, and advice; they encouraged KIPS to do systematic research and sponsored fieldwork throughout Soviet Russia. In turn, Ol'denburg and many of his colleagues quickly came to perceive their disciplinary and professional interests as compatible with the practical interests of the Soviet government. They brought to their relationship with the Bolsheviks an idealized model of expert participation in scientific government that they took in large part from the European colonial context.

The two commissions that Ol'denburg and Vernadskii had organized to support the war effort, KIPS and KEPS, worked closely with the new Soviet government. KEPS continued its systematic study of Russia's productive forces

G. K. Skriabin, "Vydaiushchiisia organizator nauki," in *Sergei Fedorovich Ol'denburg,* 9–10; and Vucinich, *Empire of Knowledge,* 104.

159. Baziiants, "Dve vstrechi S. F. Ol'denburga s V. I. Leninym," 23. The Academy's president, Aleksandr Karpinskii, told Ol'denburg to negotiate for the Academy. Bailes, "Natural Scientists and the Soviet System," 270.

160. Kol'tsov, *Lenin i stanovlenie Akademii nauk,* 37, 47–48. The KIPS members were Karskii, Shakhmatov, and D'iakonov.

161. Ibid., 114–15. Also A. V. Lunacharskii, *Vospominaniia i vpechatleniia* (Moscow, 1968), 206.

and helped the Bolsheviks to determine how best to organize new industries and exploit the county's resources.[162] KIPS continued its ethnographic research and provided the Bolsheviks with maps and detailed information not just about the population of the borderlands, but about all of the former Russian Empire's nationalities and tribes.[163] The KIPS ethnographers helped the new Soviet government to negotiate peace treaties and borders with other states. They also served as expert-consultants on the nationality question, and helped the Bolsheviks bring the socialist revolution to the non-Russian regions of the former Russian Empire.[164]

The alliance between Bolsheviks and former imperial experts shaped the very formation of the Soviet Union. Stalin, of course, was the Soviet government's Commissar of Nationality Affairs and its recognized expert on the nationality question. As such, he gave Soviet nationality policy its theoretical contours. But Ol'denburg and the other KIPS ethnographers fundamentally affected that policy through their work on maps, censuses, and inventories of the population. This revolutionary alliance—revolutionary because of its origins and because of its goal of transforming Russia into a modern state—was based on a shared appreciation for scientific rule. It was not, however, based on a shared faith in Marxist ideology or socialism—and was therefore tenuous from the start. Ol'denburg and his colleagues were state patriots who saw scientific government as a desirable end in and of itself and also as a means of promoting Russia's national and imperial interests. The Bolsheviks, by contrast, saw scientific government as a tool with which to carry out a more radical revolution.

Over the course of the next decade, Bolsheviks and experts would work together to spread Soviet rule. During and after the civil war, the KIPS ethnographers would lead dozens of ethnographic expeditions, make new maps, and participate in deliberations about the administrative-territorial form of the Soviet state. In the mid-1920s, the ethnographers would help produce the First All-Union Census of the population, allowing the Bolsheviks to attain the conceptual conquest of the lands and peoples of the former Russian Empire. The choices that the ethnographers made—about how to determine an individual's

162. Kol'tsov, *Lenin i stanovlenie Akademii nauk*, 40–41, 71; Vucinich, *Empire of Knowledge*, 101–6; Baziiants, "Dve vstrechi S. F. Ol'denburga s V. I. Leninym," 24–25; and Lunacharskii, *Vospominaniia i vpechatleniia*, 204–6.

163. In 1917 KIPS was renamed the Commission for the Study of the Tribal Composition of the Population of Russia. In the 1920s it was renamed the Commission for the Study of the Tribal Composition of the Population of the USSR and Contiguous Countries.

164. Rossiiskaia Akademiia nauk, *Izvlecheniia iz protokolov zasedanii komissii v 1917 i 1918 godakh, Izvestiia Komissii po izucheniiu plemennogo sostava naseleniia Rossii*, vol. 2 (Petrograd, 1919), and D. Zolotarev, "Komissiia po izucheniiu plemennogo sostava naseleniia SSSR (KIPS) pri Akademii nauk SSSR," *Etnografiia*, no. 1 (1927): 213–14.

"nationality" in the "Asiatic" versus "European" regions of the former Russian Empire, about which peoples to include on a "List of the Nationalities of
the USSR," and about how to delimit borders in ethnographically mixed regions, for example—influenced Soviet policies and practices in fundamental
ways.

CHAPTER 2

The National Idea versus Economic Expediency

The era of great discoveries has long since passed, but is not the transformation of old Russia into the USSR the discovery of a new continent?

—N. Mikhaylov, *Soviet Geography*, 1935

Between 1917 and 1924 the Red Army pushed its way across thousands of miles, pro-Bolshevik forces waged successful uprisings in the peripheries, and the Soviet government marked the revolution's territorial gains with new borders and an official constitution. The Bolsheviks achieved the physical reconquest of most territories of the Russian Empire, but the formation of the Soviet Union was just beginning.[1] The new leaders of Soviet Russia did not aspire only to establish formal political control over the lands and peoples of the former Russian Empire. They aimed to mark a break with the imperial past and implement a revolutionary agenda. In particular, the Bolsheviks wanted to overcome the problem of "historical diversity": to build socialism in an immense territory with lands and peoples "at the most diverse levels of historical development."[2]

The Bolshevik leaders and liberal experts who came together in late 1917 had a shared orientation toward Western Europe and a shared faith in the potential of scientific rule. Both groups drew inspiration from the Enlightenment idea that modern governments could use expert knowledge to revolutionize economic production, social structures, and human consciousness.[3] And both

1. Here I take a different approach from Richard Pipes, who maintains that "the process of formation of the Soviet Union" was "brought to an end" with the ratification of the Constitution of the USSR on January 31, 1924. Richard Pipes, *The Formation of the Soviet Union: Communism and Nationalism, 1917–1923*, rev. ed. (Cambridge, MA, 1997), 293.

2. G. I. Broido, "Nasha natsional'naia politika i ocherednye zadachi Narkomnatsa," *Zhizn' natsional'nostei*, no. 1 (1923): 5–13 (esp. 5). In discussing "historical diversity," they used the term *mnogoukladnost'*.

3. This idea gained an audience during the Enlightenment, gathered steam after the French Revolution, and became something of a truism during the European "age of empire." On the Eu-

groups sought to use such knowledge to transform the former Russian Empire. By establishing a rational administrative structure and a centralized economic plan, the new regime and its experts would attempt to convert the former empire and its "underdeveloped expanses" into a "federation of cotton and flax, coal and metal, ore and oil, agriculture and machine industry."[4] By eliminating traditional institutions and ancient loyalties, they would attempt to speed up "evolutionary time"—turning the nomads of the Kirgiz steppe, the indigenous tribes of Siberia, and the illiterate peasants of central Russia into cultured socialist citizens.[5] The historian E. H. Carr has argued that "the disappearance of the old landmarks and the old names, the delimitation of new divisions and subdivisions, the arrival from Moscow of specialists and experts in planning, were a visible symbol of the consolidation of the revolution in the countryside."[6] These measures were more than symbolic. With new landmarks, new administrative-territorial borders, and new ambitious economic plans, the Soviet regime set out to transform people's lives.

Concerns about time, geography, and the revolution's future converged in deliberations about the administrative-territorial structure of the new Soviet state. It was by no means a given that the Soviet state would take the shape of an ethnoterritorial union. In the wake of 1917, neither the Bolshevik Party nor the regime's "specialists and experts in planning" had a singular vision for reorganizing the vast lands of the former Russian Empire. Instead, two paradigms vied for supremacy between 1918 and 1924 and found supporters among Bolsheviks and experts alike. These were the ethnographic paradigm and the economic paradigm. The former took the "ethnographic principle"— or the "principle of nationality" as it was called in the Paris Peace Conference—as its starting point and drew inspiration from the European nation state. Arguing that administrative-territorial divisions should conform to ethnographic boundaries, its supporters attempted to apply the "national

ropean case see Michael Adas, *Machines as the Measure of Men: Science, Technology, and Ideologies of Western Dominance* (Ithaca, 1989); Eric Hobsbawm, *The Age of Empire, 1875–1914* (New York, 1989); and George W. Stocking Jr., *Victorian Anthropology* (New York, 1987). On Enlightenment ideas about expert knowledge and the "art of government" in the European context see Michel Foucault, "Governmentality," in *The Foucault Effect: Studies in Governmentality,* ed. Graham Burchell, Colin Gordon, and Peter Miller (Chicago, 1991), 87–104. On the connection between Enlightenment thought and the Bolshevik Revolution see the introduction to Stephen Kotkin, *Magnetic Mountain: Stalinism as a Civilization* (Berkeley, 1995).

4. S. Dimanshtein, "Slozhnost' raboty novogo Narkomnatsa," *Zhizn' natsional'nostei,* no. 17 (74) (June 9, 1920): 1.

5. On "evolutionary time" and the Soviet project see Stephen E. Hanson, *Time and Revolution: Marxism and the Design of Soviet Institutions* (Chapel Hill, 1997). In some respects, Soviet-style modernization was similar to the French Republic's efforts to "civilize" its peasants and imperial subjects. But in the Soviet case, all peoples (Russian and non-Russian, urban and rural) were to at once participate in and be subject to state-sponsored modernization. All former tsarist subjects were to be remade as Soviet citizens. On the French case, see Eugen Weber, *Peasants into Frenchmen: The Modernization of Rural France, 1870–1914* (Stanford, 1976).

6. E. H. Carr, *Socialism in One Country, 1924–1926,* vol. 2 (New York, 1959), 301.

idea" to the Soviet context.[7] The economic paradigm, by contrast, was motivated by the "principle of economic expediency" and drew inspiration from
the European colonial economies.[8] Its advocates maintained that the Soviet
state should be organized into specialized economic-administrative units based
on a scientific evaluation of local "productive forces" (defined in Marxist
terms as raw materials, instruments of production, and labor power).[9] Dismissive of "national rights," they argued that nationalism would dissipate once favorable economic conditions were established through the state-sponsored colonization of backward territories within Soviet borders. Ultimately, it was the
attempt to reach a compromise between these two paradigms that gave the Soviet Union its unique form.

The debate about the administrative-territorial organization, or regionalization, of the new Soviet state was in essence a debate about the road to socialism. It closely paralleled discussions within the Bolshevik Party about the
nationality question and internationalism. Addressing Russia's nationality
question before 1917, Vladimir Il'ich Lenin had suggested that the peoples of
the Russian Empire were at different stages on the Marxist historical timeline:
that the peoples of Asiatic Russia were still in the "feudal era," while the nationalities of the western borderlands had entered the era of "developing capitalism." Reflecting on the population's historical diversity, Lenin had argued
that the road to internationalism would require patience—and had criticized
those Bolsheviks who assumed that a socialist revolution would instantly eradicate Russia's nationality question. He had called for careful studies of the
population's ethnographic makeup, arguing that the boundaries of a new Russian socialist state could not be drawn to meet "the requirements of production" alone.[10] In spite of Lenin's position, the Bolsheviks remained divided
about the nationality question—even after October 1917. Controversial
enough was the party's promise of national self-determination, which some
Bolsheviks (such as Georgii Piatakov) condemned as a betrayal of Marxist internationalism.[11] Even more contentious was the question of how to deal with

7. On the Paris Peace Conference and the national idea see C. A. Macartney, *National States
and National Minorities* (London, 1934); Arno Mayer, *Wilson vs. Lenin: Political Origins of the
New Diplomacy, 1917–1918* (Cleveland, 1964); Margaret MacMillan, *Paris 1919: Six Months
that Changed the World* (New York, 2001); and Mark Mazower, *Dark Continent: Europe's
Twentieth Century* (New York, 1999).

8. It also drew inspiration from plans for the regionalization of the former Russian Empire—
whose authors also looked to the European colonial economies for ideas.

9. For a discussion of Marx's use of the term *productive forces* see G. A. Cohen, *Karl Marx's
Theory of History: A Defense* (Princeton, 2000).

10. V. I. Lenin, "Itogi diskussii o samoopredelenii," in *Polnoe sobranie sochinenii*, vol. 30
(Moscow, 1962), 18, 21.

11. Piatakov and Nikolai Bukharin led the charge against the Bolshevik promise of national
self-determination at the Eighth Party Congress in spring 1919. For Bukharin's arguments and
Lenin's response see *Vos'moi s"ezd RKP(b): Protokoly* (Moscow, 1959), 75–116. Discussed in
Yuri Slezkine, "The USSR as a Communal Apartment, or How a Socialist State Promoted Ethnic
Particularism," *Slavic Review* 53, no. 2 (1994): 420.

the "backward ethnic groups" of the former Russian Empire that lacked, or were experiencing the first stirrings of, national consciousness.[12] Was it necessary for all of the peoples of the former Russian Empire to go through a "national" stage of development? Or could rapid economic development eradicate all traces of nationalism (zealous or incipient) and speed the way to communism?

The classic works on the Bolshevik Revolution describe a party that had decisive leadership and clear aims. Working from this premise, a number of scholars have concluded that the Bolsheviks devised the Soviet Union's complicated administrative-territorial structure as a means to divide and rule.[13] This chapter, by contrast, makes the case that the Soviet Union took shape as it did precisely because the party did not fully control the process of regionalization—and in fact could not even agree on the approach to take in the beginning.[14] Instead, regionalization was a process of trial and error. It took place with the input of a coterie of administrators and experts, who were themselves engaged in an interinstitutional competition for influence and resources. The staunchest institutional supporter of the ethnographic paradigm was the People's Commissariat for the Affairs of the Nationalities (Narkomnats)—a government agency whose official role was to win non-Russians over to the side of the revolution. The main champion of the economic paradigm was the State Planning Commission (Gosplan)—a government commission staffed predominantly by non-party academics and engineers whose job it was to put together a centralized economic plan.[15] Former imperial ethnographers served as expert-consultants for both Narkomnats and Gosplan, shaping a new field of applied Soviet ethnography and influencing the very formation of the Soviet Union.

The Principle of Nationality

As World War I came to an end in 1918, the era of the multinational dynastic states also drew to a close. The Allies marked their victory by dismantling the

12. Slezkine, "USSR as a Communal Apartment," 420. On this point, Slezkine is citing A. P. Nenarokov, *K edinstvu ravnykh: Kul'turnye faktory ob"edinitel'nogo dvizheniia sovetskikh narodov, 1917–1924* (Moscow, 1991), 91–92.

13. See, for example, Hélène Carrére d'Encausse, *The End of the Soviet Empire: The Triumph of the Nations* (New York, 1993), and Olaf Caroe, *Soviet Empire: The Turks of Central Asia and Stalinism* (London, 1953). I discuss the "divide and rule" literature and the national-territorial delimitation of Central Asia in detail in chapter 4.

14. Stalin did not weigh in on the regionalization debate during the civil war. According to Stephen Blank, he neglected Narkomnats, which soon "lapsed into torpor." See Stephen Blank, *The Sorcerer as Apprentice: Stalin as Commissar of Nationalities, 1917–1924* (Westport, 1994), 52. In fact, Narkomnats was quite energetic during these years—even without Stalin's attention.

15. Many of the economists and engineers who worked in Gosplan were former Mensheviks. For a discussion of the makeup of Gosplan see Alec Nove, *An Economic History of the U.S.S.R.*, rev. ed. (London, 1989).

Austro-Hungarian and Ottoman Empires. By this time, the Russian Empire had already ceased to exist in both political and territorial terms. The Bolsheviks had ceded Russia's western borderlands to Germany in the Treaty of Brest-Litovsk of March 1918. After the German defeat, these and other territories exercised what local leaders (seizing the slogan of the day) proclaimed to be their right to national self-determination.[16] By late 1918, Ukraine, Belorussia, Georgia, Armenia, Azerbaijan, Latvia, Lithuania, and Estonia had signed peace treaties with foreign powers and had attained international recognition as independent states. In fact, all of these states remained embroiled in civil war until at least 1921, and came at various points under foreign occupation.

Between 1919 and 1921, the Bolsheviks used military force, intrigue, and diplomatic measures in attempts to form alliances with and exert control over the newly independent states of the former Russian Empire. In a number of cases, Soviet leaders signed treaties with local communists, who then declared their states to be independent soviet socialist republics. The actual status of these territories changed several times, however, as White armies, Polish forces, and Allied interventionists challenged the Bolsheviks and their claims. Meanwhile, separatist forces were also at work in "Asiatic Russia" and other parts of the former empire. Self-described national leaders created local militias and launched movements for national liberation in Turkestan, the Far East, and the Volga region. Whenever possible, the Bolsheviks forged ties with local radicals. In many regions, though, the Bolsheviks had no indigenous support whatsoever.[17]

The Bolsheviks' success in reuniting almost all of the former empire's disparate parts into a single Soviet state by 1922 was nothing less than remarkable.[18] In part, this accomplishment was an extension of the Red Army's military victory. But the reverse was also true: the Bolsheviks' adept handling of the nationality question helped them to build alliances with non-communists and win the civil war. While the imperial regime, the Provisional Government, and the Whites had attempted to ignore the national idea, the Bolsheviks integrated it into their ideology and their vision of the Soviet socialist state.

Before the revolution, the Bolsheviks had rejected the two "solutions" to the nationality question favored by nationality-based political parties—federalism and extraterritorial autonomy. Shortly after seizing power, however, the Bolsheviks declared the "Soviet Russian Republic" to be a federation: the Russian

---

16. In the midst of World War I, Woodrow Wilson, Lenin, and the German government had all declared that nations had the right to self-determination. See chapter 1.

17. See E. H. Carr, *The Bolshevik Revolution, 1917–1923,* vol. 1 (London, 1950); Pipes, *Formation of the Soviet Union;* and Blank, *Sorcerer as Apprentice.*

18. Several provinces (*gubernii*) of the western borderlands (including Latvia, Lithuania, and Estonia), the principality of Finland, the Congress of Poland, and part of the southern borderlands would remain outside of Soviet borders at this time.

Soviet Federation of Socialist Republics (RSFSR).[19] Against the backdrop of war and revolution, much had changed. Previously, Lenin had criticized federalism as a force that would destroy the unity of the state. But faced with the empire's dissolution in 1918, and forced to recognize the establishment of "independent" (in fact German-controlled) Belorussian and Ukrainian republics, he envisioned ethnoterritorial federalism as the most effective means to reunite Russia's lands and peoples—and as a first step toward the long-term aim of the merger of nations in a socialist union.[20] In late 1918, a Bolshevik Constitutional Commission affirmed Joseph Stalin's recommendation to base the Soviet "federal system" on the principle of "national-territorial autonomy."

The idea of an ethnoterritorial federation had not gone unchallenged in the Constitutional Commission's deliberations. Commissar of Justice Mikhail Reisner had argued that the Russian Soviet Federation should be organized into economic regions, maintaining that the "national factor was secondary, and should be limited to cultural matters."[21] A sizeable faction within the Bolshevik Party had supported Reisner's position and continued to denounce the idea of a socialist federation of nationalities as ridiculous.[22] But, for some time at least, the ethnoterritorial model prevailed; holding a tenuous military and political position, the Bolsheviks could not afford to alienate local leaders whose allegiance was contingent on Soviet support for their independent national-territorial status.

Through the civil war years, the Bolsheviks attempted to learn about the peoples of the former Russian Empire—with the goals of winning them over and bringing them under Soviet rule. The revolutionaries, lacking even the most basic information about the languages and cultures of many of the former empire's subjects, looked to ethnographers from the imperial regime for assistance. The Commission for the Study of the Tribal Composition of the Population of Russia (KIPS) played a particularly important role in the Bolsheviks' struggle to bring the revolution to non-Russian regions. In the midst of the civil war, the Bolsheviks commissioned KIPS ethnographers to travel to recalcitrant regions and survey their populations and terrain. For example, during the summer of 1920, the ethnographer Aleksei Petrov led a small expedition to the North Caucasus, using a KIPS-generated questionnaire to map

19. *S"ezdy sovetov RSFSR v postanovleniiakh i rezoliutsiiakh* (Moscow, 1939), 44–45. Cited in Pipes, *Formation of the Soviet Union,* 111.

20. Pipes, *Formation of the Soviet Union,* chapter 3, and John Stephen Reshetar, *The Ukrainian Revolution, 1917–1920: A Study in Nationalism* (Princeton, 1952).

21. G. S. Gurvich, *Istoriia sovetskoi konstitutsii* (Moscow, 1923). Cited in Pipes, *Formation of the Soviet Union,* 111. Reisner, an expert in legal philosophy, believed that national rights could be safeguarded through the law. On the contest between the "ethnographic" and "economic" principles, also see Jeremy Smith, *The Bolsheviks and the National Question, 1917–1923* (Houndmill, UK, 1999).

22. This group included Piatakov and Bukharin. See the discussion in Slezkine, "USSR as a Communal Apartment," 420.

out the lands and peoples along his route; the questionnaire asked for a description of important mountains, rivers, and "natural boundaries," for "the exact name (or names) of each population group," and for information about the population's national consciousness, kinship ties, native languages, knowledge of Russian, and religious and folk beliefs.[23] A number of Soviet institutions relied on the ethnographic knowledge that KIPS provided. The party used KIPS reports about local languages and cultures to deploy emissaries from Moscow who could better communicate with local populations, while Narkomnats used KIPS ethnographic maps to delimit ethnoterritorial borders within the RSFSR. The People's Commissariat of Foreign Affairs enlisted KIPS to provide evidence supporting Soviet claims to contested territories in the eastern and western borderlands, and later to assist in its peace negotiations with Poland.[24]

The Bolsheviks' efforts to reunite the territories of the former Russian Empire were also furthered by their willingness to collaborate with nonsocialist local elites in non-Russian regions. Narkomnats played an important role in this area. It reached out to local populations and helped the Bolsheviks broker alliances with new self-identified national leaders; it also helped facilitate local-level coups, installing local leaders who were either sympathetic to the Bolsheviks or prepared to trade their allegiance for Bolshevik backing.[25] Through these efforts, the Bolsheviks gained a foothold in regions without local communists. In Turkestan, for example, Narkomnats drew young Muslims with a secular orientation (the Jadids) into local government and party institutions. The new "Muslim communists" supported Bolshevik claims to power, and the Bolsheviks supported their claims to leadership against those of traditional Muslim authorities.[26] As part of its efforts, Narkomnats established local-level national commissariats throughout Soviet Russia. Beginning in February 1918, these national commissariats sent representatives to participate in a general Narkomnats collegium, which met once a week to discuss issues of concern for the localities.[27] Through the collegium, new national rep-

23. The St. Petersburg Branch of the Archive of the Russian Academy of Sciences (PFA RAN) f. 2, op. 1–1917, d. 31, ll. 13–14. The expedition went from May through August.

24. On KIPS and its responsibilities see PFA RAN f. 135, op. 1, d. 3, ll. 1–3, 6, 17, 42–43, 52–53; d. 9, ll. 26, 70. Also see A. V. Kol'tsov, *Lenin i stanovlenie Akademii nauk kak tsentra sovetskoi nauki* (Leningrad, 1969). On Ol'denburg's involvement in the negotiation of peace treaties see "Osnovnye daty zhizni i deiatel'nosti S. F. Ol'denburga," in *Sergei Fedorovich Ol'denburg*, ed. G. K. Skriabin and E. M. Primakov (Moscow, 1986), 121. Samoilovich participated in a diplomatic mission to Anatolia, Turkey, and did research to support Soviet claims for contested territories on the Turkish border. PFA RAN f. 2, op. 1–1917, d. 31, l. 39.

25. On Narkomnats see G. P. Makarova, *Narodnyi komissariat po delam natsional'nostei RSFSR, 1917–1923 gg.: Istoricheskii ocherk* (Moscow, 1987), and Blank, *Sorcerer as Apprentice*.

26. See the epilogue to Adeeb Khalid, *The Politics of Muslim Cultural Reform: Jadidism in Central Asia* (Berkeley, 1998).

27. The collegium was later renamed the Soviet of Nationalities. See M. Kalinin and A. Enukidze, "Novoe polozhenie o Narkomnatse," *Zhizn' natsional'nostei*, no. 17 (152) (August 21,

resentatives began to participate in the Soviet government apparatus—bringing their own ethnographic knowledge about the former empire's lands and peoples to the table, and adding their voices to the discussion about the form of the Soviet state.

The national idea thus became an integral part of Soviet Russia's physical and conceptual makeup over the course of the civil war years. The Bolsheviks upheld the principle of national-territorial autonomy, and administrators and ethnographers characterized the delimitation of borders along ethnographic lines as a means to integrate non-Russian territories into a Soviet state. During this period, Narkomnats oversaw the establishment within the Russian Soviet Federation of a number of ethnoterritorial units: autonomous soviet socialist republics such as the Bashkir ASSR, autonomous national oblasts such as the Chuvash AO, and national communes.[28] Narkomnats even discussed delimiting ethnoterritorial units in parts of the Far East and Turkestan where local populations did not seek autonomous national status. Significantly, neither the party nor Narkomnats ever seriously discussed giving "the Great Russians" their own ethnoterritorial unit. To do so would have been gratuitous; the working assumption was that the Russians, as the state-bearing people of the former Russian Empire and the most dominant nation of the Russian Soviet Federation, did not need their own ethnoterritorial unit. All of the territories that remained outside of the official ethnoterritorial units were understood to be "Russian" by default.[29]

Even as the principle of nationality took hold, many Bolsheviks remained uncertain about relying on the ethnographic paradigm alone to organize the state's administrative-territorial structure. And as the civil war wound down in 1921, a group of Moscow-based economists and engineers also urged caution. While Narkomnats encouraged the regime to stand by its commitment to the national idea, these experts warned that the wholesale application of the ethnographic paradigm would result in economic underdevelopment. Could the principle of nationality and the principle of economic expediency coexist?

1922): 14–16. In 1924 Narkomnats was eliminated and the Soviet of Nationalities became a second branch of the Soviet government.

28. In March 1921 the RSFSR had within it six soviet socialist republics (the Turkestan, Bashkir, Tatar, Kirgiz, Dagestan, and Mountaineer ASSRs), four autonomous national oblasts (the Chuvash, Votiak, Mari, and Kalmyk AOs), and two national communes (the Volga German and Karelian communes). The list would grow. In 1923, *Zhizn' natsional'nostei*, the official newspaper of the Soviet of Nationalities, was turned into a journal. The first issue featured articles about all of the national-territorial units within the RSFSR and about the allied national republics. See "Avtonomnye natsional'no-territorial'nye ob''edineniia i natsional'nye men'shinstva za 5 let Revoliutsii (1917–1922)," *Zhizn' natsional'nostei*, no. 1 (1923): 25–273.

29. Terry Martin has argued that "Affirmative Action for all non-Russians necessarily implied reverse discrimination against Russians." But this misses the point. The Soviet state did not make the Russians give up their language or culture, and the Russians remained the dominant nationality in the nonnational territories of the Soviet Union. See Terry Martin, *The Affirmative Action Empire: Nations and Nationalism in the Soviet Union, 1923–1939* (Ithaca, 2001), 25.

Which would take precedence in the administrative framework of the Soviet state? The regionalization debate was born.

The Regionalization Debate

The Bolsheviks devoted significant effort to the work of state-building during the civil war years. Against a backdrop of massive dislocation and destruction, the revolutionaries began to create new institutions and delimit new borders—marking their victories and claiming the lands of the former Russian Empire as their own. The establishment of official guidelines for the creation of a "rational" administrative-territorial framework became an official project in December 1919, when the Seventh All-Russian Congress of Soviets declared that the All-Russian Central Executive Committee (VTsIK) of the government should "work out the practical question" of the regionalization (*raionirovanie*) of the RSFSR.[30] The congress suggested that VTsIK set clear guidelines for the future establishment of all administrative-territorial units, including national republics, oblasts, and communes. It also called for the logical reorganization of all local government organs and institutions (such as schools, hospitals, and courthouses) within these administrative-territorial units.[31]

Regionalization was supposed to "put an end to the chaos" of the preceding few years through a major reform of the federation's infrastructure. Describing the existing system of administrative organization as "anarchic," VTsIK officials Timofei Sapronov and Mikhail Vladimirskii (both members of the party elite) had regaled the Congress of Soviets with tales of administrative disorder.[32] According to these officials, the RSFSR's existing administrative structure combined the inadequacies of the imperial *guberniia* system (which had divided the Russian Empire into ninety-seven provinces without regard to either ethnographic or economic considerations) with the "spontaneous" changes that were taking place during the civil war. In the midst of the fighting, armies, local leaders, soviets, and villages were acting on their own volition to create administrative units. In the Far East and Siberia, in particular, local struggles with foreign interventionist forces were resulting in the im-

---

30. *S''ezdy sovetov RSFSR*, 152. Cited in Carr, *Socialism in One Country*, vol. 2, 274. Also E. N. Bashkova, "Raionirovanie SSSR: Istoricheskaia spravka," in *Voprosy ekonomicheskogo raionirovaniia SSSR: Sbornik materialov i statei (1917–1929 gg.)*, ed. G. M. Krzhizhanovskii (Moscow, 1957), 304. The Soviet regime inherited from the Russian Empire a system of *sela* (villages), *volosty* (rural districts), *uezdy* (counties or regions), and *gubernii* (provinces).

31. K. D. Egorov, ed., *Raionirovanie SSSR: Sbornik materialov po raionirovaniiu s 1917 po 1925 godu* (Moscow, 1926), 10–13, 17.

32. Ibid. Sapronov captured the absurdities of the existing administrative-territorial system when he described the plight of a peasant forced to travel to one city to appeal to a judge when his cow was stolen and then to a different city to appeal to another judge when someone plowed up his field.

promptu creation of new administrative units as territories were gained and lost in battle.[33]

In the wake of the Congress, VTsIK set up an Administrative Commission and directed it to work out general principles for the administrative-territorial organization, or regionalization, of the RSFSR.[34] Initially, the commission would evaluate all existing administrative units and decide whether or not they were viable from economic, military, administrative, and geographical perspectives. It would devote special attention to the recently established national-territorial units, assessing their long-term potential as administrative units. To facilitate this work, in February 1920 the VTsIK Administrative Commission and the People's Commissariat of Internal Affairs (NKVD) distributed a questionnaire to all local-level government organs, seeking "materials useful" for the possible administrative remapping of the state. The questionnaire requested a detailed account of each region's economic enterprises (especially those with military or industrial significance), natural-geographical conditions, transportation infrastructure (railroads, roads, ports), and economic ties to nearby regions. It also requested information about the population's "national composition" and "economic orientation." Perhaps most significantly, the questionnaire attempted to gauge the potential response to administrative remapping, asking whether the issue of "creating new administrative-economic units" had "come up." "If so," it inquired, "how did the matter end?"[35]

Thus, even as the Soviet regime continued to voice its commitment to the principle of nationality, it explored the idea of reorganizing the RSFSR according to other criteria. The following month, at the Ninth Party Congress, Bolshevik leaders proposed "a single economic plan" for all territories of the federation. In response, the VTsIK Administrative Commission began to discuss in earnest a form of regionalization based on the "economic principle."[36] Following the party congress, the VTsIK commission appealed to KIPS and to the Commission for the Study of the Natural Productive Forces of Russia (KEPS), the two Academy of Sciences commissions engaged in systematic research on the federation's lands and peoples, for assistance on a possible plan to divide Russia into economic regions. KEPS, whose Committee for the Description of Russia by Region (established to aid the imperial regime in World War I) was already working on an analysis of Russia's natural productive forces, sent the commission detailed notes and recommendations. KIPS, which was providing Narkomnats and other institutions with ethnographic maps, agreed to work with KEPS to inventory the population's productive potential.[37]

---

33. Ibid., 16–17; P. M. Alampiev, *Ekonomicheskoe raionirovanie SSSR* (Moscow, 1959), 62–70; and Blank, *Sorcerer as Apprentice*, 82.

34. Egorov, *Raionirovanie SSSR: Sbornik*, 17–19.

35. The State Archive of the Russian Federation (GARF) f. 5677, op. 1, d. 7, ll. 5–7.

36. Carr, *Socialism in One Country*, vol. 2, 274.

37. PFA RAN f. 135, op. 1, d. 3, ll. 4–6, 18; d. 1, l. 6.

In interinstitutional deliberations about the federation's form, Narkomnats was the most vocal defender of the ethnographic paradigm, arguing that nationality was "a fact" demanding primary consideration during the transitional period to socialism.[38] Many of the commissariat's national representatives had given their support to the Soviet regime with the expectation that the Bolsheviks would recognize their demands for national self-determination and grant them national-territorial autonomy. With Stalin, the head of Narkomnats, at the front or preoccupied with other pressing issues during the civil war—and silent on the question of regionalization—lower-level Narkomnats administrators took up the fight. Up through December 1920, these administrators were confident that the ethnographic paradigm would prevail. A November 1920 article in the Narkomnats newspaper *Zhizn' natsional'nostei* (*Life of the Nationalities*) celebrating the formation of the Mari, Votiak, and Kalmyk autonomous national oblasts stated that the ethnographic principle reflected "the essence" of the regime's approach to "the nationality question." According to the author, the creation of a full-fledged ethnoterritorial federation would be the most efficient means to introduce all the nationalities of the former Russian Empire "to a universal socialist culture." The author looked forward to the ethnoterritorial regionalization of Siberia and the Caucasus (anticipating the Soviet reconquest of all of Transcaucasia), adding that such a task awaited the completion of new ethnographic maps.[39]

Despite Narkomnats's optimism, the formal institutionalization of the principle of nationality was still being hotly contested. In December 1920, the Eighth All-Russian Congress of Soviets proposed an alternative to the Narkomnats vision: a federation organized solely along administrative-economic lines.[40] As if on cue, a front-page article in the Narkomnats newspaper proclaimed what had just become obvious: "The federation is still far from having taken its final form!"[41] The timing of the December resolution was not accidental. Red forces had all but emerged the victors in Russia's civil war. With the defeat of the Whites, the return of Azerbaijan, Ukraine, and Belorussia to the Soviet fold, and the recognition that world socialist revolution was perhaps not imminent, Soviet leaders and experts began to search for the model of administrative-territorial organization that would best facilitate economic recovery.

The most serious challenge to the ethnographic paradigm came from the offices of Gosplan. In May 1921, with the introduction of the New Economic Policy (NEP), Gosplan's Council of Labor and Defense established a Regional-

38. S. K., "Ekonomicheskoe raionirovanie i problemy avtonomno-federativnogo stroitel'stva," *Zhizn' natsional'nostei*, no. 25 (123) (November 12, 1921): 1.

39. I. Gertsenberg, "Natsional'nyi printsip v novom administrativnom delenii RSFSR," *Zhizn' natsional'nostei*, no. 37 (94) (November 25, 1920): 1.

40. S''ezdy sovetov RSFSR, 179. Cited in Carr, *Socialism in One Country*, vol. 2, 275.

41. S. Kotliarevskii, "O razvitii federatsii," *Zhizn' natsional'nostei*, no. 41 (97) (December 24, 1920): 1.

ization Commission and directed it to come up with a concrete plan for the economic-administrative organization of the Soviet federation. The new Regionalization Commission began its work in the summer of 1921, as a major famine was devastating much of Russia and Ukraine. The commission was staffed largely by professional economists and engineers who had worked in imperial ministries before 1917—and who had long aspired to use their expertise to modernize Russia's economic infrastructure. The head of the commission, the economics professor Ivan Aleksandrov, had earned Lenin's respect in 1920 with his work on a major project to promote the electrification of Russia. He, like most members of the commission, was not a party member.[42] The commission consulted with a number of government institutions that had already been discussing alternatives to ethnoterritorial regionalization, such as the People's Commissariat of Agriculture, the Central Statistical Administration, and the VTsIK Administrative Commission.[43] It also studied past proposals for the regionalization of the Russian Empire, including those produced by the geographers Dmitrii Rikhter in 1898 and Veniamin Semenov-Tian-Shanskii in 1911 and by KEPS in 1920.[44] In addition, the commission reviewed detailed reports about the RSFSR's lands and peoples that had been compiled, in part, by KIPS and KEPS.

The Gosplan Regionalization Commission sought a plan to promote the rational reorganization of the state's administrative infrastructure and the best use of the RSFSR's productive forces.[45] As such, it discussed different possible criteria for delimiting economic regions. Some commission members advocated that Russia adopt the model of the French administrative *département* and delimit regions to correspond with river basins. But others criticized this attempt to transfer "the French experience" with its "completely different economic and political conditions" to Soviet Russia.[46] Aleksandrov proposed that the Soviet regime take "a completely new" approach to regionalization based

42. Aleksandrov had been a member of the State Commission for the Electrification of Russia. Anne D. Rassweiler, *The Generation of Power: The History of Dneprostroi* (New York, 1988), 18–24.

43. The resolutions are published in Gosplan R.S.F.S.R., *Ekonomicheskoe raionirovanie Rossii: Materialy podkomissii po raionirovaniiu pri Gosudarstvennoi obshche-planovoi komissii S.T.O.* (Moscow, 1921). On the commission's origins and meetings see Alampiev, *Ekonomicheskoe raionirovanie SSSR*, 88–108.

44. For a discussion of past plans and recommendations see Egorov, *Raionirovanie SSSR: Sbornik*, 28–35; Z. Mieczkowski, "The Economic Regionalization of the Soviet Union in the Lenin and Stalin Period," *Canadian Slavonic Papers* 8 (1966): 88–90; and Alampiev, *Ekonomicheskoe raionirovanie SSSR*, 46–56.

45. Egorov, *Raionirovanie SSSR: Sbornik*, 12, 26–27; V. Ul'ianov (Lenin) et al., "Polozhenie o gosudarstvennoi obshcheplanovoi komissii," in *Ekonomicheskoe raionirovanie Rossii*, 3–4; and G. M. Krzhizhanovskii, *Khoziaistvennye problemy R.S.F.S.R. i raboty Gosudarstvennoi obshche-planovoi komissii (Gosplana)*, vol. 1 (Moscow, 1921), 92–100. (Ivan Aleksandrov wrote this section of the volume.)

46. I. G. Aleksandrov, "Ekonomicheskoe raionirovanie Rossii," in *Ekonomicheskoe raionirovanie Rossii*, 31–32.

on "the production trait": that it delimit economic-administrative oblasts in accordance with their natural resources, their potential economic specialization, and their population's *byt* (way of life).[47]

Aleksandrov's "new" approach essentially involved appropriating elements from the European colonial economies and adapting them to the Soviet context—a point that his critics raised repeatedly. He and some of his colleagues imagined Turkestan as a cotton oblast, Arkhangelsk as the base for a "forest-exploiting colony," the Caucasus as an oil and mineral procurement oblast, Moscow as the base for a central-industrial oblast, Ekaterinburg as the base for a Urals industrial oblast, and so on.[48] Aleksandrov spoke enthusiastically about "the natural division of labor" among agricultural, industrial, and natural resource oblasts.[49] He envisioned that Moscow-based economists and administrators would direct economic transactions among the different (agricultural, industrial, and raw-material) oblasts, and plan production, trade, and consumption for the federation as a whole. Making room for some local autonomy, Aleksandrov suggested that individual oblasts be delimited according to "the principle of economic completeness": that each contain "a complex of resources" able to meet its inhabitants' basic needs. Thus, industrial oblasts and natural-resource oblasts would have agricultural subregions to supply foodstuffs to workers, and each agricultural oblast would have a "proletarian" subregion to exert a positive cultural influence on the rest of the population.[50]

The existence of the national republics, oblasts, and communes that had been created during the civil war years presented a formidable challenge to plans for economic-administrative regionalization. Aleksandrov and his colleagues at Gosplan thought of the Soviet state as one unified landmass, including not just the RSFSR but also the allied national republics. Most of the economists assumed that the existing national territories would be incorporated into new economic-administrative units. This assumption had some basis; the economic unification of the RSFSR with the allied national republics was already in progress in 1921. The Bolsheviks had overseen the establishment of treaties between the RSFSR and the Ukrainian, Belorussian, and Azerbaijan SSRs that affirmed the autonomous status of these republics while providing for their inclusion in a centralized economy and military. But Aleksandrov and his colleagues imagined a far greater degree of unification, raising an impor-

47. Ibid., 32.

48. Ibid., 38–42. Also "Programmy razrabotki raionov," in *Ekonomicheskoe raionirovanie Rossii*, 55–58.

49. Aleksandrov, "Ekonomicheskoe raionirovanie Rossii," in *Ekonomicheskoe raionirovanie Rossii*, 31–33. On economic oblasts and the division of labor see also S. V. Bernshtein-Kogan, "K voprosu o programme i metode sostavleniia poraionnykh obzorov i khoziaistvennykh planov," in *Ekonomicheskoe raionirovanie Rossii*, 25–26.

50. Aleksandrov, "Ekonomicheskoe raionirovanie Rossii," in *Ekonomicheskoe raionirovanie Rossii*, 42. See the discussion in Egorov, *Raionirovanie SSSR: Sbornik*, 39–42.

tant question: How would national-territorial units preserve their autonomous status in a state that was reorganized along economic-administrative lines?

The Gosplan Regionalization Commission had a ready, if dismissive, response to what it saw as the bothersome question of national rights. Ethnoterritorial units would *not* retain their autonomous status. Instead, their lands and peoples would be integrated directly into economic-administrative units.[51] Aleksandrov acknowledged that this contradicted the idea of national self-determination. But, echoing those Bolsheviks who continued to criticize the party's official position on the nationality question, he argued that rapid economic development would eradicate the need for national territories altogether. "National tendencies were always quite limited" among the masses and "manifest themselves only in the face of unfavorable [economic] circumstances," Aleksandrov argued.[52] Describing economic regionalization as a "revolutionary method of economic uplift," he predicted that the nationality question would soon become irrelevant.[53]

In September 1921, Aleksandrov presented to Gosplan the Regionalization Commission's proposal for the organization of the RSFSR and allied republics into thirteen European and eight Asiatic economic-administrative oblasts.[54] Each economic-administrative oblast would be "an actual administrative unit," not just a "paper oblast" for statistics and economic planning.[55] Each would represent "a link in the chain" of the national economy, a component part of a "complete state organism."[56] Aleksandrov conceded that small national territories might remain intact upon their integration into the twenty-one economic-administrative oblasts. But he advocated that larger ethnoterritorial units, such as the Ukrainian SSR and the Kirgiz ASSR, be broken up into oblasts based on their potential economic specializations.[57] For example, his plan called for the division of the Ukrainian national republic into the indus-

51. Aleksandrov, "Ekonomicheskoe raionirovanie Rossii," in *Ekonomicheskoe raionirovanie Rossii*, 33.

52. Ibid., 33–35.

53. Cited in Alampiev, *Ekonomicheskoe raionirovanie SSSR*, 133.

54. I. G. Aleksandrov, "Ekonomicheskoe raionirovanie Rossii," in Krzhizhanovskii, ed., *Voprosy ekonomicheskogo raionirovaniia SSSR*, 66–86, and Mieczkowski, "Economic Regionalization of the Soviet Union," 98–100. This proposal was published in *Ekonomicheskaia zhizn'* in September 1921. There were several different versions of the plan. One version listed twelve European and eight Asiatic oblasts, another version fourteen European and four Turkestani oblasts. See for example I. Trainin, "Ekonomicheskoe raionirovanie i natsional'naia politika," *Zhizn' natsional'nostei*, no. 21 (119) (October 10, 1921): 1. Also Alampiev, *Ekonomicheskoe raionirovanie SSSR*, 104–8; Carr, *Socialism in One Country*, vol. 2, 276; Krzhizhanovskii, *Khoziaistvennye problemy R.S.F.S.R.*, 96–97; and Aleksandrov, "Ekonomicheskoe raionirovanie Rossii," in *Ekonomicheskoe raionirovanie Rossii*, 33–41.

55. Aleksandrov, "Ekonomicheskoe raionirovanie Rossii," in *Ekonomicheskoe raionirovanie Rossii*, 32.

56. Krzhizhanovskii, *Khoziaistvennye problemy R.S.F.S.R.*, 94.

57. The Kirgiz ASSR, established in 1920, was renamed the Kazakh ASSR in 1925.

trial Southern Mining oblast and the agricultural Southwestern oblast.
Demonstrating an awareness of Ukraine's ethnographic composition (and
making a small nod toward ethnographic considerations), Aleksandrov asserted that these two parts of Ukraine were "ethnically" distinct from one another: that the projected Southwestern oblast was dominated by Ukrainians,
while the projected Southern Mining oblast was inhabited by "representatives
of all the main *narodnosti* of Russia," including Great Russians, Ukrainians,
Greeks, Bulgarians, Germans, Jews, and Tatars.[58]

Aleksandrov and his colleagues purported to take an innovative approach
to the problem of backwardness, one based on rational economic planning
and "not on the vestiges of lost sovereign rights."[59] But for local national leaders and for most Narkomnats administrators, the commission's dismissal of
"national rights" was an expression of economic and political imperialism.[60]
Aleksandrov insisted that economic-administrative regionalization would not
interrupt "the development of the cultural-customary particularities of different nationalities."[61] But local leaders, concerned about protecting their populations' right to native-language schools and institutions, were not so sure. Nor
were they worried only about language and culture.[62] Ukrainian representatives protested that the division of Ukraine into two economic-administrative
oblasts would mean the loss of its *political* autonomy. Narkomnats expressed
similar concerns and felt obliged to remind Gosplan that "Ukraine is an independent state."[63] The Narkomnats administrator Il'ia Trainin cautioned that
"the substance" of autonomy would decrease for all nationalities if economic-
administrative oblasts usurped administrative functions.[64]

Moreover, Trainin asserted that Gosplan did not realize that Narkomnats
was also concerned with Soviet economic goals. According to Trainin,
Narkomnats had been delimiting ethnoterritorial units with *both* the national
idea and economic rationalism in mind:

> We did not simply draw a line on the territory of each nation and say,
> 'Please, here is your territory and its borders. Figure things out.' No! We
> studied the economic situation of each oblast, its main economic and cul-

58. Aleksandrov, "Ekonomicheskoe raionirovanie Rossii," in *Ekonomicheskoe raionirovanie
Rossii*, 38, 40–41.

59. Ibid., 33.

60. For an argument about the vestiges or survivals (*perezhitki*) of an "imperialistic ideology"
see I. Iamzin, "Natsional'nye interesy i voprosy kolonizatsii," *Zhizn' natsional'nostei*, no. 16 (151)
(July 31, 1922): 3.

61. Aleksandrov, "Ekonomicheskoe raionirovanie Rossii," in *Ekonomicheskoe raionirovanie
Rossii*, 38.

62. I discuss the economic, political, and cultural stakes of border-making in greater detail in
chapters 3 and 4.

63. S. K., "Ekonomicheskoe raionirovanie i problemy avtonomno-federativnogo stroitel'stva,"
1.

64. Trainin, "Ekonomicheskoe raionirovanie i natsional'naia politika," 1.

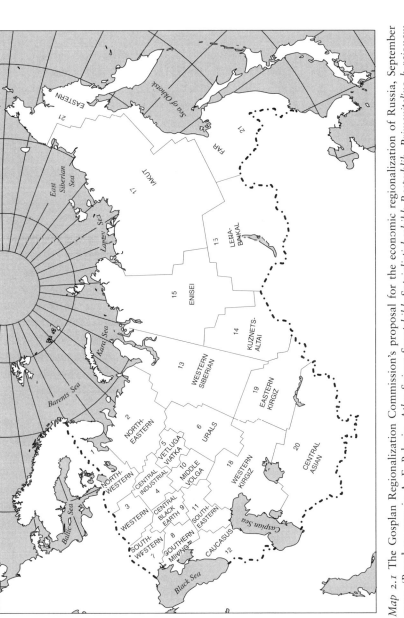

Map 2.1 The Gosplan Regionalization Commission's proposal for the economic regionalization of Russia, September 1921. (Based on map in A. F. Belavin, *Atlas Soiuza Sovetskikh Sotsialisticheskikh Respublik: Primenitel'no k raionam ekonomicheskogo raionirovaniia Gosplana SSSR* [Moscow-Leningrad, 1928], 13)

tural centers, and set out to put things together in such a way that [people with similar] national-cultural particularities are settled in one autonomous region.

Such an approach, Trainin argued, was not a conciliatory measure taken at the cost of progress. On the contrary, it had "maximum economic and cultural benefit"; it would give "backward" nationalities the chance to thrive and to participate in the Soviet campaign "on the economic front." Trainin acknowledged the practical advantages of an economic plan that placed all resources under a "central command." But he argued that such a plan need not forfeit the ethnographic principle. Gosplan could set overall "production targets" for the Soviet state but allow the autonomous national territories to use their "experiences and resources" to work toward plan goals.[65]

It was not just the Regionalization Commission's disregard for the principle of nationality but also its position on the "colonization question" that alarmed Narkomnats. As revolutionaries in imperial Russia, the Bolsheviks had condemned all forms of colonization as exploitative. Not long after the Bolsheviks seized power, however, they began to argue that the state-sponsored colonization of resource-rich regions was critical for economic progress—and thus imperative for the transition to socialism. Bolshevik leaders explained that it was simply not possible for Soviet Russia to "do without the petroleum of Azerbaijan or the cotton of Turkestan."[66] The Gosplan Regionalization Commission reiterated this argument in the 1920s. Characterizing colonization as a program of state-sponsored agricultural and industrial development, it took for granted the regime's right to organize, use, and develop *all* land, mineral deposits, forests, and water sources in Russia and the allied republics.[67] Such an approach was consistent with Soviet law, which did not recognize the private ownership of property.[68]

Aleksandrov and his colleagues did not apologize for their colonization agenda, but instead insisted that colonization was not by its nature exploitative. The Gosplan economists argued that late-imperial efforts to colonize Turkestan and the Caucasus had provoked "anti-Russian sentiment" because they had been accompanied by a "crude Russification policy, with measures deeply insulting" for some of "Russia's *narodnosti*." According to Aleksandrov, "the sharp expression of national tendencies and the mobilization of the native population" in Turkestan before the revolution (for example, the revolt of the Kirgiz population in Semirech'e in 1916) had been "provoked" by "certain individuals in the Resettlement Administration" of the imperial regime who had mistreated the region's indigenous peoples. Under different circum-

65. Ibid.

66. Walter Russell Batsell, *Soviet Rule in Russia* (New York, 1929), 117.

67. Egorov, *Raionirovanie SSSR: Sbornik*, 7–14.

68. This point about property law is made in Allan Laine Kagedan, "The Formation of Soviet Jewish Territorial Units, 1924–1937," Ph.D. diss., Columbia University, 1985.

stances, "national feeling probably never would have taken such a sharp form" since "most natives in Turkestan" recognized that their connection with Russia meant "economic and cultural advances."[69] Aleksandrov insisted that the Gosplan recommendations were neither economically nor culturally oppressive, arguing that Russians and non-Russians alike would benefit from the full development of the country's productive forces.

The Kalinin Commission

Between 1921 and 1923, regionalization remained a focal point in deliberations about the new Soviet state. In November 1921, Gosplan's Council of Labor and Defense discussed the Aleksandrov plan; Lenin presided at the session. While the council evaluated the plan favorably, it also gave consideration to Narkomnats's warning that economic-administrative regionalization would spark hostility to Soviet rule. The council called for further discussion, acknowledging that regionalization would have a serious impact on the national republics and oblasts.[70] At this point, party representatives from the RSFSR and the allied republics were still debating the basic federal structure of the Soviet state: whether the allied national republics would be included in an expanded RSFSR or maintain separate status. (The idea of a Union of Soviet Socialist Republics was not considered until September 1922.)

Subsequent events illustrate just how seriously the regime took the work of consensus-building in those early years. The Council of Labor and Defense directed Aleksandrov to publish a brochure about the Gosplan proposal and to send it, with a map, to all the provinces of the RSFSR and to all the allied republics for comment. It also directed VTsIK to create a commission to evaluate the proposal, assess Narkomnats's concerns, and suggest possible revisions. A few weeks later, VTsIK set up its own regionalization commission under the leadership of Mikhail Kalinin (the head of VTsIK); this commission included Aleksandrov and other representatives from Gosplan, as well as representatives from most of the all-union commissariats (including Narkomnats).[71] VTsIK also invited representatives from the national republics and oblasts who

---

69. Aleksandrov, "Ekonomicheskoe raionirovanie Rossii," in *Ekonomicheskoe raionirovanie Rossii*, 35–36.

70. Alampiev, *Ekonomicheskoe raionirovanie SSSR*, 106–7, and Mieczkowski, "Economic Regionalization of the Soviet Union," 109.

71. The commission was formed by decree of the Council of Labor and Defense of the RSFSR on November 4, 1921. Other represented institutions included the NKVD, the People's Commissariat of Agriculture, the People's Commissariat of Enlightenment, the Central Statistical Administration, the People's Commissariat of Production, and the All-Union Council of Trade. GARF f. 6892, op. 1, d. 1, ll. 1–30. A special four-member Preparatory Commission (including Aleksandrov from Gosplan and representatives from Narkomnats and VTsIK) debated how autonomous national oblasts and national regions might be integrated into the proposed economic-administrative oblasts.

happened to be in Moscow to participate in commission sessions; the Kalinin Commission thus became a forum for local national leaders to present their "written protests and verbal objections" to the Aleksandrov plan.[72]

Representatives from groups that considered themselves "developed nations," like the Georgians, as well as members of former *inorodtsy*, like the Bashkirs, characterized the Aleksandrov plan as a throwback to late-imperial colonialism. Georgian communists argued that the commission's proposal to combine the Georgian, Armenian, and Azerbaijan republics with the North Caucasus into a single economic-administrative oblast that specialized in oil and mineral procurement was an attempt to subordinate "the Georgian nation" to Moscow.[73] Bashkir representatives maintained that the inclusion of the Bashkir ASSR in the proposed Urals economic-administrative oblast would promote a colonial relationship between Russian workers and Bashkir peasants. The Bashkir leader and Narkomnats representative Sharif Manatov attacked Gosplan's assumption that Bashkir "cattle and bread" should feed the Russian workers of Ekaterinburg. For Manatov it was not essential that the Bashkirs have their own ethnoterritorial unit, only that they not be integrated into a Russian-dominated oblast; he recommended the unification of the Bashkir ASSR and the Kirgiz ASSR into one oblast.[74]

Even as national representatives characterized the Aleksandrov plan as exploitative, the Gosplan economists continued to assert that they were acting in the best interests of the federation's non-Russians. Aleksandrov argued that underdeveloped nationalities in particular would benefit from being attached to "existing and rising industrial centers": "cultured" workers would have a positive influence on these nationalities and would help to "liquidate" their "age-old backwardness." To "raise the economic and cultural level" of the Bashkirs, he insisted, it was critical to include them in the Urals oblast with its sizeable population of Russian workers. Gosplan and VTsIK cautioned that the regime should under no circumstances unite "backward regions with backward regions": to unite the Bashkir ASSR with the Kirgiz ASSR, for example, would be to doom both to backwardness.[75]

In February 1922, the Kalinin Commission produced a revised regionalization plan that purported to honor the principle of nationality within the general framework of economic-administrative regionalization. The new plan proposed twelve European and nine Asiatic oblasts. Like the Aleksandrov plan, it was premised on the integration of ethnoterritorial units into

---

72. Alampiev, *Ekonomicheskoe raionirovanie SSSR*, 106–7, 110.

73. Ibid., 128–29. Tension between Moscow and Georgia over related issues erupted in the so-called "Georgian Affair" several months later. See Jeremy Smith, "The Georgian Affair of 1922— Policy Failure, Personality Clash or Power Struggle?" *Europe-Asia Studies* 50, no. 3 (1998): 519–44, and Moshe Lewin, *Lenin's Last Struggle* (New York, 1968), 43.

74. Alampiev, *Ekonomicheskoe raionirovanie SSSR*, 112, 128–29. On Manatov, also see Blank, *Sorcerer as Apprentice*, 84.

75. Alampiev, *Ekonomicheskoe raionirovanie SSSR*, 113.

economic-administrative oblasts. But it differed in its recognition of the borders of national republics as inviolable. No national republic would be divided between two or more administrative units. Small ethnoterritorial units, which "due to their economic weakness" could not form separate economic oblasts, would constitute "internal subregions" in economic-administrative oblasts. Large, developed ethnoterritorial units would constitute separate economic-administrative oblasts in themselves. The most expansive and diverse ethnoterritorial units (such as Ukraine) would constitute two or more economic oblasts, but would be unified in one administrative unit. In short, ethnoterritorial units would either overlap with or exist as subunits of economic-administrative oblasts. Kalinin acknowledged that the commission still had not worked out important "technical issues"—many of which had real political significance—such as which administrative bodies, those of the economic-administrative oblasts or those of the ethnoterritorial units, would have the authoritative voice on economic and political questions.[76]

Alluding to Lenin's pre-1917 writings about the relationship between oppressor and oppressed nations, Kalinin maintained that for regionalization to succeed, the Soviet government had to "build trust" between Russians and non-Russians. To do so, he suggested, it had to guarantee that nationalities retained "national rights" upon their integration into economic-administrative oblasts. Kalinin warned state planners to be sensitive to "the particularities of custom and culture," and proposed that the regime appoint Narkomnats representatives to defend the interests of each ethnoterritorial unit entering an economic-administrative oblast. At the same time, Kalinin argued that it was imperative for local national leaders to support Soviet plans for economic and political unification.[77] He recommended that VTsIK involve in regionalization national representatives who "know the nationality policy of the party" and who understood that economic-administrative regionalization would result in the "economic and cultural development of all the nationalities" of the RSFSR and the allied republics.[78]

For local national leaders, questions about the Soviet state's political and economic form were especially charged—and the Kalinin Commission's proposal did not satisfy their concerns. This became apparent as Aleksandrov discussed the new proposal with local national representatives in February 1922 and at a session with Narkomnats three months later.[79] Local national leaders argued that even the revised plan compromised "the political rights and com-

76. Egorov, *Raionirovanie SSSR: Sbornik,* 47–50.

77. Ibid., 47–48.

78. Alampiev, *Ekonomicheskoe raionirovanie SSSR,* 113–14. (Kalinin made these points before his colleagues at VTsIK meetings.)

79. On the April Narkomnats meeting see GARF f. 1318, op. 1, d. 9, ll. 4–7. On the February meeting (of the All-Russian Conference of Local Regionalization Workers) see Alampiev, *Ekonomicheskoe raionirovanie SSSR,* 130–31. On both meetings see Mieczkowski, "Economic Regionalization of the Soviet Union," 109–10.

petencies" of the national republics and oblasts and was thus "in fundamental contradiction" with the party's nationality policy.[80] Narkomnats expressed particular concern about "weak nationalities," which "strong nationalities" might "swallow up" in the economic-administrative oblasts. Narkomnats administrators predicted that in the push for economic modernization, state resources would be focused on the "more developed subregions" of each economic-administrative oblast, and "backward nationalities" in "backward" subregions would fall "under the thumb" of their neighbors.[81] Local national leaders concurred with this assessment. The head of the Chuvash oblast's Executive Committee, for example, complained that Gosplan's work from the start had been guided by "general considerations" about the RSFSR and ignorance of "the economic position of the peoples earlier called *inorodtsy*."[82]

While the Kalinin Commission responded to criticism of its regionalization program, Soviet leaders forged ahead with the formal political unification of the RSFSR and the allied republics. In December 1922 the party rejected a controversial proposal advocated by Stalin to include the allied republics in an expanded RSFSR. Instead, on December 30 at the All-Russian Congress of Soviets, the RSFSR, the Ukrainian SSR, the Belorussian SSR, and the Transcaucasian Soviet Federative Socialist Republic (made up of the Georgian, Azerbaijan, and Armenian republics) entered a new Union of Soviet Socialist Republics, centralized through Moscow.[83] As the republics were integrated into this union, the regionalization debate remained charged. The economic and ethnographic paradigms proved difficult to reconcile: It was not clear, for example, how the two proposed Ukrainian economic oblasts would be integrated into the Ukrainian SSR from an administrative standpoint. Moreover, the regime still had to decide whether to delineate lower-level administrative subunits within the RSFSR and the other republics on the basis of ethnographic or economic criteria. Narkomnats and Gosplan continued to defend competing paradigms; in making their cases, and in arguing against one another, each came up with a unique approach to Soviet-sponsored development.

Narkomnats, the Central Ethnographic Bureau, and State-Sponsored Evolutionism

The regionalization debate was not just about the administrative-territorial organization of the Soviet state. Institutions on both sides characterized their proposals as the best means to build socialism. Narkomnats and Gosplan both maintained that it was imperative to resolve the nationality question and to eliminate economic backwardness. At issue was how best to do so. Narkom-

---

80. S. Korichev, "K voprosu ob ekonomicheskom raionirovanii RSFSR," *Zhizn' natsional'nostei*, no. 12 (147) (June 15, 1922): 4–5.

81. "Iz deiatel'nosti Narkomnatsa," *Zhizn' natsional'nostei*, no. 10 (16) (May 19, 1922): 12.

82. Korichev, "K voprosu ob ekonomicheskom raionirovanii RSFSR," 4.

83. Carr, *Bolshevik Revolution*, vol. 1, 396–97.

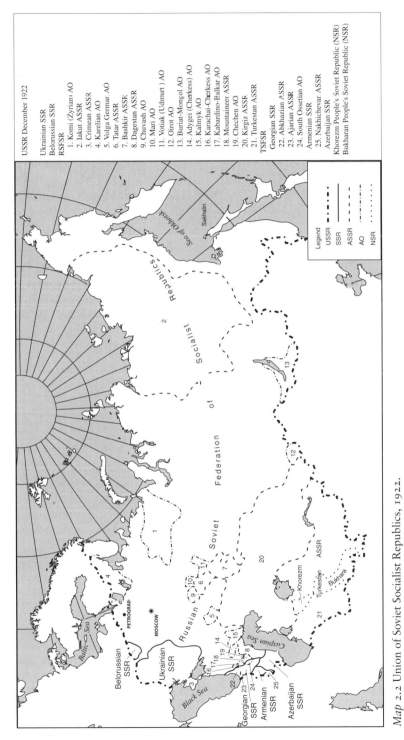

Map 2.2 Union of Soviet Socialist Republics, 1922.

nats agreed with Gosplan that the ideal federation was one in which nationalities disappeared through a "great synthesis" and economic units formed "a
large harmonious whole: the mighty socialist state." But where Gosplan economists saw such an outcome as imminent, Narkomnats administrators such as
Semen Dimanshtein imagined it as the end result of a "long process, which will
hardly come to a close before our planet dies off." According to Dimanshtein,
the "great synthesis" could result only when nationalities that were equals
chose voluntarily to "merge" and "enrich one another." Echoing Lenin's famous polemic against imperialism, he suggested that disregard for the ethnographic principle in the interim would result in the economic exploitation of
less-developed peoples.[84]

In important respects, Gosplan and Narkomnats shared a common approach. Both institutions looked outside Soviet borders for inspiration, and
both relied on professional ethnographers from the imperial regime for ethnographic knowledge about the lands and peoples of the former Russian Empire.
Both hoped to win central and local institutional support, and both attempted
to validate their positions on scientific and ideological grounds. Moreover,
each institution adjusted its proposals and arguments in response to the other's
criticism. Reacting to the Narkomnats critique of the economic paradigm,
Gosplan argued that its proposals were not "imperialistic" and made a small
nod toward ethnographic considerations. Responding to the Gosplan critique
of the ethnographic paradigm, Narkomnats argued that its regionalization
proposal reflected a concern for economic rationalism.

As Gosplan touted the scientific basis of economic regionalization,
Narkomnats looked to ethnography, and to KIPS in particular, to bring scientific authority to its arguments for the ethnographic paradigm. The ethnographers, who also advised Gosplan, had divided loyalties; while many KIPS
ethnographers sympathized with Narkomnats (the defender of national minorities), some, like Veniamin Semenov-Tian-Shanskii, had a longstanding interest in economic regionalization. It was in this context in late 1921 (just as
the Kalinin Commission was beginning its work) that Narkomnats proposed
to establish its own council of scholars to conduct ethnographic research in
the national republics and oblasts.[85] A series of articles appearing in the
Narkomnats journal around this time noted the importance of such research
for protecting and developing the Soviet state's most important resource: its
population.[86]

84. S. Dimanshtein, "Slozhnost' raboty novogo Narkomnatsa," 1. Lenin's polemic, "Imperialism, the Highest Form of Capitalism," was written in 1916.

85. I. Borozdin, "Odna iz ocherednykh zadach Narkomnatsa," *Zhizn' natsional'nostei*, no. 28
(126) (December 3, 1921): 1.

86. See for example D. Ianovich, "K voprosu ob izuchenii byta narodnostei RSFSR," *Zhizn'
natsional'nostei*, no. 29 (127) (December 14, 1921): 1; I. Iamzin, "Sovetskaia Rossiia i otstalye
narodnosti," *Zhizn' natsional'nostei*, no. 30 (128) (December 23, 1921): 1; and I. Borozdin,
"Odna iz ocherednykh zadach Narkomnatsa," 1.

In subsequent months, the original Narkomnats proposal was upgraded into a plan to establish a Central Ethnographic Bureau in Moscow, which would oversee the "systematic ethnographic investigation" of all territories within Soviet borders. This bureau, under the auspices of Narkomnats, would include professional ethnographers in its ranks. It would initiate its own expeditions and also collaborate with KIPS and other institutions that engaged in ethnographic research. A number of KIPS ethnographers, such as Sergei Rudenko, Vladimir Bogoraz, and Nikolai Iakovlev, attended the bureau's organizational sessions.[87]

The Ethnographic Bureau was intended to serve an important propaganda role, celebrating the diverse national makeup of Soviet Russia through civic education and outreach programs and thus building support for the ethnographic paradigm. It would publish a popular encyclopedia of the "Peoples of the RSFSR" and would organize ethnographic exhibits (on the model of world's fair expositions) spotlighting the "national life" and "economic enterprises" of the nationalities.[88] Some Narkomnats representatives advocated the construction of a new ethnographic museum in Moscow to house these exhibits; there was even talk of bringing "an actual family" from Central Asia or Siberia "with its genuine belongings and dwelling" to live in the museum yard for a month "under the open sky."[89] Of even greater importance, the bureau would have a hands-on role in national-cultural construction and state-building. Its experts would act as mediators between Soviet authorities and indigenous populations; they would bring information about local cultures to government institutions, while introducing agricultural techniques, health care, sanitation, and literacy in native languages to local populations.[90]

Narkomnats wanted to make clear that its agenda for the Ethnographic Bureau—like its plan for ethnoterritorial regionalization—was not an unscientific "humanitarian" scheme that would impede local development, but rather a bulwark of economic modernization. An August 1922 Narkomnats memo about the bureau characterized "the collection and analysis of information about the lives of the nationalities" of the RSFSR as having "enormous scientific, social, and administrative significance": "Without scientific knowledge about geographical conditions and familiarity with national particularities IT IS IMPOSSIBLE TO GOVERN TO THEIR BENEFIT different peoples and not waste strength and resources on unneeded experiments."[91] The KIPS ethnographer Iakovlev reaffirmed this point in a speech at the bureau's first organizational session. "Not sentimentality but strict economic calculations"

87. PFA RAN f. 135, op. 1, d. 1, ll. 224–26; GARF f. 1318, op. 1, d. 19, ll. 9–10.
88. PFA RAN f. 135, op. 1, d. 1, ll. 224–26; GARF f. 1318, op. 1, d. 17 (1), ll. 57, 62–64.
89. GARF f. 1318, op. 1, d. 17 (1), ll. 62–63.
90. PFA RAN f. 135, op. 1, d. 1, ll. 218–26.
91. The memo was signed by the Moscow-based ethnographer Daniil Ianovich and the head of the Narkomnats Department of National Minorities Plich. GARF f. 1318, op. 1, d. 17 (1), l. 62.

compelled the government to become well-informed about and assist all of the peoples within Soviet borders, he argued. "Every living person should be valued as a source of state revenue, as living capital which yields a determined amount of profit to the state through productive labor."[92]

If Narkomnats seemed to give the upper hand to Gosplan by arguing in economic terms, the commissariat continued to insist that its own version of regionalization was most in line with the party's nationality policy. Narkomnats administrators argued that the phenomenon of historical diversity was pronounced in Soviet territories because the policies of the imperial regime had stunted the development of "productive forces" in the Russian Empire's colonies and had left the inhabitants of these regions "at backward historical stages." Within Soviet borders one could "encounter the clan and tribal insularity" of the peoples of the Caucasus, Turkestan, and Siberia as well as more-developed peoples already "on the road to capitalism," explained the Narkomnats administrator Georgii Broido in a 1923 article that set out the commissariat's position. Broido suggested that state-sponsored efforts to promote the population's national-cultural development would further the goals of Bolshevik nationality policy and economic policy. Such efforts would "emancipate the consciousness" of backward *narodnosti* by fostering their ethnohistorical development through the stages on the Marxist timeline: from feudalism to capitalism to socialism, and eventually to communism.[93]

Broido and his colleagues at Narkomnats went beyond the usual arguments for national self-determination and asserted that the Soviet government should delimit national-territorial units for peoples lacking national consciousness. They advocated what might be described as a program of "state-sponsored evolutionism": a Soviet version of the civilizing mission that combined the idea of cultural evolutionism (which presumed that all peoples evolved through progressive stages on a universal ladder of culture) with the Marxist theory of history (which presumed that different cultural forms corresponded to different economic forms found at particular stages on a timeline of historical development) and added to it the Leninist conceit that revolutionary actors could speed up historical progress.[94] Ethnographic knowledge about the population was absolutely critical to this endeavor. For example, Narkomnats was considering the ethnoterritorial regionalization of Turkestan, even though the region's "three main peoples—the Uzbeks, Kirgiz, and Turkmen . . . have not reached that stage of political and economic development when it can be said with full certainty how their national interrela-

92. PFA RAN f. 135, op. 1, d. 1, ll. 222–23.

93. Broido, "Nasha natsional'naia politika," 5–6. For a similar articulation of this argument, see I. Trainin, "O plemennoi avtonomii," *Zhizn' natsional'nostei*, no. 2 (1923): 19–26.

94. All modern states have ideologies of progress. The Narkomnats approach was distinctive in its focus on accelerating the development of ethnohistorical groups. This approach was by no means programmed into Marxism, but could not have taken its particular form without Marx's theories about historical evolution.

tionships are developing."[95] The commissariat looked to ethnographers as well as to local national leaders to determine which tribes and clans "belonged to" which nationality-in-formation—with an eye to delimiting national territories that would unify the related clans and tribes and accelerate their transition to nationhood.[96]

Gosplan, Goskolonit, and Soviet Colonization

While Narkomnats attempted to prove that its vision of ethnoterritorial regionalization was economically sound, Gosplan endeavored to prove that its project for economic-administrative regionalization was not imperialistic. Around the same time that Narkomnats was organizing its Ethnographic Bureau, Gosplan turned to a new Moscow-based organization, the State Colonization Research Institute (Goskolonit), asking it to formulate a philosophical framework for "Soviet colonization [*kolonizatsiia*]." Goskolonit, established in April 1922, was made up of experts on the "colonization question," including former imperial economists, geographers, and historians of empire. The head of Goskolonit, professor Arsenii Iarilov, was a historian and agricultural-geographer and a member of Gosplan; in the mid-1920s he would become the head of a new Gosplan commission to study the Soviet Union's productive forces.[97]

Goskolonit's work was both practical and theoretical. Like KEPS, it conducted geographical and demographic research on Soviet territories. It surveyed the "productive forces of land, water, oil, and forests" and recommended economic specializations for the Gosplan-proposed economic-administrative oblasts. Some Goskolonit experts plotted out railroad routes; others discussed irrigation and sowing methods; still others studied "backward social groups" (such as nomads and tribes) and worked on a Soviet "colonization code." All worked toward the goal of socialist construction. Unlike KEPS, Goskolonit took a comparative historical approach. Its experts studied European and North American colonization policies, publishing articles about the

95. G. Safarov, "K voprosu o prisoedinenii Syr-Dar'inskoi i Samirechenskoi oblastei k Kirrespublike," *Zhizn' natsional'nostei*, no. 10 (16) (May 19, 1922): 4. In 1920, Lenin had mandated the preparation of a new ethnographic map of Turkestan, that identified the region's Uzbek, Kirgiz, and Turkmen parts. "Zamechaniia na proekte Turkestanskoi komissii," *Leninskii sbornik* 34 (1942): 323–26.

96. See for example PFA RAN f 135, op 1, d 3, l 43. See the discussion in chapters 3 and 4.

97. It was organized under Glavnauka, the science division of the Commissariat of Enlightenment, by decree of Sovnarkom RSFSR. "Gosudarstvennyi kolonizatsionnyi nauchno-issledovatel'skii institut, ego zadachi, organizatsiia i deiatel'nost' (Kratkii otchetnyi ocherk)," *Trudy Gosudarstvennogo kolonizatsionnogo nauchno-issledovatel'skogo instituta*, vol. 1 (Moscow, 1924), 299–30. Also I. Iamzin, "Natsional'nye interesy i voprosy kolonizatsii," 3. Members of Goskolonit included David Grimm, Mitrofan Dovnar-Zapol'skii, and Dmitrii Egorov. Grimm, a former member of the Kadet Party, was a historian of the Roman Empire; Egorov was a historical-geographer and an expert on German colonization policies. On the formation of Goskolonit also see E. H. Carr, *Socialism in One Country*, vol. 1 (New York, 1958), 522–23.

French colonization of North Africa, the British colonization of India, the American colonization of the Great Plains, and so on.[98] Some Goskolonit researchers analyzed the geographical and climatic similarities and differences between particular European and American colonies and "colonizable" territories within Soviet borders, making (direct or implicit) recommendations to Soviet planners.[99] Goskolonit researchers also studied imperial colonization policies, and in some cases built on the unrealized plans of progressive reformers like Georgii Gins, a resettlement administrator who in 1913 had advocated "a new colonization program" that would "draw into economic circulation" the "little-used productive forces" of the empire.[100]

It was one of Goskolonit's tasks to explain how, in a Soviet socialist context (without an exploiter capitalist class), Soviet colonization policies would enable indigenous peoples such as the former *inorodtsy* to "attain a higher level of material and spiritual culture." In the civil war years, some Bolsheviks had used an old-fashioned civilizing-mission rhetoric to justify Soviet economic policy. In a 1920 speech, Grigorii Zinoviev had declared that the Soviet regime takes "these products which are necessary for us, not as former exploiters, but as older brothers bearing the torch of civilization."[101] Most Bolshevik leaders worried, however, that the population did not perceive the difference between colonization (*kolonizatsiia*) and colonial exploitation (*kolonizatorstvo*). Bolshevik concerns heightened as the regime's political opponents (Mensheviks and liberals) argued in articles published abroad that Soviet Russia was conducting "colonial politics of oppression" in Turkestan and the Far East.[102]

In order to differentiate Soviet practices from those of the "imperialistic" European and Russian empires, Goskolonit decided that it was necessary to define its terms. The experts focused on two terms that were often used interchangeably: *kolonizatsiia* and *pereselenie*. According to Goskolonit, these terms in fact referred to different processes: *Pereselenie* was the "agricultural

98. "Otchet o deiatel'nosti Gosudarstvennogo kolonizatsionnogo nauchno-issledovatel'skogo instituta za 1924–1925," *Trudy Gosudarstvennogo kolonizatsionnogo nauchno-issledovatel'skogo instituta*, vol. 2 (Moscow, 1926), 21–36. The institute published these articles in its *Trudy*. See for example P. D. Voeikov, "Razvitie proizvoditel'nykh sil frantsuzskikh kolonii," in *Trudy Gosudarstvennogo kolonizatsionnogo nauchno-issledovatel'skogo instituta*, vol. 1, 384–85.

99. "Gosudarstvennyi kolonizatsionnyi nauchno-issledovatel'skii institut," 305–6.

100. G. Gins, "Pereselenie i kolonizatsiia," *Voprosy kolonizatsii*, nos. 12, 13 (1913): 73–120, 39–99. The Goskolonit experts repeat many of Gins's ideas (at times almost verbatim) without attribution.

101. Cited in Batsell, *Soviet Rule in Russia*, 117.

102. Soviet leaders noted that British journals, as part of an anti-Soviet propaganda campaign, were reprinting excerpts of these articles. *Dvenadtsatyi s"ezd Rossiiskoi kommunisticheskoi partii (bol'shevikov), Stenograficheskii otchet, 17–25 aprelia 1923 g.* (Moscow, 1923), 565. On *kolonizatorstvo*, see 473–74. Also "Kolonizatorstvo v Turkestane i bor'ba s nim," *Zhizn' natsional'nostei*, no. 9 (101) (April 23, 1921): 1, and Kara Ikul, "K roli Vneshtorga v nezavisimykh Vostochnykh Sovetskikh respublikakh," *Zhizn' natsional'nostei* no. 11 (17) (June 1, 1922): 1–2.

settlement of uninhabited territories," whereas *kolonizatsiia* was a process of agricultural or industrial development. *Pereselenie* could be spontaneous or state-sponsored and did not have an enlightenment agenda. *Kolonizatsiia*, by contrast, was always state-sponsored and aspired to foster the cultural development of backward peoples and to develop local productive forces.[103]

Discussion about these two terms was not simply a matter of semantics. The experts wanted to establish that local populations in Turkestan and other regions were resisting Soviet *kolonizatsiia* because they associated it with late-imperial *pereselenie*. They maintained that in most cases what the imperial regime had called *kolonizatsiia*—such as the internal migration of Russian peasants to Asiatic Russia—was in fact *pereselenie*. According to one Goskolonit expert, professor Ivan Iamzin, late-imperial colonization had been misguided because the regime had "followed the peasant," whose goal was simply to resettle where it was "easiest, closest, and the land was best." Russian peasant settlers had gone as far as the Kirgiz steppe, where they found fertile land and a vulnerable nomadic population that did not engage in agriculture. The imperial regime had used force to confiscate "so-called land surpluses" from the natives and redistribute them to the Russian settlers. In so doing, "it dug a chasm between natives and settlers" that "the revolution could not totally heal."[104] The term *kolonizatsiia* came to be associated with these exploitative practices which had "worsened the chronic agricultural crisis" and which were responsible for an anti-Russian mood in many national territories. The term *kolonizatsiia* was still "considered so odious that in some parts of the country it is urgently recommended to abstain from using it."[105]

Should the Soviet state, which had "established its authority on the basis of national self-determination," reject the concept of colonization altogether? Iamzin and his colleagues asked. They answered with a decisive "no."[106] Invoking the rhetoric of progress, they argued that the destruction of old economies was "unavoidable." "In order to live, the state must develop, go forward."[107] The Goskolonit experts maintained, however, that colonization

103. A. A. Iarilov, "Kolonizatsiia i pereselenie," in *Trudy Gosudarstvennogo kolonizatsionnogo nauchno-issledovatel'skogo instituta*, vol. 1, 50–53.

104. [I.] Iamzin, "Kolonizatsiia v usloviiakh Sovetskoi Rossii," *Zhizn' natsional'nostei*, no. 2 (131) (January 17, 1922): 1. Also I. L. Iamzin and V. P. Voshchinin, *Uchenie o kolonizatsii i pereseleniakh* (Moscow-Leningrad, 1926).

105. A. A. Iarilov, "Puti kolonizatsionnogo stroitel'stva," in *Trudy Gosudarstvennogo kolonizatsionnogo nauchno-issledovatel'skogo instituta*, vol. 1, 3; Iarilov, "Kolonizatsiia i pereselenie," 54–55; and "Gosudarstvennyi kolonizatsionnyi nauchno-issledovatel'skii institut," 337–38. On Goskolonit's efforts to define the term *kolonizatsiia* in the 1920s, see A. N. Petrov, "K vyiavleniiu organizatsionnykh form industrial'no-promyslovoi kolonizatsii," in *Problemy promyshlenno-promyslovoi kolonizatsii, Trudy Gosudarstvennogo nauchno-issledovatel'skogo instituta zemleustroistva i pereseleniia*, vol. 11 (Moscow, 1930), 58–77.

106. Iamzin, "Kolonizatsiia v usloviiakh Sovetskoi Rossii," 1.

107. Iarilov, "Puti kolonizatsionnogo stroitel'stva," 7. Iamzin gave the example of Turkestan, where only "two percent of cotton-producing land is used" and "future cotton-growing farmers" are waiting "to leave their names in history."

under the Soviet regime would not be "an act of warlike imperialism" or an exploitative policy (*kolonizatorstvo*) carried out by "a dominant people." Instead, it would be a policy for "the organization of all the territories and economies of the Union in coordination with a state [economic] plan."[108] Describing colonization as a "platform for the greatest economic conquests," Goskolonit researchers sketched out their vision for the modernizing state. The state would "take the role of *khoziain* [master]" of its country's economic life; it would evaluate the productive potential of all the territories within its domain from a scientific perspective, relying on qualified experts. The goal, the researchers explained, was the "full development of local productive forces," the optimal use of all territories with their "natural riches and economic particularities."[109]

Of course, the Soviet Union was not just any state. In order to set it apart from the European colonial empires, Goskolonit experts argued that "Soviet *kolonizatsiia*" was premised on a new relationship between metropole and colony. European theorists, they explained, "view the colony as a territory across the ocean" which "serves the economic and imperialistic goals" of the metropole.[110] The Russian Empire had tried to emulate this model: in the late nineteenth century, educated Russians imagined that the Ural Mountains divided European Russia from its colonies in Asiatic Russia. The October Revolution, however, had placed the "colonization question in a new light" by radically changing the relationship between the "Great Russian metropole" and its colonies.[111] "*Kolonizatsiia* as we understand it now within the borders of the USSR" is not the "robbery of parts of the Union, of former colonies, by the RSFSR, the former metropole"; nor is it the "movement of Great Russian peasants to the Siberian or other expanses" to satisfy their land hunger. Soviet *kolonizatsiia*, they explained, "flows from the needs" of colonized regions. It was the role of the state-*khoziain,* the Goskolonit experts suggested, to coordinate the needs of colonized regions with "state interests as a whole," "with the interests of all federated republics," and finally "with the interests of all laboring humanity."[112]

Iarilov and his colleagues thus characterized the Soviet project in universalistic and humanist terms. They argued that the very division of the earth's surface into "metropoles" and "colonies" was illegitimate since it was premised

108. Iamzin, "Kolonizatsiia v usloviiakh Sovetskoi Rossii," 1, and "Natsional'nye interesy i voprosy kolonizatsii," 3. Also Iarilov, "Kolonizatsiia i pereselenie," 54.

109. Iamzin, "Natsional'nye interesy i voprosy kolonizatsii," 3, and Iarilov, "Puti kolonizatsionnogo stroitel'stva," 5–6. The term *khoziain* has a number of meanings, including master, head of the household, and husband. It implies an active, managerial approach.

110. Iarilov, "Puti kolonizatsionnogo stroitel'stva," 4–5.

111. Iarilov, "Kolonizatsiia i pereselenie," 54. On the idea of the Urals as the dividing line between "metropole" and "colony" see G. Gins, "Pereselenie i kolonizatsiia," *Voprosy kolonizatsii,* no. 12 (1913): 102–8, and Willard Sunderland, "The 'Colonization Question': Visions of Colonization in Late Imperial Russia," *Jahrbücher für Geschichte Osteuropas* 48 (2000): 210–32.

112. Iarilov, "Puti kolonizatsionnogo stroitel'stva," 6–7, and "Kolonizatsiia i pereselenie," 55.

on the existence of private property; instead, they claimed, the earth represented a "common dwelling place" and all its territory, "no matter which side of the ocean" it lay on, was "the property of humanity." Initially, the state-*khoziain* would determine how best to use the "vast expanses of free territories" within the "Union of Soviet Republics." Ultimately, the state-*khoziain* would oversee *kolonizatsiia* "on an international scale." The rational use of all "available" territories through the process of *kolonizatsiia*, the experts explained, would "broaden the area of the earth's surface used by human beings in their interest." This, in turn, would increase the "quantity and quality" of "human beings on this earth" and "would raise the level of human culture."[113] In effect, the experts offered their own rendition of world revolution as a Soviet-sponsored world development project.

A final distinguishing feature of Soviet *kolonizatsiia* rested on a redefinition of the relationship between colonizer and colonized. In the Soviet context, the "local indigenous population" was to be recognized as "the most valuable resource" and "as the most valuable colonist[s]." Citing the research of the KIPS ethnographer Vladimir Bogoraz, Goskolonit experts maintained that native peoples who "know the flora and fauna" and the precious metals and minerals of a region were "best suited" to "exploiting that region's natural riches." They suggested that natives and outsiders work together to further the "economic and cultural development" of the Union's "outlying territories."[114] Goskolonit experts agreed with Narkomnats that ethnographic knowledge—local knowledge as well as scientific knowledge prepared by experts—was imperative for state planning. But unlike Narkomnats, which was using this knowledge to delimit ethnoterritorial borders, Goskolonit wanted to use it to determine which peoples were most suited to further particular economic goals: to construct roads and irrigation systems, to engage in agricultural work, and to work in industries. In arguing that the population should be organized "not on the basis of local nationalism," but in accordance with its economic orientation, Goskolonit touched on the issue at the heart of the regionalization debate.[115]

By the eve of the Twelfth Party Congress of April 1923, institutions on both sides of the regionalization debate had developed philosophical arguments and had gathered scientific evidence to prove that their proposals for the administrative-territorial organization of the Soviet state would best enable the regime to overcome the problem of historical diversity and build socialism. While Narkomnats argued that the socialist future was contingent on a program of state-sponsored evolutionism (best achieved through ethnoterritorial regionalization), Gosplan argued that it depended on rapid economic modernization (best facilitated by economic-administrative regionalization and Soviet

113. Iarilov, "Puti kolonizatsionnogo stroitel'stva," 5–8.

114. Iarilov, "Kolonizatsiia i pereselenie," 54–55.

115. Iamzin, "Natsional'nye interesy i voprosy kolonizatsii," 3, and "Kolonizatsiia v usloviiakh Sovetskoi Rossii," 1.

kolonizatsiia). Yet even as Narkomnats and Gosplan continued to clash on fundamental issues, some of their individual members began to find common ground. Some economists and state planners conceded that attention to the population's national-cultural development—helping clans and tribes to overcome their "feudal-era" backwardness and achieve national self-realization, for example—could lead to an increase in productive forces. At the same time, some Narkomnats administrators imagined a type of benevolent colonization in which colonizers "assist local populations" and promote their economic and cultural advancement.[116]

The Regionalization Debate and the KIPS Ethnographers

By 1923, the KIPS ethnographers were shaping a new field of applied Soviet ethnography that conceptualized the population in both ethnohistorical and economic-productive terms.[117] For Narkomnats, KIPS assessed the ethnographic composition of Soviet territories and recommended borders for potential ethnoterritorial regions. The ethnographers studied subnational identities in Turkestan and the North Caucasus, advising Narkomnats which tribes or clans were "part of which *narodnost'*."[118] They also helped Narkomnats evaluate appeals from local populations (such as the Komi-Permiaks) requesting national-territorial status, providing Narkomnats with maps and ethnographic analyses and in some cases participating directly in deliberations about the creation of autonomous national republics and autonomous national oblasts.[119] For Gosplan, KIPS, along with the KEPS Committee for the Description of Russia by Region, inventoried the former empire's "human productive forces" or biopower. Taking a lead from nineteenth-century "race science," the ethnographers argued that each nationality had a different economic orientation based on its physical type and *byt*.[120] They attempted to understand the correlation between physical traits and economic activities—agriculture, cattle-breeding, hunting, and so on—in order to help Gosplan and Goskolonit determine which population groups might work best in which enterprises.

As Narkomnats organized its own Ethnographic Bureau, the KIPS ethnographers became anxious about their continued role as expert-consultants to the government. Narkomnats invited members of KIPS to participate in its proposed bureau. But the ethnographers, understandably, were concerned

116. A. Skachko, "K voprosu o kolonizatsii okrain," *Zhizn' natsional'nostei,* no. 2 (1923): 13–18.

117. In the late 1920s, the party would argue that this discipline was not sufficiently "Soviet" and needed to be reformed on Marxist-Leninist lines. See chapters 3 and 5.

118. PFA RAN f. 2, op. 1–1917, d. 30, l. 188; d. 31, ll. 13–14; f. 135, op. 1, d. 1, ll. 199–200.

119. GARF f. 1318, op. 1, d. 14 (1), ll. 33, 34, 60–610b; d. 20, l. 218, 220, 225; PFA RAN f. 135, op. 1, d. 9, ll. 140–1400b. Also see B. G. Bogoraz-Tan, "Ob izuchenii i okhrane okrainnykh narodov," *Zhizn' natsional'nostei,* no. 3–4 (1923): 168–80.

120. On KEPS and KIPS see PFA RAN f. 135, op. 1, d. 1, l. 6; d. 3, l. 18; f. 2, op. 1–1917, d. 30, ll. 40–42. On KEPS see GARF f. 5677, op. 1, d. 7, ll. 64–66.

about what this new Moscow-based institution would mean for KIPS.[121] To ensure KIPS's continued participation in the work of state-building, a number of the commission's ethnographers traveled to Moscow to attend Narkomnats meetings and forged close professional relationships with Narkomnats administrators. Several KIPS ethnographers worked with Trainin, Dimanshtein, and Broido on a major project to create written languages for Russia's former *inorodtsy*.[122]

KIPS also seized on the occasion of the upcoming First All-Union Census of the population to strengthen its ties with Narkomnats. The census, slated for 1925 (and ultimately held in 1926), was a main topic of discussion at a March 1923 Narkomnats meeting that several KIPS ethnographers, including Sergei Rudenko, attended. Rudenko argued that KIPS—which had used data from the 1897 census to produce ethnographic maps and knew the data's flaws—could prevent Narkomnats and the Central Statistical Administration from making critical mistakes.[123] Rudenko's bid to involve KIPS in the census was successful. As KIPS assumed more responsibilities in connection with the census, it started to take on the role of a central ethnographic bureau of the Soviet state.[124]

Meanwhile, KIPS also began to collaborate with Goskolonit. In March 1923, Gosplan brought together representatives from KIPS, KEPS, Goskolonit, and other scientific institutions for the First All-Russian Conference for the Study of Natural Productive Forces. Aleksandrov, Iarilov, Rudenko, Sergei F. Ol'denburg, Dmitrii Anuchin, and roughly 150 other scholars and administrators convened in Moscow for the week-long conference, whose aim was to discuss the organization of "the socialist economy on scientific grounds."[125] Aleksandrov, who headed the conference's Organizational Bureau, saw the conference as an opportunity to mobilize support for economic-administrative

121. GARF f. 1318, op. 1, d. 17 (1), ll. 62–64. From December 1921, the KIPS ethnographers discussed how best to ensure their role in state affairs. See, for example, PFA RAN f. 135, op. 1, d. 3, ll. 36–37.

122. PFA RAN f. 135, op. 1, d. 3, ll. 43, 52. GARF f. 1318, op. 1 d. 14 (1), ll. 60–600b; d. 19, ll. 9–10, 12. Ol'denburg, Rudenko, Anuchin, Shternberg, and other KIPS ethnographers attended Narkomnats sessions.

123. GARF f. 1318, op. 1, d. 19, ll. 9–10. PFA RAN f. 135, op. 1, d. 9, l. 62.

124. PFA RAN f. 2, op. 1–1917, d. 31, ll. 127–1270b; f. 135, op. 1, d. 3, l. 65; d. 9, ll. 174–75. Later that month, Trainin and Broido successfully appealed to the Council of People's Commissars to provide KIPS with an increased budget. PFA RAN f. 135, op. 1, d. 3, l. 53; d. 9, l. 70. The Narkomnats-based Ethnographic Bureau, in turn, adopted a more modest agenda. It was reorganized as the Historical-Ethnological Subsection of the Association of Oriental Studies. GARF f. 1318, op. 1, d. 18 (3), l. 175; d. 19, ll. 1–2.

125. "Konferentsiia po izucheniiu estestvenno-proizvoditel'nykh sil Rossii: Otkrytie konferentsii," *Ekonomicheskaia zhizn'*, no. 62 (1292) (March 21, 1923): 3; N. Gorbunov, "Nauka i sovetskoe khoziaistvennoe stroitel'stvo," *Ekonomicheskaia zhizn'*, no. 61 (1291) (March 20, 1923): 3. The conference was held from March 20 to March 26, 1923. Twenty representatives from Gosplan, fifty from Moscow, fifty from Petrograd, and thirty from the provinces attended. On KIPS and the conference see PFA RAN f. 135, op. 1, d. 3, l. 46.

regionalization; sessions were held on regionalization, colonization, soil science, agriculture, forest industries, oil and mineral industries, and population
policy.[126] While Goskolonit representatives discussed plans for agricultural
and industrial colonization, the KIPS ethnographers lectured on how to "uti-
lize the human being as a productive force." Ol'denburg and Anuchin argued
that new anthropological research, studying the influence of "physical, racial,
and hereditary" factors on the "physiological development of the population,"
would enable the government to use its human resources to maximum economic benefit.[127] The ethnographers proposed (and soon after began to plan)
research expeditions to support the Goskolonit agenda of Soviet colonization.

The KIPS ethnographers, characterizing economic orientation as an important ethnographic trait and ethnographic composition as a critical economic
factor, contributed to both paradigms for regionalization. It was not up to
KIPS to determine which of the competing paradigms was most appropriate
for the Soviet state. But the work that the ethnographers did for Narkomnats,
Gosplan, and Goskolonit—predicting which peoples would merge into which
nationalities and sketching out the economic proclivities of different population groups—would have a profound impact on the Soviet regime's approach
to its population for decades to come.[128]

The Compromise

Not just administrators and experts, but also Communist Party leaders, found
themselves caught between two competing paradigms for administrative-
territorial regionalization in the 1920s. During these years, Party leaders could
not reach a consensus about how best to organize the Soviet state, let alone
dictate all aspects of state-building in the RSFSR and the union republics. During and immediately following the civil war, the party did not take an official
position regarding regionalization. To be sure, high-ranking members of the
party followed the regionalization debate at all stages, and many participated
in the deliberations through their positions in government institutions. But it
was not until March 1923—once regionalization had been debated in local-
level party and government organizations as well as at nonparty conferences

126. "Uchet prirodnykh bogatstv Rossii (Beseda s chlenom prezidiuma Gosplana, Prof. I. G.
Aleksandrovym)," *Ekonomicheskaia zhizn'*, no. 61 (1291) (March 20, 1923): 3; "Konferentsiia po
izucheniiu estestvenno-proizvoditel'nykh sil Rossii: Ob"edinennoe zasedanie sektsii raionirovaniia
i sektsii cheloveka," *Ekonomicheskaia zhizn'*, no. 64 (1294) (March 23, 1923): 3.

127. "Izuchenie cheloveka, kak ekonomicheskogo faktora (Beseda s nepremennym sekretarem
Akademii nauk, Akademikom S. F. Ol'denburgom)," *Ekonomicheskaia zhizn'*, no. 26 (1296)
(March 26, 1923): 5. "Konferentsiia po izucheniiu estestvenno-proizvoditel'nykh sil Rossii: 2-e
plenarnoe zasedanie," *Ekonomicheskaia zhizn'*, no. 65 (1295) (March 24, 1923): 3. The same issues of *Ekonomicheskaia zhizn'* featured articles about the future colonization of Siberia, the Far
East, and the North. See for example M. Bol'shakov, "Kolonizatsionnye meropriiatiia na 1923
god," *Ekonomicheskaia zhizn'*, no. 62 (1292) (March 21, 1923): 2.

128. I explore this in later chapters.

for peasants and for non-Russian speakers—that the Politburo and the Central Committee formally weighed in on the issue. They approved the revised regionalization plan "in principle." But, reacting to regional dissent, interinstitutional conflict, and continuing disagreement within the party about the road to socialism, they urged "great caution."[129]

Aleksei Rykov spoke about the party's position in April 1923 at the Twelfth Party Congress. "In spite of its 'technical' name, the question of the administrative-economic division or regionalization of the state has colossal, gigantic significance" for "the entire transitional period of the October Revolution, for the entire transitional period from NEP to communism," asserted Rykov. In practical terms, regionalization would entail the total reorganization of government and party organs. Arguing that the regime did not have enough "knowledge of local conditions" to take on such a major endeavor all at once, Rykov called the VTsIK-approved Gosplan proposal a "preliminary working hypothesis" that would have to be revised "on the basis of experience." He announced the party's decision to introduce regionalization "over a protracted period of time" and suggested that Gosplan begin by delimiting two "trial regions."[130]

The party congress's deliberations on both regionalization and the nationality question are striking in their attempt to balance all-union economic and national (ethnographic) concerns. On the one hand, the party denounced prominent national leaders (such as the Narkomnats administrator and Tatar leader Mirsaid Sultan-Galiev) for subordinating Soviet priorities to "local nationalist" interests.[131] On the other hand, the party affirmed the right of all "nationalities to their own state formations" and embraced the Narkomnats position on nonimperialistic development. The counterexamples of the European colonial empires loomed large in the congress's discussions. Pointing to "colonial states such as Great Britain and old Germany," the party noted an "irreconcilable contradiction" between the "economic unification of peoples" (which party leaders described as a progressive process) and the "imperialistic" practices often associated with economic unification (such as "the exploitation of less developed peoples by more developed peoples"). For the European powers, the establishment of colonial empires had had "positive historical significance," in that it had facilitated the "international division of labor" and the

---

129. Alampiev, *Ekonomicheskoe raionirovanie SSSR*, 137.

130. *Dvenadtsatyi s''ezd Rossiiskoi kommunisticheskoi partii*, 429–31, 574, 651. Cited and discussed in Egorov, *Raionirovanie SSSR: Sbornik*, 56–59, and Carr, *Socialism in One Country*, vol. 2, 279.

131. At a secret conference in June 1923, the party censured Sultan-Galiev. In part, he was charged with attempting to undermine the inclusion of the Tatar ASSR in an economic-administrative oblast and advocating instead the creation of a Soviet Muslim national republic under Tatar leadership. *Chetvertoe soveshchanie TsK RKP s otvetstvennymi rabotnikami natsional'nykh respublik i oblastei v Moskve 9–12 iiunia 1923 g. (Stenograficheskii otchet)* (Moscow, 1923).

"colossal development of productive forces"—and thus had established the "material prerequisites" for socialism. At the same time, however, the economic unification of diverse peoples under the "conditions of capitalism" had facilitated "national oppression," "colonial robbery," and the competition for colonial expansion that had exploded in the First World War.[132]

To differentiate the Soviet Union from the European colonial empires and also from the Russian Empire, a number of high-ranking party leaders called for an "emancipatory" nationality policy.[133] Some of these leaders recommended that the party introduce economic measures to spark the industrial development of former colonial peoples. For example, Turar Ryskulov, from Turkestan, proposed that the regime transfer factories from Moscow to former "raw material regions" in Central Asia. Others argued for extensive political and cultural measures to defend and aid "backward" peoples.[134] Stalin took this second position, arguing that economic measures were not enough. According to Stalin, the Soviet regime was obligated to struggle against the "chauvinism" of "dominant nationalities" such as the Great Russians and the Georgians.

Stalin cautioned that to allow some nationalities to benefit at the expense of others would be to replicate an "old system" of imperial government in which the ruler "gives privileges to some nationalities" and "oppresses others through them." He gave the example of the Austro-Hungarian Empire, which had designated several nationalities "to manage the others." He also gave the example of British India: "England decided that rather than deal with 600 nationalities [natsional'nosti]" it would be preferable to choose some, "give them certain privileges and through them rule the others." While the Austro-Hungarian and British approaches had certain administrative benefits (such as channeling the dissatisfaction of subordinate peoples against dominant peoples instead of against the state), both were indefensible from the Soviet perspective, Stalin argued.[135] In the wake of the conference, Stalin began to advocate an approach to the former Russian Empire that combined the Goskolonit vision of Soviet colonization with the Narkomnats vision of state-sponsored evolutionism: a program of intensive economic development coupled with a

132. *Dvenadtsatyi s"ezd Rossiiskoi kommunisticheskoi partii*, 642–44.

133. The Bolsheviks frequently used the formulation "osvoboditel'naia natsional'naia programma [emancipatory nationality program]." Ibid., 644.

134. Ibid., 465–71.

135. Ibid., 446–50. Stalin addressed the two main forms of nationalism that threatened "backward peoples." The first, Great Russian chauvinism, was a consequence of the "former privileged position of Great Russians" in the Russian Empire. The second, the "national chauvinism" of other developed nationalities (such as the Georgians), often originated as a "defensive" response to Russian chauvinism. This "defensive nationalism" often turned into "aggressive nationalism" against smaller nationalities. Ibid., 447–50, 596–600. The Bolsheviks were working from the assumption that most Russians had national consciousness. The 1926 census would show that this was not necessarily the case.

program of promoting nationhood among the Soviet Union's "feudal-era" and "former colonial" peoples.[136]

Neither Narkomnats nor Gosplan "won" the regionalization debate. In the aftermath of the Twelfth Party Congress, the party directed Gosplan to oversee the regionalization of two trial economic-administrative oblasts in the RSFSR: the agricultural North Caucasus oblast and the industrial Urals oblast. At the same time, the party and the new Central Executive Committee (TsIK) of the Soviet government upheld the general framework of the Soviet state in its existing form: union republics, autonomous national republics, autonomous national oblasts, and national regions. Significantly, the party and TsIK declared that union republics (such as the Ukrainian SSR) were "sovereign states" that could not be included in an economic-administrative oblast, and that autonomous national republics (such as the Bashkir ASSR) and autonomous national oblasts (such as the Chuvash AO) were "sovereign in their internal affairs" and had the right to refuse to be included in an economic-administrative oblast.[137] In August, TsIK established a Commission for the Regionalization of the USSR; it directed this new commission to review the borders of existing national-territorial units, to evaluate the possible delimitation of additional national-territorial units, and to mediate border disputes.[138]

It was through the deliberations that followed that the ethnographic and economic paradigms both became part of the structure of the Soviet Union. Between 1924 and 1929, Gosplan worked toward the delimitation of economic-administrative oblasts throughout the RSFSR and the union republics. Its plans were compromised again and again as the leaders of autonomous national oblasts refused to integrate their national territories into proposed economic-administrative oblasts. The Urals oblast, for example, was supposed to include the Bashkir ASSR in addition to Ekaterinburg, Cheliabinsk, and Perm provinces. But Bashkir leaders argued for the exclusion of their autonomous national unit, and Soviet leaders upheld the Bashkir position as a matter of national rights.[139] In order to make up for the loss of the Bashkir territories, Gosplan added several Siberian provinces with agricultural and forest specializations to the oblast.[140] This in turn ruined plans to establish a sep-

136. I explore this further in later chapters.

137. A national region, by contrast, had no such right. P. M. Alampiev, *Ekonomicheskoe raionirovanie SSSR* (Moscow, 1963), vol. 2, 135–36. On the administrative and budgetary rights of these different national-territorial units see GARF f. 6892, op. 1, d. 47, ll. 1–5.

138. GARF f. 6892, op. 1, d. 1, ll. 1–3, 12, 15–17. Sapronov and Avel Enukidze headed the commission. The commission included representatives from the Belorussian and Ukrainian SSRs, the RSFSR, and the Transcaucasian SFSR.

139. Most of the Bashkir ASSR was excluded, but a small part without a Bashkir majority was included on ethnographic and economic grounds.

140. GARF f. 6892, op. 1, d. 47, ll. 8–10. As a general rule, if autonomous national republics or autonomous national oblasts refused to enter planned economic-administrative oblasts, Gosplan adjusted the plan and added other regions with similar economic profiles.

arate Western Siberian oblast. Such examples were commonplace.[141] The original plan for the North Caucasus oblast also fell apart in the face of local demands for national self-determination. In its place, a North Caucasus *krai* was established in 1924, containing within it the Dagestan ASSR and six autonomous national oblasts.[142] The *krai* was a compromise solution. It was an administrative unit whose component national territories were united in a regional economic plan but also had some control over their own budgets, economies, and "national affairs"—which included education, healthcare, and judicial and land issues. In 1925 and 1926 the Siberian and Far Eastern *kraia* were also organized on this model.

Even as Gosplan modified its plans for economic-administrative regionalization to take into account the principle of nationality, TsIK and the party adjusted the borders of the union republics and autonomous national republics with economic considerations in mind. The populations of the Bashkir ASSR, the Ukrainian SSR and other union and autonomous national republics quickly learned that their exclusion from economic-administrative oblasts did not exempt them from integration into the all-union economic plan. Over the course of the 1920s, Gosplan defined economic specializations for all of the union republics, autonomous national republics, and autonomous national oblasts. To ensure that these national-territorial units were viable economically and administratively as well as ethnographically, the TsIK regionalization commission investigated—and in most cases redrew—their borders. On numerous occasions, ethnographic precision was sacrificed for the sake of all-union economic (and other) goals—an issue that is explored in depth in chapter 4.

By 1924, the Soviet regime had achieved the formal political unification of the territories within its borders. Soviet experts and administrators had begun the work of conceptual conquest and had elaborated a revolutionary approach to overcoming the problem of historical diversity. Moreover, the economic and ethnographic research completed for the regionalization projects had facilitated the integration of resources, peoples, and territories into the Soviet whole. But much remained unresolved. The tension between the economic and the ethnographic paradigms for regionalization would remain at the heart of Soviet state-building throughout the next decade.

---

141. Ibid., ll. 10–11, 20–22, 25–26. For example, the leaders of the Buriat-Mongol ASSR opposed their republic's inclusion in the Lensko-Baikal economic-administrative oblast, and the leaders of the Tatar ASSR protested their republic's inclusion in the Middle Volga economic-administrative oblast.

142. These were the Adygei, Ingush, Kabardino-Balkar, Karachai, North Ossetian, Cherkess, and Chechen AOs. Kraevoi komissii po ucheta opyta raionirovaniia pri Severo-Kavkazskom kraevom ispolnitel'nom komitete, *Severnyi Kavkaz posle raionirovaniia (Itogi i vyvody)* (Rostov-on-Don, 1925).

PART 2

Cultural Technologies of Rule and the Nature of Soviet Power

CHAPTER 3

The 1926 Census and the Conceptual Conquest of Lands and Peoples

> Most of these peoples have nothing in common except the fact that before they were all part of the Russian Empire and now they have all been liberated by the revolution. . . . [T]here are no internal connections among them.
>
> —Semen Dimanshtein, Narkomnats, 1919

> Complete enumeration, and the possibility of assigning at each point the necessary connection with the next, permits an absolutely certain knowledge of identities and differences.
>
> —Michel Foucault, *The Order of Things,* 1970

On January 31, 1924, the All-Union Congress of Soviets ratified the Constitution of the USSR, officially creating the Soviet Union. This was not the end of the process of Soviet state formation, but only its beginning; despite the official declaration, the transformation of the Russian Empire into a multinational socialist state was just getting under way. As the Congress of Soviets met in Moscow, a group of KIPS ethnographers gathered at the Academy of Sciences in Petrograd to discuss an important assignment KIPS had recently received from the Soviet of Nationalities: to come up with an "exact definition" of "nationality," to determine rational criteria for classifying the population in the First All-Union Census, and to present its findings to the Central Statistical Administration (TsSU) as soon as possible.[1] The ethnographers, who had become involved in preliminary work on the census during the previous year, were about to become official consultants to the regime on questions about the census registration of nationality.

---

1. The St. Petersburg Branch of the Archive of the Russian Academy of Sciences (PFA RAN) f. 135, op. 1, d. 3, l. 65; d. 13, l. 1; d. 11, ll. 115–16. Semenov-Tian-Shanskii notes that "representatives of the regime in Moscow" asked KIPS "to elucidate the idea of *natsional'nost'* for the rational formulation of suitable questions" for the census.

The classification of all Soviet citizens under the rubric "nationality" in the First All-Union Census, which was conducted in 1926, constituted a critical step in the process of internal transformation that shaped the Soviet state. The ethnographers, statisticians, and linguists who formulated questionnaires and drew up lists of nationalities for the census had to define the terms *natsional'nost'* and *narodnost'* in the new Soviet context. Through a Herculean intellectual and physical effort, these experts worked out definitions, classified diverse peoples, and helped the Bolsheviks to introduce "Soviet power" in the most remote villages, towns, and mountain regions of their domain.[2] Their effort was a tremendous success. By the late 1920s the Soviet regime would have enough expert knowledge about the peoples within its borders to step up its transformative agenda—waging an attack on "backward" population groups and denouncing the "old regime" ethnographers who had served the revolution so well. In an effort to save their field, the ethnographers would participate in a dual process of Sovietization: of the population and of their discipline.

The process of census categorization highlights important similarities and differences between the Soviet Union and other modernizing empires. The Soviet Union, like the European colonial empires, used the census to achieve the intellectual and actual mastery of diverse lands and peoples. Soviet experts, like their British and German contemporaries, used their expertise to place their subjects into standardized knowable categories (a definitional grid) that facilitated centralized rule. But Soviet-style classification was far more ambitious than the classificatory projects described by scholars of the colonial census. Several decades after Europe's "age of empire," the Soviet regime used the census not just to achieve the conceptual conquest of its population, but also to deliberately transform its subjects' identities. In his study of British census-taking in India, Bernard Cohn suggests that the British used caste categories at least in part because they thought that each Indian had a "true" caste; in other words, British anthropologists believed that their census categories mirrored a meaningful sociological truth.[3] By contrast, Soviet administrators and ethnographers used nationality categories knowing full well that

2. Ethnographers and census takers boasted about how they had risked life and limb "with enthusiasm" to do preliminary research and conduct the census in inaccessible regions like the mountains of the Caucasus (The Russian State Archive of the Economy [RGAE] f. 1562, op. 336, d. 46, ll. 117, 228) and "by foot, through a typhoon. . . . almost perishing" in and around Vladivostok (RGAE f. 1562, op. 336, d. 4, l. 108). This drive to reach out to and transform even the most remote areas within Soviet borders was a striking feature of Soviet nationality policy in general. On the ethnographers' role in spreading the revolution to non-Russians see Yuri Slezkine, *Arctic Mirrors: Russia and the Small Peoples of the North* (Ithaca, 1994). On the juncture between nationality politics and "politicized ethnography," see Bruce Grant, *In the Soviet House of Culture: A Century of Perestroikas* (Princeton, 1995).

3. Bernard Cohn, "The Census, Social Structure, and Objectification in South Asia," in *An Anthropologist Among the Historians and Other Essays* (New Delhi, 1990). Also see Cohn, *Colonialism and Its Forms of Knowledge: The British in India* (Princeton, 1996), and Arjun Appadu-

the very concept of nationality was not (yet) meaningful for some of the peoples they were registering. Elaborating on this aspect of Soviet policy in June 1925, the Central Committee member Anastas Mikoian explained that the Soviet regime was "creating and organizing new nations [*sozdaet i organizuet novye natsii*]."[4]

How should we understand the Bolsheviks' interest in the national categorization of all of their subjects, including those without national consciousness? In recent years, historians have described Soviet nationality policy as a form of "affirmative action," adopting "the contemporary American term for policies that give preference to members of ethnic groups that have suffered from past discrimination."[5] Positioning themselves against a previous generation of scholars who characterized the Soviet regime as a "breaker of nations," these historians have documented how the Bolsheviks promoted the creation of "national territories, languages, elites, and identities" and "assumed leadership over the usual process of national formation" in an effort "to construct Soviet international nations."[6] Although the term *affirmative action* has some descriptive power, it is also misleading—disconnecting Soviet policies and practices from their actual historical context. Soviet nationality policy was not a precursor to American race policy of the twentieth century, but rather an attempt to adapt evolutionary paradigms of the late nineteenth century to the Soviet context. It was grounded in a tradition of European thought that saw nationalism as a necessary but transient phase in the development of a more universalistic identity. As I argued in the previous chapter, Soviet nationality policy is best understood as a policy of state-sponsored evolutionism. Its ultimate goal was not to promote "national minorities" at the expense of "national majorities," but to speed *all* peoples, minorities and majorities alike, through the imagined stages on the Marxist historical timeline from feudalism and capitalism to socialism, and on to communism. Its more immediate goal was to promote the economic and cultural development of the population as a whole—to lay the groundwork for a socialist economy and society—while

rai, "Number in the Colonial Imagination," in *Orientalism and the Post-Colonial Predicament: Perspectives on South Asia*, ed. Carol Breckenridge and Peter van der Veer (Philadelphia, 1993). On the German colonial census see Peter Uvin, "On Counting, Categorizing and Violence in Burundi and Rwanda," in *Census and Identity: The Politics of Race, Ethnicity, and Language in National Censuses*, ed. David Kertzer and Dominique Arel (Cambridge, 2002).

4. The speech is printed in Umar Aliev, *Natsional'nyi vopros i natsional'naia kul'tura v Severo-Kavkazskom krae (Itogi i perspektivy): K predstoiashchemu s"ezdu gorskikh narodov* (Rostov-on-Don, 1926), 9.

5. The quote is from Terry Martin, who makes this argument in *The Affirmative Action Empire: Nations and Nationalism in the Soviet Union, 1923–1939* (Ithaca, 2001), 17. Ronald Suny writes about what he calls the Soviet Union's "affirmative action" policies. Suny, *The Revenge of the Past: Nationalism, Revolution and the Collapse of the Soviet Union* (Stanford, 1993), 109.

6. Martin, *Affirmative Action Empire*, 18. Following Martin, a number of scholars have adopted this term. Robert Conquest famously called the Soviet Union a "breaker of nations." See Conquest, *Stalin: Breaker of Nations* (London, 1991).

proving that the terms *metropole* and *colony* could no longer be applied to the territories that comprised the Soviet Union.[7] In the 1920s, in pursuit of these ends, Soviet leaders and experts attempted to determine which clans, tribes, and peoples were "related" in order to intervene in the process of national consolidation and speed up the population's ethnohistorical development.[8]

The Soviet regime aspired to control the enumeration and classification of its population into nationality categories. In practice, however, these processes were replete with unexpected outcomes. The census classification of the population by "nationality," together with policies that entitled nationalities (as opposed to tribes or clans) to land, resources, and rights, encouraged local elites and experts to project their own aspirations onto the census and to interfere in the registration process. Representatives of peoples with their own national-territorial units (union and autonomous national republics and national oblasts) used coercion and deception to manipulate the census registration of nationality in order to ensure their dominant position and maintain their local monopolies on land, water, and other resources. Representatives of peoples without national territories or with small national territories used the census as a vehicle for national realization. Through the census they attempted to increase their group's official numbers and document that it lived in a "compact mass" in particular regions, and thus lay claim to desirable land.[9] Hotly politicized, the census showed the diverse peoples of the Soviet Union the extent to which national categorization could affect their day-to-day lives. Instead of settling territorial disputes conclusively, the process of categorization often led to an escalation in local conflicts and tensions.[10]

Nationality in the New Soviet Context

The First All-Union Census of December 1926 was an event of phenomenal proportion that involved the entire Soviet population. As such, it was a critical instrument of Soviet power and guarantor of Soviet knowledge. Attempting to

7. See A. Skachko, "Vostochnye respubliki na Vserossiiskoi S.-Kh. Vystavke SSSR v 1923 godu," *Novyi Vostok*, no. 4 (1923): 485.

8. An interesting comparison can be made with the new nation states of the nineteenth century, which used statistics to "create" or "produce" the nationalities they purported to describe. See Silvana Patriarca, *Numbers and Nationhood: Writing Statistics in Nineteenth-Century Italy* (Cambridge, 1996).

9. Letters to the newspaper *Krest'ianskaia gazeta* (*The Peasant's Paper*) in the 1920s, written in response to articles about the upcoming census, give a sense of how people throughout Russia began to mobilize around the category "nationality" in the months before the census was taken. While a few letters expressed hope that the registration of nationality would guarantee minority rights, a greater number complained that rumors about the allocation of land on the basis of nationality had fostered local conflict. For example RGAE f. 396, op. 4, d. 28.

10. On the census and map in nation formation see Benedict Anderson's chapter "Census, Map, Museum," in *Imagined Communities: Reflections on the Origin and Spread of Nationalism*, rev. ed. (London, 1991).

rule an expansive land mass and establish a viable administrative framework, the new regime sought data about the nationality, sex, native language, occupation, literacy level, marital status, and physical and mental handicaps of all Soviet citizens.[11] In previous years, the Bolsheviks had conducted two demographic censuses: the general census of 1920 and the city census of 1923. Both were taken against a turbulent backdrop, as borders changed, populations moved, and the fledgling Soviet state struggled to survive. As a consequence, both had excluded numerous territories. The 1920 census, taken in the midst of the civil war and the Soviet-Polish war, left out sizeable regions that at the time were occupied, contested, or outside of Soviet borders: the Crimea and most of Transcaucasia; large parts of Ukraine, Belorussia, the Far East, and Central Asia; and smaller parts of Siberia, the Far North, and central Russia. The 1923 census limited its scope to urban areas, as one of its main objectives was to provide information about the economic and sociological problems of cities.[12]

Even after data from the 1920 and 1923 censuses were tabulated, Soviet leaders and administrators lacked essential knowledge about the population. This became clear in a number of contexts. For example, when Communist Party and government commissions began the national delimitation of Central Asia in 1924 (redistributing the territories of Turkestan and of the former Bukharan and Khorezm emirates among a number of new national republics and oblasts), the new Commission for the Regionalization of Central Asia reported with dismay that there were national majorities and minorities in the region about which it knew "almost nothing at all." In particular, the commission noted its ignorance about the populations of Bukhara and Khorezm, and those of the Afghan and Chinese borderlands.[13] Such ignorance was not without consequences. Soviet leaders hoped to accelerate the consolidation of clans and tribes into nationalities—to "make nationalities" out of related ethnographic groups. But they stated repeatedly that it was not their aspiration to

11. The "personal form" (*lichnyi listok*) of the census included questions about the above. In urban regions, the census also included a "family card" and a "property list"; the former requested economic and demographic information about each family, the latter information about each family's living space. See N. Osinskii, "Printsipy i praktika vsesoiuznoi perepisi naseleniia," *Sovetskoe stroitel'stvo*, no. 3–4 (1927): 37–38. On the goals of the census see RGAE f. 1562, op. 1, d. 349, l. 57; d. 433, ll. 1–24. Also see M. Krasil'nikov, *Doklad Obshchesoiuznomu s"ezdu statistikov, 1–7 dekabriia 1926 g.* (Moscow, 1926), 1–23.

12. On the exclusion of certain territories from the census due to the war see PFA RAN f. 135, op. 1, d. 50, l. 28, and Krasil'nikov, *Doklad Obshchesoiuznomu s"ezdu statistikov*, 1. For a discussion of both of these censuses see G. G. Melik'ian and A. Ia. Kvasha, eds., *Narodonaselenie: Entsiklopedicheskii slovar'* (Moscow, 1994), 310–11. The statisticians Vasilii Mikhailovskii and Olimpii Kvitkin had important roles in the production of the 1920, 1923, and 1926 censuses. (Mikhailovskii died in October 1926.)

13. GARF f. 6892, op. 1, d. 42, ll. 3–8. Bukhara and Khorezm were still independent republics at this point.

create "false nationalities" out of peoples who did not share "ethnographic traits" or "historical origins."[14] Acknowledging the shortage of reliable information, in 1924 party officials distributed a memo to administrators and experts throughout the Union, proclaiming the need for basic facts about the population's national composition, everyday-life (*bytovye*) particularities, spoken languages, cultural level, and occupations.[15]

The formulation of a census question about nationality was particularly important for the Soviet state and was especially fraught with difficulty. As discussed in chapter 1, the 1897 All-Russian Census had classified most of the Russian Empire's subjects according to native language and religion, which contemporaries had characterized as the essential components of nationality.[16] With the delegitimization of religion after the October Revolution and with the Soviet regime's recognition that many peoples of the former Russian Empire had "lost" their native languages as a result of the imperial government's policies of linguistic and cultural Russification, Soviet officials and experts called this formula into question.[17] In contrast to prerevolutionary censuses, the Soviet censuses of 1920 and 1923 had sought the national self-definition (*samonazvanie*) of respondents; both Soviet censuses had used the term *natsional'nost'*, defining it as "a population group united into a nationally self-conscious community."[18] Almost as soon as these censuses were completed,

---

14. M. Reisner, "Sovet Natsional'nostei," *Sovetskoe stroitel'stvo*, vol. 1 (Moscow, 1925): 192–207. Reisner argued that the regime should not "resurrect the dead" or "create a living ethnographic museum" by protecting the "ethnographic particularities" of peoples that had all but disappeared. Participants at a November 1926 meeting of the "national" (non-Russian) members of VTsIK and TsIK maintained that the regime was not interested in creating "artificial nations" (even if it "seemed like it on the surface"). The State Archive of the Russian Federation (GARF) f. 3316, op. 16a, d. 212, ll. 97–99.

15. The Central State Archive of Historical-Political Documents of St. Petersburg (TsGAIPD SPb), f. 9, op. 1, d. 223, ll. 3–6.

16. The Imperial Census Commission had used the terms *narodnost'* and *natsional'nost'* interchangeably. It had used data about native language and confessional group to produce a list of the Russian Empire's nationalities, listing 104 nationalities in table 22 of the census. (This table tabulated data for "occupational groups by *narodnost'*.") Melik'ian and Kvasha, *Narodonaselenie*, 310, and A. I. Gozulov, *Perepisi naseleniia SSSR i kapitalisticheskikh stran* (Moscow, 1936), 189–201. Also see Patkanov's introduction to N. A. Troinitskii, ed., *Obshchii svod po imperii rezul'tatov razrabotki dannykh Pervoi vseobshchei perepisi naseleniia proizvedennoi 28 ianvaria 1897 goda,* vol. 2 (St. Petersburg, 1905). Data about language and confessional group were recorded according to each respondent's self-definition for estate owners and urban residents, but according to the census taker's judgment for peasant households in rural regions. See David W. Darrow, "Census as a Technology of Empire," *Ab Imperio*, no. 4 (2002): 145–76.

17. The tsarist regime's approach to its population varied considerably. In some regions and time periods, it endorsed a policy of religious and cultural toleration and administrative integration. In others, it advanced a policy of Russification, characterized by linguistic and cultural assimilation. See Dietrich Geyer, *Russian Imperialism: The Interaction of Domestic and Foreign Policy, 1860–1914* (Leamington Spa, UK, 1987). The Soviet regime emphasized the coercive aspect of Russification in making the case that it was more enlightened than its predecessor.

18. After 1920 other Soviet documents (birth, death, marriage, divorce and adoption certificates) also had a line for nationality. Between 1920 and 1925 birth certificates requested the *nat-*

their data on nationality became a subject of contention. Conflict about the accuracy of the 1920 and 1923 censuses heated up further in 1924, after the official formation of the Soviet Union. Soviet officials were using data on nationality from both of these censuses in their deliberations about the national-territorial borders of the Ukrainian, Belorussian, and other Soviet republics. Representatives from Belorussia and Ukraine argued that the 1920 census had produced unreliable data due to the circumstances of civil war. Experts and officials from both republics explained that when the census was being taken in the western borderlands, it had been unclear whether entire towns and villages "would go to Poland or remain in Russia." They suggested that census takers had schemed to inflate the numbers of Great Russians (and underestimate the numbers of Poles, Belorussians, and Ukrainians) in these regions in order to bolster Soviet Russian claims.[19]

The KIPS ethnographers, who were using data from the 1920 and 1923 censuses to prepare new ethnographic maps of the Soviet Union to be used in deliberations about contested borders, offered an even more fundamental critique: that these censuses were inaccurate because the TsSU had mistakenly equated nationality with membership in a nationally-conscious community.[20] Both the 1920 and 1923 censuses had asked respondents to state their *natsional'nost'*. Both had used a list of fifty-three *natsional'nosti*, which had been compiled by statisticians and administrators. (This list in fact included far more than fifty-three names—in some cases listing numerous peoples as members of each *natsional'nost'*.[21])

As Soviet leaders and administrators began deliberations about a future All-Union Census, they too expressed dissatisfaction with the existing census data on nationality. Back when the Bolsheviks were an underground revolutionary party, Joseph Stalin had characterized a nationality (*natsional'nost'* or *natsiia*) as a "historically developed" people.[22] But in 1923, as a government-in-power with an "emancipatory nationality policy," the Bolsheviks looked to catego-

---

sional'nost' of the mother. Between 1926 and 1927 official documents requesting *natsional'nost'* provided a list of possible choices: Great Russian, Ukrainian, Belorussian, Jewish, Armenian, Georgian, Tatar, Kirgiz, Mordva, Bashkir, Chuvash, German, Votiak, Uzbek, Turkmen, Tajik, Latvian, Polish, Other. Beginning in 1928 official documents requested the *natsional'nost'* "to which the person concerned identifies [himself or herself]." During the late 1920s, official documents asked for the bearer to provide his or her "*natsional'nost'*, that is *narodnost'*." Melik'ian and Kvasha, *Narodonaselenie*, 581, 591, 597. The instructions explained that *natsional'nost'* was not to be confused with religion or the name of the territory in which the respondent lives: "for example a Tatar must not identify as a Bashkir simply because he lives in Bashkiria." RGAE f. 1562, op. 20, d. 6, ll. 31–33.

19. These issues were discussed at a December 1923 meeting of the TsIK Subcommission for Changing the Borders Between the RSFSR and the BSSR. GARF f. 3316, op. 16, d. 206, ll. 35–45.

20. See the discussion below.

21. For this list see "Statisticheskii ezhegodnik 1922 i 1923 gg.," *Trudy Tsentral'nogo statisticheskogo upravleniia* 8, no. 5 (Moscow, 1924), 48–53.

22. See chapter 1.

rize as members of nationalities even "backward" peoples (individuals and entire groups) lacking national consciousness. Having made the decision to use "nationality" as a standard rubric of classification for the Soviet Union, the Bolsheviks sought a formula for determining the actual or potential nationality of *all* Soviet citizens. It was with this goal in mind that Soviet officials looked to professional ethnographers.

The KIPS Census Subcommission

In early 1923, Sergei F. Ol'denburg, Sergei Rudenko, Lev Shternberg, and other KIPS ethnographers had participated in discussions about a future All-Union Census through their work with Narkomnats. But it was after the official formation of the Soviet Union—which precipitated the elimination of Narkomnats and the concomitant dissolution of its Ethnographic Bureau—that KIPS took on a fundamental role in the production of the census. In 1924, KIPS began to function as a de facto ethnographic bureau of the regime. Around the same time, Soviet leaders turned the Soviet of Nationalities (which had been a collegium within Narkomnats) into the second branch of the Soviet government.[23] In the wake of this major reorganization, the Soviet of Nationalities presented KIPS with the urgent request to define nationality and come up with a formula for census registration.[24] In response, KIPS created a new census subcommission under the leadership of Veniamin Semenov-Tian-Shanskii, who was an active member of KIPS, KEPS, and the Russian Geographical Society.[25] Experts from all three institutions (including ethnographers, economists, and statisticians) attended the subcommission's meetings.[26]

What was the "essence" of *natsional'nost'*? Could one formula for registering nationality be effective throughout the Soviet Union? Semenov-Tian-Shanskii posed these questions at the census subcommission's first meeting in

23. Soviet leaders explained that Narkomnats had fulfilled its original purpose of drawing non-Russian regions into the Soviet state and was no longer needed. See G. P. Makarova, *Narodnyi komissariat po delam natsional'nostei RSFSR, 1917–1923 gg.: Istoricheskii ocherk* (Moscow, 1987), and Stephen Blank, *The Sorcerer as Apprentice: Stalin as Commissar of Nationalities, 1917–1924* (Westport, 1994).

24. This is the episode with which this chapter began.

25. Members of the KIPS census subcommission were Sergei F. Ol'denburg, Nikolai Marr, Vasilii Bartol'd, Fedor Shcherbanskii, Lev Berg, Aleksandr Samoilovich, Petr Mashtakov, David Zolotarev, Sergei Rudenko, Lev Shternberg, Vladimir Bogoraz, Vasilii Shibaev, and Veniamin Semenov-Tian-Shanskii. Semenov-Tian-Shanskii directed the proceedings and Rudenko served as the KIPS liaison to Moscow. PFA RAN f. 135, op. 1, d. 11, l. 114. Semenov-Tian-Shanskii's father, Petr Petrovich, had directed the proceedings of the 1897 census.

26. Semenov-Tian-Shanskii had leadership roles in all three institutions. In addition to the ethnographers, other experts at the first session included the statisticians and economists Ivan Mainov, Andrei Dostoevskii, Viktor Stepanov, A. D. Poliakov, Nikolai Berezin, Viktor Shtein, and Sergei Shvetsov. On the subcommission and its initial meetings see PFA RAN f. 135, op. 1, d. 8, ll. 174–75; d. 23, ll. 1, 2; d. 11, l. 114. The first meeting was held on January 4, 1924.

Figure 3.1 Veniamin Semenov-Tian-Shanskii in a group photo of the Olonets scientific expedition in Segozero, Karelia, 1921. Semenov-Tian-Shanskii is seated fourth from right in the front (with white hair and beard). (Archive of the Russian Academy of Sciences, St. Petersburg Branch f. 893, op. 2, d. 66, l. 2)

January 1924 and then attempted to answer them. He suggested that *natsional'nost'* could be likened to a collection of traits "arising under the joint influences of anthropological, geographical, and historical causes." From "a strictly scientific point of view," there were two possible ways to define the term: as an "anthropological concept, indicated by a given person's physical breed," or as a "cultural concept, indicated by the type of geographical and ethnological environment in which a given person lived and lives his or her mental life." Each definition had its own set of implications. Semenov-Tian-Shanskii gave his colleagues an example to contemplate: What is the nationality of a woman who has always lived in the part of Russia populated by the Finnish peoples, whose parents are English and German, but who herself was educated in Russian schools and speaks English and Russian? In other words, can a woman "without a drop of Russian blood" be Russian?[27] Members of Russia's educated elite had pondered such questions before. But the decision to use "nationality"

27. PFA RAN f. 135, op. 1, d. 11, ll. 115–16. Also see the Archive of the Russian Geographical Society (RGO) f. 48, op. 1, d. 147, ll. 1–10b.

as a standard category of identity, which would establish people's rights to economic and cultural resources, increased the stakes of the debate.[28]

In preparation for the subcommission's discussions, Semenov-Tian-Shanskii had circulated a proposed formula of five questions to help census takers ascertain respondents' nationalities:

> 1. To which nationality [*natsional'nost'*] does or did (if they are not alive) the given person's father and mother belong? (to determine the person's anthropological type)
> 2. To which religion was the given person born?
> 3. Does the person regard himself or herself as a member of any religion today? If yes, then to which one in particular?
> 4. What conversational language did the given person speak in childhood, and which does he or she use today at home?
> 5. Is the given person able to express himself or herself in Russian?[29]

This formula, with its focus on religion, language, and anthropological type, inspired spirited debate at the January meeting and afterward. The ethnographer and subcommission member Nikolai Marr criticized the proposed questions, arguing that in the modern age *natsional'nost'* could not be extrapolated from "blood, territory or physiological type," but was a reflection of group consciousness.[30] Other experts maintained that Semenov-Tian-Shanskii's approach was "too scientific" and that his suggested questions were too diffuse. The statistician Andrei Dostoevskii suggested that "Moscow" should try a more straightforward approach if its aim was to use the census to "determine most precisely the national composition of the state's population." Census takers should ask respondents directly: "In which nationality do you include yourself?" Dostoevskii maintained that the Soviet leadership's promise of national self-determination, combined with the "division of the whole state into [national] republics and communes," provided "the most opportune and favorable" conditions for "obtaining a correct answer to a direct question about *natsional'nost'*." He conceded that Semenov-Tian-Shanskii's formula (or a variation of it) might be useful in those instances when respondents "had difficulty answering the question" as posed.[31]

Dostoevskii assumed that most people would be able to answer a direct question about their nationality. But other commission members and KIPS

---

28. After 1924 the KIPS ethnographers participated in ethnographic expeditions to identify and study "the many disputed points" which resulted after national delimitation. For example, PFA RAN f. 135, op. 1, d. 18, l. 3.

29. PFA RAN f. 135, op. 1, d. 11, ll. 115–16. Semenov-Tian-Shanskii precirculated the questions to commission members and other interested experts. (The experts used gender-neutral language.)

30. Ibid., ll. 123–27.

31. Ibid., l. 117.

correspondents were not so sure. Experts on Central Asia insisted that religion and clan were the key components of local identity in their region of focus, while experts on Siberia maintained that tribal identities remained most significant in their region.[32] Vasilii Chernyshev, a KIPS correspondent in central Russia, argued that "uncultured folk" throughout Soviet Russia had difficulty answering a direct question about nationality. Chernyshev explained that peasants often did not distinguish among Belorussians, Great Russians, and Ukrainians, but simply called everyone "Russian" or named the town they were from; he and his colleagues had encountered a number of self-described "Vladimirians" and "Kostromians."[33] Local leaders might define the people they claimed to speak for in "national" terms, but it did not necessarily follow that "nationality" was a meaningful or readily translatable concept for the general population. Arguing that a census question about nationality left too much room for honest mistakes, as well as for abuse by local leaders with their own political aspirations, Chernyshev proposed that the question about nationality be replaced with a "simpler and more meaningful question about native language."[34]

Closely connected to the discussion about the most effective formula for registering nationality was the question about which term to use in the census questionnaire: the term with the Russian root, *narodnost'*, or the term with the foreign root, *natsional'nost'*. For decades, educated elites had used both terms, often interchangeably, to signify nationality. But in the aftermath of the revolution, some ethnographers suggested that the terms corresponded to two different positions on a timeline of evolutionary development. They argued that *natsional'nost'* was a meaningless concept for the more "backward" peoples they encountered since it implied "an understanding of one's ethnohistorical origins."[35] There was some discussion about using both terms in the census, in order to differentiate between nationalities at different levels of development: The members of a "cultured" (or "civilized") *natsional'nost'* could identify themselves through a direct census question, while the members of an "uncultured" (or "uncivilized") *narodnost'* could be identified through a formula that used "objective" traits.[36] But the subcommission—and ultimately the TsSU—rejected this proposal, on the grounds that the division between the cultured and uncultured did not wholly follow national lines. As Chernyshev had indicated, the "general masses" of the Russians (presumed to be an advanced nationality) had as much trouble with a direct question about nation-

---

32. See, for example, PFA RAN f. 135, op. 1, d. 18, l. 3; d. 21, l. 42; d. 22, ll. 9–25.

33. PFA RAN f. 135, op. 1, d. 11, ll. 134–37. Chernyshev noted that "the well-known joke, 'A person from Pskov is not a Russian,' quite truthfully defines our national consciousness." Chernyshev's written statement, sent to KIPS, was dated February 26, 1924.

34. Ibid.

35. Ibid., ll. 109–11.

36. See the discussion about the Georgians below.

ality as the indigenous tribes of Siberia did. Uncertain about how this issue would be resolved, the KIPS census subcommission used both terms, and sometimes the designation *"natsional'nost'/narodnost',"* in its work.

While many KIPS ethnographers doubted the population's ability to answer a direct census question about nationality, they also rejected the idea that census takers could determine a respondent's nationality on the basis of "objective criteria" like language and confessional group. Some insisted that local conceptions of identity were far too particular to apply one formula to all Soviet territories. After extensive discussion, the KIPS census subcommission suggested that limited self-definition—that is, self-definition circumscribed by regionally-specific directions and control questions—might be the most effective approach. The census taker would ask each individual to state his or her nationality. Then, with the aid of detailed explanatory materials and questionnaires, census takers could make sure that responses were appropriate.[37]

Over the course of the next two years, in keeping with the subcommission's recommendations, KIPS drafted regionally specific materials for census takers.[38] Marr wrote up a report for census takers in the Caucasus, admonishing them to "note religion as control data" in communities where respondents were uncertain of their "national membership (tribal origins)."[39] Shternberg wrote a short note for census takers in Siberia, directing them to record the "self-definition" of all adults in each house or hut and also to make a list of all the local names for each *narodnost'*.[40] David Zolotarev drafted a report for census takers in European Russia with detailed region-by-region instructions; he directed census takers in the northwest oblast, for example, to determine if self-identified "Finns" were Izhora, Suomi, Leningrad Finns, Chukhars, Vods, or Karelians.[41] The ethnographer and Turkologist Ivan Zarubin prepared extensive notes for census takers in the territories of former Turkestan, Bukhara, and Khorezm, citing about twenty special cases in which census takers should ask respondents control questions about native language, conversational language, religion, and kinship group in order to ascertain whether they had given "correct" responses to the question about nationality. To differentiate between Iranians and Tajiks, Zarubin recommended that census takers "pay attention to the religion of the subject"; he noted that in Bukhara and Khorezm most "Iranians are Shiites and Tajiks are Sunni."[42] According to the ethnographers, census registration would be particularly challenging in the territories of former Turkestan due to the fact that many of the region's inhabi-

---

37. PFA RAN f. 135, op. 1, d. 23, ll. 5–60b.

38. KIPS organized this work through its four main departments: European Russia, Siberia and the Far East, the Caucasus, and Central Asia. See PFA RAN f. 135, op. 1, d. 23, ll. 14–17.

39. PFA RAN f. 135, op. 1, d. 21, ll. 36–37. He also suggested that census takers note the "tribal" affiliation of self-identified Turks and Georgians.

40. Ibid., l. 47.

41. PFA RAN f. 135, op. 1, d. 23, ll. 21–22; d. 320, l. 1.

42. PFA RAN f. 135, op. 1, d. 21, ll. 42–420b.

tants identified with several categories at once. In Fergana, for example, communities of people called themselves "Kirgiz-Kipchak" or "Uzbek-Kipchak." Until the national-territorial delimitation of Central Asia in 1924, the terms *Uzbek, Kirgiz,* and *Kipchak* typically denoted linguistic or kinship affiliations, not nationality. Zarubin suggested that census takers ask respondents a series of direct questions, including: "Are you Kirgiz? Are you Uzbek?" He advised them to register only people replying "no" to both questions as "members of the Kipchak nationality." The others, he argued, should be registered as Uzbeks or Kirgiz, with "Kipchak noted in parentheses as a clan designation."[43]

Potentially complicating census registration even further, the ethnographers also explained that not all answers to the question about nationality were acceptable. The term *Teptiar* was a case in point. In his instructions for census takers in Bashkiria, Zolotarev asserted that "Teptiar" was not the name of a people, but the name for a tenant on Bashkir land.[44] The term *Sart* was another example. Zarubin and other Turkologists maintained that "Sart" was not a suitable response to the census question, arguing that the term designated people of a particular economic orientation and not a nationality or ethnographic group. The ethnographers, nonetheless, predicted that there would be "many cases" in which respondents "call themselves Sarts" either "in separate instances or in entire regions." Zarubin recommended that census takers register self-identified Sarts who speak Uzbek as Uzbeks, adding "the term *Sart* in parentheses."[45] The question of the Teptiars and the Sarts was extremely controversial. Representatives from other nationalities were attempting to claim the Teptiars and the Sarts as their own in order to establish their right to lands that the self-identified members of these groups inhabited.[46]

In early 1926, Semenov-Tian-Shanskii combined all of these materials into a first draft of the "Instructions for the Registration of Nationality in the 1926 Census."[47] Copies circulated among ethnographers, statisticians, and officials throughout the Soviet Union and became the subject of interinstitutional discussion. The instructions directed census takers to ask each respondent "to which nationality he or she belongs" and to write his or her testimony "exactly as given" in the census form. To ensure that responses were "sufficiently

43. Ibid.

44. PFA RAN f. 135, op. 1, d. 22, l. 142; d. 23, ll. 21–22.

45. PFA RAN f. 135, op. 1, d. 21, ll. 42–42ob. The KIPS ethnographers debated the term amongst themselves. Samoilovich argued for the elimination of the term on the grounds that the Sarts were not a "pure" ethnic group, but a combination of different peoples of a particular economic orientation. Zarubin opposed the elimination of the term. See I. I. Zarubin, *Spisok narodnostei Turkestanskogo kraia, Trudy Komissii po izucheniiu plemennogo sostava naseleniia Rossii i sopredel'nkh stran,* vol. 9 (Leningrad, 1925). On the Sarts see John Samuel Schoeberlein-Engel, "Identity in Central Asia: Construction and Contention in the Conceptions of 'Ozbek,' 'Tajik,' 'Muslim,' 'Samarquandi' and Other Groups," Ph.D. diss., Harvard University, 1994.

46. This case is discussed in chapter 4.

47. PFA RAN f. 135, op. 1, d. 21, ll. 48–49; d. 23, ll. 21–22. KIPS sent the instructions and draft list to the Central Statistical Administration in mid-May.

accurate from a scientific point of view," they recommended that census takers refer to the supplementary notes and instructions that the ethnographers were preparing.[48] The instructions did not spell out whether or not census takers had the right to change respondents' testimonies if, after consulting the supplementary materials, they deemed them to be inaccurate. Semenov-Tian-Shanskii, for his part, seems to have imagined the census interview as a conversation in which census takers who knew local conditions and enjoyed the trust of the local population helped respondents to determine their "true" national identities. As a further aid to census takers, the KIPS ethnographers drafted lists of nationalities for different regions of the Soviet Union. These lists were supposed to help census takers as well as statisticians evaluate whether or not responses to the question about nationality were acceptable.[49] To facilitate this work, the ethnographers worked with experts and administrators throughout the Soviet Union.

Setting the Terms of the Census

Preparations for the All-Union Census involved correspondence among an extensive network of institutions.[50] Between January 1924 and December 1926, KIPS was in constant communication with statisticians at the TsSU's Commission for the Production of the Census, officials with the Soviet of Nationalities and TsIK, economists at Gosplan, party and government officials in Moscow and the regions, and ethnographers at Moscow State University. Party leaders were kept well-informed of all proceedings. Valerian Osinskii, candidate member of the Central Committee of the Communist Party and head of the TsSU, served as an important intermediary between the experts and party leaders, giving briefings about the census at Politburo and TsIK meetings.[51] In addition, the Commission for the Production of the Census forwarded protocols from its meetings directly to Stalin, Aleksei Rykov, and Valerian

48. PFA RAN f. 135, op. 1, d. 23, ll. 21–22.

49. KIPS sent commission members to Central Asia, the Caucasus, Ukraine, Belorussia, Moscow, and other locales to collect information for the preparation of these lists. The commission borrowed statistical and cartographical materials from republic- and local-level statistical bureaus, the People's Commissariat of Internal Affairs, the Military-Topographic Administration of the Red Army, the Commission for the Regionalization of Central Asia, and other institutions. KIPS had reciprocal relationships with many of these institutions. See, for example, PFA RAN f. 135, op. 1, d. 18, ll. 36–37; d. 22, l. 149.

50. For a discussion of the relationship between center and regions in the formulation of the 1926 census see Juliette Cadiot, "Les relations entre le centre et les régions en URSS à travers les débats sur les nationalités dans le recensement de 1926," *Cahiers du monde russe* 38, no. 4 (1997): 601–16.

51. The Russian Center for the Preservation and Study of Documents of Modern History (RTsKhIDNI) f. 17, op. 3, d. 546, 580, 599, 601, etc. Also Tsentral'nyi ispolnitel'nyi komitet, *Zasedanie TsIK SSSR*, 3 sessiia, Stenograficheskii otchet (Moscow, 1927), 196–242. Stalin, Bukharin, and other Bolshevik leaders were present at these meetings. Osinskii's original surname was Obolenskii. He published as N. Osinskii and V. Obolenskii.

Kuibyshev.[52] Piles of memos and reports reveal the efforts of the different institutions to achieve a common language.[53] They also show points at which central party and government officials overruled the ethnographers' and statisticians' recommendations.

In early February 1926 Semenov-Tian-Shanskii and Rudenko joined representatives from many of these institutions for nine days at the Fourth All-Union Statistical Conference in Moscow. The aim of the conference was to lay the groundwork for the upcoming census. Entire sessions were devoted to establishing an official lexicon of identity categories.[54] Statisticians, ethnographers, and officials again debated which term to use in the census: *natsional'nost'* or *narodnost'*. Many made the case for the term *narodnost'*, arguing that *natsional'nost'* was a "cultural and political category" that did not necessarily reflect "ethnic" or ethnographic type.[55] Those present also hashed out the language of class, defining "worker," "peasant," and "kulak." They discussed the term *family*, arguing about whether it was an "economic" or a "biological" unit: whether the term applied to all members of a household, or just those who were related. Finally, the conference participants debated the census question about language, asking whether "native language" should be understood as the language of one's ancestors or the language of conversation. Although the TsSU originally had not planned to include a question about language in the census, Soviet officials had argued that information about language was critical for "the practical implementation of nationality policy." Administrative organs sought a breakdown of the population's "native languages" in order to establish schools and print books. Statisticians wanted data about "native languages" in order to put together a "more accurate" picture of the Union's national composition. Participants in census deliberations attempted to define the term with both ends in mind: While some suggested that "native language" should be understood as "the language of [the respondent's] mother" or "the language of [the respondent's] nationality," others argued that it was "the language in which the respondent speaks with the people closest to him" or "the language in which he thinks." Several statisticians proposed that respondents define the term for themselves, but this suggestion was dismissed as dangerous and unacceptable.[56]

Discussions about terminology had serious implications for the shape of the Soviet Union. Experts, administrators, and local leaders recognized that the

52. RTsKhIDNI f. 17, op. 85, d. 168, ll. 23–29. The party's secret section also received protocols of the meetings. The Politburo, the Council of People's Commissars, and TsIK funded and approved plans for statistical work.

53. See PFA RAN f. 135, op. 1, d. 23.

54. RGAE f. 1562, op. 1, d. 433, ll. 1–71. The conference was held February 1–9.

55. RGAE f. 1562, op. 1, d. 433, ll. 25, 29 (Comments of Vasilii Mikhailovskii). For a discussion of this question also see V. B. Zhiromskaia, "Vsesoiuznye perepisi naseleniia 1926, 1937, 1939 godov: Istoriia podgotovki i provedeniia," *Istoriia SSSR*, no. 3 (1990): 93.

56. RGAE f. 1562, op. 1, d. 433, ll. 25–27, 63–64.

decision to use particular terms could manipulate census results; this in turn would affect the distribution of land and national-language schools and institutions. Indeed, a number of national republics and oblasts awaited census results about nationality in order to settle border disputes with their neighbors.[57] Consequently, representatives from the localities (especially nationally-conscious government administrators and statisticians) approached issues of categorization with interests to defend. Representatives from the Ukrainian and Georgian republics campaigned against proposals to use the term *narodnost'* in the census questionnaire. Georgian representatives from the Transcaucasian government preferred the term *natsional'nost'*, insisting that the Georgians were already a developed nation.[58] Many Georgian government and party elites, who had opposed Georgia's inclusion in the Transcaucasian federated republic (the TSFSR) in 1922, were still bristling about Georgia's diminished status. Ukrainian elites expressed similar concerns, insisting that the Ukrainians were a *natsional'nost'*, and not a *narodnost'*.[59] They undoubtedly remembered the 1897 census in which the "Little Russian" language had been included as a sublanguage of Russian and did not want the Ukrainian *narodnost'* to be categorized as a subgroup of a Russian *natsional'nost'*.

Several statisticians from the Ukrainian branch of the TsSU protested the very inclusion of a direct question about *narodnost'* or *natsional'nost'* in the census. Arguing (as Chernyshev had) that "native language" was the most reliable indicator of nationality, they recommended that census takers inquire about a "respondent's self-consciousness" only in "extreme cases." In order to make their point, the statisticians compared data about self-reported *natsional'nost'* from the 1920 census with data about "native language" from the 1897 census. Noting that the registration of nationality "suffers most" when "political conditions do not favor the census," they asked: Was it really possible that 2 million Ukrainians in the Kuban region alone had "become Russians" between 1897 and 1920? Moscow-based experts, in turn, rejected the Ukrainian statisticians' interpretation of the data from the 1897 census and warned against conflating native language with nationality.[60] The ethnographer Vladimir Bogdanov, a Moscow-based expert who had helped to delimit the borders between the Ukrainian SSR and the Belorussian SSR and the RSFSR in 1919, weighed in on this discussion. According to Bogdanov, the delimitation commission had used "language as the main determinant of *narodnost'*" because ethnographers at that time had considered it to be "one of the most reliable traits of ethnicity." But, he added, ethnographers had not considered language to be an indicator of nationality outside of European Russia.

57. See, for example, RGAE f. 1562, op. 336, d. 53, l. 30; d. 8, ll. 114–15.

58. RGAE f. 1562, op. 336, d. 433, l. 1770b; d. 43, l. 89.

59. Osinskii relates this narrative in his "Printsipy i pratika," 46–47. Osinskii writes that "Ukrainian comrades considered it politically awkward not to note that *narodnost'* in Soviet Russia acquired the position of *natsional'nost'*."

60. RGAE f. 1562, op. 1, d. 433, ll. 79–81.

Moreover, they were no longer certain about its efficacy even in Ukraine, as the Ukrainians were attempting to linguistically and culturally Ukrainize all peoples within their republic's borders.[61]

In response to the Georgian and Ukrainian protests, the TsSU attempted to clarify the goals of the census registration of nationality. Moscow-based statisticians and officials affirmed that the census aimed to gather information about the "ethnographic (ethnic) composition" of the Soviet Union, regardless of national consciousness, and argued that *narodnost'* was preferable to *natsional'nost'* for this reason.[62] Analyzing the relationship between *narodnost'* and *natsional'nost'*, Osinskii described the former as the ethnographic foundation for the "cultural-political superstructure [*nadstroika*] which turns a *narodnost'* into a *natsional'nost'*." Osinskii argued that "not all *narodnosti*" of the Soviet Union "have succeeded in creating this superstructure."[63] For those that had (like the Georgians), he added, *narodnost'* and *natsional'nost'* could be understood as equivalents. Using the rhetoric of state-sponsored evolutionism, Osinskii described the census as a tool for promoting the evolution of the population. He explained that the regime would use the ethnographic knowledge it attained through the census to further the transformation of *narodnosti* into *natsional'nosti*.[64]

The TsSU next grappled with the question of how to ascertain the nationality of people lacking national consciousness. This was the main focus of a September 1926 meeting at its headquarters, at which statisticians from the Commission for the Production of the Census and the Moscow-based ethnographers Bogdanov and Aleksandr Maksimov evaluated materials prepared by the KIPS census subcommission.[65] All agreed that the *narodnost'* of each respondent would be determined through an interview with a census taker. At issue was who would have the last word if the census taker believed that the respondent had answered the question incorrectly: the census taker or the respondent. Bogdanov asserted that the testimonies of respondents were "notoriously unreliable" and it would be better to "take a chance" on the census taker; he recommended that experts train census takers to "decipher what is

61. RGAE f. 1562, op. 336, d. 8, ll. 105–1050b. The Moscow-based ethnographers Vladimir Bogdanov and Aleksandr Maksimov, like the KIPS ethnographers, served as consultants to the Soviet of Nationalities. Bogdanov and Maksimov were affiliated with Moscow State University and the Society of Enthusiasts of Natural Science, Anthropology, and Ethnography.

62. Osinskii, "Printsipy i praktika," 40–41. Also see the stenogram of the TsSU's September 1926 discussion on this topic. RGAE f. 1562, op. 336, d. 8, ll. 105–16.

63. Osinskii, "Printsipy i praktika," 41. Osinskii contended that some *narodnosti*, such as the Jews, due to "objective conditions" such as not having their own "compact territorial unit," could not create their own superstructure in full.

64. Ibid.

65. RGAE f. 1562, op. 336, d. 8, ll. 104–16. The statisticians who participated were Kvitkin, Mikhailovskii, Volkov, Iosif Trakhtenberg, E. V. Pashkovskii, Vasilii Nemchinov, and M. N. Fal'kner-Smit. The ethnographers Bogdanov and Maksimov attended as did a representative from the TsIK Department of Nationalities.

going on" in the regions. Vasilii Mikhailovskii, a Moscow-based statistician from the Commission for the Production of the Census, agreed. He argued that national minorities in particular often "confuse residence in a national republic with *narodnost'* "—and that representatives of the main (titular) nationalities in the republics encourage them to make such mistakes.[66] Mikhailovskii proposed that census takers explain to respondents that *narodnost'* does not have to correspond with residence in a particular national republic or oblast and help respondents give an appropriate answer to the question. Mikhailovskii argued that census takers should intervene even in cases when members of national minorities chose to register themselves as members of titular nationalities. When other statisticians protested that this was a violation of national rights, Mikhailovskii insisted that his aim was to protect, not unmask, respondents. To illustrate his intentions he explained that "giving the census taker the right to intervene" does not give him the right to try to "certify by physiognomy" that a respondent is "a Jew, Latvian, or German."[67]

Other experts were wary about giving census takers too much power, cautioning that it would "create great confusion" if census takers changed respondents' answers. "One census taker will see one *narodnost'* where another registrar sees an altogether different *narodnost'*," contended Maksimov.[68] The head of the Commission for the Production of the Census, Olimpii Kvitkin, agreed, arguing that *narodnost'* was a subjective category and therefore *had* to be based on the respondent's self-definition. "What should the census taker do if a respondent answers that he is a Muslim?" one of Kvitkin's colleagues challenged. Kvitkin responded that in such a case the census taker should "explain that Muslim 'is a confessional group' and the question asks for 'your *narodnost'*.' " If, however, the respondent answered that he belonged to an actual *narodnost'*, "the census taker does not have the right to insist 'that you do not belong to this *narodnost'* but to another.' "[69] Kvitkin and Maksimov advocated rephrasing the census question to ask "to which *narodnost'* do you count yourself (*prichisliat'*)?" instead of "to which *narodnost'* do you belong (*prinadlezhat'*)?" This would compel census takers to rely on the subjective testimony of each respondent. They argued that census takers should write down respondents' answers "exactly and clearly," but that after the census was completed, ethnographers might review the data and "make corrections."[70]

Some of the statisticians argued that the principle of national self-definition should be understood as an extension of the principle of national self-

66. RGAE f. 1562, op. 336, d. 8, ll. 108–1090b.

67. Ibid., l. 108.

68. Ibid., ll. 1070b–108. Maksimov argued that census takers should record the respondents' exact answers, but in "extreme cases" (if it was completely obvious that a response was inaccurate) might also note their doubts on the census form.

69. Ibid., ll. 1060b–107.

70. Ibid., ll. 1060b–108.

determination. It might be possible to differentiate among nationalities ("the Turkmen," "the Ukrainians") on the basis of "objective traits" such as physical type, language, and *byt,* they argued. But the nationality of an individual should at least to some degree take into account his or her consciousness. The TsSU statistician Aleksandr Volkov presented the most eloquent exposition of this argument, explaining that national self-determination had been a political ideal "from the beginning of the revolution" and should translate on an individual level into self-reporting in the census. While arguing for "subjective testimony," Volkov also acknowledged the hazards of such an approach. He warned of "different dangers in different territories," including "very strong, divergent . . . political and economic interests." He elaborated on political tensions in Ukraine, noting that minorities such as the Bulgarians, Poles, Romanians, and Jews "each have their own special concerns," such as whether they would get their own national territories or be included in Ukrainian regions. Acknowledging that the dominant nationalities often pursued a nationalist agenda through the census, Volkov recommended that the regime take measures to protect the national minorities in the registration process.[71]

While some experts were sympathetic to Volkov's argument, others pointed out that there were cases in which national self-determination and national self-definition did not necessarily coincide. An official representative of the national minorities argued that only the registration of "*narodnost'* by origins (*proiskhozhdenie*)," and not by self-definition, could counteract the "legacy of Russification" and the ongoing attempts of other dominant nationalities (such as the Ukrainians) to forcibly assimilate neighboring peoples.[72] But the idea of a question about "national origins"—which presumed "the hardening of national barriers forever"—also made most of the experts uncomfortable. The ethnographer Maksimov argued that such an approach would lead to an archaic "picture of that which had existed thousands of years ago." He explained, for example, that the inhabitants of Smolensk province "had been Ukrainians in the seventeenth century" but since then had become Russians. He argued that it would be wrong to register them as Ukrainians "on the basis of historical memory." Emphasizing the "dynamic" nature of nationality, Maksimov suggested that national identity could and would change as a result of cultural contact.[73] (KIPS ethnographers, such as Lev Berg, had reached a similar conclusion. Berg had studied a group of "Little Russians" who became "Romanized" after living among Moldavians; the people he interviewed insisted that they were Moldavian, even if their parents and grandparents were Little Russian.)[74]

71. Ibid., ll. 110–11.
72. Ibid., ll. 112, 114.
73. Ibid., l. 1140b.
74. L. S. Berg, *Naselenie Bessarabii: Etnograficheskii sostav i chislennost', Trudy Komissii po izucheniiu plemennogo sostava naseleniia Rossii,* vol. 6 (Petrograd, 1923).

The issue of Russification was highly politicized for a regime with an expressed commitment to an "emancipatory nationality policy." While many officials and experts who participated in census deliberations shared Maksimov's reluctance to rely on "national origins," they also dismissed the assumption that all forms of assimilation were alike. In particular, they suggested that the (presumably forced) Russification or Ukrainization of an undeveloped nationality was qualitatively different from the (presumably natural) assimilation of a dominant nationality such as the Ukrainians. The KIPS ethnographers were facing the issue of Russification head on in their attempt to sort out the "Meshcheriak and Misher question." The Meshcheriaks and Mishers of Bashkiria both derived from the "Meshars," which were a Mordva subgroup subject to Volga Tatar influence. The Meshcheriaks of Bashkiria had been linguistically and culturally Russified under the imperial regime; they had adopted the Russian language and Orthodox religion, and referred to themselves as "Russians."[75] By contrast, the Mishers of the region spoke the Tatar language and practiced the Sunni Muslim religion. The question was as follows: Should the two groups be unified, so that the Meshcheriaks could "reclaim" their lost identity? Or were the Russian-speaking Meshcheriaks a separate *narodnost'*?[76] After much debate, the ethnographers concluded that the Meshcheriaks were a subgroup of the Misher *narodnost'*—and had been deprived of their true identities through Russification. Individuals would have the right to register themselves as Meshcheriaks in the census; but when the data were tabulated, Meshcheriaks would be counted as Mishers.[77]

At the close of the September 1926 meeting, the Commission for the Production of the Census was still debating the finer points of the census question about nationality. It did, however, resolve to edit the KIPS-recommended question and instructions, suggesting three major changes. First, making the case for the subjective self-reporting of nationality, the experts argued that the census question should ask: "To which *narodnost'* do you count yourself?" Second, in order to ensure that the question elicit "the type of information we envisioned," the experts recommended that the instructions explain that a respondent's *narodnost'* did not "have to correspond" with his or her native language, *grazhdanstvo* (roughly translated as "citizenship"), or residence in a particular national republic or oblast, and that *narodnost'* was not the same as religion. Finally, the experts maintained that if a respondent had "difficulty" answering a direct question about his or her *narodnost'* (by ascribing himself or herself to a group that did not appear on the "List of the Nationalities of

75. See James Stuart Olson, ed., *An Ethnohistorical Dictionary of the Russian and Soviet Empires* (Westport, 1994), 554.

76. PFA RAN f. 135, op. 1, d. 21, l. 107.

77. Tsentral'noe statisticheskoe upravlenie SSSR, *Vsesoiuznaia perepis' naseleniia 1926 goda*, vol. 4, *Narodnost' i rodnoi iazyk naseleniia SSSR* (Moscow, 1928), and Tsentral'noe statisticheskoe upravlenie SSSR, *Programmy i posobiia k razrabotke Vsesoiuznoi perepisi naseleniia 1926 goda*, vol. 7, *Perechen' i slovar' narodnostei* (Moscow, 1927).

the USSR"), census takers should ask additional questions about his or her national (or clan or tribal) origins.[78] The KIPS ethnographers were already preparing supplemental questions for different regions.

The "List of the Nationalities of the USSR," like the census question itself, was subject to intense debate. In August 1926, KIPS had sent a draft list to the TsSU, which forwarded it to Bogdanov and Maksimov as well as to local experts for review.[79] The list, which KIPS had whittled down to some two hundred entries (from an initial draft of more than six hundred names), had real implications for the population. Only groups included on the list would be recognized as official nationalities and entitled to national rights. Those that were omitted would be amalgamated into other nationalities—and not just on paper. Drafts circulated to local experts and administrators around the Soviet Union and were returned to KIPS covered with comments and question marks. KIPS made revisions and sent the list back to the TsSU; in November, Timofei Semenov from the Commission for the Production of the Census went to Leningrad in order to work with KIPS on a final version.[80]

The notes from the Leningrad meeting suggest a close collaboration between the TsSU and KIPS.[81] Semenov and the KIPS ethnographers worked together on a (nearly) final version of the "List of the Nationalities of the USSR" as well as on a "Dictionary of Nationalities" with the synonyms and local names of all *narodnosti*.[82] Semenov also asked KIPS to prepare a list of foreign nationalities represented in the population of the Soviet Union; data about foreigners would not be worked out according to *narodnost'*, but data about subjects of the Soviet Union of foreign descent would be. For his part, Semenov shared with KIPS drafts of the statistical forms that would be used to tabulate census data about *narodnost'*, native language, and literacy.[83] He also informed KIPS of the TsSU's decision to include an additional "household form"

---

78. RGAE f. 1562, op. 336, d. 8, ll. 115–16; op. 1, d. 433, l. 155. In the Central Asian republics and parts of Siberia, the census included an additional form with questions about tribal and clan ties.

79. RGAE f. 1562, op. 336, d. 8, ll. 22–230b. PFA RAN f. 2, op. 1–1926, d. 33, l. 10. For a copy of the list, comments from Bogdanov and Maksimov, and KIPS's response see PFA RAN f. 135, op. 1, d. 23, ll. 92–1220b, 227–29.

80. On Semenov's trip see PFA RAN f. 135, op. 1, d. 23, ll. 25–27, 29. KIPS also forwarded instructions and lists to republic-level and provincial-level statistical bureaus for comment.

81. PFA RAN f. 135, op. 1, d. 23, ll. 25–27; d. 18, ll. 40–41. The KIPS ethnographers Rudenko, Samoilovich, Shvetsov, Zolotarev, Aron Akuliants, Zarubin, Anna Troitskaia, and Semenov-Tian-Shanskii attended the meeting.

82. Ibid., ll. 26–27, 61–630b, 233–34. Semenov presented KIPS with a list of all of the *narodnosti* found in the TsSU's materials and correspondence. He asked the ethnographers to review it and note mistakes.

83. Ibid., ll. 26–27. The statisticians would tabulate data on *narodnost'* (*poddanstvo* for foreigners); *narodnost'* and native language; native language; and *narodnost'* and literacy. They would use additional forms to tabulate data for the Soviet Union's "major nationalities" (*glavnye narodnosti*). Semenov noted that the TsSU might seek the ethnographers' assistance in tabulating the data on *narodnost'* for regions with a "complicated ethnographic composition."

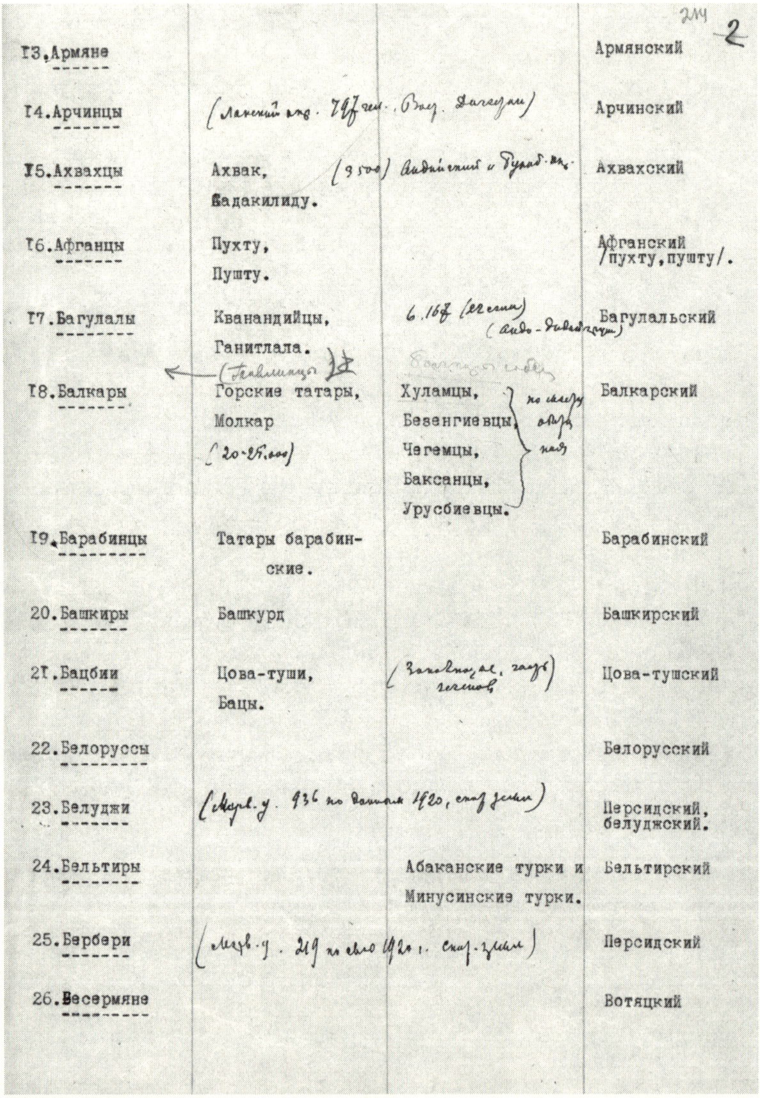

I3. Армяне			Армянский
I4. Арчинцы	*(Лакский окр. 74 чел. Вост. Дагестан)*		Арчинский
I5. Ахвахцы	Ахвак, Бадакилиду.	*(3500) Андийский и Дурад. окр.*	Ахвахский
I6. Афганцы	Пухту, Пушту.		Афганский /пухту, пушту/.
I7. Багулалы	Кванандийцы, Ганитлала.	*6.167 (человек) (Анд.-Дагестан)*	Багулальский
I8. Балкары	← *(Балкары)* Горские татары, Молкар *(20-25.000)*	*Барлакская окр.* Хуламцы, Безенгиевцы, Чегемцы, Баксанцы, Урусбиевцы. } *по смыслу один народ*	Балкарский
I9. Барабинцы	Татары барабин- ские.		Барабинский
20. Башкиры	Башкурд		Башкирский
2I. Бацбии	Цова-туши, Бацы.	*(Закатальск. газ. чечен.)*	Цова-тушский
22. Белоруссы			Белорусский
23. Белуджи	*(Мерв. у. 936 по данным 1920, стар. земли)*		Персидский, белуджский.
24. Бельтиры		Абаканские турки и Минусинские турки.	Бельтирский
25. Бербери	*(Мерв. у. 219 по спис. 1920 г. стар. земли)*		Персидский
26. Весермяне			Вотяцкий

Figure 3.2 Page from a draft of the "List of the *Narodnosti* of the USSR" that KIPS prepared for the 1926 All-Union Census. The four columns are for name of *narodnost'*, synonyms, names of subgroups or geographical designations, and native language. (Archive of the Russian Academy of Sciences, St. Petersburg Branch f. 135, op. 1, d. 23, l. 214)

with the census in nonurban regions to record (along with other information) the *narodnost'* of the head of each household; he promised KIPS copies of the completed forms for its work on ethnographic maps.[84]

As the census date approached, deliberations continued about the list of nationalities. Semenov and his colleagues at the TsSU, responding to complaints about the list from statisticians and government officials in the national republics, asked KIPS to clarify the relationships among a number of peoples. For example, addressing Georgian grievances about the inclusion of the Mingrelians and the Svans on the list of nationalities, they asked the ethnographers whether "Mingrelian" and "Svan" were "synonyms for Georgian" (as the Georgians claimed) or separate nationalities.[85] Some local government and statistical organs turned directly to KIPS with questions about the list. In one case, administrators from the Bashkir branch of the TsSU challenged KIPS's decision to omit the Teptiars.[86] In another instance, officials from the North Caucasus insisted that "the Cossacks" should be counted as a *narodnost'* in the census.[87] As the census began, the fates of a number of groups—including the Mingrelians, Svans, Cossacks, and Teptiars—remained in question.

Classification in Practice

The staging of the First All-Union Census was an extraordinary feat, mobilizing experts, government and party personnel, and census takers (teachers, students, unemployed workers, and others) throughout the Soviet Union.[88] The civil war had officially ended some five years earlier and the Soviet regime was now engaged in the work of state-building and economic restructuring. But, in fact, there was still significant fighting in Central Asia and the Caucasus, and economic and social turmoil persisted in Russia and all of the national republics. In the wake of World War I, two revolutions, and a civil war, the Bolsheviks now faced the challenge of establishing order and building socialism.

84. The ethnographers had proposed the inclusion of a household form in their early discussions with the statisticians. RGAE f. 1562, op. 336, d. 10, l. 18.

85. The ethnographers argued that the Mingrelians and the Svans were related to the Georgians but were "pronounced ethnic units" with national consciousness and should therefore be listed as separate *narodnosti*. PFA RAN f. 135, op. 1, d. 23, l. 64.

86. PFA RAN f. 135, op. 1, d. 21, l. 158; d. 19, l. 24. KIPS put together a subcommission (which included Samoilovich and Mashtakov) to do fieldwork on the Teptiars in response to these inquiries (PFA RAN f. 135, op. 1, d. 21, l. 107). The KIPS ethnographers suggested that respondents who stated that their *narodnost'* was Teptiar should be asked if they also considered themselves a member of another *narodnost'*, such as Bashkir, Tatar, or Chuvash (PFA RAN f. 135, op. 1, d. 23, ll. 21–22).

87. GARF f. 1235, op. 71, d. 384, l. 29. The KIPS ethnographers disagreed.

88. The census cost more than 14 million rubles. *Zasedanie TsIK*, 196, and Osinskii, "Printsipy i praktika," 36. The census was carried out by republic-level, provincial-level, and oblast-level statistical bureaus.

The same tumultuous conditions which made census-taking difficult also made the compilation of accurate data about the population extremely pressing.

The census aimed to take a "momentary photograph" of the population on one "critical day," December 17, 1926.[89] Officials and experts alike acknowledged, however, that the actual registration of the population would take several months. The Commission for the Production of the Census planned for census takers to spend one week in each urban region, two weeks in each agricultural region, and up to two months in regions with nomadic populations. This is just one example of the ways in which the general census plan was in tension with the chosen method of registration. It was impossible for census-takers—who showed up a week or two after December 17—to conduct one-on-one interviews with all household members who had been present on the "critical day." [90]

On the eve of the December 17 kickoff, the Soviet press heralded participation in the census as every citizen's revolutionary duty. Eye-catching posters and radio announcements in dozens of languages broadcast the census as a test of the population's consciousness and level of cultural development (*kul'-turnost'*).[91] Party pronouncements and articles in local newspapers informed the population that the census taker was an official representative of the Soviet regime who should be received in every home "as a welcome guest." They explained that the census taker would ask each household member a set of questions specifically designed to help the Soviet state "build bread factories and schools." Such articles assured the population that the formal registration of nationality would guarantee the right of "each people [*narod*]" to "establish its life in its own way [*ustraivat' svoiu zhizn' po svoemu.*]"[92] Moscow-based officials recognized that people throughout the Soviet Union were apprehensive about the census. In an attempt to appease people's concerns about the registration of nationality, the TsSU issued special bulletins, reassuring the population that the census would "bring no harm."[93]

89. Statisticians explained that the census was not an inventory of the population in its place of "constant residence." Osinskii, "Printsipy i praktika," 36, 38–39. In polar regions and several mountainous regions, census registration took longer and was on a different timetable. See, for example, RGAE f. 1562, op. 1, d. 433, ll. 177, 218ob.

90. Census takers depended on family members for information in such cases. Osinskii, "Printsipy i praktika," 40.

91. See the accounts of preparations for the census in Belorussia and Tatarstan. RGAE f. 1562, op. 336, d. 46, ll. 13–14, 86ob–87.

92. These quotes are from a December 24, 1926 article in *The Peasant's Path* (*Krest'ianskii Put'*). RGAE f. 1562, op. 336, d. 47, l. 64.

93. RGAE f. 1562, op. 336, d. 48, l. 106. Meetings at the statistical administration were devoted to the question of "winning the trust of the masses." See PFA RAN f. 135, op. 1, d. 23, ll. 5–6ob. The party sent political workers to conduct agitation in national republics and oblasts to prepare the population for the census. It published pamphlets in local languages on themes such as "Why is the census taken?" See RGAE f. 1562, op. 336, d. 46, l. 23.

The Soviet government and party had approved the census questions and instructions in early December, accepting the case for the subjective self-definition of nationality. In most regions, the census taker was to ask each household member in the appropriate language: "In which *narodnost'* do you count yourself?" and record the answer as given.[94] In some regions, in response to protests, the statistical administration approved a slightly different version of the census question. In Transcaucasia, census takers would ask respondents "In which *narodnost'*—that is *plemia* [tribe], *narodnost'*, *natsional'nost'*—do you count yourself?"[95] In Ukraine, census takers would ask respondents "In which "*natsional'nost' (narodnost')* do you count yourself?"[96] In both cases, responses would be recorded in the standard form under the heading *narodnost'*.

Participants in the KIPS census subcommission had noted in their deliberations that the "ideal" answer to the census question was a "completely heartfelt one" in which the respondent answers "without any sort of difficulty and doubt."[97] But the Commission for the Production of the Census and KIPS had prepared for all sorts of contingencies. If the respondent clearly "did not understand what was expected," the census taker was to intervene. For example, he or she was to prevent people from answering the question about *narodnost'* with testimony about their native language, religion, place of residence, or *grazhdanstvo*.[98] In some regions, the instructions admonished census takers under "no circumstances to write Muslim, Christian, Bekhaist, or Orthodox," in the census form, "since these are not *narodnosti* but religions."[99] Instructions for most regions suggested that respondents (especially children) with parents of different nationalities who were unsure how to answer the question take their mother's *narodnost'*.[100]

After ascertaining a respondent's *narodnost'*, the census taker was to move on to the next question: "What is your native language [*rodnoi iazyk*]?" The directives defined "native language" as the language that the respondent by his

94. *Zasedanie TsIK*, 98, 99. The TsSU subsequently adopted the same formula for the registration of nationality in birth, death, marriage, divorce, adoption, and other official documents. The census instructions and forms were printed in the "major languages" of each population point. See, for example, RGAE f. 1562, op. 20, d. 5, ll. 31–33. For examples of the forms see Tsentral'noe statisticheskoe upravlenie SSSR, *Vsesoiuznaia perepis' naseleniia 1926 goda*, vol. 12, *Ukrainskaia SSR* (Moscow, 1928).

95. RGAE f. 1562, op. 336, d. 44, l. 1100b; *Vsesoiuznaia perepis' naseleniia 1926 goda*, vol. 14, *Zakavkazskaia SSR* (Moscow, 1929), iii; and Osinskii, "Printsipy i praktika," 46.

96. *Vsesoiuznaia perepis' naseleniia 1926 goda*, vol. 12, *Ukrainskaia SSR* (Moscow, 1929), 468, and Osinskii, "Printsipy i praktika," 46.

97. PFA RAN f. 135, op. 1, d. 11, l. 117.

98. *Vsesoiuznaia perepis' naseleniia 1926 goda*, vol. 17, *SSSR* (Moscow, 1929), 98.

99. RGAE f. 1562, op. 336, d. 26, l. 157.

100. *Vsesoiuznaia perepis' naseleniia 1926 goda*, vol. 17, *SSSR*, 98. This recommendation reflected the belief that women, who did most of the child-raising in traditional households, passed on language and *byt* to the next generation.

or her "subjective determination" speaks best and uses most frequently, and noted that *narodnost'* and native language need not correspond.[101] Together, the census questions about nationality and native language were supposed to shed light on the Union's "ethnographic dynamic" and on the current distribution of language. A combination of both data sets would reveal which peoples had been victims of linguistic Russification.[102]

As an acknowledgment of regional particularities, the TsSU approved supplementary census materials for certain localities. These materials included detailed directives excerpted from ethnographers' instructions and research notes and were designed to help census takers navigate through potential pitfalls. Instructions for Kirgizia, for example, noted that the "Uigurs" would not be recognized as a separate nationality, taking into account the ethnographers' pronouncement that the Uigurs were a "mixed group" made up of several "tribal peoples." Individuals stating "Uigur" as their *narodnost'* were to be asked "if they were in fact Kashgars, Dungans, Kalmyks, or Taranchi."[103] Instructions for Turkmenistan and Uzbekistan adopted many of Zarubin's recommendations for former Turkestan. As control data, census takers in Turkmenistan were to record each respondent's tribe (*plemia*), clan (*rod*), and subclan (*koleno*).[104] This reflected ethnographers' assertions that clan and tribal affiliations remained most meaningful in Central Asia.[105]

While some directives circumscribed self-definition, others reaffirmed it. Supplemental instructions for the Central Asian republics and Dagestan—regions with large Muslim populations—reminded census takers that in mixed-marriage households, husbands and wives were to register their own *narodnost'*. Supplemental instructions for the Caucasus and a number of other regions stipulated that if parents and a son identified as members of different *narodnosti*, "the son should be registered as a member of that *narodnost'* to which he counts himself."[106] Central government and party organs, which had hoped for a standardized census questionnaire, accepted these supplementary materials with some misgivings.[107]

---

101. Ibid., 98, 102. Some of the statisticians characterized native language in this context as the language of "later cultural deposits." RGAE f. 1562, op. 336, d. 8, l. 106.

102. RGAE f. 1562, op. 1, d. 433, l. 178, and *Vsesoiuznaia perepis' naseleniia 1926 goda*, vol. 17, *SSSR*, 101.

103. RGAE f. 1562, op. 336, d. 47, ll. 49–51. The directives also emphasized the importance of differentiating among Kirgiz, Kazakhs, and Kara-Kirgiz.

104. RGAE f. 1562, op. 336, d. 11, ll. 87–87ob; d. 26, l. 157; d. 8, ll. 121–22; and *Vsesoiuznaia perepis' naseleniia 1926 goda*, vol. 17, *SSSR*, 101. KIPS prepared genealogical tables for this purpose.

105. Such supplemental information would prove useful several years later, when the regime established clan-based collective farms in the Central Asian republics.

106. RGAE f. 1562, op. 336, d. 26, l. 151ob. Instructions for other regions had a similar clause.

107. Osinskii, "Printsipy i praktika," 45–47.

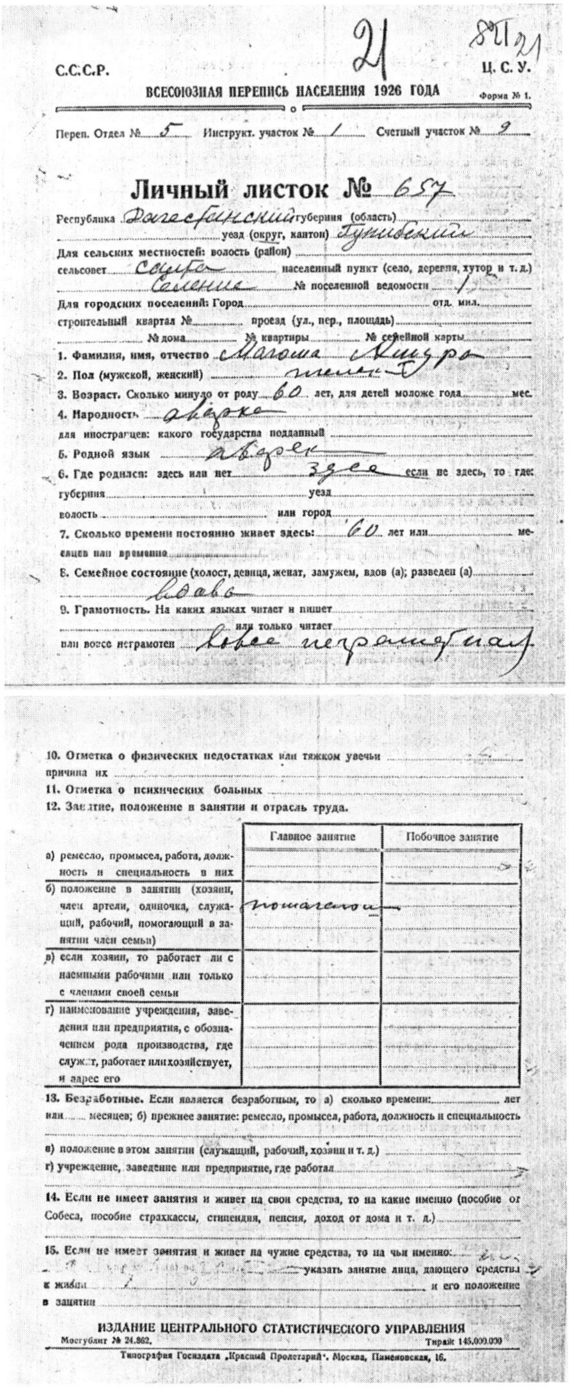

21 8/II 21

С.С.С.Р. Ц. С. У.

ВСЕСОЮЗНАЯ ПЕРЕПИСЬ НАСЕЛЕНИЯ 1926 ГОДА

Форма № 1.

Переп. Отдел № 5 Инструкт. участок № 1 Счетный участок № 9

Личный листок № 657

Республика Дагестанский губерния (область)
уезд (округ, кантон) Гунибский
Для сельских местностей: волость (район)
сельсовет Согра населенный пункт (село, деревня, хутор и т. д.)
Селение № поселенной ведомости 1
Для городских поселений: Город отд. мил.
строительный квартал № проезд (ул., пер., площадь)
№ дома № квартиры № семейной карты
1. Фамилия, имя, отчество Магома Ашура
2. Пол (мужской, женский) женск.
3. Возраст. Сколько минуло от роду 60 лет, для детей моложе года мес.
4. Народность аварка
для иностранцев: какого государства подданный
5. Родной язык аварек
6. Где родился: здесь или нет здесь если не здесь, то где:
губерния уезд
волость или город
7. Сколько времени постоянно живет здесь: 60 лет или месяцев или временно
8. Семейное состояние (холост, девица, женат, замужем, вдов (а); разведен (а)
вдова
9. Грамотность. На каких языках читает и пишет
или только читает
или вовсе неграмотен вовсе неграмотная

10. Отметка о физических недостатках или тяжком увечьи
причина их
11. Отметка о психических больных
12. Занятие, положение в занятии и отрасль труда.

	Главное занятие	Побочное занятие
а) ремесло, промысел, работа, должность и специальность в них		
б) положение в занятии (хозяин, член артели, одиночка, служащий, рабочий, помогающий в занятии член семьи)	помогающ.	
в) если хозяин, то работает ли с наемными рабочими или только с членами своей семьи		
г) наименование учреждения, заведения или предприятия, с обозначением рода производства, где служит, работает или хозяйствует, и адрес его		

13. Безработные. Если является безработным, то а) сколько времени: лет или месяцев; б) прежнее занятие: ремесло, промысел, работа, должность и специальность
в) положение в этом занятии (служащий, рабочий, хозяин и т. д.)
г) учреждение, заведение или предприятие, где работал
14. Если не имеет занятия и живет на свои средства, то на какие именно (пособие от Собеса, пособие страхкассы, стипендия, пенсия, доход от дома и т. д.)
15. Если не имеет занятия и живет на чужие средства, то на чьи именно:
указать занятие лица, дающего средства к жизни и его положение в занятии

ИЗДАНИЕ ЦЕНТРАЛЬНОГО СТАТИСТИЧЕСКОГО УПРАВЛЕНИЯ

Мосгублит № 24.862. Тираж 145.000.000

Типография Госиздата „Красный Пролетарий", Москва, Пименовская, 16.

Figure 3.3 "Individual form" from the 1926 All-Union Census. Point four asks for *narodnost'* and point five asks for native language. This particular form was filled out in Dagestan. (Russian State Archive of the Economy f. 1562, op. 336, d. 47, ll. 21–21ob.)

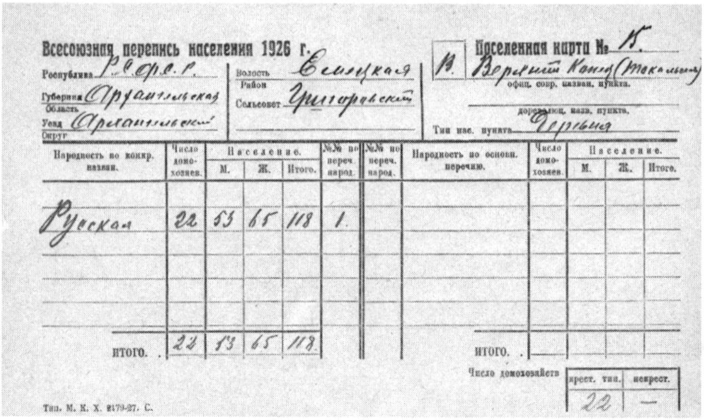

Всесоюзная перепись населения 1926 г.

Поселенная карта № 15.

Республика Р.С.Ф.С.Р.

Губерния Архангельская

Область

Уезд Архангельский

Округ

Волость Емецкая

Район

Сельсовет Григорьевский

офиц. сокр. назван. пункта.

дореволюц. назв. пункта.

Тип нас. пункта Деревня

Народность по конкр. назван.	Число домохозяев.	Население. М.	Ж.	Итого.	№№ по переч. народ.	№№ по переч. народ.	Народность по основн. перечню.	Число домохозяев.	Население. М.	Ж.	Итого.
Русская	22	53	65	118	1.						
Итого.	22	53	65	118			Итого.				

Число домохозяйств: крест. тип. 22; некрест. —

Тип. М. К. Х. 2179-27. С.

Figure 3.4 Form used during the 1926 All-Union Census to tabulate the number of adult members of each *narodnost'* residing at a particular population point (village, agricultural soviet, and so on). Only Russians were living in this village in Arkhangelsk *guberniia* of the RSFSR. (Archive of the Russian Academy of Sciences, St. Petersburg Branch f. 135, op. 3, d. 2, l. 15)

In practice, detailed directives often did little to help census takers circumvent problems or address local specificities. This became apparent as the census takers, a veritable army of nearly 200,000 people, began their work. The census takers were for the most part teachers and students from Moscow and other cities; many were self-defined Russians with a halting command of local languages.[108] The TsSU had organized seminars to train census takers, but these had been poorly attended.[109] This lack of training, along with time constraints (each census taker was expected to conduct one hundred interviews a day in the countryside or seventy-five a day in cities), complicated the registration process.[110] Administrators reported that census takers often rushed through interviews, in many cases neglecting altogether to ask respondents to state their nationality. In one region of Siberia, census takers routinely wrote "*inorodets*" (alien) in the space for *narodnost'*.[111] In other regions, census takers simply asked "the respondent's last name, and if the last name seem[ed] Russian [wrote] Russian" in the space for *narodnost'*.[112] In non-Russian regions throughout the Soviet Union, in the absence of translators, embarrassing "blunders" were made. Confounded by the communication barrier, census

108. Ibid., 36. The statistical administration made numerous attempts to recruit students, teachers, and other educated (or literate) individuals from the localities. See RGAE f. 1562, op. 1, d. 408a, l. 45ob. On the use of the unemployed as census takers see RGAE 1562, op. 336, d. 9, l. 19.

109. RGAE f. 1562, op. 336, d. 4, l. 92.

110. RGAE f. 1562, op. 1, d. 433, l. 3.

111. RGAE f. 1562, op. 336, d. 10, l. 45.

112. Reported by a Chuvash representative from the Soviet of Nationalities. *Zasedanie TsIK*, 227.

takers unwittingly recorded as nationalities the local language equivalents for "from here" and "from there."[113]

Most egregious, however, were active campaigns for assimilation that the main (titular) nationalities of the national republics and oblasts launched by means of the census.[114] A number of regions awaited census results in order to continue with the work of regionalization or settle border disputes—and census takers sometimes used the enumerative process to advance local ("nationalist") agendas. In regions where members of the titular nationalities served as census takers, a disproportionately small number of people were registered as members of minority nationalities. For example, in one region of the Bashkir ASSR, census takers registered everyone "as Bashkir" without asking respondents to state their nationality.[115] The TsSU reprimanded those responsible for the "premeditated falsification of census data" and directed census takers to redo the census in affected regions.[116]

In many cases, local conditions and particularistic understandings of nationality, and of identity in general, complicated the registration process. Census takers in Dagestan wrote that in mixed-marriage households, the men, "who typically give the information . . . do not allow the child to take the *natsional'nost'* of the mother."[117] (Representatives of the national minorities had cautioned that in many regions *narodnost'* was patrilineal.[118] The TsSU had ignored their advice.) Census takers in and around Tashkent noted the tendency of Kurama, Tajiks, and Kazakhs to identify themselves as Kurama-Uzbek, Tajik-Uzbek, and Kazakh-Uzbek. According to the census takers, if they registered someone as "Kurama" without adding that he or she was also "Uzbek," they risked "insulting not just the head of the household but all of his relatives."[119] Census takers in the Far East reported that in one region the majority of the population identified themselves as "Sibiriak"—even though ethnographers did not recognize the existence of a "Sibiriak" *narodnost'*. The census takers noted: "In our hearts we fully agree with them, because we think there is such a northern *narodnost'*. But we had to redo the census in the region."[120]

113. Ethnographers reported similar problems in their work on maps in 1927. PFA RAN f. 135, op. 1, d. 38, ll. 5–50b.

114. Osinskii noted numerous instances in which census takers had disregarded instructions for the registration of *narodnost'* and had thereby "deviated from the general principle of national self-determination" and "from the spirit of Soviet policy in general and nationality policy in particular." GARF f. 3316, op. 20, d. 148, l. 4.

115. On border disputes in general see RGAE f. 1562, op. 336, d. 53, l. 30. On the Bashkir example see GARF f. 3316, op. 20, d. 148, ll. 1, 4. In another region of the Bashkir ASSR, Bashkir-identified instructors from the local statistical administration told census takers to register all people calling themselves "Teptiars" as "Bashkirs."

116. RGAE f. 1562, op. 336, d. 4, l. 123; d. 10, l. 2.

117. RGAE f. 1562, op. 336, d. 52, ll. 68–680b.

118. RGAE f. 1562, op. 336, d. 8, l. 113.

119. RGAE f. 1562, op. 336, d. 47, l. 77.

120. RGAE f. 1562, op. 336, d. 4, l. 112. The journalist Maurice Hindus, who traveled through the Soviet Union in the 1920s and 1930s, reported that "the Siberian . . . considers him-

In some instances, rifts between official and local identity categories were settled by compromise: In Kirgizia, so many people had asked to be registered as Uigurs that the TsSU eventually added the category to a special list of "questionable" (later "provisional") nationalities.[121]

It was not just in response to the question about "nationality" that respondents gave undesired or unexpected answers. Census takers in Ukraine explained that data about "literacy" were inaccurate since Ukrainians who attended Russian schools "understand literacy as literacy in Russian" (and "do not answer that they are literate in Ukrainian").[122] The question about "occupation" also was cause for concern. Census takers from one region noted that they were unsure what to do when a group of women gave the answer "prostitute."[123]

In some regions it proved impossible to secure an accurate population count at all. In Ufa, Bashkirs and Teptiars refused to answer questions if census takers were not accompanied by local leaders.[124] Census takers in contested border regions reported similar difficulties. Kazakh-identified census takers in the Uzbek SSR and Uzbek-identified census takers in Karakalpakia noted that local populations, regarding them as outsiders, refused to speak with them.[125] In some parts of Central Asia, where civil war was still raging, census takers reported that the presence of the Basmachi, anti-Soviet resistance fighters, impeded census-taking altogether. In one instance, they noted, the local population is "so terrorized by the Basmachi" that "one part lies in hiding" and another part had migrated to different regions.[126] Even in relatively peaceful regions, census takers reported obstacles to counting. They complained, for example, that men hid wives and children in villages where polygamy was common.[127]

Of course, it is difficult to know how much these accounts reflected or misrepresented local life. They do, however, give a sense of the frustration and mistrust, on the part of census takers and respondents, that accompanied the registration process. To say the least, census takers from the outside were sel-

---

self as of a group, if not a race, all his own . . . He is a Siberiak [sic]—a Siberian—and, even when also a Bolshevik and not supposed to cherish special local loyalties, he glories in the word." Maurice Hindus, *The Great Offensive* (New York, 1933), 339.

121. *Vsesoiuznaia perepis' naseleniia 1926 goda*, vol. 17, *SSSR*, 101, 107.

122. RGAE f. 1562, op. 336, d. 4, ll. 97–98.

123. RGAE f. 1562, op. 336, d. 47, l. 61.

124. RGAE f. 1562, op. 336, d. 4, l. 123. Complaints of this sort were lodged all over the Soviet Union. Even if census takers spoke the native language of respondents, they were shunned. RGAE f. 1562, op. 336, d. 4, l. 102.

125. See, for example, RGAE f. 1562, op. 336, d. 48, ll. 1–8. Also see chapter 4.

126. RGAE f. 1562, op. 336, d. 48, ll. 10b, 30b.

127. In deliberations about the census questionnaire, some Moscow-based statisticians had proposed that census takers ask the heads of households in certain regions how many wives they had. The TsSU ruled against this, fearing that such an "offensive question" would deter people from participating in the census. RGAE f. 1562, op. 336, d. 9, l. 190b.

dom received as "welcome guests." Concerns about the "nationality question" and about the collection of information that would be used for administrative purposes complicated census-taking in general and exacerbated local tensions.

The List of Nationalities Revisited

In late January 1927, as census takers finished collecting data in most regions and as the TsSU prepared to convert the millions of completed questionnaires into information for the regime, statisticians, ethnographers, and government officials gathered at an all-union statistical meeting in Moscow to discuss the census and the official list of nationalities.[128] Rudenko and Semenov-Tian-Shanskii represented KIPS; Semenov, from the Commission for the Production of the Census, led the session.[129] In 1926, the TsSU had distributed regional versions of the list to local statistical administrations. In practice, as is clear from the example of the "Siberiaks," census takers often ignored the list or did not receive copies of it and recorded responses as given. In such cases, upon tabulating census data, statisticians and statistical workers in Moscow and the regions used the "Dictionary of Nationalities" to determine the "concrete names of *narodnosti*" and recategorize respondents into official nationality categories.[130] (It was at this stage in the process, for example, that self-described Meshcheriaks were recategorized as Mishers.)

Much of the meeting was devoted to deliberations about a special sublist of "questionable" nationalities. This list included groups such as the Khakass, Uigurs, Teptiars, Chala-Kazakhs, Oirots, and Sarts, whose places on the list of nationalities were still being debated. Some, such as the Khakass, the ethnographers argued, were geographical groups made up of several "constituent peoples." According to the experts, the term *Khakass* referred to a group of western Siberian clans and tribes that lived in the Khakass *okrug*. (The experts maintained that when the government created the *okrug* in 1923 these tribes and clans did not define themselves as part of one distinct group, but that at the time of the census local leaders began to mobilize them around the idea of a Khakass *narodnost'*.)[131] Others, such as the Uigurs, Teptiars, Chala-Kazaks, and Sarts, the ethnographers characterized as "mixed peoples" without clearly identifiable national or tribal origins.[132] The Chala-Kazakhs were in their estimation "a mix of Kazakhs with Russians or with Tatars." While some experts and administrators argued that "mixed peoples" should be omitted from the

---

128. The meeting was held from January 28 through 31, 1927. Preliminary totals for most of European Russia were complete, with the exception of a few regions including Karelia, Komi oblast, and Iakutiia. The census in Central Asia would not be completed until mid-March. RGAE f. 1562, op. 336, d. 10, l. 9.

129. PFA RAN f. 135, op. 1, d. 23, l. 231.

130. RGAE f. 1562, op. 336, d. 16, ll. 150b–16.

131. GARF f. 3316, op. 23, d. 1296, l. 5.

132. RGAE f. 1562, op. 336, d. 4, ll. 4–6.

final list, others argued for their inclusion, noting that "mestizos or mulattos" were counted in the American census.[133] Some experts (working from the assumption that nationalities could have "mixed origins") speculated that some of the groups on this list might have become nationalities in the aftermath of 1917: "It is said that several years in the revolutionary period is equal to one hundred years" of ordinary time when it comes to the development of national groups, Semenov noted.[134]

The classification of Jews also was discussed at the January meeting, but was considered "questionable" for the opposite reason. Ethnographers maintained that all Jews shared the same tribal origins. Nonetheless, because Georgian Jews, Central Asian Jews, Crimean Jews, and European Jews (from Russia, Ukraine, and Belorussia) spoke different languages and had different customs, the ethnographers were unsure how to count them. Some statisticians and ethnographers argued for the unification of all Jews into one census category. Others argued for separate categories and even recommended adding another group, the "Mountain Jews," to the final list.[135] The so-called "Jewish question" was already a subject of much contention. Between 1924 and 1927 the Soviet government officially opposed the creation of a Jewish national republic or oblast, but sponsored the establishment of Jewish agricultural settlements in southern Ukraine, the Crimea, and Belorussia.[136] While some Soviet officials advocated the creation of a separate Jewish territory, others argued that the Jews, as a dispersed people, were not entitled to "national rights." Some officials, such as Commissar of Justice Mikhail Reisner, argued that only "backward" groups of Jews—which had preserved their ancient language and practiced their traditional culture and religion—could claim recognition as a nationality or national minority. Reisner asserted that the creation of a united Jewish nation with a "specially designated territory thrust upon it in the spirit of a new Zion" would have a negative impact on the Union's "advanced" Jews, who formed an important "vanguard of internationalism."[137]

The classification of the peoples of Transcaucasia was the most controversial topic in discussions about the official list of nationalities. Georgian representatives from the Transcaucasian government and the Transcaucasian branch of the TsSU complained that a number of peoples designated as separate nationalities on the list (the Mingrelians, Svans, Batsbi, Laz, and Ajars) were really religious or tribal subgroups of the Georgians. They berated central authorities and experts for attempting "to break up the Georgian nation,"

133. Ibid., l. 36. Semenov reminded his colleagues that the census would not provide "exact data" about the Soviet Union's nationalities. But he maintained that it was no worse than the Austrian attempt to measure *narodnost'* or the American attempt to measure race. (l. 1.)

134. RGAE f. 1562, op. 336, d. 4, l. 6.

135. Ibid., ll. 29–30.

136. Allan Laine Kagedan, "The Formation of Soviet Jewish Territorial Units, 1924–1937," Ph.D. diss., Columbia University, 1985.

137. Reisner, "Sovet Natsional'nostei," 193–94.

maintaining that the "false division" of the Georgians was reminiscent of tsarist colonial politics, which had sought to divide and rule. The Georgian representatives maintained that Ajars were Georgians who had once been Muslims—and asserted that the Soviet regime had created the Ajarian ASSR with the explicit goal of promoting Ajar separatism. They argued that "Mingrelian" and "Svan" were regional names for Georgians from different localities.[138] The national-political stakes gave these discussions a high emotional pitch; the previous year party leaders had accused the Georgians of pursuing the "physical liquidation of national minorities" in their republic.[139]

As it turned out, more than half of the people thought by ethnographers to be Mingrelians had registered themselves in the census as Georgians. Ethnographers wondered aloud whether census takers in Transcaucasia had engaged in foul play or whether the census results reflected the population's self-definition. The Georgian representatives maintained that more Mingrelians would have registered themselves as Georgians if census takers had not intervened and insisted that they were Mingrelians. But the ethnographers and statisticians in attendance were not so sure; one of the experts asked his colleagues if they could "with calm hearts" take responsibility for the consolidation of Transcaucasia's smaller nationalities with the Georgians.[140] Rudenko noted that if peoples were excluded from the list now, "it would become too difficult" to tabulate data for them—and thus champion their national rights—later.[141]

In the final version of the list, Soviet experts and officials gave some 172 peoples official recognition. They eliminated from the list a number of smaller peoples (groups with fewer than fifty registered members); in the census results these peoples were counted as members of neighboring groups. The fates of a number of "questionable nationalities" were also settled. The Jews were not consolidated (yet) but were divided into five *narodnosti* based on geographical location. The Mingrelians, Ajars, Svans, and Laz were listed as subgroups of the Georgians, but separate census data would be tallied for each.[142] The Cossacks were included on the list, but the TsSU asserted that the Cossacks would not be counted in future censuses.[143] The Sal'tkalmaks were omitted from the list, as were the Sarts (although the Sart-Kalmyks were temporarily included); self-identified Sarts speaking Uzbek were counted in the census as Uzbeks. Teptiars who had given another *narodnost'* on request were counted as members of that second (presumably more legitimate) nationality. However, so many people had insisted that their *narodnost'* was Teptiar that the group was

138. RGAE f. 1562, op. 336, d. 4, ll. 30–32. Also see GARF f. 3316, op. 19, d. 834, l. 26.
139. GARF f. 6892, op. 1, d. 42, l. 30.
140. RGAE f. 1562, op. 336, d. 4, ll. 30–32. He was unnamed in the stenogram.
141. Ibid., l. 28.
142. GARF f. 3316, op. 19, d. 834, ll. 26–30; RGAE f. 1562, op. 336, d. 12, ll. 12, 14–16; and *Vsesoiuznaia perepis' naseleniia 1926 goda*, vol. 17, SSSR, 106–7.
143. RGAE f. 1562, op. 336, d. 10, ll. 20–21. The Oirots and Uigurs were also on this list.

included on a short list of provisional nationalities. Census figures were tallied for the peoples on this list.[144] The provisional nationalities were the subject of further ethnographic research during the late 1920s.[145]

The inclusion of a group on the 1927 "List of the Nationalities of the USSR" did not ensure its continued recognition as an official nationality.[146] But peoples with slots on the census list and national territories of any size (republic, oblast, region) fared better than others in the 1930s, when the Soviet regime began a process of consolidating the 172 *narodnosti* identified in the 1926 census into a significantly smaller number of larger, economically developed, and historically "evolved" *natsional'nosti*.

Toward a List of "Major Nationalities"

In February 1927, shortly after the "List of the Nationalities of the USSR" was finalized, the TsSU began work on a list of the Soviet Union's major nationalities (*glavnye narodnosti*). While the initial round of census calculations was based on an "exhaustive list" of nationalities prepared by KIPS, the Sector for Social Statistics now sought a shorter list for additional statistical work.[147] It asked republic-level, oblast-level, and some provincial-level statistical bureaus to prepare lists of six or fewer "major nationalities" for their regions.[148]

144. The census explanatory notes state that there were 184 *narodnosti*. This figure includes twelve smaller nationalities (peoples with fewer than fifty registered members) that had been eliminated from the list in 1927. A version of the list that includes these twelve smaller nationalities and the four Georgian subgroups (188 peoples in all) plus the provisional nationalities was published with the census results. This published list includes footnotes that explain how and why the smaller nationalities lost their spots. *Vsesoiuznaia perepis' naseleniia 1926 goda*, vol. 17, *SSSR*, 106–7. Some 188 peoples were noted, with asterisks next to those that had been eliminated or consolidated with other nationalities. For an earlier version of the list see Tsentral'noe statisticheskoe upravlenie SSSR, *Programmy i posobiia k razrabotke Vsesoiuznoi perepisi naseleniia 1926 goda*, vol. 7, *Perechen' i slovar' narodnostei*. In 1927 KIPS published a slightly different version, which included 169 peoples. Some of the "provisional *narodnosti*" such as the Ui-gurs and Oirots were not included, while the Teptiars were.

145. In the 1930s most appeared on a new list of official nationalities.

146. In the late 1920s, Gosplan, arguing for the consolidation of the Komi-Permiak *okrug* of the Urals oblast with the Komi (Komi-Zyrian) AO, maintained that the Komi-Permiaks and Komi-Zyrians were parts of one *narodnost'* and should be combined. KIPS stood its ground, asserting that the Komi-Permiaks and the Komi-Zyrians have "substantive linguistic, ethnographic, and customary differences," and that "it would be completely incorrect" to unite them as "one *narodnost'*." PFA RAN f. 2, op. 1–1929, d. 33, ll. 58, 60, 65–66; f. 135, op. 1, d. 79, l. 80. KIPS's decision was upheld, but the two groups were consolidated in the 1930s.

147. PFA RAN f. 135, op. 1, d. 79, l. 8. Additional work included calculations of the correlation between nationality and class and profession. *Zasedanie TsIK*, 222.

148. RGAE f. 1562, op. 336, d. 4, ll. 175–76; op. 336, d. 10, l. 30; and *Zasedanie TsIK*, 222. The initial round of census tabulations (for data on *narodnost'* alone) took about nine months. The statistical administrations put together their lists of *glavnye narodnosti* in tandem with this work.

Moscow-based statisticians, with input from ethnographers and local and central officials, used these local lists to put together a composite list.[149] The idea of a "major nationality" was vague and subject to interpretation: some statisticians defined it as an important nationality, others as a nationality with "significant territory not smaller than a province," and others as a nationality with a large number of members.[150]

On the one hand, the creation of a new census list of major nationalities could be seen as a practical decision. The statisticians explained that time and resources would permit detailed data to be produced for only the major nationalities of each territorial region.[151] The statisticians, who frequently compared the Soviet census with the censuses of other countries, including the United States, noted that it was common practice throughout the world to work out detailed statistical calculations for only the largest and most important population groups.[152] In actual practice, however, the compilation of a list of major nationalities turned out to be not just a matter of noting the largest, most numerous, or most important nationalities of the Soviet Union. It also involved uniting or amalgamating peoples who shared ethnographic similarities (so-called related *narodnosti*). For example, upon preparing a list for the Karelian ASSR, administrators and experts consolidated the Karelians, Veps, and Finns into the "Finnish group."[153] Upon preparing a list for the North Caucasus, administrators and experts united the Cherkess, Kabardinians, and Beskesek-Abaza into the "Circassian group."[154] The implication was that these "related *narodnosti*" were on the road to national consolidation.

Another element of the creation of a list of major nationalities threatened the official national status of peoples spread out across the Soviet Union. The new list was to note the major nationalities of chosen "population points" and not of the Soviet Union as a whole. This meant that only the most dominant nationalities of each officially designated region were included on the list, while nationalities spread thinly across multiple regions were left out.[155] For the RSFSR, lists of major nationalities were composed for each autonomous republic, oblast, and *okrug*.[156] Other geographical regions, however, were divided into fewer population points. Belorussia was considered one population

149. RGAE f. 1562, op. 336, d. 10, l. 75; d. 13, ll. 45–46.

150. RGAE f. 1562, op. 336, d. 4, ll. 6–8, and *Zasedanie TsIK*, 222.

151. *Zasedanie TsIK*, 222.

152. RGAE f. 1562, op. 336, d. 4, ll. 1–4.

153. RGAE f. 1562, op. 336, d. 11, ll. 48–48ob. Also *Vsesoiuznaia perepis' naseleniia 1926 goda*, vol. 17, *SSSR*, 105.

154. RGAE f. 1562, op. 336, d. 11, l. 730b. Also *Vsesoiuznaia perepis' naseleniia 1926 goda*, vol. 17, *SSSR*, 105. The Balkars were added to the Circassian group on this list.

155. RGAE f. 1562, op. 336, d. 10, l. 75; d. 11, ll. 48, 590b.

156. RGAE f. 1562, op. 336, d. 11, ll. 30. 760b. For example, the Tatars, Russians, and Chuvash were listed as the major nationalities of the Tatar ASSR, and the Kirgiz, Russians, Uzbeks, and Ukrainians as the major nationalities of the Kirgiz ASSR. For each territory, totals for the re-

point, and figures were calculated for only the major nationalities of the entire republic.[157] The same was true for Turkmenistan.[158]

Through their participation in the creation of a list of major nationalities, representatives of the dominant nationalities attempted to push forward the process of national consolidation and pursue other goals. For example, officials from the Ukrainian branch of the TsSU proposed that Ukrainians, Russians, and Jews be listed as Ukraine's major nationalities, despite the fact that the Polish and German populations were slightly more numerous than the Jewish population. They noted that a full set of results for Poles, Germans, Greeks, and Bulgarians was needed to resolve "political, national, and economic questions," but they requested that such results be tallied informally, and that the four groups be excluded from Ukraine's official list of major nationalities.[159] Their chosen methodology seems to have had a specific national-political goal: to prevent Germans and Poles from being recognized officially as dominant nationalities in areas of Ukraine where they were concentrated and thus to thwart possible German and Polish claims to land and resources.

In other regions as well, deliberations about major nationalities brought into sharp focus the conflicting interests of national majorities and minorities. In Transcaucasia the same issues that plagued deliberations about the KIPS list of *narodnosti* reemerged, as Georgian representatives contended that the Laz, Mingrelians, and Svans were all part of the "Georgian *glavnaia narodnost'*." Georgian representatives also continued to characterize the designation of the Ajars as a separate *narodnost'* as "inaccurate," but conceded that it would be necessary to tabulate data for the Ajars, who were the titular people of the Ajarian ASSR.[160] This time, the Georgians largely got their way. The TsSU declared the Georgians, Turks, Armenians, and Russians to be the major nationalities of the Georgian republic, and the Laz, Mingrelians, and Svans to be part of the "Georgian *glavnaia narodnost'*." To ensure that data were tabulated for all titular nationalities, the TsSU approved slightly different lists of major nationalities for autonomous national republics and national oblasts within the Georgian SSR (for the Abkhazian and Ajarian ASSRs and the South Ossetian AO). For example, it included the Ajars as one of the major nationalities of the Ajarian ASSR.[161]

For their part, official representatives of the national minorities questioned whether the consolidation of smaller nationalities with more dominant nation-

---

maining *narodnosti* (those not included on the list of *glavnye narodnosti*) would be tabulated under the category "Others" (*prochie*).

157. RGAE f. 1562, op. 336, d. 11, l. 590b.

158. Ibid., l. 990b.

159. Ibid., ll. 64–67.

160. RGAE f. 1562, op. 336, d. 4, ll. 8–12; GARF f. 3316, op. 18, d. 834, l. 26; op. 13, d. 8, pt. 1, l. 24.

161. RGAE f. 1562, op. 336, d. 12, ll. 14, 16; d. 11, ll. 87–870b.

alities ran counter to the promise of national self-determination.[162] These concerns were justified. It was unclear what would happen to national minorities that made up a majority in some towns and rural regions. Beginning in the late 1920s, data about the major nationalities were used for administrative purposes: to adjust national-territorial borders, parcel out land, and set up national-language schools. The data were used to justify the actual amalgamation of smaller nationalities with their more dominant neighbors, as well as the unification of smaller nationalities into composite nationalities. The list of major nationalities thus had more than statistical significance: it had major repercussions for people's everyday lives.[163]

This shift from the general conceptual conquest of the population to the consolidation of nationalities in no way followed a preexisting plan or blueprint. The state-building process was very much influenced by changing circumstances, such as Stalin's rise to power. The resilience of traditional culture and religion among "less-developed" nationalities was an embarrassment for the Soviet regime, which had redoubled its efforts to industrialize with the introduction of the First Five-Year Plan in 1927. It became all the more so in 1929 as Stalin proclaimed a "great break" (*veliku perelom*) with the past and strove to accelerate the economic, social, cultural, and political transformation of the country.[164] By amalgamating "small" or "weak" *narodnosti* into "larger" and "more-developed" *glavnye narodnosti,* first on paper and then through its land and language policies, the regime attempted to speed the ethnohistorical evolution of the population—to usher the peoples of the USSR through the feudal and capitalist stages on the Marxist historical timeline and move toward the communist future. While the consolidation of nationalities was connected to Stalin's program, it—and arguably the "great break" itself— was made possible by the completion of the first round of census calculations, which gave the regime crucial information about its population, territory, and resources. Volumes of census data were published beginning in 1928; they included data about age, sex, language, and literacy for 166 *narodnosti,* 4 subgroups, and 6 "provisional nationalities."[165]

The KIPS ethnographers expressed their misgivings about the statistical and actual consolidation of *narodnosti.* In correspondence with government and

---

162. RGAE f. 1562, op. 336, d. 4, ll. 11–12.

163. On the use of census data in border deliberations in Central Asia see chapter 4.

164. See the discussion in David Joravsky, *Soviet Marxism and Natural Science, 1917–1932* (New York, 1961), 233.

165. *Vsesoiuznaia perepis' naseleniia 1926 goda,* vol. 17, SSSR, 106–7 and table 7 (26–33). The published census tables include fewer peoples than had been noted on the 1927 revised list of nationalities. The list for the census tables looks like a replica of the 1927 list and appears to feature the same number of peoples. But the numbers are not consecutive; nationalities are missing along with their originally designated numbers. The final volumes were published in 1933. A slightly revised list of *narodnosti* and list of major nationalities by region were used.

party institutions, the ethnographers argued that without a complete statistical analysis of all available data it would be impossible to compose accurate ethnographic maps, which had been requested by government committees to settle border disputes.[166] Some commission members, such as Zolotarev, also censured efforts to amalgamate *narodnosti* "by decree," arguing that "the unification of *narodnosti*" can only occur through "complicated life processes."[167] The ethnographers were realists and recognized that government and party institutions could and would ignore their advice—even while continuing to seek it. KIPS had finished its most important service to the state; it had helped provide the Soviet regime with volumes of detailed information about the peoples and territories of the Soviet Union. Now it was up to government and party officials to decide how to use that information.

Political Power, Scientific Knowledge, and the Fate of KIPS

In 1928, Stalin introduced the First Five-Year Plan, and several months later the Soviet regime embarked on a violent campaign for rapid economic and social transformation. Vowing to eliminate backwardness—to "change the lives of millions of people" by "pulling poverty, darkness, and slavery out by the roots"—the regime set out to industrialize, collectivize agriculture, and build socialism in record time.[168] Stalin's "great socialist offensive," or what some historians have aptly called his "revolution from above," brought about tremendous upheaval in all spheres of life throughout the Soviet Union.[169] As the regime attempted to accelerate the revolution, it built new cities, declared war on the peasantry, intensified the search for "class enemies," attempted to create a new proletarian socialist culture, and sought greater control over the Soviet Union's scientific institutions.[170]

166. See, for example, PFA RAN f. 135, op. 1, d. 79, l. 8.

167. PFA RAN f. 2, op. 1–1929, d. 33, l. 58. Zolotarev made this statement in an exchange with Gosplan about the proposed consolidation of the Komi-Permiak and Komi-Zyrian *narodnosti*.

168. M. Ilin, *New Russia's Primer: The Story of the Five-Year Plan* (Boston, 1931), 121.

169. The term *revolution from above* was coined by Robert Tucker. See Robert C. Tucker, "Stalinism as Revolution from Above," in Robert C. Tucker, ed., *Stalinism: Essays in Historical Interpretation* (New York, 1977), 77–108.

170. On the "Great Break" and "the building of socialism," see Stephen Kotkin, *Magnetic Mountain: Stalinism as a Civilization* (Berkeley, 1995). For a discussion of the impact of the "Great Break" on other Soviet professions see Susan Gross Solomon, "Rural Scholars and the Cultural Revolution," in *Cultural Revolution in Russia, 1928–1931*, ed. Sheila Fitzpatrick (Bloomington, 1978), 129–53; Kendall E. Bailes, *Technology and Society under Lenin and Stalin: Origins of the Soviet Technical Intelligentsia, 1917–1941* (Princeton, 1978); and Joravsky, *Soviet Marxism and Natural Science*. Following in the footsteps of Sheila Fitzpatrick, many scholars have referred to the Bolsheviks' attempt to take over the cultural and scientific spheres between 1928 and 1931 as "*the* cultural revolution" and have focused on the "struggle" between "non-Party intellectuals" and "workers and worker-communists." My own interpretation is more in line with that of Joravsky, who prefers to call these years the period of "the great break" or "the revolution from above" and argues that the turmoil in the sciences "whirled about a void, the lack of a Marxist-

Soviet leaders were acutely attuned to the connection between political power and scientific knowledge. From 1917, the alliance between liberal experts and Bolsheviks had been founded on a shared appreciation for scientific government, but not on a shared ideology or shared long-term goals. Now, with the basic work of conceptual conquest accomplished, the party endeavored to rein in those institutions and individuals engaged in the production of knowledge. The party was determined to demonstrate that it, and not former imperial experts, was overseeing the work of socialist construction, and that scientific socialism and not "liberal-bourgeois" social science was leading the way to the future. As the party began a major campaign to restructure scientific and cultural institutions that were dominated by former imperial experts, it focused its attention on the Academy of Sciences—condemning it as a "sanctuary for counterrevolutionary work against Soviet power."[171]

The party's campaign against the Academy of Sciences began in the spring of 1928 with the Politburo's interference in elections to the Academy's General Assembly.[172] The campaign became more virulent in the summer of 1929, when, under direct orders from the Politburo, the party's Leningrad Regional Committee established a special government commission headed by Iurii Figatner, a high-ranking figure in the People's Commissariat of Workers' and Peasants' Inspection, to investigate the Academy and purge it of so-called counterrevolutionaries.[173] While the Academy had scholars within its ranks who were critical of Soviet policies, it was by no means a site of anti-Soviet activities. Throughout the 1920s scholars and scientists had helped the Bolsheviks to create a secular government grounded in scientific knowledge. But in 1929, the regime broadened its definition of anti-Soviet thought, blurring "the former distinction between political loyalty and ideological solidarity."[174] It in-

---

Leninist position" and the all-out effort to establish one. See Sheila Fitzpatrick, "Cultural Revolution as Class War," 8–40, and David Joravsky, "The Construction of the Stalinist Psyche," esp. 105–9, both in *Cultural Revolution in Russia*. For a discussion of the term *cultural revolution* see Michael David-Fox, "What is Cultural Revolution?" *The Russian Review* 58, no. 2 (1999): 181–201.

171. The quote is from Iu. Figatner, "Proverka apparata Akademii nauk," *VARNITSO* (February 1930): 75. Quoted in Loren R. Graham, *The Soviet Academy of Sciences and the Communist Party, 1927–1932* (Princeton, 1967), 120. On the party's "seizure" of the Academy of Sciences also see Loren R. Graham, *Science in Russia and the Soviet Union: A Short History* (Cambridge, 1993), and Alexander Vucinich, *Empire of Knowledge: The Academy of Sciences of the USSR (1917–1970)* (Berkeley, 1984). Also see V. P. Zakharov et al., eds., *Delo po obvineniiu akademika S. F. Platonova, Akademicheskoe delo 1929–1931 gg.*, vol. 1 (St. Petersburg, 1993).

172. Zakharov et al., *Delo po obvineniiu akademika S. F. Platonova*, xvii—xxiii. On the party's interference in the elections also see Vucinich, *Empire of Knowledge*, 123–27, and Ronald Grigor Suny, *The Soviet Experiment: Russia, the USSR, and the Successor States* (New York, 1998), 210–12.

173. Zakharov et al., *Delo po obvineniiu akademika S. F. Platonova*, xxiv–xxix. Also Graham, *Soviet Academy of Sciences and the Communist Party*, 120–22, and Vucinich, *Empire of Knowledge*, 127.

174. The quote is Joravsky's. *Soviet Marxism and Natural Science*, 236.

sisted that all scientific knowledge correspond with (or at least not contradict) the premises of "scientific socialist thought."[175]

The party assigned a number of prominent academics to serve on the Figatner commission and facilitate its investigation of the Academy of Sciences and its personnel. One of these academics was Ol'denburg, permanent secretary of the Academy of Sciences and head of KIPS. In 1917 Ol'denburg and Vladimir Il'ich Lenin had formed an alliance, bringing together scholars and Bolsheviks; the Academy had provided the regime with expert knowledge and had been granted in exchange funding, protection, and a considerable degree of scientific freedom. This alliance had always been somewhat tenuous. Now that the party had achieved the actual and conceptual conquest of its domain it abruptly changed the terms—demanding that the Academy become a "Marxist-Leninist institution." Ol'denburg initially cooperated with the Figatner commission, helping it to investigate the Academy's scholars. He defended the new party line to his colleagues and tried to convince them that a compromise with the party was necessary.[176] But the party soon turned on Ol'denburg himself, accusing him in October 1929 of "obstructing the reconstruction of the Academy of Sciences." Ol'denburg was dismissed from his post as permanent secretary and relieved of his administrative duties. Unlike some of his colleagues, however, he did not lose his academic position and was not arrested.[177]

As it continued its investigation, the Figatner commission also organized a number of smaller commissions to investigate and restructure institutions within the Academy of Sciences. In the fall of 1929 it set up the Commission for the Reorganization of KIPS and the Museum of Anthropology and Ethnography (MAE), comprised of local party and government representatives and Moscow- and Leningrad-based ethnographers, including Vladimir Bogoraz. The commission subjected KIPS and the MAE to "socialist criticism."[178] It reproached some of the ethnographers for exhibiting "great power [Russian] chauvinism," and others for fostering "national separatism."[179] It reproached Rudenko for both. The commission also criticized KIPS's organizational struc-

175. Vucinich, *Empire of Knowledge*, 127, and Graham, *Soviet Academy of Sciences*, 122. On the tension between the Academy of Sciences and the Communist Academy in the 1920s see Michael David-Fox, *Revolution of the Mind: Higher Learning Among the Bolsheviks, 1918–1929* (Ithaca, 1997).

176. Graham, *Soviet Academy of Sciences*, 122, and Zakharov et al., *Delo po obvineniiu akademika S. F. Platonova*, xix, xxvii.

177. The quote is cited in Graham, *Soviet Academy of Sciences*, 122. Graham cites Ermakov, "Bor'ba kommunisticheskoi partii za perestroiku raboty nauchnykh uchrezhdenii v gody pervoi piatiletki," Kandidatskaia diss., Moscow State University, 1956, 156. Also see Vucinich, *Empire of Knowledge*, 127, and Zakharov et al., *Delo po obvineniiu akademika S. F. Platonova*, xxviii, xxxi.

178. PFA RAN f. 135, op. 1, d. 29, ll. 32–33; d. 79, ll. 45, 102–10.

179. PFA RAN f. 135, op. 1, d. 29, ll. 32–33. The commission criticized the KIPS ethnographers for their ignorance of local languages and failure to recruit national minorities into their ranks. The first charge is unfair, the second somewhat accurate. For critiques of commission members see M. Khudiakov, "Kriticheskaia prorabotka Rudenkovshchiny," *Sovetskaia etnografiia*, no.

ture, asserting that each of its departments had "proclaimed itself to be an independent republic" and "worked as it wanted, disconnected from the rest of the commission."[180] (Here, the "failings of KIPS" read like a metaphor for the failings of the Soviet multinational state. The First Five-Year Plan was supposed to end the Union's decentralization, but critics complained that it was not doing so.) The popular press covered and furthered the attack on KIPS, publishing articles which characterized the commission as a "closed corrupt circle" of old-regime experts that was resistant to progress.[181] At the same time, members of a younger generation of ethnographers and other experts in Leningrad and Moscow—all of whom had at least some training in Marxist-Leninist theory—organized conferences and published articles that questioned the future of ethnography in more general terms. They asked: Should ethnography be outlawed as a "bourgeois science," or was it possible to create a Marxist ethnography?[182]

In an effort to save their discipline and themselves—and in some cases to advance their own careers—some of the KIPS ethnographers (among them Marr, Bogoraz, and Mikhail Khudiakov) censured KIPS and its leaders. They attacked Ol'denburg and Rudenko as holdovers from the old regime who paid insufficient attention to "political questions" and had refused to adopt a Marxist approach to the population.[183] Marr and Bogoraz called for the reorganization of KIPS, while insisting that a commission like it was essential for the work of "Soviet state construction." The ethnographers contended that the TsSU needed KIPS's assistance in the classification of the Soviet Union's nationalities.[184] Marr proposed that KIPS become a "scientific research institute" dedicated to promoting the economic and cultural development of the peoples of the USSR.[185] He recommended that the commission include within its ranks Russian and non-Russian experts trained in Marxist-Leninist theory and ethnography.[186] In December 1929 the restructured Academy of Sciences appointed Marr to replace Ol'denburg as the head of KIPS, and Khudiakov to replace Rudenko as the commission's scientific secretary.[187]

1–2 (1931): 167–69, and S. N. Bykovskii, "Etnografiia na sluzhbe klassovogo vraga," *Sovetskaia etnografiia*, no. 3–4 (1931): 3–13.

180. PFA RAN f. 135, op. 1, d. 79, l. 36.

181. PFA RAN f. 2, op. 1–1929, d. 33, l. 91. One such article, "A Quiet Intelligentsia Family," was published in the popular daily *Vecherniaia Moskva*.

182. See, for example, V. G. Tan-Bogoraz, "K voprosu o primenenii marksistskogo metoda k izucheniiu etnograficheskikh iavlenii," *Etnografiia*, no. 1–2 (1930): 4–56. Bogoraz is sometimes referred to as Tan-Bogoraz or Bogoraz-Tan.

183. PFA RAN f. 135, op. 1, d. 79, ll. 32–33.

184. Ibid., ll. 46, 47.

185. Ibid., ll. 32–34, 47. Ol'denburg and Rudenko defended KIPS, arguing that the commission did not have a unified plan because it organized its research in response to urgent questions that arose in the process of state-building.

186. Ibid., ll. 102–9.

187. PFA RAN f. 135, op. 1, d. 44, l. 19. Marr, Bartol'd, Bogoraz, Semenov-Tian-Shanskii,

The published sources suggest that this assault on ethnography heralded the end of ethnographers' influence on state-building, and the "fall" of the profession.[188] But the archival sources tell a more complicated story. To be sure, the party's seizure of the Academy of Sciences and its attack on former imperial experts had tragic consequences for many individuals and an enormous impact on all the social sciences, including ethnography. Party and government officials reorganized scientific institutes and commissions; they arrested dozens of prominent scholars and dismissed others from their posts. Between 1929 and 1931 Ol'denburg was demoted and other KIPS ethnographers, including Zolotarev, were publicly denounced for "anti-Soviet" views and activities. Rudenko was arrested after the Figatner commission falsely charged him with using ethnographic expeditions to organize "anti-Soviet activities in the peripheries of the USSR."[189] Yet perhaps what is most striking is that ethnographers and other experts continued to forge ahead with their research, which the government and party continued to depend on.[190]

Indeed, even as the Figatner commission attacked KIPS, government and party officials in central institutions and commissariats (TsIK, the Soviet of Nationalities, the TsSU, Narkompros, the NKVD, and others) continued to work with the KIPS ethnographers and to seek their expertise. It was precisely between 1929 and 1931 that the KIPS ethnographers participated in a number of important projects. They mediated border disputes, served as expert-consultants for the collectivization effort in non-Russian regions, and organized and participated in dozens of expeditions. As it turned out, the party still needed professional ethnographers. Ol'denburg and Zolotarev remained active through this period, in spite of the attacks against them; in 1934, Rudenko was released from prison and resumed his research.[191]

The party's takeover of the Academy of Sciences initiated not the fall but rather the invention of "Soviet" ethnography. By working to transform "back-

---

Shibaev, Zarubin, and Khudiakov occupied leadership roles in the reorganized commission. Niko-lai Matorin, Sergei Bykovskii, and a number of other ethnographers with training in Marxist-Leninist theory joined the commission.

188. Such published sources include the journals *Etnografiia* (up to 1930) and *Sovetskaia etno-grafiia*. Yuri Slezkine, drawing on these and other published sources, tells the narrative of a break that left ethnographers "bewildered" and led to the eventual "fall" of the discipline. See Yuri Slezkine, "The Fall of Soviet Ethnography, 1928–1938," *Current Anthropology* 32, no. 4 (1991): 476–84. Elsewhere, Slezkine notes that the "banning" of ethnography was "inconclusive." See Yuri Slezkine, "N. Ia. Marr and the National Origins of Soviet Ethnogenetics," *Slavic Review* 55, no. 4 (1995): 845.

189. Zakharov et al., *Delo po obvineniiu akademika S. F. Platonova*, viii.

190. Graham makes a similar point about the Academy of Sciences as a whole, arguing that "the fact that the Academy was purged and coerced was not so remarkable as the fact that within its battered framework it preserved the seeds of fruitful research." Graham, *Soviet Academy of Sciences and the Communist Party*, 149.

191. On institutional changes during this period, and on the arrest and release of Rudenko, see Frédéric Bertrand, *L'anthropologie soviétique des années 20–30: Configuration d'une rupture* (Pessac, 2002).

ward clans and tribes" into "developed Soviet nations," and by articulating their research goals and results in "Marxist-Leninist" terms, professional ethnographers engaged in a dual process of Sovietization—of the population and of their discipline.[192] In February 1930, the Academy of Sciences reorganized KIPS and renamed it the Institute for the Study of the *Narodnosti* of the USSR (IPIN). Marr, the head of the institute, explained that the term *tribal* was dropped from its name because tribes "are only of historical significance in the Soviet context," where "all tribal forms, including those with little or no literacy, have received or are receiving the right to national self-determination."[193] Criticizing the "feudal-bourgeois understanding" of nationality as an "unchanging social category," and characterizing nationality as a "superstructural category" based on "socioeconomic factors" (and not on race), Marr explained that IPIN would study the process of ethnohistorical transformation that was "taking place before our eyes."[194] Comprised of former KIPS ethnographers as well as younger scholars with training in both Marxist-Leninist theory and ethnography, the new institute would trace how collectivization, industrialization, and other programs to revolutionize the Soviet economy and society were furthering the ethnohistorical development of the population.[195]

The processes of national-territorial state formation and the consolidation of nationalities continued throughout the 1930s. Indeed, the amalgamation of clans and tribes into *narodnosti,* and of *narodnosti* into *glavnye narodnosti,* provides an important context for evaluating the regime's efforts in the 1930s to amalgamate *narodnosti* into a smaller number of "advanced" *natsional'nosti.* This policy of the 1930s marked an attempt to control and *further* accelerate the process of state-sponsored evolutionism—and the revolution itself.[196] Whereas in the 1920s the creation of "official" nationalities and national-territorial units was somewhat haphazard and often connected to the

---

192. I agree with T. D. Solovei, who argues that the creation of "Soviet ethnography" took place between 1929 and 1936. See T. D. Solovei, *Ot "burzhuaznoi" etnologii k "sovetskoi" etnografii: Istoriia otechestvennoi etnologii pervoi treti XX veka* (Moscow, 1998). Vucinich discusses the "Sovietization of the Academy," noting that the Academy's survival depended on its willingness to become "a true Soviet institution." He characterizes Sovietization as the reworking of the Academy's "administrative procedures, staffing methods, and philosophical-ideological orientation" as well as the creation of a "new intelligentsia loyal to the Soviet system" and "imbued with the spirit of the new society." Vucinich, *Empire of Knowledge,* 124, 126. Vucinich does not discuss the process through which members of the "old intelligentsia" (like the KIPS ethnographers) underwent a process of Sovietization.

193. PFA RAN f. 135, op. 1, d. 44, ll. 23–25.

194. PFA RAN f. 135, op. 1, d. 79, l. 112.

195. PFA RAN f. 135, op. 1, d. 44, ll. 23–25. IPIN focused on the Soviet Union's "seven main national-economic regions" and the nationalities that lived in each.

196. See chapter 7. Here I am arguing against Martin and other historians who have suggested that this shift represented a "retreat" from the initial goals of Soviet nationality policy. Martin, *Affirmative Action Empire,* 26.

aspirations of local leaders, during the 1930s it became part of an explicit policy managed by central administrative organs. Moreover, the consolidation of nationalities and the official discourse that validated this shift was the impetus behind a general turn to consolidation—of languages, national territories, cultural institutions, and administrative structures.

CHAPTER 4

Border-Making and the Formation of Soviet National Identities

> There is no doubt that the Uzbek *narodnost'* at the present time is only at the stage of taking form. . . . The establishment of the Uzbek republic after the delimitation of 1924, and the rise in national consciousness connected with it, should accelerate this process of forming a people [*narod*] from a conglomeration of tribes.
>
> —Commission for the Regionalization of Central Asia, 1926

> The map is almost as close to becoming the center of the new Russian iconic cult as Lenin's portrait.
>
> —Walter Benjamin, "Moscow," 1927

In 1921, in the midst of the civil war and in the wake of the census of 1920, ethnographer-consultants to the Soviet government noted that people in large expanses of the former Russian Empire were unsure of how to answer when asked a direct question about their nationality. Some five years later, during the All-Union Census of 1926, the ethnographer-consultants reported that the inhabitants of nonurban regions continued to identify themselves primarily in terms of clan, tribe, religion, or place of origin, while local elites attempted to manipulate the registration of nationality to advance their own agendas. By the early 1930s, however, a qualitative shift had occurred. Even rural and no-madic populations that previously had not exhibited "national consciousness" were describing themselves as members of nationalities—and were using the language of nationality to argue for economic, administrative, and political rights. Nationality had become a fundamental marker of identity, embedded not just in the administrative structure of the Soviet Union, but also in people's mentalities. How did this happen?

Throughout the 1920s the census and the map had pivotal roles in the work of conceptual conquest, helping Soviet leaders to order individual and group identities. Border-making, like census-taking, was an identity-transforming process that changed the categories that people used to describe themselves. Through one-on-one interviews with census takers—and through the institutionalization of a multitude of official documents asking for one's *narodnost'*—Soviet citizens learned that they were supposed to define themselves as members of an official nationality. But it was the creation of new national republics, oblasts, and regions, along with the Soviet policy of *korenizatsiia* (indigenization), which called for the promotion of indigenous people in these national territories, that *activated* nationality categories by demonstrating that nationality, resources, and local political power were officially linked. Indeed, it was against the backdrop of Soviet border-making that local elites throughout the Union originally came to see the census, with its question about nationality, as instrumental to their struggles for land and influence. In time, the peoples that these local elites claimed to represent also came to understand the potential benefits of nationhood—and the hardships that could ensue if one's village ended up on the "wrong" side of a national-territorial border, where the official language and culture were different from one's own.

Historians of the European empires have described census-taking and border-making as "cultural technologies of rule," which facilitated and sustained centralized rule as much as "the more obvious and brutal modes of conquest."[1] The Soviet regime too consolidated power over the lands and peoples of its domain not just through the army but also through these more subtle mechanisms of control. In the 1920s, the Soviet government used the census and the map to facilitate a process that might be called "double assimilation": the assimilation of diverse peoples into nationality categories and, simultaneously, the assimilation of nationally categorized groups into the Soviet state and society. Soviet leaders aimed to turn the "feudal" and "colonial" peoples of the former Russian Empire into nationalities that would participate in local national soviets and "further the work of socialist construction."[2] To facilitate this goal, the Soviet government advocated different policies toward different national territories depending on their populations' presumed place on the Marxist historical timeline. The national republics and oblasts of "less-developed" peoples were entitled to special assistance, while the republics and oblasts of "mature nations with mature classes" were to be monitored for

1. Cited from Nicholas B. Dirks's foreword to Bernard S. Cohn, *Colonialism and Its Forms of Knowledge: The British in India* (Princeton, 1996), ix. According to Dirks: "Colonial knowledge both enabled conquest and was produced by it; in certain important ways, knowledge was what colonialism was all about." Also see the essays in Nicholas B. Dirks, ed., *Colonialism and Culture* (Ann Arbor, 1992). The term *cultural technologies of rule* is particularly fitting for the Soviet case—where revolutionaries and experts *intentionally* used census-taking and border-making (along with other means of classification and delimitation) to transform local identities.

2. The State Archive of the Russian Federation (GARF) f. 3316, op. 16a, d. 212, ll. 97–99. Representatives from the union republics, autonomous national republics, and oblasts, and "national members of VTsIK and TsIK" (that is, the non-Russians in these institutions) discussed this issue on November 12 and 14, 1926.

signs of bourgeois nationalism.[3] This approach to the population was markedly different from that of the Russian Empire, which had pursued a policy of direct assimilation (Russification) in some regions and a policy of "association" or noninterference (religious and cultural toleration and administrative integration) in others.[4]

Double assimilation, like Soviet state formation in general, was not simply a top-down process. Its success depended on mass participation. Soviet leaders and institutions introduced new vocabularies and structures, and then worked to make sure that people found them meaningful. Thus, government and party commissions relied on the input of experts and local leaders, and gave serious consideration to correspondence (petitions, appeals, and letters of grievance) from people throughout the Soviet Union. Participation of this type made Soviet rule all the more insidious.[5] Local elites and peasants who appealed to central authorities about disputed national-territorial borders—even those actively "resisting" official decisions—learned to frame their protests in the language of the state and to direct them to the appropriate government organs; most accepted the official assumption that nationalities and territories were linked.[6] This had mixed results. On the one hand, it led to a proliferation of local "national" conflicts that threatened the regime's agenda for economic modernization. On the other hand, and in the longer term more importantly, it

3. Ibid., 98–99. The Kazakh, Bashkir, and Buriat-Mongol ASSRs were noted as examples of the former and the Tatar ASSR as an example of the latter.

4. On Russian imperial policy see Adeeb Khalid, *The Politics of Muslim Cultural Reform: Jadidism in Central Asia* (Berkeley, 1998); Dietrich Geyer, *Russian Imperialism: The Interaction of Domestic and Foreign Policy, 1860–1914* (Leamington Spa, UK, 1987); Richard A. Pierce, *Russian Central Asia, 1867–1917: A Study in Colonial Rule* (Berkeley, 1960); and Daniel Brower, "Islam and Ethnicity: Russian Colonial Policy in Turkestan," in *Russia's Orient: Imperial Borderlands and Peoples, 1700–1917,* ed. Daniel R. Brower and Edward J. Lazzerini (Bloomington, 1997), 115–35. On the general concepts of "association" and "assimilation" and European colonial policy see Martin D. Lewis, "One Hundred Million Frenchmen: The 'Assimilation' Theory in French Colonial Policy," *Comparative Studies in Society and History* 4, no. 2 (1962): 129–53. Also see Raymond R. Betts, "Association in French Colonial Theory," and Hubert Jules Deschamps, "Association and Indirect Rule," in *Historical Problems of Imperial Africa*, ed. Robert O. Collins (Princeton, 1996), 154–64 and 165–78 respectively.

5. On the importance of mass mobilization and participation to the success of the Soviet project see Hannah Arendt, *The Origins of Totalitarianism*, rev. ed. (San Diego, 1979). Also see Stephen Kotkin, *Magnetic Mountain: Stalinism as a Civilization* (Berkeley, 1995), and Peter Kenez, *The Birth of the Propaganda State: Soviet Methods of Mass Mobilization, 1917–1929* (Cambridge, 1985).

6. In other words, even people "resisting" the system strengthened it by using the regime's basic conceptual categories and institutions. This is a point often overlooked in the literature about "resistance" under Stalin. In an article about "local resistance" in Uzbekistan, Douglas Northrop has argued that "Soviet courts and procedures were manipulated to become an instrument working against stated Soviet goals." But the very fact that local populations were *using* Soviet courts and procedures to settle local grievances shows the extent to which those populations were being successfully integrated into the Soviet whole. See Douglas Northrop, "Subaltern Dialogues: Subversion and Resistance in Soviet Uzbek Family Law," in *Contending with Stalinism: Soviet Power and Popular Resistance in the 1930s,* ed. Lynne Viola (Ithaca, 2002), 135.

served as an effective mechanism to anchor the population more firmly in the Soviet state and society.

Whereas the previous two chapters focused on interinstitutional deliberations about the organization of the Soviet state and the formulation of a definitional grid of nationalities, this chapter takes up the issues of implementation and local response. It asks three key questions. First: How were the ethnographic and economic paradigms translated in practice into principles for border-making? Second: What were the consequences of using "nationality" as a standard category of state organization in regions where many people lacked national consciousness? Third: What role did the 1926 census—with its new data about *narodnost'*—have in the evaluation (and reevaluation) of border disputes in the late 1920s?

From Principles to Paradigms

With the ratification of the new Soviet constitution in 1924, Soviet administrators and experts reinterpreted the ethnographic and economic paradigms for regionalization as the ethnographic and economic *principles* for border delimitation; this reflected the compromise between the competing Gosplan and Narkomnats models for administrative-territorial regionalization (discussed in chapter 2). Out of deference to the "principle of nationality," Gosplan excluded all union republics and most autonomous national republics from its economic-administrative oblasts. It worked instead to integrate these national-territorial units into the all-union whole as separate economic-administrative units. For example, while Gosplan had formerly proposed the inclusion of the Belorussian SSR in the Western economic-administrative oblast, the inclusion of the Bashkir ASSR in the Urals economic-administrative oblast, and the division of the Ukrainian SSR into two economic-administrative oblasts, it now set out to make the Belorussian SSR, the Bashkir ASSR, and the Ukrainian SSR into separate economic-administrative oblasts of their own.

At the same time, the new Central Executive Committee (TsIK) of the Soviet government established its own Commission for the Regionalization of the USSR to oversee the continuing work of border delimitation and to mediate border disputes.[7] Following the decision to exclude union republics and autonomous national republics from larger economic-administrative oblasts, the Politburo mandated that the borders of all national-territorial units be reevaluated with broader economic, administrative, and ethnographic considerations in mind. The new commission's first deliberations involved the Ukrainian SSR, the Belorussian SSR, and the RSFSR.[8] The initial borders among these three republics had been delineated by an All-Russian Central

7. Hereafter referred to as the TsIK regionalization commission.
8. See GARF f. 6892, op. 1 (TsIK SSSR Commission on Regionalization, 1923–1927).

Executive Committee (VTsIK) subcommission in 1919 on the basis of "nationality determined by language."[9] Beginning in 1923, the TsIK regionalization commission investigated these borders for ethnographic, economic, and administrative viability.

The TsIK regionalization commission's approach was twofold. It solicited expert knowledge from ethnographers, economists, and all-union commissariats; simultaneously, it invited local leaders from both sides of a projected or disputed border, as well as Moscow-based officials, to participate in a border-resolution subcommission.[10] The commission reviewed the expert reports and local arguments, and weighed the relative importance of ethnographic, economic, and administrative considerations. Whereas local leaders usually took a local perspective (arguing, for example, that a particular region was economically oriented toward their republic), the regionalization commission took an all-union approach and evaluated ethnographic, economic, and administrative considerations in the context of the "political factor" (*politicheskii moment*)—shorthand for domestic, international, and ideological concerns.[11] The commission then sent its recommendations to the TsIK Presidium and to the Politburo.[12]

The Belorussian Case

From the start, the creation of the Belorussian republic was an example of nation-making "from above"—based on ethnographic data, but with limited popular support.[13] Although a small self-described "Belorussian intelligentsia" had enthusiastically supported the establishment of the republic, the so-called "Belorussian people" had been indifferent or opposed. Administrators and experts who helped delimit the initial borders of the Belorussian Soviet Socialist Republic (BSSR) in 1919 reported that it was impossible to distinguish between Belorussian and Russian villages, which were linguistically and ethni-

9. In part, it had used KIPS's ethnographic maps, which were based on data from the 1897 census. The Russian State Archive of the Economy (RGAE) f. 1562, op. 336, d. 8, l. 105.

10. All-union institutions included the People's Commissariat of Agriculture and the People's Commissariat of Finance.

11. Terry Martin has argued that "foreign policy goals" (what he calls the Piedmont Principle) were responsible for the regime's approach to the formation and revision of the Soviet Union's national territories. Terry Martin, *The Affirmative Action Empire: Nations and Nationalism in the Soviet Union, 1923–1929* (Ithaca, 2001). My materials suggest that foreign policy goals were just one aspect of the "political factor"; other administrative and ideological goals were equally important, and in some cases more so.

12. See GARF f. 3316, op. 16, d. 206, l. 8.

13. The German Occupation Army created the first Belorussian national territory in the midst of World War I. On the details see Nicholas P. Vakar, *Belorussia: The Making of a Nation* (Cambridge, MA, 1956), 93–106.

cally intermixed.[14] In 1921, two years after the Belorussian SSR was definitively brought into the Soviet fold, some party members expressed concern that the party was "artificially cultivating" a Belorussian nationality which otherwise did not exist.[15]

Such expressions of concern did not trouble Joseph Stalin and other Soviet leaders, who saw the creation of a Belorussian republic as a means of transforming the local population and accomplishing important political ends. They suggested that a Belorussian republic on the western border would serve as a buffer between the Soviet Union and an independent Poland, and as a counterbalance to the Ukrainian republic (whose "nationalist tendencies" were considered a threat to all-union stability). Soviet leaders further argued that a Belorussian republic would advance the cause of world revolution, by demonstrating to the world—and in particular to "the millions of Belorussians inhabiting Poland"—the Soviet regime's commitment to "non-Russian" peoples.[16] The fact that a sizeable percentage of the people included in the Belorussian republic defined themselves as "Russians" did not deter Soviet leaders. Ethnographers such as Evfimii Karskii (a member of KIPS) argued that most of the inhabitants of the Belorussian republic were "ethnographically Belorussian," even if they currently lacked national consciousness.[17]

Soviet leaders remained committed to the idea of a Belorussian republic even though Gosplan challenged its economic and administrative viability. In 1921, after the Soviet state was forced to relinquish a sizeable strip of Belorussia to Poland in accordance with the Treaty of Riga, Gosplan proposed that the BSSR be included, along with Smolensk, Briansk, and Gomel *gubernii* of the RSFSR, in the Western economic-administrative oblast. Soviet leaders considered, but ultimately rejected, this proposal—and shortly thereafter ruled that union republics could not be integrated into economic-administrative oblasts.[18] The Gosplan proposal was not forgotten, however, and provided some of the inspiration in 1923 for a new plan to enlarge the Belorussian re-

14. Discussed in GARF f. 3316, op. 22, d. 129, ll. 42–43.

15. Noted in E. H. Carr, *The Bolshevik Revolution, 1917–1923*, vol. 1 (New York, 1950), 311.

16. The quote is from Enukidze. GARF f. 3316, op. 16, d. 206, ll. 40–41.

17. For Karskii's analysis of the region see E. F. Karskii, *Etnograficheskaia karta Belorusskago plemeni, Trudy Komissii po izucheniiu plemennogo sostava naseleniia Rossii*, vol. 2 (Petrograd, 1917). Jeremy Smith and Yuri Slezkine also note Karskii's influence on the delimitation of Belorussia's borders. See Slezkine, "The USSR as a Communal Apartment, or How a Socialist State Promoted Ethnic Particularism," *Slavic Review* 53, no. 2 (1994): 428–30, and Smith, *The Bolsheviks and the National Question, 1917–1923* (London, 1999), 71–72. Anatolii Lunacharskii noted in his memoirs that the Academy of Sciences had "created by our order more precise ethnographic maps of Belorussia and Bessarabia." A. V. Lunacharskii, *Vospominaniia i vpechatleniia* (Moscow, 1968), 206.

18. GARF f. 6892, op. 1, d. 47, ll. 21–22. On the Treaty of Riga see Vakar, *Belorussia: The Making of a Nation*, 116–18.

public: if Belorussia could not be integrated into the proposed Western economic-administrative oblast, then some of the territories of that proposed oblast—in particular, those with large ethnographically Belorussian populations—could be integrated into the Belorussian SSR.

Once the Politburo decided to enlarge the BSSR, it wanted the appeal to come from the republic itself. In the fall of 1923, it organized a new Commission on the Enlargement of the Territory of Belorussia under the leadership of Aleksandr Osatkin-Vladimirskii, the head of the Belorussian Communist Party. As this new commission began its deliberations, it looked to the work of Karskii, whose ethnographic research suggested that the "present administrative borders" of Belorussia were incorrect and that certain territories in the neighboring republics were actually Belorussian.[19] Karskii, a linguist by training, maintained that the Belorussian language—and thus the Belorussian *narodnost'*—predominated in "Gomel, Vitebsk, and almost all of Smolensk *gubernii.*"[20] To support Karskii's analysis, the commission compiled census data. The 1920 census showed that large swaths of Vitebsk and Gomel *gubernii,* as well as two western *uezdy* (Gorets and Mstislav) of Smolensk *guberniia,* had Belorussian majorities.[21] The commission argued that an even greater proportion of these *gubernii* was ethnographically Belorussian: that the 1920 census, conducted "at the end of the Polish war, when it was still unclear where the border would be delimited with Poland," had intentionally registered Belorussians as Russians. The commission proposed that the regime use data from the 1897 census—which showed almost all of Vitebsk and Gomel to be ethnographically Belorussian—as a corrective. The commission also reviewed Gosplan's economic analysis of Vitebsk, Gomel, and Smolensk; it noted that the three *gubernii* included cultivated agricultural land, some factories, and a strip of the railroad—all of which would support the economic development of the BSSR.[22]

In November 1923, the Osatkin-Vladimirskii commission reported back to the Politburo. Noting the "disproportionately small size" of the Belorussian SSR in relation to the Ukrainian SSR and the RSFSR, it recommended that the latter two republics cede to Belorussia parts of *gubernii* "that were related to it in *byt* and ethnographic and economic type."[23] It presented ethnographic and economic data to advocate the transfer of Gorets and Mstislav *uezdy* from Smolensk *guberniia,* all eleven *uezdy* from Vitebsk *guberniia,* and eight (out of

19. GARF f. 3316, op. 16, d. 206, l. 2.
20. Ibid.
21. Ibid. An *uezd* is a regional administrative unit (or county). The commission noted that according to the data most of Vitebsk (except for the northern *uezdy* of Velizh, Nevel, and Sebezh), and much of Gomel (except for the southeastern *uezdy* of Gomel, Rogachev, Klintsy, Starodub, Novozybkov, Mglin, and Pochep) were more than 50 percent Belorussian.
22. GARF f. 3316, op. 16, d. 206, ll. 3–4.
23. Ibid., l. 8.

thirteen) *uezdy* from Gomel *guberniia*. The commission noted with optimism that the unification of these ethnographically Belorussian regions into a "greater Belorussia" would facilitate the republic's economic and ethnohistorical development. It added that "often in history, the national consolidation of a country promotes its industrial enlightenment."[24]

As expected, the Politburo upheld the general position of the Osatkin-Vladimirskii commission. But it asked the TsIK regionalization commission to review "in detail" the territories in question and to "resolve which *uezdy*" of which *gubernii* "should be included in which republic."[25] In response, the TsIK regionalization commission established a Subcommission for Changing the Borders Between the RSFSR and the BSSR, under the leadership of Avel Enukidze (the head of the TsIK Secretariat and a member of the party's Central Committee). This subcommission included members of the Ukrainian SSR, Belorussian SSR, and RSFSR governments, as well as representatives from Smolensk, Gomel, Vitebsk, and Briansk *gubernii* and a representative from the VTsIK Administrative Commission.[26] It reported to a Politburo subcommission headed by Iakov Peters.[27] Significantly, some members of the RSFSR-BSSR subcommission questioned whether their deliberations would influence the actual borders of the Belorussian republic, or whether the Politburo would make such decisions on its own. Enukidze insisted that while the Politburo had "resolved decisively to enlarge Belorussia," it had not determined "the exact borders" and would leave that to the TsIK commission.[28]

The representatives from Gomel, Vitebsk, and Smolensk all maintained that their *gubernii* should remain in the RSFSR—and invoked both the economic and the ethnographic principles to argue their cases. The Smolensk representative emphasized economic considerations, arguing that Gorets and Mstislav *uezdy* were economically oriented toward Smolensk *guberniia* and that it would thus "be harmful" to transfer them to the BSSR.[29] The Vitebsk representative, by contrast, focused on the ethnographic principle; presenting data from the 1920 census, he contended that a number of the *uezdy* in question were less than 35 percent Belorussian, and that some were less than 5 percent Belorussian.[30] The Vitebsk representative further argued that most people who registered themselves as Belorussians in the census were "Belorussian by tradition," and not by language, *byt,* or national consciousness—and that the Be-

---

24. Ibid., ll. 2, 5–6.
25. Ibid., l. 1.
26. Ibid. Konstantin Egorov was the representative.
27. Peters later headed several TsIK subcommissions that adjudicated border disputes in Central Asia.
28. GARF f. 3316, op. 16, d. 206, ll. 43, 45. Enukidze also was a member of the Orgburo commission. GARF f. 3316, op. 64, d. 551, l. 34.
29. GARF f. 3316, op. 16, d. 206, l. 44.
30. Ibid., ll. 35–36. These were some of the *uezdy* for which the Osatkin-Vladimirskii commission had recommended the use of data from the 1897 census.

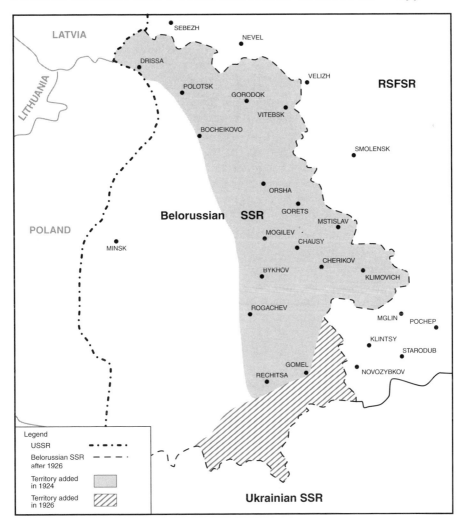

Map 4.1 The Belorussian SSR in 1922, 1924, and 1926. The map shows the contested *uezdy* of Vitebsk, Gomel, and Smolensk *gubernii*. Vitebsk *guberniia*: Sebezh, Nevel, Velizh, Drissa, Polotsk, Gorodok, Vitebsk, Bocheikovo, and Orsha *uezdy*. Gomel *guberniia*: Mogilev, Klimovich, Chausy, Cherikov, Bykhov, Rogachev, Gomel, Rechitsa, Mglin, Pochep, Klintsy, Starodub, Novozybkov *uezdy*. Smolensk *guberniia*: Mstislav and Gorets *uezdy*.

lorussianization of the *guberniia* "would be a blow to the peasant population" in particular.[31] Representatives from all three *gubernii* focused on the issue of national self-determination. The Vitebsk representative noted that the transfer of his *guberniia* to Belorussia had been debated at local "soviets, among school workers, and in the press," and "everywhere at all forums there was a

31. Ibid.

negative attitude toward the Belorussian question (even among the intelligentsia)." The Smolensk and Gomel representatives reported similar opposition, noting that people were worried about "the forced introduction of the Belorussian language."[32]

The Belorussian representatives and the Moscow-based officials on the TsIK subcommission took different approaches to counter these impassioned arguments against "forced Belorussianization." The Belorussian representatives went on the offensive and argued that local party and government leaders were manufacturing local resistance to the transfer of their *gubernii* to the BSSR. One Belorussian representative maintained that Gomel peasants had welcomed the idea of their inclusion in the BSSR until local party leaders "led a campaign" against the transfer and told the population that "within two weeks after their unification with the BSSR everything will be translated into the Belorussian language, Russian schools will be closed, and so on"; only after this campaign did the local population decide that it wanted to remain within the RSFSR. The Vitebsk local government had led a similar campaign "to leave its borders alone" as soon as it had learned about the Politburo's interest in enlarging the BSSR, the same Belorussian representative added.[33]

The subcommission members from TsIK, by contrast, argued that local self-determination was irrelevant. Noting that he would "speak completely openly" since "only communists are present," Enukidze acknowledged that most of the inhabitants of Smolensk, Vitebsk, and Gomel *gubernii* considered themselves "Russian" and "would vote for remaining within the boundaries of the RSFSR if a plebiscite were taken." But Enukidze insisted that most of these people were in fact Belorussians who, as a result of "historical circumstances" (such as the legacy of Russification), "had attached themselves to the Great Russian culture, language, and *byt*." "Present political considerations," he argued, mandated the inclusion of *gubernii* with large ethnographically Belorussian populations in an expanded Belorussian republic.[34]

Arguing that Russified Belorussians were entitled to Belorussian nationhood—whether they wanted it or not—the TsIK subcommission ruled to transfer most of the territory in question to the BSSR.[35] The subcommission noted that it would "not force" regions in which "Great Russians predominated" to enter the BSSR.[36] But it relied on ethnographic data—and not national consciousness or national self-definition—to make this determination. It suggested by example that the Soviet regime would use ethnographic data to impose nationhood on people who either "hid" or did not know their "true"

32. Ibid., ll. 35–37.

33. Ibid., ll. 37–38.

34. Ibid., ll. 40–41, 46.

35. It recommended that Sebezh, Velizh, and Nevel *uezdy* of Vitebsk *guberniia*, and Starodub, Novozybkov, Mglin, Pochep, Gomel, Rechitsa, and Klintsy *uezdy* of Gomel *guberniia* remain in the RSFSR. The BSSR protested and the question went before the Politburo.

36. GARF f. 3316, op. 16, d. 206, l. 41.

nationality. And it made clear that "self-determination" in the Soviet context did *not* necessarily mean that people would have a say in the *political* choices that were linked to identity. In the end, the commission was somewhat more conservative in its recommendations than the Osatkin-Vladimirskii commission had been, advocating the transfer of sixteen *uezdy* (with almost 2 million people) to the BSSR.[37] The party followed through on these recommendations and later ruled to transfer two more of the disputed *uezdy* from Gomel *guberniia* to Belorussia.[38]

The Ukrainian Case

Deliberations about the borders of the Ukrainian republic also demonstrate that the Soviet regime evaluated the ethnographic and the economic principles in the context of all-union interests. But unlike the Belorussian case, the Ukrainian case illustrates how Soviet authorities responded when they perceived nationalities as too nationalistic. Self-identified Ukrainian elites had pushed for the formation of a Ukrainian national territory from the revolution's earliest moments. After the establishment of the Ukrainian SSR, Ukrainian leaders argued for the expansion of the republic's borders—and acquired part of the former Don oblast.

In 1924, as the Politburo redrew the borders of Belorussia, the borders of Ukraine again came under reconsideration. Representatives from the newly formed North Caucasus *krai* in the RSFSR put in their own claim to the territories of the former Don oblast, which they argued were economically oriented toward the North Caucasus.[39] Soviet leaders established a Parity Commission, which reviewed the competing claims of Ukraine and the North Caucasus *krai*.[40] While North Caucasus representatives focused on the region's economic orientation, Ukrainian representatives focused on its ethnographic composition. The North Caucasus representatives conceded that the majority of the population of this oblast was "undoubtedly Ukrainian." But they argued that the population had lost the "Ukrainian language and does not want to return to it."[41] The North Caucasus representatives submitted petitions from the local population supporting their argument. Several months before, Vitebsk and Gomel representatives had made a similar claim about the limited role of the Belorussian language in their *gubernii*—in an *unsuccessful* attempt to pre-

37. The transferred territories were: Gorets and Mstislav *uezdy* of Smolensk *guberniia*; Vitebsk, Polotsk, Bocheikovo, Orsha, Drissa, and Gorodok *uezdy* of Vitebsk *guberniia*; Mogilev, Rogachev, Bykhov, Klimovich, Chausy, Cherikov, Gomel, and Rechitsa *uezdy* of Gomel *guberniia*.

38. Noted in Martin, *Affirmative Action Empire*, 277.

39. Ibid., 278.

40. GARF f. 3316, op. 1, d. 19, ll. 1–2. It was headed by TsIK member Aleksandr Cherviakov.

41. Ibid., l. 3.

vent their transfer to the BSSR. But because Soviet leaders considered the Ukrainian SSR to be more developed than the North Caucasus *krai* (or the Belorussian SSR), they did not argue in this case that the population's ethnographic origins should trump its self-determination.

Under pressure from Moscow, the Ukrainian leaders gave in to some of the North Caucasus' territorial claims. But they objected to giving up their claim to Taganrog *okrug,* which past censuses had shown to have a sizeable Ukrainian-speaking population. The Ukrainian leaders also made some additional territorial claims of their own. Demanding tit for tat, they argued that the RSFSR should hand over large and economically important regions from Kursk and Voronezh *gubernii* (as well as smaller regions from Briansk and Gomel *gubernii*) to the Ukrainian SSR.[42] All four *gubernii* were on Ukraine's northeastern border. Invoking the ethnographic principle, the Ukrainian leaders argued that large parts of these regions "have majority Ukrainian populations"; they presented data from the 1920 census, as well as petitions from the local population, to support their position. The Ukrainian leaders argued that the transfer of these ethnographically Ukrainian regions was politically imperative. They explained that news of Ukraine's territorial concessions to the RSFSR was sparking "political dissatisfaction among certain people" in the Ukrainian SSR, who were concerned that "the RSFSR is beginning to storm Ukraine."[43]

At the Politburo's request, the TsIK regionalization commission, still under Enukidze's leadership, took up the question of Ukraine's borders in late 1924. Following the Belorussian precedent, the commission solicited the opinions of economists, ethnographers, statisticians, and a number of all-union commissariats.[44] It also formed a subcommission and invited representatives from the Ukrainian SSR and RSFSR governments, from the *gubernii* in question, and from the VTsIK Administrative Commission to participate.

As deliberations began, representatives from the RSFSR set out to discredit the Ukrainian claims as unfounded. A member of the RSFSR delegation, Mikhail Boldyrev, argued that the Ukrainian demands could not be justified on the basis of the ethnographic principle, the economic principle, or "the principle of administrative order." Boldyrev spoke at length about the ethnographic principle, which had proven decisive in the Belorussian case. He argued that there "remain no signs of Ukrainian *byt* and language" in regions that "Ukraine wants to appropriate." He further charged that the Ukrainian

---

42. Ukrainian leaders requested large regions in the southern parts of Kursk and Voronezh *gubernii.* They also requested Semenovka *volost'* from Gomel *guberniia* and Klintsy and Novozybkov *uezdy* from Briansk *guberniia.* See GARF f. 5677, op. 1, d. 9, ll. 2–20b, and f. 6892, op. 1, d. 19, ll. 1, 3–4. (Klintsy and Novozybkov had formerly been part of Gomel *guberniia* but became part of Briansk in 1924.)

43. GARF f. 3316, op. 1, d. 19, l. 2.

44. These included the commissariats of finance, agriculture, health, internal trade, labor, enlightenment, and worker-peasant inspection. See GARF f. 5677, op. 1, d. 9, ll. 1–3.

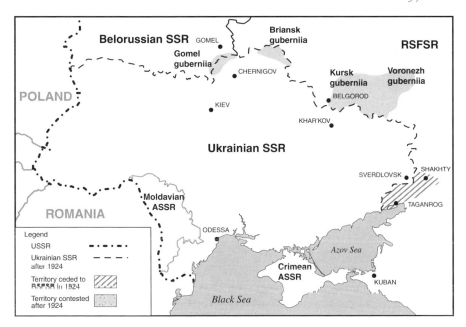

Map 4.2 The Ukrainian SSR in 1924. The map shows the territories that were ceded to the RSFSR in 1924 and the parts of Kursk, Voronezh, Gomel, and Briansk *gubernii* that Ukraine had demanded from the RSFSR and Belorussian SSR.

petitions were false documents: that the petitions' authors and sole supporters were "three teachers and a few people of indeterminate professions" and that the petitions' demands did not represent the will of the masses. He urged TsIK to ignore such "false statements" for unification with Ukraine that had been produced "artificially" by a handful of Ukrainian nationalists.[45]

Ethnographers also questioned Ukraine's claims—but on the grounds that it was difficult to evaluate the ethnographic principle in the contested *gubernii* due to their complicated ethnographic mix. The border region between the Ukrainian SSR and the RSFSR had been settled at the same time from the north and south.[46] As a result, Kursk, Voronezh, and Briansk did not contain large homogeneous areas of Great Russians and Ukrainians but were instead "dotted with interspersed settlements."[47] A decision about the border that satisfied one part of the population was sure to disappoint the other. Statisticians from the Central Statistical Administration contended that the region had ex-

45. GARF f. 6892, op. 1, d. 19, l. 5. Boldyrev was the secretary of the RSFSR Council of People's Commissars.

46. For a discussion of the settlement of the region see GARF f. 6892, op. 1, d. 21, ll. 30–32; d. 4, l. 143.

47. GARF f. 6892, op. 1, d. 4, l. 330b. S. N. Vvedenskii from the Moscow Archeological Institute and Dmitrii Bagalei (an expert on Ukraine) compiled ethnographical materials for these deliberations.

perienced "the Ukrainization of the Great Russian population and the Russification of the Ukrainian population"; they argued that the regime could not
undertake the "exact delimitation" of this area "in accordance with the ethnographic principle" due to "the presence of *narodnosti* of the transitional
type."[48] The statisticians also called into question the data from the 1920 census that the Ukrainians had presented to argue for Kursk and Voronezh. They
maintained that census takers in the republic had based their determination of
natsional'nost' on "native language" and not on national consciousness. (Of
course, Soviet authorities and experts had not had a problem equating native
language with nationality in the Belorussian case.) The statisticians further argued that the 1920 data were inconclusive even as a determinant of native language: census takers had interviewed only the heads of households, while "the
younger generation speaks a different language" from the elders, "often Russian."[49]

Economists based in Voronezh and Kursk concurred with the ethnographic
analysis of the contested *gubernii,* but they also argued that ethnographic data
were irrelevant in the face of the overwhelming economic argument for leaving
these *gubernii* in the RSFSR.[50] The economists explained that both Voronezh
and Kursk were part of the Central Black Earth economic-administrative
oblast, which served as the granary for Moscow region; furthermore, Kursk
was a major site of sugar manufacture, with large sugar factories that served
much of Russia. Asserting that these *gubernii* were integral to the RSFSR's
economic enterprises and that a change in their borders would have negative
economic consequences for the entire Union, Gosplan argued against their
transfer to the Ukrainian SSR.[51] Most of the all-union commissariats agreed
with Gosplan and noted that the RSFSR could meet the economic needs of
these *gubernii* for fuel, scientific expertise, and goods.

For Enukidze and other TsIK leaders, it was the question of ethnohistorical
development that most differentiated the Ukrainian case from the Belorussian
case: while the Belorussians "lacked" national consciousness, the Ukrainians
had too much. Enukidze noted that the Soviet regime sometimes put ethnographic considerations over all-union economic considerations in order to further the development of weak tribes and nationalities. "This was done for the
Kirgiz republic and for our northern national oblasts." But the Ukrainian SSR
was already "a republic strong in its own right, and a powerful nation," and
did not need such treatment. To transfer "Ukrainian populations from Great
Russian oblasts" to Ukraine would economically weaken both the RSFSR and
the Ukrainian SSR. The "republics of a united union cannot base decisions on
the national principle alone"—and the Soviet government should not weaken

---

48. GARF f. 5677, op. 1, d. 9, ll. 1–10b.
49. GARF f. 6892, op. 1, d. 21, l. 16.
50. GARF f. 6892, op. 1, d. 4, ll. 147–48.
51. Ibid., l. 3; d. 19, ll. 9–14.

important regions to redraw borders according to "some kind of dubious and obscure pure national trait," Enukidze maintained.[52] In an aside that seemed calculated to anger Ukrainian leaders, Enukidze added that there was little difference between Ukrainians and Great Russians; they had a "common root," closely resembled one another "in culture and language," and had "lived interspersed for many centuries."[53] (Of course, Enukidze and his colleagues could have made the same argument with regard to the Belorussians, had they so wished.)

While Enukidze was dismissive of the ethnographic principle in this case, he was nonetheless reluctant to base the regionalization commission's decision solely on the economic orientation of the contested *gubernii*. Russia and Ukraine shared numerous economic enterprises, and the RSFSR representatives argued that much of Ukraine was economically oriented toward Russia. Enukidze expressed concern that to invoke the economic principle alone would invite endless disputes between the republics and bring "economic destruction" to the entire region. He continued to maintain that the economic principle was the "most important" consideration in the Ukrainian case. But he argued that some ethnographically Ukrainian regions—defined as "regions where a Ukrainian population now predominates and where the conversational language is Ukrainian"—should be "given to Ukraine" so as to prevent a "heated battle" with dire administrative and economic consequences. In particular, he recommended that the RSFSR cede to Ukraine much of Voronezh *guberniia*.[54] TsIK and the party gave serious consideration to Enukidze's recommendations. Ultimately, Ukraine lost most of Taganrog *okrug* to the North Caucasus *krai,* but was granted slightly more than half of the territory that it had requested from the RSFSR.[55]

By 1924, all three principles—ethnographic, economic, and administrative—had become the criteria (sometimes explicit, sometimes unstated) for border-making and for the resolution of border disputes. Deliberations about the Ukrainian and Belorussian borders set important precedents, which Soviet leaders, experts, and local elites (who became familiar with these cases through the press, political meetings, and word of mouth) cited when they turned their attention to other parts of the Soviet Union. It bears mentioning that the League of Nations also considered economic, ethnographic, and administrative criteria in its discussions about the borders of the new European nation states in the aftermath of the Paris Peace Conference.[56] But where the

52. GARF f. 6892, op. 1, d. 19, ll. 16–17.

53. Ibid.

54. Ibid., ll. 8, 17.

55. See Martin, *Affirmative Action Empire,* 279. Kursk, Voronezh, and Briansk remained part of the RSFSR and Gomel remained part of the Belorussian SSR even as some of the *uezdy* from these *gubernii* were transferred to Ukraine.

56. On the national idea in the aftermath of World War I see C. A. Macartney, *National States and National Minorities* (London, 1934); Margaret MacMillan, *Paris 1919: Six Months that*

League of Nations evaluated the European nation states as autarkic units, the TsIK deliberations made it clear that the Soviet national republics and oblasts would be evaluated as interconnected parts of a larger political, economic, and administrative whole. The TsIK deliberations also suggested that the relative weight given to the economic, ethnographic, and administrative principles would shift in relation to the perceived place of a given region or people on the timeline of historical development.

There was another important difference between the Soviet and European-Wilsonian approaches to the question of national minorities. While the Paris Peace Conference participants aimed to protect the rights of national minorities in the new European states through a series of laws and treaties, TsIK approached this goal by calling for the delimitation of small national-territorial units within larger ones "where there are compact nationalities [natsional'nosti]."[57] Thus, as the new borders of the Ukrainian and Belorussian republics were established, TsIK embarked on the "internal" or "lower-level" regionalization of these republics. It evaluated the economic orientation and the ethnographic composition of the republics and created administrative subunits or institutions for national minorities. For example, within the Ukrainian SSR, the Soviet government established German, Bulgarian, Polish, Belorussian, Albanian, Moldavian, Jewish, Czech, and even Russian village soviets and/or national territories.[58] The supranational structure of the Soviet state, together with the lower-level administrative subunits, were supposed to safeguard the rights of national minorities within each republic (by limiting the power of the titular nationalities over them) and facilitate the Sovietization of all of the Union's peoples.

Border-Making in Central Asia

Much of the older Western scholarship about the national-territorial delimitation of Central Asia asserts that "Moscow" drew the new borders in 1924 without local participation, and on the basis of "neither ethnographical nor economic principles."[59] Indeed, while historians have characterized the creation of the Ukrainian and Belorussian republics as an expression of the "na-

---

Changed the World (New York, 2001); and Mark Mazower, *Dark Continent: Europe's Twentieth Century* (New York, 1998).

57. GARF f. 6892, op. 1, d. 42, l. 31.

58. GARF f. 6892, op. 1, d. 27, ll. 35–37. On lower-level regionalization see P. M. Alampiev, *Ekonomicheskoe raionirovanie SSSR* (Moscow, 1959).

59. Quoted from Robert Conquest, *The Last Empire* (London, 1962), 29. Works appearing after the breakup of the Soviet Union have repeated this myth. Olivier Roy writes that the Soviets "amused themselves" by purposefully making borders that bore little correlation to the ethnographic composition of the population. Olivier Roy, *The New Central Asia: The Creation of Nations* (London, 2000), 68. The Roy quote is cited in Adrienne Lynn Edgar's excellent review of the book in *Kritika: Explorations in Russian and Eurasian History* 3, no.1 (2002): 182–90. Ahmed Rashid has argued that Stalin drew "arbitrary boundary divisions" and "created republics that

tional idea," they have characterized the Central Asian delimitation—which eliminated Turkestan, Bukhara, and Khorezm and reorganized their territories into a number of new national republics—as an example of "divide and rule."[60] The archival record suggests, however, that the Soviet approach to Central Asia was consistent with its approach to the Belorussian and Ukrainian republics. In all of these cases, Soviet administrators and experts evaluated ethnographic, economic, and administrative criteria, while giving priority to larger all-union concerns. The archival record further suggests that the classic argument about the delimitation, which asserts that Soviet leaders set out to subordinate Central Asia by drawing borders in a way that would intentionally sow discord, misses the mark.[61]

First, there is significant evidence that the delimitation was not just Moscow-driven but was in large part a collaborative effort between Moscow-based leaders and local (national) communist elites from former Turkestan, Bukhara, and Khorezm who had made common cause with the Bolsheviks in the early 1920s. Many local communists—and the Jadids in particular—saw "the nation" as a means for promoting economic and cultural modernization.[62] Some of them helped shape the national delimitation of 1924 through their participation in the Territorial Committee of the Central Asian Bureau (of the party's Central Committee). Having learned from the Ukrainian and Belorussian cases, they framed their claims in ethnographic, economic, and administrative terms.[63] Like Ukrainian and Belorussian leaders, they mobilized

had little geographic or ethnic rationale." Rashid, *Jihad: The Rise of Militant Islam in Central Asia* (New Haven, 2002), 88.

60. The delimitation created the Turkmen SSR, the Uzbek SSR, and the Tajik ASSR (within the Uzbek SSR). It also created the Kara-Kirgiz AO, which was renamed the Kirgiz AO in 1925 and turned into an ASSR in 1926; and it created the Kirgiz ASSR, which was renamed the Kazakh ASSR in 1925. For an excellent account of the national delimitation see Arne Haugen, *The Establishment of National Republics in Soviet Central Asia* (Basingstoke, 2003). Also see Shoshana Keller, "The Central Asian Bureau: An Essential Tool in Governing Soviet Turkestan," *Central Asian Survey* 22, no. 2–3 (2003): 281–97. For an account of the making of the Turkmen SSR see Adrienne Lynn Edgar, *Tribal Nation: The Making of Soviet Turkmenistan* (Princeton, 2004). For a summary of the Soviet literature on the delimitation see R. Vaidyanath, *The Formation of the Soviet Central Asian Republics* (New Delhi, 1967). On the Kazakhs and the Kirgiz see I. I. Zarubin, *Naselenie Samarkandskoi oblasti, Trudy Komissii po izucheniiu plemennogo sostava naseleniia SSSR i sopredel'nykh stran,* vol. 10 (Leningrad, 1926), 19.

61. The "divide and rule" argument is repeated (in various forms) in many works on the delimitation. See, for example, Olaf Caroe, *Soviet Empire: The Turks of Central Asia and Stalinism* (London, 1953); Hélène Carrére d'Encausse, *The End of the Soviet Empire: The Triumph of the Nations* (New York, 1993); and Steven Sabol, "The Creation of Soviet Central Asia: The 1924 National Delimitation," *Central Asian Survey* 14, no. 2 (1995): 225–41.

62. On the role of local elites in the delimitation see Haugen, *Establishment of National Republics in Soviet Central Asia,* and Edgar, *Tribal Nation.*

63. See Islamov's speech at a 1924 VTsIK meeting about the delimitation. "Natsional'noe razmezhevanie Srednei Azii: Zasedanie vtoroi sessii VTsIK 14 oktiabriia 1924 g.," *Narodnoe khoziaistvo Srednei Azii,* no. 4 (1924): 187–92. Also see I. Khodorov, "Natsional'noe razmezhevanie Srednei Azii," *Novyi Vostok,* no. 8–9 (1925): 65–81; M. Nemchenko, *Natsional'noe*

local populations for the Soviet project, integrated local lands and peoples into the Soviet Union, and subjugated themselves to Moscow in exchange for national-territorial status and local power.[64]

Second, economists, ethnographers, and other expert-consultants also left an imprint on the national delimitation of 1924, both directly and indirectly.[65] In part, these experts influenced the delimitation through the Commission for the Regionalization of Central Asia, a branch of the TsIK regionalization commission that collected maps, economic inventories, census data, and other materials for the Central Asian Bureau to use for the delimitation.[66] Economists from Gosplan and Goskolonit provided the commission with a region-by-region economic assessment of Turkestan; ethnographers from KIPS provided the commission with ethnographic maps and reports.[67] Furthermore, even before there was a concrete plan to delimit Central Asia on national lines, the ethnographers shaped how Moscow-based officials and local national leaders viewed the region.[68] In 1918 Ivan Zarubin had worked with Soviet administrators in Turkestan to produce lists of the region's nationalities; in 1920,

---

razmezhevanie Srednei Azii (Moscow, 1925), 27; and Haugen, *Establishment of National Republics in Soviet Central Asia.* The Central Asian leaders also learned from the example of the Caucasus. In 1918, Transcaucasian leaders pursued their own national delimitation to establish the Azerbaijan, Georgian, and Armenian republics. Each republic also began its own internal regionalization. After the integration of these republics into the Soviet Union, TsIK began to reevaluate their borders. The Georgian deliberations were the most contentious, as Soviet leaders and experts argued for the delimitation of Abkhazian, Ossetian, and Ajarian national subunits within the Georgian republic. GARF f. 6892, op. 1, d. 42, ll. 28–36.

64. The Territorial Committee and its Turkmen, Uzbek, Kazakh, Kirgiz, and later Tajik national subcommittees worked on proposals for the prospective borders of new national republics and oblasts. See Haugen, *Establishment of National Republics in Soviet Central Asia,* chapters 6–8, and Rakhim Masov, *Tadzhiki: Istoriia s grifom "sovershenno sekretno"* (Dushanbe, 1995), 158–91.

65. Haugen and Keller, focusing on the proceedings of the Territorial Committee, discuss the involvement of local elites in the delimitation process. Haugen argues that experts were not involved in the delimitation. See Keller, "Central Asian Bureau: An Essential Tool in Governing Soviet Turkestan," and Haugen, *Establishment of National Republics in Soviet Central Asia,* 184.

66. GARF f. 6892, op. 1, d. 42, ll. 1–4. Hereafter referred to as the Central Asian regionalization commission.

67. GARF f. 6892, op. 1, d. 42, l. 21. See Komissiia po raionirovaniiu Srednei Azii, *Materialy po raionirovaniiu Srednei Azii,* vol. 1, pt. 1, *Territoriia i naselenie Bukhary i Khorezma: Bukhara* (Tashkent, 1926). Nemchenko quotes Bartol'd's work at length in his *Natsional'noe razmezhevanie Srednei Azii.*

68. Zarubin noted that famine, civil war, and the Basmachi made it impossible to do ethnographic research. On the Basmachi see Richard Lorenz, "Economic Bases of the Basmachi Movement in the Farghana Valley," in *Muslim Communities Reemerge: Historical Perspectives on Nationality, Politics, and Opposition in the Former Soviet Union and Yugoslavia,* ed. Edward Allworth et al. (Durham, 1994). In June 1920, Lenin called for the creation of "ethnographic and other" maps of Turkestan with Uzbek, Kirgiz, and Turkmen subdivisions. See "Zamechaniia na proekte Turkestanskoi komissii," *Leninskii sbornik* 34 (1942): 323–26. KIPS was working on such maps.

Aleksandr Samoilovich, Vasilii Bartol'd, and Zarubin had provided Narkom-nats with a general, albeit incomplete, ethnographic analysis of Turkestan and the Kirgiz steppe.[69] The ethnographers had used different criteria to map out the "Asiatic" versus the "European" regions of the former Russian Empire—which ultimately affected Soviet border-making. Whereas the ethnographers relied on linguistic data to map the ethnographic borders of the Belorussian and Ukrainian republics, they took a "complex" ethnographic approach to Central Asia, studying local cultures, religions, kinship structures, *byt,* physical type, and languages.[70] (For example, Bartol'd approximated the ethnographic borders of the Kirgiz and Kazakh republics on the basis of ethnographic and historical data about *byt,* physical type, and kinship structure.)

Third, the Central Asian Bureau reevaluated contested borders *after* 1924, and continued to seek the advice of economists and ethnographers. Soviet officials with the Central Asian Bureau acknowledged from the start that Central Asia's new national-territorial borders would be provisional. Isaak Zelenskii, the secretary of the Central Asian Bureau and the chairman of its Territorial Committee, cautioned in 1924 that there were "neither sufficient statistical data about the economic and national composition of the regions nor sufficient knowledge about the indigenous workers" of the region "to make anything but preliminary decisions."[71] Administrators and experts corroborated Zelenskii's statements about the shortage of reliable data, noting that census data for Turkestan were flawed and that Khorezm and Bukhara (former protectorates of the Russian Empire) were "a completely blank page" from the "perspective of nationality" as well as "from administrative and economic perspectives."[72] After 1924, the Central Asian Bureau proclaimed that the borders of the new Central Asian republics would be revised "in accordance with

69. "Komissiia po izucheniiu plemennogo sostava naseleniia Rossii," in Rossiiskaia Akademiia nauk, *Otchet o deiatel'nosti Rossiiskoi Akademii nauk za 1919 god* (Petrograd, 1920), 304–6. Zarubin used data from the agricultural census of 1917 and statistics from former imperial institutions. He used the terms *narodnost'* and *natsional'nost'* interchangeably in his discussion.

70. Rossiiskaia Akademiia nauk, *Izvlecheniia iz protokolov zasedanii komissii v 1917 i 1918 godakh, Izvestiia Komissii po izucheniiu plemennogo sostava naseleniia Rossii,* vol. 2 (Petrograd, 1919), 8–9, 17, and "Komissiia po izucheniiu plemennogo sostava naseleniia Rossii," 304–6.

71. I. Zelenskii, "Natsional'no-gosudarstvennoe razmezhevanie Srednei Azii," in *Natsional'no-gosudarstvennoe razmezhevanie Srednei Azii,* ed. I. Vareikis and I. Zelenskii (Tashkent, 1924), 71–72.

72. GARF f. 6892, op. 1, d. 42, l. 3. Also Khodorov, "Natsional'noe razmezhevanie," 70, and I. I. Zarubin, *Spisok narodnostei Turkestanskogo kraia, Trudy Komissii po izucheniiu plemennogo sostava naseleniia Rossii i sopredel'nykh stran,* vol. 9 (Leningrad, 1925). Zarubin used data for Turkestan from the 1917 agricultural census and the 1920 census. Neither the Russian Empire nor the Soviet regime had taken a census in Bukhara and Khorezm; some data about the population's ethnographic composition existed, but the experts had less information about these regions than about others. These former protectorates of the Russian Empire became people's republics in 1920.

the will of the people," and that national minority subregions would be created, as needed, within the new national republics.[73] The Central Asian regionalization commission gave serious consideration to petitions from local communities as well as from republic- and oblast-level governments.[74] In order to evaluate these petitions, the commission solicited the expert opinions of ethnographers and economists and initiated new ethnographic and economic studies of contested regions.[75]

Most significantly, the "divide and rule" argument, with its implication that the Soviet approach to Central Asia was similar to the European approach to Africa, fails to capture what was distinctive about Soviet rule.[76] To be sure, the Soviet regime wanted to secure its hold on Central Asia. To achieve this end, it did indeed seek to eliminate traditional loyalties. But its ambitions were much greater than this. The Soviet regime aspired to reorganize and modernize Central Asia; it forged an alliance with the radical educated elites in the region and helped them to overthrow the former religious leaders in order to transform the entire region along secular, national lines.[77] Unlike tsarist Russia or the European colonial powers, which defined their metropoles in opposition to their colonized peripheries, the Soviet Union defined itself as the sum of its parts.[78] Soviet leaders argued that the fate of the revolution depended on the ethnohistorical development of *all* the lands and peoples within its borders. They chose to reorganize Central Asia along national, and not tribal, lines because they saw "the nation" as a modern (postfeudal) form of social and economic organization. By eliminating the vestiges of feudalism and reorganizing people into nationalities, the delimitation was intended to further the program of

73. Zelenskii, "Natsional'no-gosudarstvennoe razmezhevanie Srednei Azii," 71–72.

74. See the discussion below.

75. KIPS provided the TsIK regionalization commission and the Central Asian regionalization commission with copies of its maps for use in the evaluation of border disputes. See, for example, the St. Petersburg Branch of the Archive of the Russian Academy of Sciences (PFA RAN) f. 135, op. 1, d. 21, ll. 155, 157.

76. Of course, this is a generalization. There was more than one European approach.

77. On the "divide and rule" argument as applied to the African case see J. F. A. Ajayi, "Colonialism: An Episode in African History," in L. H. Gann and Peter Duignan, eds., *Colonialism in Africa, 1870–1960*, vol. 1, *The History and Politics of Colonialism 1870–1914* (Cambridge, 1969). Ajayi argues that the European powers chose to forge alliances with the "submissive chiefs" as opposed to the "radical educated elite" and aimed to sow intertribal discord (p. 505). In the past decade, historians and anthropologists in the field of colonial studies have challenged the "divide and rule" model as it was applied to the European colonial empires. See, for example, Ann Laura Stoler and Frederick Cooper, "Between Metropole and Colony: Rethinking a Research Agenda," in *Tensions of Empire: Colonial Cultures in a Bourgeois World,* ed. Frederick Cooper and Ann Laura Stoler (Berkeley, 1997). To be sure, most of the European powers also sought to reorganize and modernize vast parts of their colonial domains, and succeeded in doing so. But only the Soviets pursued nation-making so seriously and so systematically.

78. Scholars of the British and French empires have discussed the juridical and other distinctions that differentiated the metropole's citizens from the colonies' subjects. See, for example, Crawford Young, *The African Colonial State in Comparative Perspective* (New Haven, 1994), 44.

state-sponsored evolutionism: to speed the population along the Marxist historical timeline and facilitate the transition to socialism.

National Identities and Double Assimilation in Central Asia

Throughout history, the delimitation of new borders has resulted in violence, struggles over resources, and irredentist claims. The national delimitation of Central Asia was no different. Until the advent of Soviet power and the popularization of the idea that "official" nationalities could monopolize land and resources, most inhabitants of Central Asia did not define themselves in national terms. Diverse peoples lived interspersed; many had at one time been nomadic, and some still were. Ethnic, linguistic, religious, clan, and economic divisions often did not coincide, and people often claimed several identities at once.[79]

The national delimitation changed the political and social terrain of Central Asia, and led to a realignment of interests and identities. Members of the new dominant nationalities (Uzbek clans in the Uzbek SSR, for example) stood to gain access to land, water sources, and other important resources from this reorganization of the region and began to redefine their interests and concerns in "national terms." At the same time, members of the new national minorities (such as Kazakh native speakers in the Uzbek SSR) faced discrimination, forced assimilation, and the loss of land and livelihood. These new "national minorities" also began to use the language of *narodnost'* to assert their rights. In a number of cases, entire villages sent collective letters and petitions to Soviet leaders, complaining of injustices and requesting the redrawing of borders. TsIK collected dozens of these documents, had them translated into Russian, and forwarded them to the Central Asian regionalization commission for evaluation in the context of other materials pertaining to border disputes.

Self-identified Uzbeks in the new Kirgiz and Kazakh autonomous national republics and self-identified Kazakhs and Kirgiz in the new Uzbek union republic wrote petitions with almost identical grievances—suggesting that the dominant nationalities of each of the new republics behaved in a similar manner toward the minorities within their borders. Tashkent *uezd*, which was split among the Uzbek SSR, Kirgiz ASSR, and Kazakh ASSR, illustrates this point.[80]

79. Ethnographers noted that it was usually necessary to ask supplementary questions about native language, conversational language, religion, and kinship group in order to figure out a respondent's nationality. PFA RAN f. 135, op. 1, d. 21, ll. 72–72ob. On the complex nature of local identities see John Samuel Schoeberlein-Engel, "Identity in Central Asia: Construction and Contention in the Conceptions of 'Ozbek,' 'Tajik,' 'Muslim,' 'Samarquandi' and Other Groups," Ph.D. diss., Harvard University, 1994.

80. GARF f. 3316, op. 64, d. 46, ll. 5, 7, 19–21, 27–28. For a full discussion of the initial deliberations over Tashkent see Haugen, *Establishment of National Republics in Soviet Central Asia*, 194–206. For a discussion of the dispute see Khodorov, "Natsional'noe razmezhevanie," 68–70. The Soviet government gave Tashkent city to the Uzbek SSR, but split the surrounding region partly on the basis of data from the 1920 census.

In 1925, petitioners who identified themselves as "Kazakhs" from villages in Tashkent *uezd* of the Uzbek SSR sent petitions to Stalin, Lev Kamenev, Mikhail Kalinin, and Enukidze requesting unification with the new Kazakh ASSR.[81] The petitioners reported that the Uzbek government was actively violating Kazakh national rights by discriminating against Kazakhs and paying "insufficient attention" to their economic and cultural development. In distinguishing what made the villages in question "Kazakh" and not "Uzbek," the petitioners emphasized "the close economic and cultural ties of the population of the villages with Kazakhstan, the location of the villages, their national composition, and commonalities with Kazakh customs and practices."[82]

Meanwhile, Uzbek-identified residents from Tashkent *uezd* of the Kirgiz AO (soon changed to an ASSR) expressed similar concerns and voiced puzzlement about the new nationalist politics in their region.[83] An August 1925 petition sent to the Central Asian Bureau, the Soviet of Nationalities, and the Uzbek Communist Party in the name of "thirty thousand Uzbeks of Iskander *volost'*" (signed by thirteen men) stated that the sizeable Uzbek population of the *volost'* faced a wide range of abuses. The petitioners explained that the Uzbeks of Iskander at first were "not troubled" by the demarcation of new borders, believing that such formalities could not matter "under Communist Party leadership." Thus, they continued, the Uzbeks were shocked when the Kirgiz "introduced policies against Uzbek interests" and began to insult them openly.[84] The petitioners offered a detailed description of how Kirgiz officials were attempting to exclude Uzbeks from village life and force them from the region. Uzbeks had to pay higher taxes and faced police harassment and unfair judicial treatment. Moreover, all literature and official correspondence in the *volost'* was in the Kirgiz language. According to the petitioners, the Kirgiz government discriminated against Uzbek native speakers whenever economic and cultural resources were at stake. Before regionalization, nine Uzbek-language schools had served the *volost'*, but in 1925 only one remained. According to the petitioners, Kirgiz officials told them: "It is a Kirgiz state and you are obliged to study Kirgiz." But even Uzbeks who attempted to do so were

81. GARF f. 3316, op. 16a, d. 189, ll. 2–3.

82. Ibid. This case was reviewed with other border disputes in 1927 and the Kazakh claims were denied—largely on economic and administrative grounds.

83. The Kara-Kirgiz AO became the Kirgiz AO in 1925 and became the Kirgiz ASSR in 1926. (This should not be confused with the *original* Kirgiz ASSR, which was established in 1920 and was renamed the Kazakh ASSR in 1925.)

84. The *volost'*, also called Aleksandrovsk, was part of Syr-Dar'insk *guberniia*. GARF f. 3316, op. 16a, d. 189, ll. 34–36. A *volost'* is an administrative unit within an *uezd* or *raion*. Copies of the petition were sent directly to the Central Asian Bureau, the Soviet of Nationalities, and the Central Committee of the Uzbek Communist Party. A copy was forwarded to the TsIK regionalization commission.

scorned as outsiders: Uzbek youth who learned the Kirgiz language were still shut out of Kirgiz schools as "they say the allotment is filled by Kirgiz."[85]

The petitioners from Iskander recounted their interactions with Soviet institutions and their repeated attempts to seek justice. They had sent representatives to Moscow to acquaint "the appropriate organs" with Uzbek life in Kirgizia—but these representatives were arrested by Kirgiz authorities on the road. In further retaliation, Kirgiz authorities had called for the arrest of "twenty to thirty [Uzbek] peasants." "We fled to Tashkent. And there are other comrades who are hiding in the hills." The petition concluded that, as a result of political turmoil, Uzbek agriculture in the area was near ruin and the Uzbeks of Kirgizia would face "an unavoidable reversion to nomadism." To avoid such an outcome, the petitioners asked that their *volost'* be included in the Uzbek SSR; short of this, the petitioners asked the regime to resettle the Uzbeks of Iskander in Uzbekistan.[86] Intentionally or not, the petitioners echoed the regime's rhetoric about state-sponsored evolutionism: they suggested that the Soviet regime must come to their aid to prevent their backsliding to a feudal mode of existence.

Evaluating border disputes in Tashkent *uezd,* TsIK and the Central Asian regionalization commission weighed ethnographic, economic, and administrative considerations.[87] In the case of Iskander, the commission reviewed the submitted petitions, consulted with expert-consultants, and drew up a detailed response. First, it evaluated Iskander's ethnographic composition: analyzing data from the 1920 census, it concluded that the region was 47.3 percent Uzbek, 19.8 percent Tajik, 31.6 percent Kara-Kirgiz and Kirgiz-Kazakh, and 1.3 percent Russian.[88] Next, the commission evaluated Iskander from an economic perspective. It determined that it was more convenient to get from Iskander to the Uzbek economic center than to the Kirgiz economic center. It also noted that unlike most Kirgiz regions, Iskander was a settled agricultural region: that its economic orientation was similar to that of the Uzbek parts of Tashkent.[89]

However, even though ethnographic and economic data suggested that Iskander should be transferred to Uzbekistan, the Central Asian regionalization commission argued otherwise. It did so on the basis of larger administrative concerns, citing the potential conflicts that could result from such a

85. Ibid.

86. Ibid.

87. I. Magidovich, the head of the Central Asian regionalization commission, prepared the report, which had sections on "national composition," "geographical position" (which focused on administrative-territorial issues), "economic description," and "general conclusions." ibid., ll. 37–39.

88. The census had conflated the Kara-Kirgiz and Kirgiz-Kazakh so separate figures did not exist. On these groups see Zarubin, *Naselenie Samarkandskoi oblasti,* 19–21.

89. GARF f. 3316, op. 16a, d. 189, ll. 37–39.

change in borders. The commission explained that between Iskander *volost'* and the Uzbek SSR lay Kosh-Kurgan province—a part of the Kazakh ASSR that bordered the Kirgiz and Uzbek republics. If Iskander was unified with Uzbekistan, Kosh-Kurgan would be cut off from the Kazakh ASSR and unified with Uzbekistan by default. Thus, two provinces would be transferred to Uzbekistan. The commission speculated that such a transfer might provoke Kazakh officials to dishonor their side of the (already strained) agreement made between the Kazakh and Uzbek governments in 1924 at the time of the delimitation. The commission, nonetheless, acknowledged that the Uzbek petitioners' concerns were legitimate and deserved to be addressed. Attempting to come up with a compromise, it recommended that Iskander remain in Kirgizia, but as part of a separate Uzbek national region with Uzbek-language institutions.[90] The example of Iskander illustrates how efforts to mediate between local and all-union concerns gave rise over time to an increasingly complicated administrative-territorial framework.

Another region that saw intense disputes after 1924 was the Fergana Valley, a fertile cotton-growing region with rich deposits of natural resources, also on the Uzbek-Kirgiz border. This valley was of tremendous economic and cultural importance, and had an ethnographically mixed population. At the time of the delimitation, Kirgiz and Uzbek leaders had both asked for the valley's major towns. Kirgiz leaders acknowledged that none of these towns had Kirgiz majorities. But, arguing that it was essential from an economic standpoint to include commercial centers in their national territory, they requested towns that were close to Kirgiz settlements.[91] The Central Asian Bureau was sympathetic to the Kirgiz argument, and evaluated the ethnographic composition and the economic orientation of all the towns in the border region. Ultimately, it gave Jalal-Abad and Osh to the Kirgiz, and Andijan, Margilan and most other towns in the valley to the Uzbeks.[92]

Soon after the delimitation, communities on both sides of the border began to write petitions and letters of protest. In one case, the Uzbek-identified residents of six villages of Aim *volost'* within Jalal-Abad sent or hand-delivered to Soviet authorities more than sixteen petitions requesting unification with Uzbekistan. The petitioners explained that the Kara-Dar'ia river bisected Aim into two distinct national regions: the two villages on the right bank were Kirgiz, and the six villages on the left bank (where the petitioners lived) were each about 75 percent Uzbek and 25 percent Kirgiz. The petitioners claimed, however, that even Kirgiz who lived on the left bank were "by language, customs (*byt*), culture, and economic orientation more closely connected to the Uzbeks

90. Ibid. It noted that this region would be similar to Kenimekh, a Kazakh national region in Uzbekistan. On Kenimekh, see N. B. Arkhipov, *Sredne-Aziatskie respubliki* (Moscow-Leningrad, 1930), 150–51, and Khodorov, "Natsional'noe razmezhevanie," 69–70.

91. Haugen, *Establishment of National Republics in Soviet Central Asia*, 188–94.

92. Ibid.

than to the Kirgiz."[93] The petitioners suggested that the identity of their Kirgiz co-villagers had been shaped through cultural contact with Uzbeks. It was, perhaps, such a perspective about the dynamic nature of nationality that made the petitioners concerned about being cut off from the new Uzbek national republic. If Kirgiz in an Uzbek village had become Uzbeks, would Uzbeks in a Kirgiz state become Kirgiz?

The petitioners also maintained that it was an economic hardship to their villages, which were agricultural, to remain in the Kirgiz ASSR, whose economic focus was cattle breeding. They noted that the Uzbek government "provides its population with agronomical help, tractors, and help with inventories," while the Kirgiz government "gives no economic aid" to Uzbek peasants engaged in agriculture. The petitioners further explained that the Uzbek-Kirgiz border had become a real barrier: that the citizens of the Kirgiz ASSR were forced to use the administrative, economic, and medical institutions in their own republic. In particular, the petitioners complained that the delimitation disrupted "close economic ties" between Aim and a neighboring region, Andijan, which had ended up in the Uzbek SSR.[94]

The petitioners from Aim framed their petitions in the language of the Soviet regime and quickly learned how to direct them to the appropriate government organs. Like practiced bureaucrats, they documented the appeals process. A spring 1927 petition to Stalin, for example, recounted all previous interactions with Soviet officials.[95] According to the petition, Uzbek representatives from Aim first presented their case to the Central Asian regionalization commission and the Central Asian Bureau in Tashkent. The Central Asian Bureau redirected them to the TsIK regionalization commission in Moscow, where the representatives went (twice) with petitions in hand. In February 1926, a representative from the TsIK regionalization commission came to Aim to assess the situation; he recommended that Aim and Andijan be included together in the same republic—either in the Uzbek SSR or the Kirgiz ASSR.[96] Dissatisfied with this response, the petitioners sent another representative to Moscow. Soon thereafter, Iakov Peters and two other members of a regionalization subcommission came to Aim. Peters reassured the petitioners that the question would be settled in their favor—and in September 1926 TsIK did in fact resolve to cede the six villages of Aim to Uzbekistan. But in the face of protests from the Kirgiz government, the TsIK resolution was not implemented. Instead, in January 1927 Bashim Kul'besherov and two other mem-

93. GARF f. 3316, op. 64, d. 411, ll. 9–11.

94. Ibid.

95. Ibid., ll. 6–8. The Secret Department of the Central Committee forwarded the petition to Enukidze. The petition had 380 signatures and claimed to represent 18,000 people. Also see GARF f. 6892, op. 1, d. 29, ll. 12, 15.

96. GARF f. 3316, op. 64, d. 411, ll. 6–8. The representative was Chanyshev. On his visit, Chanyshev also went to Andijan, where Kirgiz communities had been petitioning for their inclusion in the Kirgiz ASSR.

bers of a new TsIK Parity Commission showed up in Aim. Kul'besherov gave the villagers cause to be hopeful. But in March, he announced that the question could not be decided until the next meeting of the Congress of Soviets.[97]

What is most clear from the Aim petitioners' narrative is that the stakes increased over time. While Soviet authorities were deliberating on the fate of the petitioners' villages, the Kirgiz government had started to imprison Uzbek peasants and "engage in hostile acts" against the local Uzbek population. Initially, the petitioners expressed concern about a loss of land and resources. Later, they expressed anxiety about their safety and survival as "Uzbeks" in a Kirgiz republic.[98] Through the active process of appeals and the struggle for fundamental rights, petitioners developed a heightened sense of what Soviet officials defined as "national consciousness." Did all the petitioners really consider themselves to be members of a discrete Uzbek nationality? It is impossible to say. The point is that the petitioners used the language of nationality in their interactions with the state, and in doing so helped to make official nationality categories real. The petitioners did not question the official assumption that "nationality" was linked to land and other resources. Instead, the petitioners argued that they were entitled to such resources as a matter of national rights.

From their villages in the Kirgiz ASSR, the Aim petitioners did not understand why it was taking Soviet leaders so long to reach a decision about their *volost'*. But in Moscow and Tashkent, Soviet officials were drowning in a sea of claims and counterclaims to contested regions on or near the Uzbek-Kirgiz, Uzbek-Turkmen, Uzbek-Kazakh, and Uzbek-Tajik borders. As it attempted to mediate disputes between Uzbekistan and Kirgizia, the TsIK Parity Commission (formed in December 1926 and comprised of representatives from both republics and from all-union organizations) evaluated a long list of disputed territories.[99] Indeed, Kul'besherov's visit to Aim in January 1927 was part of a larger trip that included stops in a number of other contested regions in the Fergana Valley.[100] After his visit, Kul'besherov had concluded that the six villages of Aim *volost'* should be transferred to the Uzbek SSR. But he postponed the resolution of the Aim question because of concerns about parity; he sought to evaluate all of the Uzbek-Kirgiz territorial disputes as a whole in order to come up with a compromise suitable to both sides.

---

97. Ibid. Kul'besherov, the head of the Soviet of Nationalities, was the head of this commission. The other representatives were Ali-Khodzhaev from the Uzbek SSR and Mendeshev from the RSFSR.

98. Ibid. In 1925, the Presidium of the Soviet of Nationalities of TsIK warned the Kirgiz government to "take measures to stop the repression" of the "citizens of Aim *volost'*." GARF f. 6892, op. 1, d. 29, l. 12.

99. GARF f. 6892, op. 1, d. 45, ll. 5–6. These institutions included TsIK, VTsIK, the Central Asian regionalization commission, and the International Water-Use Commission.

100. The Uzbek government requested parts of Osh and Jalal-Abad *okruga* from Kirgizia, while the Kirgiz government requested parts of Fergana and Kokand *uezdy* from Uzbekistan.

Whereas Kul'besherov had considered the Aim question to be relatively straightforward, he was less certain how to resolve other, more complicated territorial disputes in the Fergana Valley. Uch-Kurgan, a settlement of some six thousand people in the valley, was a case in point.[101] The Kirgiz government and the Uzbek government agreed that Uch-Kurgan, though located far from the Tajik ASSR, was predominantly "Tajik in national composition." But they disagreed about what to do as a result. Uzbek leaders attempted to claim the Tajiks of Uch-Kurgan on ethnographic grounds—arguing that the "language, customs, culture, and economic orientation" of the Tajiks did not differ from that of the Uzbeks, and that it would be a mistake to unite Tajiks with "Kirgiz-nomads." But Kul'besherov and other Parity Commission members were skeptical of this argument; they agreed that Tajiks and Uzbeks "have many common customs," but maintained that the Tajik and Uzbek languages were quite different and that Kirgiz and Tajiks could understand one another as well as Uzbeks and Tajiks could. Kul'besherov further argued that the Tajiks were a "poorly served" national minority in Uzbekistan—due in large part to Uzbek attempts to forcibly assimilate them—and that they would be better off in the Kirgiz ASSR.[102]

The Parity Commission also evaluated the economic orientation of Uch-Kurgan. Uzbek leaders argued that the transfer of Uch-Kurgan to Kirgizia would hurt Uzbek cotton production, since Uch-Kurgan was the site of a major irrigation canal used by a number of Uzbek *volosty*. Kirgiz leaders, in turn, argued that Uch-Kurgan was the sole economic center for two important *volosty*, with some twenty thousand people, in the Kirgiz ASSR. Because Uch-Kurgan had a Tajik (and not an Uzbek or a Kirgiz) majority, the Parity Commission made its decision on the basis of each side's economic claims. It declared the Kirgiz case stronger, and noted that Uch-Kurgan also had "great economic significance" for the development of coal mines in the Kirgiz ASSR. The commission did not ignore the ethnographic principle, however, calling for the establishment of Tajik-language schools and other Tajik institutions in the settlement. The commission also noted that the transfer of Uch-Kurgan to Kirgizia would have an administrative benefit, as it would straighten out part of the Kirgiz-Uzbek border.[103]

By spring 1927, TsIK and its various commissions had reviewed numerous appeals to contested territories on or near the Uzbek-Kirgiz border. In the end, both republics gained and lost. Evaluating the Kirgiz claims, TsIK ruled that Uch-Kurgan and several other settlements should be transferred to the Kirgiz ASSR.[104] But it ruled that a number of other contested territories, which were oriented toward the Uzbek economy and had majority-Uzbek populations,

101. It was located in Auval'sk *volost'* of Fergana *uezd*.
102. GARF f. 6892, op. 1, d. 45, ll. 5, 8, 14–17; f. 3316, op. 64, d. 411, ll. 29–300b.
103. GARF f. 6892, op. 1, d. 45, ll. 5, 14–18.
104. Ibid., l. 6.

should remain in the Uzbek SSR.[105] Evaluating Uzbek claims, TsIK argued that the left bank of Aim *volost'* should be transferred to the Uzbek SSR; however, it denied Uzbek claims to other regions that were ethnographically intermixed.[106] (Uzbek leaders would continue to fight for these regions; many years later some of them, including Iskander, would be transferred to the Uzbek SSR.)[107]

Whether borders were changed or remained in place, the stage was set for further conflicts—which began immediately.[108] The examples from the Fergana Valley demonstrate, however, that it was *in spite of* Soviet efforts to resolve conflicts that these tensions escalated. There is no evidence that Soviet leaders "amused themselves" by drawing "arbitrary" boundary divisions.[109] To the contrary, Soviet authorities actively attempted to organize the population into national-territorial units that were economically and administratively viable and stable. After borders were drawn, they did research, surveyed local opinion, and attempted to resolve local conflicts—which, after all, would have negative political and economic consequences for the Soviet Union as a whole if not addressed. It was the very decision to use "nationality" as a rubric of administrative-territorial organization throughout the Soviet Union that led to an increase in "national" tensions—by giving local leaders and local populations a new vocabulary in which to pursue their own interests vis-a-vis other groups. And it was the process of pursuing these interests that bound these local leaders, and with them their populations, more closely to their own national republics as well as to the central Soviet state.

In the spring of 1927, the TsIK regionalization commission and Parity Commission drafted a document describing the new "borders between the union republics in Central Asia."[110] With new maps in the making, TsIK declared that the "mutual territorial claims" of the Uzbek SSR, Kirgiz ASSR, and Kazakh ASSR were to be considered "decisively settled for three years."[111] There seem to have been three reasons for the regime's decision to prohibit further border revisions. First, the Central Statistical Administration had just completed the 1926 census, and it would take time to analyze new data about nationality and native language. Second, the process of border revision was creating additional instability and conflict in a number of regions; Soviet leaders recognized that continued border changes would result in still more dis-

105. Ibid., ll. 5, 12–14.

106. GARF f. 3316, op. 64, d. 411, l. 21.

107. See the maps in E. Murzaev, *Sredniaia Aziia: Fiziko-geograficheskii ocherk* (Moscow, 1957).

108. GARF f. 3316, op. 64, d. 411, ll. 270b–29.

109. The quotes are from Roy, *New Central Asia*, 68, 72, and Rashid, *Jihad*, 88.

110. GARF f. 6892, op. 1, d. 47, ll. 68–75. For correspondence between the Central Committee and TsIK on these matters see GARF f. 3316, op. 64, d. 411, ll. 4–5.

111. GARF f. 3316, op. 64, d. 411, l. 27. TsIK reported that it would not review additional petitions until 1930.

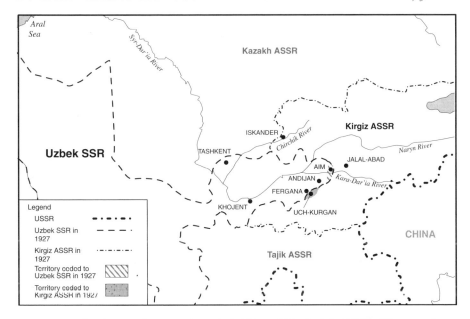

Map 4.3 Border disputes between the Uzbek SSR and Kirgiz AO (ASSR). The map shows how the borders were changed around Aim *volost'* and Uch-Kurgan settlement in 1927. It also shows Iskander *volost'*.

putes—and that there was no possible way to satisfy all sides. Third, the Soviet government needed stable borders to accomplish the next phase of the regionalization process: the "internal" or "lower-level regionalization" of the Central Asian republics into administrative subunits.

Internal Regionalization and the Problem of National Minorities

Internal regionalization represented a different approach to solving the problem of national minorities—by creating national subunits and institutions for national minorities within the national republics whenever possible.[112] In practice, this approach posed real difficulties, often exacerbating local tensions. Even as national identities were gaining political, and thus local, importance, tribal and clan identities continued to endure throughout much of Central Asia. Communities often claimed different identities for different audiences or occasions. When the Central Asian regionalization commission turned its attention to the internal regionalization of the republics, it reported that local communities had initiated a process of "spontaneous" internal regionalization on their own: that without sanction from Tashkent or Moscow, the leaders of

112. For a discussion of the principles and practices of internal (or lower-level) regionalization see GARF f. 6892, op. 1, d. 42, ll. 1–61; d. 47, ll. 1–67. On the internal regionalization of the Central Asian republics and the Caucasus see GARF f. 6892, op. 1, d. 42, ll. 10–61.

villages and communities had delimited administrative subunits based on the "clan" or "tribal" principle. As the commission set out to eliminate these subunits and create new ones, it experienced significant resistance, coming into conflict with Kirgiz clans in the Kirgiz ASSR, Turkmen tribes in the Turkmen SSR, and other groups who demanded "to be organized as independent units." To make matters worse, different branches of the same tribe sometimes demanded their own administrative subunits; for example, the commission noted that the Dzhafarbaevi and the Atabaevi of the Iomud tribe of the Turkmen *narodnost'* were mortal enemies and could not live together.[113]

As communities pushed for tribe- or clan-based subunits within the national republics, republic-level leaders attempted to "nationalize" the territories within their borders—and in particular to establish standardized national languages. Thus, even as some Turkmen tribes lobbied for separate status, Turkmen government and party officials embarked on the "Turkmenization" of the republic's population—and assured TsIK that the "monolithic" ethnographic and linguistic composition of the republic would facilitate this process.[114] Party and government leaders in Moscow, for their part, favored the amalgamation of clans and tribes into nationalities. This, after all, was in line with the program of state-sponsored evolutionism, in which nationhood was seen as a cure to feudal-era backwardness. But the consolidation of nationalities in this manner also had its dangers. First, republic-level leaders, who wanted to lay claim to as much land as possible, were attempting to assimilate into their *narodnost'* all the tribes and clans that resided in their republic—including those that "belonged to" other *narodnosti.* Second, it was often difficult for the regionalization commission to determine to which *narodnost'* certain clans and tribes belonged.

Difficulties faced by residents of Tajik territories within the Uzbek SSR demonstrate how internal regionalization sometimes failed to resolve the problem of national minorities on the local level. In 1924, the Soviet regime had established the Tajik ASSR as a subregion within Uzbekistan. At the time, several important regions with numerous Tajik native speakers (Samarkand, Bukhara, Khojent, Surkhan-Dar'ia) remained part of Uzbekistan, outside of the Tajik ASSR. Uzbekistan was supposed to deal with this "Tajik question" through internal regionalization—through the establishment of Tajik subregions and institutions. Instead, Uzbek authorities attempted to assimilate the Tajik native speakers into the Uzbek *narodnost'.* Not long after the national delimitation of 1924, self-identified Tajiks living in Uzbekistan in areas outside of the Tajik ASSR barraged Soviet leaders in Moscow and Tashkent with letters and petitions complaining about forced "Uzbekization." Petitioners com-

---

113. Komissiia po raionirovaniiu Srednei Azii, *Materialy po raionirovaniiu Srednei Azii,* vol. 1, pt. 1, *Territoriia i naselenie Bukhary i Khorezma: Bukhara,* 2–6; GARF f. 6892, op. 1, d. 42, ll. 1–13. In 1926, the commission questioned "whether there is a Turkmen *narod*" (l. 13).

114. GARF f. 3316, op. 64, d. 397a, protocol 4.

plained that education and political life were conducted in the Uzbek language, and that Tajik native speakers had been denied their own schools in spite of "the party's decree that each people has the right to speak its native language."[115] Responding to such petitions, Uzbek officials insisted that the regions in question were Uzbek and that the people who lived there spoke the Uzbek language.[116]

In the late 1920s, Tajik-identified government and party officials throughout Uzbekistan (both within the Tajik ASSR and outside of its borders) launched a campaign for Tajik national rights. Using dozens of petitions from Tajik native speakers in Uzbekistan to demonstrate the failure of internal regionalization, these officials argued that the Soviet government should revisit the national delimitation, granting the Tajik ASSR the status of a union republic (SSR) and including within it all "predominantly Tajik" territories from Uzbekistan. In 1929, leaders of the Tajik ASSR asked the Politburo directly to free the "Tajik population" from Uzbek oppression.[117] The Politburo agreed to hear the case for secession on the grounds that the Tajik ASSR was "by economic, national, and geographical indications isolated from Uzbekistan."[118] It instructed TsIK to appoint a new commission to reconsider the borders of Uzbekistan and determine which of its territories might be included in a new Tajik SSR.[119] Some historians have argued that Soviet leaders decided to expand the Tajik republic at this time in order to attract the attention of "Tajik elements" in Persia.[120] But there is strong evidence that economic considerations were the main factor behind the reconsideration of the borders; it was right around this time that state planners from the reorganized Goskolonit proposed turning Khojent—a part of the Uzbek SSR with a large Tajik-identified population—into a model cotton-production region. The planners suggested that the regime resettle Tajiks from the mountainous regions of the Tajik ASSR onto new cotton-oriented collective farms in this region. The expansion of the Tajik ASSR to include Khojent provided a national-political rationale (Tajik nation-building) for this resettlement operation.[121]

Ethnographic Knowledge and the Making of Tajikistan

The making of the Tajik SSR between 1929 and 1930 provides an ideal context to examine the influence of census data on Soviet border-making. Soviet

115. GARF f. 3316, op. 22, d. 129, ll. 54–55; d. 128, l 1.

116. See, for example, GARF f. 3316, op. 22, d. 129, l. 54.

117. GARF f. 3316, op. 22, d. 127, l. 38a; d. 129, l. 54.

118. GARF f. 3316, op. 22, d. 127, l. 38a. The timing of the decision to hear the Tajik case was connected to larger all-union political concerns.

119. GARF f. 3316, op. 22, d. 129, l. 9; d. 127, l. 132.

120. See, for example, Geoffrey Wheeler, *The Modern History of Soviet Central Asia* (London, 1964).

121. See chapter 6.

leaders and experts who had been involved in the All-Union Census of 1926 had proclaimed that new census data would be used to settle border disputes. But instead of making the reevaluation of borders easier, new census data complicated matters further. The census had been conducted in Central Asia in the midst of ongoing discussions about contested territories and resources. Now, with so much at stake, debate ensued about whether the new data were correct. This, in turn, led to a more general discussion about what constituted accurate ethnographic knowledge. Should the regionalization commission give greater weight to expert knowledge or to local knowledge? Should it trust current data or historical data, data based on ethnic "origins" or data reflecting present cast of mind? And what if present cast of mind was the result of assimilation? How these questions were answered would have tremendous consequences for the delimitation of new borders throughout the region.

The deliberations about the secession of the Tajik ASSR from Uzbekistan proceeded in a manner similar to that of the earlier border disputes. In June 1929 TsIK established a Commission on the Separation of the Tajik ASSR from the Uzbek SSR and included in it representatives from TsIK and other all-union institutions, as well as representatives from the Tajik ASSR and Uzbek SSR.[122] TsIK directed the commission to sort out Tajik demands and determine what territories might be included in a new Tajik SSR. Tajik representatives requested a number of important territories from the Uzbek SSR, including Samarkand, Bukhara, and Khojent *okruga*. The commission evaluated ethnographic, economic, and administrative criteria. It resolved that Khojent, which had sizeable Tajik and Uzbek populations, should be united with the Tajik ASSR on economic grounds. It rejected Tajik claims to Bukhara and Samarkand, but noted that parts of these *okruga* with Tajik majorities might later be ceded to the Tajik ASSR.[123]

In mid-December 1929 Soviet leaders formally announced the creation of the Tajik SSR.[124] Around the same time, a new TsIK Commission to Resolve Border Disputes Between the Uzbek and Tajik SSRs began its deliberations, holding a series of closed sessions. This commission too was comprised of representatives from TsIK, other all-union institutions, and from the Uzbek and Tajik SSRs.[125] The official who presided over the commission, Iakov Peters, had played an important role in deliberations about the enlargement of the Be-

122. GARF f. 3316, op. 22, d. 127, ll. 40, 43–45, 57–570b, 193; d. 129, l. 10. Kuprian Kirkizh, the secretary of the Central Committee of the Uzbek Communist Party, led this commission's proceedings.

123. GARF f. 3316, op. 2, d. 129, l. 10. For a more detailed account of these events and of the subcommissions that preceded the formation of the TsIK commission see Rakhim Masov, *Istoriia topornogo razdeleniia* (Dushanbe, 1991).

124. GARF f. 3316, op. 22, d. 130, l. 1.

125. GARF f. 3316, op. 22, d. 127, ll. 131, 135. The commission held its first meeting on December 12, 1929. Its members were Iakov Peters, Kirkizh, Tadzhiev, Tursun Khodzhaev, S. A. Anvarov, and Akimov. Present were leaders from the Uzbek SSR (Akhun-Babaev, Rustan Uslamov, and Matskevich) and from the Tajik SSR (Nusratullo Maksum, Abdurakhim Khodzhibaev,

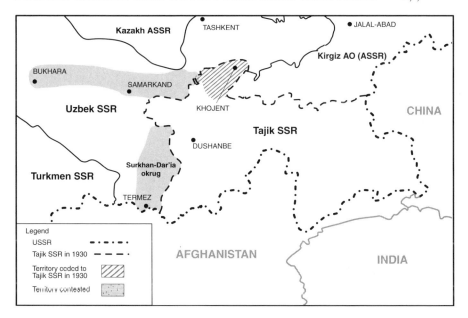

Map 4.4 The Tajik SSR. Khojent *okrug* was added to the Tajik SSR in late 1929. The Tajik leadership continued to ask for Samarkand and Bukhara and for Surkhan-Dar'ia *okrug*.

lorussian SSR and the delimitation of the Central Asian republics.[126] This new regionalization commission solicited expert information about the contested regions from KIPS, Gosplan, the Central Statistical Administration, and other institutions.[127]

The commission's deliberations proved contentious because the Tajiks continued to claim Samarkand and Bukhara *okruga* and also asked for part of Surkhan-Dar'ia *okrug*.[128] The Uzbek representatives, who resented these claims, showed up late to sessions and at first refused to cooperate with the commission at all.[129] According to the Uzbek representatives, the Uzbek SSR had agreed to give up Khojent *okrug* in order "to help Tajikistan"—and the Tajik leaders were unappreciative.[130] The Uzbek representatives asked Peters

Malakhov, and Shirinsho Shotemor). Also present was a representative from the Central Asian Economic Council.

126. Peters, who also had a prominent role in the Eastern Department of the secret police, was in frequent communication with Joseph Stalin during this period. On Peters see K. A. Zalesskii, *Imperiia Stalina: Biograficheskii entsiklopedicheskii slovar'* (Moscow, 2000), 35.

127. The discussion that follows is from the December 12 and 22, 1929 meetings. For the stenograms see GARF f. 3316, op. 22, d. 127, ll. 132–35; d. 129, ll. 9–51.

128. GARF f. 3316, op. 22, d. 129, l. 10.

129. For example, GARF f. 3316, op. 22, d. 127, l. 135.

130. GARF f. 3316, op. 22, d. 129, ll. 11–12, 250b.

to disregard petitions that Tajik leaders had presented from communities that asked to be included in the Tajik SSR: "We have petitions from Uzbek regions in Tajikistan," Uzbek representatives claimed. "The only difference is that the Tajiks presented this material [to the commission] and the Uzbeks did not." Peters emphasized that the commission would not "trade" territories or engage in the "politics of compensation," but would decide the fate of the contested regions on the basis of their ethnographic composition and economic orientation.[131]

The Tajik and Uzbek representatives focused primarily on the ethnographic principle in their presentations to the commission. Each side marshaled census data to prove that their *narodnost'* predominated in the contested regions. The Tajik representatives presented data from pre-Soviet and early Soviet censuses and argued that data from the 1926 census were "biased and unfair." This was a strategic move, since earlier population counts (such as the 1897 and 1917 censuses) had shown a much greater percentage of "Tajiks" in Samarkand, Bukhara, and Surkhan-Dar'ia *okruga* than had the 1926 census.[132] Shirinsho Shotemor, the chief secretary of the Tajik Oblast Committee of the Uzbek Communist Party, attempted to discredit the 1926 census altogether, describing it as a tool of Uzbekization. According to Shotemor, soon after the delimitation of 1924, Uzbek newspapers claimed that Tajiks could be found only in the Pamir (in the Tajik ASSR), and that "people who believe there are Tajiks in the rest of Central Asia are insane." Shotemor described how Uzbeks engaged in the systematic "persecution of Tajiks and the Tajik language." The situation became so bad, he argued, that at the time of the 1926 census "it was impossible to step forward and say that Tajiks existed in Uzbekistan," let alone tell a census taker that you were one.[133] Other Tajik leaders agreed that such circumstances had led to false census totals. Bukhara and Samarkand were famous throughout the east as Tajik cities, but the 1926 census showed them to be Uzbek. "Did all the Tajiks die?" asked Abdurakhim Khodzhibaev. "If so, it must be as a result of un-Soviet policies."[134]

The Uzbek representatives, by contrast, maintained that the 1926 census—which showed Uzbek majorities in most of the contested territories—was more accurate than past population counts.[135] They acknowledged that there were

131. Ibid., ll. 12, 22, 24–240b.

132. GARF f. 3316, op. 22, d. 127, ll. 134–1340b. The Tajiks used data from 1897 and 1917 for Samarkand and Bukhara, and from before 1917 for Surkhan-Dar'ia. (The 1897, 1917, 1920, and 1923 censuses did not cover Surkhan-Dar'ia.) These data showed the cities of Samarkand and Bukhara to have Tajik majorities. (The Tajiks asked for the cities *and* contiguous regions.) The pre-1917 data showed the contested parts of Surkhan-Dar'ia to have Tajik majorities.

133. GARF f. 3316, op. 22, d. 129, ll. 26–270b. Shotemor was also a member of the TsIK of the USSR. In the mid-1920s he served in the Central Committee's Central Asian Bureau and in the Narkompros of the Uzbek SSR. On Shotemor see Boris Levytsky, ed., *The Stalinist Terror in the Thirties: Documentation from the Soviet Press* (Stanford, 1974), 303–6.

134. GARF f. 3316, op. 22, d. 127, ll. 203–4; d. 129, ll. 18, 34.

135. GARF f. 3316, op. 22, d. 129, ll. 13, 23.

some mistakes in the 1926 data, but maintained that these were unintentional—and, moreover, that mistakes affected both sides. "Why would a Central Statistical Administration worker register a Tajik as an Uzbek?" asked the Uzbek representative and leader Rustam Islamov. "We do not have an intelligentsia that could have been mobilized for this business."[136] Islamov noted that Russian students (with no interest in Uzbekizing the population) had served as census takers throughout Uzbekistan.[137] According to the Uzbek representatives, it was the pre-Soviet censuses—which had tabulated data about *narodnost'* on the basis of native language—that had produced false results. The Uzbek leader Akhun-Babaev explained that although "the Bukharan Emir was Uzbek," he had pursued the "Tajikification" of the population"—so that under his rule Tajik was spoken "everywhere." Thus, just because people spoke Tajik did not mean that they were Tajik. According to the Uzbek representatives, the Soviet regime had helped redress the mistakes of the past: People who had been recorded in earlier censuses as Tajiks "turned out to be Uzbeks."[138]

In deliberations about contested borders, the Tajik representatives made historical arguments and the Uzbek representatives focused on the present. According to the Tajik representatives, the Tajiks were the "aboriginals" of Samarkand, Surkhan-Dar'ia, and Bukhara, descended from ancient Iranian tribes. The Tajiks had not left these regions voluntarily, they argued, but had been "driven from all good places" several hundred years ago, when Uzbek invaders had forced the Tajiks into the mountains and "Turkicized" those who remained.[139] The Tajik position hinged on two connected points. First: People of "Iranian origins" had lived in the contested regions for more than fifteen centuries before the "Turks arrived." Second: "These Iranians" were "the long-ago ancestors of the present-day Tajiks."[140] The Uzbek representatives, by contrast, emphasized that currently Uzbeks—and not Tajiks—predominated in the disputed regions. It was irrelevant whether contested regions had been Uzbek all along or had become Uzbek as a result of migration or assimilation, Islamov argued: if a Tajik lost his Tajik "cast of mind" and became an Uzbek, the regime could not force him to call himself a Tajik. Some territories such as Samarkand might have been Tajik regions some three hundred or four hundred years ago, but "there is no reason to return to the past."[141]

The Tajik representatives criticized Uzbek efforts to force "Tajiks to assimilate into Uzbeks."[142] But claims about forced Uzbekization became more complicated as the Uzbek representatives implicated a number of Tajik leaders, in-

136. Ibid., l. 34.
137. Ibid., l. 13.
138. Ibid., ll. 14, 24–25.
139. Ibid., l. 31.
140. GARF f. 3316, op. 22, d. 127, ll. 219, 220. Mukhamedov is quoting Bartol'd.
141. GARF f. 3316, op. 22, d. 129, ll. 16, 36.
142. Ibid., l. 30.

cluding Khodzhibaev, as former Uzbek nationalists.[143] In late December 1929, Nisar Mukhamedov, a leading member of the Tajik government, attempted to shed light on this subject. Mukhamedov outlined in an official statement to the commission how "historical circumstances" had prompted the "Tajik intelligentsia" to help Uzbek leaders assimilate the "Tajik population" of the currently contested territories into the Uzbek *narodnost'* at the time of the national delimitation of 1924. As recounted by Mukhamedov, at the start of World War I, Tajik and other non-Turkic leaders had supported the pan-Turkic movement, which aspired to form a united front of "eastern" peoples against "western" powers and end European domination.[144] After the Bolshevik Revolution, the pan-Turkic forces united with anti-Soviet forces (the Basmachi) and "re-sisted Soviet infiltration into Turkestan." But when it became clear that Turkestan would become part of the Soviet Union, local Turkic leaders (the Jadids) shifted alliances and began to collaborate with the Soviet regime. The local pan-Turkic movement evolved into a pan-Uzbek movement: Turkic leaders "put on a Soviet mask" and promoted the idea of an autonomous Uzbek nation within a Soviet federation. Members of "the Tajik intelligentsia" supported the Uzbek movement, "renamed themselves Uzbeks," and encouraged other Tajiks to do the same.[145]

As long as borders were unfixed, "Uzbeks" and "Tajiks" were able to unite for common goals. But the national delimitation of 1924 created a new relationship among nationality, access to resources, and political power. Mukhamedov maintained that after the delimitation, Uzbek leaders began to assert that "there was room only for Uzbeks" in Uzbekistan and that people who claimed Tajik as a native language or "considered themselves Tajiks" had to go live in the Tajik ASSR. The Tajik ASSR, still the site of fighting between Soviet forces and the Basmachi, was described in such horrible terms that it became "synonymous with prerevolutionary Siberia." At the same time, administrators, as well as teachers, doctors, and other professionals, who did not "accept Uzbek as their official language" were dismissed and reassigned to menial labor.[146] According to Mukhamedov, "Soviet and party workers and teachers" began "to call themselves Uzbeks" in order to keep their jobs in Uzbekistan and avoid being sent to the Tajik ASSR. The Tajik masses saw such behavior and "began to conceal their nationality." Mukhamedov argued that this "Uzbekization" campaign was reflected in the results of the 1926 census— which had been "conducted under the influence of Uzbek chauvinists" who

143. Ibid., l. 25. They also pointed out that at the time of the 1926 census Khodzhibaev was the head of the Uzbek SSR Commissariat of Agriculture.

144. GARF f. 3316, op. 22, d. 127, ll. 205–27. He noted that they hoped to unite the countries of the east (Afghanistan, India, Turkey, and Turkestan) under "Turkic rule" and form a Muslim state "united in defense of Islam."

145. GARF f. 3316, op. 22, d. 127, ll. 205–7.

146. Ibid., ll. 205–6.

did not want to provide national-territorial subunits or native language schools and institutions to self-described "Tajiks" or Tajik native speakers.[147]

As the TsIK border dispute commission considered the Tajik and Uzbek arguments, it debated sending a special subcommission to the contested regions to interview local populations about their national identities.[148] Peters, for his part, argued that such fieldwork could not help but prove inconclusive in the current political context. In the Belorussian case too, Peters noted, there had been a considerable divergence between pre-Soviet and Soviet statistics. But when TsIK representatives went to Gomel *guberniia* and other contested regions, it had proven difficult to determine whether communities were "Belorussian or Russian": in conversation people used "some Russian words, some Belorussian words." Peters explained that when he had asked the inhabitants of these regions if they wanted to be unified with Belorussia, they had given a resounding no. "Why should I learn the Belorussian language?" they had asked. "I can travel one-sixth of the earth's surface with the Russian language." According to Peters, these people had responded "on the basis of material interests," concealing their "Belorussian" origins.[149] Noting that TsIK and the Politburo had decided to unite most of these regions with the Belorussian SSR on the basis of ethnographic data, instead of national consciousness, Peters recommended a similar approach to Tajikistan.[150]

With census data and the principle of self-definition in question, the Peters commission looked to other sources of information about the population. When deliberations about Tajik borders had begun in mid-December, the Peters commission had asked experts to send information about the ethnographic composition of contested regions. As the deliberations continued, the commission sent KIPS several urgent memos, requesting that the ethnographers send their analysis as soon as possible. The memos explained that in order to determine "the borders betwcen the Uzbek and Tajik SSRs," the commission needed information about the relationship "between the main nationalities (*natsional'nosti*), the Uzbeks and the Tajiks, of Surkhan-Dar'ia, Samarkand, and Bukhara *okruga* not just at the time of the last census but also from a historical perspective." TsIK asked the ethnographers to report which of the two "is indigenous to each *okrug*" and to provide general historical information about "Tajik and Uzbek settlement patterns."[151]

Thus, in December 1929—shortly after the party had embarked on its investigation of the Academy of Sciences and the press had criticized KIPS as a "closed corrupt family"—the Peters commission appealed to KIPS for urgent

147. Ibid., ll. 203–5.
148. GARF f. 3316, op. 22, d. 129, ll. 45–56.
149. Ibid., ll. 42–43.
150. Ibid., l. 45.
151. For correspondence among KIPS, Peters, and Akimov about KIPS's analysis see GARF f. 3316, op. 22, d. 127, ll. 140, 141, 176, 235, 240, 250, 265–66, 267.

assistance. Mikhail Khudiakov (the new permanent secretary of KIPS, who had just replaced Sergei Rudenko) assured Peters of KIPS's cooperation. He proceeded to send the TsIK commission ethnographic reports and maps of Surkhan-Dar'ia, Samarkand, and Bukhara based on pre-Soviet and Soviet ethnographic fieldwork and censuses. Among other materials, Khudiakov sent ethnographic analyses of Turkestan that Zarubin had written before the All-Union Census, a 1924 report from the Central Asian regionalization commission, and a historical evaluation of Uzbek-Tajik relations that Bartol'd had prepared in response to TsIK's request.[152]

The ethnographic reports and maps supplied by KIPS provided another lens through which to examine the competing claims of Uzbek and Tajik leaders. When pre-Soviet and Soviet census figures for the contested regions of Surkhan-Dar'ia did not match up—because communities that had been formerly categorized as "Tajik" were registered in 1926 as "Uzbek"—Tajik leaders maintained that Uzbek chauvinism was responsible for the falsification of census data. But Khudiakov suggested in his report that the new census data were inconsistent because a large number of respondents did not fit into the Soviet regime's definitional grid. To support his point, Khudiakov gave the example of the "Chagatai"—who spoke Tajik, were members of an Uzbek clan subgroup, and sometimes went by the name "Tajik-Chagatai." Regions with large Chagatai populations (such as Kashkadar in Surkhan-Dar'ia) were classified as "Tajik" or as "Chagatai" in pre-1926 population surveys, but as "Uzbek" in the 1926 census results. (The Chagatai had not been included on the "List of the Nationalities of the USSR.")[153] Khudiakov suggested that the Chagatai were neither fully Uzbek nor fully Tajik, but were probably "Tajik tribes at one or another stage of Turkization" or "Uzbeks who had acquired the Tajik language."[154]

Zarubin's materials on Turkestan also emphasized that the relationship between the Tajiks and the Uzbeks did not reflect clear ethnic, linguistic, or religious divisions. According to Zarubin, the Uzbeks were not "a unified and separate ethnic group" but included a diverse mix of Turkic peoples. The Tajiks, too, he argued, did not constitute a cohesive whole. The term *Tajik* sometimes referred to a non-nomadic Muslim, regardless of language, and sometimes referred to a person who spoke a dialect of the Farsi language, regardless of religion. Zarubin maintained that settled Tajiks had little in common with "mountain Tajiks," aside from a shared base language. Settled Tajiks, he suggested, had more in common with the part of the region's settled

152. Khudiakov, the new KIPS academic secretary, was a former member of the Commission for the Regionalization of Uzbekistan. GARF f. 3316, op. 22, d. 127, ll. 160–68, 244–48; d. 128, l. 31.

153. GARF f. 3316, op. 22, d. 127, ll. 161–62, 166–67.

154. Ibid., ll. 161–62.

Turkic population "that lack clan ties, are known as Sarts, and presently comprise the main core of the Uzbek *narodnost'*."[155]

According to Zarubin, the question of Sart identity was even more complicated. Zarubin characterized the Sarts as an Uzbek-Tajik mix: Uzbek in culture and Iranian in origin—and descended from the same Iranian tribes as other Tajiks. Zarubin explained that when "Turkicized Iranians were surrounded en masse by long-settled Uzbeks who did not differ from them culturally," the former sometimes took the name of the latter, but remained outside of the clan structure. In other instances, the Turkicized Iranians called themselves Turks or accepted the name "Sart," which is what their neighbors often called them.[156] The "Sart question" had become a major point of contention in Tajik-Uzbek border disputes. Since self-identified Sarts comprised a sizeable population in contested parts of Samarkand, Bukhara, and Surkhan-Dar'ia, and since a Sart *narodnost'* did not officially exist, Uzbek and Tajik leaders were both attempting to claim the Sarts—and the territories that the Sarts inhabited—as their own.

The materials that Khudiakov supplied to TsIK suggested that the KIPS ethnographers themselves were far from unanimous in their opinions—and advocated different approaches to the population and to the delimitation in general. Zarubin, who urged care and caution, criticized some of his colleagues for "accelerating" the assimilation of Sarts into Uzbeks. According to Zarubin, the creation of the Uzbek SSR in 1924 had acted as a catalyst to Uzbek nation formation; in the aftermath of the delimitation, Sart communities began to "cast off the name Sart" and call themselves Uzbeks.[157] He noted that some ethnographers—such as his colleague Samoilovich—had been eager to speed this process along. Samoilovich had advocated eliminating the term *Sart* from ethnographical studies and statistical reports and replacing it with *Uzbek*.[158] This had become a point of debate as ethnographers prepared the list of nationalities for the 1926 census. Ultimately, the ethnographers had omitted the Sarts from the list; census instructions had recommended that

---

155. Zarubin, *Spisok narodnostei Turkestanskogo kraia*, 5–7, 14–15. On the categories "Tajik" and "Uzbek" see Bert G. Fragner, "The Nationalization of the Uzbeks and Tajiks," in *Muslim Communities Reemerge*; Ingelborg Baldauf, "*Kraevedeniia*" and *Uzbek National Consciousness*, (Bloomington, 1992); Khalid, *Politics of Muslim Cultural Reform*, chapter 6; and Schoeberlein Engel, "Identity in Central Asia."

156. Zarubin, *Spisok narodnostei Turkestanskogo kraia*, 6. Zarubin argues that "Sart," which had been a pejorative term for settled townspeople and traders, took on "ethnic significance" in regions where Sarts lived "in small islands among other peoples." According to Brower, in imperial Russia "confusion surrounding the term 'Sart' produced scientific debates that lasted throughout the tsarist period" ("Islam and Ethnicity," 129).

157. Zarubin, *Spisok narodnostei Turkestanskogo kraia*, 14–15. He noted that the term had "unpleasant connotations."

158. Ibid., 20–21. Samoilovich argued that "Sart" designated people of a particular economic orientation.

census takers register self-identified Sarts who spoke Uzbek as members of the Uzbek *narodnost'*, adding "the term *Sart* in parentheses."[159]

While Samoilovich had taken up the cause of Uzbek nation formation and Zarubin saw the consolidation of the Uzbek nation as inevitable, Bartol'd was more critical—as evidenced in his report to TsIK. First, Bartol'd criticized the naiveté of those who contended that an "attraction to the mountains" was a "characteristic national trait of the Tajiks." He argued that the Turks had forced "the settled Iranian agricultural population"—the "ancestors of the Tajiks"—"out of the plains and into the mountains."[160] Bartol'd had made this point numerous times in his published studies of the region. In fact, Tajik leaders, in their own appeals to the Peters commission, cited from Bartol'd's works to argue that the Tajiks were the descendents of Iranian tribes that were indigenous to contested parts of Uzbekistan.[161] Second, Bartol'd criticized the national delimitation in more general terms—arguing that it was based on a "nineteenth-century Western European" idea, the national idea, that was "completely alien" to the region. He expressed particular regret at the destruction of existing political units such as Khorezm.[162]

Most important, Bartol'd emphasized the point that the Tajik and the Uzbek leaders refused to concede: that Tajiks and Uzbeks were so ethnographically intermixed that in some regions it was difficult even for locals to differentiate between them. According to Bartol'd, both the "Uzbeks" and the "Tajiks" were a Turkic-Iranian mix: the product of several centuries of migration, conquest, and cultural contact. He described the initial subordination "of Turks to the influence of Islam and Iranian-Muslim material and spiritual culture" and "of Iranians to the influence of the Turkic language"; he explained how the Turkic state later adopted "Iranian" as its official language of administration and culture, and how the Iranians had been forced to accept Turkic political institutions.[163] The implication of Bartol'd's analysis was that peoples like the Sarts and Chagatai—who could not be neatly categorized as either Tajiks or Uzbeks—were more the rule than the exception.

The ethnographers and the Tajik and Uzbek elites, in spite of their differences, shared a focus on the ethnographic principle. But as the Peters commission attempted to reach a decision about Tajik demands in January 1930, its own deliberations followed a familiar format. It evaluated the contested territories in terms of ethnographic, economic, and administrative considerations—and gave primary importance to larger all-union con-

---

159. This is discussed in chapter 3.
160. GARF f. 3316, op. 22, d. 127, ll. 164–65.
161. For example, ibid. ll. 218–19.
162. Ibid., ll. 164–65.
163. Ibid.

cerns.[164] Taking up the cases of Samarkand and Bukhara, the commission concluded that the Tajik claims "had no foundation from an economic, national, geographical, or any other perspective." The commission members agreed with Tajik leaders (and with Bartol'd) that the Tajiks had ended up in the mountain regions and the cities as a result of "past events." But the commission argued that Tajik claims still could not be "justified": while pre-Soviet censuses and ethnographic data showed Tajiks to be numerous and "perhaps predominant" in the *cities* of Samarkand and Bukhara, these same materials showed that "Uzbeks predominate in the *okruga* overall." The commission further noted that the unification of "Uzbekistan's largest cities" with Tajikistan would cut through non-Tajik territories and create administrative and economic difficulties. The "chaos and disorder" that would ensue would "bring benefit to no one, including the Tajiks."[165]

The commission reached a different conclusion, however, about Surkhan-Dar'ia—arguing that the entire *okrug* should be transferred to the Tajik SSR "on the basis of historical, ethnographic, physical-geographical, and economic data as well as political considerations."[166] The commission agreed with ethnographers that the ethnographic data were inconclusive—that "the process of mutual cultural and *bytovoi* influence" between the Tajiks and Uzbeks was so "deep" that it was often impossible to determine the "national membership" of a given region of the *okrug*. What most differentiated the case of Surkhan-Dar'ia from those of Samarkand and Bukhara was the commission's conclusion that its transfer to the Tajik SSR had economic and administrative benefits. The commission noted that Surkhan-Dar'ia had a strong economic connection to Tajikistan—in part through a shared river system. The commission also discussed the "political significance" of the unification of Surkhan-Dar'ia with the Tajik SSR; it noted that the *okrug* bordered the northern part of Afghanistan, where the main population was comprised of "Tajiks, or those who speak the Tajik language."[167]

In early February, the commission ruled that Surkhan-Dar'ia *okrug* should be transferred "in its present borders" to the Tajik SSR in the next two months.[168] Even before this decision was formally announced, Uzbek leaders launched a protest campaign, arguing that the commission "did not fully consider the ethnographic and economic data."[169] In the end, Surkhan-Dar'ia was not transferred. This, of course, raises the question: Why not? While the archival materials available do not provide an answer, it is possible to speculate. Rahim Masov proposes in his history of Tajikistan that Soviet leaders

164. Ibid., ll. 256–63. It referred to administrative considerations as "physical-geographical" considerations.

165. Ibid., ll. 260–62, 274.

166. Ibid., l. 256.

167. Ibid., ll. 256–57, 274.

168. Masov, *Istoriia topornogo razdeleniia*, 100.

169. GARF f. 3316, op. 22, d. 127, ll. 277, 307.

might have reconsidered the decision to transfer Surkhan-Dar'ia for administrative reasons: in accordance with Soviet law, in order for the Uzbek SSR to
retain its status as a union republic, it had to have "a border with foreign
states." Masov notes that "Uzbekistan could have a border with a foreign state
only through the city of Termez, located in Surkhan-Dar'ia *okrug*."[170] There
are also additional possible reasons for the decision to leave Surkhan-Dar'ia in
the Uzbek SSR. First, it was not clear that the *okrug* had a predominantly
"Tajik" population; based on the census data and ethnographers' reports, a
case could have been made for the inclusion of the *okrug* in either republic.
Second, as TsIK was evaluating this question in 1930, the party had already
embarked on a campaign to set up collective farms in Khojent—and was experiencing significant difficulties. Soviet leaders suggested that Tajikistan needed
to develop its present resources, and not concern itself with the integration of
new land and people.

The case of the Tajik and Uzbek national republics suggests how even an
unsuccessful or a partially successful campaign to adjust borders could have
long-term effects. Even as Moscow-based officials and members of the party
elite made the final decisions about disputed territories, hostilities between the
Uzbek and Tajik governments escalated. Moreover, leaders on both sides
noted that "the dragging out of this question" was "increasing the antago-
nism" between the Uzbek and Tajik populations.[171] Most significantly, as local
elites argued about the national identities of "mixed peoples" living in contested territories, these "mixed peoples" came under increasing pressure to define themselves as either "Uzbeks" or "Tajiks" in their everyday interactions.
Clans and tribes continued to exist, but local conflicts were reconfigured along
national lines—in the language of the Soviet state.

By 1930, TsIK and the party had reviewed and adjusted the borders of the Soviet Union's national-territorial units on the basis of ethnographic, economic,
and administrative criteria. People throughout the Soviet Union were using the
language of the Soviet state—and the vocabulary of nationality in particular—
to fight for resources and assert their rights. Through a process of double assimilation, the clans, tribes, and *narodnosti* of the former Russian Empire were
taking on Soviet national identities and becoming integrated into the Soviet
Union. However, as the next chapter will show, the process of Sovietization
was just beginning.

170. Masov, *Istoriia topornogo razdeleniia,* 100.
171. GARF f. 3316, op. 22, d. 129, l. 240b.

CHAPTER 5

Transforming "The Peoples of the USSR": Ethnographic Exhibits and the Evolutionary Timeline

> Anthropology promoted a scheme in terms of which not only past cultures, but all living societies were irrevocably placed on a temporal slope, a stream of Time—some upstream, others downstream.
>
> —Johannes Fabian, *Time and the Other,* 1983

> Comrades, come visit the Ethnographic Department of the State Russian Museum and see how the Votiaks of northern Siberia, the Samoeds of Novaia Zemlia, the Soiots of the Altai, the Kirgiz of Central Asia, the Georgians of the Caucasus, the Tatars of the Crimea, the Lopars of Kol'sk peninsula, the Ukrainians of Podoliia and the Russian peasants of Murmansk lived and live. Pay attention to their economic tools, their diet, homes, beliefs, and customs, and you will see how much there is for the conscious worker to do in the far-off corners of our enormous country, where the power of old *byt* is still strong.
>
> —Flyer advertising a workers' education course on "The Peoples of the USSR," 1930

In 1923, ethnographers' lectures and ethnographic exhibits celebrated the exotic dress, traditional culture, and religious beliefs of the diverse peoples that could be found within Soviet borders. In the 1930s, these lectures and exhibits presented a different characterization of the peoples of the USSR—as peoples who were "experiencing a period of unusually rapid economic and cultural uplift" but still needed assistance to overcome the powerful pull of traditional beliefs and customs (*byt*).[1] This shift from an "exoticizing" to a "moderniz-

---

1. Archive of the Russian Ethnographic Museum (REM) f. 2, op. 1, d. 283, l. 190b. (Transcript of a December 1929 lecture about the Central Asian republics).

ing" discourse came on the heels of Joseph Stalin's declaration in November 1929 that the Soviet Union was "advancing full steam ahead" toward socialism and would overcome its "backwardness" in record time.[2] Because the Soviet Union defined itself as the sum of its parts, the Soviet socialist future depended on the rapid economic and social modernization of *all* the lands and peoples within Soviet borders. The revolution had promised to turn "empty spaces" into "green pastures and cultivated lands"[3] and "primitive" clans and tribes into modern Soviet citizens. If, after more than a decade of Soviet rule, the peoples of Central Asia and Siberia were still steeped in "feudal-era backwardness," then the revolution was not fulfilling its promise.

The Ethnographic Department of the Russian Museum in Leningrad was one of the Soviet Union's most important museums devoted to the lands and peoples of the USSR. As such, it provides a venue for exploring the production, dissemination, and reception of official narratives about a new type of multinational state that shared some similarities with the European empires but defined itself in anti-imperial terms. The previous two chapters analyzed the importance of census-taking and map-making to Soviet rule. This chapter examines the ethnographic museum as another cultural technology of rule—one with a critical role on the "ideological front."[4] The Ethnographic Department was a microcosm of the Soviet Union, and it provided ethnographers and political-enlightenment activists with a venue to work out and disseminate an idealized narrative about the socialist transformation of the Soviet Union—minus the violence and the setbacks. It also served as an important institution of civic education that provided Leningraders, Muscovites, and people from other regions who had neither the time nor the resources to travel throughout the Soviet Union with the experience of "virtual tourism."[5] At the museum it

2. I. Stalin, "God velikogo pereloma," *Voprosy Leninizma* (Moscow, 1932), 432–41. On the discourses of representation see Ivan Karp, "Culture and Representation," and Curtis M. Hinsley, "The World as Marketplace: Commodification of the Exotic at the World's Columbian Exposition, Chicago 1893," in *Exhibiting Cultures: The Poetics and Politics of Museum Display,* ed. Ivan Karp and Steven D. Lavine (Washington, 1991), 11–24, 344–65.

3. M. Ilin, *New Russia's Primer: The Story of the Five-Year Plan* (Boston, 1931), 120. This shift was in the making before the November 1929 speech. An April 1929 article in *Vsemirnyi turist* about summer tourism packages to the national republics proclaimed that "against a backdrop of brilliant nature and distinctive *byt*" it would be "easy to trace the rapid growth of the economy and culture of formerly oppressed nationalities." "Ekskursii po SSSR letom 1920 g.," *Vsemirnyi turist,* no. 4 (1929): 1920.

4. On the importance of the ethnographic museum to the "ideological front" see the St. Petersburg branch of the Central State Archive of Historical-Political Documents (TsGAIPD SPb) f. 4406, op. 1, d. 1, ll. 1–3.

5. Expositions of progress also provided an experience of virtual tourism. On Soviet expositions of progress see Greg Castillo, "Peoples at an Exhibition: Soviet Architecture and the National Question," in *Socialist Realism without Shores,* ed. Thomas Lahusen and Evgeny Dobrenko (Durham, 1997), 91–119. On international colonial expositions and world's fairs see Herman Lebovics, *True France: The Wars over Cultural Identity, 1900–1945* (Ithaca, 1992), and

was possible to visit all the "lands and peoples of the USSR" in the course of a few hours. Ethnographers, museum workers, and activists monitored the responses of Soviet citizens to their tours of the changing Soviet Union through discussion groups and through comment books that were placed throughout the museum.

The Ethnographic Department was a nexus of Soviet cultural production and state-building between 1923 and 1934—a critical period that saw the rise of Stalin and an effort to accelerate the revolution through a violent campaign for economic and social transformation. For more than a decade, the department's influence reached regions far beyond Leningrad. Exhibits throughout the Soviet Union were based on the department's approach, dubbed the "Leningrad model"; representatives from provincial- and republic-level museums traveled to the department to see the museum's collections and exhibits, and parts of the department's collection traveled to the provinces in the summer.[6] The Ethnographic Department was also a major research center and served as an institutional base for ethnographers who organized and participated in research expeditions throughout the Soviet Union. A number of prominent KIPS ethnographers—Sergei F. Ol'denburg, Sergei Rudenko, Aleksandr Samoilovich, David Zolotarev, Vasilii Bartol'd, Boris Kryzhanovskii, and others—held important positions in both institutions; Rudenko was the department's director during the 1920s.[7] These ethnographers were simultaneously organizing the First All-Union Census (the first census to categorize all Soviet citizens by "nationality"), drawing up ethnographic maps and reports for Soviet institutions engaged in the work of border delimitation, and producing exhibits for the Ethnographic Department. The fact that the same experts were involved in all three of these projects made discussions about which nationalities to include in or exclude from the ethnographic exhibits all the more politicized.

And yet for many years there was a major disjuncture between the department's museum work and other elements of Soviet state-building. Indeed, Benedict Anderson's much-cited argument that census, map, and museum comprise "a totalizing classificatory grid" does not hold up when tested in the Soviet context.[8] Even in the authoritarian Soviet Union, the overlap among

---

Robert W. Rydell, *All the World's a Fair: Visions of Empire at American International Expositions, 1876–1916* (Chicago, 1984). Of course, this form of virtual tourism predates the computer age.

6. See, for example, "Muzeinye s"ezdy, Kazanskii s"ezd," *Kraevedenie* 4, no. 2 (1927): 391.

7. Ol'denburg and Bartol'd were members of the museum soviet (council). Rudenko was curator of the Siberia collection, Zolotarev of the Finnish collection, and Kryzhanovskii of the Ukrainian and Belorussian collections. The museum also served as an institutional base for the regional studies (*kraevedenie*) movement. See T. V. Staniukovich, *250 let Muzeia antropologii i etnografii imini Petra Velikogo* (Moscow-Leningrad, 1964), 103–4.

8. Benedict Anderson, *Imagined Communities: Reflections on the Origin and Spread of Nationalism*, rev. ed. (London, 1991), 184.

census, map, and museum was far from seamless or "total." Soviet experts and administrators used the census and the map to amalgamate clans and tribes into nationalities—in an effort to facilitate the process of state-sponsored evolutionism. By contrast, the ethnographic museum, with its rich collection and exhibits about traditional culture, devoted significant attention to the "pre-Soviet" present and the past.[9] The Ethnographic Department's activists and experts worked hard to close this gap and come up with a heroic narrative about the evolution and development of the peoples of the USSR. This proved excruciatingly difficult. Newspapers and speeches could trumpet the revolution's successes in the countryside and steppe; it was much more challenging—and often impossible—to document these successes in a museum exhibit, where artifacts and evidence of the "new life" and its "new culture" were expected.

Beginning in 1927, the Communist Party and the People's Commissariat of Enlightenment (Narkompros) attempted to take control of the department, the museum experience, and the narrative of Soviet state formation. But they had limited success. It was not until the early 1930s that ethnographers and political-enlightenment activists came up with a template for a new series of ethnographic exhibits that successfully reconciled "the ideal" with "the real."[10] Instead of attempting to gloss over the revolution's setbacks, these new exhibits set out to explain them; they suggested that living "survivals" (*perezhitki*) from the Russian Empire's feudal and colonial past—clan leaders, shamans, and other class enemies—were hindering the process of revolutionary transformation.

The Ethnographic Department in the Period of Conceptual Conquest

The Ethnographic Department of the Russian Museum was founded in 1902, but did not open to the public until 1923. Initially, it was to have been imperial Russia's first public museum devoted to the lands and peoples of the Russian Empire; the initial exposition, slated for 1915, was supposed to demonstrate the breadth of tsarist rule and the influence of Russian language, thought, and *byt* on the empire's other tribes and *narodnosti*.[11] The start of

---

9. George Stocking has noted that all ethnographic museums are "institutions in which the forces of historical inertia (or 'cultural lag') are profoundly, perhaps inescapably, implicated." George W. Stocking, Jr., *Delimiting Anthropology: Occasional Essays and Reflections* (Madison, 2001), 251.

10. On the Soviet project and the tension between "the ideal" and "the real" also see Eric Naiman, *Sex in Public: The Incarnation of Early Soviet Ideology* (Princeton, 1997).

11. N. Mogilianskii, "Russkie etnograficheskie muzei i sobraniia: Etnograficheskii Otdel Russkogo Muzeiia Imperatora Aleksandra III," *Zhivaia starina* 20, no. 3–4 (1911): 473–98. On the early history of the museum also see Gosudarstvennyi Russkii muzei, *Otchet Russkogo muzeia za 1922 goda* (Petrograd, 1923), 3–47. The Ethnographic Department was supposed to replicate the model of the "public museum" found at the time in France and Germany; such museums served explicit civic education roles. See B. Adler, "O 'natsional'nykh' muzeiakh," *Zhizn' natsional'nostei*, no. 1(7) (February 25, 1922): 2–3.

Figure 5.1 Anatolii Lunacharskii and Sergei F. Ol'denburg at the Ethnographic Department of the Russian Museum. (From the collection of the Russian Museum of Ethnography, St. Petersburg, Russia)

World War I postponed the opening of the exhibit—and facilitated the collapse of the very empire that the museum celebrated. Ethnographers continued to use the department as an institutional base for their research and were able to preserve much of the collection during the chaos of war and revolution.[12] In the aftermath of the civil war, Lenin, Anatolii Lunacharskii (the head of Narkompros), and other Soviet leaders recognized the potential of the museum as a tool to educate the masses and allocated funds to the Ethnographic Department.[13] Six years after imperial Russia had ceased to exist, the department finally opened its doors.

In June 1923, on the eve of the official formation of the Soviet Union, the Ethnographic Department invited the public to see its exhibit on "The Peoples of the USSR." Aside from the addition of some new maps, posters, and artifacts, this exhibit was more or less the one that had originally been planned for

12. A significant part of the collection was evacuated to Moscow during World War I.

13. A. B. Zaks, "Rech' A. V. Lunacharskogo na konferentsii po delam muzeev," in *Arkheografischeskii ezhegodnik za 1976 g.,* ed. S. O. Smidt et al. (Moscow, 1977), 210–16. Also I. I. Shangina, "Etnograficheskie muzei Leningrada v pervye gody sovetskoi vlasti [1918–1923 gg.]," *Etnograficheskoe obozrenie,* no. 5 (1987): 71–80.

1915.[14] Little mention was made of the revolution—and the creation of the new national republics and oblasts was not acknowledged. Instead, the exhibit was divided into four general ethnogeographical sections. The first featured the Great Russians and Finns of Russia and its northern neighbors; the second, the Ukrainians, Belorussians, and other (ethnically or culturally) related *narodnosti* of Russia and contiguous states; the third, the *narodnosti* of the Caucasus, Turkestan, the Crimea, and part of the Volga region; and the fourth, the *narodnosti,* tribes, and clans of Siberia and the Far East. The Great Russian and Ukrainian collections were each subdivided according to *guberniia,* the main administrative unit of the Russian Empire. Other *narodnosti* that also called these provinces home—such as the Finns and the Belorussians—were separated out into their own halls. The exhibit's two "non-European" ethnogeographical sections (devoted to the peoples of Turkestan, the Caucasus, Siberia, and the Far East) were organized according to a combination of "ethnic type" and *byt*; the Turkestan collection, for example, occupied three halls labeled "nomadic peoples," "semi-nomadic peoples," and "settled peoples."[15]

All four sections of the exhibit took traditional culture and *byt* as their main focus, displaying hand-woven rugs, musical instruments of wood and bone, painted masks, animal skins, and religious items from amulets to Orthodox icons. Mannequins in native dress—a Georgian knight, a "Little Russian" (Ukrainian) peasant, a Buriat hunter, and others—stood at various points throughout the museum. The exhibit also illustrated how geographical and cultural conditions affected the development of each *narodnost'*. Entering the northern-Russia hall, for example, the visitor was introduced to "a collection of items characterizing the Great Russians of the northern *gubernii* in the past and present." This section featured women's dresses and embroidered scarves, handicrafts, and tools for agriculture, fishing, and hunting for each *guberniia*. Pinned to the walls were photographs of churches, chapels, and homes. In an attempt to "enliven" the exhibit, ethnographers had reproduced a "typical" peasant hut from Olonetsk with a wood-burning stove and a samovar. The exhibit noted—with approval—that the northern Great Russians of this region still preserved a number of the distinctive *bytovye* (customary or cultural) practices and traits represented in the exhibit. Venturing "further eastward" to the Chukchi hall of the Siberia and Far East section, the visitor met the

14. The exhibit's ethnogeographical organization was based on a model that had been proposed before the war by the anthropologist-geographer Vladimir Lamanskii. See V. P. Semenov-Tian-Shanskii, "Vladimir Ivanovich Lamanskii, kak antropogeograf i politikogeograf," *Zhivaia starina* 24, no. 1–2 (1915): 9–20. Lamanskii died in 1915, but his ideas and plans endured and were championed by the ethnographers Veniamin Semenov-Tian-Shanskii, Rudenko, and Aleksandr Miller. Many of the same ethnographers affiliated with the department in the 1920s had worked on the 1915 exhibit.

15. Gosudarstvennyi Russkii muzei, *Etnograficheskii otdel Russkogo muzeia* (Petrograd, 1923), and Gosudarstvennyi Russkii muzei, *Otchetnaia vystavka Etnograficheskogo otdela za 1923 g.* (Petrograd, 1924). Parts of the description are from photographs of the exhibits, from REM's photo archive.

Figure 5.2 The Caucasus hall at the Ethnographic Department of the Russian Museum, 1924. (From the collection of the Russian Museum of Ethnography, St. Petersburg, Russia)

Chukchi warrior and the Siberian shaman. An old-fashioned wooden sled stood in the middle of the room, and tools, oil lamps, and fur pelts were laid out on shelves. Here, too, the exhibit emphasized the endurance of traditional culture, noting that in spite of Russian colonization, this indigenous people had preserved its *byt,* which had developed during its centuries-long struggle "for survival in the severe natural conditions" of the Siberian landscape.[16]

Several other halls, by contrast, explored what happened when a *narodnost'* split into two or more peoples as a result of continual pressure from other (more dominant) cultures or ethnicities. One room of the exhibit on "the Finnish peoples" compared the Komi-Zyrians with the Komi-Permiaks in order to demonstrate how one Finnic *narod* (the Komi) had split into two after part of it (the Komi-Permiaks) had been "Turkified." The Georgian halls presented a similar case, explaining that the Ajars had broken off from other ethnic Georgians after adopting Islam. They also showed the opposite phenomenon: how cultural-historical factors had united tribal groups with different ethnic origins (such as the Svans and the Batsbi) into the Georgian *narodnost'.*

Soviet leaders and pedagogues saw the museum as an institution that would educate and entertain the masses—as a "living textbook" that would teach schoolchildren, workers, peasants, and soldiers about the Soviet multinational state. The department worked with teachers to integrate the museum into the school curriculum, and arranged free—and often mandatory—tours and lec-

16. Gosudarstvennyi Russkii muzei, *Etnograficheskii otdel Russkogo muzeia,* esp. 14–16, 35–36, 40.

tures for soldiers and workers.[17] Although the department's stated purpose was to provide "a complete picture of everyday life in the USSR,"[18] its actual effect was otherwise. Visitors might marvel at the panorama of peoples with whom they shared Soviet citizenship, but they often left with the impression that the wax figures in animal hides were strange "others" from distant lands. Children became acquainted with the Chukchi warrior and the Siberian shaman, but the exhibits did not suggest what relevance either one had to their lives. Moreover, people from Leningrad and its environs were hard-pressed to see themselves even in the representations of the Russians or Finns.

To make matters worse, one of the exhibit's main messages—that geographical and climatic conditions shaped (and thus, by extension, limited) humankind—contradicted the revolution's optimism. A booklet for teachers coproduced by the museum and the Leningrad Department of Education (LONO) in 1925 explained that the museum's main exhibit would teach schoolchildren that the struggle with nature was responsible for the particularistic development of different peoples:

> Becoming acquainted with the lives of the Samoeds, Chukchi, Koriaks, Uigurs and Chuvans who are scattered in the far north of Russia and Siberia in a mire of unforgiving tundra near the cold Arctic Sea; with the Tungus and Ostiaks who wander with pack deer in search of game upon the remote taiga . . . with the peoples of the Altai and the Caucasus, cramped in the hills but stubbornly struggling for existence, we see that the human being structures its life in accordance with its natural surroundings.[19]

The booklet posited that "nature encourages certain economic activities," which in turn influence the development of social relationships, art, and even religion. The ethnographers had considered such an explanation sufficiently "Marxist," as ethnographic traits were tied to economic conditions and nationality (*narodnost'*) was embodied in the act of economic production. But the ethnographic exhibit (and booklet) gave no hint that tribes and nationali-

17. REM f. 2, op. 1, d. 174a, ll. 530b, 730b–74, 85–850b; Gosudarstvennyi Russkii muzei, *Otchet Gosudarstvennogo Russkogo muzeia za 1923 i 1924 gg.* (Leningrad, 1925); *Otchet Gosudarstvennogo Russkogo muzeia za 1925 g.* (Leningrad, 1926); and *Otchet Gosudarstvennogo Russkogo muzeia za 1926 i 1927 gg.* (Leningrad, 1928). The quote is from *Otchet Gosudarstvennogo Russkogo muzeia za 1926 i 1927 gg.*, 4. The department's ethnographers spoke with admiration about German and American ethnographic museums and about French and British colonial expositions. The journal *Etnografiia* featured numerous discussions of German, French, and American museums. See N. M. Eliash, "Etnograficheskie muzei v Germanii," *Etnografiia*, no. 1 (1927): 151–59.

18. *Otchet Gosudarstvennogo Russkogo muzeia za 1923 i 1924 gg.*, 25.

19. N. P. Popov, *Ekskursii v byt narodov SSSR* (Ekskursii po Etnograficheskomu otdelu Russkogo muzeia) (Leningrad, 1925), 3.

ties could overcome the forces of nature. Nor did they demonstrate how the Soviet regime could conquer nature and reshape identities.[20]

Between 1925 and 1927, the department's ethnographers served as expert-consultants to a number of Soviet institutions and, often in connection with this work, led research expeditions throughout the Soviet Union. They collected artifacts of local culture, took photographs, and drew sketches for new ethnographic exhibits.[21] Although all the ethnographers agreed that updating "The Peoples of the USSR" was essential, they disagreed about how best to do so. There were several key points of contention. First: Should exhibits be organized on ethnogeographical lines (according to national republic and oblast) or on ethnic lines (according to *narodnost'* or ethnic group)? For example, should the new exhibit show the Jews in each of their national republics and oblasts of residence—the Ukrainian SSR, Belorussian SSR, Georgian SSR, Kazakh ASSR, and so on—or united in one section about the Jewish *narodnost'*? (Part of the existing exhibit employed the former approach, with a corner of the Ukrainian and Belorussian section focusing on the Jews of those regions.) Second: Should a new exhibit include all of the *narodnosti* that lived within Soviet borders or just the most important ones? Some of the department's ethnographers suggested that the museum, as an institution of *Völkerkunde* (the science of national distinctiveness), should show the ethnocultural particularities of *all* the peoples of the USSR. These experts proposed that the department embark on expeditions to collect artifacts from those *narodnosti* that were not represented in the museum's collection.[22] Other ethnographers disagreed and argued that the new exhibit should focus on fewer peoples in order to chronicle in greater detail the development of their material culture and belief systems from ancient times to the present; these experts, advocates of the cultural-evolutionary school, argued that the museum's task was to document comparative cultural development.[23]

The Ukrainian expert Boris Kryzhanovskii and the Siberian expert Sergei Rudenko proposed that the new exhibit might take a cultural-historical approach that would combine elements of *Völkerkunde* and cultural evolutionism. But these two ethnographers had different ideas about what this might look like. Kryzhanovskii advocated that the department's new exhibit take *narodnost'* as its basic organizational unit; railing against the department's preoccupation with "the most exotic and colorful tribes and peoples," he recommended that each *narodnost'* receive a space "in correspondence with its

20. Ibid., 3–4.

21. For example, REM f. 2, op. 1, d. 174a, ll. 150b, 200b.

22. REM f. 2, op. 1, d. 174, ll. 200b, 37, 380b.

23. Lev Shternberg adopted this approach in exhibits at the Museum of Anthropology and Ethnography. Shternberg defined culture as "all inventions made by man for the satisfaction of different needs." T. V. Staniukovich, *Etnograficheskaia nauka i muzei (Po materialam etnograficheskikh muzeev Akademii nauk)* (Leningrad, 1978), 166–68.

size and significance."[24] In order to satisfy proponents of the cultural-evolutionary school, Kryzhanovskii suggested that the exhibit take an evolutionary-typological approach to material culture: that for each *narodnost'* it display different objects of material culture (clothing, tools, dishes) in evolutionary order.[25] He insisted, however, that the exhibit include only those items which corresponded to the culture of "expressly *ethnic* groups"—that it focus exclusively on traditional culture (in its folk forms), documenting a *narodnost'* from its "prehistory" until the moment at which "its culture loses its ethnic character" and takes on a "general European" character.[26] According to Kryzhanovskii, the "more advanced strata" of the more advanced *narodnosti*, which had "fully made the transition to European forms of life," did not have a place in the exhibit. The exhibit might display the "peasant *byt*" of such *narodnosti* (since most peasants "retain their traditional culture" longer than other classes), he conceded, but should not show the "more general urban *byt*" of workers.[27]

Rudenko, by contrast, urged his colleagues not to fetishize the past. He agreed that all nationalities had distinctive and rich folk pasts and lost much of their ethnographic distinctiveness as they became more modern. And he noted that in "revolutionary circumstances," where culture was "evolving constantly and quickly," this process of evolutionary change took place more rapidly. But Rudenko differed with Kryzhanovskii in advocating that the department "embrace these developments" and "show the evolution of humankind through its different stages" *into* its more modern stage. Rather than focus on traditional culture, the new exhibit should document "the rise of new cultural forms," he argued. For example, the new exhibit might chart the development of literacy, citizenship, public life, and new belief systems. These four spheres, he noted, created the "basic conditions" through which "ethnic groups [tribes and *narodnosti*] become nations [*natsii*]." Rudenko urged the department to take "ethnos" (which he defined as an ethnosocial formation distinguished by "a complex of historical and cultural traits")—and not *narodnost'*—as its main organizational category. According to Rudenko, an ethnos evolved over time and took on new characteristics, whereas a *narodnost'* was the expression of an ethnos at one moment on the evolutionary timeline.[28]

---

24. Kryzhanovskii suggested that the department exhibit "*narodnosti* belonging to one ethnic group" near one another. See B. G. Kryzhanovskii, *Printsipy ekspozitsii etnograficheskogo muzeia, Muzeinoe delo*, vol. 4 (Leningrad, 1926), 5–6.

25. Kryzhanovskii, *Printsipy ekspozitsii etnograficheskogo muzeia*, 10–12. On the evolutionary-typological approach see Staniukovich, *Etnograficheskaia nauka i muzei*, 190–91.

26. Kryzhanovskii, *Printsipy ekspozitsii etnograficheskogo muzeia*, 12–14. Emphasis added.

27. Ibid., 13–14.

28. The St. Petersburg Branch of the Archive of the Russian Academy of Sciences (PFA RAN) f. 282, op. 1, d. 69, ll. 2–7. For a discussion of the term *ethnos* see N. Mogilianskii, "Predmet i zadachi etnografii," *Zhivaia starina* 25, no. 1 (1916): 1–22. For a discussion about the reorganization of the Ethnographic Department see Kryzhanovskii, *Printsipy ekspozitsii etnograficheskogo muzeia*.

The department's ethnographers did not fully adopt the term *ethnos* into their discourse until the mid-1930s.[29] Instead, they tried to refine their definition of *narodnost'*. By 1926, the category *narodnost'* was becoming the leitmotif of the department's discussions, in much the same way that it had become a fundamental category of classification in the All-Union Census. The department (in some cases in coordination with KIPS) attempted to determine which of the *inorodtsy* constituted separate *narodnosti*. It also debated how to represent *narodnosti* that had been Turkified or Russified, or had otherwise mixed with other peoples and lost their original ethnocultural traits. During the summer of 1926, several of the department's ethnographers led research expeditions (under the auspices of KIPS) that focused on these questions. For example, Rudenko led an expedition to the Altai region of western Siberia, studying the "inheritance of racial traits" (in this case, physical traits) among the region's "tribes and tribal subgroups" in instances of "racial mixing [*metizatsiia*]." Zolotarev led an expedition to the central Volga region that studied the Tatarization of the Mishers and the Russification of the Meshcheriaks.[30]

Between 1923 and 1927, the department's ethnographers engaged in significant discussions and debates about reorganizing the museum, and embarked on a number of important research expeditions. But little visible progress was made within the halls of the Ethnographic Department. During these years, the new Soviet regime was most focused on the conceptual conquest of the lands and peoples within its borders; the ethnographers, occupied with the critical projects of census-taking and map-making, were able to devote only limited attention to the creation of new ethnographic exhibits.

The Anniversary Celebrations and the Campaign to Sovietize the Museum

The year 1927 marked a turning point at the Ethnographic Department and at other cultural institutions in the Soviet Union. In honor of the ten-year anniversary of the October Revolution, the party and Narkompros sponsored special events at museums and theaters in Moscow, Leningrad, and other cities. To coordinate this political-enlightenment work, the party established a greater presence in a number of cultural institutions with key roles in civic education, including the Ethnographic Department.[31] The anniversary celebra-

29. After World War II, Soviet ethnography would become the study of ethnos. This is discussed in the epilogue.

30. PFA RAN f. 135, op. 1, d. 22, ll. 82–84.

31. The Leningrad party cell of ethnography was established under the auspices of the Excursion-Lecture Base of the LONO Politprosvet. The cell discussed "methodological questions" as they related to the formulation of exhibits at Leningrad's two ethnographic museums: the Ethnographic Department of the Russian Museum and the Museum of Anthropology and Ethnography of the Academy of Sciences. For reports on the meetings of the new party cell see REM f. 2, op. 1, d. 232, ll. 1–39.

tion was an important, but not the sole, impetus behind the party's heightened interest in the ethnographic museum. With the execution of the All-Union Census, the demarcation of new national-territorial borders, and the establishment of a new administrative apparatus, the Soviet regime had completed much of the basic work of conceptual conquest. At the same time, the Soviet regime had stepped up its efforts on the ideological front, using the cultural sphere in its attempt to change mass consciousness.[32] As Soviet leaders discussed taking the revolution to the "next stage," the Leningrad branch of the Communist Party and the Political-Enlightenment (Politprosvet) Division of LONO looked to use the Ethnographic Department and its exhibits to teach the population about—and thus to further—the revolution's transformative agenda.[33] A particular goal seems to have been to teach the population of Leningrad—most of whom were ethnic Russians—about the diverse nationalities of the USSR who shared their Soviet citizenship.

In April 1927, a group of Politprosvet activists toured the Ethnographic Department and gave a scathing critique of the exhibit "The Peoples of the USSR." According to these activists, the display of Siberian shamans in lavish ceremonial robes suggested that Soviet efforts to "wipe out superstition" and "raise the population's cultural level" had failed. Furthermore, museum showcases filled with antiquated ploughs and archaic tools from Turkestan and Ukraine did not show how state-sponsored campaigns had mechanized agriculture in non-Russian rural regions. Where was the tractor? The activists asserted that ethnographers should stop dwelling on the "rare, exotic, and primitive" and should start showing the process of Sovietization.[34] These Politprosvet activists—all party members with experience in the realm of education and propaganda (and no formal training in ethnography)—were members of a new Ethnographic Bureau party cell. This party cell included in its ranks several professional ethnographers from the Ethnographic Department as well as from the Museum of Anthropology and Ethnography.[35]

---

32. The Soviet Union had become what Peter Kenez describes as "a propaganda state." See Peter Kenez, *The Birth of the Propaganda State: Soviet Methods of Mass Mobilization, 1917–1929* (Cambridge, 1985). Unlike other states that used propaganda, the Soviet regime was interested in the transformation of consciousness as opposed to the manipulation of public opinion. On the British case, see John M. Mackenzie, *Propaganda and Empire: The Manipulation of British Public Opinion, 1880–1960* (Manchester, 1990).

33. Politprosvet engaged in mass agitation work on "general political questions and practical questions" with the aim of socialist construction. For a discussion of Politprosvet's activities and goals, see TsGAIPD SPb f. 24, op. 8, d. 60, l. 98.

34. REM f. 2, op. 1, d. 232, ll. 1–20.

35. V. V. Ekimova, the head of the party cell, was a member of the party and an "experienced propagandist." Cited in T. A. Kriukova and E. N. Studenetskaia, "Gosudarstvennyi muzei etnografii narodov SSSR za piat'desiat let Sovetskoi vlasti," in *Ocherki istorii muzeinogo dela v SSSR* (Moscow, 1971), 29. Kriukova and Studenetskaia also discuss the origins of the party cell. The Politprosvet workers were connected to the LONO Politprosvet, whose job it was to coordinate the political-enlightenment work of all government and professional organizations in Leningrad. LONO reported to Narkompros. The LONO Politprosvet reported to the Methodological Bureau

Beginning in the summer of 1927, the Ethnographic Bureau party cell and the rest of the Ethnographic Department's (mostly nonparty) ethnographers embarked on a critical, albeit vague, mission: to figure out what "Soviet nationalities" looked like and how the museum should represent them in its exhibits. As this work got under way, a crisis of representation ensued. If the peoples of the Soviet Union had traded in traditional costumes for modern dress, outdated tools for state-of-the-art machines, and religious customs for Soviet practices, what was it that distinguished the different nationalities? Should mannequins continue to have racialized features, or was this in contradiction with the official line that nationality was not biologically predetermined but was instead dependent on cultural-historical variables? In their work on the All-Union Census of 1926, some of the department's ethnographers (who were also members of KIPS) had concluded that culture, language, religion, *byt,* physical type, and economic practices were all important signposts of nationality, but that an individual's subjective testimony was the ultimate determinant. This formula could not be applied to work on museum exhibits, however, since not even the most animate mannequins could express their national consciousness.

The party cell's Politprosvet activists proposed that new ethnographic exhibits highlight the achievements of the national republics and oblasts in a period of economic and social revolution. New exhibits might document the successes of unionwide industrialization and electrification; the creation of national-language schools, theaters, and clubs; the formation of national-language army divisions; and the local development of science and art.[36] The activists further suggested that Soviet nationalities should be distinguished less by ancient ethnographic particularities (such as religious rites or superstitions) and more by a combination of national-cultural forms (such as national costumes and dances) and economic practices.[37] Here, they seem to have had a specific model in mind: the Agricultural and Cottage Industry Exposition of 1923. Celebrating the formation of the Soviet Union and the transition to a peacetime economy, this Moscow exposition had featured republic-level and oblast-level pavilions set up to illustrate each ethnoterritorial region's natural resources and economic orientation.[38] This model for reworking the department's exhibit had some supporters, especially among a group of graduate students at Leningrad State University who had studied ethnography with the re-

of the Leningrad branch of the Communist Party. See, for example, TsGAIPD SPb f. 24, op. 8, d. 71a, l. 5. Party cell members also reported to the Scientific-Methodological Soviet (Council) of LONO.

36. Here they unknowingly echoed Rudenko.

37. REM f. 2, op. 1, d. 232, ll. 17, 24–28.

38. This exposition was modeled on—and against—European colonial expositions. For a general overview of the exposition and its features, see M. I. Fedorova, *Pervaia Vsesoiuznaia sel'skokhoziaistvennaia vystavka* (Moscow, 1953). Some of the Leningrad ethnographers had been consultants for the exposition. See, for example, PFA RAN f. 135, op. 1, d. 9, l. 85.

cently deceased Lev Shternberg.[39] But most of the department's ethnographers were reluctant to turn their museum into an exposition of economic achievements. They breathed a collective sigh of relief when the party cell acknowledged that the department lacked the resources to reconstruct its exhibit in time for the ten-year anniversary celebration.

With October quickly approaching, the activists and ethnographers reached a somewhat peculiar compromise: they would work together through the party cell to create a series of guided museum tours which combined the existing exhibits (those still in place from before 1917!) with new scripts about the revolution's accomplishments. New tours discussing the economic and cultural transformation of the population, the antireligious campaign, and the Soviet approach to the national and colonial questions—contrasting Soviet policies with those of the Russian Empire and the European colonial empires—were quickly prepared.[40] According to the proposed plan, trained guides (museum workers, pedagogues, and graduate students from Leningrad State University) would usher visitors from place to place in the museum, narrating the transition from the prerevolutionary past to the Soviet present. Even if the department's exhibit remained unchanged, the museum experience would be transformed; at least that was the goal.[41]

Thus began a new series of museum tours about the lands and peoples of the Soviet Union. One such tour, "October and the Peoples of the USSR," brought small groups of individual visitors as well as large groups of schoolchildren, workers, and soldiers through the museum's collections from Siberia, the Kirgiz ASSR, and the Leningrad region. The tour took a cultural-evolutionary approach in that it chronicled the progression from "less to more developed" peoples. In keeping with the Leninist idea that revolutionary actors could speed up historical progress, the tour emphasized how the Soviet regime was facilitating the development of "the cultures and economies of all the peoples of the USSR" no matter where they stood on the evolutionary timeline.[42] The first stop was Siberia, where museumgoers became acquainted with the Chukchi, Tungus, and Buriats. At a Chukchi exhibit, museumgoers beheld the bone dishes, hunting implements, fur garments, and wooden sleds "typical of a backward culture." The guide explained that the tsarist government had exploited the indigenous peoples of Siberia, but that the Soviet government had rescued them "through economic and cultural aid." Museumgo-

39. In 1927 these students started their own ethnographic journal, which was devoted to the relationship between economics and ethnography. See V. Serebriakov, "Ekonomika v etnografii," *Etnograf-Issledovatel'*, no. 2–3 (1927): 46–51.

40. See for example REM f. 2, op. 1, d. 232, l. 25.

41. REM f. 2, op. 1, d. 259, ll. 160b, 18, 24, 25, 38, 40, 42, 43, 48. For the next two years the party cell was primarily occupied with preparing, discussing, and approving potential tours.

42. REM f. 2, op. 1, d. 174a, l. 1430b. On the theory of cultural evolutionism and its application to museum exhibits, see the essays in George W. Stocking, Jr., ed., *Objects and Others: Essays on Museums and Material Culture* (Madison, 1985).

ers next looked at the ceremonial items of the Siberian shaman, while the guide explained that shamanism was "the product of a low cultural level." The guide discussed Soviet measures to enlighten the masses in Siberia, including the establishment of culture bases with medical care, schools, and educational lectures. The tour next stopped in the Kirgiz halls. Here, visitors viewed a mannequin bride and learned about Soviet efforts to eliminate the bride price and emancipate women. The last stop was "northern Great Russia" (including the Leningrad region) where museumgoers "visited" Great Russian and western Finnish peasants. As museumgoers examined traditional farming implements, the museum guide described Soviet efforts to modernize agricultural production; as they looked at fishing gear from different eras, the guide discussed the exploitation of fishermen under tsarism, Soviet measures to improve fishing, and the significance of fishing to the USSR's economy.[43] Other museum tours featuring different parts of the museum's collection took a similar approach.[44]

These new museum tours may have put the proper ideological spin on the department's exhibit, but in practice they were too dry to sustain the interest of museumgoers (most of whom had little formal education). With this concern in mind, the party and Narkompros launched a new campaign in 1928 to "Sovietize" the Ethnographic Department in a more general sense—to turn it into a museum explicitly for the masses. In June of that year, the Leningrad branch of the party and LONO established a second party cell of ethnography in Leningrad. Whereas the original cell (renamed the "methodological cell") oversaw the messages of the exhibits, the new cultural-enlightenment cell concerned itself with the role of the ethnographic museum as a Soviet institution of civic education.[45] Where the former attempted to determine what Soviet nationalities looked like, the latter asked how a Soviet museum should go about educating and entertaining the masses. This party cell also brought Politprosvet activists and ethnographers together and included nonparty ethnographers in its ranks; even if the Politprosvet activists and nonparty ethnographers did not always agree about what Soviet citizens should know, they were equally committed to making the museum more engaging, expanding the museum's audience, and raising the population's "cultural level."[46]

Perhaps the new party cell's most important innovation for introducing the masses to the peoples of the USSR was the "ethnographic evening of solidarity." Every week the department invited the workers from a different factory,

43. REM f. 2, op. 1, d. 144, ll. 16–19.

44. REM f. 2, op. 1, d. 259, l. 30b, 160b. Most of these tours visited three parts of the museum's permanent exhibit.

45. The methodological cell was later renamed the Methodological Bureau. REM f. 2, op. 1, d. 260, ll. 1–4. Also see *Otchet Gosudarstvennogo Russkogo muzeia za 1928 g.* (Leningrad, 1929), 17–19. The ethnographers Kryzhanovskii, Zolotarev, and Miller were active in this cell. The cell worked closely with the "Excursion Base" of the LONO Politprosvet.

46. REM f. 2, op. 1, d. 260, ll. 1–15; d. 250, l. 1.

club, or collective to an evening of museum tours, movies, performances, and discussions.[47] The typical evening would last for two to three hours and include some two hundred attendees. On the weekends, repeat performances were staged for Red Army units, schools, and Komsomol groups. Themes, which varied a great deal, included "Winter in the Lopar Tundra," "Chechnia and the Chechens," and "The Peoples of the USSR and the Five-Year Plan."[48] These evenings were supposed to re-create "entire episodes" from "the lives of diverse class groups in different epochs." They drew some of their inspiration from the "live exhibits" of colonial expositions and world's fairs, as well as from the "parade of nationalities" in the 1923 Agricultural and Cottage Industry Exposition—a procession of peoples in national dress who sang to the revolution's glories in their native languages.[49]

A typical "ethnographic evening" proceeded as follows: First, one of the department's ethnographers gave a short opening address or the department showed a short film on the general theme. Next, storytellers and musicians entertained the crowd with folktales and traditional music and dance. Sometimes theatrical groups from different republics appeared, and on occasion graduate students from the Institute of the Peoples of the North reenacted rituals. Often, Russian and Jewish actors from the State Experimental Theater presented their interpretations of different peoples' customs and folk cultures.[50] After the entertainment, museum guides took the visitors on one of the scripted tours of the museum; in 1927 and 1928 "October and the Peoples of the USSR" was the most repeated tour.[51] The museum guides capped the evening with a "question and answer" session—in which they quizzed the visitors. "Who helped the peasant more: the priest with the incense or the communist with the tractor?" "What is socialism and how does our country move toward it?" "From the moment of the October Revolution, what kinds of changes took

47. REM f. 2, op. 1, d. 174a, ll. 1480b–1500b; d. 259, l. 48; d. 260, ll. 10–15; d. 269, ll. 6, 12; d. 282, l. 10. Also *Otchet Gosudarstvennogo Russkogo muzeia za 1928 g.*, 20, and Kriukova and Studenetskaia, "Gosudarstvennyi muzei etnografii narodov SSSR," 30.

48. REM f. 2, op. 1, d. 269, l. 12; d. 299, ll. 10–16. Also [Gosudarstvennyi Russkii muzei], *Gosudarstvennyi etnograficheskii teatr* (Leningrad, 1931), and [Gosudarstvennyi Russkii muzei], *Etnograficheskii teatr* (Leningrad, 1930).

49. REM f. 2, op. 1, d. 260, ll. 10–15. Ethnographers in the early 1920s imagined creating an outdoor ethnographic museum with a live ethnographic exhibit. See, for example, D. Ianovich, "K voprosu ob izuchenii byta narodnostei RSFSR," *Zhizn' natsional'nostei*, no. 29 (127) (December 14, 1921): 1.

50. REM f. 2, op. 1, d. 299, ll. 29–30; d. 269, l. 25, and [Gosudarstvennyi Russkii muzei] *Etnograficheskii teatr*, 2–6. 25. In February 1929 the State Experimental Theater merged with the museum and became the Ethnographic Theater. It was shut down in 1932.

51. REM f. 2, op. 1, d. 259, l. 18, and *Otchet Gosudarstvennogo Russkogo muzeia za 1928*, 19. Other tours, such as "The Economy of the USSR in Connection with Nationality Policy: The Caucasus, Siberia, Karelia, and Turkestan," and "The Ukraine and Its Significance in the Economy of the USSR," were also given regularly. See, for example, REM f. 2, op. 1, d. 259, ll. 40, 49. In 1929, a new cycle of tours was prepared in conjunction with the antireligious campaign. See REM f. 2, op. 1, d. 319, l. 1.

Figure 5.3 In February 1929 the State Experimental Theater merged with the Ethnographic Department and became the Ethnographic Theater. Pictured above some time after the merger. (From the collection of the Russian Museum of Ethnography, St. Petersburg, Russia)

place for the Union's different *narodnosti?*"[52] The questions were supposed to elicit the "correct" responses. But if necessary, the guides provided the answers. The ethnographic evening, like the ethnographic museum in general, was intended to teach the population how to think about the past, the present, and the future, and to help the actual peoples of the USSR imagine themselves into the emerging narrative of Soviet-sponsored evolution and achievement.[53]

As the new party cell organized these evenings of solidarity, it also worked with LONO to establish a more formal program of workers' education at the department—a Workers' University course on "The Peoples of the USSR."[54] In preparation for this course, the department's ethnographers wrote lectures about "the life and *byt*" of the Soviet Union's diverse nationalities, and representatives from LONO's Politprosvet Division wrote lectures about Soviet nationality policy, the antireligious campaign, and the Five-Year Plan.[55] LONO

52. REM f. 2, op. 1, d. 282, l. 8; d. 232, ll. 26–260b.

53. On studies of the spectator see G. N. Krasilina, "Iz opyta raboty sovetskikh muzeev po populiarizatsii i izucheniiu muzeinogo zriteliia v 1920e–1930e gody," *Muzei 2 khudozhestvennye sobraniia SSSR* (Moscow, 1981). For a discussion of how the party encouraged people to imagine themselves as part of the narrative of 1917, see Frederick Corney, "Rethinking a Great Event: The October Revolution as Memory Project," *Social Science History* 22, no. 4 (1998): 389–414. On the importance of participation to the success of the "Soviet project" see Stephen Kotkin, *Magnetic Mountain: Stalinism as a Civilization* (Berkeley, 1995).

54. The three-month course, which began in December 1928, was run by the State Russian Museum and LONO. REM f. 2, op. 1, d. 261, ll. 1–4, 11.

55. For the lectures given during the first year see REM f. 2, op. 1, d. 261, ll. 15–16, 18, 21–22, 24, 28–30, 34–40, 43–54.

saw this course as a forum for recruiting new museum guides and for preparing workers for positions in other cultural institutions.[56] The ethnographers, for their part, noted that "how the course is used will depend on the students themselves" since "an understanding of the everyday-life [*bytovye*] particularities" of the population "can be applied to any area of labor." Advertisements in newspapers invited cultural workers and other individuals interested in "working in the public sphere and building new *byt*" to apply. Prerequisites for enrollment included literacy in Russian, competency in one's native language, basic math skills, "maturity," and a letter of recommendation from a party official or trade union.[57] As the course got under way, the department announced with much fanfare that it was becoming an institution for the proletariat. In truth, the majority of enrollees were not "proletarians," but teachers, students, cultural workers, and the unemployed. Moreover, in spite of the department's expressed interest in enrolling non-Russians and party members in the course (a frequent topic of discussion at party cell meetings), most students were nonparty Russians.[58]

"The Peoples of the USSR" through the "Great Break"

In 1929 the Soviet regime initiated what some scholars have aptly called the "revolution from above"—introducing new policies to promote rapid industrialization and the collectivization of agriculture, and vowing to enact a "great break" (*velikii perelom*) with the past. These efforts to accelerate the revolution were accompanied by a campaign on the ideological front. At stake was a struggle between two knowledge systems: that of former imperial experts with a Western European orientation and that of Politprosvet activists and other party members steeped in Marxism-Leninism.[59] By 1929, the party had successfully seeded cultural and scientific institutions throughout the Soviet Union; new party cells brought together ethnographers and activists, who worked in an often uneasy alliance. Over the next three years, the party sought ever greater control over the "machinery of representation," attempting to

---

56. REM f. 2, op. 1, d. 260, ll. 3–6. The course "The Peoples of the USSR" was one of fourteen civic education courses offered as part of the Workers' Sunday University in Leningrad. Other courses (on literature, music, agriculture, art, the history of the revolution, and so on) were held at other cultural institutions and at worker union headquarters. See TsGAIPD SPb f. 24, op. 8, d. 60, l. 98.

57. REM f. 2, op. 1, d. 261, l. 1; d. 326, ll. 3–6; d. 327, ll. 1–3. Ads for the course appeared in *Pravda* and *Krasnaia gazeta*. REM f. 2, op. 1, d. 283, l. 8.

58. REM f. 2, op. 1, d. 261, ll. 85–89, 164; d. 283, ll. 39, 43–48. The course attendance sheets state each student's name, age, address, place of work, occupation and party membership—but do not list nationality. The ethnographers and pedagogues spoke about the preponderance of Russian enrollees and the need to recruit more non-Russians. See, for example, REM f. 2, op. 1, d. 283, l. 11.

59. For a sense of the intensification of ideological struggle, see TsGAIPD SPb f. 4406, op. 1, d. 1, ll. 1–3, 16–18, 29.

manage more closely the representation of the Soviet Union and its peoples in exhibits, films, festivals, the press, and other cultural media.[60]

The party and Narkompros brought this campaign to the Ethnographic Department in February 1929, after issuing a series of resolutions on the role of the museum in the Soviet Union. Proclaiming that the "era of reconstruction" was over and that the era of rapid "socialist construction" was beginning, the resolutions called on all museums, including the Ethnographic Department, to focus on the "cultural reeducation of the masses." Describing the Ethnographic Department as a "powerful center of cultural revolution" (because of its important cultural-enlightenment work), the resolutions called for the radical reconstruction of its permanent exhibit on a "Marxist foundation." In particular, the department was to show how the revolution, and Lenin's approach to the nationality question, had facilitated the economic and cultural development of all the peoples of the USSR. The resolutions noted that communists, as well as nonparty people "committed to a Marxist, Soviet platform," could participate in this work.[61]

Taking its cues from the party and from Narkompros, the Ethnographic Department's methodological party cell called for the immediate and "total reconstruction" of the museum's permanent exhibit. It restated what had just become obvious: that in an era of revolutionary change, it was no longer acceptable to impose new narratives on outdated exhibits or to cover up vestiges of the past with words about progress. In response to these critiques, the department established a new ten-member commission (comprised of its most experienced ethnographers and headed by Samoilovich) and directed it to come up with a plan for a new museumwide exhibit about the peoples of the Soviet Union. The party cell directed the new Commission to Reconstruct the Exposition of the Ethnographic Department to construct the new exhibit "on a Marxist basis" and to represent the cultural and economic achievements of "formerly backward" peoples. But otherwise it left the new commission to its own devices.[62] In 1929, the official narrative about the peoples of the USSR, like the formation of the Soviet Union itself, was still a work in progress.

---

60. The term is from Timothy Mitchell, *Colonising Egypt* (Cambridge, 1988).

61. Samoilovich read these resolutions at the February 12, 1929 meeting of the main soviet of the Ethnographic Department. The ethnographers present (Zolotarev, Rudenko, Miller, and twelve others) discussed them at length. REM f. 2, op. 1, d. 281a, ll. 9–90b. The discussion about the role of museums in political-enlightenment work continued at the Conference of Leningrad and Moscow Ethnographers in April 1929. On the conference see "Soveshchanie etnografov Leningrada i Moskvy," *Etnografiia*, no. 2 (1929): 110–44, and I. I. Shangina, "Etnograficheskie muzei Moskvy i Leningrada na rubezhe 20x–30x godov XX v.," *Etnograficheskoe obozrenie*, no. 2 (1991): 72–73. For a series of Narkompros proposals and protocols about museum work in 1929 see the State Archive of the Russian Federation (GARF-TsGA RSFSR) f. A-2307, op. 14, d. 16, ll. 1–5. For a 1932 discussion of the museum as "one of the fronts of cultural revolution" which should have an active part on the "ideological front," see TsGAIPD SPb f. 4406, op. 1, d. 1, ll. 1–3.

62. REM f. 2, op. 1, d. 269, ll. 14, 24–37; d. 281a, ll. 210b–220b; d. 287, ll. 1–5.

For their part, the ethnographers who served on this commission treated the directive to re-create the department's permanent exhibit as a long-awaited opportunity. They began their deliberations in April 1929, focusing on two questions of longstanding concern to them. First, which peoples should be included in the exhibit: only the dominant nationalities or all the nationalities of the Soviet Union? Second, should the permanent exhibit be arranged according to the "ethnic trait" or according to national territory? Rudenko continued to argue that the exhibit should emphasize the links among culture, territory, and ethnos, and Kryzhanovskii continued to argue that the exhibit should be organized according to *narodnost'*. Aleksandr Miller, the curator of the Caucasus and Turkestan collection, argued that the "ethnic trait" was "the most important from a scientific perspective," but that the "territorial principle" was "the only correct principle from an exhibiting perspective."[63]

The commission's ethnographers also discussed at great length the main focus and desired "endpoint" of their new exhibit, and of ethnographic exhibits in general. The latter was also a topic of general discussion at the Conference of Moscow and Leningrad Ethnographers, held in early April in Leningrad.[64] At the conference, Kryzhanovskii presented a paper elaborating upon his earlier position that the ethnographic museum should limit its focus to the "culture of those social strata in which ethnicity is clearly expressed"—tracking "changes in culture up until the point when it has not yet lost its ethnic character and has not yet acquired an international character."[65] Boris Sokolov, representing Moscow's Central Museum for the Study of Peoples, presented a paper in which he vigorously disagreed. According to Sokolov, ethnographic museums should display "all aspects of culture and *byt*" and not just those based on ethnic particularities; echoing Rudenko's earlier remarks, he recommended that new ethnographic exhibits illustrate the "culture-*byt* complex" of peoples at "each stage in the development of society"—including the socialist stage. In particular, Sokolov recommended that the museum contrast the "old culture-*byt* complex" with the new "socialist culture-*byt* complex," whose foundations were "now being laid by socialist construction" and

63. REM f. 2, op. 1, d. 287, l. 1. He sometimes referred to the "territorial principle" as the "cultural-territorial principle."

64. PFA RAN f. 135, op. 1, d. 56, ll. 34, 45–46. The conference was held at the State Academy of the History of Material Culture. There were some eighty-six ethnographers and sixty representatives from other humanitarian disciplines in attendance. Samoilovich and Kryzhanovskii were among the representatives from the Ethnographic Department. The Central Museum for the Study of Peoples (Tsentral'nyi muzei narodovedeniia) was established in 1924 on the site of the former Ethnographic Department of the Rumiantsev Museum in Moscow. A great deal of materials from the Agricultural-Industrial Exposition of 1923 were transferred to this museum in the mid-1920s. For a discussion of this museum see A. I. Ivanov, "Tsentral'nyi muzei narodovedeniia za 15 let revoliutsii," *Sovetskii muzei*, no. 2 (1933): 68–72.

65. "Soveshchanie etnografov Leningrada i Moskvy," 135. This is a summary of Kryzhanovskii's speech, "O zadachakh etnograficheskogo muzeia." Also cited and discussed in Shangina, "Etnograficheskie muzei Moskvy i Leningrada na rubezhe 20x–30x godov XX v.," 73.

were based on "industrial technologies (tractors, machines, electrification), the collectivization of agriculture, and the cultural education of the masses."[66]

After several months of deliberations, the department's commission came up with some general principles for putting together a new permanent exhibit. Resolving that the museum should aim to "eliminate inequality," the commission recommended that the new exhibit present a "proportional and harmonious display" of all the Union's peoples. Taking up the issue of organization, it adopted Miller's position that the exhibit should adopt the "territorial principle" and display *narodnosti* in their national republics and oblasts, so that museumgoers could have the virtual experience of traveling through different regions of the Soviet Union.[67] Finally, turning to the question of content, the commission upheld Kryzhanovskii's argument that the exhibit should represent culture and *byt* in their distinctly ethnic incarnations, and therefore should focus primarily on the peasantry. But in keeping with Rudenko's argument, it proposed that the new exhibit also show the development of Soviet national (Soviet Turkmen, Soviet Georgian, and so on) cultures and the formation of national proletariats.

The ethnographers soon discovered that their proposal to radically reconstruct the exhibit was unworkable in present conditions. Representing *all* of the peoples of the Soviet Union would require extensive ethnographic research that had not yet been undertaken. Reconstructing the entire exhibit would involve transferring hundreds of artifacts from one part of the museum to another. And depicting new Soviet national cultures would depend on the rapid acquisition of new artifacts and the production of new diagrams, maps, and photographs. All of this would require significant time and financial support—neither of which was available. Rudenko suggested that the department close its doors to the public for two years in order to reorganize its collection and undertake additional research. But other commission members and the methodological party cell opposed his suggestion as impractical.[68] Faced with high expectations and limited means, the commission chose a two-tier approach: it postponed the "total reconstruction" of the museum and set out to update the museum's exhibits "in their present locations" bit by bit.[69]

Thus, as the Soviet Union forged ahead in late 1929 with a violent campaign to collectivize agriculture and "dekulakize" the countryside—and as

66. "Soveshchanie etnografov Leningrada i Moskvy," 132–34. This is a summary of Sokolov's speech, "Postroenie i deiatel'nost' sovetskikh etnograficheskikh muzeev." Also cited and discussed in Shangina, "Etnograficheskie muzei Moskvy i Leningrada na rubezhe 20x–30x godov XX v.," 73. In 1931, the journal *Sovetskaia etnografiia* published Sokolov's 1929 speech in full and declared it to be correct. B. M. Sokolov, "Postroenie i deiatel'nost' sovetskikh etnograficheskikh muzeev," *Sovetskaia etnografiia*, no. 3–4 (1931): 125–35.

67. REM f. 2, op. 1, d. 287, ll. 1–5.

68. Ibid., ll. 1–20b. The party and Narkompros provided the ethnographers with some funds to expand their collection, but the department did not have the financial means necessary to reconstruct the entire exhibit.

69. Ibid., ll. 3–30b.

Stalin declared that collective human effort could accomplish miracles of great transformation—the Ethnographic Department remained a collection of contradictions. Much of the old permanent exhibit remained in place. At the same time, the department introduced three important changes. First, it created a new subdivision devoted explicitly to the study of Soviet culture. This subdivision produced its own special exhibits on themes such as worker *byt*; it also worked with the rest of the department to prepare a series of new guided museum tours on the theme of "The Peoples of the USSR in the Struggle for the Five-Year Plan."[70]

Second, the department updated its Workers' University course on "The Peoples of the USSR"—making the type of extensive changes in the curriculum that were impossible to introduce into the museum's permanent exhibit. For the course's initial run in 1928 and 1929, the department's ethnographers had organized their lectures according to "ethnogeographical group." For its second run, from October 1929 to April 1930, ethnographers wrote new lectures about the national republics and their dominant nationalities.[71] For example, Samoilovich scrapped his lecture on "the Turkic Peoples of the USSR and Abroad" and wrote a new lecture on "Turkmeniia and the Turkmen." The initial lecture had covered the "Turkic peoples of Siberia, Central Asia, Western China, the Middle Volga and the Kama Valley, the Lower Volga and the North Caucasus, the Crimea, Bessarabia, Transcaucasia, Persia, Turkey, Belorussia, and Lithuania." The new lecture, by contrast, focused on the "culture and history of the region which is now inhabited by the Turkmen"; it reflected the new preoccupation with the idea that particular nationalities and territories went together.[72] Overall, the new lectures emphasized how the rapid economic development of the republics was resulting in a "sharp break [*rezkii perelom*]" in the culture of the Soviet Union's nationalities—and creating new Soviet national cultures.[73] The department and LONO used this new version of the course to train museum workers as well as other Soviet cultural workers, including tour guides; it brought in representatives from a local tourist organization to speak about Soviet tourism and to describe various tourist sites and routes.[74]

Third, and most important, the department closed down the halls that housed its Ukrainian and Belorussian collections, and set out to create a com-

---

70. REM f. 2, op. 1, d. 269, l. 17; d. 315, ll. 7–10, 29–33.

71. For examples, see REM f. 2, op. 1, d. 295, ll. 10–14, 25–28.

72. REM f. 2, op. 1, d. 261, l. 30; d. 295, ll. 43, 46. A small segment of the course focused on peoples without their own national republics, featuring lessons on "The Chinese, Koreans, and the Far East Problem," "The Jews and Anti-Semitism," and "The USSR's Western Neighbors." REM f. 2. op. 1. d. 283, l. 5.

73. REM f. 2, op. 1, d. 283, ll. 5–6, d. 269, ll. 13, 17–18.

74. REM f. 2, op. 1, d. 283, ll. 6, 8a, 36–37. The new version of the course (which was supposed to be more rigorous) met twice a week (on Sundays and one evening) for six months. As a result, enrollment dropped. REM f. 2, op. 1, d. 283, l. 36.

pletely new exhibit on Ukraine. Kryzhanovskii (the department's Ukrainian expert) oversaw this project, and presented the methodological party cell with his proposal for the Ukraine exhibit in March 1930—just as the actual Ukrainian countryside was being devastated by the collectivization campaign. He recommended that the new exhibit show the Ukrainian countryside at three points in time: before World War I, after the October Revolution, and in the midst of the First Five-Year Plan. Museumgoers would begin in central Ukraine and travel from there to Ukraine's border regions; these latter halls would highlight cultural similarities and differences between the Ukrainians and neighboring peoples such as the Russians, Belorussians, and Romanians. Kryzhanovskii suggested that the new exhibit take the "productive moment" as its organizational trope: that it show how tools and other artifacts were produced and used. He also suggested that the exhibit show "culture" as the product of economic conditions and relationships. Thus, the exhibit could teach the masses how the collectivization of the countryside was resulting in a new Soviet Ukrainian culture among the peasantry. The exhibit would focus primarily on the Ukrainian agricultural population, but would also show the development of a Ukrainian proletariat.[75]

The problem, of course, was that collectivization had *not* resulted in the spontaneous generation of a new Soviet Ukrainian culture in the countryside. The department's ethnographers had attempted to locate new forms of Ukrainian *byt* in the Ukrainian SSR, but with little success. As a result, the new exhibit on "The Ukrainian Village Before and After October," which opened in 1931, could not live up to its promise. The materials characterizing life before 1917 were plentiful, and included brightly dressed mannequins, objects of folk art, and traditional farming implements. But to show the Ukrainian countryside of the present, the museum relied mostly on diagrams, maps, posters, and photographs. For example, old-fashioned plows were displayed with photographs of tractors, and religious artifacts were arranged with propaganda posters from the Soviet antireligious campaign. Desperate to represent class stratification in the Ukrainian countryside, the ethnographers dressed up mannequins in a variety of traditional Ukrainian costumes, labeling those in everyday peasant clothing *bedniaki* and *seredniaki* (poor and middle peasants), and those in decorative festival clothing "kulaks."[76] But, as the ethnographers themselves knew, the same peasants might in fact wear both sets of clothing, depending on the occasion.

In spring 1931, museum workers, Politprosvet activists, and party representatives from Moscow and Ukraine visited and critiqued the new Ukraine ex-

75. REM f. 2, op. 1, d. 315, ll. 14–15. Kryzhanovskii set out some of these ideas at a June 22, 1929 session of the soviet of the Ethnographic Department. REM f. 2, op. 1, d. 281a, zhurnal 474.

76. My description is based primarily on photos from the REM photo archive. For a discussion of this exhibit see Kriukova and Studenetskaia, "Gosudarstvennyi muzei etnografii narodov SSSR," 37.

hibit. The visitors from Ukraine complained that the exhibit gave the impression that "there is still no new culture [*byt*] in Ukraine." They recommended that the department work harder to "show the transition" to socialism in the countryside.[77] The Moscow visitors' assessment was similar, and they also criticized the exhibit's organizational framework. Calling Kryzhanovskii and his colleagues "Ukrainian nationalists," they asked why the exhibit showed so little about the national minorities (Jews, Bulgarians, Greeks, and other peoples) who lived in Ukraine—"without whom it is impossible to correctly show the Ukrainian SSR." The Moscow museum workers further suggested that the ethnographers who organized the exhibit lacked a basic understanding of Marxism-Leninism. It was not enough to show "kulaks, *seredniaki*, and *bedniaki*" by dressing mannequins up in costumes, they argued. The exhibit should represent these groups at work, in their "characteristic productive moments." The visitors (and the methodological party cell) prevailed on the department to fix the exhibit.[78]

This critique of the Ukraine exhibit was all the more charged because it took place against the backdrop of an anti-expert campaign at the Ethnographic Department and at other cultural institutions throughout the Soviet Union. The attack on former imperial ethnographers gathered momentum in the summer of 1929, when a special government commission (discussed in chapter 3) undertook an investigation of the Academy of Sciences.[79] The commission subjected Academy of Sciences ethnographers—many of whom were also members of the Ethnographic Department—to "socialist criticism." The intensification of ideological struggle further politicized meetings between ethnographers and political-enlightenment activists within the Ethnographic Department. If ethnographic exhibits failed to show Soviet progress, activists suggested, it was because most of the department's ethnographers had been trained under the old regime and were unsympathetic to the revolution's agenda.[80] In 1930, Rudenko was removed from his post as head of the department and replaced with a party member (the Turkologist N. G. Talanov).[81] In

77. REM f. 2, op. 1, d. 355, ll. 10–19. This particular comment was from Comrade Solov'eva from the Korosten Museum in Ukraine.

78. Ibid., ll. 43–44. The Moscow visitors were from the Central Museum for the Study of Peoples.

79. See V. P. Zakharov et al., eds., *Delo po obvineniiu akademika S. F. Platonova, Akademicheskoe delo 1929–1931 gg.* (St. Petersburg, 1993). On the party's "seizure" of the Academy of Sciences also see Loren R. Graham, *Science in Russia and the Soviet Union: A Short History* (Cambridge, 1993), and Alexander Vucinich, *Empire of Knowledge: The Academy of Sciences of the USSR (1917–1970)* (Berkeley, 1984). Former imperial ethnographers came under fire several months earlier at the April 1929 Conference of Moscow and Leningrad Ethnographers. Valerian Aptekar (from the State Academy of the History of Material Culture) censured the "old" ethnographers as "ideological opponents of the new order" who were responsible for the miserable state of museum work. Noted in Shangina, "Etnograficheskie muzei Moskvy i Leningrada na rubezhe 20x–30x godov XX v." Also see "Soveshchanie etnografov Leningrada i Moskvy," 110–44.

80. See, for example, REM f. 2, op. 1, d. 399, ll. 15–17, 33, 47–490b.

81. REM f. 2, op. 1, d. 269, l. 39.

April 1931, the department launched a campaign against "Rudenkoism" and "Zolotarevism" in the museum. The party cell denigrated Rudenko, Zolotarev, and their followers as "apologists for colonial politics" who had borrowed from Western European ethnography "all varieties of bourgeois museum methodology"—including "evolutionism, geographism, and cultural circles," as well as "race theory" to "mask the progress" of the peoples of the USSR.[82] The next two years saw a significant turnover in the Ethnographic Department's personnel, as a number of former imperial ethnographers were censured and removed from their positions. By 1933, more than half of the department's ethnographers had been replaced.[83]

From Museumgoers to Activists

In this environment of ideological struggle, the role of the museumgoer was redefined from observer to activist. In 1929, in an attempt to monitor the success of the Ethnographic Department, the Politprosvet Division of LONO placed "response books" throughout the museum and solicited museumgoers' comments. Museumgoers of all ages and social backgrounds (schoolchildren, workers, soldiers, pedagogues, and so on) recorded their comments about the department's exhibits—and suggested how the museum might "fix" the exhibits or improve the museum experience.[84] These comment books had two important roles. First, they were an important means of supervision or surveillance. Politprosvet and the methodological party cell created a special committee to review these comment books and determine if people knew the official narrative about Soviet socialist transformation.[85] Second, they were an important tool of "socialist criticism." Beginning in 1931, the methodological party cell used the comment books—reading from them at meetings, for example—to fuel its critique of the department's ethnographers. The ordinary museumgoer thus became more than a student of the Soviet transformative experience; he or she became a participant (consciously or not) in the "revolutionary struggle" within the department's walls.

Between the summer of 1931 and the spring of 1932, as famine spread throughout Ukraine, museumgoers in Leningrad recorded their comments

82. Ibid., ll. 38–42; d. 399, ll. 15, 31, 59. On "Rudenkoism" see M. Khudiakov, "Kriticheskaia prorabotka Rudenkovshchiny," *Sovetskaia etnografiia*, no. 1–2 (1931): 167–69. Also see S. N. Bykovskii, "Etnografiia na sluzhbe klassovogo vraga," *Sovetskaia etnografiia*, no. 3–4 (1931): 3–13. Also see PFA RAN f. 135, op. 1, d. 235, ll. 32–320b; f. 2, op. 1–1929, d. 33, l. 91.

83. Shangina, "Etnograficheskie muzei Moskvy i Leningrada na rubezhe," 77.

84. I looked through about fifteen of these comment books in the archive. The comments are in different hands with numerous misspellings.

85. REM f. 2, op. 1, d. 269, ll. 24–37. The party and Narkompros worked with pedagogues and psychologists to investigate what people learned from visits to museums and other cultural institutions. See Krasilina, "Iz opyta raboty sovetskikh muzeev po populiarizatsii i izucheniiu muzeinogo zritelia."

about the new Ukraine exhibit. Most of the comments reflected a significant level of political indoctrination.[86] Some museumgoers gave the official party line about the transformation of the countryside and criticized the absence of vivid representations of "postrevolutionary everyday life [*byt*]" in the exhibit.[87] One museumgoer (a soldier) noted that "Ukraine is the granary of the Union and a republic of complete collectivization, and from this it is clear that the Ukrainian village has changed sharply." He complained that the dramatic "social advances, radical revolution [*perevorot*] in the economy of the village," and other successes of the past few years were "not reflected" in the exhibit.[88] Another museumgoer (a worker) observed that "we completed a great victory in the USSR, and also in Ukraine," but "this is little evident from the exhibit." He suggested that the exhibit document the spread of kolkhozes and the successful struggle against the kulaks.[89] Other museumgoers noted that the exhibit "artificially" separated the Ukrainian village from the city and failed to show how Ukrainian grain was supporting the industrialization effort. Where was the Ukrainian proletariat?[90] Party cell representatives sometimes wrote responses to the comments in the margins of the comment books, reasserting the party line as they understood it; in some cases, the department posted these comments and responses for museumgoers to read. When one museumgoer recommended that the exhibit "present a map of the Ukrainian SSR that shows the growth of the socialist sector of agriculture in different regions of Ukraine," the party cell responded: "The growth of the socialist sector of agriculture is so rapid that it is impossible to show on a map."[91]

Other museumgoers drew on their own firsthand knowledge of Ukraine to point out mistakes or incongruities in the exhibit or to complain that Ukraine was depicted unrealistically. An army officer from Kiev noted that the museum's representation of the typical room of a Ukrainian *seredniak* (middle peasant) was inaccurate, because "the floor should be clay, not wood." If this were corrected, "then the scene will be realistic," he added.[92] A self-identified Ukrainian peasant woman from Khar'kov complained that the exhibit misrepresented her village: "There is too little shown of Khar'kov . . . one kulak [and little else]. . . . This gives the impression that everyone there is a kulak which of course is not true."[93] Significantly, neither the army officer nor the peasant woman challenged the exhibit's—or the general Soviet—use of the terms *sered-*

86. Not surprisingly, none of the comment books contained remarks that were openly hostile to the party or to the Soviet government. If any such comments were left, they were excised from the record.

87. REM f. 2, op. 1, d. 386, ll. 13 ob, 23, 300b; d. 388, l. 220b.

88. REM f. 2, op. 1, d. 388, l. 9.

89. Ibid., l. 5.

90. Ibid., l. 19.

91. Ibid., l. 1.

92. REM f. 2, op. 1, d. 386, l. 26.

93. REM f. 2, op. 1, d. 388, ll. 60b–7.

niak and *kulak*. Instead, for example, the peasant woman (in an effort to clear the name of her native province) maintained that "most of the well-to-do people and kulaks" in Ukraine could be found in Poltava province. She added that because she herself was "a Ukrainian" her observation should be accepted as correct.[94] Another museumgoer did challenge the terms *kulak* and *bedniak* that appeared on two woven shawls. She did not reject these terms per se, but instead suggested that all women who were industrious and able could learn "to work on the machine" to weave both kinds of shawls.[95] In response, a party cell representative explained (in the margins of the comment book) that most shawls were "woven by special master craftsmen" and that "silk shawls" were "more expensive and therefore accessible only to the well-to-do and kulak stratum."[96]

Still other museumgoers commented not on the Ukraine exhibit but on the other, still unreconstructed, halls of the museum. Museumgoers identifying themselves as nationals from other republics—and claiming to have "true" firsthand knowledge of particular non-Russian regions—pointed out mistakes or gaps in the exhibit. A museumgoer from Georgia wrote that artifacts from west and east Georgia were mixed together, and that objects belonging to the Mountain Jews (Akhaltsi) were labeled as "Georgian." He also noted that an item labeled "a Khevsur women's costume" was "actually a man's *arkhaluk* [tunic]."[97] A Karakalpak student called out a "small shortcoming in the section of the eastern peoples: The Turkmen have never had a black turban, but always a bright red one," and in the exhibit "the Turkmen woman looks more like a Kazakh woman." The student also complained that there "is practically nothing in the museum showing the Karakalpaks and their *byt*."[98] A Polish worker-student from Kiev complained of the museum's tendency to idealize the national minorities:

> I know the countryside very well. I grew up in a Belorussian village in the Belorussian countryside and spent the past five years in the Urals where I saw the mass of *natsional'nosti* populating the Urals. . . . Comparing the peoples presented in the museum with reality, I have come to the following conclusion: Here in the museum the national minorities are idealized and all presented in the best light possible. People are dressed in fancy [*roskoshnyi*] holiday clothing and the type of clothing people usually wear for work is not shown at all. It is necessary to not dress up the national minorities, but to show them as they are in reality and then argue that it is important to raise their cultural-*bytovoi* level.[99]

94. Ibid.
95. REM f. 2, op. 1, d. 423, l. 14.
96. Ibid.
97. REM f. 2, op. 1, d. 387, l. 90b. The Khevsur were a Georgian tribe.
98. REM f. 2, op. 1, d. 386, l. 230b.
99. Ibid., l. 54.

A Kirgiz student from Kazakhstan noted that he was "especially interested to see our Kirgiz nation." Echoing the official line, he complained that "very little is shown about how earlier tsarist Russia and also the bey and mullah exploited Kirgizia." Moreover, he continued, the exhibit shows "little about the current changes" in the republic.[100]

Many museumgoers, non-Russians and Russians alike, complained that most of the museum remained unchanged—and that the revolutionary present seemed "pale" and unremarkable in comparison with the colorful and vivid prerevolutionary past.[101] One museumgoer (a student) noted that the museum provided no evidence of "socialist construction and cultural revolution" among "the *narodnosti* of the USSR."[102] Party cell representatives reassured visitors that the Soviet Union was changing so rapidly that the department was having difficulty keeping up. But for museumgoers who saw the Ethnographic Department as a microcosm of the Soviet Union, the transformative power of the revolution was not self-evident.

Indeed, even the museum's physical space was a reminder of the harsh conditions and deprivation that still prevailed. A number of visitors complained that the museum was cold, uncomfortable, and unhygienic. One worker noted that he was "not a Ukrainian" and had come to see the Ukraine exhibit because he "wanted very much" to "become acquainted with Ukrainian *byt*" and economic practices. He complained that it had been "impossible to do this satisfactorily" because the museum was too cold. He asked "the administration to eliminate this defect—either to allow people to visit the museum in their overcoats and galoshes or to heat the museum."[103] Another museumgoer noted that "the museum is cold and it is very good that there is a snack bar with tea." He observed that it "would be preferable if the tea was served hot" and "in clean and not in dirty unwashed glasses that are passed from one visitor to another."[104] Still other museumgoers complained that tickets to visit the museum independently (not as part of an organized tour) were prohibitively expensive.[105]

Party cell representatives also responded to these more general complaints in the margins of the comment book, explaining that the museum was still in a period of transition. In 1932, the party cell posted a typewritten note:

> Comrade-visitors, your reproaches are fair, but all the same you will have to wait a little while. The restructuring of the museum is not an easy

---

100. Ibid., l. 50b.
101. REM f. 2, op. 1, d. 388, l. 50b.
102. REM f. 2, op. 1, d. 386, l. 18.
103. REM f. 2, op. 1, d. 388, l. 70b.
104. Ibid., l. 14.
105. REM f. 2, op. 1, d. 386, l. 8; d. 462, l. 6.

affair. It demands a great deal of time, financial means, and strength, all of which there are not enough of in the museum.[106]

By this time, a younger generation of ethnographers, along with Politprosvet activists, had taken over the department's museum work and faced the daunting task of reorganizing the rest of the museum's permanent exhibit. The same experts and activists who several months earlier had been calling for radical and rapid change—and had chastised Rudenko and his colleagues for not moving quickly enough—were now asking for patience.

"The Peoples of the USSR" on the Road to Socialism

The assault on ethnography between 1929 and 1932 had a significant impact on the discipline. Research commissions, institutes, and journals were reorganized and brought under greater party control; prominent scholars were dismissed from their posts, and several were arrested.[107] At the same time, a new generation of ethnographers, untainted by the prerevolutionary past, quickly rose up through the ranks of cultural and scientific institutions. These younger ethnographers were not uneducated hacks or inexperienced outsiders. Many of them had studied ethnography or related disciplines at the Academy of Sciences or at Leningrad or Moscow State University and had worked closely with the older generation of ethnographers.[108] An example was Leonid Potapov, who received a degree from the Ethnographic Department of the Geographical Faculty at Leningrad State University—where he had worked with Lev Shternberg and Vladimir Bogoraz, two of the most important ethnographers of the older generation. In 1928, when he was a student, Potapov accompanied Samoilovich and Rudenko on an expedition to the Altai.[109] Between 1930 and 1933 Potapov did graduate work in ethnography, studying the indigenous peoples of Siberia. He and several other graduate students took on important roles in the Ethnographic Department precisely during these years.[110]

Although there was a major shakeup in the profession, no irreconcilable conceptual differences existed between the old and the new ethnographers. The new ethnographers dutifully critiqued their former teachers. But more important, they brought their teachers' ideas into a difficult political climate and adapted them to the times. As argued in chapter 3, these events initiated not

106. REM f. 2, op. 1, d. 423, l. 12.

107. See Yuri Slezkine, "The Fall of Soviet Ethnography, 1928–1938," *Current Anthropology* 32, no. 4 (1991): 476–84.

108. See the discussion in chapter 3.

109. PFA RAN f. 135, op. 1, d. 28, ll. 173–74.

110. For Potapov's biography and a list of his publications see A. S. Myl'nikov and Ch. M. Taksami, eds., *Leonid Pavlovich Potapov: K 90-letiiu so dniia rozhdeniia* (St. Petersburg, 1995).

the fall, but rather the invention, of "Soviet" ethnography. Those ethnographers (new and old) who were willing to help "build socialism"—even if they were not party members—led and participated in major expeditions with practical, scientific, and ideological goals. For example, between 1931 and 1934, ethnographers at the Academy of Sciences and the Ethnographic Department joined forces with the People's Commissariat of Agriculture's Kolkhoz Center to monitor, study, and participate in the collectivization of agriculture throughout the Soviet Union. The department's ethnographers had become involved with the Kolkhoz Center through their collaboration on the Workers' University course about "The Peoples of the USSR." In December 1930, as the course began its third run, the department turned it into a program that prepared worker-activists to participate in collectivization and kolkhoz construction.[111] Shortly thereafter, brigades made up of ethnographers, linguists, economists, and other experts began working with the Kolkhoz Center to study the course of "cultural revolution" on collective farms throughout the Soviet Union. In the ethnographers' usage, "cultural revolution" was part of the Soviet "civilizing mission"—aiming to create new structures, institutions, territories, and people through the introduction of new habits and practices. These brigades took an active part in kolkhoz construction and provided Soviet officials with critical information about local languages, cultures, and kinship structures.[112]

Around the same time, the party asked ethnographers to deal with a burgeoning external ideological threat: Nazi race science.[113] As national socialism gained ground in German universities after 1930 and as racial biology began to squeeze out physical anthropology, the Soviet regime prevailed on its ethnographers and anthropologists to build an international coalition of scholars

---

111. REM f. 2, op. 1, d. 328, ll. 1–12; d. 327, l. 2. Ethnographers lectured on the "cultural-*by-tovye* particularities" of the nationalities of each national republic. Political-enlightenment activists and LONO representatives taught enrollees how to instruct kolkhoz members in new agricultural techniques and matters of culture. When the course came to an end in June 1931, the Kolkhoz Center set up its own classes for worker-activists—which it taught with the assistance of the ethnographers. The Russian State Archive of the Economy (RGAE) f. 260, op. 1, d. 3, ll. 3–5.

112. PFA RAN f. 135, op. 2, d. 99, l. 233; d. 117, ll. 2, 29. One May 1932 program to research "cultural revolution in kolkhoz regions" described cultural revolution as a movement for "political enlightenment" that aims to "alter people's consciousness." PFA RAN f. 135, op. 2, d. 1029, ll. 10–100b, 21–210b. In this usage, cultural revolution was not "class war," although mass enlightenment through "cultural revolution" was supposed to awaken "backward" populations and precipitate class struggle (against mullahs and kulaks, for example) in the localities. For a discussion of cultural revolution in Kazakhstan, see Paula A. Michaels, "Medical Propaganda and Cultural Revolution in Soviet Kazakhstan, 1928–41," *The Russian Review* 59, no. 2 (2000): 159–78. For the classic articulation of the argument of cultural revolution as "class war," see Sheila Fitzpatrick, "Cultural Revolution as Class War," in *Cultural Revolution in Russia, 1928–1931*, ed. Sheila Fitzpatrick (Bloomington, 1978), 8–40.

113. On the rise of national socialist ideas in German universities, see Robert Proctor, *Racial Hygiene: Medicine under the Nazis* (Cambridge, MA, 1988). For more on the German ideological threat, see chapter 6.

against race theory and to challenge on scientific grounds the claims of German anthropologists that the indigenous peoples of Siberia and Central Asia were made up of inferior racial stock and destined for extinction. Brigades made up of ethnographers, physical anthropologists, and doctors studied the populations of Siberia and Central Asia, attempting to determine why revolutionary progress was slower in these regions than in others without resorting to racial explanations.[114] The ethnographers also used opportunities like these to collect materials to update other parts of the department's permanent exhibit.[115]

What did all this mean for the Ethnographic Department and its virtual tours of the Soviet Union? Did the ethnographers find artifacts that represented the development of new Soviet national cultures and *byt?* Were they able to set up new exhibits that satisfied political-enlightenment activists and museumgoers? No and yes: the ethnographers did not find sufficient evidence of revolutionary transformation, but, working with the Politprosvet activists, they were able to adapt the message of the exhibits to suggest why this was the case. The department's new western Siberia exhibit—which became a template for a number of later exhibits—exemplified this new approach. Potapov, a rising star among the younger generation of ethnographers, led the work on this exhibit from start to finish.

Beginning in May 1931 (as museumgoers were visiting and critiquing the Ukraine exhibit), Potapov worked with the department's ethnographers and with the methodological party cell to put together a new research program, "The Survivals of Clan Structure: A Hindrance to Socialist Construction in Oirotiia."[116] In the summer of 1931, Potapov accompanied a larger research team of Academy of Sciences economists, geographers, topographers, botanists, and other experts to the Oirot autonomous national oblast in western Siberia. While some research team members surveyed the region's economic resources and "productive potential," Potapov and his assistants studied how "class enemies" (such as Russian and native kulaks) were attempting to undermine collectivization by encouraging local populations to organize kolkhozes according to the "clan principle." All of the expedition's experts served as activists in the field, explaining the importance of collectivization to the local population. Potapov documented these efforts. He also collected archeological and ethnographical materials for the museum.[117] The research team, which had a clear political goal, found the evidence of class war that it was looking for.

The Ethnographic Department's new exhibit—which used materials from Potapov's expedition to the Oirot autonomous national oblast—chronicled the

114. See, for example, PFA RAN f. 174, op. 2, d. 156, ll. 172–77. These expeditions are discussed in detail in chapter 6.

115. REM f. 2, op. 1, d. 355, ll. 78–80; d. 399, ll. 66–68. PFA RAN f. 135, op. 1, d. 99, l. 1; d. 154, l. 10; d. 155, ll. 25–27.

116. REM f. 2, op. 1, d. 355, ll. 20–21ob.

117. Ibid., ll. 20–21ob, 24–25.

process of state-sponsored evolutionism in the Altai-Saian region of western Siberia. The exhibit suggested that with the help of the Soviet regime the peoples of the USSR were actively developing through the main points on the Marxist historical timeline in accordance with the "law of development by stages [*po zakonu stadial'nosti*]."[118] Tracing the evolution of the region through the stages of primitive communism, feudalism, capitalism, and socialism, it showed that clans and tribes had become nationalities, and it described how nationalities were starting the process of becoming Soviet nations. The exhibit relied on archeological materials to illustrate the prefeudal period (of primitive communism) and on ethnographic materials, photographs, and maps for its sections on feudalism, capitalism, and socialism. The Soviet scenes featured life-size dioramas of "The Agricultural Soviet in Altai," "Cooperative Shops," and "The Present-Day Dwelling of an Altai Hunter."[119]

This exhibit shared its basic narrative with the Ukraine exhibit that had been fiercely critiqued, and like the Ukraine exhibit, it highlighted collectivization as a critical transitional moment. But it differed from the Ukraine exhibit in two important respects. First, it exaggerated the "feudal-era backwardness" of pre-Soviet Altai-Saian in order to emphasize Soviet achievements in the region.[120] Second, it did not attempt to show the Soviet transformative process as an unequivocal success. Instead of glossing over the revolution's setbacks, it set out to explain them in nonracial terms. In particular, it documented how "survivals" (*perezhitki*) from the Russian Empire's feudal and colonial past were actively hindering the process of revolutionary transformation.

The ethnographers derived the idea of "survivals" from the work of the British cultural evolutionist Edward B. Tylor. In his 1871 book *Primitive Culture*, Tylor argued that "elements of culture" that "no longer had any meaning or function" were often "carried on by force of habit into a new state [or stage] of society."[121] According to Tylor, these "survivals" could be found in the most advanced societies and were not a sign that a population was doomed to backwardness or had degenerated. Beginning in the 1890s, Russia's ethnographers had debated Tylor's anthropological theories. In the aftermath of the

118. REM f. 2, op. 1, d. 453, l. 150b; d. 399, l. 54. In coming up with this approach, the ethnographers drew on the linguistic theories of Marr and on the ideas of Friedrich Engels.

119. L. Potapov, "Saiino-Altaiskaia vystavka (Leningrad)," *Sovetskaia etnografiia*, no. 3 (1932): 93–96. Also Kriukova and Studenetskaia, "Gosudarstvennyi muzei etnografii narodov SSSR," 38–39. The capitalism section showed the region's native peoples subjected to "Russian and Chinese trade-usurer capital."

120. Potapov, "Saiino-Altaiskaia vystavka (Leningrad)," 93–96.

121. E. B. Tylor, *Primitive Culture*, vol. 1 (Boston, 1874), 16. Cited in Robert Geraci, "Ethnic Minorities, Anthropology, and Russian National Identity on Trial: The Multan Case, 1892–96," *The Russian Review* 59, no 4 (2000): 539. On Tylor's ideas, see George W. Stocking Jr., *After Tylor: British Social Anthropology, 1888–1951* (Madison, 1995), and John J. Honigmann, *The Development of Anthropological Ideas* (Homewood, IL, 1976). On the study of "survivals" in the Soviet Union, see Yuri Slezkine, *Arctic Mirrors: Russia and the Small Peoples of the North* (Ithaca, 1994), 257–60, and Slezkine, "The Fall of Soviet Ethnography, 1928–1938."

revolution, some of them had discussed religion and superstition as Tyloresque "survivals of belief."[122] In the Soviet Union of the 1930s, the ethnographers looked to some of the "classics" of cultural evolutionism—and to Tylor in particular—to prove that the scientific as well as the ideological assumptions at the heart of the Soviet project were correct. Tylor was favored for several reasons. First, he had the proper ideological lineage: Marx and Engels had praised his work and had described the process of development through stages in similar terms.[123] Second, he had explicitly challenged the idea that humankind was divided into higher and lower races. Third, his theory of "cultural survivals" provided a nonbiological, sociohistorical explanation for the persistence of traditional socioeconomic forms and cultures.

In this period of "the great break," Tylor's ideas merged not only with the Leninist conceit that individuals could intervene in the historical process, but also with the Stalinist idea that "internal enemies" were attempting to undermine the revolution. "Survivals" included not just old forms of belief or culture that were obstacles to "socialist construction." They also included the people who held onto those beliefs and cultures, and the class enemies who manipulated them to their advantage.[124] The Altai-Saian exhibit showed two main groups of "living" survivals. The first group was made up of "former colonial peoples" who still preserved "the rudiments" of past eras in their "*byt* and consciousness" and maintained "ancient feudal and clan social relations." The second, more dangerous, group consisted of class enemies—including the priest, the shaman, the kulak, and the mullah—who were working behind the scenes to sabotage the revolution.[125] According to the ethnographers, the development of the first group was slower than expected in new Soviet conditions because of the continuing negative influence of the second group. As soon as class enemies were eliminated (through class struggle), all former colonial peoples would resume their evolution toward communism.[126]

Work on the Altai-Saian exhibit, like work in the field, was a collaborative effort among "old" and "new" ethnographers. According to the new head of

122. Ethnographic expeditions from the late 1920s often cataloged and studied "survivals" of belief, *byt,* and culture. See for example REM f. 2, op. 1, d. 260, ll. 12–15.

123. Lenin, drawing on Marx and Engels, had expressed a similar vision, noting in 1917 that "remnants of the old, surviving in the new, confront us in life at every step, both in nature and in society." V. I. Lenin, "The State and Revolution," in *The Lenin Anthology,* ed. Robert C. Tucker (New York, 1975), 381.

124. N. M. Matorin, "Sovremennyi etap i zadachi sovetskoi etnografii," *Sovetskaia etnografiia,* no. 1–2 (1931): 3–38, and N. M. Matorin, "Piatnadtsat' let sovetskoi etnografii," *Sovetskaia etnografiia,* no. 5–6 (1932): 4–14.

125. Potapov, "Saiino-Altaiskaia vystavka (Leningrad)," 93–96. Also REM f. 2, op. 1, d. 460, l. 1; d. 355, l. 24.

126. See for example L. P. Potapov, *Poezdka v kolkhozy Chemal'skogo aimaka Oirotskoi Avtonomnoi Oblasti, Trudy Instituta po izucheniiu narodov SSSR,* vol. 1 (Leningrad, 1932). Most research expeditions after 1932 had questionnaires or ethnographic programs to study living survivals. See, for example, PFA RAN f. 135, op. 2, d. 1029, ll. 10–11, 21–210b.

the Ethnographic Department (Talanov), this work was supposed to provide "the old men [*stariki*] with the opportunity to methodologically rearm themselves [*metodologicheski perevooruzhat'sia*]" with the knowledge of Marxism-Leninism, and the younger generation with the experience to "master museum work."[127] (To supplement this retraining, LONO's Politprosvet Division and the department held special seminars on historical materialism for the museum's ethnographers during this period.)[128] The department worked on the exhibit for more than two years, during which time Politprosvet activists, ethnographers from other institutions, and museumgoers offered their "socialist criticism." There was serious discussion about whether or not to eliminate the exhibit's shamanism section—but the department ultimately resolved to use this section as a vehicle for antireligious education.[129] There was also considerable debate about how to show the "role and significance of Altai-Saian," with its hunters and herders, in the general economic life of the Soviet Union.[130] In the end, the department decided to show the collectivization of these occupations. The exhibit opened to mixed reviews, but by 1934 was hailed as a success and adopted as the model for the reconstruction of the museum's Central Asian halls.[131]

The Altai-Saian exhibit established the new role of the Soviet ethnographic museum—presenting a passion play about good and evil that seemed to prescribe a new, more proactive role for the museumgoer. The museumgoer did not simply travel through the museum and visit its peoples, either randomly or according to their level of cultural development. Nor did the museumgoer take a straightforward journey from the pre-Soviet past to the Soviet present. Instead, he or she embarked on an "evolutionary" adventure through the stages on the Marxist historical timeline. Along the way, the museumgoer learned about the differences among feudal, capitalist-colonial, and Soviet social structures, economic practices, and cultures. The museumgoer also learned that the Soviet regime had encountered, and was still encountering, significant obstacles. Taking the idea of "survivals" as a main theme, exhibits explained that feudal-era and capitalist-era enemies still abounded in the present—and were actively working against the forces of progress.[132] Becoming acquainted with kulaks, mullahs, and other class enemies in the museum, the museumgoer would then be able to identify them through their clothing, culture, and prac-

127. REM f. 2, op. 1, d. 399, l. 60.

128. Ibid., ll. 80–81. These seminars included sessions on "classes and class war," "productive forces and productive relations," "cultural revolution," and so on.

129. REM f. 2, op. 1, d. 355, ll. 4–9.

130. Ibid.

131. Kriukova and Studenetskaia, "Gosudarstvennyi muzei etnografii narodov SSSR," 38–39. Also REM f. 2, op. 1, d. 399, ll. 15–18. On the new Central Asian exhibits see S. M. Abramzon, "Sredniaia Aziia v Leningradskikh etnograficheskikh muzeiakh," *Sovetskaia etnografiia*, no. 6 (1935): 136–39, and L. Potapov, "Gosudarstvennyi muzei etnografii," *Sovetskaia etnografiia*, no. 2 (1936): 126–29.

132. REM f. 2, op. 1, d. 460, l. 1.

tices—and participate in the campaign to eradicate them—outside of the museum's walls. Significantly, the museum even provided museumgoers with opportunities to take their activism to the countryside, recruiting Russians and non-Russians alike to work as assistants on department-led expeditions to research and transform non-Russian regions.[133]

The Problem of Advanced Nationalities

Between 1932 and 1934, the department worked to update other parts of the museum, focusing first on the Central Asian and Belorussian halls.[134] According to the methodological party cell, the Ethnographic Department had entered a period of major restructuring (*perestroika*).[135] The ethnographers, with the assistance of Politprosvet activists, endeavored to trace the ethnohistorical evolution of the peoples of the USSR according to the "law of development by stages" and to capture the important changes in the population's material and spiritual culture and cast of mind that were taking place under Soviet power. Most new museum exhibits continued to document the development of the population through the Marxist historical timeline—highlighting precapitalist social relations and cultures, the "destructive influence" of capitalism and colonial policies on backward peoples, and the development of new social relations and cultures among the peoples of the Soviet Union during the "era of socialist construction."[136] Thus a new Uzbek exhibit, which opened in 1934 (and received enthusiastic reviews from the Leningrad soviet), showed the Uzbek tribe "under feudalism," the Uzbek *narodnost'* struggling for national realization "under colonialism," and the Uzbek nation "building socialism." The feudalism and colonialism halls of the exhibit included scenes of a bazaar, a feudal court, and the "typical" homes of a peasant and of a landowner; the hall on socialist construction featured Uzbeks dressed in national (non-European) clothing in recognizably "Soviet" settings, such as a sulfur mine, a textile plant, a cotton field, a classroom, a kolkhoznik home, and a red teahouse.[137]

And yet the situation in the Ethnographic Department remained fraught. Heated debate continued about how to reconstruct major parts of the mu-

133. REM f. 2, op. 1, d. 300, ll. 2, 5–7, 10, 29, 40.

134. REM f. 2, op. 1, d. 269, l. 105.

135. According to the methodological party cell, the department was making the transition from a "museum of things" to a museum of historical development. REM f. 2, op. 1, d. 269, ll. 121–28; d. 462, l. 200b; d. 453, ll. 15–17. On the transition of the Ethnographic Department into the State Ethnographic Museum see Kriukova and Studenetskaia, "Gosudarstvennyi muzei etnografii narodov SSSR," 40–41.

136. PFA RAN f. 142, op. 1 (1932), d. 48, l. 7.

137. REM f. 2, op. 1, d. 269, l. 148, and Kriukova and Studenetskaia, "Gosudarstvennyi muzei etnografii narodov SSSR," 42–43. The exhibit is also described in Potapov, "Gosudarstvennyi muzei etnografii," 126–29; Abramzon, "Sredniaia Aziia v Leningradskikh etnograficheskikh muzeiakh," 136–39; and M. V. Sozonova, *Putevoditel' po vystavke Srednei Azii* (Leningrad, 1934).

Figure 5.4 Scene "Feudal Court" from the Uzbek exhibit at the Ethnographic Department. The exhibit opened in 1934. (From the collection of the Russian Museum of Ethnography, St. Petersburg, Russia)

Figure 5.5 Scene "At a Tashkent Textile Plant" from the Uzbek exhibit at the Ethnographic Department. (From the collection of the Russian Museum of Ethnography, St. Petersburg, Russia)

Figure 5.6 Scene "Red Teahouse" from the Uzbek exhibit at the Ethnographic Department. (From the collection of the Russian Museum of Ethnography, St. Petersburg, Russia)

seum's permanent exhibit. In particular, the experts and activists were uncertain how to represent the Soviet Union's most "advanced" nationalities: those (like the Russians, Belorussians, Ukrainians, and Moldavians) who had long been "under the influence of general European culture," had experienced a significant degree of urbanization and industrialization, and had thus lost much of their national distinctiveness.[138] Indeed, most of the museum's experts agreed that the model of the Altai-Saian exhibit worked best for exhibiting the "former colonial peoples" of Siberia, the Far East, Central Asia, and the North Caucasus. According to ethnographers, most of these peoples had not developed "bourgeois national" cultures and, with Soviet assistance, would be able to make a direct jump from the "feudal stage" to the "socialist stage" on the Marxist historical timeline.[139] As a result, the experts argued, these peoples could experience the direct transformation and consolidation of their traditional cultures into Soviet national cultures.

The road from traditional culture to Soviet national culture was somewhat less straightforward for the Soviet Union's more "developed" nationalities—

138. See Kriukova and Studenetskaia, "Gosudarstvennyi muzei etnografii narodov SSSR," 43–45.

139. Some ethnographers argued that these peoples were following a "noncapitalist path of development."

especially for those who had experienced the Europeanization of their cultures *before* the establishment of Soviet power. According to the experts, there were two main issues of concern. First, how should the museum and its experts differentiate "Soviet national culture" from "bourgeois national culture"? Second, would Sovietization lead to homogenization?

The Ethnographic Department's ethnographers and activists were familiar with Stalin's argument that the "abolition of national oppression" had allowed the "regenerated nations" of the Soviet Union "to revive and develop their national cultures." They also understood that the national cultures of "Soviet nations" were supposed to be "in content, socialist cultures."[140] But the experts and activists were uncertain how to depict the national cultures of developed Soviet nationalities versus those of bourgeois nationalities. This issue came into stark relief as the department began work on a small exhibit on Soviet Moldavia in 1932 and 1933. The department's ethnographers debated, without total resolution, how best to depict the Soviet Moldavians versus the Romanian Bessarabians. These peoples derived from the same ethnic group; but while the Romanian Bessarabians had attained nationhood under capitalism, the Soviet Moldavians had attained nationhood under socialism. The ethnographers rejected the idea (espoused by German anthropologists) that these two peoples had a common "race culture," but acknowledged that they had certain "cultural similarities" as a result of their common past. Most important, the experts emphasized, was the fact that these two peoples had developed different national cultures as a result of living under different types of states. The ethnographers maintained that the exhibit could best capture this by comparing Soviet Moldavian and Romanian Bessarabian peasant culture. Noting that the peasant was the "main productive force" of both countries, the experts suggested that the exhibit show the Moldavian *bedniaki* and *seredniaki* engaging in active class struggle against kulaks and attaining a proletarian culture and consciousness, and the Bessarabian *bedniaki* and *seredniaki* being crushed by class oppression and bowing before kulak culture.[141]

The question of homogenization drew even greater attention, especially as the department unveiled its new exhibit on "Belorussia and the BSSR" in August 1933. This exhibit was organized into three main sections. The "pre-1917" section depicted the primitive communist, feudal, and capitalist eras,

140. In a March 1929 exchange on "The National Question and Leninism," Stalin tweaked his definition of a nation—defining it as "a historically constituted, stable community of people, formed on the basis of the common possession of four principal characteristics, namely: a common language, a common territory, a common economic life, and a common psychological makeup manifested in *common specific features of national culture.*" Emphasis added. Stalin's comments were published for the first time in 1954. There is no evidence that the ethnographers were privy to this particular exchange, but Stalin's ideas about "national culture" were well known at this time. I. V. Stalin, "Natsional'nyi vopros i leninizm," *Sochineniia,* vol. 11 (Moscow, 1949), 333.

141. REM f. 2, op. 1, d. 399, ll. 3–6.

with halls devoted to "the exploitation of the population of the pre-reform village" and "belief and religion as a means of exploitation and oppression." The
"October Revolution and civil war" section focused on the topic of "class
struggle before and after October." The Soviet section—the largest and the
most elaborate—showed the socialist reconstruction of agriculture, class struggle on the kolkhoz, the development of socialist industries, and national-
cultural construction in the republic.[142] This exhibit, like the Altai-Saian exhibit, used materials that ethnographers had brought back from recent
research expeditions to national kolkhozes; also like the Altai-Saian exhibit, it
showed the continuing struggle against "survivals." But because the Belorussians were considered an advanced nation—struggling against "capitalist-era"
(not "feudal-era") survivals—the Soviet section showed Belorussian workers,
peasants, and students dressed in plain "European" clothing.

Therein lay the problem for the experts and local party representatives who
viewed and critiqued the exhibit: there was far too little "national form" to
balance out the Belorussians' "socialist content." In one published critique, the
ethnographer Nina Gagen-Torn railed against the exhibit and the museum for
taking a nonethnographic approach as well as for forgetting that national
forms were flourishing under socialism. According to Gagen-Torn, the exhibit's life-size dioramas of a Young Pioneer (communist youth) eating in a
kolkhoz cafeteria and of a medical worker in a smock examining a sick woman
at a medical station were bland and uninteresting—and "homogenized" the
Belorussian people.[143] Gagen-Torn conceded that the plates and the smock
had no doubt been taken from Belorussia, but noted that such things "also
exist in Ukraine, and in the Crimea, and in Siberia, and near Moscow."[144]
Without the appropriate national markers, such as national clothing or other
artifacts of Belorussian national culture, it was not clear what was "Belorussian" about Soviet Belorussia.

For the rest of the decade, the Ethnographic Department (renamed the State
Ethnographic Museum in May 1934) would struggle to satisfactorily represent
the Soviet nationalities and their cultures as "national in form and socialist in
content." The museum's new Soviet Folk Theater and Music Hall (which
opened in late 1934 and was based in part on the museum's defunct ethnographic theater) helped it to hedge its bets. In the summer of 1934 the museum's directors had asked Narkompros to support such a folk theater, which
would complement the museum's exhibits, "enliven" its political-educational
work, and allow the museum to present "a more complete representation of
the life of one or another people at one or another stage" on the historical

142. For a description of the exhibit see A. K. Supinskii, *Belorussiia i BSSR (Putevoditel' po
vystavke Gosudarstvennogo etnograficheskogo muzeia)* (Leningrad, 1934). Also see Kriukova and
Studenetskaia, "Gosudarstvennyi muzei etnografii narodov SSSR," 37–38.

143. N. Gagen-Torn, "Belorusskaia vystavka Etnograficheskogo otdela Russkogo muzeia v
Leningrade," *Sovetskii muzei*, no. 1 (1934): 65–68. She was a former student of Lev Shternberg.

144. Gagen-Torn, "Belorusskaia vystavka," 69.

timeline.[145] The Soviet Folk Theater debuted with Belorussian, Ukrainian, and Russian evenings—focusing on those very nationalities that the museum itself was having the hardest time representing. The performers wore Belorussian, Ukrainian, and Russian national costumes and performed traditional and Soviet national folk songs, comedies, and dramas for museumgoers; favorite themes included the civil war and socialist construction.[146] To be sure, this type of portrayal of the peoples of the USSR also had its dangers, especially against the backdrop of Nazi Germany. Members of the Soviet Folk Theater emphasized that their goal was to use "Marxist-Leninist teachings" to evaluate the "genesis and class composition of different forms of folklore in relation to the history of the peoples of the USSR."[147] But in the effort not to homogenize the Belorussians, Russians, and Ukrainians, such performances ran the risk of erring in the other direction—of essentializing the national cultures of these peoples and thus seemingly giving credence to Nazi claims about primordial race cultures. The museum's experts and activists found themselves walking a very fine line.

The example of the ethnographic museum suggests that the Soviet regime worked out its official narrative about Soviet state formation and transformation in tandem with, and as part of, its other (often violent) efforts to further the revolution. The Soviet regime cared a great deal about the ideological front—and about the dissemination of a heroic narrative about the evolution and development of the peoples of the USSR. That said, for most of the 1920s and 1930s, the party was unable to exert full control over the Ethnographic Department's narrative and over the museum experience. Indeed, the ethnographic museum was not so much a mirror of an official ideological position as it was a venue in which experts and Politprosvet activists attempted to actively reconcile "the ideal" with "the real." The Soviet regime used the cultural sphere in its attempt to change mass consciousness. In the Soviet Union, where all spheres were politicized, all forms of participation—going to a museum, critiquing an exhibit, writing in a comment book—were political acts. The regime and its political-enlightenment activists brought Soviet citizens from Leningrad and other regions into the museum in order to teach them about the diverse peoples of the USSR and about the historical timeline and the road to socialism. Beginning in 1929, the regime went a step further and enlisted museumgoers as "socialist critics"—asking them to evaluate the exhibits while continuing to give them instruction. Some museumgoers from non-Russian regions presented themselves as "local experts" and made suggestions for improving the exhibits. But, more important, museumgoers from throughout the

145. REM f. 2, op. 1, d. 299, l. 52.
146. Ibid., ll. 41–42. The folk theater also performed worker ballads (either about work or sung at the time of work) in the national languages of all three peoples.
147. Ibid., l. 52.

Soviet Union affirmed the regime's conceptual categories and rhetoric—parroting official views about kulaks, class struggle, and the wonders of socialist construction. The museumgoers were learning to speak the language of Soviet progress, even as the "real" experts were trying to figure out how to show such progress in a context where visual evidence was essential.

The need to develop a workable narrative of Soviet development and to document the process of Soviet socialist transformation shaped the ethnographers' research agenda, giving rise to a new subfield of research on "survivals" as well as another subfield on the formation of Soviet national cultures. The ethnographers who researched "survivals" in the 1930s conducted research expeditions that produced a nonbiological, sociohistorical explanation for the persistence of traditional culture and *byt*. Those who researched national cultures evaluated national-culture formation and collected folklore on national kolkhozes. Both types of expeditions helped shape the Soviet response to the external ideological threat of Nazi race science. How they did so is the subject of the next chapter.

PART 3

The Nazi Threat and the Acceleration of the Bolshevik Revolution

State-Sponsored Evolutionism and the Struggle Against German Biological Determinism

> We are dealing here with a revolution which maintains that with it and through it the old world ceases and a new humanity begins.
>
> —René Fulop-Miller, *The Mind and Face of Bolshevism,* 1926

The Soviet approach to the population developed in the late 1920s and 1930s in response to Joseph Stalin's push to accelerate the revolution and in reaction to major events abroad—one of the most significant being the rise of German national socialism with its "scientific" theories about biological determinism. In 1929, Stalin launched his campaign for rapid economic and social transformation, proclaiming the power of nurture over nature and promising to enact a "great break" with the past. In 1930, national socialism began to gain ground in German universities, and German anthropologists argued that humankind could not advance without a "racial-biological revolution."[1] The confluence of these events shaped the research agenda of Soviet ethnographers and anthropologists for the next decade.

The German anthropologists' assertions about human development would not have mattered to the Soviet regime were it not for a combination of three factors. First, the German claims tapped into Soviet leaders' own anxieties about the difficulties of building socialism in lands inhabited by a multiethnic population "at the most diverse levels of historical develop-

---

1. On the rise of national socialism in German universities see Robert N. Proctor, *Racial Hygiene: Medicine under the Nazis* (Cambridge, MA, 1988), and Paul Weindling, *Health, Race, and German Politics between National Unification and Nazism, 1870–1945* (Cambridge, 1989). On "the biological" and "the social" in the Soviet Union see Amir Weiner, "Nature, Nurture, and Memory in a Socialist Utopia: Delineating the Soviet Socio-Ethnic Body in the Age of Socialism," *The American Historical Review* 104, no. 4 (October 1999): 1114–55, and Peter Holquist, "To Count, to Extract, to Exterminate: Population Statistics and Population Politics in Late Imperial and Soviet Russia," in *A State of Nations: Empire and Nation-Making in the Age of Lenin and Stalin,* ed. Terry Martin and Ronald Grigor Suny (New York, 2001), 111–44.

ment."[2] The collectivization of agriculture was supposed to accelerate the
process of state-sponsored evolutionism and speed the road to socialism; instead it seemed to be resulting in the physical "degeneration" of the rural
population.[3] Second, German anthropologists challenged the very premises
of the Soviet project and made direct reference to the Soviet population. In
the German order of things, "culture" was a reflection of racial traits, which
derived from "immutable genetic material," and neither social reform nor
socialist revolution could improve the human condition. Even more offensive
was the German suggestion that nature "established a division into higher
and lower races" and that the peoples of the Soviet Union could never catch
up to the "Nordic" or "Aryan" Germans.[4] Third, during the mid-1920s, the
Weimar and Soviet governments had established strong scientific ties—as a
result of which German anthropologists and pathologists had cataloged
racial traits and conducted experiments in the realm of constitutional medicine (*Konstitutionslehre*) on Soviet soil in Buriat-Mongolia and Central Asia.
This had the unfortunate effect of making German assertions about the Soviet population seem all the more credible.[5]

Against this backdrop, in 1931 the Soviet regime prevailed on its anthropologists and ethnographers to disprove German race theories. In particular,
the Soviet experts were to wage a war against biological determinism: to prove
to audiences at home and abroad that "all *narodnosti* can develop and flourish" and that "there is no basis whatsoever for supposing the existence of
some sort of racial or biological factors" that would make it impossible for
certain peoples to participate in "socialist construction."[6] Soviet ethnographers and anthropologists, most of whom were themselves troubled about
the German turn to "Nordic race science," and none of whom wanted to be
accused of anti-Soviet tendencies, set out to refute German claims in scientific
terms and prove that the Marxist vision of historical development—grounded
in sociohistorical, not sociobiological, laws—was the correct one.

Combining physical-anthropological and ethnographic research, the Soviet
experts took a two-pronged approach. Soviet anthropologists did physical and

2. This quote is from G. I. Broido, "Nasha natsional'naia politika i ocherednye zadachi
Narkomnatsa," *Zhizn' natsional'nostei*, no. 1 (1923): 5.

3. On state-sponsored evolutionism see chapters 2 and 3.

4. On German claims and the Soviet response see S. Bykovskii's introduction to G. I. Petrov,
"Rasovaia teoriia na sluzhbe u fashizma," *Izvestiia Gosudarstvennoi akademii material'noi kul'-
tury* 95 (1934): 4–14; A. I. Iarkho, "Protiv idealisticheskikh techenii v rasovedenii SSSR,"
Antropologicheskii zhurnal, no. 1 (1932): 9–23; and M. S. Plisetskii and B. Ia. Smulevich, "Rasovaia teoriia—klassovaia teoriia," *Antropologicheskii zhurnal*, no. 1–2 (1934): 3–24.

5. On these German expeditions see Paul Weindling, "German-Soviet Medical Co-operation
and the Institute for Racial Research, 1927–c. 1935," *German History* 10, no. 2 (1992): 177–206,
and Weindling, *Epidemics and Genocide in Eastern Europe, 1890–1945* (Oxford, 2000). Also,
Susan G. Solomon, "The Soviet-German Syphilis Expedition to Buriat Mongolia, 1928: Scientific
Research on National Minorities," *Slavic Review* 52, no. 2 (1993): 204–32.

6. The St. Petersburg Branch of the Archive of the Russian Academy of Sciences (PFA RAN) f.
174, op. 1, d, 71, ll. 3–4.

constitutional studies throughout the Soviet Union in order to prove that even the most "backward" tribes and nationalities were physically "able" and could develop when placed in favorable economic and social conditions. At the same time, Soviet ethnographers studied the population's culture and *byt*—and explained the phenomenon of "backwardness" in sociohistorical terms. In particular, the ethnographers invoked the idea of "survivals" (which originated in the theories of Edward B. Tylor and took on a new life in the Soviet Union), arguing that progress was slow in some regions because beliefs, economic relationships, social structures, and "class enemies" from "earlier historical eras" had not yet been altogether eliminated.[7] The experts not only provided Soviet institutions with expert knowledge, but also actively participated in the campaign to eradicate survivals—which the ethnographers (appropriating the language of the Communist Party) referred to as a campaign for "cultural revolution."[8]

Whereas previous chapters have focused on the concept of "nationality," this chapter examines the relationships among "nationality," "culture," and "race" in the Soviet Union, looking at the nature-nurture debate as it unfolded through the years of the "great break." It explores three related issues. What were "race" and "culture" in the Soviet context, and how did these concepts change over time? How was the Soviet approach to the population shaped by the broader international context—and by the German ideological challenge in particular? And, finally, to what degree did Soviet social scientists (who are often portrayed as the hapless victims of Stalinism) legitimate and perpetuate the Soviet hunt for enemies through their efforts to explain and wipe out "backwardness"?

Soviet Applied Science in the 1920s: The "German Model" Idealized

The Soviet and Nazi regimes, and their visions for transforming their societies, were built on dramatically different ideological foundations. These ideologies, in turn, were grounded in irreconcilable social science theories regarding the relationship between the biological and the social.[9] The breakdown in Soviet and German scientific relations in the late 1930s is thus not surprising—but it makes the strength of the collaboration between Soviet and German social scientists in the 1920s all the more striking in retrospect. On the Soviet side, this collaboration was grounded in a deep respect for the German model of applied science. Sergei F. Ol'denburg, Vladimir Vernadskii, and Vladimir Il'ich Lenin himself had long admired the German approach to the scientific management

7. On the theory of "survivals," and class enemies as "living survivals," see chapter 5.

8. PFA RAN f. 135, op. 2, d. 1029, ll. 21–210b. Also see Akademiia nauk SSSR, *Otchet o deiatel'nosti Akademii nauk SSSR za 1931 g.* (Leningrad, 1932), 354.

9. For a thoughtful discussion about science and ideology see Helen E. Longino, *Science as Social Knowledge: Values and Objectivity in Scientific Inquiry* (Princeton, 1990).

and use of productive forces, which German scientists had developed in South West Africa (a former German colony) and had used to their government's advantage during World War I.[10] The Commission for the Study of Natural Productive Forces (KEPS), which Vernadskii had organized in Russia in 1915, and the Gosplan Bureau for the Study of Productive Forces, which Arsenii Iarilov had helped establish in 1926, were both based in part on the German model. Iarilov (the former head of the State Colonization Research Institute) maintained that the bureau would further the work of "Soviet colonization [*kolonizatsiia*]," which he continued to define as a program for the economic and cultural development "of the entire Soviet Union in agreement with a general plan." In this case, Iarilov had in mind the First Five-Year Plan, which Gosplan was developing and which Stalin would introduce in 1928.[11]

Soviet economists and other experts with the new Gosplan Bureau were on the whole enthusiastic about using applied science to promote planned economic development. Most also welcomed the chance to work with and learn from German scholars. By June 1926, when the Soviet government sent Ol'denburg (the permanent secretary of the Academy of Sciences) to Berlin to meet with German scientists, such collaboration was already under way.[12] Ol'denburg's host was the Emergency Association of German Science (the Notgemeinschaft der Deutschen Wissenschaft).[13] Some ten months earlier, Friedrich Schmidt-Ott, the head of the Notgemeinschaft, had been in Leningrad, where he, Ol'denburg, and prominent members of the Soviet government (including Mikhail Kalinin, Anatolii Lunacharskii, and Nikolai Gorbunov) had discussed the establishment of Soviet-German scientific collaboration.[14] As a result of this initial meeting, a group of Soviet and German anthropologists and physicians were spending the summer in the Buriat-Mongol ASSR, doing preliminary work for an expedition to investigate the effects of syphilis on the Buriats.[15] At the Notgemeinschaft, Ol'denburg discussed potential areas of German-

10. PFA RAN f. 208, op. 2, d. 104, l. 5.

11. Ibid., d. 114, ll. 112–1140b, 153. On the origins of the State Colonization Institute (Goskolonit) see chapter 2. In the late 1920s, Goskolonit became the State Research Institute for Land-Tenure Regulations and Resettlement and participated in the organization of large-scale collectivized agriculture.

12. Solomon, "Soviet-German Syphilis Expedition," 207–10, and Weindling, *Epidemics and Genocide in Eastern Europe,* 183–88.

13. PFA RAN f. 208, op. 2, d. 104, ll. 1–14. The Notgemeinschaft was created in 1920 to facilitate the rebuilding of postwar Germany. On its history see Solomon, "Soviet-German Syphilis Expedition," and Weindling, *Epidemics and Genocide in Eastern Europe.* Schmidt-Ott was the former Prussian Minister of Culture.

14. Schmidt-Ott was in Leningrad for the 200th anniversary of the Academy of Sciences. Noted in Solomon, "Soviet-German Syphilis Expedition," 207–8, and Weindling, *Epidemics and Genocide in Eastern Europe,* 188.

15. Solomon, "Soviet-German Syphilis Expedition," 209–10. Also see Karl Wilmanns, *Lues, Lamas, Leninisten: Tagebuch einer Reise durch Russland in die Burjatische Republik im Sommer 1926* (Pfaffenweiler, 1995), with an introduction by Susan Gross Solomon and documents from the Soviet and German archives.

Soviet research with Schmidt-Ott and other prominent German scholars (among them geographers, anthropologists, and geologists). The German scholars expressed a strong interest in doing fieldwork in the Caucasus and Central Asia.[16] As a result of the Treaty of Versailles, Germany had lost its colonies in Africa and East Asia, which had been important sites of German fieldwork. Schmidt-Ott and his colleagues saw the "Russian Reich with its range of racial differences," and Russia's "colonial hinterland" in the east in particular, as a promising place to continue their research agenda.[17]

The 1926 meeting inaugurated a period of intensive collaboration between Soviet and German scientists, which the Soviet and the Weimar governments considered of great diplomatic and scientific importance. In the spirit of scientific exchange, Soviet experts traveled to Germany to learn more about its techniques for studying and using productive forces. Most significantly, in the summer of 1927, the mineralogist Aleksandr Fersman—the vice president of the Academy of Sciences—toured German economic enterprises in order to learn about new methods for extracting and processing raw materials. Fersman was impressed with German technologies, and was even more taken with the German government's commitment to the scientific reconstruction of the economy and of society.[18] After returning to Leningrad, he recommended a number of revisions to Gosplan's proposal for the First Five-Year Plan. In particular, he suggested that Gosplan take a more serious "region-by-region" approach to economic development (following the German model), and that Gosplan call for the more extensive development of the Soviet Union's natural mineral wealth (lest the Soviet Union fall further behind Germany). Fersman also called for including in the plan measures for improving the population's health and cultural level, arguing that this in turn would further the work of economic construction.[19] Fersman reminded Gosplan that it was embarking on a "grand experiment . . . not in a laboratory but on one-seventh of the earth with a population of 140 million people."[20]

Of course, Fersman was not the first Soviet scientist to stress the importance of considering "the population" in plans for economic development. Soviet economists, ethnographers, and anthropologists had for years discussed the population as an economic resource that should be studied and utilized as efficiently as possible. In deliberations about the creation of KEPS and KIPS during World War I, Dmitrii Anuchin had described the population as a "powerful productive force," and Sergei Rudenko had argued that anthropological

16. PFA RAN f. 208, op. 2, d. 104, ll. 4–8.

17. The quote is from Solomon, "Soviet-German Syphilis Expedition," 204–5. Solomon is citing an August 1927 letter from Schmidt-Ott to the Foreign Office. Also see PFA RAN f. 208, op. 2, d. 104, l. 5.

18. PFA RAN f. 208, op. 2, d. 114, ll. 3–5.

19. Ibid., ll. 2–7.

20. Ibid., ll. 260b–27. On the creation of the Gosplan Bureau and its "Human Being" group see ll. 31–320b.

studies of physical type could elucidate "the degree of suitability" of different nationalities "for the execution of military and other state obligations."[21] The First All-Russian Conference for the Study of Natural Productive Forces, in 1923, had held special sessions on "the human being as a productive force"— and after the conference, Gosplan had established its own "human being" working group, in which Ol'denburg, Rudenko, and Veniamin Semenov-Tian-Shanskii had assumed leading positions.[22] In 1926 this working group became a subdivision of the new Gosplan Bureau for the Study of Productive Forces, and set out to determine which particular nationalities were most suited to further specific economic goals. Physical anthropologists played a prominent role in the subdivision's work.[23]

In the 1920s, as KIPS was compiling its list of nationalities for the First All-Union Census, Soviet physical anthropologists were doing intensive studies of racial (physical and constitutional) traits among the same population groups.[24] KIPS had in its ranks several physical anthropologists, including Rudenko (who served as KIPS's liaison to the Commissariat of Health).[25] But Soviet anthropologists, like Soviet linguists and geographers, also had their own institutions and journals—and pursued their own research agendas. Before 1917, most anthropologists in Russia had subscribed to the "French school" of physical anthropology, and had used anthropometry (with its tools and techniques for measuring the human body) to map out racial (physical) variation. After the revolution, these experts reoriented themselves toward German applied anthropology, with its focus on constitutional medicine, and began to work closely with pathologists, biologists, and physicians to compare health, illness, blood group, morphological type, intelligence level, and physiological functions among different population groups.[26] Soviet anthropological research—

21. D. I. Anuchin, "Izuchenie proizvoditel'nykh sil Rossii," in D. I. Anuchin, *Geograficheskie raboty*, ed. A. A. Grigoriev (Moscow, 1954), 335–42, and PFA RAN f. 2, op. 1–1917, d. 30, ll. 40–42. On the link between Anuchin and later efforts in the Soviet Union to evaluate the human being as a productive force, see M. Plisetskii, "Dmitrii Nikolaevich Anuchin: Po povodu desiatiletiia so dniia smerti," *Antropologicheskii zhurnal*, no. 3 (1933): 110–12.

22. PFA RAN f. 135, op. 1, d. 11, l. 22; d. 14, l. 20.

23. PFA RAN f. 208, op. 2, d. 114, ll. 31–320b, 112–1140b. Also PFA RAN f. 135, op. 1, d. 21, ll. 312–33, and V. P. Semenov-Tian-Shanskii, "Chelovek kak proizvoditel'naia sila," *Chelovek*, no. 1 (1928): 60–62.

24. Physical anthropology was considered a subfield of ethnography in the Soviet Union, but also had the status of a separate discipline.

25. KIPS worked on anthropological questionnaires for the Commissariat of Health's Institute for Social Hygiene. See D. Zolotarev, "Rabota Komissii Vsesoiuznoi Akademii nauk po izucheniiu plemennogo sostava (1917–1927)," *Nauchnyi rabotnik*, no. 12 (1927): 48–50, and Akademiia nauk SSSR, *Nauchnye uchrezhdeniia Akademii nauk SSSR: Kratkoe obozrenie ko dniu desiatiletiia, 1917–1927* (Leningrad, 1927), 127–28.

26. The history of the profession in Russia and the Soviet Union is recounted in A. I. Iarkho, "Osnovnye problemy Sovetskoi antropologii: Ocherednye zadachi Sovetskogo rasovedeniia," *Antropologicheskii zhurnal*, no. 3 (1934): 3–20. For an account of anthropologists' activities in the 1920s see S. I. Rudenko, "Glavneishie uspekhi antropologii v SSSR za vremia revoliutsii," *Nauchnyi rabotnik*, no. 2 (1926): 33–42. Also L. Godina, M. L. Butovskaya, and A. G. Kozintsev,

and in particular the charting of blood groups and constitutional traits, often using German indices, within the Soviet population—made an important contribution to the growing international field of racial anthropology.[27]

Defining Race and Culture

But what *was* race? And what role did Soviet physical anthropologists ascribe to nature versus nurture before the Soviet regime enlisted them in 1931 to criticize German race theories? During the 1920s Soviet physical anthropologists characterized races as distinct physical or biological types within humankind—and, like their Western European and American counterparts, participated in an international dialogue about the significance of race and the causes of physical and constitutional differentiation. In particular, Soviet anthropologists debated (both among themselves and with colleagues abroad) whether the physical and constitutional characteristics associated with different population groups were indelible and immutable, or developmental and dynamic. This debate ran parallel to an international discussion about the relative importance of nature versus nurture and the potential effect of "hereditarian" racial hygiene versus "environmentalist" social hygiene on human progress. Soviet anthropologists shared with French anthropologists an interest in neo-Lamarckian inheritance, and both Soviet and French anthropologists borrowed from British and German colleagues new techniques to evaluate constitutional traits such as blood group. Soviet anthropologists, physicians, and biologists, like their colleagues abroad, did studies to determine which physical and constitutional characteristics were transgenerational (that is, followed Mendelian law), and whether "acquired traits" such as muscle mass could be transmitted to future generations as neo-Lamarckian theories posited.[28]

In the Soviet Union, as elsewhere, these studies of constitutional traits were

History of Biological Anthropology in Russia and the Former Soviet Union (Newcastle upon Tyne, 1993).

27. On the use of German indices see Akademiia nauk SSSR, *Chuvashskaia respublika*, part 1, *Predvaritel'nye itogi rabot Chuvashskoi ekspeditsii Akademii nauk SSSR po issledovaniiam 1927 g.*, *Materialy Komissii ekspeditsionnykh issledovanii*, vol. 10 (Leningrad, 1929).

28. *Russkii evgenicheskii zhurnal*, published by the Russian Eugenics Society in the 1920s, featured articles about and transcripts of these debates. On Soviet social hygiene and eugenics, see Susan Gross Solomon, "Social Hygiene and Soviet Public Health, 1921–1930," and Mark B. Adams, "Eugenics as Social Medicine in Revolutionary Russia: Prophets, Patrons, and the Dialectics of Discipline Building," in *Health and Society in Revolutionary Russia*, ed. Susan Gross Solomon and John F. Hutchinson (Bloomington, 1990), 175–99, 200–223. For a discussion of the international debate about Lamarckian and Mendelian theories, see Proctor, *Racial Hygiene*, 30–38, and William Schneider, *Quality and Quantity: The Quest for Biological Regeneration in Twentieth-Century France* (Cambridge, 1990). On constitutional medicine as it was practiced in Germany and the United States see Sarah W. Tracy, "George Draper and American Constitutional Medicine, 1915–1946: Reinventing the Sick Man," *Bulletin of the History of Medicine* 66 (1992): 53–89.

connected to new experimental research in the area of eugenics—a field as yet untainted by the absolute biological determinism and sociobiological claims of Nazism. Some Soviet physicians and scientists advocated a new field of "socialist eugenics" grounded in Lamarckism; these researchers took a social-hygiene approach and sought to understand the effects of economic and social conditions on health and disease.[29] Others, such as Aleksandr Serebrovskii (a leading researcher at the Commissariat of Health's Biomedical Institute), promoted a new field of "anthropogenetics" which was based on Mendelian genetics, but included the proviso that environmental influences might change genetic traits. Serebrovskii, for his part, described "anthropogenetics" as the foundation for a Soviet version of eugenics, which would eliminate "harmful genes" and thus wipe out inherited diseases and "maximize" the human productive forces of the Soviet Union.[30]

During these years, Soviet ethnographers, like Western European and American cultural anthropologists, were also engaged in a similar discussion about the origins and transmission of culture. To what degree was culture an expression of a people's innate character and abilities, and to what degree was it the product of environment? Before the revolution, some of Russia's ethnographers had characterized culture as the expression of the *Volksgeist* or "unique spirit" of a people (*narod*), while others had defined it as the product of a combination of anthropological, geographical, and economic factors.[31] In the mid-1920s, the latter, less essentialist, definition prevailed in the Soviet Union. Soviet ethnographers argued that culture (in both its spiritual and material manifestations) developed in connection with a people's economic life, which itself was a product of climate and geography. In other words, to use the Marxist language which ethnographers themselves were adopting in the 1930s, "culture" was part of the "superstructure," which changed in response to changes in the "economic base."[32]

29. Adams, "Eugenics as Social Medicine in Revolutionary Russia"; Mark B. Adams, "The Soviet Nature-Nurture Debate," in *Science and the Soviet Social Order*, ed. Loren R. Graham (Cambridge, MA, 1990), 94–138, and Solomon, "Social Hygiene and Soviet Public Health." A Bureau of Eugenics was established under KEPS in 1921 with ties to the Commissariat of Health. B. A. Lindener, ed., *Raboty Rossiiskoi Akademii nauk v oblasti issledovaniia prirodnykh bogatstv Rossii: Obzor deiatel'nosti KEPS za 1915–21 gg.* (Petrograd, 1922), 40–41.

30. Adams, "Eugenics as Social Medicine," 215–17.

31. See chapter 1. Also see L. Ia. Shternberg, "Sovremennaia etnologiia: Noveishie uspekhi, nauchnye techeniia i metody," *Etnografiia*, no. 1–2 (1926): 15–43. In the mid-1920s Vladimir Bogoraz taught courses in ethnogeography, which he defined as "the history of culture as a 'resultant of geographical, anthropological, and economic factors.'" Cited from Yuri Slezkine, *Arctic Mirrors: Russia and the Small Peoples of the North* (Ithaca, 1994), 249. For a discussion of "the double potential (racial as well as cultural) of the Herderian *Volksgeist*" see Matti Bunzl, "Franz Boas and the Humboldtian Tradition: From Volksgeist and Nationalcharakter to an Anthropological Concept of Culture," in *Volksgeist as Method and Ethic: Essays on Boasian Ethnography and the German Anthropological Tradition*, ed. George W. Stocking, Jr. (Madison, 1996), 17–78.

32. For an articulation of the tasks of "Soviet ethnography," including a "dialectical-materialist approach to the question of the cultural development of peoples," see N. M. Matorin, "Sovre-

While this formula had a simple elegance, the real-life relationship between a people's economic base and its culture proved to be more complicated. First and foremost, there was considerable evidence that different nationalities could exert a powerful (positive or negative) influence on one another through a process of "cultural contact." In the Soviet Union, with its diverse peoples presumed to be at different stages on the Marxist timeline, this was no small detail. In fact, this was one of the issues that had been at the heart of the "regionalization debate" of the early 1920s: advocates of the economic paradigm had predicted that "advanced" nationalities would exert a positive economic and cultural influence on less-developed *narodnosti,* while advocates of the ethnographic paradigm had argued that backward *narodnosti* needed their own ethnoterritorial units in order to reach their economic and national-cultural potential.[33] Moreover, while working on the 1926 census, ethnographers had observed that cultural contact appeared to result sometimes in the total assimilation of one people into another, sometimes in the transmission of cultural traits from one people to another, and sometimes in the creation of altogether new nationalities and languages.[34] Ethnographers and Soviet leaders alike hoped to understand the dynamics of this process in all its variations.

Applied Science and the Study of Race and Culture

In 1927, on the eve of the First Five-Year Plan, the Soviet government allocated additional funds for scientific studies of the Union's productive forces, and Soviet anthropologists and ethnographers went to the field to further research the transmission of racial traits and the dynamics of cultural contact.[35] For the next two years, these experts—most of whom were affiliated with the Gosplan Bureau for the Study of Productive Forces—participated in more than a dozen larger "complex" or multifaceted (*kompleksnyi*) expeditions with explicit economic aims connected to the First Five-Year Plan.[36] One such expedition went to the Chuvash ASSR in the summer of 1927 in order to "elucidate the young

mennyi etap i zadachi sovetskoi etnografii," *Sovetskaia etnografiia,* no. 1–2 (1931): 3–38 (esp. 11). For Marr's articulation of the same formula for language and thought see Yuri Slezkine, "N. Ia. Marr and the National Origins of Soviet Ethnogenetics," *Slavic Review* 55, no. 4 (1996): 826–62.

33. See chapter 2.

34. See chapter 3.

35. Economists and applied geographers hoped that this research would determine whether different nationalities could adapt to "different types of labor." See A. A. Grigoriev, "Geografiia teoreticheskaia i prikladnaia, ikh sovremennoe sostoianie i namechaiushchiesiia puti razvitiia," in Akademiia nauk SSSR, Komissiia po izucheniiu estestvennykh proizvoditel'nykh sil soiuza, *Trudy Geograficheskogo otdela,* vol. 2 (Leningrad, 1930), 1–48.

36. For an account of other KIPS expeditions from 1927 see PFA RAN f. 135, op. 1, d. 22, ll. 82–84. Before 1927 KIPS's fieldwork was more limited. For an account of pre-1927 expeditions see PFA RAN f. 135, op. 1, d. 25, ll. 43–48. On *kompleksnyi* research, also see Solomon, "Soviet-German Syphilis Expedition," 208.

republic's productive forces" and promote "the development of local industries and agriculture."[37] The expedition's main detachment conducted geological and soil research, while a smaller anthropological-ethnographical detachment studied the republic's population from racial, linguistic, and social-hygiene perspectives. The anthropological-ethnographical detachment brought together physical anthropologists, ethnographers, and linguists from three Leningrad institutions: KIPS, the Japhetic Institute (which specialized in linguistics), and the Museum of Anthropology and Ethnography (MAE). The ethnographer and linguist Nikolai Marr (a member of KIPS and the head of the Japhetic Institute) led the detachment and supervised its ethnographic program. Boris Vishnevskii (a physical anthropologist from MAE) oversaw the detachment's anthropological research, which focused on the Chuvash—and in particular on the physical and constitutional similarities and differences between them and the Russians, Mordva, and Mishers of the region.[38]

Vishnevskii and his assistants examined the correlation between *narodnost'* and racial traits. They conducted blood-group studies; recorded morphological data (head measurements and height, as well as skin, eye, and hair color) on some one thousand men and women; and took photographs of representative Chuvash, Misher, Russian, and Mordva "types."[39] In his expedition report, Vishnevskii noted that, on the whole, there was a different blood group distribution among the Chuvash than among their Russian neighbors—but he pointed out that there was a continuum, and that notable differences could be found between Chuvash of different regions. He also described significant differences between the Chuvash and the Mishers in blood group distribution as well as in skin, eye, and hair color, and concluded that the two peoples belonged to "different anthropological groups."[40] Vishnevskii did not make value judgments about these anthropological groups, or attempt to link racial traits to particular cultural, behavioral, or psychological traits. He did show that the patterns of racial and linguistic intermixing in the region resembled each other, and on the basis of available historical data he argued that this was the result of migration and settlement patterns. Blood group studies, like dialect studies, Vishnevskii concluded, could provide important information about the historical interrelationships among different peoples.[41]

In the 1920s, most expeditions to research "the human being," like the Chuvash expedition, attempted to construct a "biosocial profile" of targeted population groups but made an effort to define "race" in "neutral" (or at least

---

37. Akademiia nauk, *Chuvashskaia respublika: Predvaritel'nye itogi rabot Chuvashskoi ekspeditsii*, 3–4. The expedition received funds from Gosplan, the Chuvash government, and the Academy of Sciences.

38. Ibid., 3–7, 229–32. KEPS planned the expedition's main research program. Both Marr and Vishnevskii were members of the Gosplan-based working group on the human being.

39. Ibid., 237–52 and tables.

40. Ibid., 237–44.

41. Ibid., 250–52.

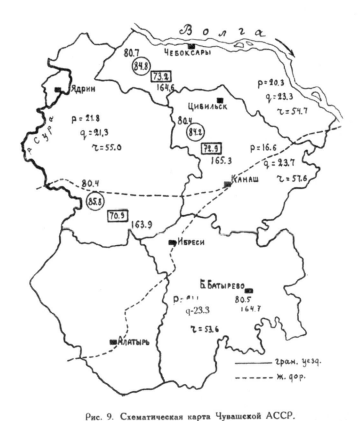

Figure 6.1 Diagrammatic map of the Chuvash ASSR from the 1927 expedition to the republic. Boris Vishnevskii oversaw the expedition's anthropological research. The map uses anthropometrical indexes to present information about the blood types (here called "biochemical races"), head shape, face shape, nose shape, and height of the populations of different *volosty*. (From Akademiia nauk, *Chuvashskaia respublika: Predvaritel'nye itogi rabot Chuvashskoi ekspeditsii Akademii nauk SSSR po issledovaniiam 1927 g.*, vol. 10, pt. 1 of *Materialy Komissii ekspeditsionnykh issledovanii* [Leningrad, 1929], 250)

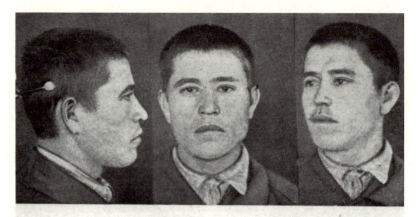

Рис. 1. Чувашин, 23 лет, род. в Больше-Батыревской волости. Цвет кожи, на внутр. стороне плеча—11 (по Лушану), волос головы—6 (по Фишеру), глаз—4 (по Мартину). Растительность на теле: грудь—0, предплечье—1, икры—2. Рост 161.1 см. головной указатель—79.78, лицевой (морфологический)—82.01, носовой—66.0. Группа крови—III.

Рис. 2. Чувашин, 27 лет, Шемуршинской волости, Батыревского у. Цвет кожи—11, волос—4, глаз—4. Отсутствие растительности на теле (грудь, живот и т. д.). Рост 163.5, головн. указ.—80.0, лицевой—80.28, носовой—77.78. Группа крови—III.

Figure 6.2 Chuvash men. Anthropological types. From the 1927 expedition to the Chuvash ASSR. (From Akademiia nauk, *Chuvashskaia respublika: Predvaritel'nye itogi rabot Chuvashskoi ekspeditsii Akademii nauk SSSR po issledovaniiam 1927 g.*, vol. 10, pt. 1 of *Materialy Komissii ekspeditsionnykh issledovanii* [Leningrad, 1929], table 1)

Рис. 1. Мордвин, 61 года, Батыревской вол. Цвет кожи—3, волос—8, глаз—16. Растительность на теле: грудь—2, живот, бедра—0, предплечье—3, икры—3. Рост—166.8, головной указ.—84.07, носовой—67.92. Группа крови—I.

Рис. 2. Русский, 29 лет, уроженец Шамкинской вол., Батыревского у. Цвет кожи—3 (серый оттенок), волос—14, глаз—10. Растительность на теле: грудь—1, живот, бедра—0, предплечье—1, икры—2. Рост—167.0, головной указ.·—80.21, лицевой—83.57, носовой—62.07. Группа крови—II.

Figure 6.3 Mordvin man (top), Russian man (bottom). Anthropological types. From the 1927 expedition to the Chuvash ASSR. (From Akademiia nauk, *Chuvashskaia respublika: Predvaritel'nye itogi rabot Chuvashskoi ekspeditsii Akademii nauk SSSR po issledovaniiam 1927 g.,* vol. 10, pt. 1 of *Materialy Komissii ekspeditsionnykh issledovanii* [Leningrad, 1929], table 4)

nonsociobiological) terms.[42] There were, however, some notable exceptions. For example, the anthropologists and ethnographers on a 1927 complex expedition to the Far East drew a direct link between biological and cultural traits, and even warned about the dangers of racial mixing. In the expedition's published report, the ethnographer Vladimir Arsen'ev argued that the Russians, Chinese, Iakuts, and Chukchi were "the most viable peoples" in the Far East and that the Tungus and other "backward *narodnosti*" of the region were doomed to extinction. In this same report, another researcher (the physician A. A. Beliaevskii) warned that the "cross-breeding" of Russians "with a lower, weaker race" was damaging to "the physical constitution of the Slavic race" and to "the Slavo-Russian *natsional'nost'*."[43] Expedition reports like this one, which gave no credence to the official line—that all races were equal and that nurture trumped nature—were the exception to the rule. But in the 1930s, officials and experts alike would invoke these examples in justifying the regime's crackdown on the social sciences and asserting the importance of fighting race theories with a unified voice.

While some expeditions to study the "human being" in the 1920s had a physical-anthropological orientation, others focused on the relationship between nationality and culture. Most of these expeditions looked at nationalities that had migrated from one part of the Soviet Union to another and found themselves in a different "ethnic milieu" and under "natural conditions that were new to them."[44] A case in point was the 1928 KIPS-Ethnographic Department expedition to the Amur-Ussuri region of the Far East. The research team, under Rudenko's leadership, studied Ukrainian settlers, evaluating changes in their economic organization and *byt*. In particular, Rudenko and his colleagues sought to determine the "degree and character of influence" that the Koreans, with their "elevated agricultural culture," had on the Ukrainians. The ethnographers also investigated how the arrival of the Ukrainians had affected the native peoples of the region, such as the Udegei, Orochi, and Manegri.[45] While Rudenko's team was in the Far East, other KIPS and Ethnographic Department ethnographers were conducting similar research in the Kuban region of the North Caucasus: studying how Ukrainian settlers were adapting to local forms of agricultural labor and evaluating the process of cultural exchange between them and the region's other *narodnosti*.[46] These studies of set-

42. See the description of the Bashkir expedition of 1928 to 1930 in Akademiia nauk SSSR, *Otchet o deiatel'nosti Akademii nauk SSSR za 1930 g.* (Leningrad, 1931), 75–76.

43. A. A. Beliavskii, "Metisatsiia zabaikal'skogo naseleniia," and V. K. Arsen'ev, "Naselenie Dal'nego Vostoka kak proizvoditel'nyi factor," in V. M. Sabitch et al., eds., *Proizvoditel'nye sily Dal'nego Vostoka, Chelovek,* vol. 5 (Vladivostok, 1927). Cited in G. I. Petrov et al., eds., *Materialy Buriat-Mongol'skoi antropologicheskoi ekspeditsii 1931 goda,* pt. 1, *Obzor rabot ekspeditsii* (Leningrad, 1933), 16–19.

44. Archive of the Russian Ethnographic Museum (REM) f. 2, op. 1, d. 233, l. 121.

45. Ibid., ll. 25, 121. (The expedition report used the term *pereselentsy* to refer to the Ukrainians.)

46. Ibid., ll. 24, 29. Boris Kryzhanovskii, the Ukrainian expert, led this expedition.

tler populations preceded the forced resettlement operations that were connected with the collectivization campaign—and there is no evidence that the
ethnographers foresaw the vicious character that these operations would take.
But the ethnographers, like other experts, did anticipate that the regime would
need to "move" people to "underpopulated regions" in order to sow fields and
extract raw materials. The idea of "the human being" as an economic resource
that could be moved and maximized—and that could adapt to a new environment—became an important part of Soviet scientific discourse during the
1920s and gave Stalin's economic policies a scientific rationale.[47]

A small but important subset of anthropological-ethnographical expeditions during these years involved Soviet and German collaboration. The meeting between Schmidt-Ott and Ol'denburg in 1926 had laid the groundwork
for collaborative expeditions to Central Asia and the Far East, some of which
had a medical-anthropological focus. For example, in the summer of 1928, a
Soviet-German team of venereologists, serologists, physicians, and other experts traveled to the Buriat-Mongol ASSR to investigate the high incidence of
syphilis among the republic's Buriats and to test the effects of a particular drug
on the course of the disease.[48] The Soviet side of the expedition had in its ranks
two ethnographers (including Kapitolina Viatkina from KIPS) who, taking a
social-hygiene approach, studied the cultural reasons for the disease's prevalence among the Buriat population. These ethnographers investigated local
health and sanitation practices and interviewed Buriats about their sexual
practices. Both the Soviet and the German researchers characterized the Buriats as a "primitive" people with a "backward" culture who were in danger of
extinction. However, only the Soviet researchers made a serious effort to evaluate Buriat culture, which Soviet ethnographers characterized as the reflection
of economic and social conditions—and thus as changeable.[49]

Even while the Buriat-Mongol expedition was under way, Soviet and German geneticists, pathologists, and other experts were putting together a still
more ambitious program for systematic collaborative research on "the human
being." In 1927, Soviet and German experts and their respective governments

47. See, for example, Ar. N. Petrov, "K vyiavleniiu organizatsionnykh form industrial'no-
promyslovoi kolonizatsii," in *Problemy promyshlenno-promyslovoi kolonizatsii*, vol. 2, *Trudy
Gosudarstvennogo nauchno-issledovatel'skogo Instituta Zemleustroistva i Pereseleniia*, vol. 11
(Moscow, 1930), 57–77. This and other articles in the volume were written in 1927 and 1928.

48. The drug was Salvarsan. Solomon, "Soviet-German Syphilis Expedition."

49. Primary funding came from the Notgemeinschaft, with some funds from the Commissariat
of Health and the Soviet Academy of Sciences. The other anthropologist was A. B. Staritskaia
from Moscow State University. Solomon, "Soviet-German Syphilis Expedition," 211, 215–20,
229–31. That same summer, another Soviet-German brigade studied the spread of tuberculosis
among the population of the Kirgiz ASSR, and a team of Soviet and German geographers and geologists surveyed the Pamir region of Tajikistan. See PFA RAN f. 4, op. 28, d. 2, ll. 5–11;
Akademiia nauk SSSR, *Otchet o deiatel'nosti Akademii nauk SSSR za 1932 g.* (Leningrad, 1933),
293; Weindling, *Epidemics and Genocide in Eastern Europe*, 188–89; and Solomon, "Soviet-German Syphilis Expedition," 206–7.

had begun negotiations about the establishment of a German-Russian Institute for Racial Research specializing in constitutional medicine and disease pathology. In late 1927, a branch was set up in Moscow, and in 1930 a second office was established in Tbilisi, in the Georgian SSR. Using the Tbilisi office as their base, German and Soviet researchers began to evaluate the prevalence of certain diseases among different nationalities in Georgia and in other parts of the Caucasus.[50]

The initiation of collaborative German-Russian racial research in the Caucasus coincided with the rise of national socialism in German universities. Over the next two years the relationship between Soviet and German scientists came under strain, as Soviet leaders came to see German race theories as an ideological threat. German pathologists and anthropologists in the Soviet Union, in discussions with their Soviet colleagues, continued to define "race" in "neutral" terms as "differentiating factors."[51] But back in Germany, anthropologists were forging close ties with the "Nordic movement," and race science was taking a pronounced turn toward sociobiologism.[52] As German anthropologists argued that there were higher and lower races—and that lower races as a matter of course had "lower cultures" which were impervious to reform—the observations of German researchers in the Soviet Union that certain nationalities, such as the Buriats, were "primitives" with "backward cultures" took on new undertones challenging the very premises of the Soviet project. It was in this context that "race" became a "problem" for the Soviet regime.

Ethnography and Anthropology through the "Great Break"

Stalin's ambitious program for economic and social transformation—his "revolution from above"—was the ultimate Promethean enterprise.[53] The campaigns for rapid industrialization and for the "total collectivization" of agriculture, launched in 1929, were intended to eliminate the gaping chasm between "the ideal" and "the real" in the Soviet Union and to speed the road to socialism. Soviet economists and theorists saw collectivization as the linchpin of this venture. The settlement of peasants and nomads onto kolkhozes and sovkhozes (collective farms and state farms) was supposed to increase

50. Weindling, "German-Soviet Medical Co-operation"; Weindling, *Epidemics and Genocide in Eastern Europe*, chapter 7; and Susan Gross Solomon and Jochen Richter, eds., *Ludwig Aschoff: Vergleichende Völkerpathologie oder Rassenpathologie* (Pfaffenweiler, 1998).

51. Weindling, "German-Soviet Medical Co-operation," 193.

52. Proctor, *Racial Hygiene*, chapter 2.

53. Much has been written about the Promethean impulse of the Soviet project, and the Promethean aspect of the Soviet applied sciences. For one example see David Bakhurst, "Political Emancipation and the Domination of Nature: The Rise and Fall of Soviet Prometheanism," *International Studies in the Philosophy of Science* 1, no. 3 (1991): 215–26.

agricultural production and support the industrialization drive, as well as increase Soviet administrative control in rural regions that thus far had eluded the grasp of the state.[54] Furthermore, collectivization, by changing the economic base and eliminating traditional forms of social organization, was supposed to accelerate the ethnohistorical development of the population. This had special significance in regions with large clan and tribal populations. Indeed, one can glean from official reports that national kolkhozes (organized according to nationality) were supposed to function as small-scale national-territorial units: as incubators of Soviet nationhood, as mechanisms of double assimilation. On national kolkhozes, clans, tribes, and *narodnosti* would become bound to particular national territories and languages, engage in collective labor, and develop "Soviet" sensibilities.[55]

In practice, the first wave of the collectivization campaign faced enormous difficulties. In 1930, officials with the Commissariat of Agriculture's Kolkhoz Center reported that peasants and nomads throughout the Soviet countryside were slaughtering their livestock, fighting the collectivizers, and fleeing their villages en masse.[56] According to the Kolkhoz Center, one of the most serious obstacles to the campaign in non-Russian regions in particular was mutual ignorance: collectivizers often lacked sufficient knowledge of "local languages and cultural and economic particularities," and most peasants and nomads did not understand "their role in the revolution."[57] To make matters worse, Kolkhoz Center officials observed, kulaks, clan leaders, and other "class enemies" were exploiting the collectivizers' ignorance and the local populations' fears. For example, during the first wave of the campaign, collectivizers (sometimes out of ignorance and sometimes in a bid to appease local populations) had allowed kolkhozes in Central Asia, Siberia, and the Far East to be organized on "traditional kinship lines." This had resulted in the widespread estab-

54. On the eve of the campaign, many regions were still organized according to pre-Soviet administrative-territorial units. On the economic goals of collectivization see Alec Nove, *An Economic History of the U.S.S.R.,* rev. ed. (London, 1989), chapters 6 and 7.

55. On "double assimilation" see chapter 4. On the administrative and cultural-enlightenment role of national kolkhozes see the Russian State Archive of the Economy (RGAE) f. 7446, op. 13, d. 8, ll. 240b–27.

56. RGAE f. 260, op. 1, d. 3, ll. 3–5. On the violent course of the collectivization campaign and the campaign's "setbacks" see Martha Brill Olcott, "The Collectivization Drive in Kazakhstan," *The Russian Review* 20, no. 2 (1981): 122–42, and Lynne Viola, *Peasant Rebels Under Stalin: Collectivization and the Culture of Peasant Resistance* (New York, 1996). The Kolkhoz Center was an official organ of the Ministry of Agriculture that coordinated collectivization and the administration of the Soviet Union's kolkhozes. See A. V. Nelidov, *Istoriia gosudarstvennykh uchrezhdenii SSSR 1917–1936,* vol. 2 (Moscow, 1962), 516–27, and Moshe Lewin, *Russian Peasants and Soviet Power: A Study of Collectivization* (New York, 1968), chapter 15.

57. A. Bogdanov, "Kolkhoznoe stroitel'stvo v natsional'nykh raionakh," *Revoliutsiia i natsional'nosti,* no. 3 (1930): 39–46. *Revoliutsiia i natsional'nosti* was the official journal of the Soviet of Nationalities. Bogdanov was the director of the Kolkhoz Center. Also RGAE f. 260, op. 1, d. 3, l. 3; f. 7446, op. 13, d. 8, ll. 10–12, 66–67.

lishment of "clan kolkhozes"—which according to the Kolkhoz Center played into the hands of clan leaders by putting them in a position to take advantage of and manipulate their own kin.[58]

In the summer of 1930, the Kolkhoz Center and its National Bureau (which assisted in kolkhoz construction in non-Russian regions) embarked on a program of reconnaissance work and political-enlightenment activities.[59] For collectivizers and political-educational workers, the Kolkhoz Center organized special courses on the local cultures and kinship structures, and sometimes the languages, of targeted regions. For kolkhozniks, the Kolkhoz Center organized political-enlightenment programs.[60] To further its efforts, the Kolkhoz Center distributed a questionnaire to regional-level kolkhoz centers throughout the Soviet Union, asking for detailed information about the ethnic, economic, and social characteristics of local kolkhozes, about "kolkhoz *byt,*" and about kolkhozniks' attitudes toward the revolution.[61] The Kolkhoz Center also recruited experts, including ethnographers, to serve as instructors and to provide it with ethnographic information about non-Russian regions that were in the midst of, or targeted for, collectivization.[62]

It was in this context that Soviet leaders called on ethnographers and anthropologists not just to provide information about the population, but also to prove that all of the nationalities of the Soviet Union were *capable* of participating in socialist construction. With the countryside in shambles, the Soviet regime was all the more sensitive to German anthropologists' claims that socialism "could never be achieved with the racial quality of present-day man."[63] Soviet leaders also hoped that new anthropological-ethnographical research would serve as a weapon against "Great Russian chauvinism" in the Soviet Union by undermining the "widespread and rooted belief among the general Soviet public, among Soviet workers, and also in literature" that certain indigenous populations, "even when placed in favorable economic and social circumstances, cannot reach the same level of physical development" or work as hard as Russians.[64]

Between 1929 and 1932, at the height of Stalin's "revolution from above," the Soviet regime reined in its scientists and scholars and insisted that all the sciences be grounded in Marxist-Leninist (scientific socialist) principles. These years saw the reorganization of important scientific institutions—including the

58. RGAE f. 7446, op. 13, d. 78, l. 12 and f. 260, op. 1, d. 36, ll. 15–17.

59. The National Bureau was created within the Organizational-Instructional Department of the Kolkhoz Center in late 1929. RGAE f. 7446, op. 13, d. 7, ll. 1–2, 6.

60. RGAE f. 7446, op. 13, d. 78, ll. 16, 19; d. 13, ll. 10–12. These were sometimes organized in coordination with the Commissariat of Enlightenment.

61. RGAE f. 7446, op. 13, d. 8, ll. 66–67.

62. RGAE f. 260, op. 1, d. 3, ll. 1–10 and f. 7446, op. 13, d. 78, l. 24.

63. This quote is by Fritz Lenz. It is quoted from Proctor, *Racial Hygiene,* 60. In the 1930s Soviet anthropologists gave Lenz and his theories a critical appraisal in their scholarly publications. See, for example, Plisetskii and Smulevich, "Rasovaia teoriia—Klassovaia teoriia," 10.

64. PFA RAN f. 174, op. 1, d. 71, l. 2.

Academy of Sciences—and a general reorientation toward applied science.[65] In 1930, KEPS and two other commissions (the Commission for Expeditionary Research and the Commission for the Study of the Republics) were merged into a new Academy of Sciences institute: the Council for the Study of the Productive Forces of the USSR (SOPS). SOPS was conceived of as a "planning body of national significance" that would better coordinate scientific research with the goals of the five-year plans.[66] It worked with Gosplan and the Gosplan-based Bureau for the Study of Productive Forces to organize complex expeditions (with geographical, geological, anthropological, and other detachments) aimed at furthering the collectivization and industrialization campaigns.[67] The SOPS agenda built on the German applied-science model that had taken root in the Soviet Union in the 1920s. But this vision of applied science was now celebrated as distinctly "Soviet," and especially suited to the unique attributes of Soviet centralized economic planning.

It was precisely during these years, as Soviet leaders endeavored to build "socialism in one country," that the borders began to close between the Soviet Union and the West. The party singled out, censured, and in some cases arrested a number of prominent Soviet scientists and scholars for their uncritical borrowing of "bourgeois ideas" and "pseudoscientific theories." It called for self-criticism and demanded constant ideological vigilance.[68] In this tense political climate, the Soviet-German scientific collaboration began to break down, albeit neither as quickly nor as completely as one would expect. Both sides had a lot invested in the relationship: Soviet administrators and experts did not want to return the expensive scientific equipment that the German government had purchased for the German-Russian Institute for Racial Research, and German experts were eager to finish their investigations. Moreover, both the Soviet and the German governments recognized the value of scientific ties as a means of keeping diplomatic channels open. For several years,

65. On the "great break" in the Academy see David Joravsky, *Soviet Marxism and Natural Science, 1917–1932* (New York, 1961); Michael David-Fox, *Revolution of the Mind: Higher Learning Among the Bolsheviks, 1918–1929* (Ithaca, 1997); Loren R. Graham, *The Soviet Academy of Sciences and the Communist Party, 1927–1992* (Princeton, 1967); and Alexander Vucinich, *Empire of Knowledge: The Academy of Sciences of the USSR (1917–1970)* (Berkeley, 1984), chapter 3.

66. Akademiia nauk SSSR, *Otchet o deiatel'nosti Akademii nauk SSSR za 1930 g.*, 73–75, and Graham, *Soviet Academy of Sciences and the Communist Party*, 165.

67. Graham states that SOPS became active in the fall of 1931, but the archival documents note that it was active from the spring of 1930. Graham, *Soviet Academy of Sciences and the Communist Party*, 166. Also RGAE f. 399, op. 1, d. 1, ll. 94, 103.

68. See, for example, S. A., "K novym zadacham sovetskoi etnografii," *Sovetskaia etnografiia*, no. 3–4 (1931): 1–13; S. N. Bykovskii, "Etnografiia na sluzhbe klassovogo vraga," *Sovetskaia etnografiia*, no. 3–4 (1931): 3–13; and M. Khudiakov, "Kriticheskaia prorabotka Rudenkovshchiny," *Sovetskaia etnografiia*, no. 1–2 (1931): 167–69. This was part of a broader "anti-expert campaign" that began with the "Shakhty Affair" of 1928 and continued with the Communist Party's siege of the Academy of Sciences. See Graham, *Soviet Academy of Sciences and the Communist Party*.

Soviet leaders tolerated the continued presence of German pathologists and other experts in the Soviet Union, and the German government continued to send funds for the institute.[69]

Meanwhile, the Soviet regime called on anthropologists and ethnographers at the Academy of Sciences in Leningrad to wage a scientific campaign against biological determinism. Much of this responsibility fell to the Institute for the Study of the *Narodnosti* of the USSR (IPIN), the successor to KIPS—which was comprised in large part of former KIPS ethnographers and their former students. IPIN's director, Marr, had established a reputation as a "Marxist thinker" for his linguistic theories (which posited that "language and thought were superstructural phenomena whose evolution mirrored the evolution of the economic base") as well as for his zealous criticism of Western European scholars who attached "culture to race."[70] IPIN continued much of the work of KIPS, but also branched out into new areas, orienting much of its research toward "promoting socialist construction" in the national republics and oblasts.[71] For example, IPIN's Division on the Union's National Composition and the Processes of Ethnogenesis studied the processes through which clans and tribes consolidated into *narodnosti* and *natsional'nosti,* and supplied the Commissariat of Agriculture with new detailed ethnographic maps of rural regions to facilitate the organization of national kolkhozes.[72]

All of the IPIN ethnographers took up the fight against "fascist race theories" after 1931—and those with IPIN's Division on Precapitalist Relations and Socialist Construction and its Division on the Human Being as a Productive Force led the charge. Both of these divisions set out to make the case that economic and social conditions, and not racial type, determined human development. The Division on the Human Being worked with Gosplan and SOPS to evaluate the population as a productive force and to further its "rational use" in economic production. It did ethnographic, medical, and anthropological fieldwork throughout the Soviet Union—evaluating the relationship between "socioeconomic conditions" and the "biological particularities of different nationalities," and assessing how this relationship affected different groups' "ca-

---

69. Weindling, *Epidemics and Genocide in Eastern Europe,* 205–6. Weindling notes that for a time the Soviets used the Institute for Racial Research as an antireligious institute. According to Weindling, efforts to keep the institute going were abandoned in October 1935.

70. Quoted from Slezkine, "N. Ia. Marr and the National Origins of Soviet Ethnogenetics," 832, 842. Slezkine is paraphrasing Marr. On Marr and his ideas also see Katerina Clark, *Petersburg: Crucible of Cultural Revolution* (Cambridge, MA, 1995), 212–22, and Boris Gasparov, "Development or Rebuilding: The Views of Academician T. D. Lysenko in the Context of the Late Avant-Garde (late 1920–1930s)," in *Laboratory of Dreams: The Russian Avant Garde and Cultural Experiment,* ed. John E. Bowlt and Olga Matich (Stanford, 1996), 133–50.

71. On the creation of IPIN see Akademiia nauk SSSR, *Otchet o deiatel'nosti Akademii nauk SSSR v 1930 g.,* 248–52. On IPIN's agenda of promoting socialist construction, see PFA RAN f. 135, op. 1, d. 162, ll. 90–91, 96–97. Also see A. D., "Khronika: Institut po izucheniiu narodov SSSR (IPIN)," *Sovetskaia etnografiia,* no. 1–2 (1931): 157–62.

72. PFA RAN f. 135, op. 1, d. 98, ll. 38–39; d. 154, ll. 21–23, 61, 62.

pacities for work." Its anthropologists recorded anthropometrical measurements, tested blood, and conducted labor experiments, evaluating the physiological functions of people from different nationalities and classes before and after working. Its ethnographers studied kinship structures, *byt,* the local organization of labor, and the relationship between labor and (class and national) consciousness. The ethnographers and anthropologists alike aimed to prove that all of the nationalities of the USSR were "able" and that the transition to new collective and mechanized forms of labor would result in positive changes in the population's constitutional makeup.[73]

Between 1930 and 1933, during the First and Second Five-Year Plans, this IPIN division sent brigades to factories, work sites, and kolkhozes all over the Soviet Union (often in conjunction with larger SOPS expeditions) in order to evaluate population groups that were in the midst of major economic changes. One of the first of these "human being" brigades went to the Far North in 1930, in connection with a SOPS expedition to explore the potential for apatite mining in the Khibinsk Mountains. The ethnographer David Zolotarev led this brigade, which studied the Lopars (Lapps), Karelians, and Russians of the Lake Imandra region.[74] Upon completing its work, the brigade's anthropologists deemed all three groups to be "able," but its ethnographers reported no real evidence of a "break [*perelom*] from the old to the new." Instead, the ethnographers reported that "tradition rules" in the region and that the Lopars in particular "do not understand" the meaning of "socialist construction." Because old customs and practices were so entrenched, the Lopars were "not being used in the planned sense as a productive force." For example, Lopars fished just for themselves and refused to join cooperatives which could provide enough food for the entire region. The Lopar expedition served as a model for future research.[75] But after 1931—when Zolotarev and other ethnographers came under fire for not taking a "class-based approach" in their research—the IPIN ethnographers began to blame "local kulaks" and other "class enemies" for impeding the development of "backward" nationalities like the Lopars.[76]

The Division on Precapitalist Relations, for its part, took as its starting point the idea that "backwardness" was a product of uneven historical development. It studied local *byt,* collected folklore, and set out to prove that cul-

73. PFA RAN f. 135, op. 1, d. 154, ll. 16, 17; d. 98, ll. 1, 2, 19, 38; d. 79, l. 113; f. 174, op. 2, d. 156, ll. 168–69. On the role of Soviet physical anthropology in fighting "the fascistization of anthropology" see M. Plisetskii, "Na antropologicheskom fronte," *Sovetskaia etnografiia,* no. 1 (1932): 91–101.

74. PFA RAN f. 135, op. 1, d. 162, ll. 48–510b. Also Akademiia nauk SSSR, *Otchet o deiatel'nosti Akademii nauk SSSR za 1930 g.,* 89–90. The expedition received funds from Gosplan, the Academy of Sciences, the State Apatite Trust, and the Colonization Department of the Murmansk Railroad.

75. PFA RAN f. 135, op. 1, d. 162, ll. 49–500b.

76. On the attack against Zolotarev, see PFA RAN f. 135, op. 1, d. 235, ll. 32–320b; d. 162, l. 91. Also see Bykovskii, "Etnografiia na sluzhbe klassovogo vraga."

ture was *not* an expression of innate racial traits (as German anthropologists were arguing), but was instead part of the "superstructure" and would evolve as the population adopted new collective economic forms. Some of its ethnographers took a hands-on approach to accelerating "the socialist reconstruction of *byt*" in the national republics and oblasts—for example, by doing cultural-enlightenment work among women and by creating alphabets for "less-developed" nationalities.[77] This division also had a Kolkhoz Subgroup, which researched, and assisted in, kolkhoz construction. In the summer of 1930, the Kolkhoz Subgroup studied agricultural, forest, livestock, cotton, and other kolkhozes in Leningrad oblast, Belorussia, the Caucasus, and the Central Asian republics.[78] Using a questionnaire drafted by the ethnographer Dmitrii Zelenin, it compiled general information about each kolkhoz—taking a special interest in kinship structures, the position of women, and "the struggle between old and new *byt*."[79]

In 1931, the Kolkhoz Subgroup joined forces with the Commissariat of Agriculture's Kolkhoz Center to research, catalog, and campaign against survivals. Over the next several years, the two groups investigated "precapitalist-era survivals" in Central Asia, Siberia, and parts of the Caucasus, and "capitalist-era survivals" in the Belorussian and Ukrainian republics and in parts of the RSFSR. In regions with large "precapitalist-era" populations, the experts focused on "clan relations" and "primitive religious beliefs" such as shamanism, and set out to prove that "the small *narodnosti* of the USSR" could, in fact, evolve and thrive once negative influences were eliminated. In regions with large "capitalist-era" populations, the experts studied the struggle for a "new proletarian culture," joined the fight against kulaks and "bourgeois nationalists," and worked to transform *narodnosti* and *natsional'nosti* into "Soviet" nations.[80] Throughout the Soviet Union, the experts studied and campaigned against "Great Russian chauvinism"—a "survival" that seemed to endure wherever there were Russian peasants. The experts differentiated between the enlightened Russian working class, which was leading the struggle for a Soviet proletarian culture, and the "bourgeois" Russian nation of the past with its treacherous kulak element.[81]

77. PFA RAN f. 135, op. 1, d. 79, l. 113; d. 99, l. 230; d. 162, ll. 143–44.

78. Its initial name was the Group for the Study of Kolkhoz *Byt*. In 1931 it was renamed the Group for the Study of Collectivization and Industrialization in National Regions. PFA RAN f. 135, op. 1, d. 117, l. 2; d. 154, l. 10. For a list of the Kolkhoz Subgroup's members see PFA RAN f. 135, op. 1, d. 98, l. 39. Also see Akademiia nauk SSSR, *Otchet o deiatel'nosti Akademii nauk SSSR za 1931 g.*, 352.

79. [Dmitrii Zelenin], *Programma etnograficheskogo izucheniia kolkhozov* (Leningrad, 1930).

80. On the expedition to the Belorussian SSR see PFA RAN f. 135, op. 2, d. 1034, l. 1; op. 1, d. 155, ll. 25–27.

81. For a list of kolkhoz expeditions see PFA RAN f. 135, op. 1, d. 99, l. 233. Also see *Otchet o deiatel'nosti Akademii nauk SSSR za 1931 g.*, 351–54. The Kolkhoz Center had presumed that Russian kolkhozniks would assist national kolkhozniks. RGAE f. 7446, op. 13, d. 8, l. 66. Much to the Kolkhoz Center's chagrin, local kolkhoz centers throughout the Soviet Union reported that

Testing the Premises of the Soviet Project

Much of IPIN's research focused on the "former colonial peoples" of the Russian Empire—whose development was of special concern during the period of the "great break." In the spring of 1931, IPIN and SOPS organized three research brigades with the explicit aim of debunking German claims that the peoples of "the Soviet east" would be unable to adapt to "new collective economic forms" and to the "demands of industrialization."[82] Two of these brigades had an anthropological-ethnographical orientation and were connected to IPIN's Division on the Human Being; one went to the Buriat-Mongol ASSR and the other to the Amgun-Selemdzhinsk mountain region of the Far East. The third brigade, which had an ethnographic focus and was connected to IPIN's Division on Precapitalist Relations, went to the Oirot autonomous oblast in western Siberia.[83]

Soviet planners and experts considered Siberia and the Far East to be important testing grounds for the Soviet project, in large part because of their status as former colonies of the Russian Empire. The expeditions to the Oirot autonomous oblast and to Amgun-Selemdzhinsk were supposed to prove that the "backward" peoples of the "East," such as the Tungus, could develop when placed in favorable economic and social conditions. According to IPIN, the "underdevelopment" of these peoples resulted not from their "racial type" but from "historical circumstances"—such as their economic exploitation under the Russian Empire—and could thus be overcome.[84] Whenever possible, the experts were to demonstrate that the revolution was turning "feudal-era" tribes and clans into nationalities who were active participants in the Soviet project, who were "doing the colonizing" of their regions and were not "being colonized."[85] In cases where the evolution of the population was not apparent, the experts were to uncover "specific survivals" from past eras and "to illuminate their role in the class struggle as weapons in the hands of our class enemies."[86]

The Buriat-Mongol ASSR, for its part, was considered to be an ideal locale for Soviet anthropological fieldwork both because it had been the site of German anthropological research and because of its substantial "mestizo" population. By 1931, "racial mixing" had become a topic of much international sci-

---

Russian kolkhozniks bullied their non-Russian neighbors and took the best land for themselves. A. Bogdanov, "Kolkhoznoe stroitel'stvo v natsional'nykh respublikakh i oblastiakh," *Revoliutsiia i natsional'nosti*, no. 1 (1931): 53.

   82. PFA RAN f. 174, op. 2, d. 156, ll. 172–73.

   83. Ibid., ll. 172–77. Also PFA RAN f. 135, op. 1, d. 162, l. 107.

   84. PFA RAN f. 174, op. 2, d. 156, l. 172.

   85. See the discussion about Goskolonit in chapter 2. This formulation was Iarilov's. PFA RAN f. 208, op. 2, d. 183, l. 1530b. According to Iarilov, the population should feel that "ono kolonizuet, a ne ego kolonizuet."

   86. PFA RAN f. 174, op. 2, d. 156, l. 138.

entific attention. That year, the German anthropologist Fritz Lenz praised
Hitler's *Mein Kampf* and the Swedish anthropologist Herman Lundborg published *Die Rassenmischung beim Menschen,* which argued that "miscegenation" produced physically and intellectually weak offspring and led to the
"decline and death of culture."[87] British, French, Italian, and American anthropologists were expounding similar theories, and European and American
politicians were using the fear of miscegenation to defend anti-immigration
policies.[88] The IPIN and MAE anthropologists criticized the arguments of
Lenz and Lundborg, as well as those of "the national-fascist Adolf Hitler"
(whose views on "the danger of crossbreeding" were well-known) and the Italian fascist Benito Mussolini (who had expressed concern about "the preservation of 'pure races' " in his 1929 address at the International Conference of
Eugenicists in Rome).[89] Even in the Soviet Union, the IPIN and MAE experts
noted, "little-grounded" and "antiscientific" theories were circulating about
the "defective" nature and "inevitable extinction" of mestizos.[90] Gathering
scientific evidence to refute such theories about racial mixing was of great ideological importance; the Soviet idea of internationalism was predicated on the
(metaphorical and actual) merger of different nationalities.

All three IPIN-SOPS brigades had significant institutional support. The
Amgun-Selemdzhinsk anthropological-ethnographical brigade was attached to
a well-funded expedition aimed at furthering the industrial colonization of the
Far Eastern *krai* and in particular at bringing Amgun-Selemdzhinsk—a remote
region near Kamchatka with "untapped natural riches" and a sparse population—into the "economic revolution." While geologists, geographers, and biologists surveyed the region's gold deposits and evaluated possible sites for
worker colonies, the anthropological-ethnographical brigade studied the local
population of Amgun-Ud.[91] The brigade's anthropologists and physicians did

87. Translated as *The Racial Mixture of Man.* Discussed in Petrov, *Materialy Buriat-
Mongol'skoi antropologicheskoi ekspeditsii,* 12–16.

88. See Daniel J. Kevles, *In the Name of Eugenics: Genetics and the Uses of Human Heredity*
(Cambridge, MA, 1985).

89. Petrov, *Materialy Buriat-Mongol'skoi antropologicheskoi ekspeditsii,* 12–16.

90. Ibid., 18–21.

91. PFA RAN f. 174, op. 2, d. 156, ll. 91–95, 168–69; d. 158, ll. 36–66. Also RGAE f. 339, op.
4, d. 14, ll. 1–2, 14; Akademiia nauk SSSR, *Otchet o deiatel'nosti Akademii nauk SSSR za 1931
g.,* 139–40; and S. Kozin, "Dal'nevostochnaia kompleksnaia ekspeditsiia," *Sovetskaia etnografiia,*
no. 3–4 (1931): 201–7. Amgun-Ud was located at the juncture of the Amgun, Nimilen, and Udsk
rivers. According to the archival sources, gold mining provided 90 percent of the national economic revenue of the Soviet Union during this period. The economist Daniil Skliarov led the
brigade. Expeditions to the Far East region in these years had ties to the Commissariat of Defense,
which had its own concerns about securing the Far Eastern border. See Jonathan Bone, "Socialism
in One Country: Stalinist Population Politics and the Making of the Soviet Far East, 1929–1939,"
Ph.D. diss., University of Chicago, 2003. Soviet leaders and experts had been interested in the industrial *kolonizatsiia* of this region from the 1920s. See P. Derber, "Demografiia i kolonizatsiia
Sovetskogo Dal'nego Vostoka," *Novyi Vostok* 7, no. 1 (1925): 103–14.

comparative constitutional and labor studies of Amgun-Ud's indigenous peoples (the Tungus and Negidals) and of its Russian and Chinese settlers—testing their motor skills, speed and strength, cardiovascular functions, and psychological state in response to different work loads—in order to prove that all of them could adapt to new labor conditions.[92] At the same time, the brigade's economists and ethnographers studied the economic practices and *byt* of these groups. The economists helped the main expedition team learn about the potential for (and scout out the best spots for) agriculture, fishing, and hunting in the region. The ethnographers collected information about the kinship networks, family relationships, *byt,* and "world outlook" of the different nationalities. The question of feudal-era survivals was of special interest to the ethnographers, who documented how "vestigial" social structures like "the clan system" were hindering the development of "socialist forms and practices."[93]

The Oirot anthropological-ethnographical brigade also investigated "clan survivals," in this case in the context of the collectivization campaign. This brigade was attached to a complex expedition, sponsored by the Commissariat of Agriculture, that aimed to further the collectivization of the Oirot autonomous oblast by mapping out meadows and fields that had not yet been "drawn into economic use" and might be used for new cattle sovkhozes.[94] Leonid Potapov (from IPIN and the Ethnographic Department) brought the Ethnographic Department's research program "The Survivals of Clan Structure: A Hindrance to Socialist Construction in Oirotiia" to ten national kolkhozes.[95] This program (discussed in chapter 5) took as its premise the Kolkhoz Center's argument that clan-based settlement patterns and the clan-specific use of "land and labor" were benefiting clan leaders and local kulaks. Potapov set out to unmask these and other "class enemies" who were "striving to insinuate clan principles" into kolkhoz construction.[96]

The Buriat-Mongol "human being" brigade, unlike the other two, was not attached to a complex expedition; it received separate sponsorship from Gosplan, the Commissariat of Health, and a number of other institutions. Anthropologists and ethnographers from IPIN and MAE (under the leadership of the anthropologist G. I. Petrov) studied the potential for drawing Buriats and Buriat-Russian "mestizos" into industrial production—in this case in leather-

92. PFA RAN f. 174, op. 2, d. 156, ll. 71–73, 136–41; f. 135, op. 2, d. 846, ll. 3–70b. The physician-hygienist Viktoriia Avvakumova, the physician Grigorii Abramovich, and the anthropologist Natal'ia Baioris led this research. Most of the Russian and Chinese settlers were either working for or providing services to the gold-mining industry.

93. PFA RAN f. 174, op. 2, d. 156, ll. 71–73, 91–95, 168–69; f. 135, op. 2, d. 846, ll. 1–2. The ethnographers Semen Kozin and Aleksandr Zolotarev led this research.

94. L. P. Potapov, *Poezdka v kolkhozy Chemal'skogo aimaka Oirotskoi Avtonomnoi Oblasti, Trudy Instituta po izucheniiu narodov SSSR,* vol. 1 (Leningrad, 1932), 5, and Akademiia nauk SSSR, *Otchet o deiatel'nosti Akademii nauk SSSR za 1931 g.,* 126–27.

95. REM f. 2, op. 1, d. 355, ll. 20–210b, 24–25.

96. Ibid., ll. 20–25. Also RGAE f. 7446, op. 13, d. 8, l. 12; f. 260, op. 1, d. 36, ll. 13–17.

tanning and glass-making factories.[97] The brigade did much of its research in the Troitskosavsk *aimak* (village); this was home to the Chikoisk leather-tanning plant, which was one of the few factories that employed both Buriat and Buriat-Russian workers. The anthropologists recorded medical histories, tested blood types, and did comparative labor studies, evaluating the muscle strength and cardiovascular functions of Buriat, Russian, and Buriat-Russian workers before and after engaging in industrial work. The ethnographers studied labor conditions and interviewed the workers about their hygiene practices. The experts also did research in the nearby countryside, studying "three living generations" of mestizo families. The anthropologists did constitutional studies of the families; the ethnographers collected information about the families' social classes and about socioeconomic conditions in the region before and after 1917.[98]

The anthropologists and ethnographers affiliated with all three research brigades went to the field with a mandate to prove or disprove particular theories. As a result, their expedition reports are rather formulaic. The reports do, however, show how the experts were drawing on—and also helping to construct—what was becoming the official narrative of Soviet development. In this narrative, which was elaborated upon in journal articles and given visual form in new museum exhibits, the peoples of the Soviet Union would resume their evolution through the Marxist timeline on the road to socialism just as soon as class enemies were eliminated. The narrative portrayed the "great break" as a decisive turning point, prompting an intensification of class struggle: kulaks, mullahs, and other class enemies (all "living survivals") were stepping up their efforts to sabotage the revolution, while the Soviet proletariat was waging a heroic struggle for the socialist future.

In Oirotiia, Potapov found what he had expected to find: evidence that class enemies were blocking the path of progress. Potapov's official account of his research, which was published in 1932, confirmed that collectivization had not yet eliminated clan survivals. Not only do "all kolkhoz members know their clan origins," he noted, but "even young children, when stating their name, add the name of their clan." Potapov gave several examples of how the "clan organization of work" prevailed in spite of attempts to "rationalize" labor. On one kolkhoz, agronomists had divided the kolkhozniks into haymaking brigades, but once the agronomists left "there was no further discussion of brigade work." The kolkhoz members abandoned the brigades and reorganized themselves along clan lines. According to Potapov, this kolkhoz, like

97. PFA RAN f. 135, op. 1, d. 162, l. 107; f. 174, op. 2, d. 156, ll. 173–74. Also Petrov, *Materialy Buriat-Mongol'skoi antropologicheskoi ekspeditsii*, and Akademiia nauk SSSR, *Otchet o deiatel'nosti Akademii nauk SSSR za 1931 g.*, 137–38. A complex expedition would go to the Buriat-Mongol republic the following year.

98. PFA RAN f. 174, op. 2, d. 156, ll. 173–74, and Petrov, *Materialy Buriat-Mongol'skoi antropologicheskoi ekspeditsii*.

other clan kolkhozes, had a poor work ethic in general; the kolkhozniks "take time off every five days," while on kolkhozes without clan influences "people work without a break for ten or fifteen days." Potapov pinned the blame on mullahs, clan leaders, and other class enemies. He noted that a young man, "20 years old or so," had been made kolkhoz chairman because "he is the only literate person on the kolkhoz." But, in practice, the young man deferred to his clan elders.[99]

Potapov described all of the victories and setbacks of collectivization in Oirotiia in Marxist-Leninist terms—maintaining that "the construction of national kolkhozes takes place in conditions of acute class struggle," an underestimation of which would be "a crude and dangerous political mistake." He criticized earlier ethnographic studies of the region that had blamed the oppression of the peoples of western Siberia on "Russian exploitation" but had "kept silent on the fact of class differentiation" among the indigenous peoples themselves. He noted that based on this " 'scientific' literature" alone, which "does not mention existing classes," it was impossible to see the current class struggle in the region for what it was—or to understand the importance of the campaign for "the liquidation of kulaks as a class." Potapov reaffirmed the Soviet position that there were local (native) kulaks in Oirotiia and that class struggle would become ever more intense among the region's native populations in the era of building socialism. He warned that "recent exploiters, having lost the basis for their activities," were attempting "to infiltrate the kolkhoz and tear it down from within." Those enemies who were unable to "infiltrate the kolkhoz themselves," he added, "act through their followers, through family members, and through relatives."[100] In the sweep of several sentences, Potapov both distanced himself from the older generation of ethnographers and provided a scientific rationale for the dispossession and arrest of a sizeable part of the Oirot population.

The published report on the Buriat-Mongol expedition also confirmed the official line, in this case about the able-bodiedness of mestizos. It noted that the expedition's data—which showed that the same physical tasks had similar effects on the physiological functions of Buriats, Russians, and Buriat-Russians—"permit a categorical denial" of arguments about the physical weakness of mixed-race peoples. It also underscored the researchers' observation that "social conditions," and not race, had the most significant impact on physical development—influencing the height, weight, and physical strength of the individuals in all three groups. Anthropological and ethnographic data from the countryside suggested that the children of Buriat-Russian mestizos who were raised with good hygiene and nutrition developed as well as, and in some cases even better than, the children of single-*narodnost'* (Buriat or Rus-

99. Potapov, *Poezdka v kolkhozy Chemal'skogo aimaka*, 37, 40–41.
100. Ibid., 42–44.

Figure 6.4 Kolkhozniks from the Oirot autonomous oblast. The banner reads, "To the best fighter for socialist stockraising—To the shockworker of the field." This photo was taken during the 1931 Oirot expedition. (From L. P. Potapov, *Poezdka v kolkhozy Chemal'skogo aimaka Oirotskoi Avtonomnoi Oblasti, Trudy Instituta po izucheniiu narodov SSSR*, vol. 1 [Leningrad, 1932], 32)

sian) families.[101] The report also discussed some of the expedition's shortcomings and made clear that all had not gone as planned on the ground. As recounted by the anthropologists, "local kulaks" had spread rumors: first that the researchers were disciples of the anti-Christ, and later that the researchers were attempting to determine who "has Russian blood" so that the regime could throw them out of Buriatiia. As a result of these rumors, part of the local population had refused to cooperate with the research team altogether. Others had interpreted the anthropologists' interest in their blood as evidence or confirmation that *narodnost'* was a biological trait that could be determined through a simple blood test. The irony of this was not lost on the researchers.[102]

101. Petrov, *Materialy Buriat-Mongol'skoi antropologicheskoi ekspeditsii*, 40–75 with charts and tables.
102. Ibid., 8.

Nature, Nurture, and Cultural Revolution

As suggested above, the same Soviet anthropological-ethnographical expeditions that set out to refute German race theories and prove that all peoples were "able" also had a nefarious effect—providing a scientific rationale for the internal deportation of Soviet citizens onto collective farms and fueling the search for class enemies. Anthropological-ethnographical research in the newly formed Tajik SSR is another case in point. In 1931, an IPIN-SOPS anthropological-ethnographical team went to mountain regions of Karategin and Darvaz in the Tajik SSR. The anthropologist Volf Ginzburg led this expedition, and Saul Abramzon (from IPIN) was second in command.[103] The research team studied the "physical development" of Tajiks, focusing on the connection between "anthropological type" and socioeconomic conditions; it did comparative constitutional and blood group studies and took anthropometrical measurements of *bedniaki, seredniaki,* workers, and "others."[104] On the basis of this research, Ginzburg concluded that there was "no basis whatsoever" for considering the Tajiks a "weak *narodnost'* " that could not "adapt to the physical and mental processes of labor." On the contrary, in spite of having suffered through difficult economic and social conditions under Bukharan rule, the Tajiks were developing, not dying out. Moreover, Ginzburg argued, Soviet "socialist construction" had already exerted a significant effect on the Tajiks: the establishment of organized collective labor and the process of "inoculating" the population with sanitary-hygiene habits had started to "render the Tajiks healthy" and "strengthen their physical development."[105]

Pointing to striking physical and constitutional differences among Tajiks of different social classes, Ginzburg made the case that socioeconomic conditions affected physiological and constitutional traits and thus shaped "racial type."[106] His report showed that Tajik peasants were shorter in height than Tajik workers; that Tajik *seredniaki* had rounder bellies and broader frames than Tajik *bedniaki;* and that Tajik workers had straighter shoulders and more developed muscles than Tajiks from all other groups.[107] Extrapolating from his own research, and from the research of other Soviet anthropologists and

---

103. Ginzburg was a graduate student at the Academy of Sciences at this time.

104. PFA RAN f. 174, op. 2, d. 468, ll. 1–60b. The "others" included teachers, cultural workers, and police officers. For a summary of this research see V. V. Ginzburg, "K antropologicheskomu izucheniiu naseleniia Tadzhikistana," Akademiia nauk SSSR, Sovet po izucheniiu proizvoditel'nykh sil, *Problemy Tadzhikistana, Trudy Pervoi konferentsii po izucheniiu proizvoditel'nykh sil Tadzhikskoi SSR,* vol. 2 (Leningrad, 1934), 212–19.

105. PFA RAN f. 174, op. 2, d. 468, ll. 5–7.

106. Ibid., ll. 3, 5–6. Ginzburg, like Vishnevskii, argued that geographical diffusion also shaped racial type. He noted that the Tajiks of Karategin and Darvaz were "a rather homogeneous group" overall, but there were notable physical differences on a continuum from southeast to northwest.

107. PFA RAN f. 174, op. 2, d. 468, ll. 2–40b.

Figure 6.5 Residents of Shul'khob village in Garm region. Photo taken during the 1931 IPIN-SOPS anthropological-ethnographical expedition to Karategin and Darvaz. The head of the expedition, Volf Ginzburg, compared the racial traits (hair color, head shape, height, and so on) of the residents of different regions. (From V. V. Ginzburg, "K antropologich-eskomu izucheniiu naseleniia Tadzhikistana," in Akademiia nauk SSSR, Sovet po izucheniiu proizvoditel'nykh sil, *Problemy Tadzhikistana, Trudy Pervoi konferentsii po izucheniiu proizvoditel'nykh sil Tadzhikskoi SSR,* vol. 2 [Leningrad, 1934], 213)

ethnographers, Ginzburg asserted that Tajik workers had more in common with other workers "from European Russia and other countries" than with co-nationals from other social classes. This idea that class trumped ethnic or na-tional origins was becoming an established Soviet maxim. Indeed, Ginzburg's characterization of physical differentiation resonated with and drew inspira-tion from Marr's theory of linguistic differentiation—which stipulated that "the language of one class will in its typological features be closer to the lan-guage of the same class in a different ethnic group than it will be to that of an-other class in the same ethnic group."[108]

Ginzburg's argument—that Tajiks were "able" in general, and that Tajiks who engaged in collective labor were healthier and "more developed" than their co-nationals—implied that the resettlement of poor Tajik peasants from the mountains to the lowlands to work on cotton-growing kolkhozes was in

108. Quoted from Katerina Clark, *Petersburg: Crucible of Cultural Revolution,* 214. Clark is paraphrasing N. Ia. Marr, "Pochemu tak trudno stat' lingvistom teoretikom," in *Iazykovedenie i materializm,* ed. N. Ia. Marr (Leningrad, 1929), 25–26. Soviet anthropologists hailed Marr as a "shining critic" of "race theory." PFA RAN f. 174, op. 1, d. 414, l. 288.

the Tajik national interest. But anthropological and medical studies of Tajiks who had been resettled from Darvaz to cotton kolkhozes in the Vakhsh River region (near Khojent) did not bear this out. According to the experts, large numbers of Tajik settlers had fallen ill with malaria at the height of cotton-processing season. This had had significant economic consequences for the republic and for the Soviet Union as a whole: the spread of malaria among Tajik settlers had ruined "all the planned measures in Tajikistan for mastering large areas for cotton," which is a labor-intensive cultivation.[109] Some anthropologists and doctors speculated that the Tajik mountain-dwellers, as newcomers to the lowlands, had been "more susceptible" to malaria.[110] But what did this mean for the anthropologists' working hypothesis that all peoples could adapt to new labor conditions?

This question inspired spirited discussion at the First Conference on the Study of the Productive Forces of Tajikistan, held in the republic in the spring of 1933. The conference's working group on "Culture and the Study of the Human Being"—which was led by Ol'denburg and included Abramzon, Petrov, Ivan Zarubin, and other experts from Leningrad, as well as representatives from the Tajik SSR Commissariat of Health—reviewed Ginzburg's findings in its session on social hygiene.[111] The experts praised Ginzburg's anthropological research, which, in their estimation, had proven that "social conditions in the broad sense of the word" were a "real factor" in "race formation [rasogenez]."[112] Turning to the spread of illness among Tajik settlers, the experts suggested that here, too, the focus should be on social and not biological factors. Whether or not the mountain Tajiks were more susceptible to malaria than local populations was a moot point: the Soviet government could eliminate the illness altogether through a public health offensive in the region. One representative from the Tajik SSR Commissariat of Health called for measures to drain swamps, move villages further from the rice fields, provide better drinking water, and teach "hygiene skills" to the population. He also called for the training of additional medical personnel, and noted the dire need for doctors and nurses who spoke local languages.[113]

This discussion about the malaria epidemic led into a general discussion at the conference session about the need for more aggressive public health and culture campaigns. According to the experts, it was imperative to introduce Soviet medicine "into the most remote corners of the Soviet Union" in order to win the struggle against folk healers (znakhari), witch doctors, mullahs, and other survivals of the pre-Soviet past. Abramzon lamented that Tajik peasants and workers continued to visit traditional healers and sacred sites to be cured of ill-

109. PFA RAN f. 174, op. 1, d. 414, ll. 290–91. Also Akademiia nauk SSSR, Otchet o deiatel'nosti Akademii nauk SSSR za 1932 g., 209, 293–300.

110. PFA RAN f. 174, op. 1, d. 414, l. 290.

111. Ol'denburg died in 1934.

112. PFA RAN f. 174, op. 1, d. 414, ll. 287ob–288ob.

113. Ibid., ll. 290–91.

nesses; he described how Tajiks in one region made pilgrimages to a large tomb near a hot spring where the soil was said to have "special healing powers." Class enemies were exploiting such beliefs, Abramzon explained, and using them to perpetuate their hold on local populations.[114] Even more of a problem, he noted, were those Tajik workers who claimed to have such healing powers themselves. Abramzon discussed the "unmasking" of one Tajik worker who was said to have "the power of the evil eye" and was selling her services as a *znakhar'*. As it turned out, this worker was a member of the local Commission for the Improvement of Worker *Byt*, which was supposed to be leading the struggle against traditional beliefs! Abramzon and Ol'denburg both argued that bringing better public health to the region was critical "from a medical as well as an antireligious perspective."[115] The population would continue "to turn to the mullah so that he can read something from the Koran or prescribe some sort of amulet" unless the regime intervened, one expert warned.[116]

In Tajikistan, the ethnographers encountered the same conundrum as elsewhere: economic change was supposed to bring about a change in culture, but entrenched cultural backwardness was hampering the process of economic transformation. In order to deal with this problem, the regime and its experts embarked on a campaign for "cultural revolution" in Central Asia and throughout the Soviet Union. Beginning in 1931, IPIN defined "cultural revolution" as a campaign to enlighten the population and eliminate those elements of beliefs, *byt*, consciousness, and culture that were "survivals of precapitalist and capitalist relations."[117] In the Central Asian republics, Siberia, and the Far East, this translated into an effort to consolidate clans and tribes into nationalities, which would ultimately become "Soviet" nations. The First Conference on the Study of the Productive Forces of Uzbekistan, held in 1932, featured a session on "cultural revolution" that included panels on Uzbekistan's "historical front," the creation of a new Uzbek alphabet and an "Uzbek Soviet literature," and "the construction of communal-living spaces and the reconstruction of Uzbek cities."[118] The 1933 Conference on the Study of the Productive Forces of Tajikistan and the 1935 Conference on the Study of the Productive Forces of the Buriat-Mongol ASSR included similar panels about the creation and standardization of national languages, literatures, and histories, the "nativization" (indigenization) of national institutions, and other aspects of Soviet nation-building.[119]

114. Ibid., ll. 285, 294.

115. Ibid., ll. 259, 285.

116. Ibid., ll. 291–2910b. (This comment was made by a representative from the Tajik SSR Commissariat of Health.)

117. PFA RAN f. 135, op. 2, d. 1029, ll. 21–210b.

118. PFA RAN f. 135, op. 1, d. 153, ll. 2–4. The ethnographer Aleksandr Samoilovich presided. Also Akademiia nauk SSSR, *Uzbekistan, Trudy i materialy Pervoi konferentsii po izucheniiu proizvoditel'nykh sil Uzbekistana, 19–28 dekabriia 1932*, vol. 4 (Leningrad, 1934), and PFA RAN f. 174, op. 1, d. 306, ll. 48–540b.

119. Akademiia nauk SSSR, *Problemy Tadzhikistana;* Akademiia nauk SSSR, *Problemy*

In these same years, IPIN also embarked on campaigns for "cultural revolution" among the Soviet Union's "more-advanced" (or "European") nationalities such as the Russians, Ukrainians, and Belorussians.[120] Among these peoples, the experts focused on eliminating national chauvinism and kulak values (capitalist-era survivals) and documenting the "Sovietization" of beliefs, social structures, identities, and *byt*. In some regions, ethnographers recorded the autobiographies of "exceptional" kolkhozniks, such as former "ignorant, downtrodden, and illiterate" peasant women who joined the women's movement, helped bring the revolution to their villages, and became kolkhoz leaders.[121] One complex expedition to the woodlands of the Ukrainian and Belorussian SSRs and contiguous parts of the RSFSR in 1932 and 1933 investigated "cultural revolution and the problem of socialist *byt*." The expedition's anthropological-ethnographical brigade participated in kolkhoz work and helped to "expose kulak elements" who were resisting the transition from capitalist to socialist forms and values. The anthropologists did constitutional studies of the population at work and conducted research in the realm of social hygiene; the ethnographers documented survivals in the kolkhozniks' economic practices, culture, and consciousness, and studied the intensification of "class struggle."[122]

The Creation of Soviet Race Science

When Adolf Hitler became chancellor of Germany in 1933, he announced that the "race question" was the most fundamental issue for the Nazi state and pledged official sponsorship to German scientists studying racial anthropology and racial hygiene (the German variant of eugenics). Many German anthropologists welcomed the chance to put their race theories into practice: to use race science (*Rassenkunde*) to facilitate "a new age of racial-biological revolution." German social science journals published articles arguing for the transformation of the "German Empire" by racial means, through the cultivation of certain racial traits.[123] The year 1933 also brought important changes to the

Buriat-Mongol'skoi ASSR, *Trudy Pervoi konferentsii po izucheniiu proizvoditel'nykh sil Buriat-Mongol'skoi ASSR*, vol. 2 (Moscow-Leningrad, 1936). Also PFA RAN f. 174, op. 1, d. 413, ll. 95–170.

120. For example, PFA RAN f. 135, op. 2, d. 1034, l. 1; d. 1029, ll. 10–100b, 21–210b. Also A. D., "Khronika: Institut po izucheniiu narodov SSSR (IPIN)," 161–62.

121. PFA RAN f. 135, op. 2, d. 1027, ll. 11–17. For an ethnographer's notes on an interview with an "exceptional kolkhoznik woman," see PFA RAN f. 135, op. 2, d. 1034, ll. 2–11.

122. For example, the ethnographers looked at the role of women and children in the kolkhoz and at "religion as an obstacle to collectivization." PFA RAN f. 135, op. 2, d. 1029, ll. 10–100b. The Woodlands Expedition was organized through IPIN and MAE. PFA RAN f. 142, op. 1 (1932), d. 35, ll. 5, 14, 29. Also REM f. 2, op. 1, d. 399, ll. 66–68, and K. Viatkina, "Ekspeditsii IPIN," *Sovetskaia etnografiia*, no. 3 (1932): 92–93.

123. Proctor, *Racial Hygiene*, 47–48.

institutional organization of the Soviet social sciences—some in reaction to these changes in Germany and others connected to the continuing "Bolshevization" of the Soviet Academy of Sciences.[124] In May the German-Russian Institute for Racial Research, at the insistence of its Soviet scientists, renamed itself the Institute for Geographical Pathology; Soviet and German scientific collaboration at this institute continued until 1937, albeit in a much more circumscribed form.[125] In the fall of 1933, IPIN and MAE were merged into the new Institute of Anthropology and Ethnography (IAE). This new institute brought together ethnographers and physical anthropologists from throughout the Soviet Union in a concerted effort to research and promote the physical-constitutional and sociohistorical development of the population.[126]

After 1933, Soviet physical anthropologists at the IAE and other institutions stepped up their efforts to establish a new field of Soviet race science (*rasovedenie*) that took an explicitly "nonracist approach" to the scientific study of race. The physical anthropologists were acting in direct response to the entreaties of Soviet leaders to define "race" in Marxist-Leninist terms and to prove that race did not have any bearing on "the historical process."[127] Some of the anthropologists had expressed concern that the creation of a Soviet field of race science would give too much credence to the Nazi worldview and its obsession with race. But Soviet leaders insisted that concrete evidence was needed in order to disarm what had become a serious ideological threat. Summing up the official position, one anthropologist explained that "if race theories were limited to the sphere of biology" it might "be possible to brush them aside." But German race theories needed to be taken on because of their application of "biological laws" to "social phenomena." Most dangerous, he noted, was the German attempt "to present race science as the scientific and ideological foundation for political theory and practice."[128]

But how should race be defined in Marxist-Leninist terms? "Races [*rasy*]," Soviet experts explained in social science journals and popular publications, were "groups of people" that as a result of the process of human evolution and "historical development" shared "external" or "physiological" traits such as hair type, skin color, height, and facial features.[129] These physiological traits did not correlate with behavioral traits and could not be used "to determine a

124. The term *Bolshevization* is taken from Joravsky, *Soviet Marxism and Natural Science*.

125. Weindling, *Epidemics and Genocide in Eastern Europe*, 196, 206. According to Weindling, this collaboration broke down entirely in February 1937 when the Nazis banned scientific relations with the Soviet Union.

126. On the formation of the IAE see Akademiia nauk SSSR, *Otchet o deiatel'nosti Akademii nauk za 1933 goda* (Leningrad, 1934), 218–21.

127. Iarkho, "Osnovnye problemy," 5–6. Also Akademiia nauk SSSR, *Otchet o deiatel'nosti Akademii nauk za 1934 g.* (Leningrad, 1935), 388.

128. Iarkho, "Osnovnye problemy," 5.

129. N. Cheboksarov and M. Plisetskii, "Rasy (chelovecheskie)," in *Bol'shaia sovetskaia entsiklopediia* (Moscow, 1941), vol. 48: 285. Soviet anthropologists maintained that all humankind was one species and that it was unknown how many races existed. Also Iarkho, "Os-

political approach to one or another group of people."[130] Rejecting the "subjective-idealistic position" that race "does not exist," Soviet anthropologists argued that the "present racial face" of the earth should be understood as a "phase." The "relative [geographical] isolation" of peoples in "preclass societies" had facilitated the formation of races; distinct physiological characteristics had developed "in response to geographical and climatic conditions," and in the course of a protracted "historical period" had been "transferred from generation to generation."[131] As societies migrated or faced different economic conditions, significant changes in racial traits occurred, the experts maintained. (In this view, Soviet anthropologists found common cause with the American anthropologist Franz Boas, whose comparative studies of American-born and European-born Jews and Italians provided evidence of the influence of environment on racial traits.)[132] Moreover, as humankind evolved from primitive societies through feudal societies to class-based societies, "races mixed" and racial traits became less distinct. As societies advanced even further on the Marxist historical timeline, racial distinctions would continue to soften—and would at some point disappear altogether.[133]

Soviet anthropologists called for more scientific studies of the process of racial mixing, which the experts argued would become more pronounced in the Soviet Union with the continuing push for industrialization. Proclaiming the able-bodiedness of mestizos to be a given—that in the Soviet Union "a whole number of republics and oblasts" had populations made up of "a mixture of white and yellow races," whose achievements "on the front of economic and cultural construction are great"—the anthropologists argued that research on racial mixing could elucidate the process of inheritance and the complex interrelationship between "genetic" and "environmental" factors.[134] The experts suggested that such research might provide greater scientific knowledge about certain constitutional attributes, such as different groups' immunities to particular diseases.[135]

---

novnye problemy"; Petrov, "Rasovaia teoriia na sluzhbe u fashizma," 15–17; and A. B., "Voprosy i otvety," *Revoliutsiia i natsional'nosti*, no. 4 (1934): 91–94.

130. A. B., "Voprosy i otvety," 94. For an elaboration of this theme see T. Trofimova and N. Cheboksarov, "Rasy i rasovaia problema v rabotakh Marksa, Engel'sa i Lenina," *Antropologicheskii zhurnal*, no. 1–2 (1933): 9–32.

131. Iarkho, "Protiv idealisticheskikh techenii," 13–14; Iarkho, "Osnovnye problemy," 7–9; and Cheboksarov and Plisetskii, "Rasy (chelovecheskie)," 285–86.

132. Soviet ethnographers translated Boas's studies and reprinted excerpts in the journal *Sovetskaia etnografiia*. In the 1930s, the "Race Division" of Moscow State University's Museum of Anthropology (devoted to disproving fascist race theories) featured an exhibit on Boas's work. See N. Cheboksarov, "Rasovyi otdel Gosudarstvennogo muzeia antropologii MGU," *Antropologicheskii zhurnal*, no. 2 (1936): 252.

133. Iarkho, "Osnovnye problemy," 7–9, and Cheboksarov and Plisetskii, "Rasy (chelovecheskie)," 289–90, 293–97.

134. A. I. Iarkho, "Kritika i bibliografiia: O tom kak ne sleduet zanimat'siia antropologiei," *Antropologicheskii zhurnal*, no. 1 (1935): 147.

135. Iarkho, "Osnovnye problemy," 14–15.

Whereas German anthropologists of the 1930s tended to conflate races and nationalities (or nations), Soviet experts endeavored to explain the distinctions among these categories. According to Soviet anthropologists and ethnographers, the same historical process that was responsible for the gradual "disappearance" (*sniatie*) of racial distinctions also promoted the "unification of peoples" into new complex sociohistorical units—nationalities and nations—that were based on shared language, culture, and cast of mind (consciousness).[136] The experts backed up the arguments of Soviet leaders that races and nationalities were altogether different: that peoples of one race could be members of different nationalities; that all nationalities were comprised of people of various racial origins; and that "racial types" were "abstractions" extrapolated from the "variations of racial traits" found within nationalities. Soviet anthropologists proposed that race scientists take up "the biological problem of race formation"—that they evaluate the racial traits still present within nationalities in order to elucidate the sociohistorical processes of ethnogenesis (which led to the formation of modern nationalities and nations). Observing, as Vishnevskii had several years earlier, that racial differentiation often paralleled linguistic differentiation and migration patterns, the anthropologists noted that race scientists might work with historians and linguists to trace the "origins" of different nationalities and nations back to the "prehistorical era" of primitive communism.[137]

The "Law of Development by Stages"

While Soviet anthropologists contemplated the role of *rasovedenie* in shedding light on the genesis of nationalities and nations, Soviet ethnographers reflected on the links among national consciousness, culture, and origins. The members of a *natsional'nost'* or nation were united in the present through a number of characteristics, including national consciousness, the experts noted. But the nationalities and nations themselves were the products of a long process of sociohistorical evolution—which proceeded according to the "law of development by stages."[138] A 1934 article in the journal *Revoliutsiia i natsional'nosti* (*Revolution and Nationalities*) explained the main attributes of a *natsiia, natsional'nost'*, and *narodnost'* in such sociohistorical terms. According to the article, the term *natsiia* referred to a state-bearing people with its own territorial region and "other state attributes," among them a common language, eco-

136. Cheboksarov and Plisetskii, "Rasy (chelovecheskie)," 295–96, and Iarkho, "Protiv idealisticheskikh techenii," 12–14.

137. Iarkho, "Protiv idealisticheskikh techenii," 13; Iarkho, "Osnovnye problemy," 9; A. B., "Voprosy i otvety," 93–94; and A. I. Iarkho, "Metodika antropologicheskikh issledovanii: O nekotorykh voprosakh rasovogo analiza," *Antropologicheskii zhurnal*, no. 3 (1934): 43–69.

138. On evolution according to the "law of development by stages [*po zakonu stadial'nosti*]" see REM f. 2, op. 1, d. 453, l. 15. Also see Dana Prescott Howell, *The Development of Soviet Folkloristics* (New York, 1992), 371.

nomic life, and culture, that it had "attained over the course of its entire historical process of development." The term *natsional'nost'* referred to a people that had national consciousness but had not yet attained all of the other essential attributes of a nation: a common land, language, economic life, and culture. The term *narodnost'* signified a people with "national particularities," whether or not it had national consciousness.[139] By 1934, providing evidence that the process of sociohistorical evolution was continuing and accelerating under Soviet rule—that *narodnosti* were amalgamating into *natsional'nosti,* and *natsional'nosti* into Soviet nations—had already become an important means of demonstrating the revolution's success.[140]

Indeed, even as Soviet leaders continued to maintain that at some point in the future (after the achievement of socialism on a *world* scale) national differences would fade and nations would merge, there was widespread agreement that in the meantime—in the "long transitional period"—Soviet nations with distinct national cultures would develop and flourish.[141] Beginning in 1936, the State Ethnographic Museum began to discuss plans for a new permanent exhibit called "USSR: Fraternal Union of Peoples," which would trace the evolution of all the Soviet nationalities and nations through the Marxist historical timeline and showcase the "blossoming" of their national cultures and economies in the conditions of socialist construction.[142] Significantly, during these years there was a concerted effort at the State Ethnographic Museum and other cultural institutions to highlight the evolution of the Russians and the creation of a Soviet Russian national culture. Soviet leaders and experts had originally characterized the Russians, the state-bearing people of the former Russian Empire, as "great-power chauvinists." In the mid-1930s, the Soviet regime proclaimed that national oppression had been all but abolished within Soviet borders, and that all of the fraternal peoples were experiencing the development of their national cultures. In these new conditions, in the wake of the "great break," to continue to treat the Russians as an "oppressor nation" would be anachronistic—and would support the Nazi position that nations had essential traits.

Against this backdrop, the regime and its experts attempted to show how the Russians, like the other peoples of the USSR, had evolved through the

139. A. B., "Voprosy i otvety," 91–94. The article cited with reverence Stalin's 1913 definition of a *natsiia.*

140. In the mid-1930s, new ethnographic exhibits at the State Ethnographic Museum in Leningrad and at the Museum of the Peoples of the USSR in Moscow (formerly the Central Museum for the Study of Peoples) documented this process and represented each Soviet nation's "official" national culture.

141. On the idea of the "socialist nation" and Stalin's position on the development of national cultures see Gerhard Simon, *Nationalism and Policy toward the Nationalities in the Soviet Union: From Totalitarian Dictatorship to Post-Stalinist Society* (Boulder, 1991), 136–38, and Walker Connor, *The National Question in Marxist-Leninist Theory and Strategy* (Princeton, 1984), chapter 10.

142. REM f. 2, op. 1, d. 607, ll. 1–12.

stages on the Marxist timeline and had taken their present form under the aegis of Soviet power. To that effect, Soviet historians and ethnographers produced new textbooks that narrated the transition from the Great Russian past to the Soviet Russian present.[143] This new historical narrative was not a glorification of the imperial Russian past, nor did it mark a "retreat" from the Stalin revolution.[144] It called out both the achievements and the misdeeds of the tsarist state. But most importantly, it celebrated the Russian proletariat—the most "progressive" part of the former "oppressor nation," the part that had been the vanguard of the revolution and had become the heart of the new Soviet Russian nation. The national culture of the Soviet Russian nation differed a great deal from traditional Russian national culture, which had been based in large part on the Russian Orthodox religion and peasant culture.[145] Exhibits and history texts that celebrated the Soviet Russian nation as "the first among equals" were hearkening not to the Russian national past or to the Russians' innate traits but to the Russian proletariat's "historical role."

In the face of the Nazi threat, Soviet experts were under considerable pressure to demonstrate that "national culture" was the expression not of primordial racial traits, but of the sociohistorical process. This accrued increasing political importance as the Nazis used German "homeland nationalism" (which considered "transborder Germans" to be "full members" of the German nation) as a political weapon in its effort to establish a *grossdeutsches Reich* (Greater German state).[146] At the First All-Union Folklore Conference (held in Leningrad in 1936), Soviet ethnographers and folklorists criticized their German counterparts not just for equating races with nations and for idealizing "kulaks" as the source of national culture, but also for appealing to ethnic Germans throughout the world to return to the German fatherland.[147] German experts' characterization of German culture as an expression of primordial Germanness that was linked to "blood descent" took on menacing tones as the Nazi state declared its right to intervene in the affairs of all "ethnic Germans"—including those within Soviet borders.[148]

Aware of the danger in essentializing national culture, ethnographers at the IAE and the State Ethnographic Museum emphasized that music, literature,

143. See for example A. V. Shestakov, ed., *Kratkii kurs istorii SSSR* (Moscow, 1937).

144. Here I am arguing against Terry Martin, The *Affirmative Action Empire: Nations and Nationalism in the Soviet Union, 1923–1939* (Ithaca, 2001), and David Brandenberger, *National Bolshevism: Stalinist Mass Culture and the Formation of Modern Russian National Identity, 1931–1956* (Cambridge, MA, 2002).

145. Martin Malia, *The Soviet Tragedy: A History of Socialism in Russia, 1917–1991* (New York, 1994), 235–36.

146. Rogers Brubaker, *Nationalism Reframed: Nationhood and the National Question in the New Europe* (Cambridge, 1996), 132–34.

147. Howell, *Development of Soviet Folkloristics*, 371–73.

148. For a critique of German arguments about *Volksgeist* (*rasovaia dusha*) and national culture see G. Soboleva, " 'Volk und Rasse': Kriticheskii obzor," *Antropologicheskii zhurnal*, no. 1 (1936): 110–16.

dance, and other modes of cultural expression could not be divorced from their sociohistorical context. These experts argued that it was imperative to give special attention to the distinct characteristics of (Russian, German, Uzbek, and other) national cultures that resulted from having evolved through the historical timeline *under* Soviet power.[149] For example, it was critical to show that Uzbek national culture was a product not of primordial "Uzbekness," but of the historical process of Uzbek development as it unfolded in the Soviet context. For the rest of the decade, Soviet ethnographers and other experts looked for elements of national cultures that embodied the formula "national in form and socialist in content." Under pressure to document this aspect of sociohistorical evolution, the experts in some cases intervened in the process of cultural production themselves.

The field of Soviet folklore, which had been folded into the field of Soviet ethnography in the early 1930s, provides a vivid example of this phenomenon. Beginning in the 1920s, Soviet folklorists had traveled throughout the Soviet countryside looking for songs, dances, and tales about the revolution, the civil war, Lenin, Stalin, and the "new life." These efforts had had limited success. Then in the mid-1930s, despite their protestations that it was not possible to "produce folk songs and tales the way one produces grain and manufactures tractors," folklorists at the IAE Folklore Division and other institutions began to take on a direct role in "folklore production."[150] These experts accompanied national folk poets on visits to collective farms and factories in search of new material, and helped them to produce new works. For example, one folklorist (Viktorin Popov) helped the northern folk poet Marfa Kriukova "place certain events in their correct historical sequence" and even taught her the biographies of Lenin, Stalin, and the civil war hero Chapaev.[151] These new works, which were presented as the original creations of the peoples of the USSR, provided proof of the revolution's achievement on the cultural front—and of the ethnographers' theories.

The most impressive product of such efforts was the collection published in 1937 (under the auspices of the *Pravda* editorial staff) titled *Creative Works of the Peoples of the USSR*. The collection featured some six hundred pages of stories, songs, and poems, which were said to have been translated from the languages of almost all of the official nationalities.[152] Several subthemes ran

149. Howell, *Development of Soviet Folkloristics*, chapter 7.

150. The quote is from Robert Magidoff, *In Anger and in Pity* (Garden City, 1949), 153. On the collaboration between the IAE folklorists and other folklorists, see Howell, *Development of Soviet Folkloristics*, 308–15.

151. Frank J. Miller, *Folklore for Stalin: Russian Folklore and Pseudofolklore in the Stalin Era* (Armonk, NY, 1990), 19–23. On the IAE folklore division also see Akademiia nauk SSSR, *Otchet o deiatel'nosti Akademii nauk za 1933 g.* (Leningrad, 1934), 219, and Akademiia nauk SSSR, *Otchet o deiatel'nosti Akademii nauk za 1934 g.*, 388. On expert intervention in folklore production also see Magidoff, *In Anger and in Pity,* 151–54.

152. A. M. Gor'kii and L. Z. Mekhlis, eds., *Tvorchestvo narodov SSSR* (Moscow, 1937).

throughout the volume and were intended to underscore the common experiences of the Soviet nationalities during the era of building socialism. One popular theme was the emergence of "new people." A Ukrainian ode to four female tractor drivers, "Tractorists"; a collection of Russian songs (*chastushki*) about a kolkhoz brigade leader, "Songs of the Shockworkers"; and the Uzbek song "Girl—Kolkhoz Worker" all celebrated the roles that men and women could fill in the Soviet Union.[153] The most often-repeated theme, however, was transcendence. Poems and songs that were said to have originated in almost all of the national republics and oblasts characterized the revolution and the collectivization of agriculture as important moments of transformation and enlightenment. The Evenk tale "Now It Is Light in the Taiga," the Armenian song "Electric Light in the Countryside," and others described how the Bolsheviks had liberated the peoples of the USSR from darkness and hardship.[154]

Folk songs and tales about Lenin, like Turkmen rugs embroidered with Stalin's image and folk dances about collectivization, were illustrations of the dictum "national in form and socialist in content." A 1939 English-language (Soviet-produced) volume, *Soviet Folk Art*, featured a section about folk dance that was in fact a lucid metaphor for how national and socialist elements were fusing together in the Soviet Union. The author described the creation of new dances in new cities where "people from various provinces and republics" exhibited their "native dances" to each other and adopted "new steps and superior technique." These dances were said to capture the nationalities' experiences after the revolution. One such dance, which was said to have been created and popularized "in the mountain villages of North Ossetia," was the Dance of the Collective Farm Brigade Leader. The volume included photos of an Ossetian in "national dress" demonstrating the dance sequence. Each of the six main steps mimed a different aspect of collective farm work: plowing, driving a tractor, husking corn, binding the sheaves, lifting the sheaves, and loading the sheaves.[155] These folk dances suggested that the national cultures of the peoples of the USSR were evolving and becoming more similar to one another in conjunction with the process of Soviet-sponsored development. Indeed, while German folklorists of this era were venerating the "pure" and "primordial" nature of the German nation, Soviet folklorists were celebrating the ethnohistorical evolution and "internationalization" (or cultural hybridization) of the peoples of the USSR.[156]

153. Ibid., 439–43, 447.
154. Ibid., 46–51, 417–18, 525–26.
155. Vsesoiuznyi tsentral'nyi sovet professional'nykh soiuzov, *Soviet Folk Art* (Moscow, 1939), 14–15.
156. Terry Martin has argued that the mid-1930s saw the "primordialization" of nationality in the Soviet Union. See Terry Martin, "Modernization or Neo-traditionalism? Ascribed Nationality and Soviet Primordialism," in *Stalinism: New Directions,* ed. Sheila Fitzpatrick (New York, 2000). While the regime emphasized the importance of national culture during this period, it con-

Figure 6.6 Turkmen rug with Joseph Stalin's face, 1930s. (A. M. Gor'kii and L. Z. Mekhlis, eds., *Tvorchestvo narodov SSSR* [Moscow, 1937])

The rise of national socialism in Germany and the spread of race theories in the international scientific community in the early 1930s presented the Soviet regime and its program of state-sponsored evolutionism with a serious ideological challenge. The regime and its experts faced this challenge head on, in part by further developing and clarifying an official Soviet position on race, nationality, and culture. Soviet ethnographers and anthropologists defined all three concepts in sociohistorical terms, did extensive fieldwork to document

tinued to characterize it as a product not of origins but of the *experience* of ethnohistorical development—and thus as part of the superstructure.

Figure 6.7 "Dance of the Collective Farm Brigade Leader." The sequence of photos shows: preliminary steps; plowing; driving a tractor; husking corn; binding the sheaves; lifting the sheaves; loading the sheaves; and final steps. (From Vsesoiuznyi tsentral'nyi sovet profes-sional'nykh soiuzov, *Soviet Folk Art* [Moscow, 1939], 14–15)

the primacy of nurture over nature, and blamed all instances of "degenera-tion" or "stagnation" on the machinations of class enemies.[157] The experts worked with the regime to advance the campaigns for economic and cultural (as opposed to racial-biological) revolution and provided a scientific rationale for police measures targeting "class enemies."

By the late 1930s, as Hitler consolidated power, the Soviet regime found it-self facing not just an ideological threat, but also a major geopolitical one. Against this backdrop, Soviet leaders became increasingly concerned about the potential danger of German (and other types of) homeland nationalism and about the loyalties of the so-called "diaspora nationalities" (Germans, Poles, Greeks, and so on) who had states and cultures outside of Soviet borders. The next chapter examines how the Soviet regime and its experts confronted these issues in the late 1930s, and how their response was shaped by the need to counter the German geopolitical and ideological threats simultaneously.

157. For example, PFA RAN f. 174, op. 1, d. 71, ll. 3–4.

CHAPTER 7

Ethnographic Knowledge and Terror

Ideologies pretend to know the mysteries of the whole historical process—
the secrets of the past, the intricacies of the present, the uncertainties of the
future—because of the logic inherent in their respective ideas.

—Hannah Arendt, *The Origins of Totalitarianism*, 1951

We now have a fully formed multinational socialist state, which has stood
all tests, and whose stability might well be envied by any national state in
any part of the world.

—Joseph Stalin, "On the Draft Constitution of the USSR," November
1936

By 1933, the Bolsheviks had brought the revolution to the Soviet Union's
farthest corners, and had created a new type of state that looked like an empire
of nationalities but defined itself in anti-imperial terms. This state was comprised of a combination of overlapping national-territorial and economic-
administrative units, all unified through a web of unionwide institutions and
plans. Nevertheless, the Soviet Union was still a work in progress. As it continued to take form in the 1930s, it responded to the pressures of a dual threat:
the ideological challenge of Nazi race theories and the geopolitical danger of
"imperialist encirclement" from the Germans in the west and the Japanese in
the east.[1]

The Nazi ideological challenge was an embarrassment for the Soviet regime.
The success of the Soviet project was premised on the belief that nurture
trumped nature. German race scientists were loudly proclaiming that the in-
verse was true—and were publicizing their appraisals of the "inferior races" of

1. On the international climate of the late 1930s and the fear of "imperialist" or "capitalist"
encirclement see William J. Chase, *Enemies within the Gates? The Comintern and the Stalinist Repression, 1934–1939* (New Haven, 2001).

the Soviet Union. Further, the danger of "imperialist encirclement," a long-held preoccupation of the Soviet regime, loomed large after the signing of the Polish-German pact in 1934 and the signing of the Japanese-German pact in 1936. Then, in 1938, Adolf Hitler laid claim to Austria and to Czechoslovakia's Sudetenland on the grounds that these territories had large ethnic German populations—raising immediate concerns about Nazi interference in the Soviet Union's western borderlands. Compounding Soviet fears, the Nazi regime had cut off scientific relations with the Soviet Union in 1937, calling home its experts—who, it turned out, had been mapping the locations of ethnic German populations in Russia and Ukraine.[2]

To counter the Nazi ideological challenge, the Soviet regime worked to prove that its vision of the historical process was correct. Joseph Stalin had predicted in the 1920s that soon after the establishment of socialism, "smaller" peoples would begin to merge into "larger" peoples, which would themselves be "incorporated into still larger nations."[3] In a November 1936 speech about the new constitution, Stalin announced that socialism had been established in the USSR. This announcement in turn precipitated an all-out effort to further accelerate the revolution and its program of state-sponsored evolutionism. As the decade came to a close, ethnographers began to anticipate—and to help bring about—the rapid *completion* of the consolidation of clans, tribes, and nationalities into Soviet socialist nations.[4]

To secure its borders, the Soviet regime drew a distinction between "Soviet" nations and "foreign" nations—labeling the latter as "unreliable elements." Throughout the 1920s and 1930s the peoples of the former Russian Empire had been integrated into the Soviet whole through their official national identities and territories, via a process of double assimilation. In the late 1930s, in the face of a major geopolitical threat, the regime attempted to stir up among the population a heightened sense of double patriotism—to "their" socialist nation and to the Soviet whole. In this context, the People's Commissariat of Internal Affairs (NKVD) questioned the allegiance of the "diaspora nationali-

---

2. On the fate of Soviet-German scientific relations in the late 1930s see Paul Julian Weindling, *Epidemics and Genocide in Eastern Europe, 1890–1945* (Oxford, 2000).

3. Quoted from Walker Connor, *The National Question in Marxist-Leninist Theory and Strategy* (Princeton, 1984), 395–96. Connor is paraphrasing Stalin. Also see Gerhard Simon, *Nationalism and Policy toward the Nationalities in the Soviet Union: From Totalitarian Dictatorship to Post-Stalinist Society* (Boulder, 1991), chapter 6.

4. On Stalin's claim that socialism had been established in the Soviet Union and on the subsequent effort to accelerate the revolution see Amir Weiner, *Making Sense of War: The Second World War and the Fate of the Bolshevik Revolution* (Princeton, 2001). On the importance of the Marxist timeline to the Soviet project see Yuri Slezkine, *Arctic Mirrors: Russia and the Small Peoples of the North* (Ithaca, 1994), and Igal Halfin, *From Darkness to Light: Class, Consciousness, and Salvation in Revolutionary Russia* (Pittsburgh, 2000). Here I disagree with Terry Martin, who argues that a primary goal of Soviet nationality policy was "affirmative action," and thus characterizes the 1930s, which saw official sponsorship of a smaller number of larger nationalities, as a period of "retreat." See Terry Martin, *The Affirmative Action Empire: Nations and Nationalism in the Soviet Union, 1923–1939* (Ithaca, 2001).

ties": peoples who comprised national minorities in the Soviet Union but had homelands outside of Soviet borders. At issue was whether the members of these nationalities could ever be true Soviet citizens. The Germans, Poles, and Japanese in particular were characterized as part of a potential fifth column. In 1937, invoking the danger of "homeland nationalism," the NKVD began deporting diaspora nationalities en masse from the borderlands.

An NKVD passport decree of April 1938 circumscribed national self-definition and facilitated this campaign against the diaspora nationalities. The decree's explicit aim was to ferret out members of "suspect" nations who, the NKVD claimed, were "concealing" their true identities. The internal passport system had been introduced in late 1932, adding yet another layer to the Soviet Union's complex administrative-territorial form.[5] It had divided the USSR into three types of zones: "regime zones" (regions of geopolitical or economic significance, including territories within one hundred kilometers of the USSR's European and Far Eastern borders), "nonregime zones" (rural regions and smaller provinces), and "extra-administrative zones" (such as the Gulag).[6] All people age sixteen and older who worked or lived in a regime zone had to obtain an internal passport, inscribed with their name, address, occupation, and nationality. Whereas the original passport instructions of 1932 had called for the registration of each passport recipient's *narodnost'/natsional'nost'* according to his or her self-definition, the 1938 decree required the registration of each passport recipient's *natsional'nost'* to be in accordance with that of his or her parents. This decree, affecting all regime zones, went into effect even as the Second All-Union Census trumpeted the right to national self-definition as a fundamental element of being "Soviet."

This chapter examines the tension between the census and the passport, two cultural technologies of rule that had critical roles in the creation of a new definitional grid of nationalities in the 1930s. The census and the passport had different institutional bases, served different purposes, and used different tech-

5. The State Archive of the Russian Federation (GARF) f. 9401, op. 12, d 137, ll. 1–2, 129–129ob. The passport instructions noted that *natsional'nost'* should "not be confused with the name of the place where the recipient of the passport lives." On the introduction of passports in general see *O vvedenii edinoi pasportnoi sistemy v SSSR* (Moscow, 1933).

6. GARF f. 9401, op. 12, d. 137, ll. 78–81. The list of regime zones also included all territories within a one-hundred-kilometer radius of Moscow and Leningrad, and within a fifty-kilometer radius of Kiev and Khar'kov. It was soon expanded to include regional centers and major agricultural settlements. In 1937 it was extended to Soviet territories bordering Iran and Afghanistan. On the passport system as a form of social control see Gijs Kessler, "The Passport System and State Control over Population Flows in the Soviet Union, 1932–1940," *Cahiers du monde russe* 42, no. 2–4 (2001): 477–503; Nathalie Moine, "Passeportisation, statistique des migrations et contrôle de l'identité sociale," *Cahiers du monde russe* 38, no. 4 (1997): 587–600; Viktor Zaslavsky, *The Neo-Stalinist State: Class, Ethnicity, and Consensus in Soviet Society* (Armonk, NY, 1994); and Mervyn Matthews, *The Passport Society: Controlling Movement in Russia and the USSR* (Boulder, 1993). On the Gulag as an administrative zone see Jonathan Bone, "Socialism in One Country: Stalinist Population Politics and the Making of the Soviet Far East, 1929–1939," Ph.D. diss., University of Chicago, 2003.

niques to gather information about the population. The NKVD (the secret police apparatus) used the passport to "unmask" and monitor members of diaspora nationalities and other "undesirable elements." At the same time, party and government institutions used the census to track the Soviet population's self-definition and to publicize the difference between the Nazi idea of "race" and the Soviet idea of "nation." Soviet leaders saw no immediate need to smooth out the differences between the passport and the census—recognizing that each served an important function. But in the late 1930s, in the midst of "the Great Terror," Soviet ethnographers and statisticians were themselves anxious to be in compliance with the NKVD.[7] A feedback loop developed between terror and ethnographic knowledge—and ethnographers ended up giving scientific backing to the NKVD's extralegal division between Soviet and diaspora nationalities.

Accelerating the Work of State-Sponsored Evolutionism

The Second All-Union Census of 1937—the first demographic census conducted "under socialism"—was to be an event of great significance, providing evidence of the revolution's achievements and a definitive response to the Nazi ideological challenge. Census preparations, which began in earnest in 1934, were similar to those for the 1926 census. Olimpii Kvitkin, who had directed the 1926 Census Commission, headed the new Census Bureau, and kept the Central Committee, the Council of People's Commissars, and TsIK (the Supreme Soviet after 1937) informed of its work.[8] Viacheslav Molotov and Stalin set the general tone and signed off on plans, but did not oversee the deliberations themselves. Their involvement did not preclude statisticians and ethnographers from engaging in intensive debate about the formulation of census materials—such as a new list of the nationalities of the USSR.

Even before Stalin's momentous 1936 speech, Soviet experts understood that the 1937 census was expected to show that the revolution had facilitated the ethnohistorical evolution of the population. Thus, much attention went into making sure that the new list of nationalities took stock of "the positive

---

7. On "the Great Terror" see Robert Conquest, *The Great Terror: A Reassessment* (New York, 1990), and Gabor Tamas Rittersporn, *Stalinist Simplifications and Soviet Complications: Social Tensions and Political Conflicts in the USSR, 1933–1953* (New York, 1991).

8. For the Census Bureau's 1935 secret report to the party on its work preparing for the census see the Russian State Archive of the Economy (RGAE) f. 1562, op. 329, d. 116, ll. 143–46. The Census Bureau was under the auspices of the Central Administration of the National-Economic Inventory (TsUNKhU), formerly the Central Statistical Administration. On the Census Bureau in the 1930s see V. B. Zhiromskaia et al., *Polveka pod grifom "sekretno": Vsesoiuznaia perepis' naseleniia 1937 goda* (Moscow, 1996); V. B. Zhiromskaia, "Vsesoiuznye perepisi naseleniia 1926, 1937, 1939 goda: Istoriia podgotovki i provedeniia," *Istoriia SSSR*, no. 3 (1990): 84–104; and Alain Blum and Martine Mespoulet, *L'anarchie bureaucratique: Statistique et pouvoir sous Staline* (Paris, 2003).

developments" in the formation and consolidation of nationalities that had occurred "since the 1926 census."[9] Beginning in 1934, two different institutions worked on separate drafts. The first, the Soviet of Nationalities' new Scientific-Research Institute of Nationalities (under the leadership of former Narkomnats administrator Semen Dimanshtein), took as its task the creation of a list of "developed *narodnosti*."[10] It used the list of *narodnosti* from the 1926 census as its starting point—first expunging all tribal, clan, and regional names (which, the experts argued, should never have been included in the first place), and next eliminating the names of all "smaller *narodnosti*" that had amalgamated into "larger *narodnosti*" over the course of the previous decade.[11] The second institution, the Institute of Anthropology and Ethnography (IAE), worked on a list of *natsional'nosti*, using "the trait of national (not ethnic) belonging" and taking stock of the amalgamation of *narodnosti* into *natsional'nosti*.[12] The IAE, now under the leadership of Ian Koshkin, included a number of former KIPS ethnographers in its ranks, such as Dmitrii Zelenin and Ivan Zarubin.[13]

By late 1935, the Institute of Nationalities had enumerated 121 *narodnosti*, whereas the IAE had enumerated 113 *natsional'nosti*. There was significant overlap between these two lists, with some 90 names included on both. As it turned out, the Institute of Nationalities' idea of a developed *narodnost'* was more or less equivalent to the IAE's idea of a *natsional'nost'*.[14] For example, while the Institute categorized the Telengit as a subgroup of the Oirot *narodnost'*, the IAE categorized them as part of the Oirot *natsional'nost'*. Both institutions held up the Oirots as an ideal example of Soviet-sponsored nation formation, noting that in less than one decade some ten western Siberian *narodnosti* and tribes had consolidated into the Oirots.[15]

9. B. Grande, "Materialy dlia utochneniia spiska narodov SSSR," *Revoliutsiia i natsional'nosti*, no. 4 (1935): 77–87 (esp. 77).

10. On the Scientific-Research Institute of Nationalities see A. Khatskevich, "Postanovlenie Prezidiuma Soveta Natsional'nostei TsIK Soiuza SSSR," *Revoliutsiia i natsional'nosti*, no. 7 (1935): 85–86.

11. GARF f. 3316, op. 28, d. 865, ll. 29–30, and Grande, "Materialy dlia utochneniia," 77. This list enumerated "smaller *narodnosti*" as subgroups.

12. The IAE's Ethnographic Division was responsible for work on the list. The St. Petersburg Branch of the Archive of the Russian Academy of Sciences (PFA RAN) f. 142, op. 2 (1935), d. 34, ll. 63–63ob. This list enumerated some *narodnosti* as subgroups of *natsional'nosti*.

13. Koshkin was a former student of Lev Shternberg. A number of other former KIPS and IPIN ethnographers were involved in this project, including Aleksandr Samoilovich, Vladimir Bogoraz, and Kapitolina Viatkina. PFA RAN f. 142, op. 1 (1935), d. 34, ll. 63–63ob. Koshkin (also known as Al'kor) was a party member from 1917 and had fought in the civil war. PFA RAN f. 142, op. 1 (1935), d. 31, l. 57.

14. Grande, "Materialy dlia utochneniia," 86–87, and PFA RAN f. 142, op. 1 (1935), d. 34, ll. 106–30. Both of these lists were significantly shorter than the 1926 list of *narodnosti*, but included a number of peoples that had been omitted from the 1927 list of *glavnye narodnosti*.

15. GARF f. 3316, op. 28, d. 865, l. 30; PFA RAN f. 142, op. 1 (1935), d. 34, ll. 63–63ob; Grande, "Materialy dlia utochneniia," 77–78; and L. Krasovskii, "Chem nado rukovodstvovat'sia pri sostavlenii spiska narodnostei SSSR," *Revoliutsiia i natsional'nosti*, no. 4 (1936): 67–71 (esp.

The two lists differed the most when it came to those peoples for whom the process of national consolidation was "just beginning." Both the Institute and the IAE conceived of nationalities as ethnohistorical groups that took form through a process of ethnogenesis, and both had attempted to determine which clans, tribes, and *narodnosti* had evolved and amalgamated into which *narodnosti* or *natsional'nosti*. Both agreed that it was impossible to "determine with decisiveness" how the processes of nation formation would continue to unfold.[16] But both made predictions—and used different criteria to do so. The Institute of Nationalities, drawing on the research of the ethnographer and linguist Nikolai Marr, assumed that the future amalgamation of clans, tribes, and *narodnosti* would transpire "on the basis of closeness of languages." The IAE, bringing to bear its own fieldwork experience, took a more heterodox approach: it used a combination of ethnic, linguistic, cultural, and historical data to forecast the population's future development.[17]

These approaches, based on different understandings of the process of ethnogenesis, had led the Institute and the IAE to make different decisions about which peoples were entitled to national rights. In the Caucasus, the Institute had enumerated the Mingrelians, Laz, Svans, and Georgians as separate *narodnosti*, on the grounds that these four peoples spoke different languages and thus would continue to grow further apart. It had amalgamated the Ajars into the Georgians, however, explaining that the Ajars spoke Georgian and that ancient religious differences between the Ajars (who were Muslims) and "other Georgians" (who were Christians) had become irrelevant.[18] The IAE, for its part, had amalgamated the Mingrelians and Svans into the Georgians on the basis of their cultural similarities and historical ties. It had given the Ajars and the Laz separate status as *natsional'nosti* since both had their own national territories: the Ajars had an ASSR in the Georgian SSR and the Laz had a national homeland outside of Soviet borders.[19]

For similar reasons, the Institute and the IAE had also come to different conclusions about the peoples of the Tajik SSR—and in particular about the Shugnans, Vakhans, and Ishkashims (who populated the republic's Gorno-Badakhshan autonomous oblast) and the Iagnobs and Iazguls (who lived near

---

70–71). The Oirots at first had been excluded from the 1926 "list of *narodnosti* of the USSR" but were added to a list of "provisional *narodnosti*" in 1927.

16. GARF f. 3316, op. 28, d. 865, ll. 56, 90–900b. On ethnogenesis see Yuri Slezkine, "N. Ia. Marr and the Origins of Soviet Ethnogenetics," *Slavic Review* 55, no. 4 (1996): 826–62.

17. For a discussion of the divergent methodologies see GARF f. 3316, op. 28, d. 865, l. 56. On the Institute's approach, see Grande, "Materialy dlia utochneniia," 77–85. Marr, who died in 1934, had founded the Institute of Language and Thought and, drawing on the ideas of Friedrich Engels and Edward B. Tylor, had pioneered an approach to language formation based on the "law of development by stages." See B. Grande, "N. Ia. Marr i novoe uchenie o iazyke," *Revoliutsiia i natsional'nosti*, no. 2 (1935): 35–42. On the IAE's approach, see PFA RAN f. 142, op. 1 (1935), d. 34, ll. 63–630b.

18. Grande, "Materialy dlia utochneniia," 79–80, 86.

19. The Laz homeland was in Turkey. PFA RAN f. 142, op. 1 (1935), d. 34, l. 115.

the Iagnob and Iazgul rivers).[20] The Institute, on the basis of linguistic data, had listed the Vakhans, Ishkashims, and Iazguls as subgroups of the Shugnan *narodnost'*, and the Iagnobs as a subgroup of the Tajik *narodnost'*.[21] The IAE, using historical and cultural data, had counted the Iagnobs and Iazguls as part of the Tajik *natsional'nost'*, and the Shugnans, Vakhans, and Ishkashims as part of the Pamiri *natsional'nost'*; it conceived of the Pamiri as a new *natsional'nost'* that had formed through the "mutual assimilation" of the inhabitants of Gorno-Badakhshan.[22]

The Institute and the IAE also disagreed about which diaspora nationalities to include on the list. The issue of diaspora nationalities came to the fore because Soviet leaders resolved that the Second All-Union Census (unlike the 1926 census) would record the national identities of *all* residents of the Soviet Union, including foreigners. It was a given that the census would include those "foreign" nationalities that had their own national republics or oblasts on Soviet soil (such as the Germans) or had their own national soviets or kolkhozes in the Soviet countryside (such as the Poles and the Greeks). But debate arose about whether or not to include peoples such as "the English and the Madiars," who did not live in compact masses but were dispersed "often in significant numbers" throughout Soviet cities.[23] Whereas the Institute included these peoples on its list, the IAE did not.

Decisions about which peoples to include on the list of nationalities were not just academic. Experts at both institutions understood that the list would serve as the official menu of options for the census, and most believed that it would have use beyond the census. But while some experts expressed the concern that the exclusion of a group from the list of nationalities would precipitate the loss of its national rights, others insisted that omitting a group was *not* the same as denying its "right to existence."[24] Most of the ethnographers, at least, seem to have understood from the precedent of the 1926 census that

20. All five groups had been included on the 1926 list of the *narodnosti* of the USSR.

21. Grande, "Materialy dlia utochneniia," 79, 86.

22. PFA RAN f. 142, op. 1 (1935), d. 34, ll. 109–10, 112. For a discussion of mutual assimilation, see N. Tiurakulov, "Spisok narodnostei SSSR," *Revoliutsiia i natsional'nosti*, no. 8 (1936): 73. For a discussion about assimilation that predates Stalin's 1936 speech see S. Dimanshtein, "Otnoshenie marksizma-leninizma k voprosu ob assimiliatsii natsional'nostei," *Revoliutsiia i natsional'nosti*, no. 7 (1935): 57–63. Dimanshtein (not anticipating Stalin's speech and the subsequent push to accelerate the amalgamation of nationalities) noted that "for our period comrade Stalin firmly established as the main trend not assimilation, but on the contrary, the growth of the number of *natsional'nosti* and languages" (p. 62).

23. Krasovskii, "Chem nado rukovodstvovat'sia," 69–70. Also B. Grande, "Spisok narodnostei SSSR," *Revoliutsiia i natsional'nosti*, no. 4 (1936): 74–85. A version of the Institute list published with this Grande article included some diaspora nationalities, such as the Bulgarians, Chinese, Germans, and Poles. A number of other diaspora nationalities (the Madiars, English, Italians, Serbs, Swedes, Romanians, French, Indians, Norwegians, and Japanese) were moved to a separate list of "foreign nationalities."

24. See, for example, Krasovskii, "Chem nado rukovodstvovat'sia," 70–71, and Tiurakulov, "Spisok narodnostei SSSR," 73.

once a group was omitted from the list of nationalities, it would be all but impossible to tabulate data needed to champion its right to land, schools, or other resources.

As 1936 began, the Institute of Nationalities and the IAE had not worked out their differences. Recognizing that these institutions had reached an impasse, the Soviet of Nationalities created a subcommission with representatives from both institutes as well as from the Census Bureau and several other institutions, and directed it to come up with a final list before the summer.[25]

Self-Definition against the Nazi Backdrop

By 1936, the Nazi propaganda machine was in full gear and German anthropologists were pronouncing their findings that the peoples of the USSR were of inferior racial stock and destined to degeneration. Against this backdrop, the Soviet regime became ever more intent on showing the world the successes of Soviet-sponsored development. Up until this point, the Census Bureau had been undecided about which term to use for the census questionnaire: some drafts used the term *narodnost'*, others *natsional'nost'*, and still others used *narodnost'/natsional'nost'*.[26] But in 1936 the Census Bureau resolved to use *natsional'nost'* in all census materials—proclaiming that it presumed a higher level of ethnohistorical development and was thus more fitting for the Soviet population.[27]

With this issue resolved, the debate then turned to another matter of great importance: how to determine an individual's *natsional'nost'*. From the time of the 1926 census, national self-definition had been the norm in the Soviet Union. Beginning in 1928, most official documents—birth certificates, marriage licenses, and so on—requested the nationality in which the recipient "counts" himself or herself.[28] In 1936, with the Nazi counterexample of racial categorization looming large, the Census Bureau invoked the precedent of the 1926 census and announced that the Second All-Union Census would record *natsional'nost'* on the basis of self-definition. The census taker was to write down each respondent's *natsional'nost'* according to how he or she "says it"

---

25. GARF f. 3316, op. 28, d. 865, ll. 3, 6, 20–27. Participants included Dimanshtein and Grande (from the Institute of Nationalities), Koshkin (from the IAE), Kvitkin (from the Census Bureau), Anatolii Skachko (from the Committee of the North), and Vladimir Bogoraz (from the Antireligious Museum in Leningrad).

26. Zhiromskaia et al., *Polveka pod grifom "sekretno,"* 7, 16–17, and Iu. A. Poliakov et al., eds., *Vsesoiuznaia perepis' naseleniia 1937 g.: Kratkie itogi* (Moscow, 1991), 9. Also RGAE f. 1562, op. 329, d. 151, l. 187.

27. See Gozulov, *Perepisi naseleniia SSSR i kapitalisticheskikh stran* (Moscow, 1936), 121–23.

28. G. G. Melik'ian and A. Ia. Kvasha, eds., *Narodonaselenie: Entsiklopedicheskii slovar'* (Moscow, 1994), 591. Viktor Zaslavsky notes that "the testimony of persons who received their first passports in 1933–35 reveals that nationality was recorded on passports on the basis of oral declarations." Zaslavsky, *Neo-Stalinist State,* 92.

and was "forbidden" from intervening unless the respondent, "having misunderstood the question," named something other than a *natsional'nost'*, such as "a religion, former estate, or place of birth."[29] In mixed-nationality families, the parents were to decide together how to register their children.[30]

The principle of national self-definition also shaped the census questions about native language and religion. To register native language, the census taker was to "write down the name of the language which the respondent himself or herself considers his or her native language." The instructions reminded census takers that native language did not have to coincide with *natsional'nost'*.[31] The question about religion—the first of its kind in a Soviet census—attempted to elicit information about the respondent's "actual beliefs," and not about his or her relationship to religion before the revolution or "formal membership" in a confessional group. First, the census taker was to ask the respondent: "Do you consider yourself a believer or nonbeliever?" Then, after recording the response, the census taker was to ascertain whether or not the "believers" ascribed "to a defined confessional group" and, if so, "to which one."[32]

Some Soviet officials expressed concern that the Census Bureau's reliance on self-definition would lead to false results: that some respondents would misunderstand the question and that others would attempt to "hide" their "true" identities and beliefs. For example, officials from the Kazakh ASSR argued that it would be "difficult to ascertain the *natsional'nost'*" of the large Kazakh population that lived outside of the Kazakh ASSR with a question that relied on self-reporting. According to the officials, Kazakhs in Russian regions, in an effort to help administrators and census takers, frequently referred to themselves as "Kirgiz"—which until 1925 had been the "official name" for the Kazakhs. At the same time, Kazakhs in the other Central Asian republics often attempted to "hide their *natsional'nost'*" and "assimilate" into the dominant (titular) *natsional'nost'*: "Kirgiz, Uzbek, Turkmen, Karakalpak, Bashkir, Tatar, and so on."[33] The Kazakh officials—worried that the census would show a precipitous drop in the Kazakh population, for which Soviet leaders would blame the Kazakh ASSR government—argued that the Census Bureau

29. RGAE f. 1562, op. 329, d. 116, l. 71. In such cases, the census taker was supposed to explain the respondent's mistake to him or her and "obtain a correct answer."

30. Ibid., and RGAE. f. 1562, op. 336, d. 92, ll. 25–26. This marked a change from the 1926 census, which had directed census takers to register the children of mixed-*narodnost'* families according to the *narodnost'* of the mother.

31. The questionnaire used gender-neutral language. RGAE f. 1562, op. 329, d. 116, l. 72. For "children unable to speak" the census taker was to record "the language which is usually spoken in the family."

32. Ibid., and RGAE f. 1562, op. 336, d. 92, l. 27. Census takers were to ask this question to respondents age sixteen and older. The 1897 All-Russian Census had included a question about confessional group (*veroispovedanie*), but not belief.

33. RGAE f. 1562, op. 329, d. 116, ll. 149–1490b. The officials explained that Kazakhs understood that "Russians are accustomed to thinking of Kazakhs as Kirgiz."

should "take special measures" to ensure that all Kazakhs would be registered as Kazakhs.[34]

The Census Bureau did not take "special measures" to deal with the Kazakh question per se—on the grounds that it *was* possible for Kazakhs to become Uzbek or Kirgiz (for example) through the processes of cultural contact and ethnic mixing. Upholding this position had become a matter of ideological importance. However, the Census Bureau, with the assistance of the IAE ethnographers, did prepare supplemental questions and instructions to help census takers determine the *natsional'nost'* of peoples who continued to define themselves by tribe, clan, region, or confessional group. These materials, which were to be utilized if a respondent's national consciousness was deemed to be undeveloped, focused on language, origins, and kinship. Thus a tension between cast of mind and "objective factors" remained: the *natsional'nost'* of respondents with "sufficient" national consciousness would be ascertained on the basis of self-definition, whereas the *natsional'nost'* of respondents lacking national consciousness would be determined on the basis of other criteria. Of course, national self-definition was already circumscribed even before census takers went into the field: the Census Bureau only recognized as *natsional'nosti* those peoples that were included on its official list.

The 1937 List

While the Census Bureau was finalizing the census questionnaire, the census subcommission was completing its work on a new list of the nationalities of the USSR, sending its final draft to the Soviet of Nationalities in June 1936. This draft, which took *natsional'nost'* as its term of choice, enumerated some 106 peoples—a marked contrast to the 1926 list, which had included 172 *narodnosti*.[35] The subcommission had in some cases taken into consideration the IAE's or the Institute of Nationalities' recommendations; in other cases, it ignored both. In categorizing the peoples of the Caucasus, for example, the subcommission had amalgamated the Mingrelians, Svans, and Laz into the Georgians on the basis of their ethnohistorical ties, but had given the Ajars a separate position. In categorizing the peoples of Tajikistan, it had amalgamated the Iagnobs, Iazguls, Shugnans, Vakhans, and Ishkashims *all* into the Tajiks—on the grounds that the growth of Tajik culture in the region made their future "Tajikification" inevitable.[36]

---

34. Ibid. According to the officials, between 1930 and 1933 a significant number of Kazakhs had left the Kazakh ASSR and migrated to "neighboring *kraia* and republics" in order to work in new industries.

35. For the list, see GARF f. 3316, op. 28, d. 865, ll. 72–75. For correspondence among the subcommission, the Soviet of Nationalities, and other institutions, see GARF f. 3316, op. 28, d. 865, ll. 28, 58, 59, 67, 70, and PFA RAN f. 142, op. 1 (1936), d. 38, ll. 134, 203.

36. GARF f. 3316, op. 28, d. 865, ll. 90–900b. On the Tajikification of the peoples of Tajikistan see Tiurakulov, "Spisok narodnostei SSSR," 73.

Overall, the Soviet of Nationalities was pleased with the subcommission's work, noting with satisfaction that it had "not pursued the false subdivision" of peoples "as had been done in the past" (on the list for the 1926 census).[37] But the Soviet of Nationalities observed that in some cases the subcommission had gone too far in the opposite direction: uncertain which "foreign" peoples to include on its list, it had combined those with ethnographic similarities. The Soviet of Nationalities reproached the subcommission for ignoring Stalin's 1913 definition of a nation. If one used his definition, the officials explained, it was not possible to amalgamate the Dutch into the Germans or the Romanians into the Moldavians—both of which the subcommission had done. The Dutch and the Germans might be related from a linguistic or ethnographic perspective, the officials argued, but each had the requisite traits of a nation: a shared past, land, language, economic life, culture, and cast of mind. The Romanians and Moldavians might have the same origins, but they had developed under the auspices of different states—and their differences were now more important than their similarities. Equally indefensible, according to the Soviet of Nationalities, was the subcommission's decision to unite the Japanese and the Koreans. These two peoples had similar languages (and Korea was under Japanese occupation), but each fit the definition of a separate nation.[38]

The ethnographers took these criticisms into account and a month later presented the Soviet of Nationalities with a revised list of 107 *natsional'nosti*.[39] On this list, the Romanians, Moldavians, Koreans, Germans, and Japanese all had separate positions. The Dutch, along with the Slovaks and some 40 or so other peoples, were grouped under "Others" (number 108 on the list), on the grounds that their populations in the USSR were too small to warrant separate status.[40] In August 1936, the Soviet of Nationalities approved the revised list and forwarded it to Soviet leaders. This list mapped out which *narodnosti* had been amalgamated into which *natsional'nosti*. It would serve as an essential tool for statisticians tabulating census results; if respondents stated their *narodnost'* in the census interview, statisticians would later be able to count them as members of the *natsional'nost'* to which that *narodnost'* belonged.

Everything appeared to be settled. And then, several months later, in a speech about the new Soviet constitution at the Eighth All-Union Congress of Soviets, Stalin stated, "as is well-known there are about sixty nations, national groups, and *narodnosti* in the Soviet Union."[41] Sixty! Where had this new

37. GARF f. 3316, op. 28, d. 865, l. 94.

38. Ibid., ll. 87–88.

39. Ibid., ll. 91–92.

40. Ibid., ll. 90–900b.

41. Stalin, *Doklad o proekte konstitutsii Soiuza SSR* (Moscow, 1936), 15. Zhiromskaia argues that this statement became a type of directive for the statisticians. Zhiromskaia, "Vsesoiuznye perepisi naseleniia 1926, 1937, 1939 goda," 88. For a discussion of this speech and its implications also see RGAE f. 1562, op. 336, d. 208, l. 60b.

number come from? The new constitution recognized the RSFSR plus fifty official ethnoterritorial units.[42] The list of *natsional'nosti* that the Census Bureau had just approved included the main (titular) nationalities of these territories, as well as about twenty "foreign" nationalities, and some thirty peoples that did not have their own national-territorial units at all, such as the Izhora.

In the same speech, Stalin proclaimed that the Soviet Union had made the transition to socialism. This announcement would soon precipitate an all-out effort to show that backward *narodnosti* had completed the process of consolidating into advanced nations. The Census Bureau—not yet appreciating the significance of the speech—did not rush to further shorten the list of *natsional'nosti* for the 1937 census. (In fact, the final list included 109 *natsional'nosti*, due to a last-minute decision to add the Karaims and the Mishers.)[43] Nor did the Census Bureau concern itself with Stalin's speech as it prepared a shorter list of the Soviet Union's major (*glavnye*) *natsional'nosti* to use for further statistical tabulations. The final version of this list included some 88 peoples.[44]

Ethnographers and Statisticians in a Time of Terror

The Second All-Union Census was conducted in January 1937—the same month as the second Moscow show trial, which ended with the public condemnation and execution of a number of prominent Bolsheviks who had been falsely accused of collaborating with the Nazis and the Japanese to undermine the Soviet regime. Several months later, after the census results came in, a number of leading Census Bureau officials would meet similar fates. The census showed a decrease in the general Soviet population, as well as sharp drops in the populations of particular nationalities (such as the Kazakhs and Ukrainians). These results reflected significant population losses from the violent course of collectivization, forced migrations, and terror. But Soviet leaders were not about to admit that their policies were responsible for this tremendous loss of life. Moreover, Stalin had predicted that the census would show a

---

42. These were the ten union republics, twenty-two autonomous national republics, nine autonomous oblasts, and nine national *okruga*. Simon, *Nationalism and Policy toward the Nationalities in the Soviet Union,* 147.

43. Tsentral'noe upravlenie narodno-khoziaistvennogo ucheta SSSR, *Slovar' natsional'nostei dlia razrabotki Vsesoiuznoi perepisi naseleniia 1937 goda* ed. O. Kvitkin et al. (Moscow, 1937). Also Poliakov et al., *Vsesoiuznaia perepis' naseleniia 1937 g.,* 83–84, and Zhiromskaia et al., *Polveka pod grifom "sekretno,"* 25, 86–87. Number 110 on this list was "Others." More than forty peoples were listed under "Others," including the Yankees, Canadians, and Negroes.

44. This was a list of the most numerous or, in some cases, the most important nationalities of each national-territorial unit. The Census Bureau asked republic-level, oblast-level, and some provincial-level statistical bureaus to prepare lists of ten or fewer "major *natsional'nosti*" for their regions. (By contrast, when the TsSU had prepared a list of *glavnye narodnosti* for the 1926 census, it had requested lists of no more than *six* "major *narodnosti*" for each republic and oblast and some *kraia*.) This final list was not published. I tabulated the list from tables in Poliakov et al., *Vsesoiuznaia perepis' naseleniia 1937 g.,* 85–96.

significant *increase* in the Soviet population. Since it was not possible to contradict Stalin, Soviet leaders declared the census to be "defective" and forbade the release of its data.[45] The NKVD arrested and executed a number of prominent statisticians, including Kvitkin, as "enemies of the people" and "accomplices of fascism" for their role in the census.[46] The implication was that the Census Bureau had sabotaged the census in order to discredit Stalin and embarrass the Soviet Union before its enemies abroad.

Meanwhile, 1937 saw the expansion of a massive terror campaign throughout the Soviet Union. Hundreds of thousands of Soviet citizens were arrested (also on trumped-up charges) and sent to the Gulag or were rounded up and deported to special settlements. Hundreds of scientific and cultural institutions were closed or restructured. Ethnographers came under attack in the spring of 1937. The IAE was investigated for "anti-Soviet activities," in part for its role in the census; Koshkin, Nikolai Matorin, and several other ethnographers were ousted from their positions, arrested, and shot as "enemies of the people."[47] Most of these ethnographers were loyal to the regime and had themselves collaborated in its earlier attempts to weed out "enemies"—documenting the existence of "kulaks" in the Soviet countryside, for example, and thus providing a scientific rationale for the "dekulakization campaign." The IAE was put under the leadership of Vasilii Struve and Saul Abramzon, men who (like Koshkin and Matorin) had fieldwork experience as well as training in historical materialism—but who had not been involved in the 1937 census. The investigation of ethnographers also extended to other institutions. That summer, a party commission censured ethnographers at the State Ethnographic Museum as "wreckers" who were engaging in the "vulgar portrayal of socialist construction." Not long thereafter the museum was closed and its directors arrested; the museum reopened several months later with new directors, one of whom was Leonid Potapov.[48]

It was in this context that the Soviet regime called for a new population count to correct the "mistakes" of the previous one. The Census Bureau reconvened—with different statisticians in charge—and began deliberations to

45. The census counted around 162 million people, whereas Stalin had proclaimed in 1933 that there were 168 million people in the Soviet Union and that the number was growing at a rapid rate. Iu. A. Poliakov et al., eds., *Vsesoiuznaia perepis' naseleniia 1939 goda* (Moscow, 1992), 4.

46. Zhiromskaia, "Vsesoiuznye perepisi naseleniia 1926, 1937, 1939 godov," 89; Zhiromskaia et al., *Polveka pod grifom "sekretno,"* 138; and Poliakov et al., *Vsesoiuznaia perepis' naseleniia 1939 goda*, 4. The head of TsUNKhU, Ivan Kraval, was also arrested and shot.

47. See Frédéric Bertrand, *L'anthropologie soviétique des années 20–30: Configuration d'une rupture* (Pessac, 2002). On changes in the profession see Yuri Slezkine, "The Fall of Soviet Ethnography, 1928–1938," *Current Anthropology* 32, no. 4 (1991): 476–84. On the "flaws" of the materials prepared by ethnographers for the 1937 census see RGAE f. 1562, op. 336, d. 211, l. 25.

48. The other new director was E. A. Mil'shtein. T. A. Kriukova and E. N. Studenetskaia, "Gosudarstvennyi muzei etnografii narodov SSSR za piat'desiat let Sovetskoi vlasti," in *Ocherki istorii muzeinogo dela v SSSR* (Moscow, 1971), 44, 53–56.

draw up a new census, which it slated for January 1939.[49] The compilation of
a new and much shorter list of *natsional'nosti* became a pressing issue on the
Census Bureau's agenda. The Census Bureau and the Soviet of Nationalities
again turned for assistance to the IAE.[50] A number of senior IAE ethnographers who had survived the 1937 purge, including Zarubin and Zelenin,
played an important role in this new round of census deliberations.[51] The IAE
used the list of nationalities from the 1937 census as its initial working draft.

The IAE's deliberations about the list of nationalities provide a vivid example of the impact that Stalin had on the production of knowledge in the late
1930s. Stalin did not dictate which *particular* peoples should or should not be
included on the list of nationalities. (Had he done so, the experts' work might
have been easier.) Instead, the experts had to work with—or somehow work
around—Stalin's November 1936 pronouncement that the Soviet Union was
comprised of "around sixty nations, national groups, and *narodnosti*"; the
number "sixty" and the phrase "nations, national groups, and *narodnosti*" became touchstones for discussions about the new list. The ethnographers
wasted little time adopting Stalin's phrasing as their own, proclaiming that the
concept *natsional'nost'*, which had been the term of choice for the 1937 list,
was in fact an umbrella term encompassing "nations, national groups, and
narodnosti."[52] Having renamed their list, the ethnographers next faced the impossible task of winnowing the number of nationalities from 109 down to 60.

The IAE found itself in a precarious position. The ethnographers were under
intense pressure to cite from Stalin's works and to explain their conclusions in
terms of the official line. And yet they had real latitude to make decisions about
the population—which in itself was frightening, since making the "wrong" decision could cost them their lives. Moreover, it was clearer than ever to the
ethnographers that their list would have real repercussions for the population:
that the exclusion of a group from the list would in all likelihood precipitate
the loss of its national rights and the closing of its national institutions.

In May 1938, the Census Bureau's new deputy director, Vladimir Starovskii, came to Leningrad to check on the IAE's progress. Starovskii praised the
ethnographers' decision to adopt Stalin's nomenclature. But he expressed
grave concern about the length of the list, which still included more than one

---

49. On the Commission for the All-Union Census of 1939 see RGAE f. 1562, op. 336, d. 69, l.
1; d. 70, ll. 107–9, 170–72. Also see Zhiromskaia et al., *Polveka pod grifom "sekretno,"* 5–6.
There is no evidence that the statisticians worked to sabotage the census.

50. RGAE f. 1562, op. 336, d. 211, l. 24.

51. For example, RGAE f. 1562, op. 336, d. 206, ll. 118–19; d. 208, l. 72.

52. RGAE f. 1562, op. 336, d. 208, ll. 25–29. Later, when explaining why the Census Bureau
had chosen *natsional'nost'* as the overarching term for its list, Starovskii would cite Molotov's argument that the use of the term *narodnost'* in 1926 had led to an "excessive splitting up" of peoples that "was not justified by circumstances" and had been used by "bourgeois nationalists" to
weaken the Soviet Union. RGAE f. 1562, op. 336, d. 79, l. 20.

hundred peoples.[53] In response, the IAE ethnographer Nikolai Iakovlev proposed one possible solution: dividing the list into two sections. The first section would include just those "nations, national groups, and *narodnosti* with national-state formations." The second section would include national and ethnographic groups that lacked their own territorial unit but were "of interest from a political and scientific point of view." Just the first section would serve as the official list of *natsional'nosti* of the USSR. Iakovlev's colleagues embraced this proposal as a means of supplying the regime with a shorter list while maintaining a longer list for future reference.[54]

Cutting the List

With the phrase "nations, national groups, and *narodnosti*" on their tongues, and the number "sixty" on their minds, the IAE ethnographers got to work. In the wake of the May 1938 meeting, the IAE created four brigades made up of its own ethnographers as well as linguists from the Institute of Language and Thought. These brigades were given the task of preparing regional lists of na tionalities, which would then be combined into a master list. Each brigade soon became embroiled in intensive debates about the status of particular peoples, often revisiting older issues.[55]

Anxious to avoid the "bourgeois-nationalist" sin of "splitting" nationalities into "nonviable" subgroups, all of the brigades reevaluated the relationships among peoples with close "ethnic ties." Zelenin's European brigade recommended the amalgamation of the Komi-Permiaks into the Komi—despite the fact that the Komi-Permiaks had their own national *okrug*, and despite the fact that ethnographers had insisted for well over a decade that the Komi-Permiaks were a separate people.[56] Nikolai Iakovlev's Caucasus brigade, on the other hand, acknowledged that the Ajars were part of the Georgians in the "ethnographic sense," but argued nonetheless that the Census Bureau should grant them a separate position "as the core population of the Ajarian republic."[57]

The issue of diaspora nationalities was another hot topic of discussion for the brigades. Zelenin's European brigade enumerated nineteen European diaspora nationalities (including the Germans, Italians, Poles, Finns, and Czechoslovaks) that it insisted should be given slots on the main list as "na-

---

53. PFA RAN f. 142, op. 1 (1938), d. 30, ll. 2–4; RGAE f. 1562, op. 336, d. 211, l. 19. Starovskii had been part of the TsSU since 1925 and had worked in central statistical organs since 1923. See V. P. Kornev, ed., *Vidnye deiateli otechestvennoi statistiki 1686–1990: Biograficheskii slovar'* (Moscow, 1993), 150–51.

54. RGAE f. 1562, op. 336, d. 211, l. 19. Iakovlev was an ethnographer and structural linguist by training.

55. RGAE f. 1562, op. 336, d. 211, l. 19; d. 208, l. 24.

56. RGAE f. 1562, op. 336, d. 206, ll. 1–4. The 1937 list of *natsional'nosti* had included both groups.

57. Ibid., ll. 14–16.

tional groups."[58] Sergei Malov's Central Asian brigade put together a less extensive list of non-European diaspora nationalities, but made a studied argument for each one. Calling for the inclusion of the Arabs on the main list, it maintained that the regime could showcase the "cultural and economic development of the Arabs" in Soviet conditions (on "Arab agricultural soviets and Arab kolkhozes") and could then contrast it with "the position of the Arab population abroad." Making a case for including the Shugnans, Vakhans, and Ishkashims on the main list—challenging the 1937 decision to amalgamate them into the Tajiks—the brigade noted that each had its own language and culture, lived in its own "compact territorial region," and had a diaspora in Afghanistan.[59] There were some cases, however, in which the brigades suggested playing down cross-border ties. For example, Malov's brigade advocated amalgamating the Sart-Kalmyks into the Kirgiz *natsional'nost'*, hoping to discourage ties between the Sart-Kalmyks of the Kirgiz ASSR and Kalmyk insurgents in Chinese Turkestan. The brigade justified this recommendation on ethnographic grounds, noting that the "younger generation" of Sart-Kalmyks had in fact "assimilated into the surrounding Kirgiz population."[60]

The four brigades included with their lists extensive recommendations for ascertaining the *natsional'nost'* of peoples lacking national consciousness. Mikhail Sergeev's Siberia and Far East brigade insisted that the Khanty, Mansi, Ket, and Sel'kup were all separate *narodnosti*, even though all four groups called themselves "Ostiaks." The brigade suggested that census takers ask self-identified "Ostiaks" to state the names for "deer," "knife," and "house" in their native language; it supplied a chart of these words in the various languages for census takers.[61] Zelenin's brigade predicted similar difficulties with registering the Evremeis and Izhora, who often called themselves "Finns." Arguing that it was imperative to separate out these indigenous groups from the actual Finns (who were a diaspora group), the brigade directed census takers to ask self-identified "Finns" about their place of birth. It maintained that respondents "who were born in Finland" should be registered as "Finns" and that all others should be registered according to "the name of their particular *narodnost'*," that is, Evremeis or Izhora.[62]

In late June 1938 the four brigades presented their draft lists of nationalities to the IAE, which combined them into a master list of thirty-one nations, twenty-eight *narodnosti*, thirty-one national groups, and thirty ethnographic

---

58. Ibid., ll. 1–4.

59. Ibid., ll. 19–20, 23–24. The brigade agreed with the earlier decision to count the Iagnobs and Iazguls as Tajiks, on the grounds that the establishment of Tajik-language kolkhozes and schools and the construction of new roads were promoting their "rapid assimilation into the surrounding Tajik population."

60. Ibid., ll. 22–23.

61. Ibid., ll. 9–11.

62. RGAE f. 1562, op. 336, d. 206, ll. 3–4; d. 208, l. 69.

groups. The IAE then forwarded this list to the Census Bureau and to the Academy of Sciences Presidium in Moscow.[63] The accompanying explanatory notes defined "nations" as "peoples making up the main population of union and autonomous republics" and *narodnosti* as "sizeable peoples" making up "the main population of autonomous oblasts and national *okruga*" or "living compactly in defined regions with literacy in their own language." The notes defined "national groups" as nations or nationalities who "live in their main mass outside of the borders of the USSR" but "within the USSR make up national minorities, interspersed among national majorities." "Ethnographic groups," the notes continued, were often the "remnants" of tribes and other peoples that had not yet amalgamated into nationalities or nations; according to the notes, the IAE was reviewing the list of ethnographic groups with an eye to shortening it.[64]

In keeping with the brigades' recommendations, the IAE listed the Arabs as a national group and the Shugnans, Vakhans, and Ishkashims as separate *narodnosti*. In several cases, however, the IAE had ignored the brigades' recommendations; for example, it listed the Sart-Kalmyks as a separate ethnographic group.[65] The IAE also included a list of questions that it considered still "unresolved." For example: Were the Ajars part of the Georgians or a separate nation? Were the Komi-Permiaks part of the Komi or a separate *narodnost'*? Should the Germans, who had their own Volga German ASSR in the USSR, be categorized as a nation or a national group? Should the Jews, who in 1934 had received their own autonomous national oblast (Birobidzhan) in the Soviet Far East, be considered a *narodnost'* or a national group?[66] These questions were also the topic of high-level discussion. The Ajar question had drawn sharp comments from the Georgian leaders Lavrentii Beria and Valerian Bakradze, who maintained that the separation of the Ajars from the Georgians was in "fundamental contradiction with the Stalinist definition of a nation," since "the Ajars are united with the Georgian nation by common language, territory, economic life, and culture."[67]

While the combined number of nations and *narodnosti* now totaled fifty-nine and was more or less in line with Stalin's sixty, the rubric "nations, national groups, and *narodnosti*" still encompassed ninety peoples. On reviewing this list at a meeting of the Academy of Sciences Presidium, a group of ethnographers from Moscow State University proclaimed that it must be wrong. After all, the Moscow ethnographers noted, Stalin "in his historic speech about the constitution of the USSR" had "indicated that there were

63. RGAE f. 1562, op. 336, d. 208, ll. 45–51. For an earlier draft with handwritten notes and comments see PFA RAN f. 142, op. 1 (1938), d. 43, ll. 138–54.
64. RGAE f. 1562, op. 336, d. 206, ll. 80–82.
65. RGAE f. 1562, op. 336, d. 208, ll. 46–47, 49.
66. Ibid., ll. 50–51, 63–64.
67. RGAE f. 1562, op. 329, d. 151, l. 93.

around sixty," not ninety, "nations, national groups, and *narodnosti*" in the Soviet Union. Trying to be helpful, these ethnographers suggested that the IAE might have conflated "national groups" with "national minorities"—and that *all* "national minorities" (the Romanians, Japanese, Lithuanians, and more than two dozen other peoples) should be removed from the main list.[68] The IAE went back to work, and in late July presented the Academy of Sciences Presidium with a revised draft of the fifty-nine "nations, national groups, and *narodnosti*" of the USSR, as well as separate lists of twenty-eight national minorities and thirty-nine ethnographic groups.[69]

The ethnographers had tweaked their terms in order to get this job done. According to the explanatory notes to the new list, "nations" were peoples possessing all of the traits that Stalin had enumerated in his 1913 article. "National groups and *narodnosti*" were peoples that had most of these traits but that, at their present stage of "historical development," had not yet "succeeded in consolidating" into nations. "National minorities" were peoples that had national territories outside of Soviet borders, and in the Soviet Union lived (either compactly or dispersed) in one or more of the republics, oblasts, or *okruga* "without making up the main population" of any of them. "Ethnographic groups" were small peoples that lived compactly in the Soviet Union and, unlike national minorities, did not have their own states outside of Soviet borders.[70] The most significant change was that "national groups" and "national minorities" were no longer synonyms. "National groups," like *narodnosti*, were peoples that might evolve into Soviet nations. "National minorities," on the other hand, were the diasporas of foreign nations whose allegiance lay elsewhere.

The revised list incorporated some significant changes. A considerable number of *narodnosti* (including the Izhora and the Veps) were demoted to ethnographic groups. Others were amalgamated into nations; in this manner, the Shugnans, Vakhans, and Ishkashims were again combined into the Tajiks. At the same time, a number of ethnographic groups (including the Sart-Kalmyks) were amalgamated into other ethnographic groups or into *narodnosti*. The revised list also documented the fates of those peoples whose status had been "unresolved" in June. The Ajars were listed as a subgroup of the Georgians and the Komi-Permiaks as a subgroup of the Komi—demonstrating that having an ethnoterritorial unit did not guarantee a group separate status. The Germans were listed as a nation and the Jews as a *narodnost'*. The most sweeping change affected those peoples enumerated on the earlier list as "na-

68. Recounted in RGAE f. 1562, op. 336, d. 208, ll. 6–60b. The Academy of Sciences and its Presidium had moved to Moscow in 1934 and had absorbed the Communist Academy.

69. RGAE f. 1562, op. 336, d. 205, ll. 86–8/0b, PFA RAN f. 142, op 1 (1939), d. 38, ll. 3–30. This list was published in *Perechni otraslei narodnogo khoziaistva i truda, proizvodstv, zaniatii, natsional'nostei i tipov uchebnykh zavedenii vydeliaemykh pri razrabotke materialov Vsesoiuznoi perepisi naseleniia 1939 goda* (Moscow, 1939), 14–16.

70. RGAE f. 1562, op. 336, d. 208, l. 33; d. 206, l. 71.

tional groups." Most of them were relabeled "national minorities" and either moved to the separate list or omitted altogether.[71]

Through their efforts, the IAE ethnographers had drawn on *and* given scientific backing to an extralegal division between Soviet and diaspora nationalities. This division was already a fact of life in the regime zones. In 1937, the NKVD, citing "strategic considerations," had initiated its "national operations"—deporting diaspora nationalities en masse from the border regions to the interior of the Soviet Union. It oversaw the deportation of the Koreans and Japanese from the Far Eastern *krai,* and the deportation of the Germans, Poles, Estonians, Latvians, Finns, Bulgarians, and Greeks (as well as a number of other peoples) from the western borderlands.[72] At the same time, the Soviet government had passed a series of resolutions that stripped the diaspora nationalities of their national regions, national village soviets, and national kolkhozes. The government turned what it now deemed to be "artificial national institutions" into "regular institutions," which were to publish newspapers, run schools, and conduct government affairs in either Russian or the official language of the national republic or oblast in which they were located.[73]

By 1938, the distinction between "Soviet" and "foreign" nations had also become part and parcel of an official narrative about the "friendship of peoples." Beginning in late 1936, the regime and its experts began to discuss the "great" and "mutual" friendship that existed among the Soviet socialist nations and nationalities. Stalin himself addressed this theme in his November 1936 speech about the new constitution.[74] The friendship theme also received prominent attention in the first official Soviet history textbook: Andrei Shestakov's *Short Course of the History of the USSR.*[75] Published in 1937, this

71. RGAE f. 1562, op. 336, d. 208, ll. 34–43. The Finns, Bulgarians, and Greeks were not moved to the list of national minorities at this time, but would be six months later.

72. On these deportations see Michael Gelb, "An Early Soviet Ethnic Deportation: The Far Eastern Koreans," *The Russian Review* 54, no. 3 (1995): 389–412; N. F. Bugai, ed., *Iosif Stalin— Lavrentiiu Berii: "Ikh nado deportirovat'": Dokumenty, fakty, kommentarii* (Moscow, 1992); Amir Weiner, "Nature, Nurture, and Memory in a Socialist Utopia: Delineating the Soviet Socio-Ethnic Body in the Age of Socialism," *The American Historical Review* 104, no. 4 (1999): 1114–55; and Terry Martin, "The Origins of Soviet Ethnic Cleansing," *Journal of Modern History* 70, no. 4 (1998): 813–61.

73. GARF f. 7523, op. 65, d. 397, ll. 3–18, 25–38. For example, about twenty German and Greek village soviets in Krasnodar oblast, a dozen Finnish and Latvian village soviets in Leningrad oblast, and an unspecified number of Chinese village soviets in Khabarovsk oblast were all turned into "ordinary" Russian-language institutions. In the Ukrainian SSR, German and Greek village soviets were turned into Ukrainian-language institutions. TsIK had established these national regions and institutions in the late 1920s and early 1930s. Martin also discusses the closing of national institutions in the western borderlands. Martin, *Affirmative Action Empire,* 332–34.

74. Stalin, *Doklad o proekte konstitutsii Soiuza SSR,* 16.

75. Work on a new textbook began in earnest in 1934 and reached a critical point in 1936 with the kick-off of a unionwide campaign celebrating the great friendship. On the textbook, see Lowell Tillett, *The Great Friendship: Soviet Historians on the Non-Russian Nationalities* (Chapel Hill, 1969), 44–49; Konstantin F. Shteppa, *Russian Historians and the Soviet State* (New Brunswick, 1962), 128–29; and David Brandenberger, *National Bolshevism: Stalinist Mass Cul-*

textbook explained that in "no other country of the world" had there ever been "such friendship among diverse peoples as in the USSR." Significantly, this friendship did not include "foreign" nationalities; those mentioned—the Poles, Germans, Swedes, Lithuanians, and Japanese—were presented in the worst possible light, as former conquerors.[76] In late 1937, the State Ethnographic Museum also devoted itself to the friendship theme. It began working in earnest on a museumwide exhibit, "USSR: Fraternal Union of Peoples," which was to highlight the "blossoming of the national cultures of the peoples of the USSR, national in form and socialist in content," as well as the unifying force of "Soviet patriotism." The main objects of representation would be the Soviet nations and nationalities in their national republics and oblasts. Foreign nationalities and nations—even those comprising large national minorities in the Soviet Union—were to be excluded altogether.[77]

The IAE ethnographers, relieved to have hit the magic number of sixty, did not dwell on the potential consequences of moving the diaspora nationalities to a separate list. But at a time when the Soviet regime was obsessing about the dangers of homeland nationalism and foreign infiltration, the decision to expunge diaspora nationalities from the official list of Soviet nationalities was no small matter. Under duress, the IAE ethnographers had taken the path of least resistance. In doing so, they provided a scientific justification for the NKVD's treatment of diaspora peoples as suspect outsiders. In July 1938, the IAE forwarded its revised lists and notes to the Census Bureau, the Soviet of Nationalities, and the Supreme Soviet (formerly TsIK).[78] The next month, when Starovskii (the deputy director of the Census Bureau) announced at a Census Bureau meeting that the Academy of Sciences had completed a list of the "sixty main *natsional'nosti*" of the Soviet Union, he was referring to the ethnographers' list of fifty-nine "nations, national groups, and *narodnosti*."[79]

ture and the Formation of Modern Russian National Identity, 1931–1956 (Cambridge, MA, 2002), chapter 3. The Central Committee distributed some 10 million copies of the Shestakov textbook throughout the Soviet Union.

76. V. Shestakov, ed., *Kratkii kurs istorii SSSR* (Moscow, 1937), 3. The textbook stated that "about 50 different peoples live in the 11 Soviet Union republics" (p. 7). It made no mention of the numerous *narodnosti* that had been amalgamated into *natsional'nosti* and expunged from the official list between the 1926 and 1937 censuses.

77. Archive of the Russian Ethnographic Museum (REM) f. 2, op. 1, d. 607, ll. 1–12. The museum did not finish its work on this new exhibit before the start of World War II; the exhibit would be unveiled (with the inclusion of the Latvian, Lithuanian, and Estonian republics) in the late 1940s.

78. RGAE f. 1562, op. 336, d. 208, ll. 16–23.

79. RGAE f. 1562, op. 336, d. 79, ll. 20–22. This list included a sixtieth item, "Others." On the final version of the list, the "Others" group includes some of the larger ethnographic groups.

Self-Definition and the New Passport Directives

In 1938, as Hitler's armies marched into Austria and the Sudetenland, the Soviet approach to the population was becoming more and more contradictory. Even as ethnographers were drastically cutting the official list of nationalities—and thus circumscribing the menu of options for the census—the Census Bureau was proclaiming national self-definition to be a fundamental right of all Soviet citizens. In 1938 the Census Bureau adopted the same formulas for registering *natsional'nost'* and native language that had been used in 1937, calling for self-reporting.[80] The Census Bureau also invoked the ideal of self-definition when it explained its decision to drop the census question about religious belief, calling the question too charged to elicit respondents' honest reactions. It maintained that many people who had registered themselves as "believers" in 1937 had done so out of deference to their elders or fear of repercussions.[81] In one instance, it reported, people had registered themselves as "believers" after "anti-Soviet elements" had cautioned that "soon Hitler will come and exterminate nonbelievers."[82]

Most glaring was the contradiction between the NKVD's treatment of diaspora nationalities and the party's propaganda campaign against the Nazi concern with racial origins. Even children's stories contrasted the Soviet registration of nationality (based on self-reporting) with the Nazi registration of race (based on blood). One such story, "A Tale of Numbers," followed the electrical engineer Anna Markovna, a volunteer census taker. On a train, Markovna meets two kolkhozniks—a young boy and his grandfather—and tells them about the upcoming census. As the train pushes through the countryside, she explains that the Soviet census guarantees all citizens the right to declare their national identities "according to their conscience and not their birth." In one burst of enthusiasm, Markovna asserts that the right to self-definition is what distinguishes the Soviet Union from "tsarist Russia" and from "the capitalist countries" abroad. She describes how fascists in Nazi Germany were arresting people after "rummaging through all kinds of old documents" in an effort to determine "who belongs to which nation by blood." In the Soviet Union, she tells them, census takers were prohibited from asking for verification of an individual's *natsional'nost'*, since the Soviet leadership was interested in "national consciousness." By the end of the train ride, Markovna has convinced the boy and his grandfather that "no one should fear" the Soviet census.[83] But the parents of young readers had reason to be skeptical: by 1938 the NKVD too was interested in old documents that could shed light on people's origins.

80. RGAE f. 1562, op. 336, d. 71, l. 10. These questions were discussed at length at a February 1938 Census Bureau meeting. RGAE f. 1562, op. 336, d. 70, ll. 67, 73.
81. RGAE f. 1562, op. 336, d. 216, l. 16.
82. RGAE f. 1562, op. 329, d. 143, l. 53.
83. RGAE f. 1562, op. 336, d. 1439, ll. 1–24. For other stories see ll. 25–105.

In fact, even as the Census Bureau was enshrining the right to national self-definition in the formal ritual of the census, the NKVD Department of Passport Registration had issued a decree that circumscribed national self-definition in the passport—and was particularly damaging for diaspora nationalities. The NKVD introduced this decree in April 1938, directing registrars to write the nationality of a passport recipient's parents—and *not* the self-defined nationality of the passport recipient—in newly issued passports. Passport recipients were to provide their birth certificates or other official documents for verification. If a person's parents belonged to two different nationalities and one "belonged to a foreign state," the registrar was to write the nationality of both parents in the passport: "Father Polish, Mother Russian" or "Father Belorussian, Mother German," for example. Even Poles and Germans who had lived in Russia for generations were designated as people who "belonged to" a foreign state; it made no difference that the Germans had their own autonomous national republic (the Volga German ASSR) within Soviet borders.[84]

The 1938 passport directives marked a major departure from the original passport instructions, which had been in place since 1932 and which had been based on the principle of self-definition. The new directives retained extralegal status and were not made part of the passport law—but in the late 1930s the extralegal mode became the dominant one. According to the NKVD, the directives were intended to deal with specific "strategic considerations" and would not be extended to the registration of nationality in other official documents.[85] In particular, they were aimed at "unmasking" members of the diaspora nationalities in the Soviet Union's border regions who, according to the NKVD, were lying about their national identities. If these people were lying, it was with good reason, given the ruthless nature of the NKVD's national operations.

To some extent the NKVD's passport decree, like the NKVD's national operations, was motivated by real geopolitical concerns. The First World War had shown the national idea to be an effective political weapon: all of the combatants had attempted to use it to their advantage. Now, more than two decades later, the Nazis were using the national idea to buttress their irredentist ambitions—claiming the right to interfere in the affairs of states with ethnic German minorities. The League of Nations, in refusing to act, seemed to recognize the German claim as legitimate. The Soviet regime, concerned that the Nazis and their allies might attempt to claim Soviet territories on the basis of their populations' ethnic origins, began to move diaspora nationalities from the borderlands to less vulnerable regions.[86]

84. GARF f. 7523, op. 65, d. 304, l. 1.
85. Ibid.
86. On this point see Mark Mazower, *Dark Continent: Europe's Twentieth Century* (New York, 1998). On German homeland nationalism see Rogers Brubaker, *Nationalism Reframed: Nationhood and the National Question in the New Europe* (Cambridge, 1996), chapter 5. During the 1930s, France introduced policies to monitor "foreigners" and citizens of "foreign de-

The NKVD was worried not just about the claims of foreign states, but also about the loyalties of the diaspora nationalities themselves: if enemies advanced onto Soviet soil, for whom would the diaspora peoples fight? This suspicion of the diaspora peoples was connected to the Soviet regime's broader concern about the place of "foreign" nationalities in the Soviet Union—a concern that had an ideological dimension. From the time of the revolution, Bolshevik leaders had described "bourgeois nationalism" and "spontaneous nationalism" as dangerous threats. But the regime's anxieties about these nationalisms surged in the 1930s, in tandem with the NKVD's worries about the cross-border ties of the Poles, Germans, and Japanese. Soviet leaders and experts anticipated the amalgamation of nationalities into socialist nations as well as the integration (and eventual merger) of those nations into a single Soviet whole. The peoples of the former Russian Empire were supposed to become Soviet *through* their official national identities, cultures, and territories, via a process of double assimilation. Because the diaspora nations had homelands outside of Soviet borders, and because the Soviet regime could not fully reinvent their histories, traditions, and cultures, the regime and its experts questioned whether these peoples could in fact become "Soviet" at all.

The NKVD's approach to ascertaining an individual's nationality, privileging proof of origins over self-reporting, did not represent a wholesale shift in the Soviet conceptualization of national identities or a "dramatic turn" to "Soviet primordialism" as some historians have suggested.[87] The tension between origins and self-definition had been embedded in the Soviet understanding of *natsional'nost'* from the 1920s. Soviet ethnographers conceived of *natsional'nosti* as ethnohistorical groups whose origins could be traced back to the "prehistorical era"—but whose members were united in the present through a shared cast of mind. In the 1920s, government commissions overseeing the delimitation of new ethnoterritorial borders had evaluated the origins *and* cast of mind of local populations to determine which groups had rights to which territories. Even the Census Bureau did not rely on self-definition alone, but used supplemental questions about origins and kinship for peoples lacking national consciousness. Even so, the difference between the NKVD's and the Census Bureau's overall approaches was striking. After 1938, these two institutions—with different agendas and responsibilities—found themselves championing two very different elements of the Soviet understanding of *natsional'nost'*.

---

scent." See Gerard Noiriel, *The French Melting Pot: Immigration, Citizenship, and National Identity* (Minneapolis, 1996).

87. Here I am disagreeing with Martin, who argues that this period saw a shift from a "constructivist" to a "primordialist" approach: that "there was a dramatic turn away from the former Soviet view of nations as fundamentally modern constructs and toward an emphasis on the deep primordial roots of modern nations." Martin, *Affirmative Action Empire*, 442–43.

The fact that the Census Bureau and the NKVD were advocating different approaches for registering nationality was not lost on the statisticians at the Census Bureau. Most of these statisticians, still shaken after the recent arrest and execution of their colleagues, were anxious to not contradict the NKVD. At an August 1938 Census Bureau meeting, several statisticians proposed that the Census Bureau adopt the NKVD's method for registering nationality, or at least that it direct census takers to request verification (such as a birth certificate or passport) if a respondent seemed to be "masking" his or her real identity.

Starovskii (the Census Bureau's deputy director) addressed these concerns by reaffirming the Census Bureau's original approach. Defending the principle of self-definition, he emphasized how the Soviet Union differed from capitalist and colonial countries, which categorized their populations into racial or ethnic groups on the basis of blood or skin color. In Nazi Germany, the main goal of the census was to determine "the number of persons with German blood and other such bigoted things," he explained. In the United States, "if a respondent has even a drop of black blood," he or she is registered as a member of the "black race." In the Soviet Union, by contrast, "if a person by blood is a Negro and was brought up in such a society and with such a language and culture that he calls himself Russian there is nothing incorrect about this, even if his skin color is black."[88]

Starovskii described national self-definition as subjective but not random, explaining that a person's *natsional'nost'* was supposed to be a "reflection" of belonging to a particular culture and consciousness. Thus, "if a person calls himself an Uzbek that means he is attached to the Uzbek culture." He added, "It would not be correct if I suddenly called myself Chinese since I have no ties whatsoever with Chinese culture." Starovskii continued to maintain, however, that self-definition would trump "precision" in the census—and that census takers must write down the *natsional'nost'* stated by the respondent. Some statisticians challenged Starovskii on this point. Shouldn't the census taker intervene in cases of "hooliganism": if a respondent "declares that he is Chinese and is not?" What should the census taker do if a respondent "whom he knows to be Ukrainian says that he is Tatar"? One statistician alluded to a recent government decree which stipulated that the Soviet regime would prosecute citizens who "gave false information" in the census interview.[89]

Again, Starovskii stood his ground. Although a person claiming to be Tatar "should be knowledgeable about the Tatar language and culture," it was "outside of the census taker's domain to request verification." The census taker "must register such a person as a Tatar."[90] Starovskii acknowledged that up-

88. RGAE f. 1562, op 336, d. 79, ll. 18–20.
89. Ibid., ll. 19–22. The statistician was referring to the July 26, 1938 decree from the Council of People's Commissars, "About the All-Union Census of the Population of 1939." This decree is discussed in Zhiromskaia, "Vsesoiuznye perepisi naseleniia 1926, 1937, 1939 goda," 90.
90. Ibid., l. 22.

holding the principle of self-definition would allow "suspect elements [*som-nitel'nye elementy*]" (such as Poles, Germans, and Japanese) who "prefer assimilation" to "conceal themselves" in the census: that Poles would attempt to pass themselves off "as Ukrainians" and Japanese "as Koreans." (It is not clear if he was aware that the Koreans were also being deported from the Far Eastern *krai* at this time.) But Starovskii explained that he had brought this concern to the Soviet government—which had affirmed that documents should not be "verified" and that some "false self-reporting" was an acceptable price for upholding the principle of self-definition, which was the right of all Soviet citizens.[91]

Nationality and Citizenship

The NKVD passport directives of 1938 based an individual's *natsional'nost'* on that of his or her parents, and were in this narrow sense biological. But the directives were not biological in the Nazi racial sense.[92] The Soviet regime was not worried that Poles and Germans were degenerate or flawed from a biological perspective, but that Poles and Germans could not become loyal Soviet citizens because of their "alien" culture and consciousness. This was an important difference between the Soviet and the Nazi projects. But it was little solace to those inhabitants of regime zones who were registered against their will as members of one of the diaspora nationalities—losing their functional citizenship as a result.[93] Diaspora nationalities remained Soviet citizens in the formal legal sense, but were stripped of their native-language institutions, land, and possessions, and were deported from regime zones. Individuals who were accused of masking their membership in one of the diaspora nationalities lost their jobs and party membership, and were also deported or arrested. People facing such treatment sent letters to Stalin, Mikhail Kalinin, and other Soviet leaders in 1938 and 1939 with questions of consequence. "How is *natsional'nost'* determined?" "Is it possible to change one's *natsional'nost'*?" "Can someone challenge my *natsional'nost'* and citizenship?"[94]

A number of the letter writers, like the statisticians at the Census Bureau, expressed real confusion about the divergence between the rules for census and passport registration. Some of the letter writers cited Stalin's 1913 definition of a nation. Others explained their understanding that *natsional'nost'* was not to

91. RGAE f. 1562, op. 336, d. 79, ll. 22–24.

92. Here I am arguing against Eric Weitz, who has suggested that the new passport directives marked the wholesale biologicization of nationality in the Soviet Union. See Eric D. Weitz, "Racial Politics without the Concept of Race: Reevaluating Soviet Ethnic and National Purges," *Slavic Review* 61, no. 1 (2002): 1–29.

93. On the idea of functional citizenship see Jürgen Habermas, "Citizenship and National Identity: Some Reflections on the Future of Europe," in *Theorizing Citizenship*, ed. Ronald Beiner (New York, 1995), 255–81.

94. For example, GARF f. 7523, op. 9, d. 99, ll. 45–450b.

be confused with place of birth, religion, or native language. All attempted to use the official promise of national self-definition, prominent in census propaganda, to defend their rights. Most of the letter writers understood that as a result of their presumed status as a member of a diaspora *natsional'nost'* their allegiance to the Soviet Union was suspect. With this in mind, they included detailed autobiographical information intended to prove their identification with one of the "Soviet" nationalities and to convince Soviet leaders of their devotion to the revolution.

One self-defined Ukrainian, V. S. Shuneiko, who had been registered against his will as Lithuanian in his passport, touched on issues of language, citizenship, religion, and national consciousness in a 1939 letter to Kalinin. Shuneiko explained that he was born in Kiev in 1913 and from 1914 onwards lived in Odessa. His mother was born in Kurland (a former Baltic province) and his father in Minsk. Shuneiko maintained that he did not know the Lithuanian language and considered his native language Russian. He also maintained that he had no close relatives abroad and that none of his "parents, grandfathers, and so on had foreign citizenship." To be as forthright as possible, he mentioned that he had a distant cousin "in the small town of Shavil" in Lithuania, but then explained that he and his other relatives "have no ties" with this person. The question of religion was more muddled. Shuneiko admitted that his parents had been religious and that he had been baptized Roman Catholic—and he speculated that "this fact alone" had resulted in his classification as a Lithuanian. But Shuneiko contended that he could not be held accountable for his parents' choices, and that he had been taught that "the determination of *natsional'nost'* was not based on confessional group." In order to prove his devotion to the Soviet Union, Shuneiko chronicled his experiences as a Stakhanovite metalworker, Komsomol leader, and political education worker. In conclusion, he asserted: "I was born in the Ukraine. I am a citizen of the Soviet Union. I am absolutely loyal to the Soviet regime." He then asked: "May I consider my *natsional'nost'* Ukrainian?"[95]

In a 1938 letter to Kalinin, S. M. Lozovskii of Leningrad used his knowledge of the Soviet constitution and the Soviet census to challenge the new passport directives. "As far as I understand Soviet civil law, each Soviet citizen has the right to choose his *natsional'nost'* either according to his mother or father," Lozovskii wrote. He further noted that "a film connected with the census" had emphasized the right of citizens to national self-definition and had also shown that parents decide together "how to register the *natsional'nost'* of their newborn." The new passport directives were of serious concern for Lozovskii, whose mother was Polish and father was Belorussian.[96] Lozovskii noted that "for the past twenty-two years" he had considered himself to be "a

95. Ibid., ll. 19–20.

96. Lozovskii noted that he had heard rumors that passport recipients had to take their mother's *natsional'nost'*.

Belorussian." However, according to the passport directives his mother's *nat-sional'nost'* would also be listed in his passport. Lozovskii noted that he had asked "political workers," as "people more knowledgeable on this question," for clarification on this matter. But all had given "different interpretations of the passportization rules." Lozovskii observed that the new directives—which had been introduced "to coincide with the official exchange of Komsomol cards"—could have serious implications for him. He feared, with good cause, that as an "official" member of one of the diaspora nationalities, his Komsomol membership might be revoked.[97]

A self-identified Russian from Odessa, Aleksandra Mel'nik, who had been registered against her self-definition as a Pole, sent Kalinin a letter in 1939 detailing her interactions with Soviet passport authorities. Mel'nik began her letter with autobiographical information. She noted that she was born in 1885 in Poland in the city of Sandomir, but had spent much of her life in Odessa; her parents were Russian and at the time of "the imperialist war" (World War I) had moved back to Odessa, where her father had been born and raised. She explained that she did not have a birth certificate, so when she went to obtain a passport in 1938 the passport registrar had determined her *natsional'nost'* on the basis of information noted in her pre-1917 household register. The household register "did not indicate *natsional'nost',*" she explained, so the passport registrar "decided that since I was born in Poland to put my *natsional'nost'* as Polish." Mel'nik recounted that when she received her passport she protested, "I am Russian, and not Polish." But officials told her "it is all the same." Mel'nik understood that it was not "all the same," and with the goal of "restoring" her *natsional'nost'* she petitioned the regional soviet, the regional passport office, the People's Commissariat of Justice, the public prosecutor, the district judge, and the district passport office—all to no avail. She concluded her letter by emphasizing that she was Russian in both culture and origins: "In old religious times," she noted, she and her relatives had attended "a Russian church." Then she added, "I have a sister who is older than me and is Russian—so how can it be that I am Polish?"[98]

The NKVD had maintained that its 1938 passport directives should not be extended to the registration of *natsional'nost'* in other official documents. But after 1938, local branches of the party throughout the Soviet Union and economic enterprises in regime zones began checking applicants' documents to verify their *natsional'nost'*. One self-defined Belorussian, N. V. Trushkovskii from the Donbass region of the Ukrainian SSR, wrote to the Soviet of Nationalities after the party denied his petition for membership on the grounds that he had attempted to mask his true "nation"—Polish. Trushkovskii explained in his letter that his father had been born in 1883 in Poland, but had married

97. GARF f. 7523, op. 9, d. 99, ll. 31–32. The party called for periodic passport inspections. See Stephen Kotkin, *Magnetic Mountain: Stalinism as a Civilization* (Berkeley, 1995), 102.
98. GARF f. 7523, op. 9, d. 99, ll. 24–250b.

a Ukrainian Orthodox woman and because of her had "changed his nation" to Ukrainian. In 1910, Trushkovskii's parents moved to the Belorussian region of the Russian Empire, where Trushkovskii was born and lived until 1930 (when he moved to the Donbass). Trushkovskii claimed that, "having read the works of Marx," he understood that a nation was "a historically formed stable community of language, territory, economic life, and psychological cast of mind, manifesting itself in a community of culture." (Of course, this was Stalin's definition, not Marx's.) He explained that his "community of language and culture without a doubt is Belorussian," that he considered Belorussia to be his "homeland," and that he and his siblings had always written "Belorussian" in official documents. He also gave a detailed account of his devotion to the Soviet Union, describing his service in the Red Army and his work in the party. In the end, he lamented: "I do not know who I am—Polish or Belorussian." (Interestingly, he did not claim to be Ukrainian.) He added: "For me it makes no difference whether my nation is Polish, Belorusssian, Jewish, or so on as long as people think well of me at work and I devote the rest of my life to the party of Lenin and Stalin."[99]

A July 1939 letter from Viktor Zenkevich to the Soviet of Nationalities illustrates how, in regime zones, employers and employees alike differentiated between "Soviet" and "foreign" nationalities. By Zenkevich's account, he was born in 1905 in Asveia, Belorussia (part of the former Vitebsk province of Poland). He lived there until 1917, when he moved to Moscow. His parents were also born in Asveia, and spent their entire lives there. He noted: "Before 1916 and after, as far as I can recall, my whole family was considered Belorussian and I still consider myself Belorussian at the present time." Zenkevich's problems began when his employers wrote officials in Asveia for copies of his official documents (probably his birth certificate). To his surprise, the Asveian officials communicated that he was Polish-Catholic, not Belorussian. Zenkevich described how his "comrades at work" changed their opinion about his right to self-definition when they learned of his supposed "Polish-Catholic origins." Before the communication from Asveia, Zenkevich's peers thought that he was Belorussian and had even suggested that he could define himself as Russian if he wanted since "after living twenty-three years in Moscow I have assimilated all the practices, habits, and customs of a Russian." But with the revelation that Zenkevich was a member of one of the diaspora nationalities, his co-workers and employer denounced him for masking his "true" identity.[100]

These letters and others like them were of great interest to the Supreme Soviet and the Soviet of Nationalities, which considered them in the context of their own discussions about nationality and citizenship. In September 1938, soon after it began receiving such letters, the Supreme Soviet asked its Judicial

99. Ibid., ll. 15–16.
100. Ibid., l. 39.

Department to evaluate the differences between the passport and the census rules for registering *natsional'nost'*, and to determine whether or not Soviet citizens who had been categorized against their will as members of a diaspora nationality had recourse under Soviet law. The head of the Judicial Department, Konstantin Arkhipov, asked the NKVD and the Council of People's Commissars for copies of their passport and census directives. Arkhipov also consulted the All-Union Law Academy's Department of Civil Law—which in turn debated whether or not an individual whose passport nationality had been recorded in contradiction with his or her statement could file suit against local officials.[101]

Later that year, the Department of Civil Law reported to Arkhipov that its experts had split into two factions—divided first and foremost over the question of whether an individual's nationality had legal significance in the Soviet Union. One faction rejected the idea of a lawsuit on the grounds that statute 123 of the Stalin Constitution established that "the question about *natsional'nost'* does not have any juridical significance and has no legal consequences of any kind." It explained that suits about the establishment of facts were uncommon in general and "a suit about the establishment of facts without juridical significance is inadmissible." But this faction did argue that citizens of the USSR whose passports or other official documents contained "an incorrect designation of their *natsional'nost'*" (for whatever reason) "can request through an administrative procedure that these errors be corrected." Moreover, such requests "were guaranteed satisfaction," for "*natsional'nost'* is registered in documents solely on the basis of the declaration of the citizens themselves."[102] In effect, this faction dismissed the idea of a suit but upheld the principle of self-definition.

The Department of Civil Law's other faction maintained that questions about an individual's *natsional'nost'* were not "inconsequential in legal terms," since the Soviet Union "has numerous regulations to help backward nationalities, provide for national minorities' rights, and so on." This faction noted the existence of quotas to facilitate the admission of national minorities to technical colleges in large cities, as well as laws about the use of one's native language in legal proceedings. Since "national membership" was of real consequence, the experts concluded, a citizen should have the right to take legal action to redress the improper registration of his or her *natsional'nost'*.[103] Thus, in spite of their differences, both factions agreed that all Soviet citizens had a legal right to the self-definition of *natsional'nost'*. The Judicial Department forwarded the notes from this discussion to the Supreme Soviet.

---

101. Ibid., l. 14; op. 65, d. 304, ll. 3–6. It is impossible not to be skeptical about the legal implications of these deliberations, given that 1938 was a year best known for extralegal terror in the Soviet Union. But the legal experts saw themselves as professionals with real responsibilities—and looked to the Soviet constitution for guidance.

102. GARF f. 7523, op. 9, d. 99, l. 14.

103. Ibid.

Meanwhile, the Judicial Department also exchanged information with the NKVD's Division of Passport Registration. In February 1939, Ivan Serov (one of the heads of the NKVD) wrote to Arkhipov about the NKVD passport directives. He confirmed the NKVD's position that if a passport recipient had parents of two different nationalities and one belonged to a "foreign state," the passport registrar was to list *both* parents' nationalities in the passport. To illustrate his point, Serov commented on a 1938 letter from a passport recipient that Arkhipov had forwarded to him. According to Serov, "the *natsional'nost'* of A. A. Kurovskii—father Polish, mother Russian" had been written correctly in his passport, for "Kurovskii indicates in his statement that his father is Polish and that he himself was born on territory that had gone to Poland [in the 1920s]."[104] From the NKVD's perspective, Kurovskii was the child of a "foreigner" and was born in a "foreign land"—and was thus "unreliable." The fact that Kurovskii was legally a Soviet citizen did not matter.

Toward a Final List of Nationalities

The "Second" All-Union Census began, for the second time, on January 17, 1939.[105] In subsequent months, ethnographers engaged in further discussions about the list of nationalities, which would soon be used to tabulate the census's results.[106] In August 1939, the Census Bureau approved a revised list of sixty-two nations, national groups, and *narodnosti*, which included some notable changes. The Bulgarians and Greeks had been removed from this list and added to the list of national minorities, and the Crimean Tatars had been amalgamated into the Tatars. At the same time, six peoples that had been enumerated in August 1938 as ethnographic groups (the Veps, Izhora, Udegei, Uigurs, Gypsies, and Abazins) were elevated to *narodnosti* and included on the main list.[107]

As the Census Bureau completed its tabulations, it also worked with ethnographers to compile a list of the main (*glavnye*) *natsional'nosti* of the USSR—finishing a draft in early 1940.[108] The first part of this list enumerated thirty-five "nations, national groups and *narodnosti*," while the second part enumerated fourteen national minorities (nationalities "living in their main mass outside of the Soviet Union").[109] This list thus maintained the distinction between Soviet and diaspora peoples. Notably, the Germans, who were

104. GARF f. 7523, op. 65, d. 304, ll. 1–2.
105. It was conducted for seven days in the cities and for nineteen days in the countryside.
106. PFA RAN f. 142, op. 1 (1939), d. 38, ll. 1, 2; RGAE f. 1562, op. 336, d. 208, ll. 24, 30; op. 329, d. 285, l. 115. For a discussion of how the Census Bureau manipulated the results in order to hide the population losses of the 1920s and 1930s see Blum and Mespoulet, *L'anarchie bureaucratique: Statistique et pouvoir sous Staline*.
107. RGAE f. 1562, op. 336, d. 208, ll. 7–8.
108. The list included peoples with populations greater than twenty thousand in the Soviet Union. Noted in Zhiromskaia, "Vsesoiuznye perepisi naseleniia 1926, 1937, 1939 godov," 101.
109. RGAE f. 1562, op. 336, d. 221, ll. 13–14.

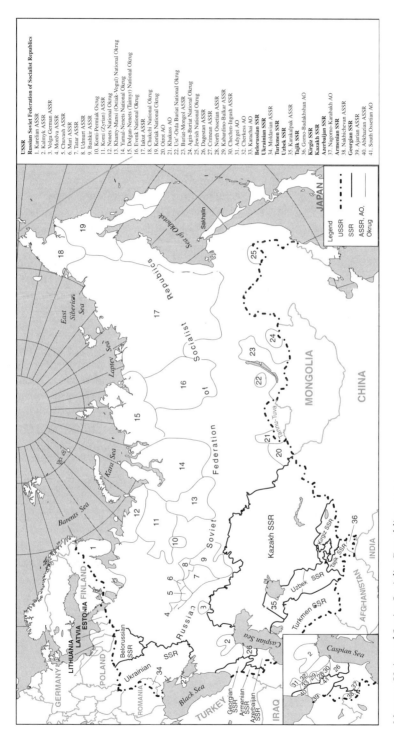

Map 7.1 Union of Soviet Socialist Republics, 1939.

treated in other respects as a foreign nation, were included on the first part of the list due to the existence of the Volga German ASSR. The experts went even further than before in amalgamating nationalities: the Mishers, Kriashens, and Teptiars were combined (with the Crimean Tatars) into the Tatars, and the Crimean Jews, Central Asian Jews, Georgian Jews, and Mountain Jews into the Jews. In addition, the Avars, Dargins, and some twenty-one other peoples were combined into a collective ethnoterritorial group and called "the *narodnosti* of Dagestan."[110] A number of "smaller *narodnosti*," such as the Izhora, Veps, Uigurs, and Gypsies, were omitted from this list altogether.

In April 1940, *Pravda* published this new list of *natsional'nosti*. Significantly, the *Pravda* version did not differentiate between Soviet and diaspora nationalities, instead enumerating all forty-nine peoples in the order of their population totals.[111] In this, it differed from the version of the list that was sent to party and government institutions. Meanwhile, the Census Bureau noted in internal documents that it had not finished tabulating data for the peoples of the Far North, and that a final, complete list of nationalities would be available in the near future.[112] This final list of the "largest *natsional'nosti* of the USSR" (which was not released for publication) included fifty-seven peoples: the forty-nine from the *Pravda* list, plus the Gypsies, Veps, Uigurs, Nogai, Buriats, Iakuts, Talysh, and the composite group "Peoples of the North" (comprised of twenty-six peoples, including the Sel'kup, Evenk, and Even).[113] The Census Bureau treated the amalgamation of peoples as a straightforward process. But a group of Moscow ethnographers—the same ones who had recommended that national minorities be expunged from the main list—expressed some unease. In particular, these ethnographers suggested that the amalgamation of "small *narodnosti*" which were "altogether different in origins and culture" into composite groups like the Peoples of the North "violated Soviet nationality policy" and could not help but compromise national rights.[114]

The Moscow ethnographers were not alone in their unease about the consequences of amalgamation. People throughout the Soviet Union experienced the amalgamation of their *narodnost'* into a *natsional'nost'*, or the demotion of their *narodnost'* to an ethnographic group, with confusion and worry. They expressed their concerns in letters to Soviet institutions and leaders. For example, a September 1939 letter from a "citizen Mikhail Timofeev of Leningrad oblast" to the Soviet of Nationalities explained that as a result of changes in Soviet policies, the peoples of Leningrad oblast were no longer sure which

110. Ibid., and Poliakov et al., *Vsesoiuznaia perepis' naseleniia 1939 goda*, 246–48.

111. "Soobshchenie Tsentral'nogo upravleniia narodno-khoziaistvennogo ucheta Gosplana SSSR o dannykh Vsesoiuznoi perepisi naseleniia 1939 goda," *Pravda*, April 19, 1940, p. 2. Number 50 on the list was "Others."

112. RGAE f. 1562, op. 336, d. 221, l. 14.

113. A version of this list was later published in Poliakov et al., *Vsesoiuznaia perepis' naseleniia 1939 goda*, 57–58.

114. RGAE f. 1562, op. 336, d. 208, ll. 2–3.

local names (Izhora, Chukhar, Ingermanlandian, Karelian, and so on) corresponded to official nationalities. He explained that the region's inhabitants,
who spoke a mix of Finnish and Estonian, did not know "to which *natsional'nost'* or *narodnost'* to register themselves." In particular, he and his neighbors wanted to know if the Soviet regime recognized "Izhora" as an official
natsional'nost'.[115] Timofeev was right to question the status of the Izhora, who
had been included on the list of *natsional'nosti* for the 1937 census, demoted
to an ethnographic group on the draft lists for the 1939 census, included as a
narodnost' on the January 1939 list of "nations, national groups, and *narodnosti,*" and then omitted from the 1940 list of the Soviet Union's *glavnye natsional'nosti* in its unpublished and published forms.

Some other letter writers, who recognized the amalgamation of nationalities
as a given, attempted to manipulate it to their advantage. A February 1939 letter from a group of self-defined "Masurians" in western Ukraine shows that
peoples without official status understood the potential benefit of being amalgamated into one of the Soviet socialist nations. The Masurians had never been included on the official list of nationalities; from late-imperial times they had been
considered to be a German or a Polish subgroup. In the late 1930s, Masurians in
the Soviet Union were persecuted for their association with these foreign nations. In an attempt to end their troubles, the Masurian letter writers asked
"Beloved Comrade Stalin" either "to affirm the existence of the Masurian nation or, if that is impossible, to count us as members of one of the other [nondi-
aspora] *natsional'nosti* of our great Soviet Union." The letter writers explained
that the Masurians "had never been German or Polish" and that they had preserved their native Masurian language. Moreover, they maintained that a hostile
relationship had long existed between the Masurians and the Germans, and that
Masurians who lived under the Nazis were suffering national persecution.[116]

As the Census Bureau was preparing its final list of nationalities for publication, high-level discussions continued about the right of Soviet citizens to
challenge the incorrect registration of their *natsional'nost'*. In January 1940—
after the NKVD completed its national operations in the borderlands—
Arkhipov sent the Presidium of the Supreme Soviet the Judicial Department's
opinion on this issue. According to Arkhipov, "based on statute 123 of the
constitution of the USSR," the practice of filling out the space *natsional'nost'*
in passports and other documents on the basis of the *natsional'nost'* of the recipient's parents "does not correspond with the demands of the law."[117] The

115. GARF f. 7523, op. 9, d. 99, ll. 42–42ob.

116. Ibid., ll. 21–22ob. On the Masurians in Poland see Michael Burleigh, *Germany Turns
Eastwards: A Study of Ostforschung in the Third Reich* (Cambridge, 1998).

117. GARF f. 7523, op. 65, d. 304, ll. 8–10. One month earlier, the Presidium of the Supreme
Soviet had also asked the Council of People's Commissars to look into the matter "in view of the
fact that the question about determining the *natsional'nost'* of people born to parents of different
natsional'nosti is not foreseen by the laws of the USSR and the union republics and the fact that
this question affects the interests of citizens of the USSR."

final decision of the Supreme Soviet on this issue (if there was one) did not make it into the archival record. The 1938 NKVD passport directives seem to have remained in force throughout the Second World War, even as the official passport law continued to suggest that an individual had the right to national self-definition.

It is important to note that the Supreme Soviet did update its passport law in other respects between April and September 1940, in response to the Soviet Union's occupation and annexation of eastern Poland and the Baltic states of Latvia, Lithuania, and Estonia.[118] The updated law extended the passport system to all of the occupied territories, declaring them to be regime zones. Reaffirming the distinction between Soviet and diaspora peoples, the law made Soviet citizenship easier to acquire for Russians, Ukrainians, and Belorussians than for Poles, Latvians, Lithuanians, Estonians, or other "foreign" nationalities. However, the law did not stipulate how registrars were to determine the national identities of the passport applicants.[119]

After German forces invaded the Soviet Union in June 1941, the NKVD had an even greater incentive to keep in place its 1938 passport directives targeting foreign nationalities. It was not until the postwar period that Soviet passport law changed and stipulated that any individual receiving a passport for the first time had to take the *natsional'nost'* of one parent or the other.[120] This new law institutionalized parental ties. But it gave people a choice: an individual with one parent from a "suspect" nationality and another from a Soviet nationality could choose the nationality of the latter. These new rules allowed the children of mixed-nationality marriages to distance themselves from their suspect parent and affirm their allegiance as "Soviet" people.

In the postwar era, the Soviet regime expanded its use of the passport to police the population. The distinction between regime zones and nonregime zones was collapsed; the passport system was extended across the entire Soviet Union. Many Soviet citizens experienced this as a positive development. Before the war, peasants living in the Soviet countryside (in nonregime zones) had not been issued passports, and thus were not allowed to travel to or through cities and other regime zones. Now, peasants were subject to the same rules as other citizens. However, the extension of the passport system provided a mechanism for the NKVD to keep tabs on the entire population, strengthen-

118. Between September 1939 and September 1940, the Soviets took advantage of the secret protocols in the Hitler-Stalin Pact of August 1939—occupying and annexing these territories, the Finnish borderlands, and the Romanian provinces of northern Bukovina and Bessarabia.

119. On passport regulations and citizenship see GARF f. 7523, op. 65, d. 304, ll. 11–16. Also see *Sobranie postanovlenii i rasporiazhenii pravitel'stva SSSR* 25, no. 24 (1940): 808–14.

120. Melik'ian and Kvasha, *Narodonaselenie*, 295–96. After 1958 *natsional'nost'* was written into other documents according to an individual's passport. If an individual did not have a passport, his or her *natsional'nost'* was determined according to the *natsional'nost'* of his or her parents. If a person had parents belonging to different *natsional'nosti,* the registrar was supposed to indicate the *natsional'nost'* of one of the parents according to the wish of the recipient.

ing the Soviet police state. In the immediate postwar period, the regime did not relax its hunt for enemies; on the contrary, it called for increased vigilance. The population had been "exposed" to "Western influences" in the course of the war. Stalin's last years saw a brutal campaign to eradicate these influences throughout the USSR.

Because the Soviet regime cared about the population's "consciousness"—not about its inherent biological traits—the list of Soviet nationalities remained subject to revision. This left some groups with the hope of "rehabilitation" and others with the fear of future persecution. During and after the Second World War, the list of Soviet nationalities underwent some important changes. Soon after the Baltic region was incorporated into the Soviet Union, the Lithuanians, Latvians, and Estonians were given official Soviet national cultures of their own and urged to become "Soviet."[121] At the same time, a number of Soviet socialist nations lost their privileged status. The Soviet regime accused the Chechens, Ingush, Balkars, and several other peoples of collaborating with German occupation forces, and added them to a list of "enemy" nations. This list was comprised of "foreign" and other "unreliable" peoples charged with anti-Soviet activities during the war. The Soviet government eliminated the ethnoterritorial units of these nationalities; the NKVD deported their populations to Central Asia and Siberia, and took additional steps to wipe out their cultures, languages, and histories.[122]

In the late 1930s, facing a dual ideological and geopolitical threat, the Soviet regime used a combination of ethnographic knowledge and terror to accelerate the revolution and consolidate the Soviet state. It pressed ethnographers and other experts to prove that the Soviet vision of historical development was correct. At the same time, it relied on the NKVD to defend regions of strategic importance from "unreliable elements"—in part through the use of the passport. The census and the passport, two cultural technologies of rule, coexisted and used different criteria to map out the population's national identities. Each served an important function. Yet the NKVD (which oversaw the passport) and Soviet ethnographers and statisticians (who worked on the census) did not exist in isolated spheres. In the midst of Stalin's terror, Soviet experts had reason to fear the NKVD. A feedback loop thus developed between terror and ethnographic knowledge. Ethnographers and statisticians expunged diaspora nationalities from their list of nationalities and provided a scientific rationale for the NKVD's population policies.

121. On the effort to integrate new territories into the Soviet Union see Jan T. Gross, *Revolution from Abroad: The Soviet Conquest of Poland's Western Ukraine and Western Belorussia* (Princeton, 1988), and Amir Weiner, *Making Sense of War*.

122. The Volga German ASSR was abolished in 1941, and the Chechen-Ingush ASSR in 1944. The Balkars lost their administrative district in the Kabardino-Balkar ASSR in 1943. See Aleksandr M. Nekrich, *The Punished Peoples* (New York, 1978), and Svetlana Alieva, ed., *Tak eto bylo: Natsional'nye repressii v SSSR 1919–1952 gody*, 3 vols. (Moscow, 1993).

Stalin's unleashing of the Great Terror had a profound impact on the production of knowledge in the Soviet Union. And yet perhaps what is most striking is that, throughout these years, ethnographers and other experts continued to play an active role in the process of Soviet state formation. To be sure, the experts worked in an environment of fear and constraint, and with the understanding that their role was to serve the regime: this was far from the type of collaboration that Sergei F. Ol'denburg and his colleagues had hoped for. But the ethnographers could no longer complain that the state disregarded expert knowledge. The Soviet Union, unlike tsarist Russia, claimed to be a scientific state—and, even at the height of the Great Terror, it continued to rely on experts to provide a scientific rationale for its policies. Thus, even Stalin (who considered himself an expert in most fields) looked to ethnographers to prepare the new list of nationalities for the 1939 census. The ethnographers, for their part, sought to fulfill the regime's demands *and* maintain a sense of themselves as professionals. They took pains to explain even the most political decisions in scientific terms—often deluding themselves in the process. Through their efforts, the experts helped subordinate the population to Soviet power and brought about the complete Sovietization of their discipline.

Epilogue

> Our socialist experiment, grand in its historical significance, was not carried out in a laboratory.
>
> —Iulian Bromlei, Institute of Ethnography, 1987

> With history encamped at its side, [the Bolshevik Party] would set out to marshal the facts of the future, and whip everyone within reach along the only true path to progress and civilization.
>
> —A. P. Thornton, *Doctrines of Imperialism*, 1965

In 1947 the legal expert and former Narkomnats administrator Il'ia Trainin published two books. The first focused on the Austro-Hungarian Empire, although its apparent purpose was to make a comparative argument about the Soviet Union. In its pages, Trainin examined the rise and fall of the Habsburg state, concentrating on the "national tensions" that had led to its collapse in 1918.[1] The second was about the Soviet multinational state. Here too, however, Trainin dwelled on the comparison between the Soviet Union and the Austro-Hungarian Empire—calling out the "flawed assumptions of the foreign press," which had characterized the Soviet multinational state as "an artificial and impracticable structure" that "awaited the fate" of Austria-Hungary.[2] Trainin noted that the enemies of the Soviet Union had clung to this comparison during the Great Fatherland War and had attempted "to sow national discord" among the Soviet population with the hope that the USSR would "implode" and "disintegrate into its component parts" as Austria-Hungary had done during World War I.[3] In both of these works, Trainin depicted the "war against the Hitlerite aggressors" as a "serious test of strength," a crucible that the Soviet socialist state had en-

1. I. P. Trainin, *Natsional'nye protivorechiia v Avstro-Vengrii i ee raspad* (Moscow, 1947).
2. I. P. Trainin, *Sovetskoe mnogonatsional'noe gosudarstvo* (Moscow, 1947), esp. 30.
3. Ibid., and Trainin, *Natsional'nye protivorechiia v Avstro-Vengrii*, 293.

dured with success—emerging all the stronger and proving itself to be a "vital state construction."[4] Trainin attributed this triumph to the Soviet approach to the nationality question, which had fostered "a friendship and brotherhood of peoples" who rallied to save their common homeland.[5]

The creation of an official narrative about the transformation of the Russian Empire into the USSR was critical to the process of Soviet state building. Trainin, a specialist in Soviet law and the nationality question, had had a hands-on role in the formation of the Soviet Union in the 1920s and 1930s, helping to define the administrative-territorial structure of the USSR and working with other administrators and experts to "bring the revolution" to non-Russian regions.[6] At the same time, he had also written numerous popular and academic works that portrayed this process of formation as natural and organic—unfolding under the guidance of Lenin and Stalin through a series of historical stages.[7] Trainin had omitted from this narrative much of the violence and terror that had accompanied the establishment of Soviet rule and the spread and acceleration of the revolution. He had also omitted those experts and administrators who had helped the Bolsheviks to attain the conceptual conquest of the former Russian Empire and to pursue an ambitious revolutionary agenda.[8] Trainin's postwar works continued to describe the formation of the Soviet Union in this vein; they cemented the earlier narrative and brought the war into it.[9]

Throughout his works, Trainin credited "the Bolsheviks" and "the socialist state" with taking charge of the process of historical development in the Soviet Union and fostering the creation of new socialist nations. According to Trainin, upon smashing the "tsarist prison of peoples" in 1917, the Bolsheviks had set out to win over the more advanced nationalities of the Russian Empire with the promise of national self-determination. But the revolutionaries had not stopped there; they also had endeavored to facilitate "the consolidation into nations" of a number of groups, such as "the Kirgiz, Turkmen, Tajiks, and Uzbeks," whom "bourgeois science had described in the past as 'nonhis-

4. Trainin, *Natsional'nye protivorechiia v Avstro-Vengrii*, 293.

5. Trainin *Sovetskoe mnogonatsional'noe gosudarstvo*, 30–31, and *Natsional'nye protivorechiia v Avstro-Vengrii*, 293–95. This theme is repeated in other postwar works such as D. Shepilov, *Velikii sovetskii narod* (Moscow, 1947).

6. Between 1922 and 1924 Trainin had edited the Narkomnats journal, *Zhizn' natsional'nostei*, which chronicled and promoted the spread of the revolution. Between 1942 and 1947 he was the director of the Academy of Sciences Institute of Law.

7. For narratives of the early years of formation see I. Trainin, *SSSR i natsional'naia problema* (Moscow, 1924), and *Imperializm na Dal'nem Vostoke i SSSR* (Moscow, 1932). For narratives that treat the formation of the Soviet Union as an ongoing process unfolding through sequential stages see I. Trainin, *Bratskoe sodruzhestvo narodov SSSR* (Moscow, 1938), and I. Trainin, *Natsional'noe i sotsial'noe osvobozhdenie Zapadnoi Ukrainy i Zapadnoi Belorussii* (Moscow, 1939).

8. Trainin did discuss the role of Narkomnats in this process, but depicted the commissariat as the instrument of Stalin. See for example *Sovetskoe mnogonatsional'noe gosudarstvo*, 15.

9. Also see I. Trainin, *Velikoe sodruzhestvo narodov SSSR* (Moscow, 1946).

torical peoples.' "[10] In the Soviet Union, the process of nation formation had taken place at a tempo "never before seen" and "altogether inconceivable in capitalist conditions," Trainin maintained. The "socialist state" had led clans, tribes, and nationalities down "the big historical road," awakening them and helping them "to stand on their feet and consolidate into nations."[11] At the same time, it had worked to eliminate "the economic and cultural inequalities" that in the past had divided "the center and peripheries." As a result of these efforts, there were "neither ruling nor oppressed nations" and "neither metropole nor colony" in the Soviet Union.[12] In effect, Trainin was celebrating the triumph of the Bolshevik programs of nonimperialistic colonization and state-sponsored evolutionism. He made no mention of the experts who had worked to develop and further these programs. Nor did he mention those clans, tribes, and nationalities that had viewed the abolishment of their traditional cultures, languages, and native-language institutions, and their forced assimilation into socialist nations, as acts of violence.

Trainin described the Great Fatherland War as a monumental event that had accelerated the consolidation of the Soviet Union and had strengthened Soviet internationalism. He had in mind a type of internationalism that looked inward—that was based on the Soviet "friendship of peoples" and was premised on a belief in "the gradual erosion of national differences" as well as on the future "merger" (*sliianie*) of the peoples of the USSR.[13] The ultimate success of this merger depended on the "elimination of bourgeois nationalism," which he described as a dangerous "survival" of the capitalist era.[14] Arguing that the war had precipitated an all-out struggle between socialist and bourgeois nations *within* the Soviet Union, Trainin offered an ideological rationale for the regime's treatment of particular groups. He suggested, for example, that the "nationalistic" Crimean Tatars and Chechens had shown themselves to be "evil enemies" of the Soviet people, and he characterized their expulsion from their homelands as a decisive blow against a major threat.[15] At the same time, Trainin presented the Russians as the "organizing force" who had rallied the other peoples of the USSR during the war—and provided a justification for their designation as "first among equals." He emphasized that the Russian socialist nation, "under the leadership of the Russian working class," had taken form *after* "the liquidation of the kulaks as a class" and was not to be confused with the Russian bourgeois nation of the past.[16]

10. Trainin, *Sovetskoe mnogonatsional'noe gosudarstvo*, and *Natsional'nye protivorechiia v Avstro-Vengrii*, 286, 288.

11. Trainin, *Sovetskoe mnogonatsional'noe gosudarstvo*, 25, and *Natsional'nye protivorechiia v Avstro-Vengrii*, 288–99.

12. Trainin, *Sovetskoe mnogonatsional'noe gosudarstvo*, 4, 26.

13. Ibid., 27.

14. Ibid., 27.

15. Ibid., 28–29.

16. Ibid., 19, 28, and Trainin, *Natsional'nye protivorechiia v Avstro-Vengrii*, 295.

The historical narrative—like the census, map, and museum—was an important cultural technology of rule, which helped the Bolsheviks pursue their transformative goals and consolidate Soviet power. Trainin's postwar works reflected the official line, telling Soviet citizens in clear ideological terms what they had been fighting for, what they had achieved, and what remained to be accomplished. His books and pamphlets were important pieces of educational propaganda that presented a simplified and cleaned-up account of the formation of the Soviet Union and reified the friendship of peoples. Over the next several decades, this basic narrative remained in place, even as the storyline stretched to accommodate changes that were taking place in the USSR and out in the wider world. During the Cold War era, the United States emerged as an important antithetical model, assuming the role that the European empires and the Nazis played in the earlier parts of the narrative. New works juxtaposed the Soviet *narod* against the American people—contrasting the harmonious relationship among the nationalities of the USSR with the antagonistic race relations of the United States. These works also discussed the impending transition to communism in the USSR and described how the Soviet people were exporting their unique approach to the nationality question to other countries in the socialist camp.[17]

The Sovietization of the Social Sciences

The Soviet Union had taken form through a process of double assimilation during the 1920s and 1930s. The diverse population of the former Russian Empire was assimilated into official nationality categories, and through those categories also became integrated into the larger Soviet whole. Ethnographers and other experts had worked to advance these processes of Sovietization, and in particular to further the transformation of clans and tribes into Soviet socialist nations. At the same time, these experts had begun to articulate and explain the ethnohistorical evolution of the population in Marxist-Leninist terms, making the case that this process was taking place according to the "law of development by stages." Drawing on Edward B. Tylor's concept of "survivals," these experts provided a nonracial explanation for the persisting "backwardness" of some populations—as well as a scientific rationale for the regime's brutal treatment of "kulaks," "bourgeois nationalists," and other alleged class enemies.

The Soviet Union was a new type of scientific state. The Bolsheviks, like the leaders of other modern states, conceived of government as an institution with the prerogative and the power to act on and transform lands and peoples. But the Soviet Union differed from these other states in that its leaders claimed to be able to understand, control, and accelerate the historical process itself. Dur-

17. See for example I. P. Tsamerian, *Velikaia epokha formirovaniia i razvitiia sotsialisticheskikh natsii v SSSR* (Moscow, 1951).

ing the 1920s and 1930s, the Communist Party had looked to social scientists to turn the ideas of Marx and Engels into scientific precepts for fostering human and social development. At the same time, it had prevailed on these experts to recast their own fields to reflect the Marxist-Leninist understanding of the world. In practice, this meant that social scientific theories had to be ideologically correct in order to be scientifically correct. This was a difficult transition to make for experts who were used to engaging multiple, often competing, discourses. But the experts soon realized that their disciplines—and also their lives—were at stake. By the late 1930s, in the wake of the Great Terror, ethnographers and other experts had Sovietized their fields from within.

The immediate postwar era saw the deepening Sovietization of the USSR and of the Soviet social sciences. A new generation of experts came of age for whom the linkage between social science and scientific socialism was automatic. Ethnography, anthropology, sociology, and other fields now had a firm ideological footing. Beginning in the 1950s, ethnographers devoted themselves to studying ethnogenesis, looking backward and describing in strict Marxist-Leninist terms how each of the Soviet socialist nations had taken form. At the same time, sociologists looked to the future, explaining how the nationalities and socialist nations of the USSR would continue to evolve until they merged into a single, unified Soviet *narod*. Experts in both of these fields did comparative-typological research with the aim of better elucidating "the general laws" of the history of humankind.[18]

For postwar Soviet ethnographers, the term of choice became *ethnos,* which was characterized as the "basic unit" of ethnic classification.[19] This was the same term that the former KIPS ethnographer Sergei Rudenko had favored in the 1920s. At the time, Rudenko had defined "ethnos" as an ethnosocial formation with "a complex of historical and cultural traits." He had suggested that KIPS and the Ethnographic Department use this term instead of *narodnost'* in their work, explaining that an ethnos evolved over time and took on new characteristics, whereas a *narodnost'* was merely the expression of an ethnos at one moment on the historical timeline.[20] The postwar ethnographers defined ethnos in a similar manner: as the "essence" or "sum total of stable ethnic features" of a people, which were retained over generations, over the course of migrations, and through the various stages on the historical timeline. These experts explained that an ethnos had both "objective and subjective properties"—that "culture" was the "main carrier" of ethnos, and that ethnic self-consciousness was an "important but not sufficient" trait. Most important, the

18. Iu. Bromlei and K. V. Chistov, "Velikii Oktiabr' i sovetskaia etnografiia," *Sovetskaia etnografiia,* no. 5 (1987): 10.

19. Iu. Bromlei, *Etnos i etnografiia* (Moscow, 1973), 25. Bromlei is citing N. N. Cheboksarov, "Problemy tipologii etnicheskikh obshchnostei v trudakh sovetskikh uchenykh," *Sovetskaia etnografiia,* no. 4 (1967): 96. Bromlei notes that the term *ethnos* had Greek origins and had long been used in the international scientific literature. Bromlei, *Etnos i etnografiia,* 21.

20. See chapter 5.

experts approached the study of ethnos from the perspective of historical materialism, looking at past and present ethnic forms "in the making."[21]

In 1955, as the idea of "ethnos" was coming into the mainstream in the USSR, Rudenko published a major work on the Bashkirs that took up the question of ethnogenesis. This work looked at the Bashkirs from a historical perspective, devoting significant attention to the various "ethnic elements" that had consolidated into the Bashkir nation. In the introduction, Rudenko at long last got some (albeit mild) revenge on Nikolai Marr, who had unseated him, Sergei F. Ol'denburg, and other KIPS ethnographers from their scientific posts more than two decades earlier. Rudenko declared that Marr was responsible for impeding the development of ethnography in the Soviet Union. He maintained that Marr's "unscientific claims" about the origins and development of languages and ethnic groups had led experts down "the wrong path" and diverted them from serious research on the problem of ethnogenesis. Particularly damaging, Rudenko asserted, had been Marr's "theory of language," which assumed that language and race were "identical" and that structural linguistics provided the key to tracing the origins of all ethnic groups.[22] Marr, who had died of natural causes in 1934, was unable to answer Rudenko's charges.

Marr's legacy was not totally erased, however. On the contrary, his conception of nationality as a "superstructural category" based on "socioeconomic factors" endured—gaining new life after the war. Beginning in the late 1960s, Iulian Bromlei, the best-known ethnographer of the Brezhnev era, expounded a "theory of ethnos" which was an elaborate version of the law of development by stages.[23] Bromlei explained that different types of ethnosocial communities corresponded to "the main historical stages" on the Marxist timeline of development: that the tribe was the "predominant form of ethnosocial organization" for "primitive social formations," the *narodnost'* for "slave-owning and feudal formations," and the nation for capitalist and socialist formations.[24] According to Bromlei, it was possible for an ethnos to "survive" several socioeconomic stages and to evolve into a more developed ethnosocial form. "The Ukrainian ethnos, for instance, existed under feudalism and capitalism, and continues to exist under socialism."[25] But Bromlei also cautioned

---

21. Bromlei, *Etnos i etnografiia*, 36–43. Also see Bromlei and Chistov, "Velikii Oktiabr' i sovetskaia etnografiia," 3–16.

22. S. I. Rudenko, *Bashkiry: Istoriko-etnograficheskie ocherki* (Moscow-Leningrad, 1955), esp. 5–8. Rudenko's work was based in part on anthropological research that he had done before 1917 and during the 1920s. On Marr's ideas, I am paraphrasing Yuri Slezkine, "N. Ia. Marr and the National Origins of Soviet Ethnogenetics," *Slavic Review* 55, no. 4 (1996): 838.

23. These ideas, which Marr propounded in 1929, were integrated into the mainstream of Soviet ethnography in the 1930s.

24. Iu. V. Bromlei, *Ocherki teorii etnosa* (Moscow, 1983), 383–84.

25. Bromlei, *Etnos i etnografiia*, 40. Bromlei also used the term *ethnikos* to refer to the "core ethnic traits" that persisted as an ethnos made the transition through different socioeconomic formations.

against ideas of "ethnic primordialism" and "national character." "No ethnos is either eternal or immutable," and none obtained its traits from God, he maintained. All ethnoses were "dynamic systems" that took shape through the process of "historical development" and that would continue to evolve in the future.[26]

Bromlei maintained that the process of ethnohistorical evolution took place through a number of "ethno-transformational processes," the most important of which were differentiation, consolidation, interethnic integration, and assimilation.[27] He further suggested that particular processes predominated at particular historical stages. Primeval and feudal societies experienced significant ethnic division and differentiation: as tribes grew in size and natural resources became depleted in a given region, subgroups "detached from tribes," moved to new territories, and became tribes of their own. Late feudalism and capitalism, by contrast, saw a trend toward ethnos enlargement in all its forms. Assimilation occurred when small peoples "dissolved" into another people; interethnic integration transpired when ethnic groups with substantial linguistic and cultural differences formed a new ethnic group; and consolidation took place when "kindred ethnic groups" with linguistic and cultural commonalities merged into a single ethnic group. Bromlei further noted that because kindred peoples in most cases had the same ethnic origins, consolidation was often the "dialectical negation" of the process of differentiation. In other words, branches of a tribe that had developed into separate *narodnosti* under feudalism came together again in a more evolved form—the nation—under capitalism.[28]

Soviet experience had shown that the process of ethnos enlargement sped up further still under socialism, Bromlei maintained. Moreover, under socialism, unlike under capitalism, the processes of assimilation and consolidation were natural and uncoerced. First, the "transitional period of building socialism" saw the gradual "elimination of antagonistic classes," and with it the transformation of "capitalist nations" into "socialist nations." Then, the establishment of socialism—with its unified economic system, high level of cultural exchange, and social homogenization—facilitated the further amalgamation of nations. Bromlei described how the establishment of socialism in the USSR in 1936 had prompted the assimilation of dozens of ethnographic groups into related nations. He explained, for example, that the Setu had "vanished" into the Estonians, the Latgalians into the Lithuanians, and the

26. This argument is neatly summarized in Yu. Bromley, "The Term Ethnos and its Definition," in *Soviet Ethnology and Anthropology Today*, ed. Yu. Bromley (The Netherlands, 1974), 5–72, esp. 66.

27. Bromlei, *Ocherki teorii etnosa*, 233–43.

28. Bromlei, *Ocherki teorii etnosa*, and Yu. Bromley, "Toward a Typology of Ethnic Processes," in Yu. Bromley, *Soviet Ethnography: Main Trends* (Moscow, 1977), 40–51. The quotes are from the latter.

Kamchadals and Kerzhaks into the Russians.[29] This same period also saw the consolidation of small *narodnosti* into larger nations, Bromlei noted, pointing to the amalgamation of the Mishers, Kriashens, and Nagaibaks into the Tatars.[30] According to Bromlei, the phenomenon of ethnos enlargement was reflected in the all-union censuses. He contended that the "absence" from the 1939 and 1959 censuses of dozens of nationalities that had been recorded in the 1926 census (such as the Mishers, Latgalians, and Kamchadals) was a "direct result" of ethnic assimilation and consolidation—and evidence of the revolution's progress.[31]

But how would the creation of larger and more-developed nations lead to internationalism? Bromlei, like Trainin and other scholars in the postwar era, maintained that the same economic and social developments that were facilitating the creation of socialist nations were also fostering the merger of those nations into the Soviet *narod*. He further contended that the Russian language, the "language of international exchange" in the USSR, was playing a decisive role in the latter—allowing for joint economic and political activities and for the creation of a general Soviet culture.[32] In effect, Bromlei was describing a process of double assimilation. To further this process, it was essential for all the peoples of the USSR to know their particular national histories, since consciousness of one's "origins" was an essential element of nationhood and contributed to "internal cohesion," Bromlei argued. At the same time, it was critical for each of the socialist nations to have a deep sense of its particular role in the revolution and its place in the Soviet whole.[33] Bromlei dismissed as "groundless" the claims of "Western Sovietologists" that the spread of the Russian language in the USSR and Eastern Europe, and the cultural integration of the socialist nations into the Soviet whole, were processes of Russification. He maintained that Soviet culture reflected the achievements of *all* of the socialist nations, and that these nations continued to use their own national languages and celebrate their own national cultures within their national territories.[34]

During the Brezhnev era, much of the conceptual work of imagining the merger of the socialist nations into the Soviet *narod* fell to sociologists. While ethnographers traced the origins of each socialist nation, sociologists charted the course to the communist future.[35] The "Leninist idea of internationalism"

29. Bromlei, *Ocherki teorii etnos*, 353. The Kamchadals were natives of Kamchatka and the Kerzheks were Old Believers (a schismatic group of the Russian Orthodox Church) who settled in Siberia. See Ronald Wixman, *The Peoples of the USSR: An Ethnographic Handbook* (Armonk, NY, 1984).

30. Bromlei, *Ocherki teorii etnosa*, 354.

31. Ibid.

32. Ibid., 363.

33. Ibid., 364–66.

34. Ibid., 363, 371.

35. See the articles in the published proceedings from the 1969 conference Soviet *Narod*. More than three hundred teachers and social scientists from throughout the USSR attended. P. M. Ro-

was grounded in "the objective sociological law of the development of na-tions," sociologists and other experts argued at a 1968 conference dedicated to the theme of the Soviet *narod*.[36] This law suggested that under socialism, as national and class antagonisms faded, developed socialist nations became in-creasingly similar to one another through a natural process of "mutual assim-ilation" or "merger." According to the experts, the merger of socialist nations differed from both "one-sided assimilation" and the consolidation of nations. The socialist nations of the USSR were not "dissolving" into the Soviet *narod*. Nor was the "Soviet-Russian nation" "swallowing up" other nations. Instead, each socialist nation was "borrowing elements" from all the others—and as a result had started to manifest a combination of its own internal traits *and* those of the entire Soviet *narod*.[37]

Reflecting on the nature of the Soviet *narod*, sociologists discussed the rela-tionship between "the parts and the whole." Whereas the American *narod* was a "conglomerate" of peoples united in a "single bourgeois state," the Soviet *narod* was an "organic whole, something more than the simple sum of its com-ponent parts," the experts argued.[38] The Soviet *narod*, like the nations that comprised it, took form through a process of historical development. But the Soviet *narod* was not a nation, and would never become one. Instead, it was a group that in its most developed form belonged to the postnational future of a "unified humankind." To get to that future, to create the "foundation for a higher phase of communism," it was imperative to eliminate "the remnants" (the survivals) of existing inequalities in the culture and material well-being of the socialist nations.[39] Sociologists maintained that the full merger of nations would happen sooner in the Soviet Union than elsewhere in the world. But the experts also warned that this process could not be rushed: that the "current stage" was not "the stage of the all-out merger of nations," but the stage of their "intensive coming together [*sblizhenie*]."[40]

During these years, ethnographers, sociologists, and other social scientists also brought their theories and narratives about the formation of the socialist nations and the Soviet *narod* to the general population. New history texts traced the origins of each of the socialist nations of the USSR. At the same time, richly illustrated books and pamphlets described the friendship of peoples

gachev et al., eds., *Sovetskii narod—novaia istoricheskaia obshchnost' liudei: Trudy mezhvu-zovskoi nauchnoi konferentsii*, vols. 1 and 2 (Volgograd, 1969).

36. Ts. A. Stepanian, "Sotsiologicheskii zakon razvitiia natsii—ob'ektivnaia osnova so-chetaniia internatsional'nykh i natsional'nykh zadach sovetskogo naroda," in *Sovetskii narod*, ed. Rogachev et al., vol. 1, 19–39 (esp. 19).

37. P. M. Rogachev and M. A. Sverdlin, "Mesto sovetskogo naroda sredi istoricheskikh ob-shchnostei liudei," and M. A. Andreev, "Sotsialisticheskaia natsiia v SSSR—sostavnaia chast' sovetskogo naroda," in *Sovetskii narod*, ed. Rogachev et al., vol. 1, 40–67, 178–82 (esp. 63–65).

38. Rogachev and Sverdlin, "Mesto sovetskogo naroda," 42, 45, and Andreev, "Sotsialistich-eskaia natsiia v SSSR," 178–80.

39. Rogachev and Sverdlin, "Mesto sovetskogo naroda," 41–44, 47.

40. Ibid., 66–67.

from the perspective of each of the socialist nations.[41] For example, a 1974 book produced in Tashkent commemorated the national-territorial delimitation of 1924 and celebrated the friendship between the Uzbeks and the other nations of the USSR. The book discussed each of the socialist nations from the Uzbek perspective: the chapter about the Russians, "First Among Equals," praised the Russian working class for the assistance that it had given to the Uzbeks after 1917; the chapter about Kazakhstan, "Brotherhood for Centuries," elaborated on the "historical roots" of Uzbek-Kazakh friendship and discussed how both peoples had consolidated into nations under the aegis of Soviet power. Meanwhile, another genre of books for the masses discussed with great enthusiasm the future merger of the socialist nations into the Soviet *narod*.[42]

Narratives about the formation of the socialist nations proved far more popular than narratives about their future disappearance or merger. Over the course of the 1920s and 1930s, membership in one of the official nationalities had become linked to land, national rights, and significant economic and cultural resources; local national leaders and their populations had learned to speak the language of *natsional'nost'*, articulating their identities and concerns in national terms in order to claim these benefits. In the postwar era, as the passport system spread throughout the USSR, nationality categories became even more embedded in the structure of Soviet life. Moreover, the division between socialist and outsider nations—and the idea that only the former were entitled to land and resources—became taken for granted. In this context, new histories which justified the special status of the socialist nations found natural audiences in the national republics and oblasts.

At the same time, pronouncements about the future merger of socialist nations provoked a hostile response. The very idea of a postnational future threatened the national leaders of the union republics and autonomous national oblasts, who had their own constituencies—and whose claims to power and successes in negotiating with Moscow were predicated on the idea that nations had rights. Moreover, for the non-Russians of the USSR, the choice of Russian as the language of international exchange looked and felt like Russification; Ukrainian and other dissidents said as much in the underground (*samizdat*) press, censuring Russia as a colonial power.[43] Feeding the resistance to the idea of merger was a growing lack of faith in the communist future.

41. For a discussion of the formation of each of the Soviet socialist nations see I. Maiatnikov, ed., *Formirovanie sotsialisticheskikh natsii v SSSR* (Moscow, 1962). This work drew on the research of Vasilii Bartol'd and other ethnographers. On the friendship of peoples see K. F. Fazylkhodzhaev, ed., *V druzhbe—nasha sila, nashe schast'e* (Tashkent, 1974).

42. See for example L. V. Metelitsa, *Rastsvet i sblizhenie sotsialisticheskikh natsii: Posobie dlia uchitelei* (Moscow, 1978), and A. I. Golovnev and A. P. Mel'nikov, eds., *Sblizhenie natsional'nykh kul'tur v protsesse kommunisticheskogo stroitel'stva* (Minsk, 1979).

43. See for example Ivan Dziuba, *Internatsionalizm chy rusyfikatsiia?* (Munich, 1968). This work was reprinted in Kiev in 1998.

For most Soviet citizens, Brezhnev's claim that the Soviet Union had achieved "developed socialism" rang hollow. As economic stagnation and corruption deepened, it became harder and harder to believe that the USSR was moving forward on the historical timeline.

The Census Lists and the Road to the Communist Future

The basic administrative-territorial structure of the Soviet state was in place by the eve of the Second World War. But the Soviet Union remained a work in progress, and the map of the USSR underwent notable changes during the postwar period. In the immediate wake of the war, the Chechens, Crimean Tatars, Volga Germans, Balkars, and other "enemy nations" were stripped of their national-territorial units; at the same time, the Latvians, Lithuanians, Estonians, and Moldavians were welcomed into the friendship of peoples as full-scale socialist nations with their own union republics. In the decades that followed, the map of the USSR also experienced a series of less dramatic changes. Representatives from the national republics and oblasts continued to petition Soviet leaders to reevaluate disputed territories, and Soviet commissions continued to adjust and readjust disputed borders—sometimes as little as several hundred feet in one direction or another. Border disputes between the Uzbeks and the Kirgiz in the Fergana Valley and around Tashkent, for example, remained contentious all the way up to (and after) 1991.

The "List of the Nationalities of the USSR," another important product of ethnographic knowledge, also sustained significant modifications during the postwar era. This was a consequence of practical as well as ideological considerations. The list, revised for each of the all-union censuses, was supposed to reflect the intensification of ethno-transformational processes in the USSR: to show that the regime's program of state-sponsored evolutionism was successful and that the population was progressing through the stages on the timeline of development. However, the timeline itself did not remain constant. Stalin's successors continued to trumpet the coming together and ultimate merger of the peoples of the USSR—but each in turn envisioned these processes happening at a more and more gradual pace. Thus, while Stalin had suggested in the late 1930s that the transition to communism (and thus the merger of nations) was imminent, Nikita Khrushchev predicted that the Soviet Union would not arrive at communism until 1980, and Leonid Brezhnev maintained that the Soviet Union would remain at its current stage of "developed socialism" for quite some time. Khrushchev and Brezhnev agreed that the merger of nations, while inevitable, should not be forced.[44]

44. For a discussion of the census lists in the postwar period also see Sergei Sokolovski, "The Kriashen Case in the 1926 and 2002 Russian Censuses: The Uses and Abuses of Anthropological Knowledge in Political Discourse," paper presented at the Ninth Annual Convention of the Association for the Study of Nationalities, April 2004.

While some experts (such as Bromlei) suggested that changes in the list of nationalities reflected the actual assimilation and consolidation of the peoples of the USSR, other ethnographers and demographers expressed skepticism.[45] Khrushchev's de-Stalinization campaign prompted an open discussion about the perversion of scientific knowledge under Stalin. Ethnographers involved in the production of the 1959 All-Union Census participated in this discussion and evaluated the impact of the Great Terror on the 1939 census. The experts concluded that the list of nationalities had been "artificially shortened" in 1939 "under the influence of Stalin's cult of personality."[46] The statistical-demographer Arkadii Isupov explained that Stalin, "making a speech about a draft of the Constitution of the USSR at the Eighth Congress of Soviets in 1936," had noted that it was "well-known" that "there are about 60 nations, national groups and *narodnosti* in the Soviet Union." As a result of this speech, experts had tabulated census data in 1939 for "only the 62 largest peoples of the USSR" and had cut other nationalities, including those who lived in their main mass "outside of the borders of the USSR," from the official list.[47]

In keeping with the political liberalization of the Khrushchev era, Soviet experts set out to undo the damage that had been done to the list of nationalities under Stalin. In particular, they endeavored to put back onto the list those nationalities that had been wrongly expunged.[48] In the late 1950s, ethnographers, linguists, and statisticians throughout the Soviet Union participated in deliberations about a new list for the 1959 All-Union Census—coming up with a final draft of 109 nationalities (78 *natsional'nosti* and 31 *narodnosti*), which they claimed corrected some of the mistakes of the Stalin era.[49] This list included a sizeable number of nationalities that had been relegated to the separate lists of diaspora nationalities and ethnographic groups in 1939. The Italians, French, Spanish, Romanians, Albanians, Japanese, Chinese, Afghans, Dungans, and Hungarians (Madiars) were among the diaspora nationalities

---

45. Bromlei, *Ocherki teorii etnosa.*

46. A. A. Isupov, *Natsional'nyi sostav naseleniia SSSR (Po itogam perepisi 1959 g.)* (Moscow, 1964), and S. I. Bruk and V. I. Kozlov, "Etnograficheskaia nauka i perepis' naseleniia 1970 goda," *Sovetskaia etnografiia,* no. 6 (1967): 6.

47. Isupov, *Natsional'nyi sostav naseleniia SSSR,* 12–13. Isupov discussed the creation of separate lists of national minorities (diaspora nationalities) and ethnographic groups.

48. Bruk and Kozlov, "Etnograficheskaia nauka i perepis'," 5–6. On the "liberalization of census procedures" under Khrushchev see Sokolovski, "The Kriashen Case in the 1926 and 2002 Russian Censuses," 4.

49. Isupov, *Natsional'nyi sostav naseleniia SSSR,* 12. For a discussion of the census program see Tsentral'noe statisticheskoe upravlenie, *Vsesoiuznaia perepis' naseleniia 1959 goda* (Moscow, 1958). For the list of nationalities, see Tsentral'noe statisticheskoe upravlenie, *Chislennost', sostav, i razmeshchenie naseleniia SSSR: Kratkie itogi Vsesoiuznoi perepisi naseleniia 1959 goda,* ed. Iu. S. Chuprova (Moscow, 1961), 35–37. Nine of the *narodnosti* are listed under the heading "*Narodnosti* of Dagestan" and 21 under the heading "*Narodnosti* of the North"; the Komi-Permiak *narodnost'* is listed under the Komi *natsional'nost'*. Sokolovski also notes that "109 groups" were enumerated in the 1959 census list; Isupov gives a different figure of "126 *natsional'nosti* and *narodnosti*," but does not cite a source.

brought back onto the main list; the Beludji, Karaims, Tats, Abazins, and Gagauz were among the peoples reincorporated from the list of ethnographic groups.[50]

Isupov, who hailed the expansion of the list of nationalities for the 1959 census as a triumph over the Stalin-era debasement of science, also called attention to the fact that the new list was still less than half the size of the list that had been used for the 1926 census.[51] In the years following the 1959 census, he and other experts, such as the ethnographers Viktor Kozlov and Solomon Bruk, offered several explanations for the divergence between the two lists—focusing in part on the nature of ethnographic knowledge. First, the experts pointed out that the 1926 and the 1959 censuses had used different criteria for their lists of nationalities. The 1926 census had taken *narodnost'* as its term of choice, so as to include peoples lacking national consciousness. The 1959 census had sought data about the population's national self-definition and had used a more exclusive list of *natsional'nosti*. According to the experts, a number of peoples that had been enumerated on the 1926 list still lacked national consciousness—and thus were not entitled to slots on the 1959 list.[52] Next, the experts maintained that the local statistical administrations which had helped put together the 1959 list had omitted some nationalities that should have been included: that local leaders and statisticians had in some cases made honest mistakes and in other cases presented false information in order to depict the main (titular) nation of their region as "more consolidated" than it was "in actual fact."[53]

But the most important reason for the divergence between the lists, according to Bruk and Kozlov, was that significant changes in the national composition of the Soviet population *had* transpired in the period between the 1926 and 1959 censuses. The ethno-transformational processes of assimilation and consolidation were undeniably taking place in the USSR, though at a slower pace than Stalin had claimed in the 1930s, they maintained. Moreover, with the excesses of the Stalin era accounted for, it was now possible to see that the Soviet population had made real progress on the road to the communist future—and that "Lenin's prediction about the coming together and merger of nations" was correct. Bruk and Kozlov offered a number of examples, pointing to the amalgamation of the Mishers, Kriashens, and Nagaibaks into the

---

50. Just about all of the nationalities that had been on the 1939 list were also included on the 1959 list, with the exception of the Oirots and Talysh.

51. Isupov, *Natsional'nyi sostav naseleniia SSSR,* 12–14.

52. Bruk and Kozlov, "Etnograficheskaia nauka i perepis'," 5–6, 9. According to Bruk and Kozlov, ethnographers had argued in 1926 that the term *narodnost'* was "more relevant" for "the broad masses of the population" since it was "more removed from the term *natsiia* which assumed national consciousness." Also see Isupov, *Natsional'nyi sostav naseleniia SSSR,* 12–13.

53. Bruk and Kozlov, "Etnograficheskaia nauka i perepis'," 8. Bruk and Kozlov noted that the Talysh, for example, had been omitted from the 1959 list because of "the mistaken idea" that they had become an "ethnographic group" of the Azerbaijani *natsional'nost'*.

Tatars; the Mingrelians, Svans, and Laz into the Georgians; and the dozen or so *narodnosti* of the Altai-Saian region into the Altai and the Khakass.[54] According to the ethnographers, these ethno-transformational processes were gradual, and it would take several generations for communities to completely lose their former national (or other group) consciousness. As a result, numerous Soviet citizens had been uncertain to which *natsional'nost'* to ascribe themselves in the 1959 census; some had attempted to register themselves as members of nationalities that were no longer on the official list.[55]

Bruk and Kozlov were members of a group of ethnographers involved in preparations for the 1970 All-Union Census—and working on yet another revised "List of the Nationalities of the USSR." The final version of this new list included 104 nationalities (73 *natsional'nosti* and 31 *narodnosti*), and, according to Soviet leaders and experts, provided evidence of the continuing progress of the ethno-transformational processes of assimilation and consolidation under Brezhnev.[56] In actual fact, the most significant difference from the 1959 list was the elimination of a number of "foreign" (diaspora) nationalities, such as the Italians, Spanish, Chinese, Japanese, Arabs, Turks, Yugoslavs, and Vietnamese. Using the diaspora nationalities in this manner— adding them to the list to "right the wrongs" of the past and omitting them to shorten the list and "prove" that the USSR was moving toward communism— was becoming a common practice.[57] Indeed, the list of nationalities was cut slightly in a similar manner for the 1979 All-Union Census. The 1979 list contained 101 nationalities—68 *natsional'nosti* and 33 *narodnosti*.[58] The most significant change was the removal of the French, Albanians, and Afghans.[59] Soviet experts, reflecting on the minimal differences between the 1970 and

54. Ibid., 7–8. Isupov gave other examples of this phenomenon. See Isupov, *Natsional'nyi sostav naseleniia SSSR*, 34.

55. Bruk and Kozlov, "Etnograficheskaia nauka i perepis'," 7–8. Isupov made a similar point, noting that some peoples belonging to the Ukrainian and Georgian nations (the Bukovinians and the Khevsurs, for example) still "define their *natsional'nost'* with local names." Isupov, *Natsional'nyi sostav naseleniia SSSR*, 11–12.

56. This list is from G. M. Maksimova, ed., *Vsesoiuznaia perepis' naseleniia 1970 goda: Sbornik statei* (Moscow, 1976), 196–98. For a discussion of the census program see B. T. Kolpakov, *Vsesoiuznaia perepis' naseleniia 1970 goda* (Moscow, 1969). This list included twenty *narodnosti* under the header "*Narodnosti* of the North, Siberia, and Far East," ten *narodnosti* under "*Narodnosti* of Dagestan," and the Komi-Permiak *narodnost'* as a group belonging to the Komi *natsional'nost'*.

57. The 1970 list saw the addition of a new collective *natsional'nost'*, the "Peoples of India and Pakistan." It also saw the "promotion" of the Aleuts and Eskimos from *narodnosti* to *natsional'nosti*, and several other changes.

58. This list is from I. P. Zinchenko, "Natsional'nyi sostav naseleniia SSSR," in *Vsesoiuznaia perepis' naseleniia 1979 goda: Sbornik statei*, ed. A. A. Isupov and N. Z. Shvartser (Moscow, 1984), 152–54. There were twenty-three narodnosti listed under "*Narodnosti* of the North" and ten listed under "*Narodnosti* of Dagestan." On this list the Komi-Permiaks were elevated to a *natsional'nost'*.

59. This list also saw the removal of the "Peoples of India and Pakistan" and the demotion of the Tofalars, Eskimos, and Aleuts to *narodnosti* belonging to the "*Narodnosti* of the North."

1979 lists, observed that the processes of assimilation and consolidation were slowing down in the conditions of "developed socialism" but undoubtedly would continue to have a significant role in the life of the peoples of the USSR.[60]

1989, 1991, and Beyond

Mikhail Gorbachev's policies of *glasnost'* and *perestroika* sparked a widespread demand in the USSR to learn the truth about—and right the wrongs of—the Soviet past. Open discussion ensued about the deportation of the Crimean Tatars, Chechens, and other nationalities, as well as about the Soviet policies of forced assimilation and linguistic Russification. Gorbachev, who was intent on making the Soviet Union a viable socialist state in the present, eschewed the longstanding Bolshevik rhetoric about the merger of nations—instead calling for mutual respect and cooperation. He further proclaimed that "even the smallest" ethnic groups were entitled to national rights.[61] In this new political climate, peoples that did not have status as official nationalities lobbied for it, and those that already had such status demanded greater autonomy. The 1989 All-Union Census took place against this backdrop.

In the spirit of the times, the 1989 census saw a still more dramatic expansion of the "List of the Nationalities of the USSR." The revised list included 128 nationalities (102 *natsional'nosti* and 26 *narodnosti*); this represented a significant increase from the 101 nationalities recognized in the 1979 census.[62] The ethnographers and statisticians who compiled this list had reincorporated many of the foreign (diaspora) nationalities that had been omitted from the 1979 list, such as the French, Italians, Spanish, Albanians, Chinese, Japanese, Arabs, and Afghans. The experts had also added several foreign nationalities that had never had their own spots on the list, such as the Austrians and Cubans. The new list also included a number of peoples that had vanished from the list in the late 1930s, such as the Mountain Jews, Georgian Jews, Central Asian Jews, and Chuvans. Perhaps most significant, groups formerly cataloged under the umbrella group "*Narodnosti* of Dagestan" (the Avars, Laks, Lezgins, and others) were separated out and recognized as full-fledged *natsional'nosti*.[63]

---

60. Bromlei, *Ocherki teorii etnosa*, 354.

61. Mikhail Gorbachev, *Perestroika: New Thinking for Our Country and the World* (New York, 1987), 104–7.

62. The twenty-six *narodnosti* were listed under the header "*Narodnosti* of the North." Gosudarstvennyi komitet SSSR po statistike, *Naselenie SSSR: Po dannym Vsesoiuznoi perepisi naseleniia 1989 g.*, ed. A. A. Isupov et al. (Moscow, 1990), 37–40. On the organization of the census see Gosudarstvennyi komitet SSSR po statistike, *Vsesoiuznaia perepis' naseleniia 1989 goda* (Moscow, 1987).

63. Gosudarstvennyi komitet SSSR po statistike, *Naselenie SSSR: Po dannym Vsesoiuznoi perepisi naseleniia 1989 g.*, ed. A. A. Isupov et al., 37–40.

The deliberations surrounding the production of the 1989 list, as well as the general attention given to the nationality question under Gorbachev, were clear indications of the immense significance of national categories in the Soviet Union. Over the previous seven decades, it had become widely understood that only the official nationalities were entitled to land, rights, and economic and cultural resources. As people used nationality-based institutions and demanded national rights—and as Soviet experts created official histories for all of the Soviet nations—"nationality" became *the* most important official category of identity for Soviet citizens. Of course, nations were still supposed to wither away in the far-off future. But as it turned out, the party-state withered away first.

Neither nationalism nor national tensions caused the collapse of the Soviet Union in 1991.[64] Overextension, economic decline, and a loss of faith in the communist future (among the general population as well as the most faithful) were far more important factors in destabilizing and bringing down "the last empire."[65] In the end, Soviet leaders and experts were unable to provide a compelling and convincing narrative of where the Soviet Union was headed. Once the collapse was in motion, however, the "principle of nationality" became a rallying point in the national republics and oblasts. Indeed, the tremendous success of Soviet nation-building efforts, combined with the fact that nations enjoyed rights on the international stage, made "the nation" seem like the natural form of organization for the post-Soviet successor states. All of the official Soviet nationalities already had their own national institutions, cultures, languages, and elites, as well as a developed sense of national consciousness; the largest socialist nations also had their own national-territorial units and governments. All of this facilitated the dissolution of the USSR along national lines and eased what many non-Russians came to hail after 1991 as a process of decolonization.

But the Soviet Union had been much more than a collection of nation-state units—and the complex legacy of Soviet rule has presented serious challenges for the successor states. First of all, despite the failure of postwar reforms, the party-state had succeeded in economically integrating the union republics through the "internationalization of the division of labor." As a result, the republics were economically dependent on Moscow and on one another, making it difficult for them to go it alone after 1991. Second, the national republics

---

64. Here I disagree with Ronald Grigor Suny, *The Revenge of the Past: Nationalism, Revolution and the Collapse of the Soviet Union* (Stanford, 1994).

65. For an argument about economic stagnation and the Soviet collapse see Stephen Kotkin, *Armageddon Averted: The Soviet Collapse, 1970–2000* (New York, 2001). For an argument about loss of faith and the collapse see David Remnick, *Lenin's Tomb: The Last Days of the Soviet Empire* (New York, 1993). On Soviet overextension during the Cold War see Jacques Levesque, *The Enigma of 1989: The USSR and the Liberation of Eastern Europe* (Berkeley, 1997). For a characterization of the Soviet Union as "the last empire" see Robert Conquest, ed., *The Last Empire: Nationality and the Soviet Future* (Stanford, 1986).

never constituted homogeneous nation states; instead, they housed ethnically diverse populations, governed through smaller national-territorial units within their borders. The collapse of the all-union framework and the transformation of the republics into self-proclaimed nation states—with rigid borders and less tolerance for minorities—created a new type of diaspora problem throughout the post-Soviet sphere.[66] Finally, in search of legitimacy, the new nation states have sought to disentangle themselves from the Soviet past with its triumphalist narrative of Soviet-sponsored development. To this end some of the successor states have taken what was most useful from their Soviet-produced histories to create new historical narratives that celebrate their victorious struggles for national independence. Others have looked to the era before 1917 for "usable pasts." For all of these states, the process of de-Sovietization remains very much a work in progress.

66. All of the new nation states have had to deal with their own nationality questions, and have had to decide whether to include a question about "nationality" in their censuses as well as whether to register "nationality" in their passports. On censuses and passports in the successor states see Dominique Arel, "Demography and Politics in the First Post-Soviet Censuses: Mistrusted State, Contested Identities," *Population* 57, no. 6 (2002): 801–28, and "Fixing Ethnicity in Identity Documents: The Rise and Fall of Passport Nationality in Russia," *Canadian Review of Studies in Nationalism* 30 (2003): 125–36. All of the successor states that have conducted censuses thus far have included a question about nationality.

APPENDIX 1

List of *Natsional'nosti* for the 1920 Census

1. Russian
2. Ukrainian, Galician, Little Russian, Rusin
3. Belorussian
4. Pole
5. Serbo-Croatian, Dalmatian, Croatian, Bosnian, Montenegrin
6. Bulgarian
7. Other Slavs[1]
8. Lithuanian, Zhmud
9. Latvian, Livonian
10. Romanian, Moldavian, Wallachian
11. Other Romanian peoples[2]
12. German, Bavarian
13. English, American, Irish, Scottish, Australian, New Zealander
14. Scandinavians[3]
15. Other Germanic peoples[4]
16. Persian, Tajik, Tat, Talysh
17. Ossetian, Digor
18. Armenian
19. Greek
20. Gypsy
21. Other Indo-Europeans[5]
22. Jew
23. Other Semites[6]
24. Esti [*Estonian*]
25. Finn[7]

1. Macedonian, Slovenian, Czech, Moravian, Slovak
2. Italian, Spaniard, Portuguese, French, Belgian, Alsatian, Argentinian
3. Swede, Norwegian, Dane
4. Flemish, Austrian, Swiss, Dutch
5. Albanian, Hindu, Arnaut, Kurd, Afghan
6. Arab, Syro-Chaldean Aisor, Syrian, Assyrian
7. Chukhon

26. Karelian, Chud, Izhora
27. Votiak
28. Zyrian
29. Permiak
30. Mordva [*Mordvinian*]
31. Mari
32. Tatar
33. Karaim
34. Chuvash
35. Bashkir, Teptiar, Meshcheriak, Besermian
36. Karachai
37. Kumyk
38. Nogai
39. Balkar
40. Kirgiz, Kara-Kirgiz, Kara-Kumyk
41. Turkmen, Trukhmen, Tekin
42. Other Tiurks[8]
43. Kalmyk
44. Mongol-Buriat
45. Samoed
46. Tungus
47. Other Ural-Altaic peoples[9]
48. Georgian, Imeretian, Mingrelian, Svan, Guri, Khevsur, Tushin, Abkhaz
49. Cherkess, Bzhedug, Abazin, Beslenei, Adygei
50. Kabardinian
51. Chechen, Ingush
52. Other peoples of the Caucasus[10]
53. Chinese, Japanese, Korean, Manchurian
54. Other *narodnosti*[11]
55. *Natsional'nosti* not noted

This list is based on the list in "Statisticheskii ezhegodnik 1922 i 1923 gg," *Trudy Tsentral'nogo statisticheskogo upravleniia* 8, no. 5 (Moscow, 1924), 48–53. For alternate spellings see Ronald Wixman, *The Peoples of the USSR: An Ethnographic Handbook* (Armonk, New York, 1988). The names in brackets and italics are synonyms that were not included on the original list.

8. Turk, Karapapakh, Nagaibak, Karagas, Iasta, Shor, Gagauz, Bukharan, Sart, Uzbek, Taranchi, Kashgar, Iakut
9. Lopar, Vogul, Ostiak, Hungarian, Madiar, Chukhar
10. Lezgin, Dagestani, Lak, Udin, Dargin, Tavlin, Tabasaran, Kiurin
11. Basque, Abyssinian, Negro

APPENDIX 2

List of the *Narodnosti* of the USSR for the 1926 Census (Published in 1927)

1. Russian (Great Russian)
2. Ukrainian
3. Belorussian
4. Pole
5. Czech
6. Slovak
7. Serb
8. Bulgarian
9. Latvian
10. Lithuanian
11. Latgalian
12. Zhmud (Zhmudin)
13. German
14. English
15. Swede
16. Dutch
17. Italian
18. French
19. Romanian
20. Moldavian
21. Greek (Ellino)
22. Albanian (Arnaut)
23. Jew
24. Crimean Jew
25. Mountain Jew (Dag Chufut)
26. Georgian Jew
27. Central Asian Jew (Dzhugur)
28. Karaim
29. Finn
30. Leningrad Finn (Chukhon)
31. Karelian
32. Tavas
33. Estonian (Esti)
34. Veps (Chukhar, Chud, Kaivan)
35. Vod (Vot, Vad, Vad'd'alaiset)
36. Izhora (Ingrian)
37. Kven
38. Lopar (Saami)
39. Zyrian (Komi)
40. Permiak
41. Votiak (Udmurt)
42. Besermian
43. Mari (Cheremis)
44. Mordva (Moksha, Erzya, Teryukhan, Karatai) [*Mordvinian*]
45. Madiar (Hungarian)
46. Gagauz
47. Chuvash

48. Tatar
49. Misher (Meshcheriak)
50. Bashkir (Bashkurd)
51. Nagaibak
52. Nogai
53. Gypsy
54. Kalmyk
55. Mongol
56. Buriat
57. Sart-Kalmyk
58. Vogul (Mansi)
59. Ostiak (Khanty)
60. Ostiako-Samoed [*Sel'kup*]
61. Samoed (Khasava, Piankhasava) [*Nenets*]
62. Iurak [*Yurak*]
63. Soiot (Soion, Uriankhai, Tuba) [*Tuvinian*]
64. Barabin (Baraba Tatar)
65. Bukharan (Bukharlyk)
66. Cherneviy Tatar (Tubalar, Tuba-Kizhi)
67. Altai (Altai-Kizhi, Mountain or White Kalmyk)
68. Teleut
69. Telengit (Telengut)
70. Kumandin (Lebedin, Ku-Kizhi)
71. Shors
72. Karagas (Tuba, Karagaz)
73. Kizil (Kyzyl)
74. Kachin
75. Sagai
76. Koibal (Kaibal)
77. Beltir
78. Dolgan (Dolgan-Iakut)
79. Iakut (Sakha, Urangkhai-Sakha)
80. Tungus (Ovenk, Murchen) [*Evenk*]
81. Lamut [*Even*]
82. Orochon
83. Goldi (Nanai)
84. Olchi (Mangun, Ulchi)
85. Negidal (Negda, Eleke Beye)
86. Orochi
87. Udegei [*Ude*]
88. Orok
89. Manegir
90. Samogir
91. Manchurian
92. Chukchi
93. Koriak
94. Kamchadal (Itel'men)
95. Giliak (Nivkhi)
96. Iukagir [*Odul*]
97. Chuvan

98. Aleut [*Unangan*]
99. Eskimo [*Inuit*]
100. Enisei (Ket, Enisei Ostiak)
101. Aino (Ainu, Kuchi)
102. Chinese
103. Korean
104. Japanese
105. Georgian (Kartvelian)
106. Ajar
107. Megreli (Mingrelian)
108. Laz (Chan)
109. Svan (Svanetian)
110. Abkhaz (Abkhazian)
111. Cherkess (Adygei)
112. Beskesek-Abaza (Abazin)
113. Kabardinian
114. Ubykh
115. Chechen (Nakh, Nakhchuo)
116. Ingush (Galgai, Kist)
117. Batsbi (Tsova-Tush, Batsaw)
118. Maistvei (Makhosh)
119. Lezgin (Kiurin)
120. Tabasaran
121. Agul
122. Archi
123. Rutul (Mykhad)
124. Tsakhur
125. Khinalug
126. Dzhek (Dzhektsy)
127. Khaput (Gaputlin, Khaputlin)
128. Kryz
129. Budukh (Budug)
130. Udin
131. Dargin
132. Kubachin (Ughbug)
133. Lak (Kazi-Kumukh)
134. Avar (Avartsy, Khunzal)
135. Andi (Andiitsy, Kwanaly)
136. Botlig (Buikhatli)
137. Godoberi
138. Karatai [*Karata*]
139. Akhvakh
140. Bagulal (Kvanandin)
141. Chamalal
142. Tindi (Tindal, Idera)
143. Didoi (Tsez)
144. Khvarshi
145. Kapuchin (Bezheta)
146. Khunzal (Enzebi, Nakhad)
147. Armenian

148. Khemshin
149. Arab
150. Aisor (Assyrian, Syrian, Chaldean)
151. Kaitak (Karakaitak)
152. Bosha (Karachi, Armenian Gypsy)
153. Ossetian (Os)
154. Kurd
155. Iezid (Yezid)
156. Talysh
157. Tat
158. Persian
159. Karachai
160. Kumyk
161. Balkar (Mountain Tatar, Malkar)
162. Karapapakh
163. Tiurk [*Azerbaijani Turk*]
164. Osman Turk (Osmanly)
165. Samarkand and Fergana Turk
166. Turkmen
167. Kirgiz (Kyrgyz, Kara-Kirgiz)
168. Karakalpak
169. Kipchak
170. Kashgar
171. Taranchi
172. Kazakh (Kirgiz-Kazakh, Kirgiz-Kaisak)
173. Kurama
174. Uzbek
175. Dungan
176. Afghan
177. Tajik
178. Vakhan
179. Ishkashim
180. Shugnan
181. Iagnob
182. Iazgul
183. Iranian
184. Djemshid
185. Beludji
186. Berber
187. Khazara
188. Hindu (Indian)
189. Other *narodnosti*
190. *Narodnosti* not noted or noted inexactly
  a) Tavlin
  b) Kriashen
  c) Teptiar
  d) Uigur
  e) Oirot
  f) Khakass
  g) Others

191. Foreign subjects

This list is based on Tsentral'noe statisticheskoe upravlenie SSSR, *Programmy i posobiia k razrabotke Vsesoiuznoi perepisi naseleniia 1926 goda*, vol. 7, *Perechen i slovar' narodnosti* (Moscow 1927), 6–7.

The names in parentheses are synonyms that were included on the original list. The names in brackets and italics are synonyms that were not included on the original list.

APPENDIX 3

Final List of the *Natsional'nosti* of the USSR (Nations, National Groups, and *Narodnosti*) for the 1939 Census

1. Russian (Great Russian)
2. Ukrainian
3. Belorussian
4. Georgian
5. Azerbaijani
6. Armenian
7. Uzbek
8. Turkmen
9. Tajik
10. Kazakh
11. Kirgiz
12. Karelian
13. Komi
14. Bashkir
15. Udmurt
16. Tatar
17. Mari
18. Mordva [*Mordvinian*]
19. Chuvash
20. German
21. Kalmyk
22. Buriat
23. Iakut
24. Jew
25. Kabardinian
26. Balkar
27. Chechen
28. Ingush
29. Ossetian
30. Avar
31. Dargin
32. Lak
33. Kumyk
34. Lezgin
35. Tabasaran
36. Moldavian
37. Abkhaz

38. Karakalpak
39. Adygei
40. Karachai
41. Oirot
42. Khakass
43. Koriak (Nymylan)
44. Mansi (Vogul)
45. Nanai
46. Nenets
47. Nivkhi (Giliak)
48. Saami
49. Sel'kup (Ostiako-Samoed)
50. Udegei
51. Khanty
52. Chukchi (Luorovetlan)
53. Shor
54. Evenk
55. Even (Lamut)
56. Veps
57. Izhora
58. Nogai
59. Abazin
60. Talysh
61. Uigur
62. Gypsy

This list is based on RGAE f. 1562, op. 336, d. 208, ll. 7–8.

APPENDIX 4

List of National Minorities (Diaspora Nationalities) for the 1939 Census

1. Albanian
2. American
3. English
4. Afghan
5. Basque
6. Belgian
7. Bulgarian
8. Dutch
9. Greek
10. Dungan
11. Iranian (Persian)
12. Spaniard
13. Italian
14. Chinese
15. Korean
16. Latgalian
17. Latvian

18. Lithuanian
19. Norwegian
20. Pole
21. Romanian
22. Serb
23. Slovak
24. Turk
25. Finn
26. French
27. Czech
28. Swede
29. Estonian
30. Japanese

This list based on RGAE f. 1562, op. 336, d. 205, l. 870b. (but with the addition of Bulgarian and Greek).

BIBLIOGRAPHY

Archival Sources

GOSUDARSTVENNYI ARKHIV ROSSIISKOI FEDERATSII (GARF). MOSCOW

f. 1235 Vserossiiskii tsentral'nyi ispolnitel'nyi komitet RSFSR (VTsIK RSFSR)
f. 1318 Narodnyi komissariat po delam natsional'nostei (Narkomnats)
f. 3316 Tsentral'nyi ispolnitel'nyi komitet SSSR (TsIK SSSR)
f. 5677 VTsIK Administrativnaia komissiia
f. 6892 TsIK SSSR Komissiia po raionirovaniiu, 1921–1929
f. 7523 Verkhovnyi sovet SSSR
f. 9401 MVD Spetsotdel

ARKHIV RUSSKOGO GEOGRAFICHESKOGO OBSHCHESTVA (RGO). ST. PETERSBURG

f. 24 Komissiia po sostavleniiu etnograficheskikh kart Rossii
f. 48 Veniamin Petrovich Semenov-Tian-Shanskii

SANKT-PETERBURGSKII FILIAL ARKHIVA ROSSIISKOI AKADEMII NAUK (PFA RAN).
ST. PETERSBURG

f. 1 Konferentsiia AN
f. 2 Kantseliariia
f. 4 Leningradskoe otdelenie AN SSSR, Sekretnaia chast', 1924–1937
f. 135 Institut po izucheniiu narodov SSSR; Komissiia po izucheniiu plemennogo
    sostava naseleniia Rossii (SSSR)
f. 142 Institut antropologii i etnografii AN SSSR (1933–1935); Institut
    antropologii, arkheologii i etnografii AN SSSR (1935–1937)
f. 174 Sovet po izucheniiu proizvoditel'nykh sil
f. 208 Sergei F. Ol'denburg
f. 282 Materialy po deiatel'nosti L. Ia. Shternberga v MAE AN, Perepiska
    nauchno-organizatsionnogo kharaktera

ROSSIISKII ETNOGRAFICHESKII MUZEI (REM). ST. PETERSBURG

f. 2 Gosudarstvennyi muzei etnografii narodov SSSR

ROSSIISKII GOSUDARSTVENNYI ARKHIV EKONOMIKI (RGAE). MOSCOW

f. 260 Nauchno-issledovatel'skii kolkhoznoi institut
f. 396 Krest'ianskaia gazeta
f. 399 Sovet po izucheniiu proizvoditel'nykh sil
f. 1562 Tsentral'noe statisticheskoe upravlenie
f. 7446 Kolkhoztsentr SSSR i RSFSR

ROSSIISKII TSENTR KHRANENIIA I IZUCHENIIA DOKUMENTOV NOVEISHEI ISTORII
(RTsKhIDNI). MOSCOW

f. 17 Tsentral'nyi Komitet KPSS

TSENTRAL'NYI GOSUDARSTVENNYI ARKHIV ISTORIKO-POLITICHESKIKH DOKUMENTOV
SANKT-PETERBURGA (TsGAIPD SPb). ST. PETERSBURG

f. 9, op. 1 Otdel agitatsii i propagandy
f. 24, op. 8 Leningradskoi oblastnoi otdel ispolnitel'nyi komitet: Otdel narodnogo
    obrazovaniia
f. 4406, op. 1 Partiinaia organizatsiia Gosudarstvennogo Russkogo muzeiia

Selected Published Primary Sources

JOURNALS AND NEWSPAPERS

Antropologicheskii zhurnal
Chelovek
Ekonomicheskaia zhizn'
Etnograf-Issledovatel'
Etnografiia
Kraevedenie
Krasnaia letopis'
Krest'ianskaia gazeta
Narodnoe khoziaistvo Srednei Azii
Nauchnyi rabotnik
Novyi Vostok
Pravda
Revoliutsiia i natsional'nosti
Russkaia mysl'
Russkoe bogatstvo
Sovetskaia etnografiia
Sovetskii muzei
Sovetskoe stroitel'stvo
Vecherniaia Moskva
Vestnik Vremennogo pravitel'stva
Voprosy kolonizatsii
Vsemirnyi turist
Zhivaia starina
Zhizn' natsional'nostei

BOOKS, STENOGRAMS, REPORTS, SCHOLARLY WORKS

Akademiia nauk SSSR. *Nauchnye uchrezhdeniia Akademii nauk SSSR: Kratkoe obozrenie ko dniu desiatiletiia, 1917–1927.* Leningrad, 1927.
——. *Chuvashskaia respublika: Predvaritel'nye itogi rabot Chuvashskoi ekspeditsii Akademii nauk SSSR po issledovaniiam 1927 g.* Vol. 10, pt. 1 of *Materialy Komissii ekspeditsionnykh issledovanii.* Leningrad, 1929.
——. *Otchet o deiatel'nosti Akademii nauk SSSR [za 1930–34 gg.]* Leningrad, 1931–35.
Akademiia nauk SSSR. Kommissiia po izucheniiu estestvennykh proizvoditel'nykh sil soiuza. Vol. 2 of *Trudy Geograficheskogo otdela.* Leningrad, 1930.
Akademiia nauk SSSR. Sovet po izucheniiu proizvoditel'nykh sil. *Materialy Buriat-Mongol'skoi antropologicheskoi ekspeditsii 1931 goda,* pt. 1. *Obzor rabot ekspeditsii,* ed. G. I. Petrov et al. Leningrad, 1933.
——. *Problemy Tadzhikistana. Trudy Pervoi konferentsii po izucheniiu proizvoditel'nykh sil Tadzhikskoi SSR.* 2 vols. Leningrad, 1933–34.
——. *Uzbekistan. Trudy i materialy Pervoi konferentsii po izucheniiu proizvoditel'nykh sil Uzbekistana, 19–28 dekabriia 1932,* vol. 4. Leningrad, 1934.
——. *Problemy Buriat-Mongol'skoi ASSR. Trudy Pervoi konferentsii po izucheniiu proizvoditel'nykh sil Buriat-Mongol'skoi ASSR.* 2 vols. Moscow-Leningrad, 1935–36.
Aliev, Umar. *Natsional'nyi vopros i natsional'naia kul'tura v Severo-Kavkazskom krae (Itogi i perspektivy): K predstoiashchemu s"ezdu gorskikh narodov.* Rostov-on-Don, 1926.
Alieva, Svetlana, ed. *Tak eto bylo: Natsional'nye repressii v SSSR 1919–1952 gody.* 3 vols. Moscow, 1993.
Anuchin, D. N. *Geograficheskie raboty,* ed. A. A. Grigoriev. Moscow, 1954.
Arkhipov, N. B. *Sredne-Aziatskie respubliki.* Moscow-Leningrad, 1930.
Belinskii, V. G. *Izbrannye filosofskie sochineniia,* ed. M. T. Iovchuk and Z. V. Smirnova. 2 vols. Moscow, 1948.
Berg, L. S. *Naselenie Bessarabii: Etnograficheskii sostav i chislennost'.* Vol. 6 of Rossiiskaia Akademiia nauk, *Trudy Komissii po izucheniiu plemennogo sostava naseleniia Rossii.* Petrograd, 1923.
——. *Vsesoiuznoe geograficheskoe obshchestvo za sto let: 1845–1945.* Moscow, 1946.
Bogdanov, V. V. *D. N. Anuchin: Antropolog i geograf (1843–1923).* Moscow, 1940.
Bol'shaia sovetskaia entsiklopediia. Moscow, 1926–47.
Bottomore, Tom, and Patrick Goode, eds. and trans. *Austro-Marxism.* Oxford, 1978.
Bromlei, Iu. *Etnos i etnografiia.* Moscow, 1973.
——. *Ocherki teorii etnosa.* Moscow, 1983.
Bromley, Yu., ed. *Soviet Ethnology and Anthropology Today.* The Netherlands, 1974.
——, ed. *Soviet Ethnography: Main Trends.* Moscow, 1977.
Petrov, G. I. *Rasovaia teoriia na sluzhbe u fashizma.* Vol. 95 of *Izvestiia Gosudarstvennoi akademii material'noi kul'tury.* Moscow-Leningrad, 1934.
Chetvertoe soveshchanie TsK RKP s otvetstvennymi rabotnikami natsional'nykh respublik i oblastei v Moskve 9–12 iiunia 1923 g. (Stenograficheskii otchet). Moscow, 1923.

Dvenadtsatyi s"ezd Rossiiskoi kommunisticheskoi partii (bol'shevikov), Stenogra-ficheskii otchet, 17–25 aprelia 1923 g. Moscow, 1923.

Dziuba, Ivan. *Internatsionalizm chy rusyfikatsiia?* Munich, 1968.

Egorov, K. D., ed. *Raionirovanie SSSR: Sbornik materialov po raionirovaniiu s 1917 po 1925 godu.* Moscow and Leningrad, 1926.

Fazylkhodzhaev, K. F., ed. *V druzhbe—nasha sila, nashe schast'e.* Tashkent, 1974.

Fülöp-Miller, René. *The Mind and Face of Bolshevism: An Examination of Cultural Life in Soviet Russia,* trans. F. S. Flint and D. F. Tait. London, 1927.

Golovnev, A. I., and A. P. Mel'nikov, eds. *Sblizhenie natsional'nykh kul'tur v protsesse kommunisticheskogo stroitel'stva.* Minsk, 1979.

Gor'kii, A. M., and L. Z. Mekhlis, eds. *Tvorchestvo narodov SSSR.* Moscow, 1937.

Gosplan R.S.F.S.R., *Ekonomicheskoe raionirovanie Rossii: Materialy podkomissii po raionirovaniiu pri Gosudarstvennoi obshche-planovoi komissii S.T.O.* Moscow, 1921..

Gosudarstvennyi kolonizatsionnyi nauchno-issledovatel'skii institut. *Trudy Gosudarstvennogo kolonizatsionnogo nauchno-issledovatel'skogo instituta.* 3 vols. Moscow, 1924–26.

Gosudarstvennyi komitet SSSR po statistike. *Vsesoiuznaia perepis' naseleniia 1989 goda,* ed. V. T. Alferov et al. Moscow, 1987.

——. *Naselenie SSSR: Po dannym Vsesoiuznoi perepisi naseleniia 1989 g.,* ed. A. A. Isupov et al. Moscow, 1990.

Gosudarstvennyi nauchno-issledovatel'skii institut zemleustroistva i pereseleniia. Vol. 11 of *Trudy Gosudarstvennogo nauchno-issledovatel'skogo instituta zemleustroistva i pereseleniia.* Moscow, 1930.

Gosudarstvennyi Russkii muzei. *Otchet Russkogo muzeia za 1922 goda.* Petrograd, 1923.

——. *Etnograficheskii otdel Russkogo muzeia.* Petrograd, 1923.

——. *Otchetnaia vystavka Etnograficheskogo otdela za 1923 g.* Petrograd, 1924.

——. *Otchet Gosudarstvennogo Russkogo muzeia [za 1923–28 gg.]* Leningrad, 1924–29.

[——]. *Etnograficheskii teatr.* Leningrad, 1930.

[——]. *Gosudarstvennyi etnograficheskii teatr.* Leningrad, 1931.

Gozulov, A. I. *Perepisi naseleniia SSSR i kapitalisticheskikh stran.* Moscow, 1936.

Gurvich, G. S. *Istoriia sovetskoi konstitutsii.* Moscow, 1923.

Iamzin, I. L., and V. P. Voshchinin. *Uchenie o kolonizatsii i pereseleniakh.* Moscow-Leningrad, 1926.

Ilin, M. *New Russia's Primer: The Story of the Five-Year Plan,* trans. George S. Counts and Nucia P. Lodge. Boston, 1931.

Isupov, A. A. *Natsional'nyi sostav naseleniia SSSR (Po itogam perepisi 1959 g.).* Moscow, 1964.

Isupov, A. A., and N. Z. Shvartser, eds. *Vsesoiuznaia perepis' naseleniia 1979 goda: Sbornik statei.* Moscow, 1984.

Karskii, E. F. *Etnograficheskaia karta Belorusskago plemeni.* Vol. 2 of Rossiiskaia Akademiia nauk, *Trudy Komissii po izucheniiu plemennogo sostava naseleniia Rossii.* Petrograd, 1917.

Kastelianskii, A. I., ed. *Formy natsional'nago dvizheniia v sovremennykh gosudarstvakh: Avstro-Vengria, Rossiia, Germaniia.* St. Petersburg, 1910.

Kolpakov, B. T. *Vsesoiuznaia perepis' naseleniia 1970 goda.* Moscow, 1969.

Komissiia po raionirovaniiu Srednei Azii. *Territoriia i naselenie Bukhary i*

Khorezma: Bukhara. Vol 1, pt. 1 of *Materialy po raionirovaniiu Srednei Azii*. Tashkent, 1926.

Kotel'nikov, A. *Istoriia proizvodstva i razrabotki vseobshchei perepisi naseleniia*. St. Petersburg, 1909.

Kraevoi komissii po ucheta opyta raionirovaniia pri Severo-Kavkazskom kraevom ispolnitel'nom komitete. *Severnyi Kavkaz posle raionirovaniia (Itogi i vyvody)*. Rostov-on-Don, 1925.

Krasil'nikov, M. *Doklad Obshchesoiuznomu s"ezdu statistikov, 1–7 dekabriia 1926 g.* Moscow, 1926.

Kryzhanovskii, B. G. *Printsipy ekspozitsii etnograficheskogo muzeia*. Vol. 4 of *Muzeinoe delo*. Leningrad, 1926.

Krzhizhanovskii, G. M. *Khoziaistvennye problemy R.S.F.S.R. i raboty Gosudarstvennoi obshcheplanovoi komissii (Gosplana)*. Moscow, 1921.

——, ed. *Voprosy ekonomicheskogo raionirovaniia SSSR: Sbornik materialov i statei (1917–1929 gg.)* Moscow, 1957.

Lenin, V. I. *Polnoe sobranie sochinenii*. Moscow, 1958–1965.

Lenin, V. I., KPSS. *O bor'be s natsionalizmom: Dokumenty i materialy*. Moscow, 1985.

Leninskii sbornik, vol. 34. Moscow and Leningrad, 1942.

Lindener, B. A. *Raboty Rossiiskoi Akademii nauk v oblasti issledovaniia prirodnykh bogatstv Rossii: Obzor deiatel'nosti KEPS za 1915–21 gg.* Petrograd, 1922.

Lunacharskii, A. V. *Vospominaniia i vpechatleniia*. Moscow, 1968.

Maiatnikov, I., ed. *Formirovanie sotsialisticheskikh natsii v SSSR: Sbornik statei*. Moscow, 1962.

Maksimova, G. M., ed. *Vsesoiuznaia perepis' naseleniia 1970 goda: Sbornik statei*. Moscow, 1976.

Marr, N. Ia., ed. *Iazykovedenie i materializm*. Leningrad, 1929.

Metelitsa, L. V. *Rastsvet i sblizhenie sotsialisticheskikh natsii: Posobie dlia uchitelei*. Moscow, 1978.

Mikhaylov, N. *Soviet Geography: The New Industrial and Economic Distributions of the U.S.S.R.*, trans. Natalie Rothstein. London, 1935.

Murzaev, E. *Sredniaia Aziia: Fiziko-geograficheskii ocherk*. Moscow, 1957.

Nemchenko, M. *Natsional'noe razmezhevanie Srednei Azii*. Moscow, 1925.

O vvedenii edinoi pasportnoi sistemy v SSSR. Moscow, 1933.

Pipes, Richard, ed. *The Unknown Lenin: From the Secret Archives*. New Haven, 1996.

Popov, N. P. *Ekskursii v byt narodov SSSR* (Ekskursii po Etnograficheskomu otdelu Russkogo muzeia). Leningrad, 1925.

Pospelov, P. N. *Lenin i Akademiia nauk: Sbornik dokumentov*. Moscow, 1969.

Potapov, L. P. *Poezdka v kolkhozy Chemal'skogo aimaka Oirotskoi Avtonomnoi Oblasti*. Vol. 1 of Akademiia nauk SSSR, *Trudy Instituta po izucheniiu narodov SSSR*. Leningrad, 1932.

Pypin, A. N. *Istoriia russkoi etnografii*. 4 vols. St. Petersburg, 1890–1892.

Rogachev, P. M. et al., eds. *Sovetskii narod—novaia istoricheskaia obshchnost' liudei: Trudy mezhvuzovskoi nauchnoi konferentsii*. 2 vols. Volgograd, 1969.

Rossiiskaia Akademiia nauk. *Ob uchrezhdenii Komissii po izucheniiu plemennogo sostava naseleniia Rossii*. Vol. 1 of *Izvestiia Komissii po izucheniiu plemennogo sostava naseleniia Rossii*. Petrograd, 1917.

——. *Izvlecheniia iz protokolov zasedanii komissii v 1917 i 1918 godakh.* Vol. 2 of *Izvestiia Komissii po izucheniiu plemennogo sostava naseleniia Rossii.* Petrograd, 1919.

——. *Otchet o deiatel'nosti Rossiiskoi Akademii nauk za 1919 god.* Petrograd, 1920.

Rudenko, S. I. *Bashkiry: Istoriko-etnograficheskie ocherki.* Moscow, 1955.

Sabitch, V. M., E. M. Chepurkovskii, and L. V. Krylov, eds. *Chelovek.* Vol. 5 of *Proizvoditel'nye sily Dal'nego Vostoka.* Vladivostok, 1927.

Semenov-Tian-Shanskii, V. P., P. P. Semenov-Tian-Shanskii, and V. I. Lamanskii, eds. *Rossiia: Polnoe geograficheskoe opisanie nashego otechestva.* 11 vols. St. Petersburg, 1899–1914.

Shepilov, D. *Velikii sovetskii narod.* Moscow, 1947.

Shestakov, A. V., ed. *Kratkii kurs istorii SSSR.* Moscow, 1937.

Shternberg, Lev. *The Social Organization of the Gilyak,* ed. Bruce Grant. New York, 1999.

Sobranie postanovlenii i rasporiazhenii pravitel'stva SSSR. Moscow, 1938–46.

Sovet Narodnykh Komissarov Soiuza SSR. *Perechni: Otraslei narodnogo khoziaistva i truda, proizvodstv, zaniatii, natsional'nostei i tipov uchebnykh zavedenii vydeliaemykh pri razrabotke materialov Vsesoiuznoi perepisi naseleniia 1939 goda.* Moscow, 1939.

Sozonova, M. V. *Putevoditel' po vystavke Srednei Azii.* Leningrad, 1934.

Stalin, I. V. *Voprosy Leninizma.* Moscow, 1933.

——. *Marksizm i natsional'no-kolonial'nyi vopros: Sbornik izbrannykh statei i rechei.* Moscow, 1935.

——. *Doklad o proekte konstitutsii Soiuza SSR.* Moscow, 1936.

——. *Sochineniia.* 13 vols. Moscow, 1946–51.

Supinskii, A. K. *Belorussiia i BSSR (Putevoditel' po vystavke Gosudarstvennogo etnograficheskogo muzeia).* Leningrad, 1934.

S"ezdy sovetov RSFSR v postanovleniiakh i rezoliutsiiakh. Moscow, 1939.

Trainin, I. *SSSR i natsional'naia problema.* Moscow, 1924.

——. *Imperializm na Dal'nem Vostoke i SSSR.* Moscow, 1932.

——. *Bratskoe sodruzhestvo narodov SSSR.* Moscow, 1938.

——. *Natsional'noe i sotsial'noe osvobozhdenie Zapadnoi Ukrainy i Zapadnoi Belorussii.* Moscow, 1939.

——. *Velikoe sodruzhestvo narodov SSSR.* Moscow, 1946.

——. *Sovetskoe mnogonatsional'noe gosudarstvo.* Moscow, 1947.

——. *Natsional'nye protivorechiia v Avstro-Vengrii i ee raspad.* Moscow, 1947.

Troinitskii, N. A., ed. *Obshchii svod po imperii rezul'tatov razrabotki dannykh Pervoi vseobshchei perepisi naseleniia, proizvedennoi 28 ianvaria 1897 goda,* vol. 2. St. Petersburg, 1905.

Tsamerian, I. *Velikaia epokha formirovaniia i razvitiia sotsialisticheskikh natsii v SSSR.* Moscow, 1951.

Tsentral'noe upravlenie narodno-khoziaistvennogo ucheta SSSR. *Slovar' natsional'nostei dlia razrabotki Vsesoiuznoi perepisi naseleniia 1937 goda,* ed. O. Kvitkin et al. Moscow, 1937.

Tsentral'noe statisticheskoe upravlenie SSSR. *Trudy Tsentral'nogo statisticheskogo upravleniia.* Moscow, 1920–27.

——. *Programmy i posobiia k razrabotke Vsesoiuznoi perepisi naseleniia 1926 goda,* vol. 7. *Perechen' i slovar' narodnostei.* Moscow, 1927.

——. *Vsesoiuznaia perepis' naseleniia 1926 goda.* 59 vols. Moscow, 1928–33.

——. *Vsesoiuznaia perepis' naseleniia 1959 goda.* Moscow, 1958.

——. *Chislennost', sostav, i razmeshchenie naseleniia SSSR: Kratkie itogi Vsesoiuznoi perepisi naseleniia 1959 goda*, ed. Iu. S. Chuprova. Moscow, 1961.

Tsentral'nyi ispolnitel'nyi komitet. *Zasedanie TsIK Soiuza SSR*. 3 sessiia. Stenograficheskii otchet. Moscow, 1927.

Tucker, Robert C., ed. *The Lenin Anthology*. New York, 1975.

Vareikis, I., and I. Zelenskii, eds. *Natsional'no-gosudarstvennoe razmezhevanie Srednei Azii*. Tashkent, 1924.

Vos'moi s"ezd RKP(b): Protokoly. Moscow, 1959.

Vsesoiuznyi tsentral'nyi sovet professional'nykh soiuzov. *Soviet Folk Art*. Moscow, 1939.

Zakharov, V. P., M. P. Lepekhin, and E. A. Fomina, eds., *Delo po obvineniiu akademika S. F. Platonova*. Vol. 1 of *Akademicheskoe delo 1929–1931 gg.: Dokumenty i materialy sledstvennogo dela, sfabrikovannogo OGPU*, ed. Zh. I. Alferov and V. P. Leonov. St. Petersburg, 1993.

Zarubin, I. I. *Spisok narodnostei Turkestanskogo kraia*. Vol. 9 of Akademiia nauk SSSR, *Trudy Komissii po izucheniiu plemennogo sostava naseleniia Rossii i sopredel'nkh stran*. Leningrad, 1925.

——. *Naselenie Samarkandskoi oblasti*. Vol. 10 of Akademiia nauk SSSR, *Trudy Komissii po izucheniiu plemennogo sostava naseleniia SSSR i sopredel'nykh stran*. Leningrad, 1926.

[Zelenin, Dmitrii]. *Programma etnograficheskogo izucheniia kolkhozov*. Leningrad, 1930.

Selected Secondary Sources

Adams, Mark B. "Eugenics as Social Medicine in Revolutionary Russia: Prophets, Patrons, and the Dialectics of Discipline Building." In *Health and Society in Revolutionary Russia*, ed. Solomon and Hutchinson, 200–223.

——. "The Soviet Nature-Nurture Debate." In *Science and the Soviet Social Order*, ed. Graham, 94–138.

Adas, Michael. *Machines as the Measure of Men: Science, Technology, and Ideologies of Western Dominance*. Ithaca, 1989.

Ajayi, J. F. A. "Colonialism: An Episode in African History." In vol. 1 of *Colonialism in Africa, 1870–1960*, ed. L. H. Gann and Peter Duigan, 497–509. Cambridge, 1969.

Alampiev, P. M. *Ekonomicheskoe raionirovanie SSSR*. 2 vols. Moscow, 1959–63.

Allworth, Edward, ed. *Muslim Communities Reemerge: Historical Perspectives on Nationality, Politics, and Opposition in the Former Soviet Union and Yugoslavia*, trans. Caroline Sawyer. Durham, 1994.

Anderson, Benedict. *Imagined Communities: Reflections on the Origin and Spread of Nationalism*. Rev. ed. London, 1991.

Appadurai, Arjun. "Number in the Colonial Imagination." In *Orientalism and the Postcolonial Predicament: Perspectives on South Asia*, ed. Carol A. Breckenridge and Peter van der Veer, 314–39. Philadelphia, 1993.

Arel, Dominique. "Demography and Politics in the First Post-Soviet Censuses: Mistrusted State, Contested Identities." *Population* 57, no. 6 (2002): 801–28.

——. "Fixing Ethnicity in Identity Documents: The Rise and Fall of Passport Nationality in Russia." *Canadian Review of Studies in Nationalism* 30, no. 1–2 (2003): 125–36.

Arendt, Hannah. *Between Past and Future: Eight Exercises in Political Thought.* New York, 1968.

——. *The Origins of Totalitarianism.* Rev. ed. San Diego, 1979.

Asad, Talal. *Anthropology and the Colonial Encounter.* New York, 1973.

——. "Afterword: From the History of Colonial Anthropology to the Anthropology of Western Hegemony." In *Colonial Situations,* ed. Stocking, 314–24.

Bailes, Kendall E. *Technology and Society under Lenin and Stalin: Origins of the Soviet Technical Intelligentsia, 1917–1941.* Princeton, 1978.

——. "Natural Scientists and the Soviet System." In *Party, State, and Society in the Russian Civil War,* ed. Diane P. Koenker, William G. Rosenberg, and Ronald Grigor Suny, 267–95. Bloomington, 1989.

——. *Science and Russian Culture in an Age of Revolutions: V. I. Vernadsky and His Scientific School, 1863–1945.* Bloomington, 1990.

Bakhurst, David. "Political Emancipation and the Domination of Nature: The Rise and Fall of Soviet Prometheanism." *International Studies in the Philosophy of Science* 5, no. 3 (1991): 215–26.

Baldauf, Ingeborg. *"Kraevedeniia" and Uzbek National Consciousness.* Bloomington, 1992.

Batsell, Walter Russell. *Soviet Rule in Russia.* New York, 1929.

Bauman, Zygmunt. *Modernity and the Holocaust.* Ithaca, 1989.

Baziiants, A. P. "Dve vstrechi S. F. Ol'denburga s V. I. Leninym i razvitie sovetskogo vostokovedeniia." In *Sergei Fedorovich Ol'denburg,* ed. Skriabin et al., 21–28.

Benjamin, Walter. *Reflections: Essays, Aphorisms, Autobiographical Writings,* ed. Peter Demetz, trans. Edmund Jephcott. New York, 1978.

Bennigsen, Alexandre, and Marie Broxup. *The Islamic Threat to the Soviet State.* London, 1983.

Bennigsen, Alexandre, and Chantal Lemercier-Quelquejay. *Islam in the Soviet Union.* London, 1967.

Bennigsen, Alexandre, and S. Enders Wimbush. *Muslim National Communism in the Soviet Union: A Revolutionary Strategy for the Colonial World.* Chicago, 1979.

Bertrand, Frédéric. *L'anthropologie soviétique des années 20–30: Configuration d'une rupture.* Pessac, 2002.

Betts, Raymond R. "Association in French Colonial Theory." In *Historical Problems of Imperial Africa,* ed. Robert O. Collins, 154–64. Princeton, 1996.

Blank, Stephen. *The Sorcerer as Apprentice: Stalin as Commissar of Nationalities, 1917–1924.* Westport, CT, 1994.

Blum, Alain, and Martine Mespoulet. *L'anarchie bureaucratique: Statistique et pouvoir sous Staline.* Paris, 2003.

Bone, Jonathan. "Socialism in One Country: Stalinist Population Politics and the Making of the Soviet Far East, 1929–1939." Ph.D. diss., University of Chicago, 2003.

Bongard-Levin, G. M. "Indologicheskoe i buddologicheskoe nasledie S. F. Ol'denburga." In *Sergei Fedorovich Ol'denburg,* ed. Skriabin et al., 29–47.

Borys, Jurij. *The Sovietization of Ukraine, 1917–1923: The Communist Doctrine and Practice of National Self-Determination.* Edmonton, 1980.

Bradley, Joseph. "Subjects into Citizens: Societies, Civil Society, and Autocracy in

Tsarist Russia." *The American Historical Review* 107, no. 4 (2002): 1094–123.

Brandenberger, David. *National Bolshevism: Stalinist Mass Culture and the Formation of Modern Russian National Identity, 1931–1956.* Cambridge, MA, 2002.

Browder, Robert Paul, and Alexander F. Kerensky, eds. *The Russian Provisional Government, 1917.* 3 vols. Stanford, 1961.

Brower, Daniel. "Islam and Ethnicity: Russian Colonial Policy in Turkestan." In *Russia's Orient: Imperial Borderlands and Peoples, 1700–1917,* ed. Daniel R. Brower and Edward J. Lazzerini. Bloomington, 1997, 115–35.

Brubaker, Rogers. *Nationalism Reframed: Nationhood and the National Question in the New Europe.* Cambridge, 1996.

Bugai, N. F., ed. *Iosif Stalin—Lavrentiiu Berii: "Ikh nado deportirovat'": Dokumenty, fakty, kommentarii.* Moscow, 1992.

Bunzl, Matti. "Franz Boas and the Humboldtian Tradition: From Volksgeist and Nationalcharakter to an Anthropological Concept of Culture." In *Volksgeist as Method and Ethic,* ed. Stocking, 17–78.

Burleigh, Michael. *Germany Turns Eastwards: A Study of Ostforschung in the Third Reich.* Cambridge, 1998.

Cadiot, Juliette. "Les relations entre le centre et les régions en URSS à travers les débats sur les nationalités dans le recensement de 1926." *Cahiers du monde russe* 38, no. 4 (1997): 601–16.

Cannadine, David. *Ornamentalism: How the British Saw Their Empire.* New York, 2001.

Caroe, Olaf. *Soviet Empire: The Turks of Central Asia and Stalinism.* London, 1953.

Carr, E. H. *Socialism in One Country, 1924–1926.* 3 vols. New York, 1958–64.

———. *The Bolshevik Revolution, 1917–1923.* 3 vols. New York, 1950–53.

Castillo, Greg. "Peoples at an Exhibition: Soviet Architecture and the National Question." In *Socialist Realism without Shores,* ed. Thomas Lahusen and Evgeny Dobrenko, 91–119. Durham, 1997.

Chase, William J. *Enemies within the Gates? The Comintern and the Stalinist Repression, 1934–1939.* New Haven, 2001.

Clark, Katerina. *Petersburg: Crucible of Cultural Revolution.* Cambridge, MA, 1995.

Clowes, Edith, Samuel Kassow, and James West, eds. *Between Tsar and People: Educated Society and the Quest for Public Identity in Late Imperial Russia.* Princeton, 1991.

Cohen, G. A. *Karl Marx's Theory of History: A Defense.* Princeton, 2000.

Cohn, Bernard. "The Census, Social Structure, and Objectification in South Asia." In *An Anthropologist among the Historians and Other Essays,* ed. Bernard Cohn, 224–54. New Delhi, 1987.

———. *Colonialism and Its Forms of Knowledge: The British in India.* Princeton, 1996.

Connor, Walker. *The National Question in Marxist-Leninist Theory and Strategy.* Princeton, 1984.

Conquest, Robert. *The Last Empire.* London, 1962.

———, ed. *The Last Empire: Nationality and the Soviet Future.* Stanford, 1986.

———. *The Great Terror: A Reassessment.* New York, 1990.

———. *Stalin: Breaker of Nations.* London, 1991.

Corney, Frederick. "Rethinking a Great Event: The October Revolution as Memory Project." *Social Science History* 22, no. 4 (1998): 389–414.

Crais, Clifton. "Chiefs and Bureaucrats in the Making of Empire: A Drama from the Transkei, South Africa, October 1880." *The American Historical Review* 108, no. 4 (2003): 1034–60.

Darrow, David W. "Census as a Technology of Empire." *Ab Imperio,* no. 4 (2002): 145–76.

David-Fox, Michael. *Revolution of the Mind: Higher Learning Among the Bolsheviks, 1918–1929.* Ithaca, 1997.

——. "What is Cultural Revolution?" *The Russian Review* 58, no. 2 (1999): 181–201.

Dawisha, Karen, and Bruce Parrot, eds. *The End of Empire? The Transformation of the USSR in Comparative Perspective.* Armonk, NY, 1997.

d'Encausse, Hélène Carrère. *The Great Challenge: Nationalities and the Bolshevik State, 1917–1930.* New York, 1992.

——. *The End of the Soviet Empire: The Triumph of the Nations.* New York, 1993.

Deschamps, Hubert Jules. "Association and Indirect Rule." In *Historical Problems of Imperial Africa,* ed. Robert O. Collins, 165–78. Princeton, 1996.

Dirks, Nicholas B., ed. *Colonialism and Culture.* Ann Arbor, 1992.

——. *Castes of Mind: Colonialism and the Making of Modern India.* Princeton, 2001.

Dumova, N. G. *Kadetskaia partiia v period pervoi mirovoi voiny i Fevral'skoi revoliutsii.* Moscow, 1988.

Edgar, Adrienne Lynn. Review of *The New Central Asia: The Creation of Nations,* by Olivier Roy. *Kritika: Explorations in Russian and Eurasian History* 3, no. 1 (2002): 182–90.

——. *Tribal Nation: The Making of Soviet Turkmenistan.* Princeton, 2004.

Edney, Matthew. *Mapping an Empire: The Geographical Construction of British India, 1765–1843.* Chicago, 1997.

Engelstein, Laura. *The Keys to Happiness: Sex and the Search for Modernity in Fin-de-Siècle Russia.* Ithaca, 1992.

Fabian, Johannes. *Time and the Other: How Anthropology Makes its Object.* New York, 1983.

Fedorova, M. I. *Pervaia Vsesoiuznaia sel'skokhoziaistvennaia vystavka.* Moscow, 1953.

Ferro, Marc. *October 1917: A Social History of the Russian Revolution,* trans. Norman Stone. London, 1980.

Fitzpatrick, Sheila. "Cultural Revolution as Class War." In *Cultural Revolution in Russia,* ed. Fitzpatrick, 8–40.

——, ed. *Cultural Revolution in Russia.* Bloomington, 1978.

——. *Education and Social Mobility in the Soviet Union.* Cambridge, 1979.

Foucault, Michel. *The Order of Things: An Archaeology of the Human Sciences.* New York, 1970.

——. *The Archaeology of Knowledge and the Discourse on Language,* trans. A. M. Sheridan Smith. New York, 1972.

——. "Governmentality." In *The Foucault Effect: Studies in Governmentality,* ed. Graham Burchell, Colin Gordon, and Peter Miller, 87–104. Chicago, 1991.

Fowkes, Ben. *The Disintegration of the Soviet Union: A Study in the Rise and Triumph of Nationalism.* New York, 1997.

Fragner, Bert G. "The Nationalization of the Uzbeks and Tajiks." In *Muslim Communities Reemerge,* ed. Allworth, 13–32.

Freeze, Gregory. "The *Soslovie* (Estate) Paradigm in Russian Social History." *The American Historical Review* 91, no. 1 (1986): 11–36.

Friedrich, Carl J., and Zbigniew K. Brzezinski. *Totalitarian Dictatorship and Autocracy.* Cambridge, MA, 1965.

Gagen-Torn, N. I. *Lev Iakovlevich Shternberg.* Moscow, 1975.

Gasparov, Boris. "Development or Rebuilding: The Views of Academician T. D. Lysenko in the Context of the Late Avant-Garde (late 1920–1930s)." In *Laboratory of Dreams: The Russian Avant-Garde and Cultural Experiment,* ed. John E. Bowlt and Olga Matich, 133–50. Stanford, 1996.

Gatrell, Peter. *A Whole Empire Walking: Refugees in Russia During World War I.* Bloomington, 1999.

Geertz, Clifford. *Local Knowledge: Further Essays in Interpretative Anthropology.* New York, 1983.

Gelb, Michael. "An Early Soviet Ethnic Deportation: The Far Eastern Koreans." *The Russian Review* 54, no. 3 (1995): 389–412.

Gellner, Ernest, ed. *Soviet and Western Anthropology.* London, 1980.

——. *Nations and Nationalism.* Ithaca, 1983.

Geraci, Robert. "Ethnic Minorities, Anthropology, and Russian National Identity on Trial: The Multan Case, 1892–96." *The Russian Review* 59, no. 4 (2000): 530–54.

Geyer, Dietrich. *Russian Imperialism: The Interaction of Domestic and Foreign Policy, 1860–1914.* Leamington Spa, UK, 1987.

Geyer, Michael. "Militarization of Europe, 1914–1945." In *The Militarization of the Western World,* ed. John Gillis, 65–102. New Brunswick, NJ, 1989.

Godina, L., M. L. Butovskaya, and A. G. Kozintsev. *History of Biological Anthropology in Russia and the Former Soviet Union.* Newcastle upon Tyne, 1993.

Golikov, G. I., ed. *Vladimir Il'ich Lenin: Biograficheskaia khronika.* 2 vols. Moscow, 1970.

Gorbachev, Mikhail. *Perestroika: New Thinking for Our Country and the World.* New York, 1987.

Graham, Loren R. *The Soviet Academy of Sciences and the Communist Party, 1927–1932.* Princeton, 1967.

——, ed. *Science and the Soviet Social Order.* Cambridge, MA, 1990.

——. *Science in Russia and the Soviet Union: A Short History.* Cambridge, 1993.

Grant, Bruce. *In the Soviet House of Culture: A Century of Perestroikas.* Princeton, 1995.

Gross, Jan T. *Revolution From Abroad: The Soviet Conquest of Poland's Western Ukraine and Western Belorussia.* Princeton, 1988.

Habermas, Jürgen. "Citizenship and National Identity: Some Reflections on the Future of Europe." In *Theorizing Citizenship,* ed. Ronald Beiner, 255–81. Albany, 1995.

Halfin, Igal. *From Darkness to Light: Class, Consciousness, and Salvation in Revolutionary Russia.* Pittsburgh, 2000.

Hanson, Stephen E. *Time and Revolution: Marxism and the Design of Soviet Institutions.* Chapel Hill, 1997.

Haugen, Arne. *The Establishment of National Republics in Soviet Central Asia.* Basingstoke, UK, 2003.

Hindus, Maurice. *The Great Offensive.* New York, 1933.

Hinsley, Curtis M. "The World as Marketplace: Commodification of the Exotic at the World's Columbian Exposition, Chicago 1893." In *Exhibiting Cultures: The Poetics and Politics of Museum Display,* ed. Ivan Karp and Steven D. Lavine, 344–65. Washington, DC, 1991.

Hobsbawm, Eric. *The Age of Empire, 1875–1914.* New York, 1989.

——. *Nations and Nationalism since 1780: Programme, Myth, Reality.* Cambridge, 1990.

Hoffman, David L. "European Modernity and Soviet Socialism." In *Russian Modernity,* ed. Hoffman and Kotsonis, 245–60.

Hoffman David L., and Yanni Kotsonis, eds. *Russian Modernity: Politics, Knowledge, Practices.* New York, 2000.

Holmes, Larry E. "Sergei Fedorovich Ol'denburg." In vol. 25 of *The Modern Encyclopedia of Russian and Soviet History,* ed. Joseph L. Wieczynski, 237–40. Gulf Breeze, FL, 1981.

Holquist, Peter. "To Count, to Extract, to Exterminate: Population Statistics and Population Politics in Late Imperial and Soviet Russia." In *A State of Nations: Empire and Nation-Making in the Age of Lenin and Stalin,* ed. Ronald Grigor Suny and Terry Martin, 111–44. New York, 2001.

——. *Making War, Forging Revolution: Russia's Continuum of Crisis, 1914–1921.* Cambridge, MA, 2002.

Honigmann, John J. *The Development of Anthropological Ideas.* Homewood, IL, 1976.

Horne, John. "Remobilizing for 'Total War': France and Britain, 1917–1918." In *State, Society, and Mobilization in Europe during the First World War,* ed. John Horne, 195–211. Cambridge, 1997.

Howell, Dana Prescott. *The Development of Soviet Folkloristics.* New York, 1992.

Janowsky, Oscar J. *Nationalities and National Minorities.* New York, 1945.

Joravsky, David. *Soviet Marxism and Natural Science, 1917–1932.* New York, 1961.

——. "The Construction of the Stalinist Psyche." In *Cultural Revolution in Russia,* ed. Fitzpatrick, 105–28.

Kagedan, Allan Laine. "The Formation of Soviet Jewish Territorial Units, 1924–1937." Ph.D. diss., Columbia University, 1985.

Karp, Ivan. "Culture and Representation." In *Exhibiting Cultures: The Poetics and Politics of Museum Display,* ed. Ivan Karp and Steven D. Lavine, 11–24. Washington, DC, 1991.

Keller, Shoshana. "The Central Asian Bureau: An Essential Tool in Governing Soviet Turkestan." *Central Asian Survey* 22, no. 2–3 (2003): 281–97.

Kenez, Peter. *The Birth of the Propaganda State: Soviet Methods of Mass Mobilization, 1917–1929.* Cambridge, 1985.

Kertzer, David, and Dominique Arel, eds. *Census and Identity: The Politics of Race, Ethnicity, and Language in National Censuses.* Cambridge, 2002.

Kessler, Gijs. "The Passport System and State Control over Population Flows in the Soviet Union, 1932–1940." *Cahiers du monde russe* 42, no. 2–4 (2001): 477–503.

Kevles, Daniel J. *In the Name of Eugenics: Genetics and the Uses of Human Heredity.* Cambridge, MA, 1985.

Khalid, Adeeb. *The Politics of Muslim Cultural Reform: Jadidism in Central Asia.* Berkeley, 1998.

Knight, Nathaniel. "Constructing the Science of Nationality: Ethnography in Mid-Nineteenth Century Russia." Ph.D. diss., Columbia University, 1994.

——. "Science, Empire, and Nationality in the Russian Geographical Society, 1845–1855." In *Imperial Russia: New Histories for the Empire*, ed. Jane Burbank and David L. Ransel, 108–41. Bloomington, 1998.

——. "Ethnicity, Nationality, and the Masses: *Narodnost'* and Modernity in Imperial Russia." In *Russian Modernity*, ed. Hoffman and Kotsonis, 41–64.

Kohn, Hans. *Nationalism in the Soviet Union*. New York, 1933.

Kojevnikov, Alexei. "The Great War, the Russian Civil War, and the Invention of Big Science." *Science in Context* 15, no. 2 (2002): 239–75.

Kolarz, Walter. *Communism and Colonialism*. London, 1964.

Kol'tsov, A. V. *Lenin i stanovlenie Akademii nauk kak tsentra sovetskoi nauki*. Leningrad, 1969.

Kornev, V. P., ed. *Vidnye deiateli otechestvennoi statistiki 1686–1990: Biografich-eskii slovar'*. Moscow, 1993.

Kotkin, Stephen. *Magnetic Mountain: Stalinism as a Civilization*. Berkeley, 1995.

——. *Armageddon Averted: The Soviet Collapse, 1970–2000*. New York, 2001.

Krasilina, G. N. "Iz opyta raboty sovetskikh muzeev po populiarizatsii i izucheniiu muzeinogo zriteliia v 1920e–1930e gody." In *Muzei 2 khudozhestvennye sobraniia SSSR*, 10–14. Moscow, 1981.

Kriukova, T. A., and E. N. Studenetskaia. "Gosudarstvennyi muzei etnografii narodov SSSR za piat'desiat let Sovetskoi vlasti." In *Ocherki istorii muzeinogo dela v SSSR*, 9–72 Moscow, 1971.

Lebovics, Herman. *True France: The Wars over Cultural Identity, 1900–1945*. Ithaca, 1992.

Levesque, Jacques. *The Enigma of 1989: The USSR and the Liberation of Eastern Europe*, trans. Keith Martin. Berkeley, 1997.

Levytsky, Boris, ed. *The Stalinist Terror in the Thirties: Documentation from the Soviet Press*. Stanford, 1974.

Lewin, Moshe. *Lenin's Last Struggle*, trans. A. M. Sheridan Smith. New York, 1968.

——. *Russian Peasants and Soviet Power: A Study of Collectivization*, trans. Irene Nove and John Biggart. Evanston, 1968.

——. *The Making of the Soviet System: Essays in the Social History of Interwar Russia*. New York, 1985.

Lewis, Martin D. "One Hundred Million Frenchmen: The 'Assimilation' Theory in French Colonial Policy." *Comparative Studies in Society and History* 4, no. 2 (1962): 129–53.

Lieven, Dominic. *Empire: The Russian Empire and Its Rivals*. New Haven, 2000.

Liulevicius, Vejas Gabriel. *War Land on the Eastern Front*. Cambridge, 2000.

Lohr, Eric. *Nationalizing the Russian Empire: The Campaign Against Enemy Aliens during World War I*. Cambridge, MA, 2003.

Longino, Helen E. *Science as Social Knowledge: Values and Objectivity in Scientific Inquiry* Princeton, 1990.

Lorenz, Richard. "Economic Bases of the Basmachi Movement in the Farghana Valley." In *Muslim Communities Reemerge*, ed. Allworth et al., 277–303.

Lunin, B. V. "Istorik vostokovedeniia (Iz nauchnogo naslediia akademika S. F. Ol'-denburga)." In *Sergei Fedorovich Ol'denburg*, ed. Skriabin et al., 58–83.

Macartney, C. A. *National States and National Minorities*. London, 1934.

Mackenzie, John M. *Propaganda and Empire: The Manipulation of British Public Opinion, 1880–1960*. Manchester, 1990.

MacMillan, Margaret. *Paris 1919: Six Months that Changed the World*. New York, 2001.

Magidoff, Robert. *In Anger and in Pity*. Garden City, NY, 1949.

Makarova, G. P. *Narodnyi komissariat po delam natsional'nostei RSFSR, 1917–1923 gg.: Istoricheskii ocherk*. Moscow, 1987.

Malia, Martin. *The Soviet Tragedy: A History of Socialism in Russia, 1917–1991*. New York, 1994.

Martin, Terry. "The Origins of Soviet Ethnic Cleansing." *Journal of Modern History* 70, no. 4 (1998): 813–61.

——. "Modernization or Neo-traditionalism? Ascribed Nationality and Soviet Primordialism." In *Stalinism: New Directions*, ed. Sheila Fitzpatrick, 348–67. New York, 2000.

——. *The Affirmative Action Empire: Nations and Nationalism in the Soviet Union, 1923–1939*. Ithaca, 2001.

Masov, Rakhim Masovich. *Istoriia topornogo razdeleniia*. Dushanbe, 1991.

——. *Tadzhiki: Istoriia s grifom "sovershenno sekretno."* Dushanbe, 1995.

Massell, Gregory J. *The Surrogate Proletariat: Moslem Women and Revolutionary Strategies in Soviet Central Asia, 1919–1929*. Princeton, 1974.

Matthews, Mervyn. *The Passport Society: Controlling Movement in Russia and the USSR*. Boulder, 1993.

Mayer, Arno. *Wilson vs. Lenin: Political Origins of the New Diplomacy, 1917–1918*. Cleveland, 1964.

Mazower, Mark. *Dark Continent: Europe's Twentieth Century*. New York, 1998.

Melik'ian, G. G., and A. Ia. Kvasha, eds. *Narodonaselenie: Entsiklopedicheskii slovar'*. Moscow, 1994.

Michaels, Paula A. "Medical Propaganda and Cultural Revolution in Soviet Kazakhstan, 1928–41." *The Russian Review* 59, no. 2 (2000): 159–78.

Mieczkowski, Z. "The Economic Regionalization of the Soviet Union in the Lenin and Stalin Period." *Canadian Slavonic Papers* 8 (1966): 89–124.

Miller, Frank J. *Folklore for Stalin: Russian Folklore and Pseudofolklore in the Stalin Era*. Armonk, NY, 1990.

Mitchell, Timothy. *Colonising Egypt*. Cambridge, 1988.

Moine, Nathalie. "Passeportisation, statistique des migrations et contrôle de l'identité sociale." *Cahiers du monde russe* 38, no. 4 (1997): 587–600.

Motyl, Alexander J. "Thinking About Empire." In *After Empire: Multiethnic Societies and Nation-Building*, ed. Karen Barkey and Mark von Hagen, 19–29. Boulder, 1997.

Myl'nikov, A. S., and Ch. M. Taksami, eds. *Leonid Pavlovich Potapov: K 90-letiiu so dniia rozhdeniia*. St. Petersburg, 1995.

Naiman, Eric. *Sex in Public: The Incarnation of Early Soviet Ideology*. Princeton, 1997.

Nekrich, Aleksander. *The Punished Peoples*, trans. George Saunders. New York, 1978.

Nelidov, A. V. *Istoriia gosudarstvennykh uchrezhdenii SSSR 1917–1936 gg.: Uchebnoe posobie*. 2 vols. Moscow, 1962.

Nenarokov, A. P. *K edinstvu ravnykh: Kul'turnye faktory ob"edinitel'nogo dvizheniia sovetskikh narodov, 1919–1924*. Moscow, 1991.

Noiriel, Gerard. *The French Melting Pot: Immigration, Citizenship, and National Identity*, trans. Geoffrey de Laforcade. Minneapolis, 1996.

Northrop, Douglas. "Subaltern Dialogues: Subversion and Resistance in Soviet Uzbek Family Law." In *Contending with Stalinism: Soviet Power and Popular Resistance in the 1930s*, ed. Lynne Viola, 109–38. Ithaca, 2002.

——. *Veiled Empire: Gender and Power in Stalinist Central Asia*. Ithaca, 2004.

Nove, Alec. *An Economic History of the U.S.S.R.* Rev. ed. London, 1989.

Olcott, Martha Brill. "The Collectivization Drive in Kazakhstan." *The Russian Review* 20, no. 2 (1981): 122–42.

Olson, James Stuart, ed. *An Ethnohistorical Dictionary of the Russian and Soviet Empires*. Westport, CT, 1994.

"Osnovnye daty zhizni i deiatel'nosti S. F. Ol'denburga." In *Sergei Fedorovich Ol'denburg*, ed. Skriabin et al., 120–21.

Patriarca, Silvana. *Numbers and Nationhood: Writing Statistics in Nineteenth-Century Italy*. Cambridge, 1996.

Pierce, Richard N. *Russian Central Asia, 1867–1917: A Study in Colonial Rule*. Berkeley, 1960.

Pipes, Richard. *The Russian Revolution*. New York, 1990.

——. *The Formation of the Soviet Union: Communism and Nationalism, 1917–1923*. Rev. ed. Cambridge, MA, 1997.

Poliakov, Iu. A., ed. *Vsesoiuznaia perepis' naseleniia 1939 goda: Osnovnye itogi*. Moscow, 1992.

Poliakov, Iu. A., N. A. Aralovets, V. B. Zhiromskaia, and I. N. Kiselev, eds. *Vsesoiuznaia perepis' naseleniia 1937 g.: Kratkie itogi*. Moscow, 1991.

Proctor, Robert. *Racial Hygiene: Medicine under the Nazis*. Cambridge, MA, 1988.

Rabinowitch, Alexander. *Prelude to Revolution*. Bloomington, 1968.

Rakowska-Harmstone, Teresa. *Russia and Nationalism in Central Asia: The Case of Tadzhikistan*. Baltimore, 1970.

Rashid, Ahmed. *Jihad: The Rise of Militant Islam in Central Asia*. New Haven, 2002.

Rassweiler, Anne D. *The Generation of Power: The History of Dneprostroi*. New York, 1988.

Remnick, David. *Lenin's Tomb: The Last Days of the Soviet Empire*. New York, 1993.

Reshetar, John Stephen. *The Ukrainian Revolution, 1917–1920: A Study in Nationalism*. Princeton, 1952.

Riasanovsky, Nicholas. *Nicholas I and Official Nationality*. Berkeley, 1959.

Rich, David Alan. *The Tsar's Colonels: Professionalism, Strategy, and Subversion in Late Imperial Russia*. Cambridge, MA, 1998.

Rittersporn, Gabor Tamas. *Stalinist Simplifications and Soviet Complications: Social Tensions and Political Conflicts in the USSR, 1933–1953*. New York, 1991.

Rosenberg, William G. *Liberals in the Russian Revolution: The Constitutional Democratic Party, 1917–1921*. Princeton, 1974.

Roshwald, Aviel. *Ethnic Nationalism and the Fall of Empires: Central Europe, Russia and the Middle East, 1914–1923*. London, 2001.

Roy, Olivier. *The New Central Asia: The Creation of Nations*. London, 2000.

Rydell, Robert W. *All the World's a Fair: Visions of Empire at American International Expositions, 1876–1916*. Chicago, 1984.

Sabol, Steven. "The Creation of Soviet Central Asia: The 1924 National Delimitation." *Central Asian Survey* 14, no. 2 (1995): 225–41.

Schapiro, Leonard. "The Concept of Totalitarianism," *Survey*, no. 73 (1969): 93–115.

Schneider, William. *Quality and Quantity: The Quest for Biological Regeneration in Twentieth-Century France*. Cambridge, 1990.

Schoeberlein-Engel, John Samuel. "Identity in Central Asia: Construction and Contention in the Conceptions of 'Ozbek,' 'Tajik,' 'Muslim,' 'Samarquandi' and Other Groups." Ph.D. diss., Harvard University, 1994.

Senn, Alfred. *The Great Powers: Lithuania and the Vilna Question, 1920–1928.* Leiden, 1966.

Serebriakov, I. D. "Po stranitsam arkhiva akademika S. F. Ol'denburga." In *Sergei Fedorovich Ol'denburg,* ed. Skriabin et al., 101–12.

Service, Robert. *Lenin: A Biography.* Cambridge, MA, 2000.

Shangina, I. I. "Etnograficheskie muzei Leningrada v pervye gody sovetskoi vlasti [1918–1923 gg.]." *Etnograficheskoe obozrenie,* no. 5 (1987): 71–80.

———. "Etnograficheskie muzei Moskvy i Leningrada na rubezhe 20x–30x godov XX v." *Etnograficheskoe obozrenie,* no. 2 (1991): 71–81.

Sherstobitov, Viktor Pavlovich. *Sovetskii narod: Monolitnaia obshchnost' stroitelei kommunizma.* Moscow, 1976.

Shteppa, Konstantin F. *Russian Historians and the Soviet State.* New Brunswick, NJ, 1962.

Simon, Gerhard. *Nationalism and Policy toward the Nationalities in the Soviet Union: From Totalitarian Dictatorship to Post-Stalinist Society,* trans. Karen and Oswald Forster. Boulder, 1991.

Skriabin, G. K. "Vydaiushchiisia organizator nauki." In *Sergei Fedorovich Ol'denburg,* ed. Skriabin et al., 4–12.

Skriabin, G. K., E. M. Primakov et al., eds. *Sergei Fedorovich Ol'denburg.* Moscow, 1986.

Slezkine, Yuri. "The Fall of Soviet Ethnography, 1928–1938." *Current Anthropology* 32, no. 4 (1991): 476–84.

———. *Arctic Mirrors: Russia and the Small Peoples of the North.* Ithaca, 1994.

———. "The USSR as a Communal Apartment, or How a Socialist State Promoted Ethnic Particularism." *Slavic Review* 53, no. 2 (1994): 414–52.

———. "N. Ia. Marr and the National Origins of Soviet Ethnogenetics." *Slavic Review* 55, no. 4 (1996): 826–62.

Slocum, John W. "Who, and When, Were the *Inorodtsy*? The Evolution of the Category of 'Aliens' in Imperial Russia." *The Russian Review* 57, no. 2 (1998): 173–90.

Smith, Jeremy. "The Georgian Affair of 1922—Policy Failure, Personality Clash, or Power Struggle?" *Europe-Asia Studies* 50, no. 3 (1998): 519–44.

———. *The Bolsheviks and the National Question, 1917–1921.* Houndmills, UK, 1999.

Sokolovski, Sergei. "The Kriashen Case in the 1926 and 2002 Russian Censuses: The Uses and Abuses of Anthropological Knowledge in Political Discourse." Paper presented at the 9th Annual Convention of the Association for the Study of Nationalities, April 2004.

Solomon, Susan Gross. "Rural Scholars and the Cultural Revolution." In *Cultural Revolution in Russia,* ed. Fitzpatrick, 129–53.

———. "Social Hygiene and Soviet Public Health, 1921–1930." In *Health and Society in Revolutionary Russia,* ed. Solomon and Hutchinson, 175–99.

———. "The Soviet-German Syphilis Expedition to Buriat Mongolia, 1928: Scientific Research on National Minorities." *Slavic Review* 52, no. 2 (1993): 204–32.

Solomon, Susan Gross, and John F. Hutchinson, eds. *Health and Society in Revolutionary Russia.* Bloomington, 1990.

Solomon, Susan Gross, and Jochen Richter, eds. *Ludwig Aschoff: Vergleichende*

Völkerpathologie oder Rassenpathologie: Tagebuch einer Reise durch Russland und Transkaukasien. Pfaffenweiler, 1998.

Solovei, T. D. *Ot "burzhuaznoi" etnologii k "sovetskoi" etnografii: Istoriia otechestvennoi etnologii pervoi treti XX veka.* Moscow, 1998.

——. "Korennoi perelom v otechestvennoi etnografii (Diskussiia o predmete etnologicheskoi nauki: konets 1920-x–nachalo 1930-x godov)." *Etnograficheskoe obozrenie,* no. 3 (2001): 101–21.

Staniukovich, T. V. *250 let Muzeia antropologii i etnografii imini Petra Velikogo, 1714–1964.* Moscow-Leningrad, 1964.

——. *Etnograficheskaia nauka i muzei (Po materialam etnograficheskikh muzeev Akademii nauk).* Leningrad, 1978.

Steinwedel, Charles. "The 1905 Revolution in Ufa: Mass Politics, Elections, and Nationality," *The Russian Review* 59, no. 4 (2000): 555–76.

Stocking, Jr., George W., ed. *Objects and Others: Essays on Museums and Material Culture.* Madison, 1985.

——. *Victorian Anthropology.* New York, 1987.

——, ed. *Colonial Situations: Essays on the Contextualization of Ethnographic Knowledge.* Madison, 1991.

——. "Maclay, Kubary, Malinowski: Archetypes from the Dreamtime of Anthropology," in *Colonial Situations,* ed. Stocking, 9–74.

——. *After Tylor: British Social Anthropology, 1888–1951.* Madison, 1995.

——, ed. *Volksgeist as Method and Ethic: Essays on Boasian Ethnography and the German Anthropological Tradition.* Madison, 1996.

——. *Delimiting Anthropology: Occasional Essays and Reflections.* Madison, 2001.

Stoler, Ann Laura, and Frederick Cooper, eds., *Tensions of Empire: Colonial Cultures in a Bourgeois World.* Berkeley, 1997.

Sukiennicki, Wiktor. *East Central Europe during World War I: From Foreign Domination to National Independence.* 2 vols. Boulder, 1984.

Sunderland, Willard. "The 'Colonization Question': Visions of Colonization in Late Imperial Russia." *Jahrbücher für Geschichte Osteuropas* 48, no. 2 (2000): 210–32.

Suny, Ronald Grigor. *The Revenge of the Past: Nationalism, Revolution, and the Collapse of the Soviet Union.* Stanford, 1993.

——. *The Soviet Experiment: Russia, the USSR, and the Successor States.* New York, 1998.

——. "Constructing Primordialism: Old Histories for New Nations," *Journal of Modern History* 73, no. 4 (2001): 862–96.

Szöllösi-Janze, Margit. "National Socialism and the Sciences: Reflections, Conclusions, and Historical Perspectives." In *Science in the Third Reich,* ed. Margit Szöllösi-Janze, 1–35. Oxford, 2001.

Terras, Viktor. *Belinskij and Russian Literary Criticism: The Heritage of Organic Aesthetics.* Madison, 1974.

Tillett, Lowell. *The Great Friendship: Soviet Historians on the Non-Russian Nationalities.* Chapel Hill, 1969.

Timasheff, Nicholas S. *The Great Retreat: The Growth and Decline of Communism in Russia.* New York, 1946.

Tracy, Sarah W. "George Draper and American Constitutional Medicine, 1915–1946: Reinventing the Sick Man." *Bulletin of the History of Medicine* 66 (1992): 53–89.

Tucker, Robert C. "Stalinism as Revolution from Above." In *Stalinism: Essays in Historical Interpretation,* ed. Robert C. Tucker, 77–108. New York, 1977.

Tylor, E. B. *Primitive Culture.* 2 vols. Boston, 1874.

Uvin, Peter. "On Counting, Categorizing, and Violence in Burundi and Rwanda." In *Census and Identity,* ed. Kertzer and Arel, 148–75.

Vaidyanath, R. *The Formation of the Soviet Central Asian Republics.* New Delhi, 1967.

Vakar, Nicholas P. *Belorussia: The Making of a Nation.* Cambridge, MA, 1956.

Velychenko, Stephen. "The Issue of Russian Colonialism in Ukrainian Thought: Dependency Identity and Development." *Ab Imperio,* no. 1 (2002): 323–67.

Viola, Lynne. *Peasant Rebels under Stalin: Collectivization and the Culture of Peasant Resistance.* New York, 1996.

Vucinich, Alexander. *Empire of Knowledge: The Academy of Sciences of the USSR (1917–1970).* Berkeley, 1984.

Weber, Eugen. *Peasants into Frenchmen: The Modernization of Rural France, 1870–1914.* Stanford, 1976.

Weindling, Paul. *Health, Race, and German Politics between National Unification and Nazism, 1870–1945.* Cambridge, 1989.

——. "German-Soviet Medical Co-operation and the Institute for Racial Research, 1927–c. 1935." *German History* 10, no. 2 (1992): 177–206.

——. *Epidemics and Genocide in Eastern Europe, 1890–1945.* Oxford, 2000.

Weiner, Amir. "Nature, Nurture, and Memory in a Socialist Utopia: Delineating the Soviet Socio-Ethnic Body in the Age of Socialism." *The American Historical Review* 104, no. 4 (1999): 1114–55.

——. *Making Sense of War: The Second World War and the Fate of the Bolshevik Revolution.* Princeton, 2001.

Weitz, Eric D. "Racial Politics without the Concept of Race: Reevaluating Soviet Ethnic and National Purges." *Slavic Review* 61, no. 1 (2002): 1–29.

Wheeler, Geoffrey. *The Modern History of Soviet Central Asia.* London, 1964.

Wilmanns, Karl. *Lues, Lamas, Leninisten: Tagebuch einer Reise durch Russland in die Burjatische Republik im Sommer 1926.* Pfaffenweiler, 1995.

Wixman, Ronald, *The Peoples of the USSR: An Ethnographic Handbook.* Armonk, NY, 1984.

Wolfe, B. D. *Three Who Made a Revolution.* New York, 1948.

Young, Crawford. *The African Colonial State in Comparative Perspective.* New Haven, 1994.

Zaks, A. B. "Rech' A. V. Lunacharskogo na konferentsii po delam muzeev." In *Arkheograficheskii ezhegodnik za 1976 g.,* ed. S. O. Smidt et al., 210–16. Moscow, 1977.

Zalesskii, K. A. *Imperiia Stalina: Biograficheskii entsiklopedicheskii slovar'.* Moscow, 2000.

Zaslavsky, Viktor. *The Neo-Stalinist State: Class, Ethnicity, and Consensus in Soviet Society.* Armonk, NY, 1994.

Zhiromskaia, V. B. "Vsesoiuznye perepisi naseleniia 1926, 1937, 1939 godov: Istoriia podgotovki i provedeniia." *Istoriia SSSR,* no. 3 (1990): 84–104.

Zhiromskaia, V. B., I. N. Kiselev, and Iu. A. Poliakov. *Polveka pod grifom "sekretno": Vsesoiuznaia perepis' naseleniia 1937 goda.* Moscow, 1996.

Zorin, Andrei. "Ideologiia 'Pravoslaviia-Samoderzhaviia-Narodnosti': Opyt rekonstruktsii." *Novoe literaturnoe obozrenie,* no. 26 (1998): 71–104.